Consumer Behavior

fundamentals & strategies

Terrell G. Williams
Department of Business Administration
Utah State University

West Publishing Company
St. Paul • New York • Los Angeles • San Francisco

PHOTO CREDITS: 1 Charles Farrow; 2 Charles Farrow; 56 Courtesy of Economics Laboratory, Inc., Alexander Liberman, artist; 112 Charles Farrow; 142 Courtesy of Southwestern Life Insurance Company/Dallas, Lee Langum, photographer; 170 Charles Farrow; 200 Charles Farrow; 230 Charles Farrow; 261 Texas Highway Department; 262 Charles Farrow; 298 Charles Farrow; 330 Charles Farrow; 376 Charles Farrow; 410 Charles Farrow; 446 Charles Farrow; 484 Charles Farrow.

COPY EDITOR: Lenore Franzen
DESIGN: Wendy Palmer
COVER DESIGN: Jack Deskin
COMPOSITION: Auto-graphics

COPYRIGHT © 1982 By WEST PUBLISHING CO.
    50 West Kellogg Boulevard
    P.O. Box 3526
    St. Paul, Minnesota 55165

Library of Congress Cataloging in Publication Data

Williams, Terrell G.
    Consumer behavior.

    Includes index.
    1. Consumers. 2. Motivation research (Marketing)
I. Title.
HF5415.3.W543   658.8'342   81-1216
ISBN 0-8299-0420-4   AACR2

To Judy

Contents

CHAPTER **8**   **Family Consuming Behavior**   **200**

CHAPTER **9**   **Consumer Research**   **230**

CHAPTER **13**   **Behavioral Concepts for Pricing**   **354**

CHAPTER **14**   **Interpersonal Communication**   **376**

Preface

Consumer Behavior: Concepts and Strategies is about consumers and why they buy. The book is also about marketing management and how consumer behavior affects marketing strategy formulation. The purpose of the book is to help you as a consumer come to understand your own buying behavior better and to help you as a prospective marketing manager to deliver to consumers more effectively the products they want. A knowledge of consumer behavior should help a marketing strategist influence consumer buying, yet at the same time marketers cannot force consumers into mindless responses to packages, displays, products, or promotional efforts. Although we can influence the behavior of others, what we know about human behavior does not allow us to control consumer response, except perhaps under highly controlled circumstances which marketers cannot generally achieve.

Consumer behavior courses have been taught in universities for only about twenty years even though the subject of why people buy has been of interest to marketers perhaps as long as marketing has been practiced. Over the years, consumer behavior has emerged as a separate discipline with a growing body of theory and its own professional organization and journal. As a teacher of consumer behavior, I have been frustrated by the lack of integration between the behavioral concepts taught in the classroom and the actual practice of marketing. Particularly, I have felt that the study of consumer behavior doesn't fit well with the preparatory marketing courses that precede the consumer behavior course. Most basic marketing texts attempt to communicate marketing knowledge through the framework of what the marketing manager does and the forces that influence that management activity, most consumer behavior texts have been organized around the various behavioral disciplines without systematically looking at how the marketing strategist might apply behavioral concepts in the formulation of the marketing mix.

My approach, then, is to begin by acquainting you with some of the major behavioral concepts that lie at the foundation of the study of consumer behavior. Although it will be helpful if you have studied some of the behavioral sciences, it is not necessary to an understanding of the first part of the book. The first nine chapters serve as an orientation to the application of behavioral theories to marketing practice. After an overview chapter, the text moves into a discussion of consumer decision making. Many comprehensive treatments of consumer behavior are built around the process by which the consumer arrives at purchase decisions. The text continues with a discussion of the contributions from psychology, social psychology, sociology, and cultural authropology. Beginning with the individual, the material covers perception, needs, motives, personality learning, and attitudes. The discussion moves from the individual to the group with emphasis on reference groups, social class, culture, sub-cultures, and family. Part I concludes with a brief overview of some of the research techniques used in examining consumer behavior.

In the second part of the book, I have tried to integrate the behavioral concepts into a discussion of the decision areas in which the marketing manager develops and implements the marketing plan. In this section, I assume that you have a background in the fundamentals of marketing. For each element of the marketing mix, product, price, distribution and promotion, some of the most important behavioral contributions are advanced. Some concepts are theoretical in nature, providing a background against which marketing decisions can be made. Other areas are more directly applicable, yielding specific suggestions for strategy planning and implementation. The text concludes with a look at some behavioral contributions for major public policy issues and a review of the consumer behavior/marketing management interface.

It has been my goal for many years to set my ideas for integrating consumer behavior and marketing strategy on paper, and the achievement of that goal has been most gratifying. However, the job is far from being complete. The study of consumer behavior is constantly yielding new insights that must be incorporated into the marketing manager's thinking. Also, the present field of consumer behavior study is so broad that many ideas were, of necessity, omitted from the book.

A textbook of this scope is not written alone. First, I have drawn heavily from the concepts and research of others, and I would like to give recognition to the many people cited in the text for their contributions to the field. Numerous poeple reviewed the various drafts. My thanks to Professor Harold Kassarjian (University of California, Los Angeles) who reviewed an early portion of the manuscript, and to Professors Michael K. Mills (University of Southern California), Edward A. Riordan (Wayne State University), Robert B. Settle (San Diego State University), and Jeffrey G. Towle (Michigan State University), who provided criticism and encouragement throughout the entire project. I also want to express my appreciation to the editors, who encouraged and cajoled me along the way and who fine-tuned the manuscript. Thanks must also go to the several people who typed the drafts: Kathy Gardner, Kay Kartchner, Barbara Marinelli, and Sandy Walker. Finally, my gratitude must go to my wife and boys who buoyed me up at times, got out of the way at other times, and were most patient in my hours of inattention to them.

Terrell G. Williams
Logan, Utah

1

Fundamental Concepts of Consumer Behavior

Consumer Behavior and Marketing Strategy

Consumer behavior is a universal phenomenon; we must consume to live. In a primitive society, people may satisfy their needs through consumption of self-produced items. In industrialized societies like the United States, Canada, Germany, and Japan, the process of satisfying those needs is more complex. The business sector of the society anticipates consumer needs and provides the necessary products and services. This sounds simple enough, but consumer needs are so complex and varied that prediction becomes extremely difficult.

At the microlevel a marketing manager is charged with the responsibility of developing a marketing strategy. The first step in formulating such a strategy is identifying and understanding the target market. This is followed by developing a marketing mix, which includes establishing product, pricing, promotion, and channel strategies. All of this requires information about and understanding of consumers.

Human behavior has long been studied, but many of the reasons for our behavior are only partially understood. Behavior, individual or aggregate, is complex and often virtually unpredictable. All of the problems that attend the study of general human behavior beset the study of consumer behavior. A quick look at your own buying behavior will begin to give you a feel for the complexity of the subject. Stop and think about the last thing you bought. What was it? Why did you buy it? What thoughts and activities led up to the purchase? How long did you deliberate before you made the purchase? Why did you buy when and where you did? How did you decide on the brand, the product features, and the price to pay? Why did you pay as you did—cash or credit? Was your behavior the same for this purchase as it was for the same item the last time you bought? Will it be the same next time? Was your behavior the same for this item as it was for other kinds of items that you have bought in the past? What people and other information sources influenced your decision, and how was it influenced? Did you buy for yourself or for someone else? How did you feel after the purchase was completed? How will that influence your next purchase?

You may begin to understand the immense complexity of analyzing your own behavior, but suppose you had to answer those same questions for other members of your family, your friends, or even for complete strangers. Seeking answers to questions like these is what the study of consumer behavior is all about. The marketing manager needs answers to these and many more questions if the firm's marketing strategy is to reach its thousands or millions of potential customers effectively and efficiently. Happily, aggregate consumer behavior is much easier to predict and understand than individual behavior, so all is not lost. By careful study of consumer behavior, the marketing manager can greatly improve the effectiveness of marketing strategy decisions.

What is Consumer Behavior?

The term *consumer behavior* is often used to refer to any behavior of people who buy and use products and services. One author defined consumer behavior as simply "the way people act in the exchange process."[1] Two recent definitions of consumer behavior are "the behavior that consumers display in searching for, purchasing, using and evaluating products, services and ideas which they expect will satisfy their needs,"[2] and "the decision process and physical activity individuals engage in when evaluating, acquiring, and using economic goods and services."[3] Essentially, these definitions say that consumer behavior involves the entire process by which people select, acquire, and use various products and services.

To understand the meaning of consumer behavior better we should carefully examine who and what are involved. In any buying activity there are at least three potential forces on the buying side of the transaction: buyers, influencers, and consumers. The buyer makes the purchase, while the consumer uses the service or product purchased. Influencers are not directly involved in buying or using the product but knowingly or unknowingly affect the decisions of the buyer.

Consider the purchase of presweetened breakfast cereal. The consumers are generally young children, although older children and parents may be at least occasional users of the product. In American households, the wife and mother has traditionally bought and decided on most of the food and other household items, performing much the same function as a purchasing agent in a business firm. As the family purchasing agent, she weighs the wants and needs of all family members, combining her own knowledge and expertise to arrive at optimum purchase decisions. Finally, there may be other family members or friends who influence the decision even though they are not users of presweetened cereal.

For example, after accompanying his wife to the grocery store, a husband might comment that he had never realized that presweetened breakfast cereals were so much more expensive than the unsugared variety. An older child might come home from school reporting that a nutrition teacher said that purchasing presweetened breakfast cereals is bad because of their relatively low food value.

Will our purchasing agent buy presweetened cereal the next time she buys groceries? We can't be sure, but the family members who eat the cereal will almost surely offer their inputs, and their desires and taste preferences may well prevail.

For our purposes, then, consumer behavior may be defined as *all purchase-related activities, thoughts, and influences that occur before, during, and after the purchase itself as performed by buyers and consumers of products and services and those who influence the purchase.* Throughout the text the term *product* will be used to mean goods, services, and ideas. In the context of this definition, what happens before and after the purchase decision is at least as important to the market strategist and student of consumer behavior as is the purchase itself. What we are most concerned with in the study of consumer behavior is not so much consumption as the process by which consumers acquire the things that they consume. This is often referred to as buyer behavior. The market strategist must be concerned with understanding, influencing, changing, and reinforcing behavior for all participants in buying/consuming activities at all levels of the process. Because researchers and writers in the field do not generally try to make a distinction between buyers and consumers in their terminology, the terms *consumer behavior* and *buyer behavior* will be used interchangeably throughout this text.

Problems in the Study of Consumer Behavior

By now you have probably reached the conclusion that the study of buyer behavior is highly complex and often deeply frustrating. You need only begin to delve into the rich and growing body of literature on consumer behavior to realize that there are considerably more questions than answers in the field. Typical of much of the theory and research on human behavior, there seems to be little agreement in consumer research. What we intuitively feel to be true is often not validated by scientific study, and often researchers seem to be diametrically opposed to one another in their explanations of various behavioral phenomena. At the outset, the student must become resigned to dealing with a high level of ambiguity. Individuals generally are not very predictable, and their behavior is caused and influenced by an overwhelming variety of internal and external factors. In the aggregate there is better predictability, but sometimes even here errors can be made. The potential range of human behavior is virtually infinite.

Somehow, out of the seeming chaos of fragmentary and often conflicting theory and data about consumer behavior, the student of marketing and the marketing manager must try to find useful tools and develop insights for formulating and implementing a marketing strategy. In the process, concepts that are unproven and even controversial must often be applied. But part of the job of the marketing decision maker is to cull the information for what seems applicable to the problem at hand. Many times uncertainties must be dealt with as intelligently as possible, given limited knowledge and information. Thus, the marketing student along with the marketing practitioner must be prepared to deal effectively with some uncertainty, ambiguity, and partial information.

Marketing managers face innumerable problems in understanding their customers. Some of these problems are well illustrated in the new product failures of numerous firms. For example, Chester M. Woolworth, president of the Woodstream Corporation, for many years had heard and believed the adage, Build a better mousetrap, and the world will beat a path to your door. Unfortunately for Mr. Woolworth, the adage is not universally true. After long research into the eating, crawling, and resting habits of mice, the company designed a trap that seemed ideal for catching mice.[4] As anyone who has tried to catch mice with the traditional trap knows, the traps are not at all reliable. The Woolworth trap was virtually foolproof; mice liked the trap. People who were asked to try the trap agreed that it was certainly superior to any trap they had previously used. The trap, which looked something like an inverted bowl, was made of molded plastic. The streamlined trap had a hole just the right size for the mouse to enter, and on nibbling the bait, the spring snapped up, choking the mouse instantly. By pressing a release on the top of the trap, the lifeless rodent fell out. Even though the price and performance were right, the new trap was a total flop in the market.

Why should such a seemingly ideal product fail so miserably? Subsequent research revealed that although the habits of mice were carefully studied, the behavior of those who would buy and use the traps was not so well understood. It seems that most mousetraps are bought by families who have few mice. The purchase is typically made by the husband, who also usually sets the trap before the family retires for the evening. The problem, it turned out, develops after the mouse is in the trap. It seems that although the husband sets the trap, he, mighty hunter, goes off to work in the morning, leaving the wife the job of emptying the trap. But the wife doesn't want to become involved with either the dead mouse or the unpredictable spring. So she has generally thrown out the mouse and trap. But our heroine is frugal above all. The old wooden trap cost about five to ten cents at the time, which was cheap enough that she didn't mind throwing it away. The new trap was about the same price as the traditional trap (twelve cents), but it *looked* so expensive that she couldn't bear to throw it away. Besides, the trap on the shelf would remind her of the awful possibility of having another mouse in the house. Rather than trying to readjust her own attitudes or convince her husband to take care of the dead mouse, the wife simply announced that the fancy new trap just wasn't satisfactory, and she wouldn't let her husband use or buy another one. Thus, the product failed, not because it wasn't a good product in a functional sense, but because the company did not adequately assess the behavior and attitudes of its consumers.

Bristol-Myers learned that consumers may report that they find a product quite satisfactory in a test situation and yet be unwilling to buy the product when it actually reaches the market.[5] After observing the large and growing sales of such analgesics as Anacin and Bufferin, the company decided to make its own market entry—a cherry-flavored, chewable pain reliever called Analoze. To make the product doubly attractive an antacid was added to make a combination pain reliever-stomach sweetener similar in effect to Alka-Seltzer or Bromo-Seltzer. Although the product was competitively priced and overwhelmingly preferred in product tests with consumer panels, Analoze failed to make a dent in the market. Why should such an apparently desirable product fail to live up to its expectations? Subsequent research led to the conclusion that the product's weakness was due to the fact that it was taken without water. Through long years of aspirin swallowing, headache sufferers had subconsciously come to associate water with pain relief, and they had no confidence in a pill that could be chewed or dissolved in the mouth without water.

Even though there is a good deal of uncertainty about how consumer motivation relates to market performance of products, there are enough success stories to suggest the potential fruitfulness of a behavioral approach to the development of marketing strategy. A few examples will help set the stage for future discussion.

A classic case goes back to the early 1950s when instant coffee was making its market debut. The Nestlé Company had rolled out its Nescafé Instant, but sales results were less than spectacular. When consumers were pressed as to why they did not use instant coffee, they replied that it just didn't taste as good as their drip grind. However, taste tests suggested that most consumers were unable to distinguish instant from regular. So the company engaged in a study to determine other reasons for product failure.[6] The study involved giving two groups of housewives shopping lists and asking them to describe the woman who might have made up the list. The two lists were identical, except that one contained Nescafé Instant coffee and the other contained Maxwell House coffee (drip grind). The results of the study showed that the woman with instant coffee on her list was seen as lazy, a poor planner, a spendthrift, and a bad wife. The woman with the regular coffee on her list was seen as a thrifty, good wife. Thus, the major selling point of the product was its downfall. With this knowledge, the Nestlé Company revised its promotional strategy to picture the wife who served instant coffee in the morning as having more time to spend with her family and more opportunity to plan her days and shopping activities. By 1955 instant coffee sales had reached twenty percent of total coffee sales.

To illustrate the complexity and dynamics of the problem of studying consumer behavior, consider the update of the shopping list study conducted in 1968.[7] By this time housewives apparently no longer had guilt feelings about serving their families easily prepared foods. On the contrary, the fact that the shopping lists contained such items as a bunch of carrots, baking powder, and a bag of potatoes led the modern housewives to see the holders of both of the shopping lists as old-fashioned. Even the notion of using a shopping list seemed to be viewed as old-fashioned. In the 1968 study, the instant coffee buyer was regarded as busy, interested in saving time, and lacking in imagination, but she was also described as quick, energetic, fast working, outgoing, friendly, physically active, and on the move. Generally, the Nescafé wife was seen as a busy, not bad, wife.

On the other hand, the Maxwell House shopper was seen as more likely to enjoy homemaking, dull, and having no spirit of adventure or elegance of taste. These comments about the shopper, however, seemed to be more influenced by items on the list other than the drip grind coffee. In any case, the housewife and her perceptions of product use patterns changed a lot in twenty years.

Once we feel that we have learned something about consumer behavior, we must continue to revise our thinking with ongoing research. However, we may be able to draw some generalizations from the study that will be of more enduring value. Three general conclusions drawn from the 1950 study still seem pertinent today.

First, many products have meaning and significance for consumers that go beyond the mere physical character of the products. Second, these underlying product values are often the major determinants of consumer behavior. Finally, determining and understanding these hidden values often requires more than simply asking consumers why they buy.

Another example of successfully applying behavioral knowledge to marketing strategy involved prunes. Prunes are, of course, well known for their superb laxative quality. This gives the fruit something of an image problem, however. Prune sales had been constant for twenty years in 1953 when Ernest Dichter's Institute for Motivation Research, Incorporated, conducted a study on the motivational patterns for purchasing and consuming prunes. The study indicated that there were six major biases in consumer minds toward prunes.[8]

1. Prunes are despised as symbols of sterile old age.
2. Prunes are suspected of being devitalized and denaturized.
3. Prunes are resented as a laxative.
4. Prunes are disliked as a symbol of parental authority.
5. Prunes are "plebeian"—a food without prestige.
6. Prunes are disparaged as food for "peculiar" or old people.

Based on the notion that the wrinkles of prunes were associated with old age and that people didn't like the messy pits, Stan Freberg launched his successful advertising campaign for Sunsweet prunes. The ad announced that Sunsweet had gotten rid of the pits and was working hard on eliminating the wrinkles ("Today the pits, tomorrow the wrinkles"), all amid stirring march music. The results were overwhelmingly successful, and sales increased fourfold in the first six months of the campaign.[9]

The Behavioral Disciplines

The student of consumer behavior must be prepared to draw heavily from a wide variety of disciplines, but the eclectic nature of the study of consumer behavior presents certain problems. First, in the early days of motivation research there was a great tendency to borrow indiscriminately from research results and techniques that were never really intended to have applicability to buying situations. Many techniques of the clinical psychologist and the psychiatrist designed for diagnosis and treatment of mental illnesses were applied directly to understanding consumer behavior. In general, these clinical tests were designed for use in one-to-one treatment and analysis sessions, but motivation researchers applied the techniques to non-randomly-selected groups and extrapolated the results to draw conclusions for consumers in general.

Although this problem has been partially solved by carefully designing specific techniques for studying the behavior of consumers, a second problem that is not easily resolved remains. Students of human behavior typically specialize in rather narrow areas of psychology, social psychology, sociology, or anthropology. The marketing practitioner or theorist who seeks to understand consumer behavior in its totality must be a generalist—that is, an expert not only in the complex field of marketing but in the several behavioral disciplines as well.

The breadth of the consumer behavior field can be appreciated from the fact that the *Journal of Consumer Research,* a periodical specializing in publication of consumer behavior research since 1974, is sponsored by eleven different professional associations.[10] In consumer research we find an excellent forum for interdisciplinary research. The study of consumer behavior provides a unique opportunity to bring together a diverse group of behavioral disciplines to study a total area of human behavior rather than an isolated facet.

The first discipline to attempt to deal directly with the problems of consumer behavior was economics. The economist seeks to understand the workings of the system that provides a society with want-satisfying goods and services. In order to build a workable theory based on economics, the consumer is viewed as a highly rational and predictable individual who reacts to nothing but price and real product differences. Also, there are no product differences, since products are assumed to be homogeneous. Under the theory of pure competition, the individual consumer is one of many who cannot individually affect the market and who is completely and perfectly informed without any effort. In spite of its rather limiting assumptions, economic theory presents many useful concepts of consumer price response.

Psychology is the study of individual behavior. The study includes needs, motivation, learning, perception, and personality, all of which potentially bear on consumer behavior. The diversity of thought in psychology has given rise to numerous theories of consumer behavior as the concepts have been applied to marketing.

From sociology's study of group behavior comes contributions to the understanding of social class, group influence, socialization, and the family. Each of these areas has contributed richly to consumer behavior literature. The suggestion is that consumers are heavily influenced by the actions of others either because they want to fit into certain groups or because they want to be accepted and looked up to by others.

Cultural anthropology leads to insights into buying behavior as influenced by subcultures, taboos, cultural imperatives, cross-cultural influence, cultural themes, and the like. The uninformed have made uncounted blunders as they tried to use the marketing tactics that worked in one culture or subculture in another setting. Many of these problems could have been avoided if significant cultural issues had been explored.

Social psychology leads to an understanding of individual behavior within groups. One aspect of social psychology as it applies to consumer behavior has concentrated specifically on the area of attitude development and change.

The job of the consumer behavior theorist is to synthesize the hodgepodge of facts and suppositions into a manageable body of thought to aid in the formation and evaluation of a marketing strategy. The student and practitioner must bring the theory of buyer behavior to the realities of the marketplace to provide the foundation for sound research and decision making.

Why Study Consumer Behavior?

Before undertaking an in-depth study of consumer behavior, it might be well to ask why such a study is worthwhile. The question of importance might be best treated from three viewpoints. First, studying consumer behavior can be valuable to you as a consumer. Second, you, as a potential marketing practitioner, will find an understanding of consumer behavior useful as you approach the problem of developing and implementing a marketing strategy. Third, makers and implementers of public policy dealing with marketing practices should have an accurate feel for consumer behavior.

Consumer Behavior and the Consumer

Have you ever made a purchase and later asked youself, "Why did I do that?" Often, motives and desires you are not fully aware of may lead you to make purchases when your more logical self might do otherwise. The salesperson who comes into your home often creates an environment in which you may buy something that you had absolutely no previous intention of purchasing. This type of seller somehow achieves the status of "invited guest." You will listen to a sales presentation that you would never tolerate in a retail store. The salesperson's message is carefully engineered to take advantage of such consumer emotional needs as acceptance, security, and cooperation. Because of this, consumers find themselves buying vacuum cleaners, movie camera outfits, cookware, book sets, and the like at prices that are often much higher than those available for similar or identical items in a retail store.

More subtle are the overtones of the love and acceptance that will be yours if only you use the "right" mouthwash, deodorant, toothpaste, or hairdressing. The individual who is aware of why and how purchases are influenced and made is in a much better position to avoid being duped into making unwanted purchases. On the other hand, an understanding of what your emotional needs are and how they are satisfied may allow you to select the products and brands that will fit your self-image and heighten your satisfaction with the things you buy.

In all buying situations, then, consumers can benefit from an understanding of consumer behavior in four ways by:

1. Becoming more aware of their needs and purchase motives.
2. Understanding the nature and effects of various promotional tactics better.
3. Appreciating the complexity of their purchase decisions and the process by which they make those decisions.
4. Making better decisions in terms of satisfying their real needs—physical and emotional.

Consumer Behavior and the Market Strategist

The thrust of this text is to provide a conceptual and practical foundation in consumer behavior so the marketer can develop and implement strategy more efficiently to meet both company goals and consumer needs. While it could be argued that knowledge of consumer behavior might be used for deception and manipulation of consumers, it could also be applied by a skillful and effective marketing manager to increase consumer satisfaction and provide for more efficient utilization and allocation of society's ever-scarcer resources. At the same time, knowledge of behavior has the potential to provide a better rate of return for investors and more rewarding and stable jobs for operatives and managers in a firm.

For many years marketers have advocated adopting the *marketing concept* as the foundation for a marketing philosophy of management. The concept is founded on the notion that the firm should concentrate its efforts on profitably satisfying consumer needs. The idea is good, but it often breaks down when applied.

Several major problems are evident here. First, consumer needs are often very difficult to discover and interpret. Consumers may not even be aware of their own needs and motives, or they may say they want things that they won't buy or use when given the opportunity. For many years users of ketchup bottles complained about the small neck that often requires using a knife to extract the contents. One enterprising company decided to answer the cries of their consumers with a wide-neck ketchup bottle. However, long years of experience with the small necks led consumers to expect a slow outpouring. What a surprise they received when they opened the new bottle, gave it a solid hit on the bottom, and found most of the contents on food, plate, and tablecloth. The new container was subsequently pulled from the market. One ketchup manufacturer handled the problem more creatively. Its product has been billed as "the slowest ketchup in the world." Success came from capitalizing on the difficulty of getting the ketchup from the bottle.

A second problem is a question of who is to define and interpret needs. In 1974 public policy makers contended that consumers "needed" to wear seat belts and passed legislation to require auto manufacturers to build cars so they would not start unless seat belts were fastened. The subsequent outcry that resulted in repeal of the regulation suggested that, while consumers might *need* seat belts, they certainly did not *want* to be forced to wear them.

The study of consumer behavior provides a sound basis for identifying and understanding consumer needs. On the strength of this recognition, the marketer can develop products with the capacity of satisfying real customer needs. If consumer theory and research are successful, the consumers themselves can communicate their needs to marketing management. Thus, the definition of consumer needs is placed where it should be in a free-choice economy—in the hands of the consumers themselves.

In a profit-based economy, however, the mere existence of a consumer need is not sufficient cause to jump into a market. Success for any business depends not only on its ability to know what consumers need but also on whether those needs represent sufficient market demand to make their satisfaction economically feasible. In addition, the firm must determine what market strategy will be required to appeal to those needs.[1] Consumer research can often help answer the vital question of whether a particular need can be economically and profitably satisfied. It can often give valuable insights into the development of effective marketing strategy as well.

For several years prior to the development of the Mustang, Ford Motor Company had received numerous requests for the return of the two-seater Thunderbird popular from 1955 through 1957. However, consumer research revealed that because of practical limitations, no more than 40,000 two-seater Mustangs could be sold, even though the two-seater design had wide appeal. This finding led the company to include a back seat as a feature in the new Mustang but to design the car to have the look of a two-seater. That was one of many features suggested by consumer understanding and research that led Mustang to a first year's sales record of nearly 420,000 units. [12] Had the company responded to the data coming informally from the market the Mustang might well have been a failure.

Markets do not consist of consumers who are alike but of persons who are quite different from one another. Thus, a single product or a single promotional appeal will likely not reach or appeal to all potential customers. Because of this, a company must often recognize the existence of numerous submarkets called market segments. Successful market segmentation strategy requires a knowledge of the bases on which to divide a large market into smaller, more homogeneous target audiences. The bases for market segmentation may be demographic—that is, they may relate to such factors as income, age, sex, and education. On the other hand, market segmentation may be based on psychographic factors, such as consumer life-style, personality, or needs. Often, the best marketing strategies grow out of a recognition and exploitation of behavioral elements common to a given market segment.

In introducing new products, market strategists face a substantial risk. Estimates of new product failures place the rate at from fifty to ninety percent. Certainly this represents a major cost and a severe waste of resources. As indicated earlier, the cause of a product demise may be in the misunderstanding of consumer needs as much as in some inherent deficiency in the product itself. Better consumer theory and research should lead to lower product failure rates and more profitable product successes.

There are, then, several marketing strategy-related reasons for studying consumer behavior.

1. Strategists may gain a better understanding of consumer needs, leading to a more effective implementation of the marketing concept.
2. Consumers themselves are allowed to communicate their needs directly to marketing strategy decision makers.
3. The profit position of a company may be improved by turning real consumer needs into effective product appeals.
4. Markets may be effectively segmented into subgroups with common behavioral characteristics.
5. The cost and resource waste associated with new product failures may be reduced.

Consumer Behavior and Public Policy

Historically, marketing-directed legislation in the United States has been aimed at indirectly protecting consumers by preserving a competitive environment and controlling specific marketing practices. More recently, the issue of direct consumer protection has become more important. There is a very real problem here, however, in that makers of public policy often do not have a clear view of consumer needs and market responses. Thus, many attempts at making the consumer purchase process easier or safer have met with very limited success. Attempts to force consumers to use seat belts have thus far failed. Consumers are given information about their loans based on the Truth in Lending Act, but they often ignore the valuable information in their rush to sign the papers and get the product home.

It is apparent that legislators and administrators in various consumer protection and education agencies must base their decisions and practices not on their own assumptions but on theoretically sound and empirically derived information about consumer behavior. For example, the fact that many consumers use little product information even when making major purchases has been of considerable concern to many consumer educators. This lack of information is an especially difficult problem for low-income consumers. The assumption of policy makers is that information is not available and must therefore be provided either by the government or at government insistance. In fact, much information is available but unused by many consumers, especially those in low income and education brackets. Readily available information, such as test reports, unit pricing, consumer installment loan disclosures, and product labeling, are much more often used by consumers in higher socioeconomic brackets than by those in lower brackets who presumably need the information more. The point is that there needs to be an understanding of who uses information, why they use it or why they do not, and what kinds of information are used before policy makers can effectively aid the consumer in making better decisions.

Often, public policy makers seem to ignore the fact that many products are legitimately purchased in order to satisfy psychological needs. New legislation requires that "real," demonstrable differences must exist for certain classes of products, such as autos, some electronic products, and over-the-counter drugs, before a company can advertise its brand as superior. A consumer who firmly believes that a new car is better than a competing model may be more satisfied with that car because psychological benefits were promoted—even when there may be little or no real physical difference. Failure to recognize this fact may lead to legislation that will ultimately result in reduced overall satisfaction with many products. For some reason many people seem to feel that it is all right to satisfy physiological needs, but somehow emotional needs should not be met.

A study of buyer behavior might, therefore, aid the public policy maker in four ways.

1. A better understanding may be achieved of how consumers meet their needs, both physiological and psychological, through product purchase and use.

2. Public policy makers may gain better insights into how to provide and protect free consumer choice.
3. Understanding ways of encouraging marketers to provide better product information could be achieved.
4. Techniques for encouraging all consumers to use available information to make better buying decisions might be developed.

Approaches to the Study of Consumer Behavior

The study of consumer behavior as a separate discipline is a relatively new phenomenon. Most universities did not teach consumer behavior as a separate course until the late 1960s. The first major textbook in consumer behavior appeared in 1968. Prior to that time, only books of collected readings or short treatises were available.

In the short time that consumer behavior has been studied, several theories and approaches to its study have appeared. Textbooks seek to take a fairly eclectic approach, but most view consumer behavior either as a problem-solving exercise or a cognitive process. In general, various topics, including attitudes, personality, learning, motivation, needs, perception, family influences, social influence, and culture, are discussed at length to provide a framework for understanding buyer behavior.

Broadly, the study of human behavior can take either a behaviorist or a cognitive approach. The behaviorist concentrates on how organisms respond to stimuli without being concerned with why they respond as they do. The cognitive, existential, or phenomenological approach is concerned as much with the process of behavior as with the outcome. Figure 1-1 suggests several significant differences between the behaviorist and cognitive schools.

Since the student of buyer behavior is at least as concerned with the process by which consumers arrive at purchase decisions as with the decision itself, the cognitive approach seems to be the general trend in the study of consumer behavior. This is appropriate since the market strategist is interested in communicating with and influencing the consumer at the various levels of behavior and cognition that precede and follow the actual purchase.

In a narrower sense, the study of buyer behavior has grown out of numerous microtheories largely based on the views of theorists in individual disciplines. Some of these theories were alluded to in the earlier discussion of the disciplines of human behavior. In general, the theories of buyer behavior that have developed and influenced our thinking can be classified into two broad areas: rational or substantive and emotional or nonsubtantive.[13]

There is a controversy and misunderstanding that surrounds the concepts of rationality and irrationality. This is partly due to the fact that behavior is often referred to as rational or irrational without precise definitions of what these terms mean. Actually, to the individual consumer, rationality may have no meaning at all. We usually consider our own behavior as rational since we normally have good, defensible reasons for our actions. Moreover, we often feel that another person's

Fig. 1-1. Behaviorist and Cognitive Schools of Psychology Compared

Behaviorist	Cognitivist
Observed behavior is all important	What goes on in the person's mind is most relevant
Behavior is predictable	Behavior is unpredictable
A person is an information transmitter	People are information generators
The world is seen as objective	The world is seen as subjective
Behavior is rational	Behavior is irrational
People are all alike	Each person is unique
Behavior is decribed in absolute terms	Behavior is described in relative terms
Human characteristics can be studied independently	A person must be studied as a whole
Emphasizes what a person is	Emphasizes what a person can be
Behavior is completely understandable	Behavior cannot be completely understood

Based on William D. Hitt, "Two Models of Man," *American Psychologist*, Vol. 24, July, 1969, pp. 651-58.

behavior is rational if we can explain it. Attribution theory is used to study the process by which we explain our own behavior and the behavior of others.

Often, consumers' economic motives are described as rational while their emotional needs are viewed as nonrational. We might say that behavioral theories that view behavior as logical, reasoned, predictable, and externally explainable are rational or substantive. On the other hand, those theories that consider behavior to be unrealistic, emotional, unpredictable, and externally nonexplainable are considered nonrational or nonsubstantive. However, from the consumer's own point of view, his or her own behavior is probably reasonable, logical, and understandable—that is, rational. Figure 1-2 lists the major theories that have been advanced as either rational (substantive) or nonrational (nonsubstantive).

Fig. 1-2 Theories of Consumer Behavior

Substantive	Nonsubstantive
Economic man	Psychoanalytic
Problem solving or decision making	Social
Risk avoidance	Impulse
Learning	Random choice or probabilistic

Substantive Theories

Essentially, substantive theories take the view that consumers approach the buying process armed with adequate information or the capability and ambition for acquiring necessary knowledge to make the decision. Given this information, consumers carefully weigh alternatives and arrive at a rational purchase decision.

Economic Man Here, the customer is completely informed about the product without significant personal cost or effort. The consumer's needs are stable and realistic—that is, he or she wants and needs the kinds of things that will satisfy physical needs. Also, this economic person is intelligent and diligent in making purchase choices and in selecting the places where purchases are made.

Problem Solving or Decision Making The problem-solving or decision-making theory suggests that the consumer does not possess all relevant information about alternatives, and the acquisition of such information requires time and effort. Some of this customer's needs are not completely stable and realistic, and most purchases involve a degree of economic and psychological risk. This buyer carefully uses information acquired to select rationally from among alternatives those that meet his or her needs. Of course, some mistakes are made, but they are generally few and insignificant.

Risk Avoidance The concept of risk avoidance also builds on the premise that customers are decision makers who try to solve buying problems through a decision process. The theory stresses the fact that customers possess relatively little information about their alternatives, and, even if they were willing to make great efforts to obtain such information, they would inevitably face considerable uncertainty about the consequences of the purchases made. The theory emphasizes that customers must take risks, often substantial risks, when they make purchases. Consumer behavior is seen in this theory as a rational response to purchase decisions that involve risk. Choices are explained as intelligent efforts to minimize risk. The theory stresses the value of brand and company reputation and suggests caution in marketing product features that are too unique.

Learning The substantive approach of learning relies heavily on the rather diverse theories posited by Pavlov and Skinner. In part, learning theory suggests that consumers learn mainly from their actual shopping experiences and gradually simplify the buying process by developing habitual purchase patterns. Differences in consumer perceptions and motives are specifically treated as they influence choice.

Nonsubstantive Theories

The nonsubstantive theories of buyer behavior differ from the substantive theories on several bases. First, they emphasize the lack of information available to customers about a large majority of products. They also argue that most customers do not go to the trouble to evaluate and compare available alternatives. Nonsubstantive theories suggest that many product and brand differences are quite intangible. Finally, and perhaps most important, they stress the emotional, unrealistic, and sometimes even destructive goals and needs that underlie many purchases.[14]

Psychoanalytic Much of the thinking embodied in the psychoanalytic school can be attributed to Sigmund Freud and his followers. Motivation research has its roots in this theory, which suggests that purchases are highly complex activities grounded in motivations of which the consumer is often not aware. According to this theory, the researcher must dig deeply into the consumer's unconscious mind to uncover the "real" reasons for purchases. These reasons tend to be highly individualistic. Thus, it is extremely difficult to predict or even to explain behavior. Data from motivation research is often interpreted in a subjective manner, and the conclusions drawn often depend heavily upon the perceptions of the analyst.

A few examples will give you a flavor of the results of psychoanalytic research, which is generally referred to as motivation research. A convertible automobile has been likened to a mistress and freedom, while a station wagon or sedan is viewed as representing the wife, family, and restrictions. Shaving is a symbolic emasculation that must be followed by a strong after-shave lotion. In one ad, the shaver was given a slap with the after-shave and responded with, "Thanks, I needed that." Baking a cake is symbolic of giving birth and is thus a highly creative experience. This led at least one packaged cake mix producer to separate the ingredients into different packages and "allow" the cook to add fresh eggs and milk from her own refrigerator.

Social Actions Each individual lives in society and is influenced by other individuals and groups within that society. Membership in or aspiration to certain groups, such as clubs or social classes, may have implied or overt requirements for acquiring and displaying certain products. Some items thus become status symbols reflecting the life-styles of various groups. The types of items purchased and even the nature of the purchase process itself are often influenced by formal or informal group affiliations.

Impulse Actions Here, purchasers are seen as making many purchases on the spur of the moment, without prior thought or planning. If no thought or information seeking precedes the purchase, the buyer may be considered nonrational.

There is some difficulty in determining whether a given purchase was made on impulse or whether an apparent on-the-spot decision was the culmination of previous deliberation or a habitual act. One attempt at measuring impulse buying asked grocery shoppers for their shopping lists as they entered the store and considered any purchase not cited on the list as an impulse purchase.[15] What the study failed to account for was the fact that many items purchased in the grocery store are staples purchased on a regular basis. These programmed purchases are certainly not acts of impulse. In addition, shoppers often use the well-organized shelf displays in the supermarket as a sort of "substitute list" to remind themselves of items to be purchased. While many retailers feel that effective displays may trigger impulse purchases, it is unclear whether such purchases are true impulsive acts or whether, in fact, purchases have been made as planned or merely earlier than anticipated. In any event, to the extent that retail sales may be enhanced for any individual store by effective display techniques, the theory may have some value for retail strategists.

Random Choice or Probabilistic Because many purchases are trivial and differences between brands are slight, some researchers hold that purchases can be best explained as random acts. Generally, research in this area has focused on predicting brand-switching behavior. There is good evidence that probabilistic models sometimes do as well as or better than more complex behavioral models in predicting brand choice.[16]

All of these theories have some merit, and each explains some facet of buyer behavior. The theories, in and of themselves, are incomplete, however, and they often contradict one another. Two assumptions seem to underlie the theories. First, they seem to assume that individuals in the marketplace all behave in essentially the same way. Second, they posit that all buying behavior is pretty much the same regardless of what the consumer is buying. Both of these assumptions are subject to challenge.

The theories discussed here, along with others that have grown out of them, provide the historical underpinning of modern consumer research and theory. We must draw upon these theories and enrich and integrate them, while adding empirical findings to strengthen their explanatory and predictive powers.

Plan of the Book

As students of marketing we are interested in designing effective marketing strategies to move goods to customers economically and profitably. The development of a marketing strategy involves identifying and understanding the target market for products and developing an effective mix of activities to get products to that target market. The marketing mix consists of all of those strategy elements that are at least partially controllable. Figure 1-3 diagrams a general model of marketing management. At the center of any marketing strategy is the consumer and his or her needs. Moving out from the center are the elements that are more or less controllable by the marketing manager. In the outer ring are those external forces and conditions that affect a marketing strategy but are more or less uncontrollable, particularly in the short run. Sometimes a portion of a marketing or corporate strategy may be aimed at modifying or influencing some of these external forces, such as public policy and consumer tastes and attitudes.

Earlier in the chapter some problems and challenges were noted that face the student of consumer behavior. Although there are major difficulties in understanding and acting upon consumer behavior, a great deal is known about how consumers behave. Over the years a significant body of theory and empirical evidence has built

Fig. 1-3. Marketing Management Model

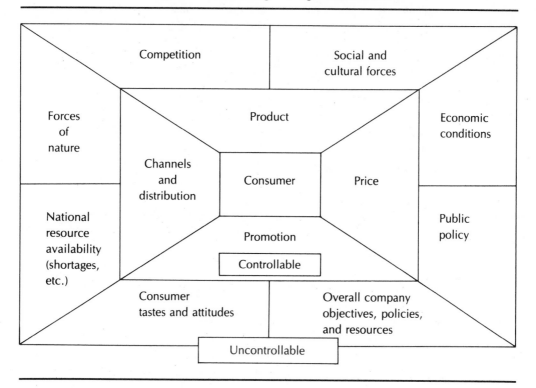

up around the study of consumer behavior. The marketing manager can and should draw heavily from this body of theory and knowledge in formulating a marketing strategy and reacting to or even shaping environmental forces. The design of this text is to help you do precisely that. As you read the text you should become aware of and sensitive to the building body of knowledge and the limitations that currently derive from corporate experience and business and academic research.

Chapter 2 provides a fundamental overview of consumer behavior, built around concepts of consumer decision making and information processing. The next six chapters summarize the major contributions of the behavioral sciences to our understanding of consumer behavior. Chapters 3 through 6 discuss internal behavioral forces at work in the consumer while chapters 7 and 8 treat broader social and cultural influences on behavior.

Chapter 3 discusses the sensory and perceptual processes by which the consumer becomes aware of and understands the environment. Since it involves the interpretation of the world around us, perception is the basis for much of our consumer behavior. The rest of the chapter treats attribution theory—the process by which we perceive the reasons why things happen.

Chapter 4 continues to look at individual behavior in dealing with consumer needs, motives, and personality. Consumer needs lie at the heart of buying behavior since buying, consuming, and influencing activities are generally aimed at need satisfaction. Motivation is the force that drives us to satisfy our needs, and personality represents the more or less consistent and predictable behavior patterns that are developed over time.

Chapter 5 is concerned with the process by which consumers learn about products and form habitual buying patterns based on learned responses. Included here are several theories of learning, all of which may contribute to our understanding of consumer behavior.

Chapter 6 moves from the realm of the psychologist to the concerns of the social psychologist. Consumers form attitudes that serve to express and organize their feelings. In general, consumers come to either like or dislike products through their experience, and these feelings at least partially guide and direct their buying behavior.

Chapters 7 and 8 are concerned with the contributions of sociologists and anthropologists to our understanding of buying behavior. Many purchases are influenced by various social forces—friends, roles, status, family, subcultures, and the overall culture.

The study of consumer behavior requires careful and effective research techniques. Chapter 9 provides a general overview of the methodology that underlies data collection and analysis relative to consumer behavior.

The emphasis in this text is on applying behavioral principles and research to the formulation of marketing strategy. Accordingly, the second part of the text looks at the various elements of the market mix and the ways in which consumer behavior affects each of these strategic elements.

Chapters 10 through 12 treat the product variable. Chapter 10 is concerned with the ways consumers accept and adopt products. Chapter 11 is particularly concerned with behavioral inputs to new and ongoing product strategy. Chapter 12 continues with a discussion of how consumer behavior influences branding and packaging decisions.

Chapter 13 deals with a behavioral view of pricing. The price of a product elicits a behavioral response and may influence consumer perceptions of products.

Chapters 14 and 15 continue with a discussion of promotional decisions and strategies. No doubt promotion, particularly advertising and personal selling, has received more attention from consumer researchers than any other single area. These two chapters develop the major behavioral contributions to these strategic elements.

The final element of the marketing mix is distribution strategy. Marketers must decide on the best way to reach consumers with their products through assorted marketing institutions. Chapter 16 investigates relevant behavioral contributions at both the overall channel strategy and the retail store level.

Chapter 17 is concerned with the problem of public policy as directed toward marketing practices and consumer information and protection. Often consumer-related policy is not well grounded in behavioral concepts. This chapter attempts to treat both problems and opportunities in the application of behavioral theory and research to public policy issues. Finally, chapter 18 provides a brief overview of the interface between behavioral concepts and marketing strategy formulation.

SUMMARY

The study of consumer behavior involves trying to understand and predict the purchase activities of buyers of all kinds of products and services. Although what we know about buyer behavior is limited at best, the development of marketing strategy demands that we begin with a knowledge of our markets. Psychology, sociology, social psychology, cultural anthropology, and economics are the major disciplines from which we draw to build a theoretical framework for understanding buyer behavior. Although difficult, the study of buyer behavior provides potential benefits to consumers, market strategists, and public policy makers. Because the study of consumer behavior is a many-faceted activity, a variety of explanations have developed. Consumer behavior has been viewed as both a substantive or rational and a nonsubstantive or nonrational activity with several theories in each area. The marketing strategist and public policy maker must work with these various theories to develop an integrated tool to aid in identifying and understanding target markets and formulating a marketing mix designed to influence buyer behavior.

CHAPTER 1 STUDY REVIEW

Important Terms and Concepts

Consumer behavior
Problems in the study of consumer behavior
Rationality
Marketing mix
Uncontrollable factors

Questions

1. Define consumer behavior.

2. What do the various behavioral disciplines contribute to the study of consumer behavior?

3. Why is it important to study consumer behavior?

4. Summarize the major theories of consumer behavior. Which seem most realistic and comprehensive to you? Why?

5. Differentiate between substantive and nonsubstantive theories of consumer behavior.

2

Consumer
Decision Making

Consumer behavior has been considered by some researchers to be virtually synonymous with consumer decision making.[1] The problem-solving theories discussed in chapter 1 emphasize the decision process. Whether the decision process is the sum total of buyer behavior or not, it is a significant phenomenon for both the consumer and the marketing strategist. The marketing manager may define the objective of promotional efforts as influencing the consumer to buy a particular product, and accomplishing that goal may involve influence of a number of activities and thought processes leading up to the actual purchase.

Buyers and sellers generally exhibit goal-directed behavior in search, promotion, and transactions. Therefore, the behavior of both parties to the marketing process may be viewed as a problem-solving activity. The consumer searches for an assortment of goods and services to satisfy a wide variety of needs and wants. The marketer provides want-satisfying products with the goal of maintaining a business and providing a return on investment. The goals of both buyer and seller can be better served through an improved understanding of the consumer decision process.

Analysis of the decision process is certainly not a new academic phenomenon. More than seventy years ago John Dewey outlined several steps in problem solving to describe the thought process of a person making a decision.[2] Since that time numerous writers have studied the decision process. The landmark work of George Katona and Eva Mueller more than twenty-five years ago preceded a large volume of research on the consumer decision process.[3] Although a number of researchers have treated consumer behavior as a decision process, there are other possible views. At the extreme, it has been suggested that a significant proportion of purchases are not accompanied by any decision process at all, even the first time an item is purchased. Actually, there are several alternative purchase strategies that may not involve decision making, including random choice, novelty seeking, conditioned behavior, and buying on impulse.[4] In any case, consumer decision making has been the topic of a great deal of theory and research.

The Nature of Decision Making

Several conditions are necessary for an activity to be considered a decision process.[5] First, a decision maker must face a problem or conflict situation that requires a solution. A decision maker can be defined as an individual or group dissatisfied with some existing state or with the prospect of a future state and with the desire and authority to initiate actions designed to alter the existing or future state.

Second, the decision maker desires to achieve some objective or objectives. These objectives are generally expressed in terms of attaining some new state or retaining an existing one. Consumer objectives generally relate to the satisfaction derived from a product or service.

Third, in order to pursue objectives, the decision maker must generate alternative courses of action that might lead to the desired goals. Consumer alternatives relate to such factors as brands, product features, and prices.

Finally, the decision maker faces some degree of uncertainty as to which altenative will lead to satisfaction. For the consumer, the uncertainty may be grounded in such conditions as a lack of complete knowledge of alternatives or a degree of unawareness of motives.

The consumer decision process is aimed at solving problems in the purchase and use of products. In effect, the consumer is trying to deal effectively with various kinds of uncertainty through information seeking and processing. The end result is selecting and implementing some alternative a marketing firm offers. The alternative selected may or may not represent the optimum solution, and decision behavior may continually be fine tuned to bring the individual closer to an optimal state.

Types and Techniques of Problem Solving

Psychologists generally consider that true problem solving takes place only when an individual faces a new situation. In analyzing consumer decisions, problem solving has traditionally been viewed as taking place anytime a purchase decision is faced. However, uniqueness of the situation is a major determinant of the degree of problem solving in which the consumer will engage. One author describes three levels of problem solving.[6] *Extensive problem solving* (EPS) involves a high degree of deliberation, undertaken when the consumer has had no experience with the product under consideration. *Limited problem solving* (LPS) represents moderate deliberation and is undertaken when the consumer has had experience with the product but is considering unfamiliar brands. *Routinized response behavior* (RRB) occurs when the consumer has had both product and brand experience and is characterized by little or no deliberation. RRB is likely to take place when brand loyalty exists or when purchases are made out of habit.

Decision-making or problem-solving strategies can be of several types.

Mechanical Mechanical solutions may be arrived at in three ways. A consumer faced with a purchase problem may proceed with *trial and error,* buying several brands more or less at random until a satisfactory one is found. *Rote* decisions result from following set decision rules. For example, "I always buy the cheapest (or most expensive) brand;" "I always buy from a large (or small) retailer." Finally, decisions can simply be reduced to *habit* (RRB), in which case a consumer automatically buys the same brand time after time with no consideration of other brands.

Understanding Many times decisions cannot reasonably be made mechanically. Cost or risk may be too high, so the first decision has to be acceptable. Usually, the consumer will first consider general properties of the product that will meet his or her needs. Then a specific brand will be selected.

Insight Insight is said to occur suddenly, after a considerable amount of unproductive thought. A consumer may wrestle for some time trying to arrive at an appropriate problem solution. Suddenly somthing will click and the solution is obvious ("Why didn't I think of that sooner?").

For example, consider the case in which my teenage son and I recently bought a set of tires for an older car. We wanted radial tires, but we wanted to economize if possible. After finding that recapped radials are of inferior quality and that no seconds were available in the required size, we were about to spend $250 on the tires when my son said, "Let's check the junkyard." His insight netted a nearly new set of radials for only $75.00.

Intuition Intuitive decisions are considered to be illogical. A consumer may buy an item because the package is a pretty color. Often, we use feelings and hunches to make decisions, especially when we have no logical information.

Information Processing In EPS and, to some degree, in LPS, the consumer must often acquire and process product and brand information prior to making a decision. This problem-solving strategy is the most complex, and a great deal of attention will be devoted to it in future sections.

Components of the Decision Process

As you have gathered by now, consumer decision making is not a discrete act but rather a sequence of steps. These steps have been variously defined by numerous writers,[7] but they can be boiled down to four activities: Problem perception, deliberation, solution, and postpurchase review. Figure 2-1 presents a simple flow diagram of the consumer decision process.

Problem Perception

What alerts you to the fact that you need something? Perception is defined in the next chapter as the process by which we become aware of and interpret the world around us. Perception of a problem comes to us through our senses and involves

Fig. 2-1.   A Consumer Decision Model

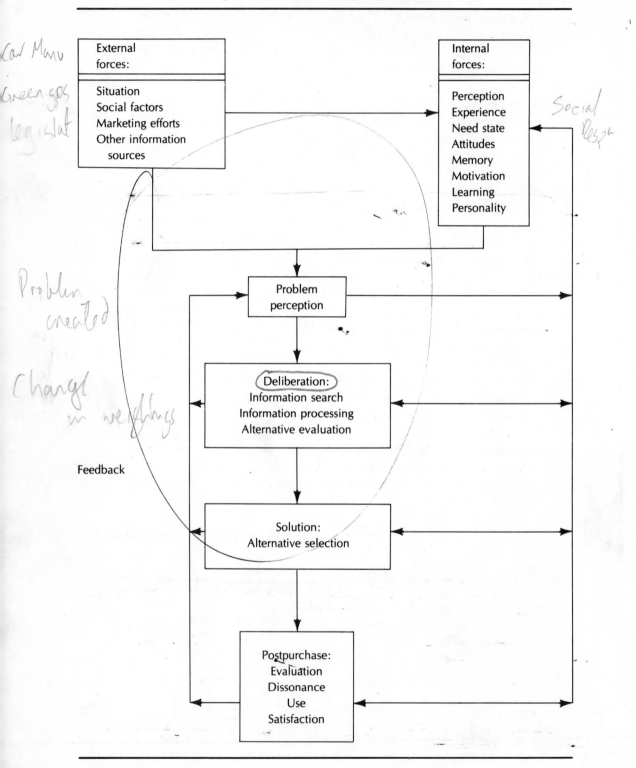

the recognition that things are not exactly as we would like them to be. Hunger represents a simple example. So long as the blood sugar level remains sufficiently high, an individual recognizes no problem. However, once the level drops below some critical level, the brain is signaled that the organism needs food. The brain signals the stomach to churn, and the individual begins to feel like eating. The problem of being hungry is thus perceived, and need arousal occurs. Of course, not all human problems are physical, and psychological needs are typically more complex than physical ones.

Consumer problems can arise from a number of sources. Various studies of consumer decision making have identified seven.

First, depletion may lead to problem recognition. Many of the products we buy are used up and replaced regularly. When we run out of the item, or perhaps slightly before, a problem is perceived.

Second, an action that we have taken to solve a problem in the past may become unsatisfactory for some reason. Sometimes this comes simply as a result of a product's wearing out. Other factors, however, may result in such problem recognition. For example, the rising price of gasoline may lead one to perceive a large automobile, which previously satisfied a variety of needs, as too costly to operate.

Third, changing family circumstances may give rise to problem perception. The birth of children, for instance, will result in new problems to solve as needs for baby food, clothing, furniture, and perhaps a new home suddenly arise.[8] As family composition changes, desired states are continually changing. Children's needs and expectations change dramatically as they grow older, influencing the entire family. A change in the place of employment of a family member can lead to a new desired state for housing, thus giving rise to problem recognition.[9]

Fourth, expectations for, or realization of, a change in financial status can affect consumer perceptions of desired states. Expectations of improved financial conditions may be very significant in triggering problem perception in young families for higher-priced items, such as furniture, appliances, and homes. Reduced buying power arising from inflationary pressures may cause consumers to redefine needs and see purchase problems in terms of "less" rather than "more."

Fifth, solving one consumer problem will often lead to the perception of other problems. As Eric Severeid once said, "The chief cause of problems is solutions." Buying a new home may lead to the recognition of any number of purchase problems—new furniture, carpets, appliances. When you buy new clothes, your old shoes may have to be replaced.

Sixth, problem recognition may occur as a result of a change in reference group. When a member of a reference group buys an article, other members of the group may feel deprived until they likewise have such an item, and joining or aspiring to a new reference group may cause an individual to perceive new needs for status symbols necessary for acceptance in that group.

Seventh, various marketing efforts, including advertising, point-of-purchase displays, and personal selling, are often designed to create dissatisfaction with the consumer's present state. To the extent that these efforts are successful, consumers may be led to recognize new problems.

Once the consumer has recognized that some dissatisfaction exists, the problem becomes what to do about it. This leads to the deliberation phase of the decision process.

Deliberation

The deliberation phase of the decision process involves several activities. First, some sort of choice criterion is developed for making the decision. Second, information relative to potential problem solutions is sought. Third, information acquired in the search process, along with information derived from past experience and stored in the memory, is processed and applied to making a choice. Finally, as the information is applied, alternative solutions are analyzed and compared against the choice criterion.

Choice Criteria When a decision is made, there is generally some sort of goal that the decision will hopefully help the consumer reach. In consumer behavior, goals are typically pretty complex. The automobile that we decide to purchse may be expected to give transportation, but we may also anticipate prestige, power, economy, safety, and a host of other satisfactions. But how can one brand or model be compared with others to offer the bundle of product characteristics that will yield satisfaction? We must seek information about alternative purchase opportunities, but the complexity of the alternatives requires that we have some way to categorize the information inputs.

The human mind often uses simple decision rules called heuristics to simplify the decision process. These heuristics are derived from perceptual cues—signals that act as simplified representations of complex phenomena (discussed in chapter 3)— that serve to summarize a variety of stimuli and facilitate the decision process. In product buying, these cues become the choice criteria against which we compare the characteristics of various brands and products.

The choice criteria and cues coming from the consumer's environment must be organized, processed, and acted upon. The structure that is used to process the incoming stimuli is composed of opinions, attitudes, and beliefs. Essentially, these represent what we know and our predisposition to act upon what we know.

If you think about a recent purchase, you can probably identify some sort of ideal or satisfactory product that you had in mind before you actually made the purchase. The ideal product would be the embodiment of all the desirable features you want or expect, including, perhaps, size, color, dependability, flavor, texture, and strength. Sometimes a purchase alternative might be compared to a number of ideal characteristics that experience has shown to be relevant. In other cases, especially when knowledge or experience is limited or when extensive evaluation is simply considered not worth the effort, surrogate quality indicators (cues), such as brand, price, or other features not necessarily directly related to quality, might become the basis for choice.

Information Search In order to compare alternative products against a choice criterion or against one another, information must be sought and processed. This section deals with the search for information, while the next is concerned with information processing. Information search is internal if the consumer calls upon past experience and accumulated knowledge, or external, involving information received from a variety of sources from the consumer's environment. Traditionally, both research and strategy have dwelt most heavily upon external search, since it is observable and directly subject to influence through various promotional efforts. Information search has typically been studied in terms of the degree of search, information sources, and types of information sought.

Degree of Information Search Consumers often engage in little or no external information search, and many purchases are made with relatively little information. The amount of information for which a consumer will search varies and depends on characteristics of the decision and characteristics of the decision maker.

Relatively extensive information search is likely to be undertaken when experience and stored information is inadequate, inappropriate, or forgotten.[10] It would seem that the demand for information should be greater when a decision is considered more important,[11] but research does not always support this idea. It has been suggested that anxiety associated with a high degree of importance may cause consumers to curtail search and rely on brand, store, or other factors as relevant decision cues.[12]

A more complex decision is thought to elicit more active information search.[13] However, it has been found that in some instances, more complex buying situations lead to the use of heuristics or cues to reduce risk, and search is thereby inhibited.[14] Information may be objective (location of a store) or subjective (the "best" brand). Subjective information search tends to be more extensive.[15] Information search is also likely to be greater: when a consumer perceives a relatively great difference among purchase alternatives; when alternatives have both positive and negative aspects; when style and appearance are significant considerations; when high perceived risk is present (discussed in chapter 3); when the consumer is dissatisfied with previous product experience; when a purchase is not considered urgent; when special buying opportunities are not present; and when information is easily accessible.[16]

The type of product purchased and the stage of the product in its life cycle are also determinants of information seeking. Durable products like automobiles and appliances, because of their price and long time commitment, are likely to be purchased after fairly extensive information-seeking activity. Low-priced convenience items would probably be the subject of relatively little information search. Using the levels of decision making identified earlier in the chapter, it has been suggested that we might expect EPS in the introductory phase of a product's life cycle, while LPS would occur in growth, and RRB would be anticipated in the product maturity stage.[17]

Several personal factors that characterize the decision maker have been investigated to determine their influence on buyer information search. Enjoyment of shopping, dependence on others for information and advice, open-mindedness, and self-confidence are personality-related variables that have been found to lead to greater information seeking.[18]

The housewife's self-perceived role has been found to influence the information search for food products.[19] The woman typed as a "mother"—characterized by her concern for family welfare—is very interested in shopping and pays a great deal of attention to advertisements. On the other hand, information search is low for the "liberal woman," interested in politics rather than housekeeping, and the "traditionalist," who tends to follow her mother's attitudes and decision style.

Higher information-seeking activity is associated with higher social class individuals and families, younger consumers, higher-income consumers, more highly educated consumers, and families with no children.[20] In addition, information search has been found to be greater when a husband and a wife make a purchase decision jointly.[21]

Sources of Information When consumers do seek external information, it may come from a variety of sources. Information can come from personal or nonpersonal sources and from marketer-controlled or independent sources.

Consumers seem to view these categories of information quite differently. As in the degree of information search, information sources utilized and those considered most important seem to be a function of the purchase situation, the consumer, and the product purchased. In general, a large number of research studies indicate that advertising represents the most often encountered information source, but it is not considered a particularly useful or effective information source by most consumers.[22] Figure 2-2 shows the results of one study that asked consumers to indicate their willingness to be guided by each of the indicated information sources in purchasing an automobile.

Dealer visits and salespeople are often utilized as information sources, but again, they tend to rank relatively low in perceived usefulness. Personal contacts with friends are generally relatively low in terms of the number of contacts, but they rank very high in terms of credibility and usefulness. Although nonpersonal, independent information sources (including consumer test reports) are seldom used by consumers, they tend to be highly regarded by those who do use them. Figure 2-3 gives you some idea of the degree to which different information sources might be used in buying small appliances.

Types of Information Sought and Used One basic question that is important in consumer information seeking is just what kind of information do consumers need? It has been observed that prior to making an informed purchase decision, consumers must know:

1. Which product set best suits their needs and the particular brand/model/seller combinations that are part of this product set.

Fig. 2-2. Sources Used in Buying Automobiles*

1. Television	25%
2. Radio	12
3. Magazines	25
4. Newspapers	30
5. Billboards	20
6. Advertising brochures	22
7. Automobile salespersons and dealers	20
8. Friends	64
9. People at work	58
10. Gasoline station attendants	43
11. Relatives	62
12. *Consumer Reports*	78

*Percentages indicate the proportion of the sample that rated each source as more than 50 on a scale of 0 to 100.

From *Consumer Behavior: Application of Theory* by John A. Howard. Copyright © 1977 (New York: McGraw-Hill) 134. Used with the permission of McGraw-Hill Book Company.

Fig. 2-3. Sources Used in Purchasing Small Appliances

Source	%Finding Helpful[a]	%Finding Most Useful[b]
Marketer-Controlled		
Newspaper advertising	25.0%	9.6%
Mail order catalogs and circulars	20.7	10.2
Magazine advertising	15.0	2.4
Television advertising	14.2	3.7
Radio advertising	7.0	0.4
Independent		
Past brand experience	50.2	33.2
Discussions with friends, relatives, neighbors, and others	33.9	18.7
Consumer rating magazines	9.1	3.0
Telephone calls to stores	3.5	1.0

[a]Percentages do not total 100% because many respondents mentioned more than one source of information; also, less frequently mentioned sources are not shown in the table.
[b]There were 10% who could recall no helpful information other than store visits.

Jon G. Udell, "Prepurchase Behavior of Buyers of Small Electrical Appliances," *Journal of Marketing* 30 (October 1966):51. Reprinted from the *Journal of Marketing*, published by the American Marketing Association.

2. How far and wide they should search for a given product (i.e., what is the appropriate market from their perspective)?
3. What is the quality of the various brand/model/seller combinations entering into the purchase decision?
4. What are the prices of the various brand/model/seller combinations?[23]

In one study of consumer information seeking for purchase of a major appliance,[24] respondents wanted to know the advantages and disadvantages of the product's specific features and have a listing of available features across all brands and models. Besides wanting to obtain general information about how the appliance operated, consumers felt they needed additional information concerning dependability, repair frequency, operating costs, operating performance, and retail prices.

Information was sought on several product dimensions, which represent the areas of the choice criteria. Apparently consumers questioned felt good about information availability since ninety-one percent of recent buyers surveyed indicated that the overall information they received met their needs.[25] Whether consumers generally get all the information they want or need may be open to question, but there is certainly more information available than most consumers use, and, according to some researchers, too much information can lead to an overload and subsequent poor decisions.[26]

Information Processing The process by which information is received, internalized, categorized, interpreted, stored, retrieved, and applied to problem solving has received increasing attention in recent years. The study of information processing in humans parallels the development of information processing in computers. The study of consumer deliberation must include an investigation of information processing; in fact, some writers treat consumer information processing and deliberation as virtually synonymous. In this book it will be discussed in a narrower sense as the mental process that occurs between overt information search and alternative evaluation but that overlaps both. Discussion in this chapter will simply introduce the concepts of information processing. Later chapters will cover information processing further and provide useful applications.

Understanding information processing is difficult because it is largely a mental activity. What consumers report when asked about their processing is likely to be distorted either because they are unable to recall or verbalize the process or because they are, for one reason or another, unwilling to describe their thoughts accurately.

Information processing can be viewed as a "series of activities by which stimuli are transformed into information and stored."[27] Figure 2-4 provides a simple model of these activities, which are defined as follows:

Perception is the process of selecting, integrating, and organizing stimuli from the environment into a meaningful pattern. *Current memory* is new information and previously acquired information that the consumer is utilizing to reach a decision. *Retention* is information that has been acquired and is not currently being utilized although it could be transferred to current memory if needed.[28]

Fig. 2-4. Information Processing Activities

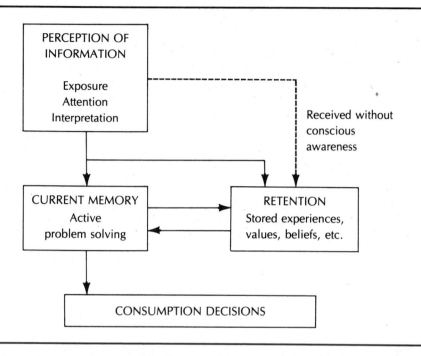

Del I. Hawkins, Kenneth A. Coney and Roger J. Best, *Consumer Behavior: Implications for Marketing Strategy*, (Dallas, Texas: Business Publications, 1980), p. 244 © 1980 by Business Publications, Inc.

Based on the activities of information processing, several principles and decision rules have been advanced. Decision strategies are categorized as compensatory or noncompensatory. In compensatory decision strategies, the consumer weighs various product attributes and averages overall attributes to form a summary evaluation. A product that is inferior on one point may be superior on another, and a superior quality can "compensate" for an inferior one. Noncompensatory rules are based on the assumption that each attribute is independent, and one cannot compensate for another.

Two compensatory strategies are the *affect-referral rule* and the *linear rule.* In the first, the consumer forms an overall attitude toward each alternative without really considering individual characteristics. Thus, a product may be selected because it's "nice" or "the best available." In the second, each alternative is evaluated on each of several dimensions, which are weighted according to importance and combined to give a summary rating. The alternative ranking highest is the one chosen.

Three noncompensatory strategies are the *conjunctive rule, disjunctive rule,* and *lexicographic rule.* In the first, the consumer forms cutoff points for each relevant dimension, and a product falling below the critical level is eliminated from consideration. For example, the consumer may shop for a new car that gets more than twenty-five miles per gallon, has front wheel drive, and seats six passengers. Any car falling below any of these standards would not be considered. Once several viable alternatives have been identified, the consumer will have to switch to another decision rule. In the second, cutoff points are established, but alternatives that pass on *any* attribute are considered. In the third, the consumer orders product characteristics according to their relative importance. The decision is made by comparing products according to the most important feature and choosing the one that is best on that dimension. Products may have other important advantages, but they are not considered. If products are alike on the most important dimension, the next most important one will become the critical one, and so on. For example, the consumer may consider price the most important factor and formulate a decision rule that says to buy the cheapest. If all alternatives are the same price, the next most important characteristic becomes the relevant choice criterion.[29]

More recently, some researchers have observed that information processing is not so much a sequentially staged activity as a set of overlapping events, as shown in figure 2-5. These events are summarized in figure 2-6.

The system consumers use to process information is complex and, as yet, not fully understood. If marketing strategists and public policy makers are to reach and influence consumer behavior effectively, they must gain the best possible insights

Fig. 2-5   Sectors of the Consumer Information Processing System

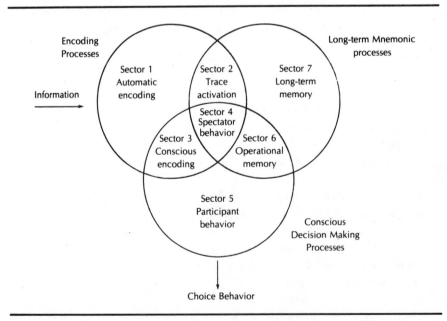

Reprinted by permission of the publisher from "Consumer Information Processing: Emerging Theory and Findings," by Robert W. Chestnut and Jacob Jacoby, in *Consumer and Industrial Buying Behavior*, by Arch G. Woodside, Jagdish N. Sheth, and Peter D. Bennett, eds., p. 124. Copyright 1977 by Elsevier North Holland, Inc.

Fig. 2-6.   Characteristics of Consumer Infomation Processing Sectors

I. Automatic Encoding
   • Effects all incoming signals (i.e., operates in parallel)
   • Operates preconsciously without requiring capacity (i.e.,attention)
   • Goes far beyond sensory recognition to create abstract (name) codes
   • Selective (extracts relevant features)
   • Elaborative (contacts memory to elaborate meaning)
   • Recodes (à la Miller) into higher order "chunks"
   • Descriptive (lists features)

II. Trace Activation
   • Operates automatically (i.e., parallel processing)
   • Provides meaning (semantic, affective, or imaginal)
   • Preconscious (only results enter consciousness)
   • Brings the contents of Long-term memory (LTM) into the perceptual process

III. Conscious Encoding
   • Involves short-term memory
   • Operates sequentially (i.e., requires attention)
   • Can transfer to sector I (via "overlearning")
   • Recodes, describes, elaborates, and selects as in sector I

IV. Spectator Behavior
   • Receives passive information
   • Little if any direct hypothesis testing
   • Leads to "intuitive" insight or solution
   • Operates in conjunction with memory to recode information

V. Participant Behavior
   • Active hypothesis testing
   • Implements "processing rules" and "heuristics"
   • Highly algorithmic
   • Available to introspection

VI. Operational Memory
   • Holding place for input from long-term memory
   • Has repeated access to LTM
   • Conscious and sequential

VII. Long-term Memory
   • Information is altered to fit previous storage
   • Recall depends on cue environment
   • Complex retrieval processes alter informational content

Reprinted by permission of the Publisher from "Consumer Information Processing: Emerging Theory and Findings," by Robert W. Chestnut and Jacob Jacoby, in *Consumer and Industrial Buying Behavior* by Arch G. Woodside, Jagdish N. Sheth, and Peter D. Bennett, eds., p. 128. Copyright 1977 by Elsevier North Holland, Inc.

into the mental processes that underlie the final decision. As was noted earlier, the topic of information processing permeates the remainder of the text as we investigate the factors that make up consumer behavior and the strategies followed to influence it.

Alternative Analysis The activities in the deliberation phase often overlap. We may enter the deliberation process with an established choice criterion, but information received during the search may change our desires and expectations, leading to a modification of the criterion. We may or may not have alternatives in mind that we want to evaluate at the outset of the decision process, but these may be continually updated through search and evaluation. Thus, the activities of deliberation (information search, information processing, and alternative evaluation) will likely be taking place simultaneously.

Determinants of Alternative Evaluation The determinants of the degree of alternative evaluation seem to be essentially the same as for information search. A possible exception was found in one study, which suggested that the number of alternatives considered tends to increase with purchase experience. It appears that previous experience in purchasing a product may, in some cases, raise the consumer's awareness of its various features, leading to choice among a larger number of product dimensions.[30] The choice criterion may be expanded with experience, leading to the necessity of more extensive alternative evaluation.

Extent of Alternative Evaluation It was noted that many consumers are not very active in information search, and alternative evaluation behavior follows a similar but more complex pattern. Numerous studies of consumer decision making indicate that a fairly large portion of consumers do evaluate alternatives. However, there is wide variability from product to product and from consumer to consumer. Alternatives may be evaluated with respect to numerous purchase dimensions, such as brand, price, store of purchase, and product features. Behavior differs from one type of alternative to another. One study found that seventy-five percent of beverage purchases, seventy-eight percent of grocery purchases, and more than ninety-five percent of washing product purchases involved consideration of more than one product alternative.[31] A study of the purchase of sport shirts and consumer durables found that seventy percent of sport shirt buyers considered more than one brand, while forty-nine percent of durable good purchasers considered alernative brands.[32] Another study of durable good purchases reported forty-one percent of respondents had considered only one refrigerator brand, forty-nine percent only one television brand, sixty-one percent considered just one brand of washing machine, sixty-five percent one brand of iron, and seventy-one percent evaluated but one brand of vacuum cleaner.[33]

The majority of consumers apparently have the price range that they consider acceptable in mind when they are involved in deliberation. One study of consumer durable purchases showed thirty-nine percent of respondents considering items in price ranges other than that of the product finally purchased. The same study found half of consumers considering sport shirts in only one price range.[34]

A study of the adequacy of purchase alternatives indicated that buyers of appliances and furniture were generally satisfied with the availability of brand and model alternatives. While ninety percent said that alternative availability was satis-factory, eight percent indicated that there were too many alternatives, and one percent felt that there were too few.[35]

Figure 2-7 gives you an idea of the product features (choice criteria) on which consumers seek to evaluate alternatives. There is a limit to the number of alternatives that consumers will consider. For example, a consumer will generally consider only a small portion of all brands available, making for greater decision efficiency. In addition, the typical consumer would probably not be aware of all brands, and even among brands the consumer is aware of, not all would be seriously considered for purchase for the following reasons:

1. Brands may be beyond the consumer's reach financially.
2. They may not be perceived as capable of meeting the consumer's needs.
3. Information may be inadequate to allow for evaluation.
4. Brand may have been previously tried and rejected.
5. Consumer may be satisfied with the brand currently used.
6. Negative feedback may have been received from various sources, such as friends or mass communication.[36]

Fig. 2-7. Alternative Features Evaluated by Consumers

Durable Goods		Sport Shirts	
Type of Feature	% of Buyers*	Type of Feature	% of Buyers*
Price	6	Price	4
Brand	21	Brand	2
Mechanical properties	21	Style, cut, color, pattern,	
Performance	9	appearance	45
Size of capacity	19	Specific fabric	34
Appearance	13	Durability	3
Durability, service,		Washability	14
guarantee, reliability	2	Special sizes	2
Operating costs	1	Other	1
No specific features	39	No specific features	23
Other	3	Not ascertained	3
Not ascertained	3		

*Percentages do not add up to 100% because some respondents mentioned more than one feature.

George Katona and Eva Mueller, "A Study of Purchase Decisions," in Lincoln H. Clark, ed., *Consumer Behavior: The Dynamics of Consumer Reaction* (New York: New York University Press, 1955), p. 49.

The brands the consumer actively considers before purchase are referred to as the evoked set. The evoked set is generally a maximum of seven brands and usually less than five.[37] This seems to hold for both low-priced convenience goods and for consumer durables, and the limits extend to the number of prices considered and the number of stores shopped, as well as to the number of brands considered.[38]

In addition, two other alternative sets, referred to as the inert set and the inept set, have been identified as part of the overall awareness set.[39] The inert set is made up of those brands for which the consumer has neither a positive nor a negative feeling. The consumer is aware of them but may not have sufficient information to evaluate them one way or the other; or information may be available, but the consumer does not perceive them to be better than the brands in the evoked set. The inept set consists of brands rejected either because of an unpleasant experience or because of negative feedback from information sources. Thus, the inept set includes brands the consumer is unwilling to consider for purchase at all in their present form.

Patterns of Deliberation Consumer deliberation activities result in a wide range of behaviors. In attempts to study information-seeking behavior, some researchers suggest that consumer decision-making strategies could be categorized according to information acquisition patterns. One study identified three basic information search patterns: (1) nonthorough (few store visits and little out-of-store information utilized); (2) store intense (numerous store visits but little additional information used); and (3) thorough and balanced (many store visits and much nonstore information utilized).[40]

A second study identified four distinct groups based on information search strategies: (1) objective shoppers, (2) moderate shoppers, (3) store-intense shoppers, and (4) personal advice seekers (see figure 2-9).[41] Objective shoppers were characterized by heavy use of retail and neutral information sources (books, pamphlets, magazines, and newspaper articles), nonuse of personal information sources (friends, neighbors, and relatives), and consideration of a wide range of brand alternatives. In addtion, they were highly educated, the purchase decision was more apt to be joint (husband-wife), and the need to purchase the item was not urgent.

Moderate shoppers visited the fewest retail stores, relied on neither neutral nor personal information sources, and considered relatively few brands. This group was older, more likely to be replacing a broken item, and less apt to be engaging in joint decision making.

Store-intense shoppers visited the greatest number of stores but relied less on neutral sources and more on personal sources. Store-intense shoppers were the youngest group, most likely to be buying the item for the first time, buying jointly, and considering more brand alternatives than any other group.

The last group, personal advice seekers, visited relatively few stores and depended primarily on personal information sources. These decision makers were somewhat younger, lowest in education, and they considered the fewest brand alternatives.

It seems that there are characteristic decision patterns. Research in this area is not well enough established to draw final conclusions, but preliminary findings suggest useful inputs to marketing strategy formulation.

Fig. 2-8

Many advertisements like this one, are designed to bring a lessor known brand from nonawareness or the inert set into the consumer's evoked set.

Courtesy of BA Cheque Corporation, BankAmerica Company.

Fig. 2-9. Patterns of Information Usage

	Objective Shoppers	Moderate Shoppers	Store Intense Shoppers	Personal Advice Seekers
		Segment*		
Retail Stores Visited				
Visited 0-1	–%	67%	–%	55%
Visited 2-3	62	33	8	45
Visited 4+	32	–%	92	–%
Total	100	100	100	100
Mean	3.42	1.18	4.44	2.0
Use of Neutral Sources				
Total using source	76%	56%	35%	24%
Main source	51	19	–%	–%
Mean	1.27	.75	.35	.24
Use of Personal Sources				
Total using source	–%	19%	81%	100%
Main source	–%	–%	21	67
Mean	0.0	.19	1.02	1.67

*Both chi square and ANOVA F - statistics for differences between segments significant beyond .001 level.

Adapted from Robert A. Westbrook and Claes Fornell, "Patterns of Information Source Usage Among Durable Goods Buyers," *Journal of Marketing Research* 14 (August 1979):309. Reprinted from the *Journal of Marketing Research,* published by the American Marketing Association.

Problem Solution

Having recognized the existence of a problem, defined desired purchase goals, and searched for and processed information relevant to potentially viable alternatives, the consumer is ready to choose the alternative that seems to have the best chance of solving the problem. The first thing to occur here is the formation of the intention to buy a particular "satisfaction bundle" (brand, product). The intention may or may not actually result in actual purchase, depending on a variety of intervening forces.

Purchase Intention Versus Realization Presumably, a consumer will attempt to match available alternatives as closely as possible with the established criterion. The feelings toward various alternatives are referred to as brand image. As noted in later chapters, consumers don't buy products, per se; rather, they buy benefits to be derived. Furthermore, these benefits must be relevant to a consumer's situation.[42] Therefore, simply having a positive attitude toward a particular brand is not sufficient reason to purchase it. As one writer observes, product attributes may be quite different from desirable purchase outcomes.

> . . . the distinction between attitude toward an object and attitude toward a behavior is a very important one, and one that has been ignored. . . . Even though I may

think some product has all kinds of good attributes, I may not believe buying or using that product will lead to valued outcomes. That is, even though I may have a positive attitude toward "Brand X," I might not have a positive attitude toward "buying Brand X," and according to behavioral decision theory, it is this latter attitude that should be related to buying behavior. For example, a woman might believe that "high pile carpeting" is "warm," "comfortable," "luxurious," and "prestigious," and since she positively evaluates those attributes, she is likely to have a positive attitude toward "high pile carpeting." However, what do you think the consequences of "buying high pile carpeting" are for that woman if she has two dogs, a cat, and three children under nine?[43]

Later chapters will be dealing more with the relationship between attitude and behavior. Suffice it to say for now that attitude often does not directly predict behavior. For this reason purchase intentions are often treated probabilistically. In one study treating intentions as probabilities of purchase, it was found that a fairly large proportion of automobile purchases followed consumers' prior probabilities of purchase fairly closely, with seventy-nine percent of those who said they were sure they would buy having purchased a car within one year.[44] Another study comparing "intent-to-buy" measures with actual purchasing behavior found that in advertising a variety of products, about half of the consumers who indicated an intention to buy an advertised item also put their names on coupons for home delivery. In addition, consumers who remembered an ad in recall testing indicated twice the intention to buy and placed twice as many coupon orders as those who could not recall the ad.[45]

Buyer confidence is important in determining whether intentions will be translated into purchase behavior.[46] Confidence may refer to the consumer's confidence in his or her ability to judge or evaluate attributes of the brands considered, or it may simply relate to the buyer's overall confidence in the brand.[47] Presumably, if the buyer has higher confidence by either definition, the probability that purchase intentions will be realized will be higher.

Situational Influences It was noted earlier that the circumstances surrounding a purchase may influence the decision. Situation has been defined as "all those factors particular to a time and place of observation which do not follow from a knowledge of personal (intra-individual) and stimulus (choice alternative) attributes, and which have a demonstratable and systematic effect on current behavior."[48] Another definition considers situation in terms of the psychology of the individual in transforming the situational input to behavioral output.[49]

Several research studies have shown that product and brand selection are, in part, determined by the purchase situation. For example, preferences for snack food and meat products were partially explained by the purchase situaton.[50] Another study identified four eating situations that led to different choices of eating places: lunch on a weekday, snack during a shopping trip, evening meal when rushed for time, and evening meal when not rushed for time.[51] The choice of eating place and the importance of several attributes of the outlets were related to the eating situations. In all but the snack during a shopping trip situation, eating place selection could be predicted with some accuracy from the situation.

A number of situational factors may influence the consumer's decision process and ultimate product choice. These factors can be grouped into five categories. First, physical surroundings, such as location, decor, sounds, aromas, lighting, and merchandise displays, will be among the most readily apparent features of a situation. Second, persons, personal characteristics, and interpersonal relationships involved in the purchase situation comprise the social surroundings. Various temporal aspects of the purchase, including time since last purchase, time between meals, and time constraints, make up the third group. The deliberation-shopping-purchase task itself is the fourth variable. This includes the intent or requirement to shop, information gathering, and various buyer and user roles, such as buying jewelry as a gift. Finally, such antecedent states as mood, cash on hand, fatigue, and illness may influence the purchase. These momentary states are immediately related to the purchase situation and do not include feelings surrounding the purchase itself.[52]

Decision Time Another aspect of the problem solution is the length of time it takes for the consumer to make the final choice. The choice can be made virtually instantaneously, as in the case of impulse buying, or it can take many years. Generally, the length of decision time is determined by the same factors that determine the extent of information search and alternative evaluation. Impulse buying is a special case that bears further discussion.

Impulse purchasing has been defined as "buying action undertaken without problems previously having been recognized or a buying intention formed prior to entering the store."[53] While some studies suggest that very large proportions of purchases made in grocery stores and drug stores[54] are impulse purchases, the validity of the figures is doubtful. For example, in a study of grocery store impulse purchase, any purchase made that was not on the consumer's written shopping list was considered an impulse purchase.[55] In fact, many grocery store purchases are routine and therefore not listed. Many decisions, such as specific types of meat to buy, are made in the store, depending on "what looks good" and "what is on sale."[56]

In order to deal with the complexity of deciding what actually constitutes an impulse purchase, a four-way definition was developed some years ago. *Pure impulse* is probably classic impulse buying and involves a complete departure from normal brand or product selection. The consumer has absolutely no idea that the purchase will take place before seeing the product displayed. *Reminder impulse* is common in the grocery store. Often consumers use the product displays as a surrogate shopping list. Walking up and down the store aisles, the consumer is reminded to buy various items. This type of purchase is often triggered when a consumer sees an item displayed and remembers that the supply at home is depleted. *Suggestion impulse* is similar to reminder impulse buying except that the item has not been seen before. The consumer sees a can of "Carpet Fresh" displayed on the shelf and remembers the careless puppy at home. The purchase is considered suggestion impulse if the consumer had not heard of the product before and bought it on the spot. *Planned impulse* buying occurs as the consumer goes into the store planning to make purchase decisions as to brand, style, etc., once having seen merchandise in the store. This behavior is especially common in buying grocery products when such factors as special prices and different cuts of meat are involved.[57]

Thus, much of what might be considered unplanned purchasing may not be so impulsive at all. Much of the purchasing that appears to be "off the wall" is really the result of carefully thought out purchasing strategy.

When impulse buying does take place, several factors seem to be important determinants. One study of impulse buying found no relationship between the economic, demographic or psychographic characteristics of those who made impulse buying decisions and those who did not.[58] However, variables were identified that did seem to influence impulse buying.[59] Unplanned purchases relative to planned purchases increased with the size of the grocery bill. Impulse purchases increased with the number of items purchased. The proportion of unplanned purchases was greater for major shopping trips as opposed to fill-in trips. Products purchased frequently were unlikely to be purchased on impulse. Shoppers with large shopping lists purchased fewer items on impulse. The number of unplanned purchases increased with the number of years a couple had been married.

Situational factors also appear to have an effect on impulse buying. One type of situation involves the consumer buying snack foods so they could later be consumed on impulse. Because the consumer plans to make the purchase decision in the store, the purchase can be considered planned impulse. For example, you are shopping for a snack that you or your family can eat while watching television in the evenings. Or, snacks around your house have become a little dull lately, and you are wondering what you might pick up that would be better. In a third situation, you are at the supermarket and notice the many available snack products. You wonder if you should pick something up in case friends drop by.

Another situation fits the notion of pure impulse buying more closely: You are in the grocery store when you get an urge for a between-meal snack.

Finally, the consumption of the product is planned, but the consumer plans to make a specific decision in the store. For example, you are planning a party for a few close friends and are wondering what to have around to snack on.[60]

Obviously, impulse buying is a complex process. It is difficult to tell from observation whether a purchase is made completely on impulse or whether making a decision in the store is part of a carefully structured buying plan. In any case, it does appear that good store layout and display can aid the consumer in decision making and perhaps trigger purchases that would not otherwise be made.

There are numerous other dimensions of choice, including brand loyalty, store choice, and nonstore buying. These factors will be considered in subsequent chapters that consider marketing strategy for influencing these areas.

Postpurchase Review

The consumer decision process is not over when the final choice is made. Once a purchase has been made, the consumer can use that product to solve the problem that was originally recognized. In so doing, the consumer will compare the product performance against the choice criterion. The result will be some level of satisfaction or dissatisfaction. This will become an input to future purchase decisions.

Postcognitive Dissonance Dissonance theory has been utilized to explain consumer postpurchase behavior.[61] Viewed in terms of dissonance theory, the consumer is faced with the necessity of collecting and evaluating information about alternatives leading to commitment to an alternative (choice). With this commitment, dissonance and the pressure to reduce it begin to exert their influence. Essentially, dissonance is psychological discomfort, and because it is uncomfortable, the consumer tries to reduce it. If the consumer's experience with the product is satisfactory, the reduction of postcognitive dissonance should lead to increased preference for the brand purchased, thus increasing the probability of repurchase.[62]

Independent of whether the consumer is satisfied or dissatisfied with the alternative selected, dissonance is likely to occur simply because the consumer can't buy everything, and rejected alternatives are likely to have attractive features. The theory says that postcognitive dissonance can occur under three conditions: (1) after making an important or difficult decision; (2) after being coerced to say or do something that is contrary to personal attitudes, opinions, or beliefs; and (3) after being exposed to discrepant information.[63]

Consumer buying decisions could conceivably fall into any of these categories. Purchases involving major financial commitments or with strong social or psychological overtones are fairly common. When you last purchased an automobile, a stereo, or new clothes, perhaps you felt some anxiety or uncertainty as to whether you made the right decision. This is sometimes referred to as buyer's remorse.

The second source of dissonance is harder to identify in buying situations,[64] but in cases where a fast-talking salesperson influences a consumer to buy, or in emergency buying situations, we may find conditions approximating forced compliance. Door-to-door salespeople who have historically used high-pressure tactics, must reevaluate their techniques in view of the seventy-two hour contract recision period applied to many sales made in homes. Postcognitive dissonance may lead a consumer to rescind a purchase contract if there is adequate opportunity to reconsider after the contract is signed.

The consumer is exposed to discrepant information almost constantly. The extreme is perhaps the health warning related to cigarette smoking, but there are other examples. How did you feel the last time you made a purchase only to find a product later that you perceived as better able to meet your needs? Or what was your reaction to seeing an advertisement for the product you bought yesterday with the product on sale for five dollars less? That feeling was postcognitive dissonance.

The way consumers handle dissonance may give marketing managers clues as to how to reduce it and thereby raise the probability of consumers' repurchasing their brands. There are numerous ways in which consumers may seek to reduce dissonance.

1. They may seek information supporting their decision.
2. They may try to convince themselves that their decision was wise by telling others what a "good deal" they got.
3. They may distort, avoid, ignore, and discount incoming discrepant information.
4. They may resolve to try another brand next time.
5. They may simply ignore the feeling until it goes away.

Marketers have tried to provide specific advertisements to dispel cognitive dissonance,[65] but any advertisement espousing the benefits of the brand could accomplish that. Adequate instructions, good warranties, and effective after-purchase service will also help dispel dissonance.

Although research results on dissonance are equivocal, the theory seems valid and applicable to purchasing decisions.[66] In any case, the marketer is well advised to consider the effects of cognitive dissonance. Specific applications will be treated in later chapters.

Purchase Satisfaction Related to the concept of dissonance is the idea of consumer satisfaction and dissatisfaction. To what degree are consumers satisfied with their purchases? What factors lead to satisfaction and dissatisfaction? Recent developments in consumerism and consumer protection suggest that consumers are often dissatisfied with business and its attempts to supply need satisfaction. In fact, buyers are often pictured by critics as being frustrated by an inability to obtain useful purchase information, resentful of a lack of personal attention in dealing with sellers, confused by a proliferation of product models and brands, and upset over the inability to find products and services that meet their needs.[67]

Consumers have expressed some dissatisfaction in studies seeking reaction to general statements negative to the marketing system.[68] These studies generally found about forty percent of respondents to be "probusiness," with about twenty to sixty percent expressing varying degrees of satisfaction.

Studies that deal with consumer satisfaction for specific purchases, however, find a different picture. High levels of satisfaction with individual purchases have been found when questioning consumers about their experiences with a wide variety of purchases.[69] In one study dealing with recent and ongoing purchases of appliances and focusing on a variety of dimensions of the purchase process, positive reaction ranged from thirty-five to over ninety percent. Generally, the study found that "consumers find enjoyment and satisfaction in their buying experiences for durables considerably more often than they find difficulty and discontent."[70]

When consumers do experience dissatisfaction in purchasing, it comes from a variety of sources. Marketers should be concerned with reducing these sources of dissatisfaction as much as possible. The more significant sources of dissatisfaction are the following:

1. Too many or too few brands
2. Inability to find desired features

3. Information availability (or lack of it)
4. Nuisance or bother to visit retail outlets
5. Difficulty in judging brand performance or product features
6. Feeling rushed or hurried in making the decision[71]
7. Dissatisfaction with manufacturers' efforts to meet consumer needs
8. Not improving products
9. Planned obsolescence
10. Insignificant differences among brands
11. Advertising not believable
12. Prices too high
13. Failure of manufacturers to back guarantee[72]

The purchase decision process is a complex activity. It may occur very quickly, or it may extend over many months or even years. We have looked at a few of the more significant aspects here, but our discussion has only scratched the surface. One important dimension of the process that has not been developed here is the decision made by the family. Buying decisions are often made not by individuals but by family units. A discussion of family decision making appears in chapter 8.

Models of Buyer Decision Making

Since the consumer decision process is so complex, several writers have attempted to reduce the process to simplified models. The purpose of a model is to identify the more significant activities or characteristics of a phenomenon, show the determinants of the phenomenon, and treat the relationships among activities, characteristics, and determinants.

Two models of buyer decision making have received extensive attention and research effort. The first of these was originally advanced in 1968,[73] has been refined through three editions of the text, and appears in its most recent form in figure 2-10.

This model is useful in that the complex decision process can be seen at a glance. The stages of decision making are similar to those just investigated. However, the model treats deliberation as two separate stages—search and alternative evaluation. The model deals with information input and processing on the far left side, which feeds through active memory to provide inputs through the problem recognition stage. Feedback to the individual's memory occurs through the loops from search and decision outcomes. Influences from the right side of the model are both internal and external. Motives and predispositions influence the evaluative criteria and the various decision stages; external forces come from cultural norms, reference groups, and situational factors, found at the extreme right of the model.

A second model was first advanced in 1963 by John Howard.[74] The model shown in figure 2-11 was refined in 1969.[75] This model gives the stages in the decision process as attention, brand comprehension, attitude, intention, and purchase. These activities correspond closely to those in the Engel-Blackwell-Kollat model and those discussed earlier in this chapter. In a later model (see figure 2-12),

Fig. 2-10. Engel-Blackwell-Kollat Buyer Decision Model

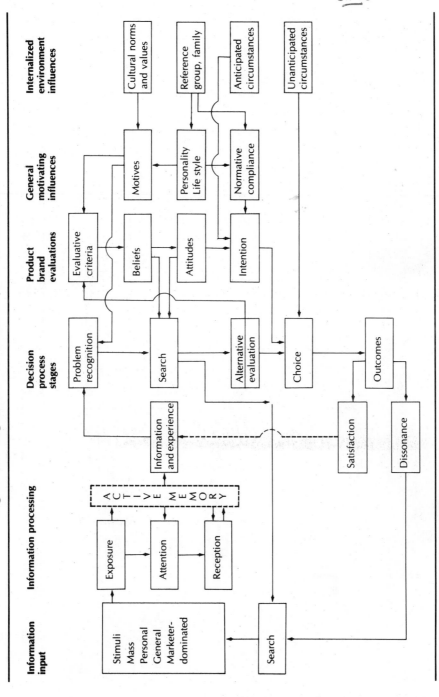

From *Consumer Behavior*, Third Edition, by James F. Engel, Roger D. Blackwell and David T. Kollat, p.492. Copyright © 1978 by The Dryden Press, a division of Holt, Rinehart and Winston. Reprinted by permission of Holt, Rinehart and Winston.

Fig. 2-11. Howard-Sheth Consumer Behavior Model

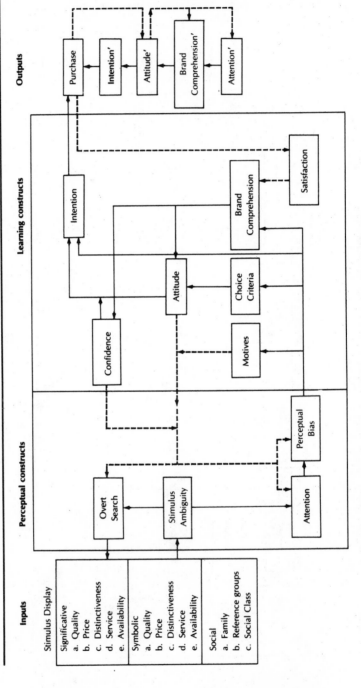

Solid lines indicate flow of information; dashed lines, feedback effects.

John A. Howard and Jagdish N. Sheth, *The Theory of Buyer Behavior*, (New York: John Wiley & Sons 1969), p. 31.

Fig. 2-12. Howard Consumer Behavior Model

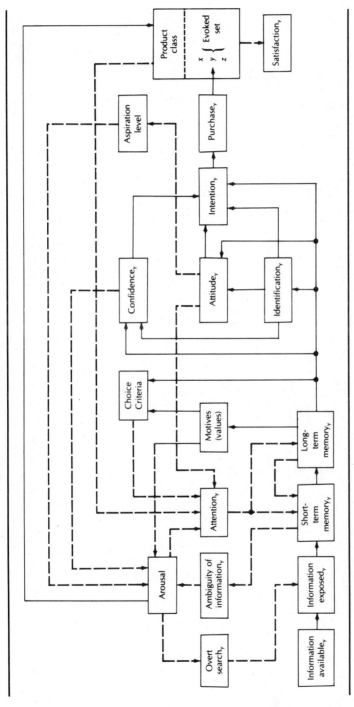

From *Consumer Behavior: Application of Theory*, by John A. Howard. Copyright © 1977 by McGraw-Hill, Inc. 138. Used with permission of McGraw-Hill Book Co.

Fig. 2-13. Effects of Exogeneous Variables

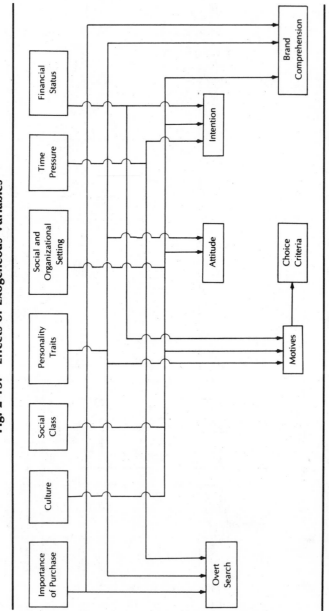

John A. Howard and Jagdish N. Sheth, *The Theory of Buyer Behavior*, (New York: John Wiley & Sons, 1969), p. 92.

Howard included arousal, evoked set, and memory, which make the model more complete.[76]

Arousal relates to problem perception, giving rise to attention, whereby the consumer becomes alert to relevant information that is acquired during overt search. Numerous inputs on the far left of the 1969 model (figure 2-11) influence the consumer. These inputs are product specific (significative and symbolic) and environmental (family, reference groups, and social class). The factors affect attention and may lead to perceptual biases. In addition, numerous exogenous variables influence the process (see figure 2-13). These are essentially the variables that were discussed earlier as determinants of deliberation.

Following figure 2-11, the information search then leads to brand comprehension. The brands are compared against choice criteria, and attitudes lead to purchase intentions and, ultimately, to the purchase itself. This act then feeds into the satisfaction element and brand comprehension (memory). Thus, the Howard-Sheth model explains the process by which internal and external determinants influence the decision process much like the earlier explanation. The development and testing of models has given valuable insights into the consumer decision process. Further refinement and empirical research should make them more valuable in the future.

The next few chapters treat the various personal and external forces that influence buyer behavior. A number of these factors were touched upon in this chapter. Following this groundwork, we will look at the activities in which marketing firms engage to attempt to influence consumer behavior.

SUMMARY

Consumer behavior is a very complex process. Treating it as a sequential decision activity helps us deal with the process and its determinants. The decision process can be characterized as a sequence of stages beginning with problem perception and proceeding to deliberation relative to an acceptable solution to the perceived problem. Deliberation activity involves searching for and processing information to evaluate alternative brands, products, and so forth. As the consumer processes information and becomes aware of the characteristics of various alternatives, the alternatives are evaluated against a choice criterion made up of expectations, opinions, attitudes, and beliefs about acceptable problem solutions. Finally, a choice is made and evaluated against needs and expectations (the choice criterion). What is learned in purchasing and evaluation becomes part of our experience to guide us in future decisions.

CHAPTER 2   STUDY REVIEW

Important Terms and Concepts

Decision process
Decision maker
Problem solving
Problem perception
Deliberation
Information search
Alternative evaluation
Information processing
Choice criteria
Information sources
Purchase intentions
Situational influences
Decision time
Impulse purchasing
Postcognitive dissonance
Purchase satisfaction
Decision models

Questions

1. What types of purchases might fit the three levels of problem solving?

2. Summarize the five decision-making strategies discussed in this chapter.

3. Using a purchase you have recently made, describe the decision process you followed, stage by stage.

4. Outline the factors that may give rise to purchase problem recognition.

5. What conditions may lead to more extensive deliberation?

6. Discuss the various patterns of deliberation.

7. To what extent are purchase intentions realized? Why?

8. What factors may lead to consumer dissatisfaction?

3

Consumer
Perception

Human behavior is grounded in need recognition and fulfillment, but perception is the initiator of behavior and the process by which we interpret our surroundings. Perception, therefore, provides a good starting point for the study of consumer behavior. Consumers are exposed to advertising, store displays, packages, and so on; and the perceptions that come from these stimuli often act as triggers and influences for buying behavior. This chapter concentrates on the process by which consumers receive and interpret information and the forces that influence that process.

The Nature of Perception

Two basic processes underlie the consumer's information acquisition: sensation and perception. Although the notion of five senses is commonly held, there are at least ten senses by which we internalize stimuli: sight, sound, taste, touch, smell, pain, cold, warmth, kinesthesis (sense of movement and position in space), and vestibular (body balance, position, and movement).[1] These senses receive information as data is gathered from the environment and sent to the brain; however, the nature of raw sensory stimuli is not sufficient to explain the coherent, organized picture of the world that we experience.[2] The brain must code and categorize the information that is received, usually from several sensory receptors simultaneously. This categorization and interpretation of sensory stimuli is referred to as perception. Look at figure 3-1. What do you see? What you sense is twenty discrete blotches; what you perceive is the figure of a dog.

Thus, sensation may be defined as "the immediate and direct apprehension of simple stimuli—the response of the sense organs to light, sound, pressure, and the like—or the experienced results of that process. So, for example, we sense or have sensations of color, brightness, shape, loudness, pitch, heat and so on."[3] Perception, on the other hand, is "the more complex process by which people select, organize, and interpret sensory stimulation into a meaningful and coherent picture of the world. We perceive a friend in a crowd or that a parking space is too small."[4]

Fig. 3-1.   Sensation versus Perception

Both sensation and perception are important to our understanding of consumer behavior. Consumers sense various promotional stimuli created by marketers and must interpret those stimuli in terms of their needs and predispositions. We sense the absence of some satisfaction and form perceptions of the nature of possible solutions to these problems. As noted in chapter 2, the purchase process generally begins with the recognition or perception of some problem state; perception continues through information acquisition and processing and plays a major role in determining whether the purchase was satisfactory.

Marketers must understand how to communicate their messages to customers so consumers will actually sense and perceive the ads. Often, advertising aims to create a problem or at least call attention to a problem that, happily, can be solved by buying and using a certain brand. This process of communication is made more complex by the natures of both sensation and perception.

The study of perception is a very broad field. There is insufficient space here to consider all dimensions of the phenomenon, so this chapter emphasizes those areas that seem most relevant to the study of consumer behavior. First, some significant attributes of perception will be investigated. Then, three specific concepts of perception relevant to consumer behavior will be treated: attribution theory, perceived risk, and subliminal perception.

Significant Aspects of Perception

There are a number of characteristics and features of perception that are relevant to the study of consumer behavior. Several attributes will be considered here: (1) thresholds of awareness, (2) selective perception, (3) cues, (4) perceptual organization, categorization, and interpretation, and (5) emotional influences.

Thresholds of Awareness

Our sensors have definite limits, referred to as thresholds, to what they can detect. Specifically, a threshold is defined as the level at which a subject can correctly perceive a stimulus at least fifty percent of the time. There are both biological and psychological thresholds.

Biological Thresholds The human ear can detect sounds pitched between a low of about 20 hertzes (vibrations per second) to a high of about 20,000 hertzes; beyond those limits most people can hear nothing. The eye also sees light within a rather narrow band, with ultraviolet waves on one end of the spectrum and infrared on the other end invisible to the human eye. Also invisible are x-rays, radio and television waves, and radar.

We can also discriminate among sensations. The trained musician can clearly distinguish between many tones, and it is estimated that the human eye is able to see more than seven million different colors.[5] An upper or lower limit is referred to as an absolute threshold, while a discriminatory limit is called a differential threshold or the j.n.d. (just noticeable difference).

Psychological Thresholds In addition to the physical limits of sensation, there are psychological ones influencing absolute thresholds. First, we tend to adapt to constant stimuli. A radio turned on while you study may soon fade from your attention. Mental set is also a factor. When you are not particularly interested in the purchase of a particular product, you may see no ads for it at all. Once you become interested in buying a new car, you are suddenly aware of advertisements everywhere. This phenomenon underlies selective perception, which will be studied in the next section.

Consumer psychology may also influence differential thresholds. Tied to the concept of mental set, expectations may cause us to fail to discriminate between stimuli. For example, the Goodrich Tire Company had an identity crisis for many years because the larger company with the similar name overshadowed them. To combat the problem, the company created the Goodrich Blimp, which of course turned out to be no blimp at all (see figure 3-2)—"Goodrich is the company without the blimp." Many consumers were then able to differentiate between the two companies.

Competitive pressures in the packaged goods field constantly lead marketers to

Fig. 3-2. Creation of Perceived Difference

BFGoodrich

"RICH LADY" :30

RICH LADY: Stop off at our Goodrich Dealer, Stanley. We must have the radial tires rotated.

HUSBAND: Have them what...?
STANLEY: Rotated, sir.

Put the front ones on the back, and the back ones on the front.

Move them, sir, so they'll wear more evenly.

RICH LADY: The Goodrich dealer says they'll last longer.

HUSBAND: How ingenious. No wonder those clever Goodrich people made that marvelous blimp.

RICH LADY: Stanley, do you ever wonder why you're up there, and he's back here?

**BFGoodrich
The Other Guys**

ANNCR: (VO) Tires you can trust. B.F. Goodrich. The Other Guys.

Courtesy of B. F. Goodrich Co.

try to keep their products fresh and new in consumers' minds. However, the words *new* and *improved* often fall on deaf ears. The question is how to break through the differential threshold without creating a totally new and unfamiliar product for the consumer. Too new a product might lead present consumers to switch to another brand because the flavor, texture, scent, or other feature is no longer desirable. Currently, advertisers create a "slice of life" where someone is asked to compare a "new" product, say a deodorant, with his or her current brand. The new product emerges as better, and only then do we learn that the "new" product is simply an improved version of the old.

Price changes, too, are subject to differential thresholds. How much do you have to reduce a price to make it appear to be a bargain? How much can you raise a price without consumers noticing? Price thresholds will be considered in chapter 13, but for now we can investigate the j.n.d., which seems to be a ratio rather than an absolute difference. The relationship, called Weber's Law, is stated thus:

$$\frac{\Delta I}{I} = K$$

Where: I is the base or established intensity

ΔI is the incremental increase that is noticeably different from I

K is a constant

Figure 3-3 shows some ratios for the various senses that were established under experimental conditions. The ratios would likely be different under noncontrolled circumstances, but the concept of the ratio suggests that the larger the base perception, the greater will have to be the differential (increase or decrease) from that base for a difference to be perceived. A can of vegetables in the grocery store selling regularly for 27¢ may go on sale at two cans for 49¢, and the consumer is likely to perceive the price cut. However, the price of an $8,000 automobile may have to be lowered several hundred dollars before the change is noticeable.

Fig. 3-3.   Weber Ratios for a Variety of Stimuli

Pitch (at 2,000 hertz)	1/333
Deep pressure (at 400 grams)	1/77
Visual brightness (at 1000 photons)	1/62
Lifted weights (at 300 grams)	1/53
Loudness (at 100 decibels or 1000 hertz)	1/11
Smell of rubber (at 200 olfacties)	1/10
Skin pressure (at 5 grams per square millimeter)	1/7
Taste, saline (at 3 moles per liter)	1/5

E. G. Boring, H. S. Longfield, and H. P. Weld, (eds.), *Psychology: A Factual Textbook* (New York: John Wiley & Sons, 1935) p. 199.

Selective Perception

Partly because our senses and brain cannot physically handle all incoming stimuli, and partly because we are more interested in some things than we are in others, we select only certain things to be perceived. This selectivity is related to the thresholds just discussed. Essentially, thresholds are raised or lowered as a result of our selective sensitivity. Because selectivity acts as a perceptual filter, determining which stimuli "get through" to a consumer, an understanding of selective perception is of vital interest to a marketing strategist.

Determinants of Selective Perception Three mechanisms are hypothesized as determining what we select and what we reject in the process of perception: perceptual overloading, selective sensitization, and perceptual defense.[6]

Perceptual overloading occurs when the organism cannot take in any more stimuli. When this occurs, certain stimuli will be mentally discarded. The average human has difficulty in considering more than seven individual items at one time,[7] leading to the evoked set concept, which states that a consumer will typically consider no more than seven and usually five or fewer brands when making a purchase decision, even when many more brands are available.[8]

Consider that we are exposed to from 600 to 800 advertising messages per day. This volume is too much to cope with, so we select out only a very few ads for our attention and fewer yet for recall. Try to recall any commercial from the last time you watched TV. Chances are pretty good that you can recall none. No wonder we have been referred to as an overcommunicated society.[9]

Selective sensitization or perceptual vigilance is the process whereby an individual becomes more tuned to stimuli that are of special interest or that are congruent with currently held attitudes, motives, personality, and so on. *Perceptual defense* represents the other extreme, where incoming stimuli that are inconsistent with self-image are selectively blocked to avoid ego threat.

Outcomes of Selective Perception Selective perception results in four kinds of selection: exposure, attention, distortion, and retention.

Selective exposure simply means that consumers can seek or avoid various stimuli. For example, a smoker is unlikely to seek out and read articles relating to the health dangers of smoking. On the other hand, if you were looking for a new personal computer, you might spend several weeks actively exposing yourself to information on the capabilities of various brands.

Selective attention is similar to selective exposure, but it is fundamentally unconscious. The consumer is "set" to give attention to relevant stimuli, a situation related to perceptual sensitization, mental set, or perceptual vigilance. As discussed in chapter 2, one of the most basic aspects of consumer decision making is the fact that it is goal directed. We tend to gather information about purchases relative to these goals and become selectively attentive to stimuli relevant to meeting purchase goals. Thus, we may have the purchase goal of avoiding high-cholesterol foods, which makes us attentive to information in ads or on package labels that would help meet that goal.

Selective attention allows us to filter through only information that is relevant to us. However, there may be vital information in the environment that does not correspond with current goals. Another aspect of selective attention explains our handling of these stimuli. Attention is also given to stimuli that are surprising, novel, and potentially physically threatening. New products, special sales, new packages and brands, cents-off offers, premiums, and contests might cause the consumer to give attention to stimuli not immediately in keeping with current goals.[10] Two forces, then, goals and unexpected important events, may lead to selective attention.

Selective distortion occurs because people tend to perceive what they want to perceive, and since perception is very subjective, it can be highly personalized. Thus, if what we want to see isn't "out there," we may mentally create it. It is entirely possible for us to see an advertisement and attribute it to the wrong sponsor or misinterpret the message.

Selective retention means that we tend to remember only those ideas that are congruent with our existing attitudes and prejudices; others are quickly forgotten. We also tend to forget unpleasant factors. Thus, we may forget the favorable features of a purchase alternative not taken and ignore or forget the negative aspects of the product we purchased.

Cues

Perception is an important part of the decision-making process. We seek information from the environment that may help us in making these decisions, but we generally do not take the time to deal with all stimuli relevant to a particular problem. We seek to simplify the search for and processing of information on the basis of our experience or some sort of introspection. Thus, certain stimuli that have been referred to earlier as cues are used to guide the consumer in forming opinions about various phenomena.

EEK & MEEK   by Howie Schneider

Reprinted by permission. © 1979 NEA, Inc.

For example, you may have used a particular brand for some time and been satisfied with it. Another product marketed by the same company may be judged according to your past experience with the brand name. In this case, the brand name acts as a cue, and you may decide to buy the new item with virtually no additional deliberation. Likewise, as noted in chapter 13, price often is used as a surrogate indicator of product quality.

Of course, there is no guarantee that a given cue is an accurate surrogate for quality or performance. In fact, consumers often make decisions on the basis of false or irrelevant cues.[11] An attractive package may lead a consumer to assume wrongly that the product within is of better quality than other products.

The important fact is that if we have no rational basis for making a decision, we are apt to create one. When presented with several stockings of equal quality, consumers unconsciously used a faint scent that had been added to some of the stockings as a surrogate for quality and judged the scented stockings as being of higher quality.[12]

From a strategic standpoint, marketers need to be aware of what cues consumers use to judge various products and promote them accordingly. Many consumers equate quality with softness in toilet tissue. Therefore, Procter and Gamble calls its toilet tissue squeezably soft. Consumers could squeeze the tissue package (if Mr. Whipple were not around) and find Charmin to be noticeably softer than competition, and it was therefore judged to be of higher quality than other brands. The perception of softness is heightened by the special paper process that blows air into the tissue as it is rolled.[13]

Perceptual Organization, Categorization, and Interpretation

In order to make sense out of their world, consumers organize incoming stimuli according to several distinct principles. Since these factors are important in determining consumer attention, they are significant in influencing perceptual thresholds. This section will look at some of the more relevant principles: color and contrast, context, similarity, figure-ground, motion, closure, position, size, intensity, isolation, and proximity.

Color and Contrast We tend to perceive color ads more readily than black and white.[14] However, because we respond to contrast, a different or unexpected stimulus may be more noticeable. A black and white ad may stand out in a magazine where all other ads are in color, and a black and white ad will often yield a better cost efficiency because of its reduced cost and heightened attention value.

Context We develop certain expectations for our world. For example, look at figure 3-4. Whether you perceive a B or a 13 depends upon the context in which the stimulus is perceived. Now select the word on this page that is closest in size to a dime. Surprised? Out of context it is difficult to make correct judgements. Products, packages, and brands are perceived in some context and with some expectations.

Would you be willing to do your laundry with a dark brown detergent? Would you buy toothpaste in a plastic bag? Marketers must be aware of what consumers expect and proceed accordingly.

Fig. 3-4. Perception in Context

A   B   C   D   E   F

11   12   13   14   15   16

Similarity Often, items that are similar are perceived as identical. In one study of perception, people in photographs were mentally given the personality traits of known people whose appearance was similar.[15] The same phenomenon is likely to extend to brands and products as well. Newcomers to a market often try to pattern their products as closely as the law will allow to existing successful products and brands.

Figure-Ground As objects are perceived, something becomes the background and something else becomes the figure. Thus, the figure stands out from the ground and is identified. However, confusion can occur if the difference is not clearly defined. Look at figure 3-5. What do you see? Two people face to face? A vase or a bird bath? What you see depends on what you perceive as figure and what you perceive as ground. Look at the figure until you can see both figures—you will not be able to see them simultaneously.

In packaging or advertising, the marketer must depend on the consumer seeing the major aspect, say the brand name, as figure and the rest of the ad or package as ground. Testing is necessary to be sure that consumers are perceiving what the marketer wants them to see. When consumers find they can remember the ad but can't remember the brand, somebody wasted a lot of money. An advertisement that has appeared on television illustrates the figure-ground problem. An attractive woman is walking down the street with the song "Pretty Woman" playing in the

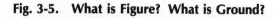

Fig. 3-5.   What is Figure?   What is Ground?

background. The woman and the song were intended as ground, while the product, Tone soap, was intended as the figure. However, it is easy to become so involved with the song and the attractive woman that they become figure, while the product is obscured as ground.

Apparent Motion Motion or apparent motion is an effective attention getter. Store displays and television commercials with movement are readily perceived. Actual motion is not necessary. Cartoons and movies are simply the rapid projection of still pictures that give the illusion of motion. When Lee Iacocca, then executive vice-president of North American Automotive Operations for Ford Motor Company, chose the clay model that was to become the 1965 Mustang, he remarked that the decision was based on the fact that the car looked like it was moving even though it was standing still.[16]

Closure When you see or hear something that is incomplete, you will likely finish it. This is the principle by which rough line drawings are recognizable. Look back at figure 3-1. Closure allows you to see the dog rather than discrete patches.

It is felt that two-way communication is more effective than one-way. However, advertising, of necessity, is generally one-way. The principle of closure, however, allows a degree of consumer involvement and feedback. Some years ago, Salem cigarette ads used the theme of freshness of taste, with the slogan "You can take Salem out of the country, but . . . you can't take the country out of Salem." The first few times the commercial ran the entire slogan was aired. But after a time, only the first half of the message was broadcast, ending with the ding of a bell. Consumers, faced with an incomplete situation, felt compelled to finish the phrase.

Of course, simply using incomplete messages may not insure better recall or product purchase. Under certain circumstances, however, getting consumer involvement may enhance learning. In chapter 11, the introduction of Vick's Nyquil is discussed. The first ads stated that Nyquil was a difficult name to remember so it would be repeated three times: "Nyquil, Nyquil . . . ." Because consumers expected Nyquil to be said the third time, they said it to finish the statement. Thus, the name *Nyquil* was strongly imprinted in consumer minds as they repeated the name (perhaps only mentally) every time they saw the ad. The marketer must take care in using the principle of closure, however. People vary widely in their ability to fill in missing elements, and if a desired closure is too subtle, many people will miss the point of the ad.[17] On the other hand, their reaction may not be the one desired. When GM ran their Buick ad "Wouldn't you rather have a Buick?" a lot of people apparently said no.

Position The position of an advertisement on a page is important in determining its attention-getting quality. Ads on the upper half of the page and on the left side of the page are more effective in getting our attention.[18] However, whether an ad is on the left- or right-hand page seems to make no difference.[19]

Size Larger phenomena tend to attract more attention than smaller. However, the relationship between size and attention is exponential rather than linear. In other words, an advertisement must be four times as large as another to achieve twice the attention-getting quality if all other factors are equal.[20] This is referred to as the inverse-square principle.

Intensity Closely related to the concept of size is intensity. Loud sounds and bright colors tend to attract attention. Again, the relationship is exponential rather than linear.

Isolation When an object is presented by itself, it may have better attention-getting capabilities than when included with other items. Many print ads present products in the midst of white space to gain singular attention for the item advertised.

Proximity We tend to perceive that things close together are related to one another. This "guilt by association" is used in promoting many products. Beer ads often use a "come let us be good fellows together" appeal, implying that having the right beer means you're having a party. If you don't like beer, open a box of Ritz crackers, and you can still have a party. Soft drinks, too, are generally portrayed in "fun" settings. The proximity of the brand shown in the ad to some favorable situation may lead to an unconscious association, which could lead to selecting that brand.

Emotional Influences

There are a number of human factors that affect what we perceive, including needs, motives, and attitudes, personality, learning, and social influences.

Needs, Motives, and Attitudes What we perceive is heavily influenced by our needs, motives, and attitudes. When we are motivated in a particular direction, our perception may become distorted. While most children tend to misperceive the size of coins, children from poverty backgrounds overestimate the size of coins more than children from higher-income families.[21] Hungry people perceive food-related stimuli more readily,[22] and thirsty people are more prone to perceive water- and drinking-oriented stimuli. The need to reduce ambiguity and indecision is a strong motivator, and the marketer who can supply strong reasons for purchasing a brand may well be the one who makes the sale.

Much of the research in perceptual reactions to persuasion has focused on attitudes. Three generalizations seem warranted, based on this research.

1. Persuasion which contradicts or otherwise is inconsistent with the predispositions of those for whom it is intended is likely to provoke a reaction of selective exposure whereby non-acceptable messages are avoided.

2. Once exposed to the message, the individual may perceive and interpret it in a manner consistent with his predisposition toward that topic, and appeals which deviate substantially from these predispositions are likely to be distorted or otherwise interpreted in a manner not intended.

3. Recipients of persuasive communication messages will tend to selectively recall appeals in a manner consistent with existing predispositions toward the topic. Unacceptable appeals are likely to be forgotten.[23]

As consumers we should be aware that our needs and motives may cause us to make poor decisions. You shouldn't shop for food when you are hungry. You should refrain from making major purchase decisions when under heavy time or other pressure. In-home salespeople have often created time pressure for consumers by saying, "I can only make this offer once; if you don't buy now, I can't come back."

Personality People's personalities differ, and personality seems to influence perception. Some personalities perceive synthetically—that is, the perceptual field is seen as an integrated whole. Others perceive analytically—where the field is broken down into its component parts or details.[24] Consumers with a low tolerance for ambiguity tend to be more influenced by such approvals as the Underwriter's Laboratory (UL) seal and the Good Housekeeping seal.[25] Many other personality types and characteristics are related to differences in perception, but since personality tends to be such an individual phenomenon, it is difficult to arrive at suggestions for marketing strategy.

Learning Perception and learning are closely related. As the consumer gains experience and learns, perceptions will likely change. Marketers should, and often do, provide information that gives consumers the opportunity for developing better perception. Essentially, these marketing activities can teach consumers how to judge, how to be more attentive to detail, and how to make effective comparisons.[26]

Perceptual learning can also contribute to the consumer's ability in leveling and sharpening. Leveling involves some forgetting. What the consumer retains from product usage and advertising tends to become shorter, more concise, and more easily understood. Sharpening is the reverse of leveling. As we forget some details, what remains carries greater importance and stands out from other pieces of information.[27] Brand loyalty may arise from the good points of a product being sharpened and the less desirable aspects being leveled.

Social Influence An individual's perception is strongly influenced by other people. A classic study showed that perceptions can be molded by social pressure.[28] A group of subjects was seated around a table and presented with two cards. One card had three lines of different lengths. The other had a single line. Subjects were asked to determine which line on the three-line card was of equal length to the single line on the other card. One member of the group was a patsy, while the rest of the group had been instructed to pick the same wrong line consistently. Even though the expected error rate in determining the correct match was only one percent, the uninformed subject agreed with the rest of the group thirty-six percent of the time.

Our product perceptions are heavily influenced by what others say and do. One of the best examples is fashion. How strange yesterday's fashions look to us now, but how right they looked then.

Social norms may also influence our perception. Ecological problems concern many people today. One study found that consumers' perceptions of laundry detergents varied according to their ecological concerns. The greater their concerns for ecology, the greater their tendency to perceive nonphosphate, biodegradable, detergent brands as similar to one another.[29]

People of different cultural backgrounds tend to have major differences in perception. Although we can distinguish seven million different colors, no culture has names for more than a relatively few colors, and these names are a function of culture. One study of ten different North American cultures found differences in the names used and in the parts of the color spectrum emphasized by the names.[30] Marketers must be aware of the fact that cross-cultural differences may influence consumer perceptions of products, packages, brands, and promotion. For example, showing pairs of anything has been taboo in Ghana, and feet could never be shown in advertisements in Thailand because they were perceived as despicable.[31] One study found that black children perceive TV commercials quite differently from white children.[32]

Social factors may influence a consumer's perceived credibility of information. A person is likely to perceive a friend as a more reliable source of product information than a salesperson or an advertisement.[33] The use of "real" people and testimonials from "credible" persons in television commercials are attempts to lend more perceived credibility to the ads. Print media tend to be perceived as more credible, while TV is generally considered least credible, so social factors are a significant issue for television advertisers.

Attribution Theory

Part of our perceptual process is aimed at interpreting the reasons for events. The underlying causes of the things we observe are very important if we are to interpret and predict the environment accurately and make effective decisions. The systematic study of the perception of causality, referred to as attribution theory, began some years ago.[34] Note that attribution theory does not necessarily deal with the "true" cause of things but rather with what a person perceives the cause to be (see Figure 3-6).[35]

Fig. 3-6.   Perceved Attributions

© 1979 United Feature Syndicate, Inc.

There are essentially three areas of study within the realm of attribution theory: person perception, self-perception, and event or object perception. The original research on attribution theory was carried out by several social psychologists (see figure 3-7), but the concepts of the theory have found wide application in consumer behavior.

Person Perception

The original work in attribution theory viewed individuals as naive psychologists who try to assess the reasons for the behavior of others by interpreting the causes of actions from the actions themselves.[36] Further research focused on the *effects* of observed

Fig. 3-7. Paradigms of Attribution Theory

Dimension	Contributors			
	Heider (1944, 1958)	Jones and Davis (1965)	Bem (1965, 1967, 1972)	Kelley (1967, 1971, 1973)
Major contribution	Originator of modern attribution theory	Made Heider's attribution theory amenable to empirical test	Extended attribution theory to self-perception	Extended attribution theory to object and generalized perception
Data used for making attributions	Others' actions or knowledge of others' actions	Perceived effects of others' actions	One's own behavior	Actions or effects of actions (events)
Treatment of others' perceptions or attributions	Implicit	Implicit	None	Explicit—specifically develops paradigm to reflect the processing of information from others
Attributable causes of action				
Personal	Intention, exertion ability	Intention/knowledge ability/possibility of action (i.e., "can")	"Tact" responses	Intention
Environmental	Task difficulty	Situation and role	"Mand" responses	Entities, modalities, persons
Basis for attribution	Naïve analysis of action, using levels of personal responsibility	Commonality and desirability of effects	Perceived freedom of choice, salience of initial attitude[a]	Covariance; causal schemata
Output of attribution	Judgment of extent actor is personally responsible for action	Intention and underlying disposition of the actor	Perception of personal or environmental causality	Cause of an action or effect
Major focus	Person-perception	Person-perception	Self-perception	Object and general perception

[a]Often operationalized through investigator inference

Richard W. Mizerski, Linda L. Golden and Jerome B. Kernan, "The Attribution Process in Consumer Decision Making," Reprinted with permission from *The Journal of Consumer Research* (1979) 6:124.

actions rather than the actions themselves and led to three basic criteria individuals use when trying to determine reasons for other persons' behavior.

1. Choice and effects—individuals are assumed to have a choice among actions (or inaction).

2. Commonality—only "noncommon effects" (those unique to specific actions) are useful for inferring personal, as opposed to environmental, causality.

3. Desirability—the more undesirable the action or the effects of the action, the more readily and more confidently causality can be inferred.[37]

An example will perhaps clarify the concepts.

> Brian walks into a car dealership, possibly to purchase a new BX-70. The car salesman spends 45 minutes discussing the purchase with Brian and, just as the sale is about to be completed, the salesman says that he is more interested in Brian's satisfaction than a sales commission. The salesman then details complaints received about the BX-70, and suggests that Brian would get a better value at a lower price with a BZ-59. Brian realizes that the salesman has invested considerable time and will make significantly less commission on the sale of a BZ-59. In light of the salesman's actions (offering information about the BX-70), Brian (the observer) infers that the salesman (the actor) is a very honest, helpful and/or credible person (the potential correspondent inferences). This inference can be explained by the criteria of Jones and Davis. [See Figure 3-7.]
>
> The salesman chose to provide unfavorable information about the BX-70, and his choice appeared to be voluntary. The effects of this choice are shown in figure 3-8. Only the noncommon effects, those unique to each course of action, are used to infer the reasons (causes) that the actual choice was made, as the common effect (in this case, "may sell the automobile") could not have been decisive in the salesman's choice of action. Therefore, Brian would base his causal inferences on effects b, c, and d (noncommon effects). Some of these multiple effects are more desirable than others to the salesman and, thus are less diagnostic of his intentions. In this example, spending more time on the sale and helping the consumer to get a better deal (and at the cost of a larger commission) prompt Brian to infer that these effects (which are "undesirable" for salesmen) must reflect an underlying personal disposition of this salesman or what Jones and Davis call "correspondence of inference."
>
> High correspondence of inference tends to occur only with certain combinations of noncommon effects and assumed desirability for the actor. When the number of noncommon effects is high, the observer finds it extremely difficult to attribute behavior to a single personal disposition, because there are many competing explanations for the behavior. Even in this example Brian could not be certain which trait best explained the salesman's "stepping out of character." Was it his honesty, his altruism, or is he simply a credible source of information?"
>
> The concepts of noncommon and desirable effects are ultimately woven into what Jones and Davis call the "action-attribute paradigm." This suggests the sequence of attribution and the influence of Heider's concepts of actor knowledge and ability. Their model states that the actor must have knowledge of the effects that will be produced from his action, as well as the ability and intention to perform the action.[38]

Thus, Jones and Davis see a person's actions as potentially attributable to a variety of motivations. An individual can influence the attributions of others. Many purchase decisions are made with relatively little information, and, under such a

Fig. 3-8. Correspondent Inferences

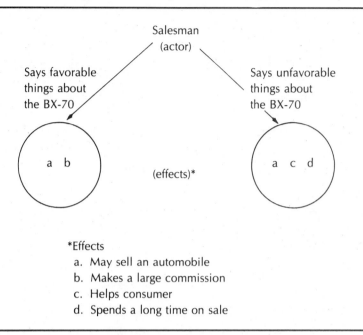

*Effects
a. May sell an automobile
b. Makes a large commission
c. Helps consumer
d. Spends a long time on sale

Richard W. Mizerski, Linda L. Golden, and Jerome B. Kernan, "The Attribution Process in Consumer Decision Making," Reprinted with permission from *The Journal of Consumer Research* (1979) 6:125.

condition, the consumer is often quite susceptible to outside influence. This may come from an "objective" statement about the product or from an opinion, in which case the character of the information source is critical. Several research studies have dealt with the attributions that consumers develop toward promotion efforts.[39] Consumers would be likely to perceive that information about a product was accurate and useful if they believed the information was attributable to the nature of the product itself. For example, a consumer would be more likely to believe an advertisement for a car's good gas mileage if the person in the ad were perceived as actually having driven the car and personally having gotten the good mileage.[40] When a celebrity endorses a product, does the endorsement come from the heart or does the paycheck have something to do with it? Some celebrities have high credibility with people, and they have capitalized on that fact by endorsing various products.

In purchasing and using products, consumers are social actors whose behavior may be open to the observation of others.[41] One thing that is often important to advertisers, then, is to make the people in their ads look like "real" consumers of the product. The slice-of-life ad is often used to give the idea that the people and their behavior are real, and "real" people (nonactors or actors acting badly enough to look like nonactors) are often used in ads featuring testimonials to lend an aura of credibility. Federal Trade Commission regulations attempt to insure that fraud is not involved in endorsement and testimonial advertising. When Joe Namath endorsed a brand of panty hose, serious questions were raised since he did not actually use the product, even though the ad was meant as a spoof. A few endorsement ads are a little questionable since viewers could easily make false attributions. Remember Carl Maulden's endorsement of American Express travelers checks? He played a tough cop in "The Streets of San Francisco," and the character in the ad is similar to the cop, even down to the hat he wore in the series. Another endorser is Robert (Dr. Marcus Welby) Young's endorsement of Sanka brand coffee. He visits a couple by himself (as he so often did in his well-remembered TV series) and talks about how Sanka has no caffeine. Young is in no way identified as a medical expert, but he was so strongly stereotyped as an MD in the series that he received a great deal of mail seeking medical advice.

Self-perception

Just as we attempt to explain the behavior of others, we try to understand and attribute causes for our own actions. Daryl Bem has argued that we interpret reasons for our own behavior from our actions or verbal reports.[42] Because we like to be perceived by ourselves and others as rational beings, we often try to explain our behavior. In effect, one might say, "I am using this product; therefore I must like it," rather than the more conventional, "I like this product; therefore I will use it." This has obvious implications for promotion. Getting the consumer to try a product through such devices as free samples, cents-off offers, test drives, and the like may well lead to a positive attitude toward the product and subsequent purchase or repurchase.

Event or Object Perception

Harold Kelley has been responsible for integrating and building upon other areas of attribution theory to develop a theory of how people establish causality for observed events.[43] Essentially, he describes attribution as an analysis of variance for two types of information: information from multiple observations over time and information from a single observation. Causality is inferred from the covariance between effects and their potential causes and is based on three dimensions of possible causality. (1) the stimulus object, (2) the observer of the effects, and (3) the context (the way in which the stimulus is presented).

The consumer/observer assesses causes of events on either the nature of the entity (for example, product) or some external or environmental factor. Four criteria are used in making the attribution.

1. Distinctiveness—the effect is attributed to the entity if it uniquely occurs when the entity is present and does not occur in its absence.
2. Consistency over time—each time the entity is present, the individual's reaction must be the same, or nearly so.

3. Consistency over modality—the reaction must be consistent even though the mode of interaction with the entity varies.
4. Consensus—actions or their effects are perceived the same way by all observers.[44]

Kelley proposes that "to the degree that a person's attributions fulfill these criteria, he feels that he has a true picture of his external world. He makes judgments quickly and with subjective confidence. . . . When his attributions do not satisfy the criteria, he is uncertain in his views and hesitant in action."[45] Another example will help to clarify this.

> If Kathy observes that her car runs smoothly (the effect) on Brand A gasoline, but knocks and misses (also effects) with all other brands, she may think that smooth operation is uniquely associated with Brand A. If Kathy further finds that Brand A is associated with smooth operation every *time* she uses this brand, she should be more confident that her initial observations were valid. Similarly, she will also be more confident if she finds that this effect is present in both city and country driving (modality). Finally, Kathy will have more confidence in her perceptions to the extent that other drivers recognize the same association between the brand and smooth engine performance (consensus).
>
> In this example, Kathy observed that smooth engine operation was distinctive with Brand A gasoline, and consistently smooth during the four times she used it in both city and country driving. Her inference that the "cause" for smooth engine operation must be something about Brand A is strengthened by the consensus information provided by other drivers.[46]

Perceived Risk

Consumers are generally forced to make purchase decisions under some degree of uncertainty and so perceive some risk in their purchasing activities.[47] Risk is comprised of uncertainty and consequences. Uncertainty is the consumer's subjective perception that the outcome (satisfaction/dissatisfaction) of a purchase is unknown, and consequences represent the potential gain or loss from making the purchase decision and using the product.[48]

Causes of Risk

Perceived risk may be caused by any one or a combination of factors. Consumers' buying goals may not be identified. Inability to identify buying goals may be the result of uncertainty about the nature of the goals, goal acceptance levels or levels of aspiration, the relative importance of achieving the goal, and the current degree of goal attainment. Consumers may also be uncertain as to which purchase alternative (place, product, brand, model, style, size, color) will best match or satisfy acceptance levels of buying goals. Consumers may perceive possible adverse consequences if the purchase is made (or not made) and the result fails to satisfy their buying goals.[49]

Other causes of perceived risk might include: limited or unsatisfactory past purchase experience; not absolutely necessary purchase; all purchase alternatives' having pros and cons; nonconformance with friends or other people's purchase behavior; economic uncertainty; high significance, as in buying gifts; social visibility; and disagreement among family members.[50]

Types of Risk

There are five important types of risk that consumers might face.[51] *Financial risk* is the risk that the money spent on the product will be wasted either because the product is unsatisfactory and must be replaced, or because it requires excessive upkeep. *Performance or functional risk* is the danger that the product may not perform as desired. *Social risk* is the risk that others may look down on the purchaser. *Psychological risk* relates to the loss of face or ego damage. *Physical risk* pertains to the potential for personal harm or health hazard.

Risk Reduction

Consumers may reduce perceived risk in a variety of ways. They can rely on: well-known brands, past experience with similar product or brands, consumer test reports or government testing agencies, testimonials or celebrity endorsements, or manufacturer or dealer warranties. Consumers can also reduce risk by buying the "best" or highest-priced model or by seeking extensive product information.[52]

Subliminal Perception

It is rare in a discussion of perception or advertising that a group doesn't raise a question about subliminal advertising. It is an interesting topic. There is something intriguing about a sinister force that can influence us without our knowledge or against our will. But just how sinister is subliminal advertising? Was Vance Packard right in his book *The Hidden Persuaders* when he suggested we are simply puppets on strings held by advertisers?[53]

The question should be treated at two levels. First, is there such a phenomenon, and, if so, what is it? Second, can consumers be subliminally influenced to buy products against their wills?

Quite a bit of research has been devoted to the study of subliminal perception. The concept specifically refers to the reception of stimuli below the limen (threshold) of awareness. This raises the first problem. The perceptual threshold is a very individual phenomenon, with the threshold varying from person to person, from time to time, and from situation to situation, even for the same person. A stimulus is defined as subliminal if it can be perceived fifty percent of the time or less, and if all persons are to be completely unaware of the stimulus, it must be much lower so that it would never be noticed. At that level there is a great opportunity for misinterpretation. However, research does indicate that subliminal stimulation does have an effect on individuals. It has been shown to affect dreams, memory, adaptation level, conscious perception, verbal behavior, emotional responses, drive-related behavior, and perceptual thresholds.[54]

Apparently, stimuli can be perceived at a subconscious level even though they are received subliminally. From our standpoint, however, the real question is, Can an individual be induced to buy something by an advertising message that cannot be consciously perceived? The basis for thinking that it might be able to do so lies in an experiment conducted in a movie theater in 1955. In this famous experiment, some 45,000 subjects were exposed over a six-week period of time to subliminal messages of 1/3,000-second duration saying "eat popcorn" and "drink Coca-Cola."[55] Supposedly, popcorn sales were up fifty-eight percent, and Coke sales were nineteen percent higher than during the previous six-week period.

Several problems make these results highly suspect. First, the experiment was conducted by a company that sold the special projectors required to display the subliminal message. Second, the movie being shown was *Picnic,* in which many scenes showed people eating and drinking in the heat of the summer.[56] Third, there were no controls set up, allowing effects of weather and other conditions to influence people's behavior. Finally, when a demonstration was given to the press, "technical difficulties" allowed subjects to become consciously aware of the stimulus.[57]

In any case, subsequent attempts to repeat the experiment under controlled conditions suggested that subliminal advertising has little or no effect on buying behavior. In one study, both subliminal and supraliminal promotional messages were broadcast during regular programming in Indianapolis.[58] Subliminal advertising by itself did not increase sales significantly. Using subliminal and supraliminal messages concurrently saw sales nearly triple, and sales increased eighteen to thirty-four times when only supraliminal ads were used. A later experiment concluded that subliminal stimulation may lead a person to some sort of action, but the action is of a general nature and not necessarily associated with the specific content of the subliminal message.[59]

It would seem, then, that whatever subliminal perception may be, it is not a useful marketing tool. If it did work, it probably ought to be illegal. However, values, needs aspirations, and motivations of individuals would likely make the perception of subliminal advertising as selective as for supraliminal advertising.[60] Apparently, subliminal advertising is not illegal anywhere,[61] but there is no valid reason for using it.

In the mid 1970s the question of subliminal advertising was raised again with the claim that advertising people were planting hidden sexual messages in print ads.[62] Numerous examples of sex symbols, four-letter words, and pornographic pictures were found hidden in a variety of ads. Perhaps the best example was the word *sex* air-brushed onto the ice cubes in a gin ad. Supposedly, these messages were designed to seduce unsuspecting consumers subconsciously. More likely, retouchers were simply adding their own humorous signatures to their artwork.[63] Viewed unemotionally, there seems to be no evidence that subtle pictures are being used in ads to influence consumers, nor is there any reason to think that they would sell products if they were used.

SUMMARY

Perception lies at the heart of consumer behavior. We must perceive such things as advertisements and products before we buy. Sensation is the fairly objective way we internalize data from our environment. Perception is the complex, subjective process by which we interpret the world we live in.

For both physiological and psychological reasons, there are levels beyond which we do not perceive. Absolute thresholds are the upper and lower limits, while differential thresholds represent the amount of stimulus change required for us to perceive a difference.

Because we cannot physically or psychologically deal with all the stimuli that come to us, we select only certain ones for our attention. Most advertising directed to us is selectively ignored, distorted, or forgotten. On the other hand, interest in a particular product can cause us to seek out and notice relevant ads selectively.

Cues signal us with data helpful in making decisions. Sometimes our interpretation of these cues is erroneous, however, leading us to make faulty decisions.

A variety of factors influence us as we process information and stimuli. These were given as color and contrast, context, similarity, figure-ground, motion, closure, position, size, intensity, isolation, and proximity.

Attribution is the process by which we perceive the causes of things that we observe. Attributions may relate to person, self, and object perception. Numerous research studies suggest that attribution theory can help us better understand the ways in which consumers respond to various marketing efforts.

Consumers perceive functional, financial, social, psychological, and physical risk in their buying decisions. They deal with that risk in a variety of ways, including relying upon experience with known brands, getting warranties and information from unbiased persons and groups, depending on price cues, and seeking additional information.

We may perceive stimuli even though they come to us below the threshold of awareness. Research indicates, though, that subliminal advertising is not effective in influencing buyer behavior.

CHAPTER 3   STUDY REVIEW

Important Terms and Concepts

Perception
Sensation
Attribution theory
Perceived risk
Subliminal perception
Thresholds of perception
Mental set
Just noticeable difference
Weber's law
Perceptual overloading
Cues
Figure-ground
Closure

Questions

1. Discuss the principles of perceptual organization, categorization, and interpretation as they influence consumer behavior.

2. Discuss the major emotional influences on perception.

3. Discuss the three types of attribution theory as they apply to consumer behavior.

4. What are the causes of perceived consumer risk, and how do consumers seek to reduce these risks?

5. What types of perceived risk face consumers?

6. Assess the nature and effectiveness of subliminal advertising.

7. How do cues influence consumer behavior? What specifically may act as cues for consumers?

4

Needs,
Motives,
and Personality

Marketers have a high stake in identifying and satisfying consumer needs. The consumer decision process outlined in chapter 2 is really the process by which consumers identify and satisfy needs. In a sense, this chapter simply looks at that process from a slightly different perspective. Chapter 2 was primarily concerned with investigating buying at the observable behavior level, while this chapter looks at ways to explain the observed behavior.

If you observe a boy in a store buying a candy bar, what can you say about the reasons for the purchase? At the lowest level you could say he bought a candy bar because he wanted one. Obviously, this is not particularly helpful, so you might suggest that perhaps he was hungry. But maybe he wasn't hungry; perhaps he was buying out of habit, to quench the cravings of his sweet tooth, or for a friend. Maybe he can get a decoder ring with just one more wrapper. By now you probably get the idea that observing behavior is often not very useful in explaining it. Of course, you could simply ask the boy, but he may be unaware of his reasons or unwilling to share them.

This chapter will review various theories that seek to explain behavior. Needs and motives provide the foundation, while personality attempts to categorize behavior systematically. The basic purpose, then, is to investigate the reasons why consumers behave as they do.

The Motivation Process

Human behavior begins with needs. Chapter 2 noted that the decision process is initiated by a perceived need, and perceived needs, in turn, lead to motivation. Needs are as consumers perceive them, and the goal objects (for example, products and brands) are what consumers *perceive* as need satisfiers. What will *really* satisfy needs is not relevant in determining what will be purchased unless consumers perceive that it will be a satisfier.

Motivation can be defined as the force that moves an organism to seek need-satisfying goals. The word *motive* is derived from the Latin *movere,* which means

81

"to move." From the same root come the words *motion* and *emotion*. Motivated activities can be thought of as beginning with a need, defined as some sort of lack or insufficiency. When needs are aroused, the psychological state or feeling called a drive is elicited. A drive activates a response, which is designed to attain a goal that will relieve the need. When the need is relieved, the motivational process ends until the need is once again recognized. The process can be simply modeled thus:

Need → Drive → Response → Goal → Goal Attainment (Need Reduction)[1]

The "law of effect" suggests that organisms tend to behave in such a way as to maximize rewards and minimize punishments.[2] Thus, when a motivation chain is established that results in need fulfillment, it tends to be repeated. There is a tendency for satisfied consumers to do what has satisfied them in the past. The marketing goal in many instances is to change the behavior of consumers. Marketers may seek to break an old motivation chain and establish a new one, or they may simply seek to maintain existing chains in the face of competitive efforts and the natural attrition of brand switching. Thus, the motivated state may be said to consist of a recognized need, a drive, and a goal object.

There is a relation between the motivation chain and personality. We seek to fulfill many needs, and research suggests that most people have fundamentally the same needs. However, there are a multitude of ways for an individual to meet needs. Also, different people seem to have quite different need strengths. Essentially, the study of personality is aimed at identifying consistent need levels and behavior patterns that individuals follow in satisfying needs. Thus, we may ask, Will a given individual tend to follow a predictable path in satisfying needs?

We can begin our discussion of motivation with the following observations:

1. Consumer motivation is based on needs.
2. Consumer motivation is goal directed.
3. Drives energize behavior.
4. Need and motivation levels vary among consumers.
5. A given need may be satisfied in a variety of ways.
6. Personality can be viewed as a set of more or less consistent need intensities and satisfaction behaviors.

Need/Motive Typologies

People exhibit a seemingly limitless number of needs and motives. In order to deal with the resulting complexity, numerous classification schemes have organized needs and motives into simplified categories.

Primary, Stimulus, Learned Motives

According to one typology, motives can be grouped into three major categories. *Primary motives* are based on unlearned biological needs that must be met if a person is to survive. The most important primary motives are hunger, thirst, and pain avoidance. *Stimulus motives* also appear to be innate, but they are not essential to survival. Their purpose appears to be to provide useful environmental information and stimulation to the nervous system. The stimulus motives are based on such needs as activity, curiousity, exploration, manipulation, and physical contact. *Learned, or secondary, motives* account for the wide diversity we observe in human activity. The most important secondary motives are related to acquired needs for affiliation, approval, status, security, and achievement. Many consumption motives are learned.[3]

Internal and Incentive Motives

Motives can also be categorized as internal and incentive. Internal motivation relates to stimuli, like hunger, that come from inside the organism, while incentive motivation comes from external goal objects. An otherwise not hungry person may be motivated to eat by the presence of appetizing food. The internal motivation pushes a person into action, while an incentive motivation pulls a person toward the goal object: drives push, incentives pull.[4] Incentive motivation is extremely important to marketers, since such marketing efforts as promotion and display involve placing goal objects before consumers in the hope of motivating them to buy.

Conscious and Unconscious Motives

Motives are also classified as conscious and unconscious. Many times our actions are sparked by forces we are not aware of. Motivation research is based on the idea that consumers are driven by unconscious, often bizarre, motives. A few of those motives were mentioned in chapter 1, but there are many others. For example, research showed that the convertible represented a substitute mistress, while the station wagon and sedan symbolized wife, family, and responsibility. It has also been posited that men wear suspenders because of an unresolved castration complex. Obviously, the Born Loser in the cartoon has a somewhat different view. While human behavior does seem to be influenced by unconscious motives, it is doubtful that a particular behavior can consistently and universally be ascribed to a given motive, conscious or unconscious.

The Maslow Hierarchy

One of the best known and most often used need typologies in thinking about consumer needs is the Maslow Hierarchy, illustrated in figure 4-1.[5] Abraham Maslow suggests that people meet needs at only one level at a time. Once needs are satisfied to some acceptable degree at one level, needs at the next highest level become primary motivators. He suggests that the basic needs (physiological and safety) are the strongest motivators. As one goes up the hierarchy, the motivating power of the needs becomes less intense. Presumably, one would not pursue ego

THE BORN LOSER   by Art Sansom

Reprinted by permission. © 1979 NEA, Inc.

needs with the same vigor as a need for food. At the same time, if a person were hungry enough, no other needs, including safety, would be of concern. Maslow labeled this ordering of needs "prepotency." Most people with whom marketing strategists are concerned have their basic needs fulfilled on a regular basis. Consequently, the higher-order needs become the basis for efforts to motivate consumers to buy. Many promotional efforts in the United States are built around affection and egoistic needs.

Fig. 4-1. The Maslow Hierarchy

Self-actualization Needs
Ego and Esteem Needs
Love and Affection Needs
Safety and Security Needs
Physiological Needs

Maslow estimates that only about ten percent of people get to the point of trying to satisfy self-actualization needs. Others, however, less convinced of the significance of prepotency, argue that a large number of people are attempting to satisfy needs at all levels simultaneously. It appears that prepotency is much more significant between basic and growth (affection, esteem, and self actualization) needs than among the growth needs themselves. If this is true, marketers might be well advised to give more attention to self-actualization needs.

Self-actualization needs are difficult to define. They, along with the needs for knowledge and beauty, represent our highest strivings. "What a person can be, he must be" represents the philosophy of this level. Maslow outlines the kinds of needs that might be sought at the self-actualization level, including wholeness, perfection, completion, justice, complexity, beauty, individuality, truth, and autonomy.[6] Although the need for self-actualization appears to be universal, Maslow feels it is fragile and easily superseded by lower needs. Once lower-level needs are regularly satisfied, there is a need to move up the hierarchy. If lower-level needs are satisfied and self-actualization needs are blocked, the individual falls into a "syndrome of decay" and experiences despair, apathy, and alienation. Thus, consumers at the self-actualization level would be seeking higher-order satisfaction, perhaps from consumption behavior. Marketing appeals to environmental protection and fuel conservation, for example, might fall into this category.

Need Arousal

We have a wide variety of needs, but we cannot seek to satisfy them all simultaneously. For example, we always need food, but we do not eat constantly. When a need becomes noticeable, we enter a motivated state. This process is referred to as arousal. There are several theories of the process by which needs are aroused. Many theories are based on the concept of tension. A need is seen as a tension or a discomfort that must be reduced to bring the individual back to a satisfactory state. Tension states may be either physical or psychological in nature.[7]

Physical balance, or homeostasis, is seen as the desired state for the lower-order needs, and imbalance leads to need recognition and motivation for action to satisfy the need. The need for food provides a relatively simple example. At the physiological level, the need for food is recognized through hunger pangs elicited as the blood sugar level drops below a critical point and signals the hypothalamus to initiate appropriate nerve impulses. When the individual eats, the blood sugar level rises and the feeling of hunger disappears for a while.

Higher-level needs are stimulated as a difference is detected between a desired and an actual psychological state. The difference generates psychological discomfort, and the individual may seek relief either by bringing the actual state into line with the desired state or by changing the perception of what is desired.

Cognitive dissonance theory can be used to explain the concept of higher-order or psychogenic needs arising from mental disequilibrium. Cognition is "any knowledge, opinion or belief about the environment, about oneself, or about one's behavior. Dissonance . . . is the existance of non-fitting relations among cognitions. . . ."[8] Cognitive dissonance, then, is the mental state that causes an individual to try to reduce any lack of consistency or conformity among cognitions.[9]

Cognitive dissonance theory is concerned with motivation and includes four stages. A person perceiving inconsistent bits of information about himself or his environment will experience psychological tension, called cognitive dissonance. Having experienced psychological tension or dissonance, the individual will react in such a way as to remove or reduce the tension. The amount of dissonance experienced by an individual from inconsistent cognitions is a function of the importance of the cognitions. Cognitive dissonance (tension) can be reduced or eliminated by bringing harmony to the dissonant information, reducing the importance of the cognitions, or by some behavior that removes the dissonant information.[10]

Leon Festinger summarizes the concept as:

> This theory centers around the idea that if a person knows various things that are not psychologically consistent with one another, he will, in a variety of ways, try to make them more consistent.
>
> A person can change his opinion; he can change his behavior, thereby changing the information he has about it; he can even distort his perception and his information about the world around him.[11]

An example by James McNeal may help to explain the process.

> Suppose an individual, while attending a movie, decides that he would like some popcorn and a coke. Unfortunately, he does not have the money to buy both. He evaluates the alternatives and decides on the popcorn. Having purchased the popcorn and returned to the movie, he begins to think of the thirst-satisfying qualities of the coke. Cognitive dissonance arises. He knows he bought the popcorn but he is also aware of the thirst-quenching qualities he could have had by buying a coke. His unrest even distracts him from the movie. What can he do to remove this unrest? He may bring harmony into his thinking by telling himself, for example, that cokes are bad for his teeth. In other words, he can rationalize away the dissonance. Or he might simply go to the water fountain when he becomes thirsty and thus reduce the importance that the coke had for him. In either case, cognitive consistency results and the tension state is removed or reduced.
>
> An important point here is that the cognitive dissonant state was a motivating force. For example, it caused the individual to leave the movie momentarily to get a drink of water. Standard theories of motivation would have explained this action by saying that the thirst motive was operative or that the person was driven by thirst.
>
> To understand cognitive dissonance as a motivating state, it is necessary to have a clearer conception of the conditions that produce it. The simplest definition of dissonance can, perhaps, be given in terms of a person's expectations about what things go together and what things do not. When such an expectation is not fulfilled, dissonance occurs.
>
> One point becomes clear about cognitive dissonance theory. Man prefers cognitive consistency—a sort of psychological homeostasis—and will take actions to maintain it.[12]

Cognitive dissonance, as was noted in chapter 2, often develops after a purchase. This is often referred to as postdecision dissonance or postcognitive dissonance, and it occurs as the consumer experiences mixed feelings because commitment to a given product or brand precludes other choices. The anxiety associated with uncertainty may be reduced by seeking or selectively attending to reinforcing information on the chosen alternative and by selectively perceiving information unfavorable to the selected product or supportive of rejected items.

These ideas are built around the tension reduction theory of arousal, which says that some sort of imbalance leads to tension, and the individual is constantly striving to eliminate tension. Marketing strategy might aim, on the one hand, at increasing tension through promotion by calling attention to needs that are not met. On the other hand, products are displayed as tension reducers. All one has to do is purchase and use the product and the tension will be gone.

Even a casual observation of human behavior, however, raises some questions about the validity of the tension reduction theory. If everyone seeks to reduce tension, why do some people jump out of airplanes that are not on fire—for fun? Why does a consumer with no money to spend engage in window shopping, arousing all sorts of desires for products that the person cannot buy—and call it recreation? The simple tension reduction theory does not explain this type of behavior at all.

One theory is that a person seeks a desirable level of arousal, which may vary a great deal from individual to individual.[13] Too high or too low a level will lead to dissatisfaction. Place a person in isolation and remove all stimulation, and the person will react negatively. Increase noise or other stimuli to a high level, and a person may seek peace and quiet. Most people seem to balance stimuli in their lives to achieve a desirable level of arousal. At times (say in athletics, sky diving, carnival rides, horror movies, and window shopping) a person may seek a high stimulus level. Arousal is temporarily raised to a high level, followed by a satisfying return to normal.[14]

Marketers, of course, have a vested interest in understanding arousal. To the extent that marketers can arouse or motivate a consumer, they stand a chance of directing purchasing behavior toward their brands. Marketing is an attempt to influence and modify tastes, preferences, and brand loyalties. Thus, marketers pursue an understanding of motivation so that they can not only predict and forecast buyer behavior but control it to some degree as well.[15]

Theories of Motivation

There have been numerous attempts to explain motivation in a broad theoretical context. At the extremes lie two fundamentally opposing philosophies. The behaviorist theories are rather deterministic, while the cognitive theories tend to be more probabilistic.

The Behaviorist School

The behaviorist school of thought describes motivation as a mechanical process. Behavior is seen as the result of stimulus-response-reinforcement. The determinist position states that all behavior is caused; all events are the inescapable result of precedent conditions. People in acts of apparent choice are in fact reflecting heredity and past experience.[16] A psychology professor expressed it eloquently when he said that behavior is fundamentally the result of glands and muscles. Muscles twitch and glands squirt. Thus, we twitch and squirt our way through life.

The behaviorist tends to ignore any element of conscious thought as being difficult to research and not particularly relevant to the real purposes of psychology as a "science." Further, B. F. Skinner argues that people can be mechanistically conditioned. He, along with other behaviorists, suggests that behavior is shaped and maintained by its outcome. By altering and adjusting the environment, largely through a reward-punishment mechanism, people can be manipulated and controlled. If such a view were correct, marketers would simply have to find the "right" reward for consumers, and they would be assured of eternal loyalty and never-ending sales.[17] Obviously, human behavior is not that simple, and the cognitive school tries to deal with that complexity.

The Cognitive School

The cognitive school of thought is almost the antithesis of the behaviorist. The cognitive approach emphasizes that behavior is goal directed and purposeful, and motivation is seen as the tendency to move toward desired goals. Unlike the behaviorist, who considers only observable stimuli and responses, the cognitive psychologist emphasizes variables that are less directly observable, such as aspiration, competency, and curiosity. The cognitive interpretation asserts that when an individual who aspires to a goal achieves it, there is satisfaction in the success.[18]

Probably the major difference between the behaviorist and cognitive schools lies in the concept of problem solving. The behaviorist sees a direct causal link between stimulus and response, with nothing intervening. However, the alternate view emphasizes that a person, having received a stimulus (need recognition), uses information to reason out a viable response. Cognitive theories of behavior see an action sequence initiated not by stimulation, per se, but by some source of information. Past behavior is reasoned, and events are encoded, categorized, and then transferred into attitudes, beliefs, or values that act as a predisposition to behavior. The cognitions do not determine behavior directly; rather, they guide, modify, condition, and shape behavior in relation to goal striving, expectancies, problem solving, and particular situations. Cognitive models of motivation emphasize that higher mental processes intervene between inputs (stimuli) and behavioral outputs (consequences). Most important is the concept that thought determines action.[19]

Cognitive processes appear to perform two functions in buyer behavior. They are *purposive* in that they are aimed at aiding the individual to satisfy needs. They are also *regulatory* in that they determine the direction the consumer takes in satisfying needs.[20] As figure 4-2 suggests, cognition ties motivation to learning and attitudes.

Given that a consumer recognizes a need, there are a wide variety of possible ways to satisfy it. Cognition takes need recognition from general to specific. A person who may feel socially inferior can take a wide variety of actions—new car, new clothes, a new house—that might meet the need. The consumer must weigh resources against feelings as to what might have the greatest impact. The thinking (cognition) will ultimately lead the consumer to a decision, but under different circumstances a consumer might arrive at quite different purchase decisions. While logically attractive, the cognitive view of motivation gives less hope for predicting or influencing buyer behavior than does behavioristic determinism.

Fig. 4-2. A Model of Cognitive Behavior Determinants

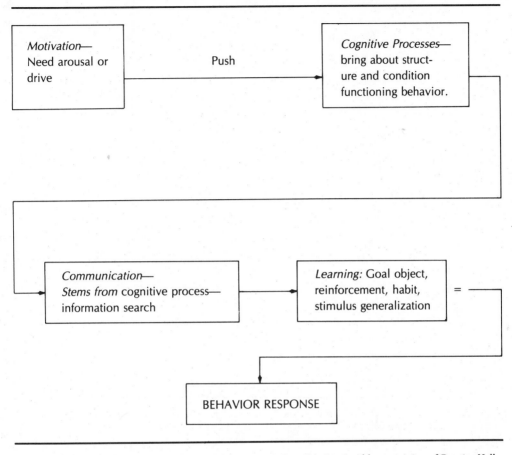

Rom J. Markin, *The Psychology of Consumer Behavior*, © 1969, p. 84. Reprinted by permission of Prentice-Hall, Inc., Englewood Cliffs, New Jersey.

Needs/Motives Multiplexity

Behavior is seldom the result of satisfying a single need. A person's needs are strongly interrelated, and attempting to attribute any given action to a single need is likely to result in oversimplification and misunderstanding.

Sources of Multiple-need Influence

Multiple-need influences in consumer behavior may be manifested in two general ways: means-ends chain and conglomerate needs. First, needs tend to be hierarchically connected, as indicated in figure 4-3. This hypothetical means-end chain shows how specific needs for products and brands may be derived from more fundamental biogenic and psychogenic needs.[21] The purchase of a given brand may be the end result of a sequence of needs. In this concept, specific needs become choice criteria that direct the individual to specific brands. Scope mouthwash has been heavily promoted as good-tasting, so if pleasant flavor is a choice criterion, an individual might be directed to this brand.

Fig. 4-3. Means-End Chain

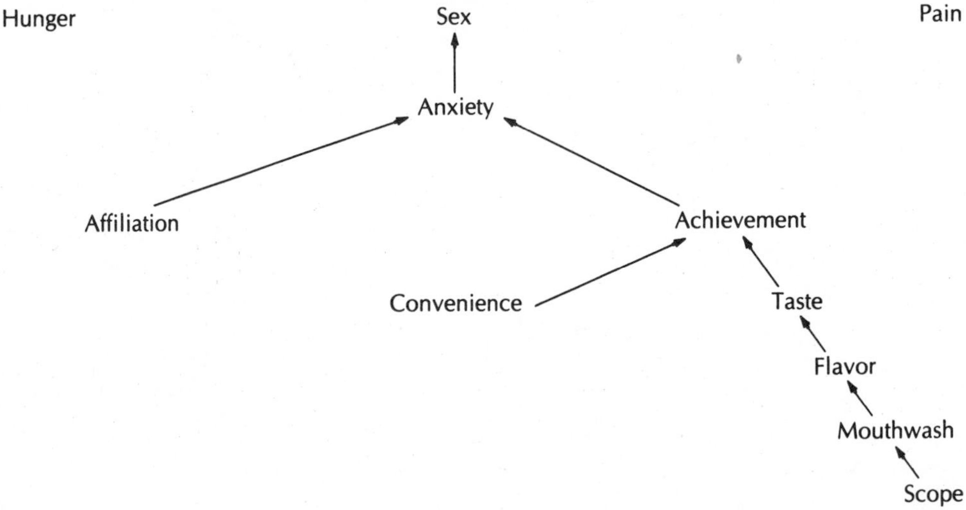

Adapted from John A. Howard and Jagdish N. Sheth, *The Theory of Buyer Behavior*, (New York: John Wiley & Sons, 1969), p. 107.

The purchase of even a relatively simple product, such as mouthwash, may also be based on a conglomeration of several needs at the same time. The purchase of mouthwash may directly and simultaneously fill needs for pleasant flavor, acceptance by others, affiliation (others use it), defendance (defending the self concept), and infavoidance (avoiding humiliation). These needs would not be a part of any hierarchy, but rather they would be independent and perhaps exert equal strength in the decision (see figure 4-4). Marketers can seek relevant needs and promote one or several to motivate consumers by showing how a given brand can satisfy these needs.

Conflicting Needs

So far, we have considered only needs that are compatible with one another. However, many purchases represent situations where needs come into direct conflict with one another. More precisely, the activities that would satisfy two or more needs

Fig. 4-4. A Conglomeration of Needs

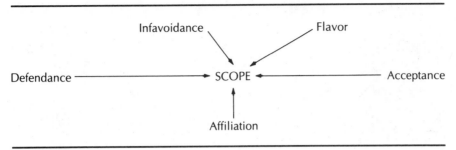

are mutually exclusive so that the individual must make a choice. Three basic conflict situations may exist.[22]

Approach-Avoidance Conflict This conflict involves both a tendency to approach an object or take some action and a tendency to avoid the object or take no action.[23] A consumer may desire a new car, but taking on several years of back-breaking payments seems like no fun at all. In a sense, all purchases represent an outlay of money or assumption of debt and, therefore, represent approach-avoidance conflicts. The action consumers take depends on the strength of the need for the product versus the need to save. Marketers seek to make the approach aspects of a purchase desirable while minimizing the avoidance side (for example, no money down, no payments for six months, twenty-four easy installments—see figure 4-5).

Avoidance-Avoidance Conflict Here, the consumer is stuck between two undesirable alternatives. Years ago as a new college graduate, I sold tires in a management training program. Very few buyers came in elated at the prospect of buying new tires; tires were viewed by most as a necessary evil. If people bought tires, they spent money on an item with little social need satisfaction. On the other hand, without the tires the car might be undrivable. Either way, the consumer perceives a loss. Promotion aimed at emphasizing safety may be helpful, but it still doesn't succeed in having the consumer perceive the opportunity for positive need satisfaction. The only satisfier is the possibility of avoiding an unpleasant outcome, and maybe the tires would hold up for another thousand miles or so anyway.

Approach-Approach Conflict The simplest conflict to resolve occurs where people must choose between two positive or desirable alternatives. Consumers may wish to see two movies, it is their last night in town, and a choice must be made. A person buying a new shirt may see two very desirable alternatives but be able to afford only one. A choice will be made, and, since both alternatives were acceptable, the consumer will presumably be satisfied. In a sense, this represents a double approach-avoidance conflict, however. If he buys one shirt, he can't have the other. Obviously, there is a good probability of postcognitive dissonance, especially if, on getting

Fig. 4-5

Now you can satisfy your sweet tooth. And still keep your sweet shape.

Figurines® let you give in to your sweet tooth without giving up your diet. Figurines Bars are a sweet, rich, and creamy diet treat. Yet they're only 138 calories a bar. And now for chocolate lovers there's new Double Chocolate Figurines—extra chocolate taste with no extra calories. It's another delicious way to a delicious figure.

© The Pillsbury Company. 1979.

Pillsbury

Try new Double Chocolate.

When consumer needs are in conflict (desire to be thin vs. the desire for sweets—approach-avoidance for sweets) an ad such as this one can show the consumer how to satisfy both needs at once—in this case, a good figure and sweets.

Courtesy of The Pillsbury Company.

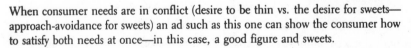

home with the selected shirt, he begins to think that its color is not quite as desirable as it seemed in the store.

Personality

People are different from one another. Consumers express their differences in the wide variety of products and brands they buy. The question is whether people with all their differences can be categorized into homogeneous groups. The study of personality is the attempt to make some organized sense out of the complexities of human behavior. Personality has been defined in a wide variety of ways. There are literally dozens of theories of personality, and virtually every writer has a slightly different definition to offer. For our purposes, personality is the system of individual attitudes, behaviors, and values that an individual exhibits and that set him or her apart from others.

Theories of Personality

There are numerous theories of personality, but this is not surprising in view of the complexity of the subject. Various theories suggest that personality is a function of instinct, socialization, body chemistry, body form, situation, needs, and learning. The large number of individual theories can be classified into a few categories. The categories are neither exhaustive nor mutually exclusive, but they do aid our understanding. The six categories are: type, trait, psychoanalytic, humanist, behaviorist, and cognitive.

Type The earliest theories of personalities attempted to identify different kinds of personalities based on some set of aspects of behavior or appearance. According to these theories, certain sets of characteristics occur together, and each group of characteristics forms a personality type.

The Greek philosopher Hypocrites believed that human behavior was influenced by four basic body fluids called humors (blood, yellow bile, phlegm, and black bile). For example, a person high in yellow bile would be high-strung, easily angered, and passionate, while a person high in phlegm would be slow moving and apathetic. Body types have also been seen as basic to personality, with people divided into endomorph (heavy), mesomorph (muscular), and ectomorph (thin). The endomorph seeks physical comfort and is friendly and slow to react, while the ectomorph is virtually the opposite.[24] In general, such theories have been refuted, although new research has suggested that body chemistry may, in fact, influence personality.

There are also theories based on psychological factors. Carl Jung posited that people were either predominantly introverted (shy, withdrawn, interested in their own subjective cognitions, and unsociable), or predominantly extroverted (realistic, conventional, sociable, and generally aggressive).[25] David Reisman typed people according to three categories: (1) inner-directed—those who have a highly developed internal set of values that guide behavior; (2) other-directed—those who are heavily influenced by external forces (for example, other people); and (3) tradition-directed —those who fundamentally behave in accordance with set patterns, are resistant to change, and are low in social class mobility.[26] Figure 4-6 gives examples of advertising appeals to inner- versus other-directed people.

Various attempts to relate consumer behavior to systems of personality types have been attempted with mixed and limited success.[27] One attempt to type consumers according to characteristics related to product selection found five behavior patterns to be relevant in determining life-styles of the consumers in the study: personal appearance, personal care, media consciousness, food preparation, and housekeeping. Six types emerged: homemakers—the traditional kitchen-bound housewife; matriarchs—surrounded by household appliances and eschewing glamour; variety girls—various roles nicely balanced; cinderellas—torn between home-making and glamour; glamour girls—concerned with appearance, enjoying life; and media-conscious glamour girls—oriented to activities external to the home.[28]

Trait Whichever theory one embraces, personality must be treated in terms of traits if it is to be measured. A trait is a particular and persistent feature of an individual's personality that can be measured and observed. Personality is therefore treated in terms of the degree to which an individual possesses a given trait.[29] There are thousands of traits; one study identified 17,953.[30] Personality tests typically use questions to determine an individual's normal behavior or attitudes. Traits can be classified as motivational (needs, attitudes, and interests) and tempermental (general, emotional, and social behavior). Motivational traits would include aggressiveness, endurance, orderliness, and vocational interests. General behavior would include confidence and impulsiveness; cheerfulness and nervousness exemplify emotional traits; social traits include ascendancy and social initiative.[31]

In profiling behavior, traits would be charted to develop trait profiles. Traits are measured according to the tendency for a person to exhibit a given characteristic in the ways various questions are answered.

The attempts to match consumer behavior with consumer personality statistically have generally been based on trait theory. One of the earliest attempts to compare brand preferences on the basis of personality traits compared Ford and Chevrolet buyers according to their scores on the Edwards Personal Preference Schedule. The owners of the two automobile brands differed little on the psychological needs: achievement, deference, exhibition, autonomy, affiliation, introspection, dominance, abasement, change, aggression, and heterosexuality.[32] In general, attempts to predict brand choice from personality have been unsuccessful. However, some relationships, mostly weak, have been found with several types of products (for example, compact versus full-size autos[33] filter versus nonfilter cigarettes[34]) and purchase decision making.[35]

Psychoanalytic Clinical observation of disturbed people provided the first psychoanalytic theories of personality. Psychoanalists view personality as the end result

Fig. 4-6. Advertising Appeals to Inner and Other Directed Personality Types

Product	Inner-directed appeal		Other-directed appeal	
	Slogan	Illustration	Slogan	Illustration
Telephone company	Just dial—Its so easy, fast, and dependable	Attractive girl holding telephone and staring into space	The personal touch for every occasion	Five separate pictures of young ladies in a variety of situations talking on the telephone
High-fidelity turn-table	Accurate, dependable, quality high fidelity equipment	Record player, AM-FM radio in quality cabinet	In selecting components use the latest high fidelity equipment	Turntable in foreground with homemade but attractive cabinet in back
Ralph's Market	Ralph's—Known for the finest quality at the right price	Food presented on extremely expensive silver serving piece	Ralph's—The supermarket with the greatest choice	Paper plates, supper napkins, many types of food in a buffet setting
Sea & Ski	For proper sun protection—Sea & Ski	Beach scene with three unrelated couples	For a desirable vacation glow—Sea & Ski	Two men and three women water skiing from the same boat
IBM Typewriter	You save time and money when you buy IBM typewriters	Typist in foreground with boss giving orders in background	Your IBM Typewriter is part of the team in progressive management	Typewriter in foreground Man and woman in background smiling and looking at some papers
Bayer Aspirin	Don't spoil your leisure time—Bayer Aspirin	Man working in "do it yourself" workshop	Don't spoil your leisure time—Bayer Aspirin	Two men holding drinks, talking at cocktail party

Fig. 4-6. Advertising Appeals to Inner and Other Directed Personality Types (continued)

Product	Inner-directed appeal		Other-directed appeal	
	Slogan	Illustration	Slogan	Illustration
Kodak	For a lasting record	Man photographing London Bridge	Share your experiences with friends at home	Man photographing women in front of building. European travel posters in foreground
Fairchild's Restaurant	The height of sophistication	Waiter in tuxedo	Good food, reasonable price, gay atmosphere	People being served in fancy restaurant
Oregon Chamber of Commerce	Oregon, a must for those who appreciate natural beauty	Single man fishing for trout	Make new friends—enjoy carefree, "crowded with fun" weeks at Oregon.	Four people camping at a lake. Two power boats in foreground.
Community organization	Take an active part in community life—do your part for your country.	Older man in foreground. Seven men sitting around a table in background.	Knowing what is going on— join a community project, etc.	Seven men in a room drinking in background. Man holding papers in foreground.
Books	Improve yourself. Read and learn.	Dozen books including: "My Life in Court," "The Outline of History," "The Valiant Years," "Conversations with Stalin."	Improve yourself; be confident in any crowd.	Illustrations of 11 books including: "Lose Weight and Live, "Women and Fatigue," "Ship of Fools," etc.

Fig. 4-6. Advertising Appeals to Inner and Other Directed Personality Types (continued)

Product	Inner-directed appeal		Other-directed appeal	
	Slogan	Illustration	Slogan	Illustration
New house	A house that makes others stop, timeless, superb construction, designed apart	Suburban house	Contemporary style, nice neighborhood, close to schools	Suburban house
Tennis shoes	Heels reinforced, arch support— the built-in heels for sportsmen	Girl standing on deck of ship	Feel happier, comfortable in fashion	Girl dressed in tennis attire
Swedish glass	You make your party unique with Swedish glass	Formal dining table set with wine glasses	You entertain in style when you serve on Swedish glass	Canapes, potato chips and dips on a counter
Umbrella	The smart sophisticated umbrella, timeless and attractive	Man and woman walking in rain, arm in arm	The choice of popular young women— in all color ranges and sizes	Four women carrying different umbrellas
Chrysler	Excellent craftsmanship, best materials—made to last a lifetime	Chrysler auto—no background	The modern, up-to-date car for active people	Chrysler auto parked in front of nightclub
Swiss watches	The watch that is dependable	Watch pictured on wrist of man	The watch that is dependable	Watches in foreground. Two boys and a girl drinking in background

Fig. 4-6. Advertising Appeals to Inner and Other Directed Personality Types (continued)

Product	Inner-directed appeal		Other-directed appeal	
	Slogan	Illustration	Slogan	Illustration
Anthony Squire Clothes	Feel smart and look smart	Young man walking in hallway	Clothing for the rising young executive	Young man and older man talking
Columbia Record Club	Select your favorite Columbia record	Illustrations of 18 albums ranging from popular to classical music	Share happy moments listening and dancing to recorded music	Two men and two women listening to records
All-State Insurance	For the finishing touch—All-State Insurance	Young man fixing motor on car	For the finishing touch—All-State Insurance	Father and son washing family car
Squibb Toothbrush Co.	For the busy man on the go. Squibb's Electric Toothbrush	Man with pleasant smile	For a natural friendly smile—Squibb's Electric Toothbrush	Man and woman smiling
Tishman Realty Co.	Maximum efficiency with a minimum of upkeeep in a modern office. Tishman Realty Co.	Secretary working hard at desk	Happy employees and pleasant working conditions in a modern office. Tishman Realty Co.	Two men in an office
Horton and Converse Vitamins	For individual all around development—Horton and Converse Vitamins	Six separate illustrations of individual sports	For outstanding achievement in your group	Illustrations of basketball, golf and bowling

Fig. 4-6.   Advertising Appeals to Inner and Other Directed Personality Types (continued)

Product	Inner-directed appeal		Other-directed appeal	
	Slogan	**Illustration**	**Slogan**	**Illustration**
RCA Television	RCA Television	Man watching television	RCA Television	Two men and two women watching television
School bonds	Your child needs the best education there is. Vote Yes on school bonds	Children and teacher in classroom	Your child wants to be part of it. Vote Yes on school bonds	Four illustrations of children in school and playground
Metropolitan Life Insurance Co.	Leave some time for relaxation. Metropolitan Life Insurance Co.	Man watching television	Leave some time for relaxation. Metropolitan Life Insurance Co.	Two couples at cocktail party
Body by Fisher	Body by Fisher	Car parked at lake. Couple in foreground	Body by Fisher	Car parked in front of house. Guests being greeted by hostess

Harold H. Kassarjian, "Social Character and Differential Preference for Mass Communication," *Journal of Marketing Research* 2(May 1965):149-150. Reprinted from the *Journal of Marketing Research*, published by the American Marketing Association.

of forces operating within the individual. Personality is a highly individualistic phenomenon, determined on a case-by-case method after learning a person's life history.

Sigmund Freud is considered the father of the theory, even though many of his early ideas are no longer generally accepted. Freud believed that emotional conflicts arise in individuals because of the interaction among the id, the superego, and the ego. The id represents the subconscious animal drive, which seeks to satisfy drives (especially sex) however it can. The superego, again subconscious, is the conscience that seeks to suppress the id. The ego is the conscious logical force that guides the libido (driving force) to socially acceptable satisfactions to placate the id. In all this, conflicts develop that may lead to neurotic or psychotic behavior and personality characteristics. Because a person may be unaware of the conflicts or the reasons for them, the personality is formed and driven by unconscious forces (motives). Motivation research is based on Freudian psychology—thus, the emphasis on subconscious motivation and sex-related motives.

Personality types may be formed as individuals move through stages of development. Freud theorized that an individual moves through four personality stages: oral, anal, phallic, and genital. Early in life, a baby's gratification comes from the mouth through sucking (oral). The anal phase occurs during toilet training as a child learns to control elimination. During the phallic stage a child's attention centers on his or her sexual organs. Finally, in the genital state an individual gains adult sexuality and psychological maturity. If a trauma of some sort occurs at an early stage, Freud felt that the personality would be affected if the individual was fixated at a particular level. An oral-fixated personality would be characterized by greed, dependence, overabundant speech, chewing, smoking, and so forth. Anal fixation produces stinginess, possessiveness, punctuality, excessive fastidiousness, and sadism. Figure 4-7 illustrates some consumer behavior characteristics that supposedly reflect fixation at one of the levels.

Other psychoanalytic theorists who followed Freud deviated from his hypotheses, especially from his emphasis on sex. Alfrec Adler felt that personality is a function of the ways in which a person overcomes feelings of inferiority. Carl Jung hypothesized that personality is purposive striving for the "unified self." Karen Horney emphasized adjustment to "basic anxiety." She classified ten basic needs that lead to conflict as falling into one of three categories: (1) compliance needs—the need to move toward people; (2) aggressive needs—the need to move against people; or (3) detached needs—the need to move away from others.[36] Harry Sullivan proposed that personality is a social product based on the need for interpersonal relations. He believed that personality is constantly changing and developing based on our experiences. There are numerous other theories, but these are representative.

Since psychoanalytic theories are highly individualistic and difficult to research objectively, it is surprising that consumer behavior theory has been so heavily influenced by them. Sex is a heavily used theme for advertising. Motivation research has ostensibly uncovered a wide variety of personality characteristics (traits, motives) on which to base product and package design and promotional efforts. For example,

Fig. 4-7. Characteristics Associated with Fixation

Oral Stage: Most pleasure comes from stimulation of the mouth; therefore, products that are sucked or chewed, such as candy, gum, mints, and cigarettes, will be significant. Promotional materials that stress the potential oral pleasures of a product should appeal to oral-fixated persons. A Pearl Drops ad showing a person licking her teeth and saying what a beautiful feeling it was is an example.

Anal Stage: People who are anal retentive should be interested in buying products that help them to be neat and orderly, such as toolboxes with separate compartments. Anal expulsive persons are likely to be more interested in products that provide them with opportunities to be disorderly and messy in a socially acceptable manner (for example, paint and mud packs) Many children's toys, such as finger paints, fit this category.

Phallic Stage: Individuals fixated at the phallic stage are particularly sensitive to phallic symbols. Packages, logos, and brand names may carry phallic symbolism.

Based on Gerald Zaltman and Malanie Wallendorf, *Consumer Behavior: Basic Findings and Management Implications* (New York: John Wiley & Sons, 1979), pp. 370-71.

Ernest Dichter hypothesized that people judge a house by its doorknob. The way the doorknob fits the hand is reminiscent of the way the thumb is tucked in the hand in the prenatal state and in early childhood. He suggested that the phenomenon carries over to the way in which we evaluate the feel of tools and other objects, even though we are not conscious of it at all.[37]

Humanist Humanist theories emphasize that people are driven toward self-fulfillment. Most important in these theories is the individual's perception of self and environment. Maslow's self-actualization theory discussed earlier fits into this category. Maslow concluded that self-actualizing people:

1. Are clear in their perceptions of reality and are able to accept ambiguities in their environment,
2. Are self-accepting and accepting of others (experience little or no guilt or anxiety about themselves),
3. Are fanciful thinkers and spontaneous behavers but not totally unconventional,
4. Are not self-centered but rather problem-centered,
5. Are able to be objective about life and often search for privacy,
6. Behave independently but are not deliberately rebellious,

7. Enjoy life,
8. Have experienced powerful and ecstatic, even mystical, events—moments when they appear to be on the brink of something new,
9. Are socially involved and identify sympathetically with the human race,
10. Can have deep interpersonal experiences but usually only with a few people,
11. Respect all people and are democratic in their attitudes toward others,
12. Know the difference between means and ends and are not annoyed by having to endure the means to arrive at the ends,
13. Have a philosophical sense of humor, spontaneity, and play, and lack hostility toward others in their humor,
14. Are uniquely creative—that is, uniquely capable of problem finding, and
15. Do not allow the culture to control them.[38]

Obviously, everybody does not fit that mold, but to the extent that there are such people, promotion can be aimed at them (see figure 4-8). Ads in this category are directed at showing that people who want to expand their frontiers and achieve their full potential use the product advertised, or vice versa.

Self-perception or self-concept has been viewed as the basis for personality.[39] The individual seeks to maintain an acceptable and constant self-concept. Behavior is regulated—perception and relationships are accepted and rejected based on selective interpretation or misinterpretation. The "ideal self" represents the goals and aims of the individual. Behavior is directed at achieving the ideal self (actualization), and products are purchased to fit the ideal self. Many products are promoted to develop strong product images that can be matched with consumer self-images. Of course, this limits the market, but it may create strong preferences among users (see figure 4-9). We will look at this more completely in later chapters, but one example will show the relationship between self-concept and brand image. This study looked at the relationship between self-concept and ownership of two different automobile brands, Volkswagen and Pontiac GTO.[40]

Owners of the two cars perceived themselves quite differently from one another and held strong stereotype perceptions of the owners of each brand. They also perceived themselves as similar to others who owned the same make of car and quite different from owners of other makes. Car owners used the scale in figure 4-10 in making their ratings. Volkswagen owners rated themselves significantly lower than GTO owners on such traits as status-conscious, fashionable, adventurous, interested in the opposite sex, sporty, style-conscious, and pleasure seeking. The respondents accepted the stereotype for both brands and felt that they fit the auto they owned and that owners of the other brand fit its stereotypes.

Behaviorist The behavioral psychologist believes that personality characteristics are learned in much the same manner as anything else is learned. Personality can be studied by analyzing the stimulus, response, and reinforcement variables. The individual's specific responses to stimuli are used to predict future behavior. This fits the behaviorist notion of motivation treated earlier in the chapter.

Fig. 4-8. Promotional Appeal to the Self-actualizing Personality

Courtesy of the Nestlé Company.

Fig. 4-9. Self-image/Brand Image

Advertisement reprinted courtesy of Prince Matchabelli Division of Chesebrough-Pond's Inc.

Fig. 4-10.   Image-rating Scale For Volkswagen and Pontiac GTO

Volkswagen Owners	GTO Owners
Thrifty	Status-conscious
Sensible	Flashy
Creative	Fashionable
Individualistic	Adventurous
Practical	Interested in the opposite sex
Conservative	Sporty
Economical	Style-conscious
Quality-conscious	Pleasure seeking

Edward L. Grubb and Gregg Hupp, "Perception of Self, Generalized Stereotypes and Brand Selection," *Journal of Marketing Research*, 5 (February 1968):60. Reprinted from the *Journal of Marketing Research*, published by the American Marketing Association.

One view sees personality as being acquired in the process of learning. The individual is driven or motivated by physiological and learned needs. If needs are satisfied by some action, the individual will seek to satisfy similar needs in the same way in the future. Since reinforcement can be both positive and negative, personality will lead the individual toward some behaviors and away from others.[41] B. F. Skinner contends that personality is a convenient fiction we invent to pretend we have explained behavior that is actually environmentally controlled. He believes that all behavior is ultimately founded on past and present rewards and punishments.[42]

Consumer personality, given behaviorist theories, would simply be the result of product experience. Purchases would not be predicted on the basis of personality in the usual sense but on satisfaction or dissatisfaction with previous purchases.

Cognitive Cognitive personality theories follow the notion that behavior is rational problem solving. Cognitive personality theory focuses on the stable components of the individual's psychological field that mediate between experience and action.[43] The approach also emphasizes the isolation of psychological predispositions (traits). The distinguishing feature of cognitive theory is the emphasis on situation and logical problem solving as influenced by predispositions. In the extreme, the cognitivist would hold that behavior is caused by goals that pull as opposed to drives that push. Buyer behavior should be ascribed largely to the situations that people encounter rather than to stable traits within the individual.[44]

Psychographics

In order to deal more effectively with personality, it has been combined with life-style and needs to form the study known as psychographics. Psychographics is based on behavioral differences among consumers that are situation and product specific.

Nonstandard measurement devices developed specifically for the case under study are utilized. Consumer activities, interests, and opinions (AIO's) become the phenomena to be measured.

A useful definition of psychographics has been proposed at three levels. Generally, psychographics may be viewed as the practical application of the behavioral and social sciences to marketing. More specifically, psychographics is a quantitative research procedure that is indicated when demographic, socioeconomic, and user/nonuser analyses are not sufficient to explain and predict consumer behavior. Most specifically, psychographics seeks to describe the human characteristics of consumers that may have bearing on their response to products, packaging, advertising, and public relations efforts. Such variables may span a spectrum from self-concept and life-style to attitudes, interests, and opinions, as well as perceptions of product attributes.[45]

Psychographic variables fall into three categories: (1) product attributes—as proposed by the marketer and/or perceived by the consumer; (2) life-style—evidenced by behavioral variables illustrating the use of time, services, and products by the consumer; and (3) psychological—often expressed as self-concept but also involving interests and opinions.[46]

A good example of application of psychographic research is found in a study of pain relievers.[47] Variables were selected for the study using the following criteria:

1. All source areas were surveyed in the initial search for independent variables (personality, life-style, physiological needs).
2. The criterion for including or discarding a variable was its relevance to brand choice or product usage.
3. All items were formulated to express a point of view that related directly to the product.
4. Four goal-fulfillment dimensions were considered important in the use of these products and were covered extensively (see figure 4-11).

The psychographic grouping appeared to split along the product's primary function into a need for extra potency and a desire for simple relief (see figure 4-12). The four groups cited had quite different characteristics. Severe sufferers are most concerned with extra potency. They are young people with children, well educated, and living at a fast pace. They are anxious and irritable and believe they suffer more severely than others. They take the ailment more seriously and pamper themselves when sick. They are the heaviest users and are constantly on the lookout for more effective products with extra potency, extra ingredients, and new formulas.

Active medicators are also interested in potency. They are typical, middle-class suburbanites, leading actives lives. They are emotionally well adjusted. They believe in getting help for all ills and look for the remedy to improve their general well-being and help them relax and recover, look better, and do better in their social activities. They tend to be brand loyal to a modern, reputable, well-advertised product with extra potency and restorative benefits.

Fig. 4-11. Four Goal-Fulfillment Dimensions of Choice Criteria In A Drug Market

Desired Benefits ⇩	Beliefs About Ailment And Its Treatment ⇩
Efficacy (product's primary function)	
Extra potency	I suffer (ailment) more severely than others do.
Long lasting relief	I take (ailment) seriously.
Fast relief	I get (ailment) more often than other people.
Extra ingredients	I like to take it really easy when I get (ailment).
Etc.	Etc.
Restorative/social end benefits	
Get physical/mental lift	(Product) helps you carry on with social activities.
Help me relax	(Product) helps you cope with responsibilities.
Modern product	(Product) helps you not to look ill.
Well-known brand	(Product) helps you perform better with others.
Etc.	Etc.
Concern about treatment	
Completely safe product	Regular use of (product) can be dangerous.
No side effects	Extra strong (product) can be dangerous.
Recommended by doctors	Taking strong (product) can be habit forming.
Etc.	I try to see a doctor when I have (ailment).
	I always ask doctor which brands of (product) to use.
	Etc.
Pragmatism	
Simple relief	All brands of (product) are much the same.
An inexpensive product	Inexpensive (product) are as good as expensive ones.
Easy to use	I use (product) as a last resort.
Suitable for all occasions	Listening to (product) advertising is wasted time.
Etc.	If left alone, (ailment) will go away.
	Etc.

Joseph Pernica, "Psychographics: What Can Go Wrong," Ronald C. Carhan, ed., *1974 Combined Proceedings of the American Marketing Association*, (1975), p. 47. Published by the American Marketing Association.

Hypochondriacs are the first on the simple relief side. They tend to be older, female, and low in education. They are deeply concerned with their health and very cautious in self-treatment. They worry about side effects and see potential dangers in heavy use, new ingredients, and too much potency. They look for products that are doctor approved and backed by a reputable company.

Fig. 4-12. Market Dichotomy on a Medication's Primary Function

Severe sufferers	Active medicators	Hypocondriacs	Practicalists

Extra potency ⟶ ⟵ Simple relief

Modern outlook:
- Active, fast life
- Cure for all ills, psycho-somatic beliefs
- Modern product with potent ingredients

Traditional outlook:
- Slower pace of life
- Mature acceptance of discomforts
- Conservative use, skeptical about "extras"

Joseph Pernica, "Psychographics: What Can Go Wrong," Ronald Carhan, ed., *1974 Combined Proceedings of the American Marketing Association*, (1975), p. 48. Published by the American Marketing Association.

The practicalists are older, well educated, and emotionally stable. Pain is accepted as a part of life. They seek a remedy as a last resort and then they want a simple, inexpensive product with proven effectiveness. You should not have too much trouble matching Exedrin (strong medicine), Bayer (simple relief), and Anacin (with the ingredient doctors recommend most for pain) with their appropriate market targets.

Personality and Marketing Strategy

If personality is a summary variable that reflects consistent human behavior, consumer behavior ought to be based on personality, but credible research proof has been scarce. As we have gone away from simply borrowing personality testing techniques and indiscriminantly applying them to relate consumer choice to personality, the track record has gotten a little better, however. Simply matching traits from a standard test to a consumer's behavior hasn't worked well; specialized instruments work better. We have a long way to go, but using specialized tests, understanding that personality may not be a useful predictor for all products or for all situations, concentrating on product type rather than brand (unless brand image is very strong), and looking at personality as a basis for consumer buying strategies could prove more fruitful.[48]

SUMMARY

This chapter has looked at the reasons why people behave as they do. Consumer behavior is rooted in needs, driven by motives, and categorized by personality. Motivation can be defined as the force that moves an organism to seek need-satisfying goals. A need is defined as some sort of lack or insufficiency. Drive is defined as the psychological state or feeling associated with need arousal.

Several typologies that have been advanced to categorize needs and motives were discussed: primary, stimulus, and learned motives; internal and incentive motives; conscious and unconscious motives; and Maslow hierarchy of needs.

Need arousal occurs as the individual becomes aware of the need's existence. Physiological needs are aroused when some body system becomes imbalanced. The human organism seeks homeostasis and will take action to reduce the imbalance or tension state. Theories of need arousal for psychogenic needs are more complex. If a person is not receiving satisfaction of a psychological need, cognitive dissonance will occur. The psychological discomfort will drive the individual to some sort of dissonance-reducing action. If the action satisfies the person, dissonance will be reduced. Some human behavior suggests that people seek both tension and tension reduction. Thus, it is theorized that different individuals will seek different ideal levels of stimulation (tension).

Two fundamental and opposing schools of thought on motivation are behaviorist and cognitive. The behaviorist emphasizes stimulus-response mechanisms that shape behavior. The cognitive school dwells upon the idea that people are thinking, striving problem solvers.

Consumers are seldom motivated to satisfy only a single need. Needs may occur in a hierarchy where one triggers another. In other cases, a wide variety of needs may occur simultaneously. A single product may satisfy many needs, or a single need may require a variety of products for satisfaction. Multiple needs may lead to situations that are referred to as approach-avoidance, approach-approach, and avoidance-avoidance conflicts.

Personality is defined as the system of attitudes, behaviors, and values that an individual exhibits and that sets him or her apart from others. Several theories of personality were discussed: type, trait, psychoanalytic, humanist, behaviorist, and cognitive. Although success in applying personality theories to marketing situations has been limited, psychographics does seem to hold some promise in pointing at promotional appeals and providing bases for market segmentation. Essentially, the technique uses specially designed instruments to provide profiles of product users based on their activities, interests, opinions, life-style, needs, and personality.

CHAPTER 4   STUDY REVIEW

Important Terms and Concepts

Needs
Motives
Law of effect
Types of motives
Maslow need hierarchy
Need arousal
Conglomerate needs
Need conflict
Personality theories
Psychographics
Freud's human development stages

Questions

1. Discuss the ways in which needs are aroused. How might this knowledge be utilized in developing promotion strategy?

2. Differentiate between the behaviorist and cognitive schools of thought in motivational theory.

3. Give an example of a consumer in each of the need conflict situations.

4. How do marketers use the Maslow need hierarchy in their advertisements?

5. To what extent do you think advertisements appeal to unconscious motives?

6. How can incentive motives be used in promoting products?

7. Summarize each of the personality theories.

8. What is psychographics, and how can it help marketers understand and apply personality concepts to marketing strategy?

9. How useful is personality theory for the development of marketing strategy? Why?

10. Outline the need/motive categories.

Learning

```
MACHINE WASH
NO CHLORINE
BLEACH
TUMBLE DRY
MEDIUM SETTING
REMOVE PROMPTLY
IF PRESSED
USE STEAM IRON
```

From the beginning to the end of life we learn. As we perceive our environment, we are motivated to understand it. Attempts to understand the process by which we learn behaviors, facts, and attitudes have probably occupied more of the psychologist's efforts than any single aspect of human behavior. Like most areas of human behavior, learning has been viewed in a variety of ways by various researchers and theorists.

What Is Learning?

One of the problems in studying learning is that it cannot actually be observed. We can observe some of the results of the process, and we can see some of the inputs, but the actual process has been something of a mystery. The earliest attempts at understanding learning sought to deal with the phenomenon at the mental level, but is was not until psychologists began to dwell on the relationship between the inputs (stimuli) and learning outputs (responses) that progress toward real understanding began. As a result, most learning research has been in the behaviorist tradition.

There are numerous definitions of learning. Most of them say that learning involves changes in behavior. One commonly cited definition says that "learning is a relatively permanent change in behavior resulting from past experience." This definition specifically excludes temporary behavioral changes such as those brought about by fatigue, disease, alcohol, injury, motivation, drugs, sleep, hunger, and physical growth. Although these forces may result in changed behavior, they do not represent learning.[1]

To understand learning fully, experience and behavior should be defined. Experience may be direct—practice or action—or it can be indirect—observation, reading, or listening. Generally, there must be some sort of feedback before experience leads to learning. If you went to the bowling alley and found no pins or a curtain over the alley so that you could not see the pins, it is doubtful that any number of lls of the bowling ball would improve your game. There are special situations, as some classical conditioning, when learning may take place without feedback.

For our purposes, behavior should be broadly defined to include attitudes, preferences, emotions, evaluative criteria, personality, stored information, and other factors that do not constitute overt behavior. Thus, *learning is more or less permanent changes in behavior and response tendencies that result from experience and environmental influences.*

Consumer behavior is learned behavior. No one is born with reflexes or instincts that control consumer buying. Therefore, in order to understand the way consumers solve purchasing problems, we must understand the ways in which they learn. In addition to using past experience and knowledge to solve new purchase problems, consumers learn patterned behavior that can be employed over and over whenever the same purchase problems recur. This routinization simplifies and speeds consumer decision making. It also makes the marketer of a new product face the prospect of causing a consumer to unlearn an old behavior and relearn a new one.

Consumers learn a wide variety of things. They learn facts and opinions (maybe even untruths) about numerous products, brands, and business firms, for example. They learn preferences and predispositions to buy certain brands and to patronize certain retailers. They actually learn to buy and use certain products. Consumer learning, therefore, takes place on three levels: knowledge, preference, and overt behavior.

Consumers often must learn limitations in seeking to satisfy various needs. Most consumers do not have the financial resources to respond to all of the behaviors they have learned are most satisfying. As a result, they may buy a brand that is less expensive or more practical than the one they prefer. They may sacrifice a new car in favor of a new washer. Consumers learn to allocate their finances in an attempt to acquire an optimally satisfying array of products and services.

As students of consumer behavior, we are interested in the ways people learn and how they apply that learning. This chapter will first look at several approaches to the study of learning. Following that, a study of retention, transfer, generalization, discrimination, and concept identification will expand on the basic approaches.

Approaches to the Study of Learning

As many people have tried to understand learning, a number of conflicting views have developed. We will look at two general approaches to learning that seem to encompass most of the major theories of learning: (1) associative or stimulus/response theories (including respondent [classical] and operant [instrumental] conditioning) and (2) cognitive theories. No one theory is a complete explanation of learning; rather, each of the theories explains different types or levels of learning. The major theories of learning along with some examples of marketing applications are summarized in figure 5-1. Several basic concepts and terms that underlie the discussion are defined in figure 5-2.

Fig. 5-1. Learning Theories and Marketing Strategy

I. Some Applications of Respondent Conditioning Principles

A. Conditioning responses to new stimuli

Unconditioned or Previously Conditioned Stimulus	Conditioned Stimulus	Examples
Exciting event	A product or theme song	Gillette theme song followed by sports event
Patriotic events or music	A product or person	Patriotic music as background in political commercial

B. Use of familiar stimuli to elicit responses

Conditioned Stimulus	Conditioned Responses	Examples
Familiar music	Relaxation, excitement, "good will"	Christmas music in retail store
Familiar voices	Excitement, attention	Famous sportscaster narrating a commercial
Sexy voices, bodies	Excitement, attention, relaxation	Noxema television ads and many others
Familiar social cues	Excitement, attention, anxiety	Sirens sounding or telephones ringing in commercials

Fig. 5-1. Learning Theories and Marketing Strategy (continued)

II. Some Applications of Operant Conditioning Principles

A. Rewards for desired behavior (continuous schedules)

Desired Behavior	Reward Given Following Behavior
Product purchase	Trading stamps, cash bonus or rebate, prizes, coupons

B. Rewards for desired behavior (partial schedules)

Desired Behavior	Reward Given (sometimes)
Product purchase	Prize for every second, or third, etc. purchase
	Prize to some fraction of people who purchase

C. Shaping

Approximation of Desired Response	Consequence Following Approximation	Final Response Desired
Opening a charge account	Prizes, etc., for opening account	Expenditure of funds
Trip to point-of-purchase location	Loss leaders, entertainment, or event at the shopping center	Purchase of products
Entry into store	Door prize	Purchase of products
Product trial	Free product and/or some bonus for using	Purchase of product

III. Some Applications of Modeling Principles

Modeling Employed	Desired Response
Instructor, expert, salesperson using product (in ads or at point-of-purchase)	Use of product in technically competent way
Models in ads asking questions at point-of-purchase	Ask questions at point-of-purchase which highlight product advantages
Models in ads receiving positive reinforcement for product purchase or use	Increase product purchase and use
Models in ads receiving no reinforcement or receiving punishment for performing undesired behaviors	Extinction or decrease undesired behaviors
Individual or group (similar to target) using product in novel, enjoyable way	Use of product in new ways

Adapted from Walter R. Nord and J. Peter Paul, "A Behavior Modification Perspective on Marketing," *Journal of Marketing* 44(Spring 1980):42-43. Reprinted from the *Journal of Marketing*, published by the American Marketing Association.

Fig. 5-2. Concepts and Terms for Learning Theories

Drive—a strong stimulus that impels action. Drives arouse individuals and keep them ready to respond; as such, they are the basis for motivation, but they are distinguished from motives in that they are not goal directed, they simply increase probability of action without specifying the nature of the activity. While primary drives are innate (thirst, hunger, pain avoidance), secondary drives (such as fear, pride, money desire) are learned. Drives lead to action, and actions that satisfy drives become learned behavior.

Cue—a stimulus object in the environment, such as a brand, display, or advertising appeal, that leads to action.

Response—a physical or psychological reaction to a drive or cue stimulus.

Reinforcement—positive or negative feedback or reward arising from the response to a stimulus. Reinforcement is positive or negative depending on the appropriateness of the response to the stimulus that elicited it.

Based on James F. Engel, David T. Kollat, and Roger D. Blackwell, *Consumer Behavior*, 2d ed. (New York: Holt, Rinehart, and Winston, 1973), p. 232-234.

Associative Theories

Essentially, the associative theories of learning are rooted in the work of Ivan Pavlov and Edward Thorndike. They attempt to explain learning as a pairing or association of a stimulus with a response. Having been paired to a particular response, the stimulus may elicit the same response at a future time. Associative theories are generally divided into respondent or classical conditioning and operant or instrumental conditioning. *Repetition* of the stimulus coupled with the response and *contiguity* (nearness or closeness in time and space of the stimulus and response) underlie the concept of associative learning. Thorndike's work is based on trial and error. Over a period of time, behaviors that lead to positive results are repeated, while those with neutral or negative results tend to be abandoned. Thus, Thorndike suggests that a response must be rewarded (reinforced) if one is to learn to repeat it.[2]

Respondent Conditioning You are probably familiar with the work of Pavlov in studying the effects of conditioning upon dogs. The conditioning is referred to as classical, Pavlovian, or respondent (because of the emphasis on reflex or respondent activities).

Pavlov discovered the conditioned reflex by accident. He was experimenting with dogs to learn about the relationship between food in the mouth and salivation. After working with the dogs for a while, he noticed that they would salivate at the sight of food and also at the sight of the experimenter who had been feeding them, whether he had food or not. Pavlov then used various stimuli, such as the musical tone of a tuning fork and a light, before the dogs were fed. After a time, the dogs would salivate with only the tone or light. Humans have also been conditioned in the laboratory by pairing a puff of air to the eye with a light or some other stimulus. Originally, the puff of air caused the eye to blink, but the other stimulus did not. After conditioning, either stimulus alone would elicit an eye blink.

In this type of conditioning there are four separate variables.

1. *Unconditioned Stimulus* (US)—a phenomenon that elicits some form of reflex or unconsciously controlled reaction. Stimulus produces response before any conditioning has taken place.
2. *Unconditioned Response* (UR)—the reflex reaction elicited by an unconditioned stimulus.
3. *Conditioned Stimulus* (CS)—a neutral stimulus that, prior to conditioning, produces no predictable reflex response.
4. *Conditioned Response* (CR)—a reflex response essentially the same as the unconditioned response, but that is elicited by the conditioned stimulus after repeated pairing between the unconditioned and the conditioned stimuli.

In classical conditioning the subject learns to respond in a new way to some previously unrelated stimulus. Figure 5-3 diagrams the classical conditioning process.

Fig. 5-3.   Classical Conditioning

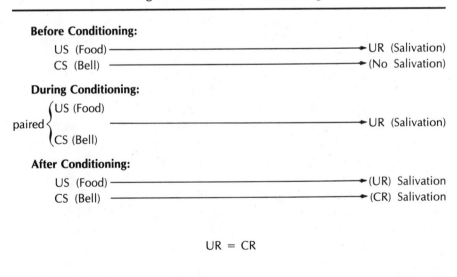

Before Conditioning:

US (Food) ————————————————————→UR (Salivation)
CS (Bell) ————————————————————→(No Salivation)

During Conditioning:

paired { US (Food) / CS (Bell) } ————————————————————→UR (Salivation)

After Conditioning:

US (Food) ————————————————————→(UR) Salivation
CS (Bell) ————————————————————→(CR) Salivation

$$UR = CR$$

In humans, direct classical conditioning can take place, but in everyday life such behavior differs from the laboratory conditioning just discussed. *Conditioned emotional responses* are important in forming our common reactions and feelings.[3] The formation of phobias is a good example. A small boy was once conditioned to fear a white rat. He came to fear anything white and furry, even though there was no reason to do so.[4] Positive or negative feelings present when a subject is exposed to a stimulus may carry over to feelings about the stimulus. If you are consuming a certain drink at a party where you are having a particularly good time, you may form a preference for that particular brand or type of drink. In-store environment or circumstances may influence a customer's feelings toward the store, its products, and its employees quite independently of the real nature of these factors.

Vicarious or secondhand conditioning can be even more significant in consumer behavior. An experiment was conducted in which subjects were divided into two groups. Group A watched while subjects in group B pretended that they were being shocked. Each pseudoshock was accompanied by a flashing light. Afterwards, the subjects in group A showed an emotional reaction, detected by a galvanic skin response (GSR), to the flashing of the light.[5] They had merely observed the reactions of others and were conditioned to react to the SC. Their reaction was not exactly the same. Group B subjects were writhing and grimacing in feigned pain. Group A did not react overtly, but an emotional feeling was present as measured by the GSR.

Vicarious conditioning may explain some of the effects of advertising. Let's say you are watching a television commercial for Coca-Cola. If it's like most Coke commercials, lots of people are singing and having fun. As a viewer, you may vicariously experience some of the feelings of gaiety. What is likely to happen the next time you see Coca-Cola in the store? Wiil you spontaneously burst into song and dance? Probably not. Remember, everyone is watching, but you may feel the inexplicable need to party, or at least you may feel a little warm and glowy inside. Will you buy Coke? Maybe, if you were going to buy some sort of soft drink anyway; perhaps, even if you weren't. Conditioning will only influence your feelings; it will not turn you into a helplessly programmed automaton.

Consider the way you feel about the ad itself. Feelings toward an ad may carry over to feelings about the product advertised. Ads that elicit positive feelings may create positive feelings for the product advertised but will not necessarily lead to purchase. They may increase purchase probability, however. There is pretty good evidence that an entertaining ad will be very limited, all by itself, in inducing people to buy unless reasons for purchase are inspired by the ad.

A question that has intrigued learning theorists for years is whether a response must be reinforced by a reward for learning to take place. Edwin Guthrie's theory of learning de-emphasized the role of reinforcement. He suggested that if a stimulus or combination of stimuli have elicited a given response in the past, that response will tend to be repeated the next time an individual is confronted with the same stimulus.[6] Further, he asserts that the stimulus-response relationship is full strength with the first pairing.[7] This presents a relatively simple theory that says that any behavior may produce learning, which will lead to similar behavior under similar circumstances in the future. Repetition and reinforcement are unnecessary. People learn simply by doing something, and learning is unrelated to success.

The immediate reaction to such a simplistic view may be negative, but at least some consumer behavior may be learned in precisely this way. The first brand in the market may develop an edge over competing products even when it is no better than, or perhaps inferior to, subsequent brands.[8] Some early models of brand choice used Markov chains, which directly predict current behavior from behavior in the immediately preceding time period. However, another study suggested that while brand choice in the immediately preceding period is a determinant, using the four previous brand selection periods greatly improved predictive power.[9]

In an attempt to account for additional variables that influence learning, Clark Hull recognized the importance of repetition and reinforcement, but he added the concept of intervening variables. He identified these variables as generalized habits, strength, drive, incentive motivation, and conditioned inhibition.[10] Hull postulated that habits are permanent connections between stimuli and responses. The connection grows stronger with each association, provided the association is accompanied by drive reduction (need satisfaction or reinforcement).

Habits may be fairly strong in buying behavior, but they can be broken if changes occur in the intervening variables. Some of these may be influenced or controlled by a marketer. For example, stimulus intensity may be tied to the power of an advertisement or display. Incentive motivation may be any reason given the consumer to modify previously set behaviors, such as free samples, price reductions, and premiums.

As you can see, the discussion has carried us away from pure Pavlovian conditioning. As we move away from reflex activity, we enter the realm of what B. F. Skinner refers to as operant conditioning.

Operant Conditioning In classical conditioning the learner is passive. An association occurs with neither the cooperation nor the knowledge of the learner. To study situations in which the learner is an active participant in the conditioning process, Skinner developed the concept of operant conditioning—so called because learning occurs as a subject actively and voluntarily *operates* on the environment.[11] Some researchers refer to operant conditioning as instrumental conditioning because the process involves an action that is *instrumental* in producing reward and that tends to be repeated.

Skinner's work was largely carried out with rats, but many of the principles are generally applicable to complex human learning. A good deal of his research was carried out with some sort of "Skinner box" (see figure 5-4). A rat is placed in the box, which contains nothing but a lever or bar on one wall and a dispenser for food. The rat will typically walk around, groom, sniff, and generally explore the box. Somewhere along the line the rat will accidentally push the bar. When that happens, food is dispensed. The rat will eat the food and return to normal behavior. After a few more pulls of the lever, the rat is conditioned and settles down to an orgy of bar pushing. After a time the rat learns to push the lever only when hungry.

The rat really has not acquired any new skill. He was already quite capable of pushing bars. What changes is the *frequency* with which the bar is pushed. Reward has led to putting existing responses together into a systematic response pattern referred to as a habit (see figure 5-5).

Fig. 5-4. The Skinner Box

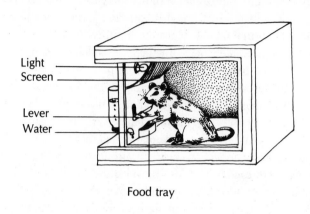

Light
Screen

Lever
Water

Food tray

Fig. 5-5. Operant Conditioning

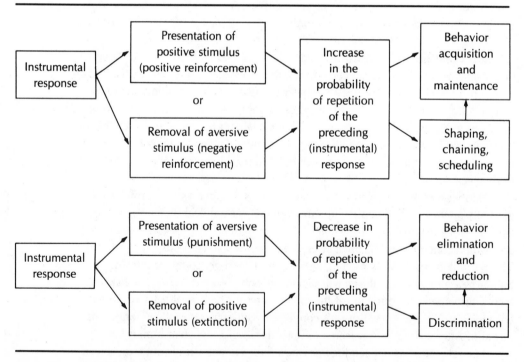

If we reward certain types of responses in sequence, we can *shape* behavior. This type of training is used to train animals. Every time the animal takes a step in the right direction, it is rewarded. By careful planning, animals can be taught rather complex behavior patterns. Skinner once taught two pigeons to play Ping-Pong through shaping.

This talk of rats and pigeons is all very nice, but few rats and pigeons are big spenders, so we must concern ourselves with operant conditioning in humans or, more precisely, consumers. Humans respond to instrumental conditioning. They tend to repeat behaviors that have, in the past, brought positive reinforcement.

Much of our repeat purchasing behavior (automatic response behavior and limited problem solving) can be explained in terms of operant conditioning. A consumer tries a product for the first time, perhaps because of a classically conditioned emotional response or because of incentive motivation. If the product performs well, the consumer's purchase choice is positively reinforced, and a second purchase becomes more likely.

Marketers may engage in shaping consumer behavior. When a life insurance salesperson is making a sales spiel, you won't be asked to sign on the bottom line right away. The salesperson will take you step-by-step through the application form. Individual questions are rather innocuous, and you readily answer. The salesperson frequently reinforces you with a nod, a smile, or an um hm. These are small reinforcers, but most of us seek and respond to approval from others. By the time you get to the commitment on the size of the policy (and whether you will take it at all), you have been shaped to answer affirmatively. What would have been a major commitment in the beginning is now a minor decision. Almost all "canned" sales presentations are designed to shape a consumer's behavior in small stages.

A bad product experience will also have a learning effect on the consumer, as illustrated in the bottom half of figure 5-5. This is referred to as aversive conditioning, and it leads to a decrease in the probability or frequency of a given action or behavior. The significance of this type of conditioning lies in the fact that, once conditioned, the subject will avoid the stimulus. A rat that learns that an electric plate gives a shock avoids the plate even when the current is turned off and never gets a chance to learn that the plate is no longer a threat. Likewise, a consumer who has a bad experience with a product will avoid it, and the marketer may never get the chance to demonstrate that the product problem has been corrected. It may take several good experiences to condition brand loyalty, but a single bad one can permanently destroy it.

Some years ago the makers of Ballentine beer changed their brewing formula, and the result was undrinkable. They changed the formula back to the original, but they couldn't get customers to come back. It took a major advertising effort under the direction of Stan Freberg to get business back. Freberg suggested to company executives that they confess their error. They asked if that wasn't a little negative. "A little negative!" he exploded. "It's a lot negative—purge yourself, they'll love you for it." Ads showed a meek Herman Ballentine confiding to his psychiatrist that his stupid relatives had changed the formula when he was on vacation, and, although he had changed it back, nobody would believe him. This ad was followed by one in which he told the psychiatrist that he had finally found something for his simpleton relatives to do—put the labels on the bottles. A shipment of 25,000 bottles with the labels on upside down followed the ad.[12]

The campaign worked, but it illustrates how much more difficult and costly it can be to reteach a dissatisfied consumer than to capture a customer the first time. Negative experience and information can be devastating to a company's marketing effort.

Reinforcement Schedules When responses are reinforced, they can be rewarded each time they occur or intermittently. The former is referred to as a continuous reinforcement schedule, and the latter is a partial reinforcement schedule. In the laboratory the reinforcement schedule can be completely controlled. However, in real-life learning situations, reinforcement is unlikely to occur with every response. This does not mean that conditioning does not take place. Establishment of a stimulus-response relationship may take longer with partial reinforcement, but once established it is very resilient. If a response goes unreinforced enough times, the S-R bond will be broken and extinction will occur. When the conditioning has taken place under partial reinforcement, unreinforced responses will not lead to elimination of the S-R bond as quickly.

There have been numerous explanations as to reasons for the effect of partial reinforcement.[13] Probably the simplest explanation is that the subject simply does not expect to be reinforced with each response. However, the subject knows that the response is sometimes rewarded and so will continue for some time without being rewarded before deciding that no reward is forthcoming.

The concept of partial reinforcement seems significant for consumer researchers. In a competitive environment, anything that will solidify buying behavior against inroads of other brands could be useful. Obviously, the idea of purposeful partial reinforcement on product quality is not particularly practical. If a consumer were accustomed to sporadic quality, a few bad items would not be so likely to lead to brand switching, but it is doubtful that brand loyalty could be established under such a partial reinforcement schedule. Brand loyalty established under continuous reinforcement would probably stand one disappointment, perhaps more, if the company always made good on the faulty product, but a change of brand would occur rather quickly if the consumer has more than a very few bad experiences.

In order to increase sales by inducing nonbuyers to purchase or current users to stock up, manufacturers of consumer packaged goods often use cents-off offers and premiums. If these offers are made intermittently, people are likely to take advantage of them each time they are offered. On the other hand, if they are offered too frequently or over too long a period of time, consumers will not respond because they will feel that the special price will be available in the future. The special price comes to be perceived as the regular price, and returning to the original price will very likely be seen as a price increase, so the new price may be resisted.

Respondent and Operant Conditioning Contrasted Respondent (classical) and operant (instrumental) conditioning are really quite different from one another. Respondent conditioning is the simplest form of learning. It takes place automatically, without the learner's awareness. Learning is the result of association, not reinforcement. Operant conditioning is a more complex, higher order of learning. It explains how we learn from our successes and failures. Learning occurs in an increase or probability or frequency of response resulting from reinforcement. Figure 5-6 summarizes some of the major differences between the two types of conditioning.

Fig. 5-6.   Classical Versus Operant Conditioning

Classical Conditioning	Operant Conditioning
1. Involves an already established response to an unconditioned stimulus	1. Involves no previous stimulus-response bond
2. Takes place without subject awareness or cooperation	2. Conscious, if accidental, action taken by subject
3. Can occur without reinforcement	3. Reinforcement required
4. Learned behavior is reflex or automatic	4. Learned behavior is conscious, goal oriented action
5. Involves changes in feelings, opinions, etc.	5. Involves changes in goal oriented behavior
6. Conditioned response is elicited each time conditioned stimulus is received	6. Increases the probability and frequency of response, but response will not necessarily occur with each stimulus

Based on David Krech, et. al., *Psychology: A Basic Course*, (New York: Knopf, 1976), p. 50-61.

Cognitive Learning

So far, the learning that has been discussed takes place in both lower animal forms and humans. Cognitive learning takes place to a limited degree in higher animals, but it is largely characteristic of human learning. Behaviorists see learning as responses consistently arising from stimuli. They emphasize what can be observed, and, while they would not argue that nothing happens in the human mind between the stimulus and the response, they largely ignore these mental processes on the ground that they are not observable. Hull's emphasis on intervening variables is an exception to this.

Cognitive psychologists, on the other hand, concentrate heavily on the intervening mental processes that occur between stimulus and response. Stimuli are perceived and information is processed and organized. Response is a reasoned, goal-oriented problem solution or a change in attitude or perception. Indeed, cognitive learning theorists see learning primarily in terms of changes in perceptions or, more precisely, as changes in the ways stimuli are perceived. The most important concepts in cognitive learning theory are insight, meaning, perception, and problem solving.[14]

Because cognitive learning is closely related to perception, Gestalt psychology contributes many basic concepts to the theory. Gestalt is a German word that means "form or shape." Kurt Lewin's field theory of learning is grounded in the Gestalt concept of field. Kurt Lewin saw the human perceptual ground as something like a magnetic field in which every part depends on every other part.[15] As learning occurs, the field changes and the learner behaves differently because perceived relationships have changed. The change in the field may occur very suddenly. Thus, the new behavior occurs as a result of insight. This follows the discussion of insight problems discussed in chapter 2. Our perceptual field of possible need satisfiers constantly changes as we become aware of new products. We must continually alter our means-ends strategy in problem solving in the marketplace.

Edward C. Tolman attempted to combine parts of associative and cognitive theories.[16] His theory is often referred to as purposive behaviorism because he emphasized goal direction along with the stimulus-response relationship. Learning activity is always directed toward a goal, and learning is the process by which one finds out what leads to what. A cognitive map (similar to Lewin's field) is developed to understand the environment by learning which responses lead to reinforcement.[17]

A consumer may have various cognitive maps that guide buying behavior. These maps may be generalized to new situations. For example, you have a mental image of where things are located in the stores you shop. But what happens when you enter a new store? Are you completely lost? Probably not. Your generalized cognitive map of all the stores you have been in will help you locate desired items rather quickly if there is any logic to the store layout. Chain stores will often help you by having all their stores arranged in essentially the same way.

Consumer learning probably exists on a continuum from unconscious learning of feelings toward brands to learning through trial and reinforcement which brands are satisfactory. The continuum would culminate in complex problem solving (EPS) behavior in which goals are identified, perception is influenced by past experience and information is brought to bear, and insight and understanding are applied to arrive at a satisfactory solution. Even when consumers operate out of habit, they are not necessarily locked into an unending stimulus-response behavior mode. Consumers continuously receive and process new information, altering their motivations and perceptions accordingly.[18]

Other Types and Conditions of Learning

We have looked at the major schools of thought concerning the ways in which learning takes place. However, there are some additional areas of learning that are relevant in our study of consumer behavior. Verbal and motor learning, concept

Fig. 5-7

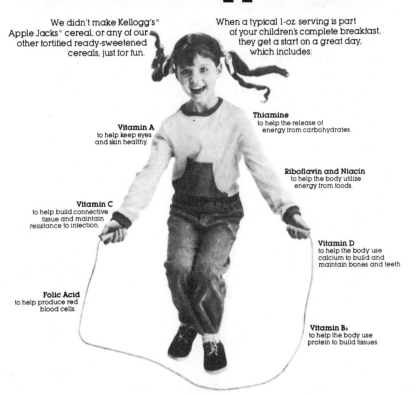

Why we put 8 essential vitamins in Apple Jacks.

We didn't make Kellogg's" Apple Jacks" cereal, or any of our other fortified ready-sweetened cereals, just for fun.

When a typical 1-oz. serving is part of your children's complete breakfast, they get a start on a great day, which includes:

Vitamin A
to help keep eyes and skin healthy.

Thiamine
to help the release of energy from carbohydrates.

Riboflavin and Niacin
to help the body utilize energy from foods.

Vitamin C
to help build connective tissue and maintain resistance to infection.

Vitamin D
to help the body use calcium to build and maintain bones and teeth

Folic Acid
to help produce red blood cells.

Vitamin B₆
to help the body use protein to build tissues.

Kellogg's
It's gonna be a great day.™

® Kellogg Company   c 1980 Kellogg Company

Cognitive learning takes place through this advertisement by Kellogg Company which helps resolve questions consumers often have about ready-sweetened cereals—are they nutritious? The ad details the fortification of Kellogg's ® ready-sweetened cereals, including the function of each vitamin, and helps consumers learn the nutritional benefits of ready-sweetened cereals as part of a complete breakfast.

Courtesy of the Kellogg Company.

formation and identification, modeling, and the special case of consumer learning among children and adolescents are covered in the following sections.

Verbal and Motor Learning

Verbal learning involves the use of language or symbols. Since most of our knowledge is stored in the form of words, verbal learning is very important. Consumers learn the names of brands and stores. Words become cues that identify the characteristics of the phenomena they perceive. As such, they become associated with feelings and images. This comes about through verbal conditioning. Words are also the stuff of which the highest order of human thinking and abstraction is made. We combine words to form ideas, often original.

Verbal learning is treated in terms of rote learning, serial memorization, paired-associate learning, and verbal discrimination. Rote learning occurs when words are learned in an unthinking, mechanical way without the aid of insight or higher cognitive processes.[19] Brand names, especially meaningless ones, may be learned in this way. Serial memorization refers to learning material in sequence. Product instructions and characteristics are often learned in sequence. Paired-associate learning is similar to classical conditioning in that two words are learned together—a store name and a brand name may be learned at the same time and be subsequently associated in the consumer's mind. A great deal of product-oriented advertising that retailers use may function to effect this type of learning. Verbal discrimination involves learning which of several words represents the "correct" response. Many times consumers see all brands as pretty much alike, so a great deal of advertising is directed at getting consumers to discriminate among brands. Comparative advertising, in which competing brands are named, shows the consumer that the name of the advertised brand represents the desired quality as opposed to the other brands mentioned.

Motor learning involves chains of responses that are joined to form physical habits. Examples are walking, driving, and riding a bicycle. Motor skills tend to be retained considerably better than verbal learning. Learning to use numerous consumer products involves motor learning. When new products are introduced, marketers must be sure that consumers have ample opportunity to learn to use them properly. Any involvement marketers can induce in promoting products will make the product and brand name better remembered. Even the simple process of entering a contest may make the sponsor better remembered. Free samples and automobile test drives follow the same principle.

Concept Formation and Identification

Many learning activities involve concepts rather than words or actions. Conceptual learning is contrasted with associative learning in that stimuli do not need to be present for learning to occur. Concepts allow us to categorize phenomena into relevant groups and can be defined as "the ability of a person to distinguish between objects so that they are classified as belonging or not belonging to a particular group of objects."[20]

Consumers learn to conceptualize product groups and identify the general character of a satisfactory product. This relates to the idea of evaluative criteria discussed in chapter 2. A consumer may not be able to list all the characteristics of the ideal product but will recognize it when it is found; the consumer has a concept of the right set of product characteristics. We will look at the measurement and application of product concepts in chapter 9, where concept testing is discussed.

Concepts have relevant and irrelevant dimensions. The relevant dimension is one that will lead an individual to a correct problem solution. If a consumer wants an economical car, the relevant conceptual dimensions might be price, fuel economy, and repair history for that particular type of vehicle. This information may be available from the sticker and consumer test reports. Irrelevant dimensions are those features of an automobile that do not consistently lead to correct decisions, such as color, interior design, body style, or brand name. Marketers should be aware of the relevant concept dimensions for various market segments—they will be different for different groups. For a teenage boy, power and styling might be the relevant dimensions of an auto.

Modeling

Social learning occurs through stimuli provided by people.[21] There are two types of social learning. Direct instrumental learning occurs when a teacher consciously and explicitly attempts to shape responses by reinforcement. Imitation or modeling occurs when an observer matches responses to cues provided by a model who may or may not be consciously attempting to influence behavior. Imitation is the process by which most children are socialized. The previous discussion has dealt primarily with instrumental training, so the following will concentrate on modeling.

Many human skills are learned by observational learning, modeling, or imitation.[22] Recent research of the effects of television violence on children's behavior suggests that modeling may be a powerful learning force.[23] Modeling has its positive side, too. Children learn socially acceptable behavior by watching their parents. (Of course, if their parents exhibit socially unacceptable behavior, children will learn that also.) Modeling is akin to the vicarious conditioning discussed earlier. It is likely that the effectiveness of movie stars, sports figures, and others in product testimonials is, in part, the result of modeling.

Albert Bandura contends that virtually all types of learning that may come from direct experience may also occur through observing the behavior of others and seeing the consequences of that behavior. In fact, he contends that most of our behaviors are learned through example.[24] He suggests four subprocesses that govern modeling.

1. Attention—the observer is exposed to the modeling stimulus, becomes aware of, and differentiates the distinctive aspects of the model's behavior. Bandura suggests that televised models are very effective in attracting attention.

2. Retention—the subject must retain the images and symbols represented by the model for a period of time, since there is typically a time lapse between exposure to the model and opportunity for imitation.

3. Motor reproduction—the observer must have the necessary resources and skills to imitate the behavior.

4. Reinforcement and motivation—receipt and anticipation of positive incentives encourage attention and determine whether observed behavior will be translated into overt behavior.

Bandura also notes several functions of modeling:

1. Observational learning—the transmission of information about ways of organizing observed responses into new behavior patterns. Demonstrations, pictures, and verbal descriptions provide models. While adults generally prefer verbal description, children respond better to behavioral demonstrations.

2. Strengthening or weakening inhibitions—observed reward and punishment induces or reduces subject inhibitions toward behavior.

3. Response facilitation—a subject's present behavior is reinforced by observation of the model's performance of an acceptable behavior.

4. Stimulus enhancement—the observer's attention is directed toward objects used by the model. As a result, the observer may use the objects, although not necessarily in the imitation of the model.

Different models will have different effects in influencing observers. When an observer perceives a model to be high in competence, expertise, power, celebrity standing, or socioeconomic status, behavior may be imitated more fully. Such factors as age, sex, and ethnic status will vary in influence depending on the observer's characteristics, since models perceived to be similar to the observer are more likely to be imitated.

Consumer Learning in Children and Adolescents

Consumers must learn buying behavior. Socialization of the buying/consuming process begins with very young children. Parents may give some attention to teaching children overtly how to be consumers, but most learning is imitative. Children learn buying behavior from parents, friends, schools, and media. Of late, public schools have taken a more active role in early consumer education. However, a good deal of conditioning through modeling has probably occurred before children start school. Television appears to be a primary modeling influence on children from preschool through adolescence.

An extensive study of the influence of television advertising on children was recently reported.[25] Charles Atkin employed the concept of modeling to structure his research results. Television commercials were found to be effective in gaining the attention of children. Younger children were somewhat more attentive than older children to ads. Public service ads (PSA's) were most frequently attended to, followed by ads for candy, hygiene, cereal, shoes, toys, and medicine, in that order.

Atkin's report noted some learning effects. When a PSA called for children to point out littering behavior to offenders, a large portion reported that they did so. Also, black children were found to be more likely to imitate the behavior of white models than black models.[26]

According to the report, commercials influenced children's inhibitions. Modeling influences were successful in changing stereotyped play attitudes (for example, girls playing with electric trains and cars). Seeing models eating candy tended to remove any inhibitions children might have for eating candy. PSA's were unsuccessful in changing children's behavior in seat belt use and smoking intentions, but short-term inhibitions were developed relative to littering. In the Atkin study, along with other studies of adults, inhibitions relative to social acts were more easily instilled than physical inhibitions.[27] Antismoking campaigns that show the smoker as being socially unacceptable have generally been more effective than health appeals.

Since most consuming behavior is inherently acceptable, the response facilitation function is relevant. Positive modeling on eating candy and cereal, for example, does seem to have a significant effect in increasing consumption. Increased brand consumption seems to be a direct function of the degree of exposure to ads.

Adolescents are also influenced in their buying behavior. Television, family, and peers seem to be the major influences in forming economic and social motivation for consumption, materialistic values, and purchasing information.

Television Television seems to affect adolescent acquisitions of *expressive* aspects of consumption directly.[28] This may extend to aspiring to have the same possessions as TV characters and to hold similar attitudes. Youngsters have been found to discuss TV ads with parents and peers.[29] One study found that peer communication about consumption declines with increased television viewing.[30]

Family Adolescents learn goal-oriented, *rational* aspects of consumption from their parents.[31] Youngsters often compare the information received from parents with the knowledge of their peers.[32]

Peers Youngsters appear to learn the *symbolic* meanings of goods from their peers.[33] Peers may also be influential in determining the extent and direction of conspicuous consumption.[34] Information and attitudes learned from peers also tend to be communicated back to parents, often influencing their behavior.[35]

Extensions of Learning Concepts

To this point, numerous specific types of learning have been considered. This section treats several general aspects of various types of learning which have application to consumer behavior. These are transfer, source and order effects, generalization, discrimination, and retention.

Transfer

Transfer is the way in which learning in one situation carries over to and influences learning and behavior in other situations. Transfer may be positive when learning in one situation facilitates learning in another. Negative transfer may also occur when learning in one situation inhibits learning in another. When prior learning influences later learning it is referred to as proactive, while the reverse is called retroactive. Thus, there may be proactive and retroactive facilitation and inhibition of learning. Experience with one brand may be transferred to other brands the company sells. Proactive facilitation occurs when a consumer transfers positive experience about a currently used brand to a new one from the same company. Retroactive facilitation may also occur when positive experience with a brand may cause a consumer to go back and try another brand from the same company that was previously tried and rejected.

A problem occurs because perception is not always accurate. All brands of a given product may be mentally lumped together. A bad experience with one brand may be transferred to all other brands of the product and even similar products. It is important that a manufacturer be aware of this in positioning products.

Source and Order Effects

It was noted in chapter 3 that the source credited with information can influence the way in which that information is perceived. When information comes from a credible source, the information is perceived as more credible, and more credible information is more readily learned.

There are also order effects in learning. Learning is subject to both primacy and recency effects. Information perceived first and last tends to be recalled better than intervening information. This may extend to an evening's television viewing. Advertisements seen early and late in the evening tend to be retained better than ads seen in midevening. A single ad may also be subject to order effects, so brand name, features, and availability of the product should be summarized and emphasized at the beginning and end of the ad. Even summarizing at the end only will be helpful in achieving retention.

Generalization

Generalization is the tendency to respond in the same manner to different but related stimuli. This, of course, relates to the concept of transfer just discussed. Learning transfers because we generalize to say, "This is like that." The more similar a new stimulus is to another one, the greater is the tendency to respond in the same manner to both of them.[36] If you place a new product in the market that is too similar to existing products, you will gain no distinctiveness, and consumers may be indifferent as to whether they select your product or another one like it. Likewise, consumers may generalize across advertisements and not perceive individual ads because they are all alike. On the other hand consumers may not perceive a product to fit existing preference and use patterns if it is too different (like the mousetrap in chapter 1).

Products are constantly being changed. Somehow, they must be perceived as different by consumers but not too different, or the brand may lose users. The change in behavior that occurs when the stimulus is changed from its original character is called the generalization gradient.

Discrimination

We learn to discriminate among similar phenomena. The experience of my young son who moved from Tuscon, Arizona, to a northern state illustrates the importance of discrimination. There are so many varieties of cacti in Arizona that the term *cactus* is not particularly descriptive. As a result, residents learn to call cacti by more specific names, such as cholla, prickley pear, and saguaro. When the boy's kindergarten teacher showed the class a picture of a saguaro and asked what it was, the boy said, "It's a saguaro." His teacher argued, "No, it's a cactus." Because the boy had a more specific verbal and mental concept than the teacher, an extended disagreement ensued. An Eskimo has as many as thirty-six different names for snow in its many variations, while other cultures may have no more than one.

Product differentiation aims at causing consumers to discriminate among competing brands. Emphasizing distinctive features, differentiated packaging and brand names, and unique advertising appeals may accomplish this.

Retention

The fact that information about products has been learned does not mean that it will be retained. Much information is forgotten very quickly after we are exposed to it. Figure 5-8 shows a typical forgetting curve. Apparently, there is a short-term memory with limited capacity from which information is quickly lost. We use this when we look up a phone number and retain it long enough to make a call; then it is quickly forgotten. Information may be transferred to long-term storage under certain conditions.[37]

In addition to their internal memory systems, consumers also have access to external memory.[38] Much information is available to consumers in the form of packages, store layout and display, shopping lists, and the like. This takes a good deal of pressure off the consumer's learning requirements and should (although it does not always seem to do so) lead to more effective consumer decisions.

The idea that there are several types or levels of learning is referred to as the multiple store concept. Some researchers argue that there is only one level of memory,[39] but the multiple store concept seems useful as a means of understanding memory.

James Bettman has identified several aspects of retention that seem relevant in the study of consumers' choice.

Fig. 5-8. Forgetting Curve

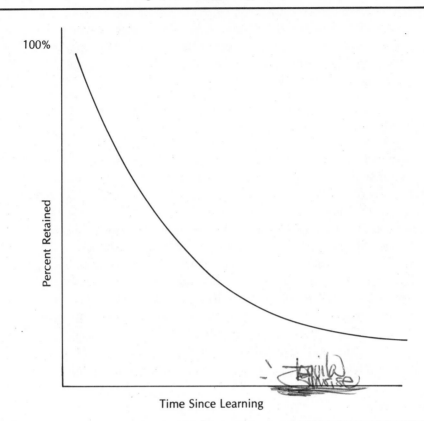

1. Factors differentially affecting recognition and recall
2. Organization of information when received by the consumer
3. Effects of a difference in context between the receipt and attempted retrieval of information
4. Effects of the total processing load on the individual
5. Memory for rules and operations
6. Effects of the modality of information presentation
7. Effects of repetition of information.[40]

A good deal of the research that has been carried out in these areas is rather far removed from real life, and often applications to consumer behavior must be the result of some heroic leaps in logic.[41] In addition, consumers generally do not make conscious attempts to memorize market information as do many of the subjects in experiments on learning.[42] For these reasons, the results discussed here must be considered indicative only of how consumer memory works.

Factors Differentially Affecting Recognition and Recall In general, it is easier for consumers to recognize learned stimuli than to recall them. Recall requires that a stimulus be *reconstructed* from memory, while recognition means that a stimulus need only be *differentiated* or *discriminated* from other stimuli. There are literally thousands of brand items in the typical supermarket. Only a few hundred may be known to a consumer, but if asked to list the known brands, probably relatively few could be brought to mind. However, going through the store, the consumer can probably recognize many times the number that could be recalled.

Words that occur less frequently seem to be more readily recognized. The opposite is true for recall.[43] Low-frequency words, because of their uniqueness, are easier to discriminate from others. More often seen words, because of their familiarity, are easier to reconstruct. Depending on whether brand choice occurs in the store (recognition) or out of the store (recall), more or less frequently seen brands may be selected.

Apparently, the consumer's plan for using information is a factor in determining whether it will be stored for recall or recognition.[44] It may be possible for advertising to carry a suggestion as to how information should be stored. For new products, the consumer may be advised to prepare for recall so that the item may be requested if not visible in the store. Other ads may simply advise the consumers to look for the product in certain locations. Simpler shopping tasks may rely on recall, while more complex ones may depend on recognition. Advertising, store layout, and packaging efforts should proceed with this in mind. In general, the consumer must give two to five seconds attention to store information for recognition and five to ten seconds for recall. Of course, the consumer's motivation will be a factor in whether information is transferred to long-term memory for any sort of future reference.

Organization of Information Input When learning information for recall, people use memory strategies in which data is organized, associated, and grouped for later retrieval.[45] However, if the organization does not correspond with usual grouping strategies, input grouping may actually hinder recall.[46] Consequently, information that is grouped or chunked in advertisements should correspond with the ways in which consumers currently group information about the product.

Effects of Context Even though information has been stored, it must be accessible to the individual if it is to be retrieved. The context in which the information is stored determines the context in which it is most readily retrieved.[47] To the extent that information in an advertisement fits the context in which the purchase is made, product information will be more readily recalled, and a brand will be more readily recognized. Often advertisements emphasize product *use* situations as opposed to product *purchase* situations. In-store recall and recognition would be facilitated by showing product purchase scenarios in ads along with consumption patterns. Simply displaying the product package prominently may be helpful. Scenes from ads or people appearing in ads are often used in illustrations on packages or in store display materials.

Effects of Processing Load The capacity of an individual's short-term memory is a function of total processing requirements at a given time. If other activities are occurring when the individual is receiving information, less memory capacity is available. Typically, there is a good deal of distraction in any consumer learning situation, so we would expect consumer memory to be less than ideal.

More complex tasks require more information processing and therefore leave less memory capacity. If a task is simple to learn, high rates of information input may be used. Consumer choice tasks vary greatly across products and situations. It is generally felt that the amount of information delivered should be minimized in advertisements. However, relatively large amounts of information may be successfully communicated if the memory task is relatively easy. This would be true where information is nontechnical, not new, and where achieving recognition rather than recall is the goal of the ad. More complex information in larger amounts may also be effectively delivered in situations where consumers already have decision rules for dealing with the information. Thus, ads for established products may present more data than those for new products.

Memory for Rules and Operations When evaluating purchase alternatives, consumers may combine knowledge of various product attributes. In general, information on the final alternative decision and on intermediate processing results relative to the various product attributes seems to be more readily recalled than the original information that was collected on the alternatives.[48] Product and brand image, then, will tend to be synthesized from numerous sources rather than from a single market communication. Even though marketers are effectively delivering information designed to create a given brand image, consumers must be constantly monitored to determine what images they have actually formed.

Effects of Input Modality In general, consumer information is received through verbal and visual modes. Research indicates that in very simple memory tasks, verbal stimuli are superior to visual ones in getting information into short-term memory. The same does not seem to be true for long-term memory.[49] In more complex situations memory seems to be enhanced by forming visual images.[50] Visual memory of the package has been shown to be a significant factor in brand choice of breakfast cereal and would be expected to extend to other products as well.[51] Musical imagery created by jingles and songs in ads is also important in children's cereal brand selection.[52]

Effects of Repetition The concept of repetition in learning has long received research attention. In general, the effects of repetition are viewed in two contexts. Learners may be perceived as more or less passive, with repeated information exposures bringing them to a higher state of awareness and understanding, but at a decreasing rate. This gives rise to the familiar learning curve (figure 5-9). The other view sees people as active information seekers and processors. Under active search, the number of trials or exposures to achieve learning may be reduced to as little as one.

Fig. 5-9. Learning Curve

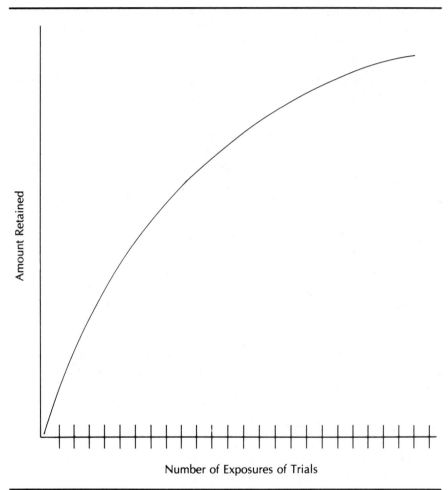

Amount Retained

Number of Exposures of Trials

In general, studies of consumer behavior show that repetition alone may be sufficient to achieve awareness.[53] In achieving recall, information inputs distributed over time are generally better than a mass of information presented all at once. If retaining information from an ad is the promotional goal, an advertising program spread over a period of time is probably the best strategy. However, if a maximum immediate response is desired, an advertising blitz may be the best approach. It should be noted that information from ads may be quickly forgotten if ads are not repeated.[54]

The consumer's plans, goals, needs, and motives may have a significant impact upon the effectiveness of advertising exposure and repetition. Interest and involvement in an advertising message may lead to more rapid learning. It has been suggested that under conditions of involvement only three exposures are sufficient to achieve retention.[55] The first exposure evokes a "What is it?" response, and a preliminary assessment of usefulness is made. If the first reaction is favorable, the second exposure will generate a more detailed evaluation and a plan for future action. The third exposure functions as a reminder to carry out the plan formulated in the second exposure. A delay reaction is hypothesized wherein the individual, having been exposed to an ad once, may ignore a large number of subsequent exposures until a need arises. At that time, the individual may again perceive the ad, and this will serve as the second exposure. Repetition may serve the function of imprinting an ad on a consumer's mind, or it may simply assure that the ad is "out there" and available for perception when the consumer is ready. Because of individual differences, it is doubtful that an exact number of stimuli can be set, but research does give limited support for the effectiveness of a small number of exposures.[56]

Thus, for low-involvement learning, sheer retention may be effective, particularly in achieving recognition as opposed to recall.[57] More elaborate information processing may occur with high involvement, and more rapid learning at a recall level may result.[58]

SUMMARY

Consumer behavior is learned behavior. Learning is defined as more or less permanent changes in behavior and response tendencies that result from experiences and environmental influences. Consumer behavior is learned on three levels: knowledge, preference, and overt behavior. As consumers learn, much of their buying behavior is reduced to habit to gain more efficiency.

Learning is generally approached as either an associative process, where connections between stimuli and responses are established, or a cognitive process, where the emphasis is on changes in perception that occur as subjects engage in goal-oriented problem-solving behavior.

Associative theories are categorized as classical and operant conditioning. In classical or respondent conditioning, a person remains passive while stimulus-response associations are established. Then, when an unconditioned stimulus is paired with a (to be) conditioned stimulus, the unconditioned stimulus comes to elicit a conditioned response much like the unconditioned response. Operant or instrumental conditioning involves overt behavior that is either rewarded and continued or punished and discontinued. Partial reinforcement leads to responses that are more resistant to extinction.

Cognitive learning occurs as consumers perceive problems and bring experience and insight to bear in order to solve the problem. Other types and conditions of learning mentioned were verbal learning, motor learning, concept formation and identification, and modeling. Subprocesses that govern modeling include attention, retention, motor reproduction, and reinforcement and motivation. The functions of modeling—observational learning, strengthening or weakening of inhibitors, response facilitation, and stimulus enhancement—were also discussed.

The extensions of learning concepts that were discussed are transfer, source effects, order effects, generalization, discrimination, and retention. The chapter concluded with a discussion of several factors that determine what will be retained.

CHAPTER 5   STUDY REVIEW

Important Terms and Concepts

Respondent or classical conditioning
Operant or instrumental conditioning
Cognitive learning
Drive
Cue
Stimulus
Response
Reinforcement
Shaping and modeling
Verbal and motor learning
Source and order effects
Generalization and transfer
Discrimination
Retention/memory

Questions

1. Summarize the learning theories discussed in this chapter, and suggest ways in which they may explain consumer behavior.

2. What is a reinforcement schedule, and how might a marketing strategy employ alternate schedules?

3. What is shaping, and how can promotional strategy shape consumer behavior?

4. What is modeling? Summarize the subprocesses that govern modeling, and discuss the functions of modeling.

5. How is the concept of modeling used in promotion strategy?

6. Describe the process by which children learn buying behavior.

7. Discuss the factors relevant to an understanding of retention. How could these factors be applied in advertising?

6

Consumer Attitudes: Formation, Structure, and Change

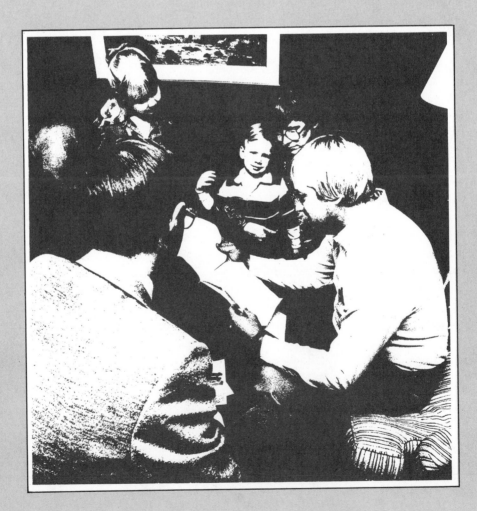

We have investigated the major contributions of the psychologist to consumer behavior. Perception, motivation, personality, and learning form the core of our understanding of individual behavior. The things that we perceive and learn must be given organization. Personality provides organization, and motives generate the driving force for behavior.

The study of attitudes takes us into the realm of the social psychologist, who is concerned with the behavior of the individual in interpersonal relationships. Attitudes, like personality, represent an interface between the individual and the environment, including other people, business firms, marketing strategies, and products. Attitudes represent the organization of beliefs, opinions, and response tendencies in an evaluative framework. Through attitudes we express what we like and dislike, and how strongly we feel toward the phenomena we evaluate. In a sense, attitudes provide a cognitive map that helps us to take and repeat actions that will satisfy our needs. We have learned to feel positively toward phenomena that satisfy us and negatively toward those that do not.

Attitudes are important to marketers at two levels. First, individual attitudes are partial determinants of the brands and products consumers buy and use to satisfy their needs. Second, general attitudes may be more or less universal and influence the consumption behavior of an entire society. Society's attitudes toward sex, leisure time, and male-female roles have changed drastically in recent years. These have given rise to dramatic changes in our life-style and, simultaneously, in purchasing patterns. We will look at these social forces in the next two chapters. This chapter is concerned with defining attitudes, investigating their formation and structure, and identifying the process by which attitudes are changed. The subject of attitude measurement will be covered in chapter 9.

Attitudes Defined

Like other behavioral concepts, attitude has numerous definitions. In spite of differences in wording, the various definitions are similar. A few of the more common definition are:

1. An attitude is a tendency or predisposition to respond in a specific manner to particular stimuli (including people, objects, and situations).[1]

2. Attitudes are relatively enduring organizations of feelings, beliefs, and behavior tendencies toward other persons, groups, ideas, or objects.[2]

3. Attitudes are learned tendencies to perceive and act in some consistently favorable or unfavorable manner with regard to a given object or idea, such as a product, service, brand, company, store, or spokesperson.[3]

4. Attitudes refer to the stands the individual upholds and cherishes about objects, issues, persons, groups, or institutions.[4]

5. Attitudes are learned predispositions to respond. Attitudes. . .are learned and relatively enduring organizations of beliefs about an object or situation disposing a person toward some favored response.[5]

There are other definitions of attitude, but these illustrate the range. Essentially, attitude definitions may be broken into three schools of thought.[6] One school views attitude as an *evaluative or feeling reaction*. Here, an attitude is seen as the favorableness or unfavorableness of feeling toward a phenomenon. Another school sees attitude as a *readiness to respond* in a particular way with regard to an attitude object. This attempts to relate attitudes closely to behavior. Finally, a third school suggests that attitudes are composed of a *constellation of cognitive, affective, and conative components*. These components are interrelated ways of understanding, feeling about, and acting toward an attitude object or issue.

Any of these definitions or schools of thought may be acceptable under different circumstances. The discussion in this chapter will draw upon all of these concepts.

Characteristics of Attitudes

Many writers contend that all evaluative feelings and tendencies to respond or behave in particular ways are not attitudes. Behavior may be grounded in beliefs and opinions. A belief may be defined as "the acceptance of a statement or proposition as a fact or a truth."[7] Opinions are described as weakly held beliefs, and thus may be quite changeable. Opinions are also defined as verbal expressions of attitudes.[8] Opinions and beliefs do not necessarily lead to behavior, nor are they always associated with evaluative feelings for or against something. They have no dynamic or driving properties. They are merely assumptions or judgments an individual believes to be true. In contrast, an attitude has motivational impact. The object of the attitude arouses a pleasant or unpleasant feeling, and this feeling is more intense with more strongly held attitudes.

Muzafer Sherif and Carolyn Sherif suggest five characteristics that typify attitudes and set them apart from other cognitive concepts.[10]

1. Attitudes are learned, not inborn. Innate needs and drives may, however, influence attitudes.

2. Attitudes are generally fairly long lasting. They do change, but they normally do not fluctuate much in the short term.

3. Attitudes are directed toward specific phenomena, such as persons, companies, or brands.
4. Attitudes can be formed toward virtually any phenomenon. Marketing efforts can influence attitudes toward any aspect of the product or purchase situation.
5. Attitudes are based on drives. Not all predispositions can be called attitudes; some may merely reflect established habits. Brand and store preferences and the like, which are based on drives, are attitudes. Repeat buying behavior that is simply habitual probably is not founded directly on attitudes.

Components of Attitudes

One school of thought holds that attitudes represent a multifaceted phenomenon. A wide range of terminology is used by different writers to describe the components of attitudes, but most agree on the nature of the three structural components of attitude: cognitive, affective, and behavioral (see figure 6-1).[11]

Fig. 6-1.   Schematic Conception of Attitudes

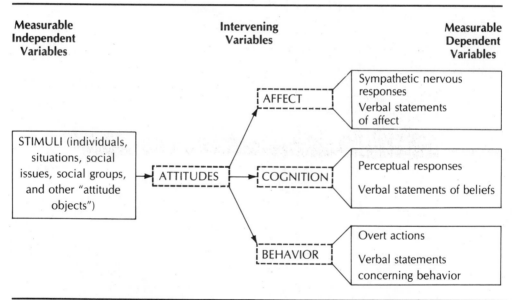

Milton J. Rosenberg, "An Analysis of Affective-Cognitive Consistency," in Milton J. Rosenberg, Carl I. Hovland, et. al., eds., *Attitude Organization and Change*, (New Haven, Conn.: Yale University Press, 1960), 3. Reprinted by permission of the Yale University Press.

Cognitive Component The cognitive component of an attitude is composed of what we know or think we know about a phenomenon, such as a brand. This component includes knowledge, beliefs, opinions, values and images that are held relative to the brand. This knowledge may come from observing others using the product, receiving information from any source, and actually using the brand. Without the other dimensions, the cognitive component alone would simply fall into the realm of opinion and belief discussed in the previous section.

Affective Component The heart of the attitude is the affective component. This dimension distinguishes attitudes from beliefs and intentions. Essentially, the affective component is an emotional construct representing how we feel about something (for example, our like or dislike of a brand). This component implies an additional attitude construct. Our feeling for or against a brand has both strength and direction. This dimension has been referred to as valence.[12] Strategically, valence is important to marketers; whether people like or dislike a brand is important information. In addition, the degree to which consumers like or dislike a brand is significant in determining how well insulated a company's brand is from competition and the likelihood of pulling business away from competition.

Behavioral Component Finally, the behavioral component is the payoff for the marketer. What a consumer does about knowledge and feelings toward a brand is most important to a firm. The behavioral component is manifested in both intentions to buy and actual purchases. The consumer may have positive information about a brand and like it but may not actually buy it for a variety of reasons. Habit toward another brand may be strong, there may be other brands the consumer likes better, or the preferred brand may be unaffordable.

There is an impetus for congruity among the components of attitude. A person will experience less dissonance if all components are in agreement. Milton Rosenberg writes:

> When the affective and cognitive components of an attitude are mutually consistent the attitude is in a stable state; when the affective and cognitive components are mutually inconsistent (to a degree that exceeds the individual's present tolerance for such inconsistency) the attitude is in an unstable state and will undergo spontaneous reorganizing activity until such activity eventuates in either (1) the attainment of affective-cognitive consistency or (2) the placing of an "irreconcilable" inconsistency beyond the range of effectiveness.[13]

Strategically, a marketer may seek to create dissonance among attitude components through various promotion activities. Dissonance reduction potential may then be provided through the marketer's promotion of desirable product features.

Functions of Attitudes

Attitudes perform several functions, and we can better understand the reasons why people hold the attitudes they do if we study the functions performed by attitudes. If we know the psychological needs that are met by holding attitudes, we are in a better position to predict when and how the attitude will change. The major functions attitudes perform can be stated in terms of their motivational bases.

1. instrumental, adjustive, or utilitarian
2. ego-defensive
3. value-expressive
4. knowledge[14]

Instrumental Function The instrumental function is grounded in behaviorist learning theory. Instrumental learning theory posits that we learn from a reward-punishment mechanism. We structure our behavior in an attempt to maximize our rewards and minimize our punishments. We develop positive attitudes toward those things that have satisfied us, and we form negative attitudes toward those things that either fail to satisfy or that punish. In this sense, our attitudes become guides to behavior that will satisfy our needs.

Experience with various products and brands leads to attitudes. The more satisfying the product, the stronger the attitude formed will be, and the more resistant the attitude will be to change.

Ego-defensive Function You are probably familiar with Aesop's fable of the fox and the grapes. The grapes were suspended in such a way that, try as he might, the fox could not reach them. At first the grapes appeared most desirable, but as it became apparent that he would be unable to have the grapes, the fox changed his attitude and finally walked away from the grapes in disgust, saying, "The grapes were probably sour anyway." With the newly formed negative attitude, he could turn his attention away from the grapes without fretting about what he had missed.

One function of attitude, then, is self-protection—not physical but ego. Consumers may form negative attitudes toward products they cannot afford or are not usable for other reasons. The low-income consumer may express a dislike for "ostentatious" luxury cars. The overweight person may develop a negative attitude toward tight-fitting jeans and shorts.

All people employ defense mechanisms to protect their egos. Some attitudes may be more defensive in function than others. People will generally be unaware of the fact that they are engaging in ego defense, but they may be aware of the fact that they are defending themselves without knowing why. Attitudes formed for defense may be fairly resistant to change, and individuals may be quite sensitive to communications directed at changing attitudes. The marketer should become aware of possible defense mechanisms. This knowledge may be difficult to apply in the case of advertising, but it may have more practical application in dealing with people face-to-face in personal selling. If a salesperson attacks a defensive attitude as old-fashioned or unrealistic, strong defense reactions may develop, resulting in a lost sale.

Value-expressive Function Ego-defensive attitudes often have the function of preventing others from seeing the individual's true nature and feelings. Value-expressive attitudes play the opposite role in that they function to communicate the individual's central feelings, values, and self-image to others. An individual may receive a great deal of ego-reinforcing reward from self-expression.

Many products are purchased to give expression to self-image and personal values. Products have meaning for their owners that go far beyond their basic functions. A person who highly values group acceptance may form positive attitudes toward and purchase products accepted by the group. A person strongly concerned about ecology and conservation will be likely to express positive attitudes toward biodegradable packaging.

Knowledge Function We are bombarded by a seemingly endless flow of facts and figures. Although we are constantly learning from our environment and our experiences, we do not learn everything we are exposed to. On the contrary, most information goes by us. Consumers are not generally motivated to be active learners about products in general, but they do want to understand the products that are particularly relevant to them.

Attitudes provide a framework for determining what information is important to learn. We perceive and store product information according to what our attitudes dictate. On the other hand, when new information comes to us in areas where no attitudes are held, new attitudes will form to evaluate and categorize the information. As we perceive new product information, it is unlikely that we will modify existing attitudes unless currently held knowledge proves to be inadequate, incomplete, or inconsistent. Marketers providing new information must often show previously held knowledge-based attitudes to be incorrect. In so doing, they must take care not to challenge ego-defensive attitudes, thereby arousing strong resistance to change.

The Relationship Between Attitudes and Behavior

Attitude formation and change are generally seen as preceding overt behavior. In particular, this notion is consistent with the logic of the Howard-Sheth model (figure 2-13) discussed in chapter 2. The product adoption models covered in chapter 10 also follow this line of reasoning. In general, the direction of attitude research and the development of marketing strategy suggest that many observers agree with the concept. Research indicates, however, that there is a far from perfect relationship between attitudes and subsequent behavior.

The question of whether attitude change will lead to predictable behavior change is an important one to advertisers since their objective in creating a message is generally to change consumer attitudes in the hope of increasing sales. (Note the connection between the discussion here and the relationship between buying intentions and actual purchase discussed in chapter 2.)

In addition to the concept that attitudes may lead to behavior, there is evidence to suggest that attitudes can be influenced by overt behavior. Once we have done something, there is considerable pressure (cognitive dissonance) to bring our attitudes into line with our actual behavior.

Looking at the relationship from the other side, we find that many early research studies suggested limited ability to predict behavior from attitudes.[15] In fact, there are a number of reasons why we may not be able to predict behavior change from attitude accurately.

To begin with, there are problems in defining and measuring attitudes. If you don't know the basis of your prediction, it is difficult to arrive at a valid prediction. In addition, shortcomings in measurement techniques may suggest a discrepancy between attitude and behavior when none actually exists.[16]

It is also important to measure the right level of attitude if behavior is to be accurately predicted. Figure 6-2 suggests that the more specific an attitude is, the more likely it will accurately predict a given behavior. Also note from the figure that the attitude toward *buying* a product is likely to better predict purchase than the attitude toward the product itself.[17]

Fig. 6-2. Attitude Specificity and Behavior Predictability

	Correlation between attitude measure and behavior	Index of the accuracy with which behavior could be predicted (Range = 0.00-1.00)
Attitudes toward environmentalism	+.12	.02
Attitudes toward air pollution	+.21	.04
Attitudes toward lead-free gasoline	+.36	.13
Attitudes toward the purchase of lead-free gasoline	+.59	.35

From Robert A. Baron and Donn Byrne, *Social Psychology: Understanding Human Interaction*, Second Edition. Copyright © 1977 by Allyn and Bacon, Inc. Reprinted by permission. Based on data from Thomas A. Heberline and J. Stanley Black, "Attitudinal Specificity and the Prediction of Behavior in a Field Setting," *The Journal of Personality and Social Psychology* 33 (1976):478. Copyright © 1976 by the American Psychological Association. Reprinted by permission.

Another reason why it is difficult to predict behavior change is that any given attitude may give rise to a variety of behaviors.[18] Liking a product may lead a person to express liking for the item verbally, to admire it in the store or in the possession of a friend, to begin saving for it, to try it on a limited basis, or to purchase the product immediately. Dislike may or may not lead to discontinuance of use.

Closely related to the previous idea is the fact that a given product will have a number of features and characteristics. We may have a negative attitude toward some and a positive attitude toward others. Whether we buy or not will depend in part on how important the features are. In competing with Listerine, Scope emphasizes its good taste. Scope commercials suggest that Listerine users have "medicine breath." Listerine countered with, "Listerine, the mouthwash that tastes terrible twice a day." The claim was that the bad taste was a testament to Listerine's strength. Many people bought and used Listerine in spite of its bad flavor.

Intervening factors may intrude, making it impossible to behave consistently with attitudes.[19] Financial restrictions would be a common intrusion. Conflicting needs among family members is another. In addition, because a person likes one brand or product does not mean that he or she doesn't like something else better. Consumers tend to develop priority systems to order products toward which they have positive attitudes so as to meet needs and express attitudes according to desirability and strength.

The degree of involvement an individual has in the attitude change process will often be a factor. It has been suggested that under conditions of high involvement, attitude change is likely to precede behavior change. In low involvement, behavior change is likely to precede attitude change.[20]

Finally, the degree of risk and anxiety associated with the purchase may be a factor in the direction of attitude/behavior influence. Attitude change seems more likely to precede behavior change for expensive items.[21] When an item can be purchased at a low price or tried for a limited time, a person with a negative or neutral attitude may be induced to buy, and satisfaction may lead to attitude change.

Attitude Formation

Marketing strategy is strongly aimed at influencing consumer attitudes. If, in fact, attitude generally precedes behavior, this is a legitimate effort. Marketing efforts enter at two phases of attitude formation. First, when a consumer has no knowledge of or attitude toward a product brand, one must be formed. (This can occur with or without intervention by market strategists.) Second, if an attitude is present, the strategist is often faced with the problem of changing the attitude. Obviously, attitude formation and attitude change are closely related. However, since products are so pervasive, the marketer seldom faces a blank attitude "slate." Attitude change is therefore more often the challenge than simple attitude formation. Initial attitude formation often occurs without conscious thought, while attitude change for products and brands will more often come about as the result of a carefully conceived and executed marketing strategy. We will briefly examine the process by which consumers form attitudes and then look at the ways in which marketing strategists seek to change these attitudes.

We are not born with attitudes; we learn them. Consumers begin to learn attitudes toward brands and products very early in their experience. Various forms of learning were discussed in chapter 5. Consumers learn attitudes like they learn anything else: by simple exposure to products or product information, by classical or instrumental conditioning, by observational learning, and by information processing/problem solving.

Exposure As noted in chapter 5, we can learn simply by being exposed to a phenomenon. When faced with a situation in which we have no basis for judgment, we may express a positive attitude for something that is familiar even though we have no objective basis for evaluation. Positive attitude may form simply through seeing a brand name or package. One goal of promotion is simply to create brand or product awareness.

Conditioning Attitudes may be classically conditioned by what happens when we do things. A consumer may develop a positive attitude toward a brand simply because it was bought in an attractive environment or because a favorite song was playing when the item was seen or purchased.

Consumers may also be classically conditioned through carefully considered strategy. The feelings elicited by a pleasant product advertisement may extend to the product itself, resulting in the formation of a positive product attitude.

Instrumental conditioning is likely to be outside the control of the marketer. Attitudes form here because various actions are rewarded or punished. Obviously, rewards would tend to create positive attitudes, and vice versa; to the extent that reward can be overtly controlled by the marketer, attitudes may be influenced. The reward needn't be great; a salesperson's nod of agreement can reward a prospective customer enough to influence product attitudes. Free samples, deals, and coupons may be used to induce a customer to try an item. In this case, attitude will follow, rather than precede, behavior.

Observation Consumers can acquire new attitudes simply by observing the behavior of others. This is, of course, similar to exposure but involves seeing the behavior of others using a product rather than simply seeing the product itself. We may learn attitudes by observing parents, friends, or people in advertisements. The earlier discussion of attribution theory concluded that consumer attitudes will be more readily influenced by observing people in an advertisement if they perceive them to be actually using and liking the product advertised.

Information Processing/Problem Solving Attitudes are formed as we seek and use information and solve problems. These attitudes develop as a result of cognitive learning. If a consumer is faced with a problem situation, a decision will have to be made among several purchase alternatives. The decision will probably be made in terms of the estimated probability that the product or brand chosen will have positive benefits and the value the derived benefits will have to the consumer.[23] Many attitudes will grow out of the instrumental relationship perceived between the attitude object (product, for example) and the consumer's goals. The closer the connection—the more strongly the consumer believes that the object will aid (or block) goal attainment—the stronger the attitude will be.[24]

Favorable attitudes may be developed toward believable and helpful information sources. Based on these attitudes, we extend our feelings to apply information from favorably viewed information sources to a wide variety of buying problems. At the same time, a workable problem solution may give rise to positive attitudes toward the problem solution and the problem-solving approach used.

Attitude Change

Marketing strategy often calls for effecting attitude changes among consumers. The ways in which attitudes may be changed are linked to the ways in which they were formed in the first place. But the marketing strategist faces the problem of getting a consumer to abandon an old attitude and adopt a new one, and attitudes are often highly resistant to change. Product attitudes are often very complex. In reality, the feelings a person has toward a product or brand are likely to be composed of a number of related attitudes. Either several attitudes must be changed, or one central attitude must be identified and influenced. This section will identify some theories of attitude change and then discuss the persuasion process in terms of persuasive communications and resistance to persuasion.

Theories of Attitude Change Many theories of attitude change have been advanced. Several of the most thoroughly developed and researched are examined here. There are similarities among the theories, and, under given circumstances, all could probably be considered accurate and useful. The five theories discussed here are: consistency, group dynamics, cognitive dissonance, attribution, and social learning.

Consistency Theory The consistency theory seems quite relevant from a strategic standpoint because it attempts to explain the effects of overt attempts to change people's attitudes through communication. The theory is related to the attitude components discussed earlier. Much of the work in this theory has been carried out at Yale University by Carl Hoveland.

An attitude is viewed as a favorable or unfavorable reaction to an attitude stimulus. Thus, attitude is the emotional affective reaction a consumer would have toward a product, brand, or store. The attitude can be changed through communication by influencing consumer beliefs (the cognitive component), consumer feelings (the affective component), or consumer behavior (the behavioral component). The theory contends that the individual seeks consistency among these components, and if one component shifts, there is pressure to bring the other two into balance. A consumer's attitude might be changed by providing new information, thereby changing beliefs; through emotional appeals or classical conditioning to influence the affective component; or by inducing the consumer to behave in a new way, as through a free sample.

An effective communication might raise questions about the product or other attitude object and then supply answers to support the sought-for attitude. Supportive statements can be made to drive the new belief home further. One significant question is, What kind of statements might be most likely to elicit attitude change?

Fig. 6-3

Mother Nature is lucky her products don't need labels.

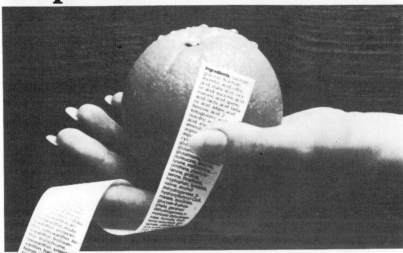

All foods, even natural ones, are made up of chemicals. But natural foods don't have to list their ingredients. So it's often assumed they're chemical-free. In fact, the ordinary orange is a miniature chemical factory. And the good old potato contains arsenic among its more than 150 ingredients.

This doesn't mean natural foods are dangerous. If they were, they wouldn't be on the market. The same is true of man-made foods.

All man-made foods are tested for safety. And they often provide more nutrition, at a lower cost, than natural foods. They even use many of the same chemical ingredients.

So you see, there really isn't much difference between foods made by Mother Nature and those made by man. What's artificial is the line drawn between them.

© Monsanto Company 1980

For a free booklet explaining the risks and benefits of chemicals, mail to: Monsanto, 800 Lindbergh Blvd., St. Louis, Mo. 63166. Dept. A3NA

Name _____

Address _____

City & state _____ Zip _____

Monsanto

Without chemicals, life itself would be impossible.

Providing new information (cognitive component) may lead consumers to change their attitudes and view chemical additives more positively.

Courtesy of the Monsanto Company

The statement about a product or brand can be couched in emotional (affective) or factual (cognitive) terminology. Research on the subject is limited, but one study indicates that in communicating promotional messages to well-educated consumers, a factual tone is superior to emotional appeals in changing beliefs and influencing the affective attitude component.[26] There is some evidence that people who hold few beliefs or who are uninformed about an attitude object tend to hold less favorable attitudes than those who are better informed.[27] It thus would seem important for a marketer to provide substantial factual information to consumers in order to establish favorable attitudes.

Four processes are seen as determining the degree to which a consumer will be persuaded by communication: attention, comprehension, acceptance, and retention.[28] Before any communication can influence attitudes, the consumer's *attention* must be gained. The principles of perception we looked at in chapter 3 apply here. Uniqueness, loudness, movement, special offers, and so forth represent ways by which marketers may gain attention.

Once attention is gained, the consumer must *comprehend* what is being said. Promotional appeals must be clear and geared for the target audience if attitudes are to be influenced.

Even if a promotional message is perceived and understood, the audience must *accept* the premise communicated. Acceptance is a function of the benefits (rewards) promised by the promotion. Also, the consumer must feel that the reward promised is relevant and worth changing attitude and behavior for. A commercial for a new dandruff shampoo may capture a woman's attention, be understood, and be accepted as factual. But if she is not troubled by dandruff, she is unlikely to be influenced one way or the other.

Finally, the attitude or the information underlying the attitude must be *retained* long enough for action to result when the opportunity arises. Advertisers use jingles, music, and slogans to make their messages more memorable.

According to consistency theory, four categories of variables influence the acceptance of persuasive communications: source, message, audience, and audience reaction.[29] Where information comes from influences its credibility and hence its persuasive power. *Source effects* may arise from the person doing the communicating or from the medium carrying the message. The two major components of credibility are expertise (factual knowledge) and trustworthiness ("good" motives). At times, nonrelevant factors may influence credibility. These might include age, race, sex, physical appearance, social standing, and batting average. Additional factors that may influence communicator credibility are power (the ability to give reward and punishment), competence (product or other relevant knowledge—for example, Mario Andretti doing an STP commercial), idealism (perceived high moral standards), similarity (the communicator perceived to have personality, attitudes, and goals similar to audience), and dynamism (charisma, speaking ability, and finesse).

The *nature of the message* itself is a major factor in influencing attitudes. A "good" advertisement may get attention, effect understanding, gain acceptance, and achieve retention, while a poorly worded or boring message may fail on all counts.

Other message factors, which are explored in the section on persuasion, are order of arguments—should the strongest one come first or last—one-sided versus two-sided arguments, explicitness of conclusions, use of fear appeals, length of the message, and hard versus soft sell.

Several *audience characteristics* are important. Among these are the audience members' intelligence, self-esteem, dogmatism, authoritarianism, store of knowledge, degree of involvement, and degree of commitment (brand loyalty). More intelligent persons may be less emotionally committed to a stand and may be converted by rational arguments. Less dogmatic (closed minded) individuals may be more easily influenced. Persons with weak brand loyalties may be more easily persuaded to hold positive attitudes toward and purchase new brands.

The *reaction of an audience* may be significant. If an advertisement or personal selling effort raises consumer defenses or leads to counter-arguing, current attitudes may be solidified and subsequent attitude change may be difficult to achieve.[30]

Group Dynamics Theory Consistency theory assumes that the individual is a more or less passive reservoir of information who processes logical arguments to arrive at a final attitude. Kurt Lewin based his social theory of attitude change on field theory. The individual is seen as a social being, heavily dependent on other people for the knowledge that underlies attitude. This dependence means that groups to which we aspire or belong have a strong influence in shaping beliefs and attitudes. Under this theory the major force leading to changes in attitudes, beliefs, and perceptions is the degree of discrepancy between an individual's attitude or behavior and group norms.[31] There is no need for persuasive arguments. The individual need only be aware that a personally held attitude is different and feel the need to be accepted by the group.

The fashions we select, the home furnishings we buy, and the automobiles we drive may be heavily influenced by the groups with which we identify. Again, persuasive efforts have little significance in this theory. Group members generally don't try to persuade others to accept their norms; they simply reject an individual who is unwilling to accept group values. There is heavy social pressure in most groups for members to conform to group standards or norms. The consistency theory takes a learning viewpoint, while the group dynamics approach emphasizes that attitude change occurs because of motivation arising from social needs. These needs might arise from a desire to compare oneself to others (My car is as good as yours); the need to evaluate one's own abilities and attitudes (Are my new jeans the "right" kind?); and the desire to reduce discrepancies between one's own attitudes and group norms by changing oneself (I'm going to have to get a new car), changing the group (Wait 'til they see my new coat—they'll all have to have one), or considering the group as irrelevant (They have no taste anyway). What people do here will depend on how much reward the group can give, their degree of independence, and their social power within the group.

Marketing strategy can benefit from applying knowledge about group dynamics. Reaching opinion leaders and showing the product to be used by "significant others" (sports figures, movie personages, and other well-known individuals) are among the means advertisers use to invoke group pressure.

Cognitive Dissonance Theory The concept of cognitive dissonance was discussed in chapter 2, but here we will look at the specific relationship between cognitive dissonance and attitude change. Leon Festinger contended that inconsistencies or discrepancies among the cognitions (opinions, beliefs, and knowledge) an individual holds create tension and psychological discomfort that he or she seeks to reduce. [32] Social forces and group pressures might play a role in creating dissonance, but the discrepancy could be entirely internal. Dissonance is a function of the relationship between elements in the individual's behavior and forces in the internal or external environment. Thus, cognitive dissonance may lead an individual to change behavior, beliefs and opinions, or the external environment (or the individual's perception of it).

As the degree of dissonance increases, the pressure for attitude change will intensify. The magnitude of dissonance is a function of three conceptual variables: importance of the cognitive elements, ratio of dissonant to consonant elements, and cognitive overlap.

If conflicting cognitions are related to needs of *importance* to the individual, the impetus to change is stronger. A commercial that says your wash is not as white as it ought to be may be greeted with a resounding, "Ho hum." On the other hand, an advertisement that illustrates a relevant need may readily stimulate the consumer. The overweight person may eagerly respond to an ad for a diet aid capsule that promises lost pounds without exercise or hunger.

People do not hold just one or two cognitions at a time. Consumers have hundreds of opinions and beliefs about products and stores, and they store a multitude of facts from experience and observation. Any brand or product may be the focus of a large number of cognitions. The degree of dissonance an individual feels at a given time is a function of the number of dissonant and consonant cognitions existing at that time. *The greater the ratio of dissonant to consonant elements at a given time, the greater the dissonance.* Few brands or products are viewed as all good or all bad. A positive attitude toward a brand is likely to exist because a consumer's positive knowledge and feelings outweigh the negative side. If a consumer holds more negative than positive cognitions toward a brand or product yet uses the product anyway, dissonance will be present and use behavior may be quite vulnerable to competitive pressures. If a few positive cognitions can be added, however, dissonance will be greatly reduced. The strategy of cigarette marketers in the face of health concerns provides a good example here. A smoker who holds the cognition "Smoking is dangerous" is in a dissonant state. Adding the cognitions "Filters reduce health hazards" and "Cigarettes low in tar/and nicotine are safer" will markedly reduce, and perhaps even eliminate dissonance, especially if the cognitions "I like to smoke" and "People who smoke are macho" are also held.

Dissonance often develops when consumers must choose one alternative over another. Dissonance may be reduced by shifting the attitude toward the rejected alternative to the negative.

Cognitive overlap refers to the degree of similarity among attitude objects or alternatives. When two alternatives share a large number of features, they have a high degree of cognitive overlap. The less two alternatives have in common, the more dissonance is likely to be aroused as a choice is made between them, and the greater is the pressure to alter the attitude toward one or both. A consumer choosing among several brands of TV sets may experience less dissonance than the consumer choosing between a new TV set and a new freezer.

The implications of cognitive overlap for marketing strategy may run in two directions. Promotion seeks to elicit attitude change. If a brand is presented as being very different from other brands, dissonance may be great, and there may be strong pressures to reduce it. If the promotion is effective, the consumer may shift attitude in the desired direction toward the new product. However, a consumer may tend to follow the path of least resistance. Given this, since the consumer is trying to reduce the dissonance created by the ad, it will be simplest to reject the new brand. Thus, when cognitive overlap is minimized in promotion, the message will have to be very persuasive if the consumer is to make a major attitude change. On the other hand, if there is a high degree of cognitive overlap, the degree of required attitude change is small, but the degree of dissonance and resulting pressure to change the attitude is also minimized.

Attribution Theory Attribution theory was discussed in chapter 3 along with the discussion of perception, but it also relates to attitude change, so the concept will be developed further here. One aspect of attribution theory attempts to explain the ways in which we interpret the motives and actions of others. The theory deals with our *perceptions* of the reasons for our own and other people's behavior. It is a cognitive theory containing no motivational constructs, such as a need to reduce dissonance or group pressure toward conformity.

The potential causes for behavior can be grouped into situational (external) and dispositional (internal) factors. A person representing a product may be perceived as selling it for the money (situational) or because he or she is really sold on the item and wants to share it with others (dispositional). Attribution theory argues that people are generally more likely to explain other people's actions by dispositional factors (intelligence, generosity, dishonesty, greed) rather than by situational factors. If that is true, the motives of people in advertisement might be perceived as nonmonetary more readily than one might think. Attitude change is more likely to occur if the change agent is perceived to be sincere, so this would be good news to advertisers. Still, the cynicism that many people feel toward advertising may swing the balance toward noncredibility. Those cynics, however, may say that advertising is not trustworthy and still might be influenced by their feelings and the tendency to attribute a degree of honesty to most other people.

Several factors will determine whether an attribution is situational or dispositional. People are more likely to make dispositional attributions when observed behavior is non-normative—that is, not characteristic of what would be expected under usual conditions. An example is the celebrity who "never" endorses a product but makes an exception in this case. A television commercial for Mocha Mix milk substitute features Steve Allen and Jayne Meadows. They had not done product endorsements before, and they make a convincing case by telling us that they began using the product years ago because of their child's milk allergy. When the company asked them to do the endorsement, they agreed only because they liked and used the product. It's easy for the viewer to forget they are getting paid for the ad.

A second factor in making dispositional attributions involves seeing the same behavior occurring in a wide variety of different situations or over an extended number of time periods. Phillips 66 has used a series of institutional advertisements in which they emphasize the "good" things they have done. For example, they have worked on a drug for arthritis victims, a blood filter for kidney machines, and other beneficial products unrelated to their gasoline business. Seeing their good deeds in a variety of situations leaves us hard pressed to come to any conclusion other than that they are "good guys," in spite of the somewhat tarnished image of the petroleum industry.

Finally, dispositional explanations are likely to occur when the observer is unable to detect possible situational causes of behavior. As was stated earlier, promotional efforts suffer from a credibility problem: the consumer knows the advertiser or salesperson is trying to make a sale. George Bernard Shaw once said of the medical profession that he had a hard time trusting a person who knew where his gallbladder was located and stood to gain $300 by removing it. The trick is to convince him that the MD is interested in his health and not his money. The same, of course, can be said for any sales effort. A salesperson might increase credibility by assuring the consumer that there is no commission on the sale. Or the salesperson may advise a prospective buyer not to purchase a particular brand that he or she sells because it will not meet the buyer's needs. We are much more likely to believe what our friends tell us about products than what salespeople say because we feel that the friends have nothing to gain or lose from our decision.

Social Learning Theory Social learning theory argues that behavior leads to consequences that feed back to the individual and influence attitudes and subsequent behavior. This is the familiar instrumental conditioning that goes on constantly, rewarding and punishing behavior and influencing attitudes. Essentially, this relates to the instrumental attitude function. We form positive attitudes toward phenomena that reward behavior, and as the reward diminishes or reverses, we experience attitude change.

Socially learned attitudes may occur through numerous modes, just as any other sort of learning. These modes include those we discussed in chapter 5—namely, direct experience, observation, reading, and listening. In order for the consequences of our behavior to influence attitudes, an individual must remember the consequence and expect it to occur again.

Persuasive Communication Persuasion is an important part of marketing strategy. Promotion is largely an influence activity. Several factors seem significant in determining whether persuasive efforts will be successful. The most important seem to relate to characteristics of the communicator, the structure and content of the message communicated, the audience, and the situation or context in which the message is delivered.

Characteristics of the Communicator Whether consumers are persuaded to change their attitudes or behavior is partially a function of the perceived credibility of the communicator. Four factors seem most significant in determining how credible people might perceive a communicator to be: expertise, intentions, likability, and enthusiasm and interest.

Research generally supports the idea that people perceived to be more *competent or expert* on an issue or product will have greater persuasive impact in effecting attitude change.[33] The argument presented by an expert generally seems more convincing and reasonable than one coming from a less expert communicator.[34] In addition, audience predisposition determines the effect of credibility. When message recipients are favorably predisposed toward an issue prior to receiving the message, a moderately credible source can bring about greater agreement than a highly credible source.[35] When respondents are negatively disposed prior to communication, a highly credible source may induce more agreement than the less credible source.

One question that research seems to leave unanswered is the degree to which expertise in one area may transfer to other areas. Advertisers use movie stars and other well-known figures to promote products about which they have no particular reason to have extraordinary expertise. Why should an expert baseball player have special knowledge about beer or razors? Prominence alone may be the major issue here. Just as we are willing to believe friends who tell us how good their car is even though they know nothing about mechanics, we may accept what people with whom we are familiar say about a product even though there is no real expertise.

A phenomenon known as the sleeper effect has long been associated with communicator credibility. The concept suggests that as time passes, the influence of low-credibility sources increases while high-credibility sources become less influential.[36] The idea is that as time passes, what was said becomes more important than who said it. However, further research suggests that while the impact of high-credibility sources may decrease, low-credibility sources do not increase in influence.[37] On the basis of the sleeper effect, some writers have suggested that advertisers should save the money they might spend on highly credible people to tout their products. However, later research suggests that the extra money could be well spent.

A communicator's perceived *intentions* will also influence a consumer's ability to be persuaded. This is, of course, related to attribution theory as it deals with the motives we attribute to others. When we perceive that communicators have little to gain from our attitude change, we are more likely to believe the message and to be influenced by it. This characteristic is referred to as trustworthiness. Evidence suggests that when we believe we are overhearing people talk about something, we are more likely to believe they are not trying to sway our opinions, and we will be more readily influenced.[38] This, of course, is the effect sought in the slice-of-life ad so often seen on television in which we seem to be observing people engaged in normal activities and using a particular brand.

How much we *like* someone is a function of several factors, and it is a major determinant in how likely we are to be influenced by that person.[39] If we like a person, we will be anxious to share his or her opinions and attitudes.[40] Two major factors that determine whether and how much we are apt to like a communicator are perceived similarity and physical attractiveness. In general, communicators who are physically attractive and seen as similar to ourselves are better liked and more persuasive.[41] The application of this in advertising is obvious. Most people who appear in ads are easy to look at. In addition, great effort is exerted to convince us that they are "regular folks," just like us.

People who are *enthusiastic and self-confident* are more likely to influence attitudes.[42] This will work best when an audience has little knowledge about the subject and no reason to think the communication is wrong.[43] In addition, the communicator's exuberance should not lead people to believe that the communicator's motive is to try to "sell" something for personal benefit. The salesperson or advertisement star who seems enthusiastic, interested, and self-confident because of belief in the product has a good chance of changing peoples' attitudes.

Characteristics of the Message The effectiveness of persuasion is influenced by the source of the message, but what is said is also a major factor in persuasion. Most research in this area has centered on the form of the message appeal and the general character of the arguments.

The form question has generally revolved around one-sided versus two-sided arguments and the degree to which the position taken by the persuader differs from that of the audience. Does presenting both sides of an argument make the communicator seem objective and therefore more credible? In general, research suggests that if an audience is favorably disposed toward the ideas of the communicator, a one-sided approach is more effective for two reasons. In the first place, a strong argument is not necessary, and in the second, introducing conflicting views will likely confuse the issue. However, when an audience is neutral or hostile, a two-sided approach is superior. Some advertisements have used a two-sided approach, but the negative side is usually pretty weak. An example is a laundry presoak ad in which the viewer was shown a number of stains and asked which one, if any, the product could not remove. It turned out that the product would not remove deck stain. But who would stain a boat in clothes they intended to get clean again? Obviously, if the communicator was willing to tell the truth about a product weakness, he must be telling the truth about the positive side of the item.

When attempting to change attitudes, there is a choice as to how strongly to state a position. This will depend, to a degree, on the position your audience is taking. Up to a point, the greater the discrepancy between the communicator's position and the audience's position, the greater the attitude change. However, beyond that point there may be a boomerang effect, in which attitude change will decrease as the gap between communicator and audience position widens.[44] The point at which the downturn occurs varies with the credibility of the communicator.[45] New product claims could be much stronger if made by a well-known person or a well-established and trusted company. If a new company presents a new product, however, its claims may have to be moderated to achieve a degree of believability.

The use of fear appeals to sell (or unsell) products has been a hotly debated issue. Early research suggested that a moderate fear appeal would be superior to a strong one in effecting attitude and behavioral changes.[46] The theory was that if you frighten people too much, they will block the fear-inducing appeal or minimize its importance. Some years ago a movie on the evils of smoking was shown to junior high school students. The hero (goat?) of the film was a heavy smoker who subsequently contacted lung cancer. The film then went through a graphic sequence in which the lung was removed and dissected to show the damage caused by smoking (in living color). Many in the audience lost consciousness or their dinners. Some were so shaken that they went outside to smoke cigarettes to calm down. Probably not many were influenced that day to stop or never start smoking.

The use of fear appeals in persuasion is complex, and several factors are significant. First, is the feared consequence sure to occur or only possible? We generally refrain from jumping from twenty-story buildings because the consequence is virtually certain (unless, of course, the consequence is sought). However, everybody knows some 100-year-old guy who started smoking when he was 14, and he doesn't even cough. Thus, the consequences of smoking are not certain—you could be one of the lucky ones.

Second, some kinds of consequences are more effective as deterrents than others. Evidence suggests that many consumers are more concerned about social than physical consequences.[47] Perhaps a life insurance salesperson would be better advised to explain to a family breadwinner that the neighbors would talk about his or her poor planning and ineptitude rather than dwelling on the problem of a starving family that would result from an uninsured death.

Obviously, the fear appeal should be relevant and the consequences believable. Many advertisements overstate the consequences of failure to use the promoted brand. The overstatement is, of course, designed to highlight the problem, but too strong a fear appeal relative to what the audience knows the likely consequences to be may cost the advertiser in terms of credibility loss. A solution often used in ads is the idea that others will recognize the feared problem but won't tell you ("Even your best friend won't tell you"). Listerine began to sell mouthwash by suggesting that people were talking behind your back about your halitosis ("He said that she said that he had halitosis"). Later ads had people anonymously awarding bottles of Scope to other people with breath problems.

Third, fear appeals seem to be more effective in changing attitudes if the audience is provided with concrete recommendations for avoiding the feared consequence.[48] Promotion using a fear appeal should clearly show the product promoted as the way to avoid the feared consequence.

Finally, certain situational and audience factors are important in determining the success of fear appeals in eliciting attitude change. The major variables suggested for segmenting a market for receipt of fear appeals are personality, usage, and socioeconomic factors.[49]

People of high self-esteem express less fear than those of lower self-esteem.[50] High fear appeals have been shown to be more successful in changing attitudes of higher-esteem persons, while low fear appeals seem more effective with low-esteem persons.[51] Anxiety level also seems to be a factor. High fear appeals have been shown to be superior to low fear appeals for people of low-anxiety level, while low and high fear appeals are of equal effect for high-anxiety persons.[52]

The usage level of the product associated with the fear appeal also determines the effectivenss of fear appeals. The person who actually uses a product appears to be less susceptible to strong fear appeals than nonusers.[53]

Relatively little research has been undertaken on the relationship between socioeconomic variables and fear appeals. Limited findings suggest that differences in age, education, and sex are factors in different reactions to fear appeals.[54] More recent research suggests that age and social class are significant factors. Older, lower social class consumers were found to be responsive to high fear appeals, while younger, higher social class consumers were not.[55]

In general, then, careful attention should be given to segmenting a market so that fear appeals can be used with consumers most likely to respond favorably and so that the appeal may be of the proper strength for the receiving audience. Response to fear is probably a function of the situation, topic, person, and criterion.[56] These factors will interact, so careful research on reactions of various segments should precede the use of fear appeals in promotion.

Audience Characteristics The personality of the recipient of a persuasive message should be a factor in determining the degree of attitude change. However, research on the persuasibility of subjects has yielded very contradictory results.[57] The reason for the confusion could lie in the fact that personality factors may influence persuasibility in two interacting ways. First, they may affect a receiver's reception or comprehension of the message. Second, they may influence willingness to change in response to the message appeal.[58] Any given personality characteristic may interact with these two influences differently and lead to very complex results.

One study of the relationship between self-esteem and persuasibility determined that persons low in self-esteem reacted to simple appeals with high levels of attitude change. Complex appeals resulted in a low degree of attitude change.[59] If the theory is correct, personality factors exert a predictable influence if recipients understand the message. Other personality factors, such as need for approval from others, are also linked to persuasibility.[60]

Situational Factors Persuasive communications are not sent and received in a vacuum. The context in which these communications occur may have significant impact on their attitude-changing capability. The two situational factors that have received the most attention are the mood of the audience and the distraction level.

The mood of receivers of persuasive messages is a significant force in determining their susceptibility to attitude change. Providing snacks and pleasant music has been shown to improve mood and raise the probability of attitude change.[61] Based on this, soft music in a store may make people more amenable to salespeople's messages, and free food samples in grocery stores may increase sales, partly because of mood change. Advertisements, particularly on television, affect our mood, but often not positively. Perhaps a pleasant soft sell would give ads more power to influence attitudes.

As was noted earlier, attention and comprehension underlie attitude change, but the environment into which a marketer sends a persuasive message is one of distractions and divided attention. Advertising messages, in particular, compete for the consumer's attention with a variety of distractions, including other advertisements, conversations with others while being exposed to the ad, daydreaming, and outside sounds and activities. On the surface it would seem that such distractions would be detrimental to any persuasive effort. However, evidence indicates that distraction may increase persuasion under some conditions and reduce it in others.[62]

Original research in the area suggested that distractions might make respondents more susceptible to persuasion because the divided attention would leave them less able to think up arguments against the message.[63] Later research, however, conflicted with this notion, revealing a complex relationship. People were found to be unlikely to accept a complicated persuasive message if they are not paying attention, but if receivers try hard to concentrate and understand the message in spite of distractions, they may be more susceptible to persuasion, and distractions may lead to greater persuasion effects if the message is a simple one.[64]

By its very nature, the marketer cannot control distraction but can compensate for it. In general, simple messages will fare better than complex ones in effecting attitude change in the face of distraction. In situations where a message is of necessity complex, some sort of incentive motivation should be presented to impel the recipient to pay attention in spite of distraction.

Resistance to Persuasion People are often quite resistant to attitude change. Even under conditions favorable to attitude change it may be quite difficult to induce people to switch allegiances. From a marketing standpoint this can be good or bad. If you are attempting to convert consumers to your brand, you don't want them to resist your persuasive efforts. On the other hand, you want users of your brand to resist the persuasive efforts of your competitors.

Factors Arousing Resistance The most important forces leading to resistance to persuasion revolve around the concept of *psychological reactance*.[65] This phenomenon occurs when we feel that someone is attempting to coerce us in some way. Arousing the defenses of respondents will cause them to become resistant.

Defenses can be aroused when our intention to change people's attitudes is announced. In Marc Antony's well-known speech to the crowd after Caesar's assassination, he first lulled his audience by saying, "Friends, Romans, and Countrymen,

I come to bury Caesar, not to praise him." Then he spent the rest of the speech praising Caesar and turning the crowd against Brutus. The theory is that if your audience knows it is about to be influenced, it is relatively easy for its members to think up counterarguments.[66] For that reason, many announcers "sneak" commercial messages into programming.

Resistance can be generated when a persuader tries to shame a recipient into changing. Often, a communicator who tries to get someone to change by belittling or ridiculing a group only raises their defenses.[67] Possible reactions include distorting the message, ignoring it, defending actions, and outright rejection, particularly if the audience feels insulted.[68] Many salespeople and advertisers try to make consumers feel guilty if they don't use the "right" product. The "Bad Mother" routine or the husband who doesn't care about his family if he doesn't carry a lot of life insurance are examples.

Communications that threaten our psychological freedom can raise resistance to the point of hostility. Under pressure, even those who agree with the position of the communicator may resist and reverse their attitude position. Salespeople or advertisers who say or imply that a recipient must buy run the risk of negative reaction. With most people, the soft sell is more successful than the hard sell.[69]

Creating Resistance to Persuasion Whenever advertisers make claims about their brands, they face the very real possibility that competitors, a government agency, or a consumer activist group will come along later to challenge their claim and attempt to change recipient attitudes. Given this, the advertiser should, if possible, persuade consumers in such a way that they will be resistant to future counterpersuasive attempts. The concept of *innoculation theory* from social psychology offers insights into the problem.[70]

Faced with possible future attempts to change recipient attitudes, the advertiser has essentially three choices: (1) say nothing about potential points of controversy (neutral), (2) mention the issues competitors might attack and support the advertiser's own view (supportive), and (3) state several weak arguments that may be raised and then strongly refute them (refutational). Research supports the concept of innoculation theory and suggests that a consumer's ability to resist future persuasion appeals is increased by exposure to refutational appeals. If no competing arguments are presented afterward, the no-defense approach is often superior because potential negative issues are not raised. But it would be difficult to predict which ads would not be the target of counterpromotion. Also, any refutational approach will tend to generalize its effect and immunize receivers against a wide range of unanticipated attack issues, but resistance is greater if the specific issues attacked are covered in the refutational message.[71]

Attitude Models

There have been numerous attempts to model consumer attitudes.[72] This chapter won't try to cover them all, but there are a few with which you should be familiar.

Essentially, the models seek to deal with consumer feelings toward various purchase attributes. Expectancy-value models, which have been most heavily researched, proceed under the assumption that a product attitude is made up of feelings toward a number of product attributes that combine to yield an attitude. The question is, How do these attribute measures combine to make up an attitude?

One type of model assumes an additive relationship among weighted attributed beliefs.[73]

$$A_{ji} = \sum_{k=1}^{k} C_{ik} B_{ijk}$$

Where: A_{ji} is consumer i's attitude toward brand j
B_{ijk} is consumer i's evaluation of brand j on a specific attribute k
C_{ik} is consumer i's importance of attribute k

The model takes the belief or feeling scores for various product attributes, multiplies each by the consumer's stated importance of the attribute, and sums all the resulting weighted belief scores. This gives a measure of the overall attitude. The result should predict the attitude expressed by the consumer toward the product. Predictive power has been low, and, in some cases, eliminating the importance variable actually increased predictability.[74]

Perhaps the best-known model is the Fishbein model.[75]

$$A_o = \sum_{i=1}^{N} B_i a_i$$

Where: A_o is the consumer's attitude toward the product
B_i is the belief about the product
a_i is the evaluation of the belief
N is the total number of beliefs

In this model, the belief score relative to a given attribute (likely/unlikely) is multiplied by the evaluative measure (good/bad) and summed over the entire range of beliefs.

The so-called extended Fishbein model was the result of Fishbein's realization that the attitude toward an object has limited predictive value relative to behavior.[76] Consequently, he substituted attitude toward the act (for example, purchase) for attitude toward the product. The model contends that attitude toward purchase of a brand would be a better predictor of purchase than attitude toward the brand itself. The second modification took explicit account of the norms governing behavior and the individual consumer's motivation to comply with those norms.[77] The model is then stated in terms of the expected overt behavior as predicted from intended behavior.

$$OB \approx IB = (A_{act})w_o + (NB)(MC)w_1$$

Where: OB is overt behavior

IB is intended behavior

A_{act} is attitude toward a given action in a given situation

NB is normative beliefs—the norms that govern the situation

MC is the consumer's motivation to comply with behavioral norms

w_o and w_1 are statistically determined importance weights for a component

The models are far from perfect, but they represent an attempt to cope with an extremely difficult and complex measurement problem. Hopefully, further research will continue to fine tune the models and make us better able to predict consumer behavior from consumer beliefs and attitudes.

SUMMARY

Much of our knowledge of attitudes has come from the research of social psychologists. Because attitude is basic to behavior and because much of promotion strategy is directed toward influencing attitudes, the study is fundamental to our understanding of consumer behavior. Attitudes are significant for the marketing strategist at two levels: (1) individual attitudes that determine product choice; and (2) societal attitudes that govern broader behavioral patterns, such as the way in which needs are satisfied through consumption, shopping activity, and the meanings of products.

Depending on the purpose, attitude could be defined in a variety of ways. Definitions generally treat attitudes in terms of: an evaluative or feeling reaction; a readiness to respond in a particular fashion; and constellation of cognitive, affective, and conative components. Attitudes have several characteristics. They are: learned, reasonably long lasting, directed toward specific stimuli, usually held toward persons, objects, institutions, ideas, and processes, and based on drives. The three structural components of attitudes are cognitive, affective, and behavioral. The functions of attitudes are instrumental, ego-defensive, value-expressive, and knowledge.

Although attitude change precedes behavior change, we cannot necessarily predict behavior from attitude. Attitudes may be formed under a variety of situations and influences, including exposure, conditioning, observation, and information processing.

The process by which attitudes change is quite complex, and attempts to understand and explain it have led to numerous theories of attitude change, including consistency theory, group dynamics theory, cognitive dissonance theory, attribution theory, and social learning theory.

Promotion is an application of persuasive communications. Four important factors determining the efficiency of attempts to persuade are the communicator, the message, the audience, and the situation. A statement of intention to persuade, attempts to shame the audience, and threats to psychological freedom may cause consumers to resist attempts to change their attitudes. A marketer may innoculate an audience against competitors' attempts to persuade them by using refutational promotional appeals.

Finally, several attitude models were presented. The models attempt to predict behavior by combining beliefs about various attributes of the attitude object.

CHAPTER 6   STUDY REVIEW

Important Terms and Concepts

Attitude
Characteristics of attitudes
Components of attitudes
Functions of attitudes
Consistency theory
Group dynamics theory
Cognitive dissonance theory
Cognitive overlap
Social learning theory
Fear appeals
Psychological reactance
Innoculation theory
Fishbein model

Questions

1. Discuss the relationship between attitudes and behavior. What is the significance of this relationship for marketing strategy?

2. Discuss the ways in which consumer attitudes are formed.

3. Discuss the theories of attitude change.

4. What factors are important in determining whether persuasive efforts will be successful?

5. How is resistance to persuasion aroused?

7

Social Forces
and Large Social Institutions

Consumer behavior is often an individual phenomenon, as evidenced in the past chapters, but it seldom occurs without the influence of other people. Our interaction with others, group buying decisions, and what we perceive that others think or expect of us are all important external factors in individual purchase decisions. This chapter and the following one examine interpersonal and group forces and institutions that shape and influence patterns of product acquisition and consumption. This chapter is concerned with basic social forces and large social institutions, while chapter 8 treats family buying behavior and social trends.

Social Forces and Concepts

The marketing manager must be concerned with the forces by which consumers are influenced by other persons. An understanding of these forces can help the manager particularly in developing promotion strategy and in creating and anticipating brand image. Among the major concepts underlying social influence are socialization, group forces, and reference groups.

Socialization

The learning of roles and expectations begins at an early age and is referred to as the process of socialization. Although people may be influenced by others all their lives, many basic attitudes and values learned in childhood stick with the individual throughout life. Socialization influence comes from such social institutions as family, friends, school, and media. Socialization may be defined as "the whole process by which an individual develops, through transaction with other people, his specific patterns of socially relevant behaviors and experience."[1] Another definition concentrates on what is learned and suggests that socialization is "the process by which individuals acquire the knowledge, skills, and dispositions that enable them to participate as more or less effective members of groups and the society."[2]

Consumer socialization may be defined as "processes by which young people

171

acquire skills, knowledge, and attitudes relevant to their functioning as consumers in the marketplace."[3] Consumer socialization, then, refers to those aspects of buying behavior that are learned from others, generally during childhood.

Some effects of socialization are delayed. This influence on future behavior is referred to as anticipatory socialization. Three types of anticipatory socialization among children have been identified.[4] First, children learn information that is not useful at the time it is learned but may become important later. For example, children may acquire basic knowledge about such things as insurance, credit cards, and auto repairs but will not apply that knowledge immediately. Second, children may acquire attitudes and values that become the basis for specific behavior patterns. Attitudes formed in childhood toward automobile brands, consumer debt, and prepurchase information seeking, to name a few, may underlie adult buying behavior. Third, children may learn general and specific skills that can be practiced at the time and throughout life, as needed. Using and counting money and buying items in a store exemplify such socialization.

Group Forces

The groups that are most significant in influencing consumer behavior are generally nonformal. As such, several forces operate within the groups to influence members in their behavior. Among the most significant forces are status, power, roles, norms, and conformity.

Status Most groups ascribe varying levels of prestige to their members. People of the same status may interact together, often to the exclusion of others. Higher-status persons may influence others to follow their lead, particularly if there is a desire among group members to achieve higher status. Status may arise from a variety of sources—including wealth, age, sex, experience, occupation—depending on the nature of the group.

Power Other people can exercise various kinds of influence over us. This influence is referred to as social power and includes reward, coercive, legitimate, referent, and expert power.[5]

We may be influenced by other people who can extend various kinds of physical and psychological reward to us. People subject themselves to an employer or a teacher so as to gain reward for various kinds of behavior. Marketers may hold reward power through the quality of products they sell, the benefits they promise, premiums, and free television and radio.

The power to coerce comes from the ability to punish or withhold reward. In general, the influencing power of coercion is less than that of reward unless the punishments are extreme. Marketers may indirectly coerce consumers by making them fearful of not using a product. Head and Shoulders dandruff shampoo has an ad in which an attractive woman sits down next to an interested man. All the time he's thinking that she's interested in him and he should ask her out, she's thinking that because he scratched his head—though no dandruff is visible—it must be indicative of latent dandruff (or maybe a flea?). So about the time he turns to speak to her, she turns her back and walks away with her nose in the air. The poor slob may be able to redeem himself if only he will use Head and Shoulders. The coercion is evident, and even though consumers are not flaking, they may be influenced to buy a dandruff shampoo.

Coercion is also evident in high-pressure selling and the more subtle pressure associated with home-party selling, the archetype of which is a Tupperware party. The atmosphere is informal with games and refreshments, and the only selling is a demonstration of various items. There is significant social pressure to buy, however, since everyone knows the hostess will receive major prizes if enough people buy. They don't want to be embarrassed in front of their friends by not making a purchase, and they don't want to let down the hostess who was kind enough to invite them to her party.[6]

Legitimate power occurs in situations where an individual or institution has the *right* to exercise influence. Churches, parents, teachers, and employers may possess such power. Appeals are couched in terms of what one ought to do or should do. Appeals to conserve energy or save for the future may involve the use of legitimate power.

The feeling of identification or admiration we may have for another person or group gives referent power—that is, we refer to another for advice or example. Referent power is widely used among marketers who have celebrities endorse products. Many times, large numbers of consumers are influenced to buy and use the advocated item. This use of referent power will be investigated more thoroughly in chapter 14.

Expert power is wielded by virtue of a person's knowledge or ability. A person with expert power may have referent power, but referent power requires that the audience desire to be like the referent person. Such a desire is not a requisite of expert power. Marketers may use real people as experts in ads, or they may create their own experts, like General Mills' Betty Crocker or General Motors' Mr. Goodwrench.

Roles People in groups perform certain roles, defined as prescribed patterns of behavior expected of a person in a given situation by virtue of the person's position in the situation.[7] The various social roles we play demand different behavior patterns and often different patterns of product acquisition, use, and display. Although many roles are informal, there may be sanctions (social punishments and rewards) to cause an individual to conform to the role requirements. As an individual moves from one role to another, different expectations must often be met. While a student, you can meet role expectations by dressing in certain ways. Those expectations are likely to change substantially as you graduate and perhaps move into a management trainee position. As is noted in chapter 8, different family members play various roles from influencer to decider in purchase decisions.

Norms Any group has certain rules, often informal, by which its members are expected to abide. If you are in a country club, you may find that you are expected to drive a certain kind of car. These expectations are called norms, defined as "general expectations about behaviors that are deemed appropriate for all persons in a social context, regardless of the position they hold."[8] Test social norms. Tomorrow, in a class where seats have not been assigned. sit in a seat someone else has occupied all term. You will violate a norm.

Conformity There is strong pressure in any group for individuals to behave like other group members. Many products are purchased because someone else in a group bought one. Abiding by role expectations is the result of conformity. Norms may specify behavior, and sanctions will enforce conformity. Many promotional efforts are based on attempts to get people to conform. In fact, simply implying in an ad that "everybody's doing it" may induce some people to buy.

Reference Groups

A reference group is a group that exerts referent power. The power may be exerted because an individual is a member of the group and wants to retain membership in it or because the individual aspires to belong to the group or emulate its members.

Types of Reference Groups One classification of reference groups identifies three types: comparative, status, and normative.[9] People seek comparison points to judge their own behavior. The consumer may look to others in a group to determine whether his or her possessions and purchases are appropriate.

People who are upwardly mobile look to reference groups of higher status for clues as to how to behave in such a way as to be accepted in the socially higher group. Many products are seen as symbols of status, and consumers may purchase and display these in order to fulfill their aspirations to be accepted in reference groups higher in status than their own.

Some groups represent what an individual should be. These groups set the norms and basic values that underlie an individual's behavior. A consumer may feel somewhat compelled to buy certain products that represent what members of a relevant reference groups ought to have. A teenage boy may belong to a hot rod club and find a certain kind of car and mode of dress to be the norm for its members.

Reference Group Influences Three motivational influences of reference groups are identified as informational, utilitarian, and value-expressive.[10] Some reference groups may play the role of providing information. This information can be transmitted in two ways. Members of the group may give direct advice, or the behavior of group members may be observed.

Reference groups may also provide various rewards to members and aspirants, and the promise of these rewards may lead to conformity with group standards. An individual might make a purchase to comply with group expectations if the group is able to reward the behavior, if the behavior will be visable to the group, and if there is motivation to receive the reward.

The individual may be influenced to associate with positive referents and disassociate with negative referents in order to enhance or support a self-image. In addition, a person may accept the influence of a group simply because he or she likes the group and its members. Membership in or aspiration to a given group is a way of communicating one's values to the world.

Levels of Social Influence

Social influence may be exerted by a wide variety of groups. We have already considered the general concept of the reference group. Any social group may be a reference group for an individual if he or she is influenced by the group. We will look at three levels of social influence in this section: culture, subculture, and social class.

Culture

Because business activity has continually moved toward internationalism, it has become necessary for marketing strategists to become aware of cultural differences among various countries. In addition, we can better operate within the confines of our own country if we understand its culture.

Culture is such a broad subject that it is impossible to cover the concept adequately here. In addition, it is difficult to pin down a viable definition of culture. It may refer to language, religion, law, customs, art, music, leisure and work, food, taboos, technology, dress, and morals. Anthropology, the behavioral discipline concerned with culture, is a far-reaching study. The word *anthropology,* derived from the Greek *anthropos* for human and *logos* for study, suggests an extremely broad orientation. Although this definition would seem to encompass all of the behavioral disciplines, anthropology can be distinguished from psychology, sociology, and social psychology in that it is aimed at people throughout the world in virtually all aspects of their life experience. Thus, it takes a holistic approach to the study of mankind in the broadest sense.

Anthropology has two general subfields, physical or biological anthropology and cultural anthropology. Cultural anthropology is further broken into archaeology, anthropological linguistics, and ethnology. Ethnology is probably the most relevant to the study of consumer behavior since it seeks to understand contemporary cultures, the ways in which they differ from one another, and the process by which they change. To most anthropologists culture is composed of the behaviors, beliefs, attitudes, customs, norms, and human artifacts of a particular society or population. Since the purchase and use of products and services is an important part of advanced societies, it follows that the culture would both influence and reflect consumer behavior.

Some Characteristics of Culture Cultures vary a great deal from one another, but there are several characteristics that seem to fit all cultures.

Culture is Shared One person does not make a culture. The customs, norms, and other cultural aspects of a society must be generally shared by all members of that society for it to be considered a culture. The choice of an automobile brand would not be considered a cultural norm, even though it might be selected by a relatively large number of persons. However, an American's perception of an automobile as more than just transportation—as a symbol of status, of personal freedom, of individuality—might be considered a cultural phenomenon since it is shared by a very large portion of the society.

Culture is Learned Many characteristics of a culture, such as dominant body type, skin pigmentation, and hair color, may be shared but are not cultural. The phenomena of culture are not innate or genetic; they are learned by members of the society. We are socialized into a culture at a very early age through the formal and informal means discussed earlier in this chapter. As was already noted, a great deal of cultural socialization is aimed at defining purchasing roles and behavior.

A major problem occurs when a marketing strategy is to be introduced into an unfamiliar culture. We learn behaviors and attitudes appropriate to our own culture through the socialization process called enculturation. Since people are enculturated without effort or awareness, they tend to become ethnocentric—that is, they consider their own cultural values to be natural, normal, and best. The process by which we learn about cultures other than our own is called acculturation. Because of our ethnocentricity, acculturation is often difficult, but marketers must carefully learn about other cultures *before* they attempt to market in them so as to avoid costly errors. If marketers are not willing to learn the foreign culture, they would be well advised to work through established foreign marketers who fully understand potential cultural problems associated with various aspects of the product and its promotion. We learn about other cultures through acculturation, and it can sometimes be traumatic.

In some instances an advertisement can be modified to fit learned cultural patterns in a number of countries. In 1976 General Motors received a CLIO (an award for outstanding advertisements) for a Chevrolet ad which carried the theme line, "Baseball, hot dogs, apple pie, and Chevrolet." The purpose of the advertisement was to illustrate that Chevrolet, "America's favorite car," was an integral part of the culture. Obviously, the ad in that form would not work elsewhere; but in Australia, where General Motors markets the Holden automobile, the theme line became "Football, meat pies, kangaroos and Holden cars."

Language problems are often significant. Cue brand toothpaste could not be marketed in France because the word *cue* is a French obscenity. In Japan Enco means *stalled car*. This may be one reason why the company changed its name to Exxon, which has no meaning in any language.

Culture Defines and Constrains Behavior Culture is a subtle external force that defines the limits of acceptable behavior. In general, we are unaware of the constraints culture exerts until we violate some cultural norm. Nobody tells you that it's rather unusual for people in our culture to shave their heads, and no one will tell you not to shave your head, but imagine the reaction if you showed up in your consumer behavior classroom with your head shaved. There are many behaviors not prohibited by law but constrained by cultural norms.

Culture is Adaptive Many customs and cultural attitudes are a result of cultural requirements. Eating customs often develop because of health requirements, and dress customs may develop in response to climate, for example. Culture may change as the result of environmental changes. American cultural values have begun to shift in response to scarce and increasingly costly energy. Automobile styles are following what the Europeans have had for many years—small and economical.

Culture is Generally Integrated The attitudes and customs that constitute culture are not random; they tend to form a consistent system. The cultural attitudes that people hold generally fit together. Thus, consuming attitudes will be consistent with other cultural norms. American attitudes toward materialism and self-indulgence have led to high levels of resource use and heavy consumer debt.

Culture is Dynamic The preceding observations that culture is adaptive and integrated suggest that culture is constantly changing. A marketer must be constantly aware of emerging cultural change, which often gives rise to new product or expanded market opportunities. New roles for women have encouraged more convenience products for cooking and housekeeping. The increasingly faster pace of American life has led to abbreviated breakfasts and fast-food outlets.

American Cultural Values Although business activity is becoming more global, the United States remains a central focus for American-based firms. In addition, an awareness of our own culture can alert us to potential points of difference between our own and other cultures. One basis for understanding a culture lies in the basic value system of its members. A cultural value may be formally defined as a conception of a desirable state that is utilized as a criterion for preference or choice or as a justification for behavior.[11] Values, then, are cognitions that underlie preference and choice in behavior. As such, many cultural values may influence buying behavior. In a sense, values are to culture as traits are to individual personality.

Because of the diversity of American culture, it is difficult to isolate universal and pervasive values. However, several fundamental values can be isolated that are shared by a significant portion of the U.S. population and that seem to influence consumer behavior.

Achievement and Success Many cultures value achievement. The major difference involves a question of what is considered to be achievement. American culture tends to value competitive occupational achievement, especially business and professional success. Individual and family status in the United States is closely tied to occupational prestige. Related to this is economic success, where emphasis is placed on monetary reward as opposed to achievement or accomplishment per se. Growing out of the emphasis on economic success is the materialistic outlook that characterizes the United States. This becomes significant to marketers since products are often purchased with the intent of reflecting economic success. In other words, some of the possessions a person owns often become symbols of status and achievement. From this same thinking comes the American preoccupation with technology and progress. Thus, we come to define "bigger" and "newer" as better.

The translation of products into status is accompanied by a search for personal comfort. All of this helps explain why U.S. consumers take shortages so hard and are so slow to conserve resources.

Activity, Work, and Time Orientation America seems to be a land of increasing human activity, where the people seem anxious to shape and control their own destinies through work and effort. The protestant work ethic seems to be with us still, and we feel somehow guilty if we are not actively engaged in doing something. Even leisure stresses activity—travel, camping, sports. The passive nature of television viewing seems to belie the active U.S. life-style, but activity is still valued, and we often feel some guilt about the time we spend in front of the "tube."

Because of the fast pace of life, Americans seem heavily preoccupied with the question, What time is it? Our lives seem to be just one long series of deadlines. A lack of punctuality is seen as a major character flaw. As noted earlier, products and services that are practical, efficient, and time saving are important to U.S. consumers. Products that are promoted to help us get more done faster often enjoy great success.

Youthfulness In many cultures of the world, age is venerated, sometimes almost worshipped. Not so in the United States. Here the emphasis is on looking, feeling, and acting young. Many products are promoted with a youth appeal. Products to help control weight and to give more pep and energy abound. Growing old is to be avoided (although the only other alternative is dying young).

Humanitarianism and Egalitarianism Although our behavior as a nation does not always demonstrate a concern for humanity, our values strongly voice such a concern. At the same time, although equality is only now beginning to emerge in the sense that *all* Americans should be equal (the founders of our nation meant that all male, white, adult, land-owning persons were equal when they said, "All men are created equal"), the concept of equality has long been an underlying principle of the nation.

Religious and Moralistic A very large proportion of the American society identifies itself with organized religion. Because of our religious orientation, we tend to be rather dogmatic in terms of what is considered right and wrong. That our everyday lives are not particularly congruent with our high moral values does not change the value. We still demand highly ethical conduct on the part of our business institutions and their communications with the public.

Individualism, Freedom, and Conformity To group individualism and conformity may seem incongruous, but they tend to be two related manifestations of the concept of freedom. Like egalitarianism, freedom is a basic tenet of our society. America is "the land of the free." Indeed, we do enjoy a high degree of personal freedom. Individuality is expressed through the products we buy—clothing, automobiles, funiture, and homes. The automobile is a manifestation of individual freedom and mobility, which explains why Americans are reluctant to end their love affair with the car in spite of its rapidly accelerating cost of ownership and operation. Getting a driver's license is an important rite of passage in our society that signifies new freedom and independence.

At the same time that we seek individuality, we also look for the comfort and reassurance of conformity. We conform to socially approved dress and grooming styles. Deviants are treated with varying degrees of ostracism. However, we generally do not see pressures to conform as particularly restrictive of freedom. We feel free to conform or not to conform, and we can select the particular group or style to which we wish to conform.

Although the foregoing are not exhaustive of American cultural values, they do serve to illustrate that the United States does have a unique value system and that the values held by individuals are significant in shaping their consuming behavior.

Subcultures

Within a complex culture we are likely to find large subgroups that share the values of the larger culture and yet have their own characteristic values. Such a subgroup is called a subculture, and it may be formally defined as a distinct cultural group that exists as an identifiable segment within a larger, more complex society.[12] Subcultures represent natural bases for market segmentation and markets for special products.[13]

Because of its size, geographic and climatic diversity, and broad population origin, the United States is a country of subcultures. The following discussion will concentrate on ethnic, age, and regional subcultures, although there are many more.

Ethnic Subcultures America is known as a country populated by people from the rest of the world. With the exception of the American Indian, everybody came here from somewhere else. Although even first-generation immigrants tend to identify themselves as Americans, many attitudes, values, and customs may remain for several generations. This is particularly true if people happen to be identifiably different from the majority in such areas as skin color, language, and neighborhood concentration.

Ethnic subcultures are generally defined in terms of national origin, race, and religion. Consumer behavior data is spotty for these groups, so this discussion will concentrate on the areas for which we have some relevant information. Minority groups in the United States (generally considered blacks and Hispanics) spent $60 billion in 1960, $116 billion in 1978, and $145 billion in 1980. In general, they spend proportionately more of their income on consumer goods than their white counterparts. [14]

Black Subculture Blacks represent the major racial subculture in the United States. They constitute approximately eleven to twelve percent of the total U.S. population, with the greatest concentrations in metropolitan cities in the Midwest and the southern states. The black population is growing faster than the white and is younger, with sixty-five percent under 35 years of age. The median age of black females in 1979 was 23.7 years as opposed to 29 for their white counterparts, while the median for black males was 21 as opposed to 27.6 for whites. [15]

Historically, blacks have lagged behind whites in education, income, and occupational prestige. That is changing, however, as the black middle class is growing rapidly. [16] Average income for blacks has risen from sixty-five percent of the white average in 1974 to eighty-five percent in 1979. [17] About half of the population may be considered middle class, accounting for roughly seventy percent of black expenditures. [18] Even so, blacks are underprivileged relative to whites. Unemployment levels are above average for blacks, and the black concentration in unskilled jobs is about twice that of whites. About twice as many whites as blacks have completed one or more years of college.

Many writers and practitioners in marketing seem to treat blacks as a monolithic market, but there are really numerous market segments in the subculture. The upper half of the population is growing in affluence, while the lower half remains under-class. The upper half may be further divided into three market segments.

1. The upwardly mobiles who tend to pattern their preferences and life-styles after general market models as seen on television.
2. Individuals who are seriously and deliberately seeking life-styles that can blend black culture and traditions with increasing material prosperity.
3. Individuals who fall somewhere in between these two groups. [19]

Studies of life-styles indicate that blacks are, in many ways, similar to whites, especially those in segment 1 in the preceding list. There are some significant differences, however. Because of a tendency toward matriarchy in black families, black women are more heavily involved in purchase decision making than their white counterparts. Black women tend to be more style-conscious than whites, and they tend to emphasize the importance of money, budgeting, and careful shopping. [20]

Blacks tend to take pride in their homes and to concentrate on cleanliness and home improvement. They are becoming more venturesome and independent with less interest in impressing whites and a greater inclination to express themselves among their peers.[21] Blacks seem to respond to "recognition, identification, and invitation (to buy products)" as fundamental market appeals.[22]

Hispanic Subculture The Hispanic subculture is receiving growing attention as a market segment. Like the black subculture, Hispanics have been subjected to various kinds of discrimination,[23] but as the second and third generations receive education and achieve middle-class perquisites, overt discrimination seems to disappear.[24]

As of 1979 there were more than twelve million Hispanics in the United States, and their population was growing at twice the annual rate of the rest of the nation. At that rate, they would represent the largest minority group in the United States by 2030.[25] The Hispanic population is heavily concentrated in a relatively few states. In general, there are three Hispanic populations: Puerto Rican—largely residing in New York; Cuban—mostly in Florida; and Mexican—concentrated in Texas, New Mexico, Arizona, California, and Colorado. For example, in 1979 twenty-two percent of Spanish-speaking Americans lived in Texas, representing twenty percent of that state's population and fifteen percent of its households with a disposable income of $7.5 billion. At the same time, the Hispanic (Cuban) market in Miami consisted of 160,000 families with incomes totalling $2.3 billion, and the Spanish-speaking population of Los Angeles reached 3.9 million persons.

A marketer must approach the various Hispanic markets according to their specific characters. Although relatively little has been published on these subcultures, there are numerous advertising agencies and consultants who specialize in marketing to Hispanics. A major complication in dealing with Hispanics as opposed to blacks is the language barrier. There are a number of Spanish radio and television stations and newspapers, but the problem is not simply to translate a message into Spanish but to tailor it for Hispanic life-styles and interests—again a problem for specialists.

Religious Subcultures A number of religions form distinct subcultures. The Jewish subculture has received the greatest research attention. Jewish families, in general, are better educated than the average market, read more books, travel more, have more disposable income, are extremely brand-conscious and brand loyal, and watch less television than the average household.[26]

While Jewish people may be found in all parts of the country, they are most heavily concentrated in ten major markets, the largest being New York City, with a Jewish population of three million.

Age Subcultures There might be an age subculture corresponding to each stage in life, but the three age groups that have received the majority of research efforts are youth, young adult, and elderly. Although designations differ, this book defines the youth market as those persons under nineteen. Young adults represent nineteen to thirty-five-year-olds, and the elderly are those sixty-five and older. Since statistical data are categorized in numerous ways, it is difficult to get information to fit any given set of designations exactly.

Youth Subculture The youth market has received a great deal of attention from marketers in recent years. Actually, the youth market as defined here is not at all homogeneous. Preteens are different from teens, and boys are different from girls. Differences lie in product attitudes, purchasing power, media consumption, and purchase influence in the family.

In general, the youth market is declining in numbers. From 1960 to 1975 the market increased by 8.7 million persons, but the U.S. Census Bureau projects a population decline of 3.5 million between 1975 and 1990. By 1985, children under fifteen are expected to represent 27.3 percent of the total population, down from 31.1 percent in 1960. As of 1979 there were 30 million teenagers in the United States with $3.5 billion in discretionary income and an influential role in $145 billion.[27]

The child market (under fourteen) is a relatively easy one for marketers to reach because of their TV viewing habits and their interest in promotion. Teens, on the other hand, are hard to isolate as a market segment. Their interests and tastes are not served by most general media. As a rule teens are not daily readers of newspapers, and only teenage girls read consumer magazines regularly. Teens do not typically have control of the TV during prime time, so that leaves radio as the major medium to reach teens.[28]

Young Adult Subculture The young adult market in the United States is a large and growing market, and it is a heavy consumption group. In 1980 more than forty percent of the adult population was between eighteen and thirty-five, and the age group will grow twice as fast as the rest of the adult population for most of the decade. One author, in assessing the economic strength of this group, observed, "Simply put, the situation is this: Never before and probably never again will one age group and one social group wield such disproportionate and newly-found economic potency in the marketplace."[29] Although this age group does not have the discretionary income of older families, households are formed during this period, so the young adult group is a significant market for furniture and appliances, among other products. Twenty-five to thirty-four-year-olds spend proportionately more on discretionary goods and services than other adults.

Old-age Subculture The elderly market is a growing segment. In 1970 consumers sixty-five and older made up 9.9 percent of the total population, and 19.5 percent of households were headed by a person over sixty-five. In 1985 more than 11 percent of consumers will be sixty-five or older with 20 percent of households headed by a person aged sixty-five or more.

The major economic story for the elderly market is its relatively low spending power. Discretionary income has been about 6.5 percent of the total for years. However, the elderly represent a significant market for some products. For example, the elderly consume 25 percent of all prescription drugs.[30]

If we back up a bit we find a special subculture in women aged fifty to seventy.[31] There are 22 million women in this category with higher per capita income, more free time, and fewer home responsibilities than younger women. Many women view these "golden years" as their last chance to buy and do all the things they denied themselves before. The mature woman's response to an increasingly hedonistic American society is, "I want mine and I want it now." These mature women are heavier viewers of TV than younger women, with the greatest concentration of viewing occurring during the daytime and early fringe hours. In prime time, women over fifty prefer general drama, variety, and informational programs rather than the situation comedies of their younger counterparts.

While this discussion doesn't give full coverage to the various age segments, it will give you some feeling for the differences. The information in figures 7-1 and 7-2 will give you some insights into attitudinal differences among age and sex groups.

Geographic Subcultures For a variety of reasons, including climate and regional heritage, people in different regions of the United States have different attitudes and often exhibit differing purchase behaviors. There are a variety of ways to divide the country for analysis, but the regional breakdowns indicated in figure 7-3 are useful.

According to the study cited, easterners are less traditional in marriage preferences, less likely to eat meat for breakfast, more likely to travel outside the United States, more likely to ride a bus, more inclined to use a bank charge card, heavier wine and cocktail drinkers, and less active in hunting than the average.

Southerners are more apt to consider children in their decision making, more likely to eat meat for breakfast, less likely to eat breakfast out, more apt to work on community projects, heavier church attenders, less inclined to travel outside the United States, less likely to return unsatisfactory products, use a cents-off coupon, go on picnics, drink wine and cocktails, and bowl, and more likely to hunt than the average.

Midwesterners are called mainstream America because their attitudes were just about average for all items in the study.

Westerners eat breakfast out more, use bank credit cards more, drink wine more often, use more spice and seasoning, visit more museums and art galleries, and hike and backpack more than the rest of the country's residents.

Southwesterners are more traditional in their marriage attitudes and less likely to use cents-off coupons and drink wine or cocktails.

Obviously, the findings of the study do not represent all regional differences, but they do effectively show that there are significant differences among consumers in various parts of the country.

Social Class

Almost all societies have a system by which some individuals and families are accorded more status or prestige than others. America has an egalitarian tradition, but in spite of the fact that all men are created equal before the law, the same is not true in terms of social standing. Prestige tends to follow those things a society values. In a primitive society an outstanding hunter may enjoy high status. In more advanced, industrialized societies the concept of social class and its determinants

Fig. 7-1. Female Interests and Opinions

Statement	Sample total	Age Group				
		Under 25	25-34	35-44	45-54	55 and older
Optimism and Happiness						
My greatest achievements are still ahead of me	64%	92%	84%	73%	52%	28%
I dread the future	23	20	18	17	24	30
I am much happier now than I ever was before	79	85	82	80	74	74
Modern—Traditional Ideas						
I have somewhat old-fashioned tastes and habits	86	78	84	87	88	89
There is too much emphasis on sex today	87	70	74	90	89	93
I like to think I am a bit of a swinger	26	43	34	26	19	15
A woman's place is in the home	46	39	39	44	49	60
The working world is no place for a woman	17	15	11	14	19	28
Young people have too many privileges	76	57	74	77	76	83
The U.S. would be better off if there were no hippies	55	32	37	46	54	82
My days seem to follow a definite routine—eating meals at the same time each day, etc.	67	59	62	61	67	75
Travel						
I would like to take a trip around the world	67	78	83	73	65	51
I would like to spend a year in London or Paris	34	38	40	34	34	25
I would feel lost if I were alone in a foreign country	68	66	66	64	68	76
I like to visit places that are totally different from my home	85	85	83	86	82	88
Mobile						
We will probably move at least once in the next five years	38	71	53	27	28	23
Our family has moved more often than most of our neighbors have	24	36	32	26	18	17

Anxious						
I have trouble getting to sleep	33	29	24	26	33	49
I wish I knew how to relax	52	51	49	49	51	59

Personal Adornment and Self

Dressing well is an important part of my life	81	84	80	78	79	83
I like to feel attractive to members of the opposite sex	85	93	91	77	82	72
I want to look a little different from others	69	71	78	70	63	72
I often wear expensive cologne	28	19	24	28	27	33
I have more stylish clothes than most of my friends	30	31	34	27	29	27

View toward Income, Personal Equity, and Spending

I will probably have more money to spend next year than I have now	45	71	70	58	53	30
Five years from now our family income will probably be a lot higher than it is now	65	87	85	75	61	26
Our family income is high enough to satisfy nearly all our important desires	74	59	66	78	78	80
No matter how fast our income goes up we never seem to get ahead	53	62	65	61	47	32
Investing in the stock market is too risky for most families	86	79	83	82	85	87
Our family is too heavily in debt today	27	36	33	37	23	11
I like to pay cash for everything I buy	77	83	79	74	71	77
I pretty much spend for today and let tomorrow bring what it will	22	33	21	22	25	18

Staying at Home

I would rather spend a quiet evening at home than go out to a party	65	50	66	64	68	78
I am a homebody	69	59	65	64	72	79
I stay home most evenings	83	81	95	80	83	83

Fig. 7-1. Female Interests and Opinions (continued)

Statement	Sample total	Age Group				
		Under 25	25-34	35-44	45-54	55 and older
Husband and Children						
A wife's first obligation is to her husband, not her children	69%	53%	65%	74%	74%	76%
When children are ill in bed, parents should drop everything else to see to their comfort	74	61	71	73	80	83
Children are the most important thing in a marriage	52	42	44	49	56	64
When making important family decisions, consideration of the children should come first	54	69	58	44	48	56
A wife should have a great deal of information about her husband's work	82	83	84	75	88	85
View toward Durable Goods						
Our home is furnished for comfort, not for style	90	83	88	88	94	94
If I must choose, I buy stylish rather than practical furniture	17	19	31	13	15	15
When buying appliances, I am more concerned with dependability than price	90	85	89	89	89	94
A subcompact car can meet my tranportation needs	66	85	74	60	61	57
Housekeeping and Cooking						
When I see a full ashtray or wastebasket, I want it emptied immediately	71	77	70	72	64	64
I am uncomfortable when the house is not completely clean	67	76	67	70	61	68
The kind of dirt you can't see is worse than the kind you can see	77	77	72	73	79	85
I am a good cook	91	93	92	88	90	91
I like to cook	87	91	88	84	85	87
I like to bake	40	43	43	42	39	38
Meal preparation should take as little time as possible	42	42	41	40	41	44

Grocery Shopping

Shopping is no fun anymore	54	49	43	58	55	51
Before going shopping, I sit down and prepare a complete shopping list	72	68	73	71	69	74
I try to stick to well-known brands	74	58	67	71	82	86
I find myself checking prices even on small items	90	89	93	92	89	86
I like to save and redeem savings stamps	75	72	70	70	75	83
I pay a lot more attention to food prices now than I ever did before	90	92	91	88	88	87
I am an impulse buyer	38	39	40	37	42	27
I shop a lot for specials	84	85	86	83	84	81

Health and Nutrition

I am very concerned about nutrition	87	87	89	87	82	89
I am concerned about how much salt I eat	56	52	55	56	50	66
I am careful what I eat in order to keep my weight under control	57	63	57	58	62	58
I try to avoid foods that are high in cholesterol	62	37	53	60	65	79
I try to avoid foods that have additives in them	56	45	52	57	53	62
I get more headaches than most people	28	30	31	28	27	22
I eat more than I should	70	68	70	75	73	69

Courtesy of Needham, Harper & Steers Advertising, Inc. *Life Style Survey*, 1975.

Fig. 7-2.   Male Interests and Opinions

Statement	Sample total	Under 25	25-34	35-44	45-54	55 and older
Optimism and Happiness						
My greatest achievements are still ahead of me	64%	98%	93%	76%	55%	25%
I dread the future	20	21	19	19	23	23
I am much happier now than I ever was before	78	87	92	97	76	74
Modern—Traditional Ideas						
I have somewhat old-fashioned tastes and habits	85	73	78	84	92	89
There is too much emphasis on sex today	66	56	65	74	81	93
I like to think I am a bit of a swinger	31	51	43	29	26	15
A woman's place is in the home	54	45	52	53	52	62
The working world is no place for a woman	27	24	20	25	26	37
Young people have too many privileges	75	60	63	77	74	88
The U.S. would be better off if there were no hippies	59	33	38	57	67	81
My days seem to follow a definite routine—eating meals at the same time each day, etc.	63	50	53	59	67	76
All men should be clean shaven every day	67	47	55	66	75	85
Travel						
I would like to take a trip around the world	67	74	73	77	68	53
I would like to spend a year in London or Paris	34	38	39	40	32	23
I would feel lost if I were alone in a foreign country	52	59	46	47	44	67
I like to visit places that are totally different from my home	72	80	73	75	73	67

Mobile

We will probably move at least once in the next five years	37	75	52	28	23	20
Our family has moved more often than most of our neighbors have	22	27	30	23	18	17

Anxious

I have trouble getting to sleep	24	20	20	23	25	30
I wish I knew how to relax	47	40	48	51	44	50

Personal Adornment and Self

Dressing well is an important part of my life	72	70	73	72	72	67
I like to feel attractive to members of the opposite sex	81	87	87	87	66	74
I want to look a little different from others	55	74	62	55	49	42
I often wear expensive cologne	14	16	14	12	15	13
I have more stylish clothes than most of my friends	25	24	26	28	24	22

View toward Income, Personal Equity, and Spending

I will probably have more money to spend next year than I have now	56	74	65	64	58	29
Five years from now our family income will probably be a lot higher than it is now	68	87	85	79	69	28
Our family income is high enough to satisfy nearly all our important desires	75	63	72	78	78	79
No matter how fast our income goes up we never seem to get ahead	58	60	68	56	52	39
Investing in the stock market is too risky for most families	83	86	82	81	87	86
Our family is too heavily in debt today	28	41	42	28	25	11
I like to pay cash for everything I buy	75	79	74	70	69	81
I pretty much spend for today and let tomorrow bring what it will	26	31	29	23	23	26

Staying at Home

I would rather spend a quiet evening at home than go out to a party	73	65	67	73	75	79
I am a homebody	72	55	67	73	79	82
I stay home most evenings	80	70	77	79	78	89

Fig. 7-2. Male Interests and Opinions (continued)

Statement	Sample total	Age Group				
		Under 25	25-34	35-44	45-54	55 and older
Husband and Children						
A wife's first obligation is to her husband, not her children	57%	43%	52%	54%	64%	66%
When children are ill in bed, parents should drop everything else to see to their comfort	70	66	68	66	73	78
Children are the most important thing in a marriage	53	37	44	50	57	78
When making important family decisions, consideration of the children should come first	53	63	54	48	49	53
A wife should have a great deal of information about her husband's work	77	74	75	73	80	82
Our family is a close-knit group	87	86	94	89	83	88
View toward Durable Goods						
Our home is furnished for comfort, not for style	93	89	92	94	95	94
If I must choose, I buy stylish rather than practical furniture	15	18	20	14	15	9
When buying appliances, I am more concerned with dependability than price	93	91	93	90	94	95
When buying appliances, the brand name is more important than the reputation of the store	56	56	53	49	55	64
A subcompact car can meet my transportation needs	59	71	57	56	58	57
Housekeeping and Cooking						
When I see a full ashtray or wastebasket, I want it emptied immediately	56	56	46	54	60	63
I am uncomfortable when the house is not completely clean	51	57	48	53	49	52
The kind of dirt you can't see is worse than the kind you can see	77	68	74	73	79	86
I am a good cook	51	63	57	50	48	41

I like to cook	50	60	58	48	48	41
I like to bake	30	34	35	27	26	30
Meal preparation should take as little time as possible	42	42	41	38	40	46

Grocery Shopping

Shopping is no fun anymore	59	54	55	55	63	64
Before going shopping, I sit down and prepare a complete shopping list	44	35	42	38	38	56
I try to stick to well-known brands	79	71	79	76	71	86
I find myself checking prices even on small items	79	78	74	75	78	84
I like to save and redeem savings stamps	43	43	31	35	42	58
I pay a lot more attention to food prices now than I ever did before	81	81	79	81	81	84
I am an impulse buyer	38	46	47	40	33	30
I shop a lot for specials	60	61	59	63	56	61

Health and Nutrition

I am very concerned about nutrition	61	66	65	60	57	63
I am concerned about how much salt I eat	40	28	32	32	46	54
I am careful what I eat in order to keep my weight under control	51	38	43	44	55	64
I try to avoid foods that are high in cholestrol	49	31	42	41	60	63
I try to avoid foods that have additives in them	44	36	35	39	49	56
I get more headaches than most people	17	18	17	19	21	12
I eat more than I should	66	57	67	68	70	64

Courtesy of Needham, Harper & Steers Advertising, Inc. *Life Style Survey*, 1975.

Fig. 7-3.   Life-style Profiles

Item	Percentage agreeing					
	Total	East	South	Mid-west	West	South-west
Prefer a traditional marriage with the husband assuming the responsibility for providing for the family and the wife running the house and taking care of the children	52%	39%	52%	59%	45%	61%
When making important family decisions, consideration of the children should come first	52	49	62	51	48	50
Every vacation should be educational	48	49	54	52	38	47
I am considering buying life insurance	19	14	30	17	17	21
I nearly always have meat at breakfast	29	14	52	22	26	34
Went out to breakfast instead of having it at home at least once last year	57	57	42	61	71	61
Worked on a community project at least once during the past year	35	39	50	34	31	34
Attended church 52 or more times last year	28	23	37	31	20	30
I like to visit places that are totally different from my home	72	79	63	72	75	65
I would like to spend a year in London or Paris	33	40	36	27	38	24
Went on a trip outside the U.S. last year	14	24	8	12	19	15
Rode a bus at least once last year	32	49	26	28	40	24
It is hard to get a good job these days	77	82	83	77	65	80
Used a bank charge card at least once last year	43	52	43	41	52	50
Returned an unsatisfactory product at least once during the past year	65	67	52	70	65	64
Used a "price off" coupon at a grocery store	63	67	50	72	60	53
My days seem to follow a definite routine—eating meals at the same time each day, etc.	62	68	66	58	53	64
Cooked outdoors at least once last year	81	86	82	84	80	84
Went on a picnic at least once last year	75	78	65	79	79	73
Had wine with dinner at least once during the past year	60	70	38	62	72	49
Had a cocktail or drink before dinner at least once last year	70	78	59	75	77	53
I am interested in spice and seasoning	43	46	44	41	54	35
Visited an art gallery or museum from 1 to 4 times in the past year	30	29	27	32	40	34
Went bowling at least once last year	36	42	20	44	34	24
Went hiking at least once during the past year	46	49	47	43	59	45
Went backpacking at least once last year	6	8	7	4	16	5
Went hunting at least once last year	32	18	43	29	32	40

Courtesy of Needham, Harper & Steers Advertising, Inc. *Life Style Survey*, 1975.

become quite complex. The discussion that follows is confined to social class in the United States, but some principles and determinants may be applicable to a wide range of complex societies.

The United States is considered an "open class" society—that is, people are, to some extent, free to move from the class into which they are born. This is contrasted to a "caste" system in which people are forced to remain in the class of their parents. In addition, the open class concept means that different factors may determine membership in different classes. Thus, the upwardly mobile middle-class in the United States tends to emphasize competitive occupational achievement and respectability. New arrivals to the upper status emphasize wealth, and the established upper class stresses lineage and certain inherited symbols of status.[32] According to American values, social position *should* be based on personal qualities and achievements. One *should* be able to move up based on personal effort. Given this, the concept of stratification becomes a logical consequence of values. This is a society of equality of opportunity and free, competitive placement ("Anyone who has it in him can get ahead"). Hence, success is solely a matter of individual merit. Those who are at the top deserve to be there; those at the bottom are there because of lack of talent or effort: it is "their own fault." Thus, the placement of individuals could not be otherwise without violating the value of individual achievement.[33] Again, however, all classes don't "play by these rules," so a system of evaluation must account for wealth, occupational status, and "quality of breeding."

By definition, social class is a hierarchy of social levels within which people are more or less equal to one another in prestige and community, are comfortable enough with one another to be able to interact readily and regularly among themselves in both formal and informal ways, and share essentially the same goals and ways of looking at life. The latter characteristic is what makes social class a useful concept for marketing strategists.[34]

In order to deal with the various factors that influence social status, a number of systems of evaluation and placement have been developed. The system that seems to have been most frequently used in consumer behavior studies is W. Lloyd Warner's *Index of Status Characteristics* (ISC). Originally, the ISC contained six variables: occupation, source of income, house type, dwelling area, amount of income, and education. Subsequent analysis, however, showed that eliminating income and education did not materially reduce the predictive power of the index.[35]

Occupation receives the heaviest weighting in the ISC, and it is generally the best single indicator of social class in all the classes except the highest. You might feel that the amount of income is the most important factor, but a little thinking about how you ascribe social standing will show you that amount of income is not the most significant determinant of social standing.

Suppose there are three families (A, B, and C) who are in different social classes, and you have to rank them in order of social standing. Each family contains a husband, wife, and two children. The husband and wife are in their mid- to late twenties, and each family has an annual income of $30,000. Can you rank them? No? What additional information would you want? If you knew that the parents in family A had completed high school, and those in the next two families had completed college, you could say that families B and C probably have higher social status than A. If you knew the occupations in each family, you could probably pinpoint the class quite easily. In family A. the husband is a cross-country truck driver and his wife does assembly work for a local manufacturer. In family B, the husband is a legal secretary and the wife is an industrial sales representative. In family C, the husband is a young attorney and the wife is currently unemployed outside the home. Now you can pretty well rank the three families from lowest to highest social status.

Again, occupation tends to be the most significant single indicator of social status. Figure 7-4 shows that the attitudes of Americans toward the status of various occupations changed little from 1947 to 1963. Subsequent research showed similar attitudes several years later.[36]

The discussion so far suggests that social class can be an individual and a family phenomenon. Historically, a family's social class derived from the class of the husband. However, as more women enter higher-level professions, we may see a change. So far, however, the traditional source of family status seems to hold. A significant portion of a family's buying behavior is influenced by its social class level, but we really can't view a social class as a homogeneous group. Actually, we might observe a wide variety of behavior within a single class, but there is enough interclass similarity and intraclass differences to analyze and segment markets. Amount of income tells us something about the buying power of a family, and it sets some limits on what the family can afford to buy and do. Social class is a determinant of family life-style, and it is accordingly a major determinant of how a family allocates its income.

Amount of income is also significant within a social class. Each class has over- and underprivileged segments, and buying behavior may vary substantially between the subsegments in each class. What constitutes a high income is relative to one's social class. An upper-middle-class family with $25,000 may be underprivileged, while the same income for a working class family might make it overprivileged relative to other members of the class. In each class the overpriviledged constitute a quality market, while the low-income segment tends to be economy oriented.

Although there is little agreement as to the number of classes that exist in the United States, a great deal of marketing analysis is based on the following divisions:

1. *Upper-upper.* Families in this class represent second or third generation wealth. High income or wealth will not get a person accepted as an equal by members of this class. The money has to have been in the family long enough for its "blood to turn blue." This is the smallest of the social classes, accounting for no more than one half of one percent of the U.S. population.[37] The basic values of this group seem to be living graciously, upholding the family reputation, and displaying a sense of community responsibility.[38] Although families in this class usually have a good deal of money to spend, they tend to spend without ostentation.

Fig. 7-4. Occupational Status: 1947 and 1963

	1947		1963	
	Score	Rank	Score	Rank
Supreme Court Justice	96	1	94	1
Physician	93	2.5	93	2
Scientist	89	8	92	3.5
College professor	89	8	90	8
Lawyer	86	18	89	11
Dentist	86	18	88	14
Civil engineer	84	23	86	21.5
Accountant—large business	81	29	81	29.5
Public school teacher	78	36	81	29.5
Building contractor	79	34	80	31.5
Artist (painter)	83	24.5	78	34.5
Electrician	73	45	76	39
Policeman	67	55	72	47
Insurance agent	68	51.5	69	51.5
Carpenter	65	58	68	53
Plumber	63	59.5	65	59
Auto repairman	63	59.5	64	60
Truck driver	54	71	59	67
Store clerk	58	68	56	70
Farmhand	50	76	48	83
Shoe shiner	33	90	34	90

In this table a score of 100 = "excellent social standing," 80 = "good," 60 = "average," 40 = "somewhat below average," and 20 = "poor social standing."

Adapted from Robert W. Hodge, Paul M. Seigel, and Peter H. Rossi, "Occupational Prestige in the United States, 1925-1963," *American Journal of Sociology* 10 (November, 1964):286-302. Reprinted from *American Journal of Sociology* by permission of The University of Chicago Press.

2. *Lower-upper.* This category is the new money class—they may have as much or more wealth than the upper-uppers, but it came within their lifetime. This class might include successful business and professional people, sports and movie stars, and other recently arrived or *nouveau riche* families. Constituting about 1 to 1.5 percent of the population, this class spends freely on symbols of status to let the world know they have arrived. Their homes, cars, and clothing are likely to be showy and expensive. This is a major market for such status symbols as swimming pools, pleasure craft, and furs. The goals of families at this social level seem to be a blend of the upper-upper pursuit of gracious living and the upper-middle drive for success and recognition.

3. *Upper-middle.* Ten to twelve percent of the population make up this professional class. The majority of this class are college educated and see that their

children are likewise privileged. Upper-middle-class families are career minded and interested in showing their career success to the world. Traditionally, the husband has been responsible for achieving the career success, while the wife has been charged with reflecting that success in home decor, dress, and social affiliations. Again this class represents a quality market: clothing and home furnishings should come from the "right stores."

4. *Lower-middle.* This class typifies mainstream America. Roughly thirty to thirty-five percent of U.S. families fit into this class, where the bywords are "respectability" and "striving." Members of this class are fundamentally white-collar workers—salespeople, office workers, and school teachers. This class strives to do a good job at work and reflect respectability in obedience to the law and church attendance. Respectability is further evidenced by middle-class homes. They tend to be neat with well-kept yards in "nice" neighborhoods. Likewise, the lower-middle class buys clothing and furniture from "nice" stores, and it follows the lead of medium-level shelter and service magazines as a guide to appropriate life-styles.

5. *Upper-lower.* The blue-collar or working class is the largest of the social classes with forty to fifty percent of the population. There are really two income segments in the blue-collar class. At one end is the family with two incomes or a high income from a well-paid union-covered job. At the other end is the family barely getting by on the income of a semiskilled or relatively unskilled breadwinner. Families at the high end of the first category will have more discretionary income than most lower-middles and even some under-privileged upper-middles. However, the income will typically be spent differently. The working class family is likely to have "more" house in "less" neighborhood than the middle-class family. In addition, they will tend to follow the times and be modern—defined as having furniture and clothing representing the latest thing to hit the mass market. The household is likely to sport more and newer appliances, a newer car, and a bigger TV than the middle class, and more income will be allocated to sporting equipment and activities, possibly including a boat and a camper.

6. *Lower-lower.* At the bottom end of the social scale are the families represented by sporadically employed, unskilled workers and perpetual welfare recipients. This class is declining in size as it becomes assimilated into the working class because of education and training and upgraded incomes. This class might encompass five to ten percent of the U.S. population, but buying power is perhaps two to five percent of the total, and discretionary income is almost nil. Apathy, fatalism, and "get your kicks when you can" describes the value system for this group. Because of its size and spending power, this class becomes more the concern of the social worker than the marketer.

It can be seen from these descriptions that families in different social class levels are likely to behave quite differently from one another in the marketplace. They often differ drastically from one another in values, attitudes, perceptions, priorities, life-style, motivation, and personality. Social classes make logical bases for market segmentation because persons in different social classes buy different products, expose themselves to and respond to different advertising media and appeals, and place significantly different meanings on the products they buy. Of course, there are many similarities among classes on these grounds, and research should be applied to determine specific class responses to various products and appeals.

SUMMARY

Individual consumer behavior is often influenced by other persons. Influence may come from individuals or groups, and buying decisions are often made in and by groups.

Socialization is the process by which children learn roles and expectations, including buying behavior. Socializing influence comes from such social institutions as family, friends, school, and media.

Several group forces may influence consumer behavior, including status, power (reward, coercive, legitimate, referent, and expert), roles, norms, and conformity.

Reference groups are those to which an individual looks for social guidance and approval. Three types of reference groups were identified: comparative, status, and normative. Reference group influence may be of three types: informational, utilitarian, and value-expressive.

Culture is defined as the behavior, beliefs, attitudes, customs, norms, and human artifacts of a particular society or population. Culture is shared, learned, adaptive, generally integrated, dynamic, and it defines and constrains behavior. Significant American cultural values were described as achievement and success; activity, work, and time orientation; youthfulness; humanitarianism and egalitarianism; religious and moralistic; and individualism, freedom, and conformity.

A subculture was defined as a distinct cultural group that exists as an identifiable segment within a larger, more complex society. Although there are many subcultures, ethnic, age, and geographic were the only ones discussed. Ethnic subcultures may be based on one's national origin, race, or religion. Three major U.S. ethnic subcultures were covered: black, Hispanic, and Jewish.

The age subcultures were youth, young adult, and old age. Easterners, southerners, midwesterners, westerners, and southwesterners form the major U.S. geographic subcultures.

Social class is a system whereby some individuals and families are accorded more status or prestige than others. In the United States, social class is a function of source of income, amount of income, education, house type, dwelling area, and occupation, with occupation being the most important single determinant. Six social class levels were identified: upper-upper, lower-upper, upper-middle, lower-middle, upper-lower, and lower-lower. Among other things, a person's social class influences products purchased, media consumed, and advertising appeals accepted.

CHAPTER 7 STUDY REVIEW

Important Terms and Concepts

Socialization
Roles
Norms
Social power
Status
Reference groups
Culture
Subculture
Social class

Questions

1. Describe ways in which each type of social power may occur in marketing strategy and consumer behavior.

2. Outline the process by which children in our society are socialized to become consumers.

3. What reference groups are relevant to you? How do they influence your buying behavior?

4. Discuss the characteristics of culture.

5. How might American cultural values influence buying behavior?

6. What differences in consumer behavior might you expect to find among different subcultures?

7. What determines social class, and how is social class likely to be reflected in consumer behavior?

8. Describe the levels of social class in the United States. How might behavior, attitudes, life-style, and buying behavior differ among the classes?

9. Compare the effects of income versus social class on consumer behavior.

8

Family
Consuming Behavior

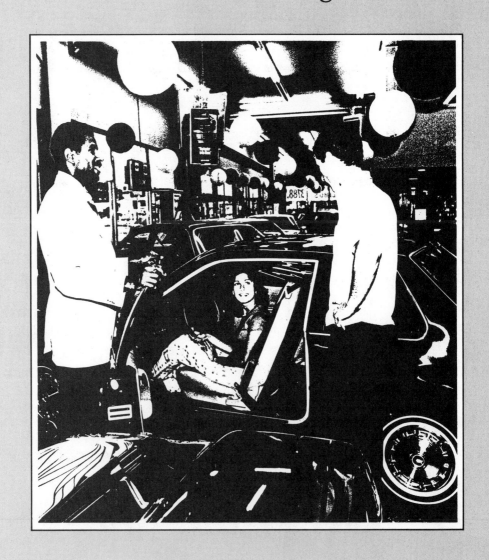

Although the exact nature of formation and composition varies widely throughout the world, the family is virtually the universal building block of a society. A family is a social entity minimally composed of a couple and whatever children they may have.[1] This definition can be qualified to include a single parent (for whatever reason) and child or children. In U.S. society, as in many others, family formation is legally sanctioned by a marriage ceremony, although common law provides for marriage without ceremony in some states. A family is characterized by common residence, economic cooperation, a sexual relationship, and (in general) reproduction. The term *household* is used as a broader term to designate a unit (individual or group) of common residence but not necessarily otherwise defined as a family.

The family plays an important role in the shaping and functioning of consumer behavior. It acts as a socializing agent to teach children necessary buying and consuming behavior. In addition, it is an economic unit that generates income (and/or direct want satisfiers, such as food), which is applied to purchase need satisfiers. Finally, it is a consumption unit that uses the goods and services acquired.

There are two levels of family. The first is the nuclear family or a husband, wife, and children. The second is the extended family, which includes grandparents or other relatives who live under the same roof as the nuclear family.

In analyzing the family and its relationship to consumer behavior, four dimensions of family structure and activities that are relevant to family buying behavior will be considered: family role structure, family life cycle, family life-style, and family decision making. The chapter concludes with a discussion of major social trends relevant to consumer behavior.

Family Role Structure

By definition, a family is composed of more than one person. Because of varying capabilities and interests, various family members will generally fill different roles to achieve efficiency. In some cases a family member may fill a variety of roles, depending upon the situation. In other instances, a family member's role may be more or less permanent. In buying behavior, roles will center around use of product or influence on its purchase. Roles will also be dependent upon the interest or expertise of individual family members.

The following list describes six consumption and influencing roles that family members may play, cycling in and out of the roles at various times:

1. *Influencers*—family members who provide information and advice and thereby affect the selection of a product or service.
2. *Gatekeepers*—family members who control the flow of information about a product or service into the family and thereby influence the decisions of other family members.
3. *Deciders*—family members who have the power to determine unilaterally or jointly whether or not to purchase a specific product or service.
4. *Buyers*—family members who actually make the purchase of a particular product or service.
5. *Preparers*—family members who transform the product into a form in which it can be consumed by family members.
6. *Users*—family members who use or consume a particular product or service.[2]

Obviously, a given family member may play a number of roles simultaneously, and role assumption will vary from product to product and situation to situation.

Traditionally, husbands and wives have played rather consistent and predictable roles in American families, with the husband the primary breadwinner and the wife the home manager. Given these roles, husbands have been primarily concerned with functional and economic (or instrumental) values, while wives were more oriented to things valued for their intrinsic nature rather than for their function (expressive values).[3] Thus, the husband would be more likely to be involved in the functional aspects of a purchase, say the mechanical or structural aspects of furniture or appliances. At the same time, the wife might look at the aesthetics of a product, including color and design.

Husbands, because of their more frequent contacts outside of the home, have traditionally been more involved with matters external to the family.[4] These might include auto repairs and insurance. The wife, on the other hand, because her domain has traditionally been the home, has been more concerned with internal factors, such as home decor and meal planning.[5]

The recent trend is for more and more women to be employed outside the home. In 1978, 46 percent of women over twenty were employed outside the home, and women made up 37 percent of the work force. During that year, total employment rose by 7.5 percent, the population of females over twenty increased by 3.5 percent, and the number of employed women increased by 10.4 percent.[6] In 1977, 27 percent of women held two or more jobs.[7] As this trend continues, we should see the traditional division of internal/external roles disappearing, and interest and expertise becoming more important.

Children and adolescents play a significant role as influencers in the purchase of certain types of products. Children under twelve are most influential in purchases of breakfast cereal, snack foods, candy, soft drinks, games and toys, clothing, records, and toothpaste.[8]

Family Life Cycle

As was noted earlier in the discussion of subculture, people of different ages behave differently in the marketplace. The same is true of families, but we need a measure other than chronological age to apply to the family. Life cycle is often used as a measure of family age. Family life cycle is a function of the age of the household head, the presence or absence of children, marital status, and the age of children. One of the problems of life cycle analysis is that there is little consistency among researchers as to which variables are determinants of the stage in cycle and the number and composition of the stages.[9] This chapter offers a composite of the various stages of life cycle to illustrate the usefulness of the concept. The stages are: single, newlywed, full nest I, full nest II, empty nest, and retirement.[10]

Single

The first stage of the life cycle occurs when a person leaves the family to strike out alone. In general, the young single will live in an apartment, often furnished. Consequently, there will be little demand for furniture and major appliances, but there may be a need for small household items and appliances. A major portion of the typically large discretionary income for singles is allocated to the purchase of clothing, recreation items, stereo equipment, and an automobile.

Newlywed

Contrary to what is found in many cultures, the extended family living under one roof is relatively rare in the United States. When children get married, they typically do not live with their parents but rather start a new household. This leads to a heavy demand for housing and the items that fill a house.

At this stage both husband and wife are likely to be working, and they have no children, so discretionary income will continue to be high. Expenditures during this stage shift to durable goods, especially furniture and appliances. The first home will often be acquired during this stage. Cars, clothing, and travel continue to be major expenditures.

Full Nest I

The addition of children to a family creates a number of changes relevant to its consuming behavior. First, discretionary income will likely drop because the needs of young children must be met, and the wife will often stop working outside the home, at least temporarily, in order to care for children.

The family will often buy a first home during this stage, or they might move to a larger home to accommodate the growing family. A family at this stage will be buying many products, and family members are fairly heavily influenced by marketing efforts, including new product introduction and advertising. Their income status makes them particularly sensitive to price promotion.

Full Nest II

At this stage the family may have younger children, but they also have older children at home. Needs for clothing, stereos, and autos for the older children now become significant. Often resources are conserved by handing items down from older to younger children.

There are heavy demands on income at this stage, but the occupational success of one or both parents is also peaking. Often a wife who has stayed out of the labor market to care for young children will take work outside the home, and in many cases, older children will also be employed.

By now family members have considerable buying experience, and they will tend to rely more heavily on that experience than on company promotional efforts. During this stage they will often be replacing worn-out durable goods, and they will be more likely to purchase more expensive, higher-line products than they did the first time around. This stage represents the "quality market" for products like furniture, appliances, and automobiles. Education and weddings for children become important expense items during this phase.

Empty Nest

At this stage children are grown and starting their own families. Income is at its peak, and the couple is interested in luxury items, travel, and recreation. Because home ownership is highest here, there is some replacement of durables, and home repair and remodeling is significant. Many times people at this stage will purchase a number of items needed at the prior cycle stages as gifts for children and grandchildren.

Retirement Age

At this stage both income and needs will decline, while needs for health-related items will increase. Several different conditions may attend this stage. If one or both family members work beyond retirement, or if financial security has been effectively achieved, income may remain high. On the other hand, many couples find themselves in financial difficulty here. It is during this stage, too, that one member of the couple will die, and the survivor will carry on with reduced financial needs and often reduced resources. In general, this final life cycle stage is a time of decline and retrenchment in the consumption of many kinds of products.

Family Life-style

Family life-style differs from social class to social class, and it also varies a great deal within classes. Family life-style may be defined as the system of attitudes and behaviors that influence how the family members spend their time and money. A family's life-style, perhaps more than any other factor, will influence what it buys, when it buys, how it buys, and what influences its buying behavior. A family's life-style is determined by such factors as the values, personalities, interests, and attitudes of individual family members, which are, in turn, influenced by culture, subculture, social class, and other reference persons and groups. Life-style is generally measured in terms of consumer AIO's (activities, interests, and opinions).

A family's life-style may be manifested in many ways. Some families are perpetually in debt as they live beyond their means, while others pay cash for virtually everything, with the exception, perhaps, of a house and car. Some families are very oriented toward family activities, such as camping, vacations, and family parties. Others will find each family member pretty much doing his or her own thing, with most social and recreational activities occurring with peers rather than family members. Some families may be oriented toward vigorous physical activities; others may go for quieter pastimes, such as parlor games, plays, and television. Some families are pretty much introverted, preferring to stay home, while others are constantly in the "social swim."

The AIO's of a family are obviously significant in determining its buying behavior. Traditionally, it has been difficult to study and classify families according to life-style—the range has been too far reaching and unpredictable. Psychographic research, however, has come to grips with the problem of identificating and measuring relevant AIO's (see chapter 9).

Family Decision Making

Many consumer decisions are made by individual consumers satisfying their own personal needs, but a very large proportion are made in the context of one individual buying to satisfy the needs of others or several individuals acting in concert to reach a buying decision that affects one or more family members. Obviously, the family decision is a more complex process than a purchase decision made by and for a single individual. Compare the model of the family decision process in Figure 8-1 with the decision models in Chapter 2. Multiple influence raises the complexity of the process considerably. The wide range of research on family decision making suggests the need to look at the family not as a set of individual consumers but as a complex interacting unit. Seldom can one family member be singled out as the chief purchaser or decision maker. Also, simply defining the roles which family members play is not realistic since roles are likely to be different from family to family, from purchase to purchase, and over the various stages of the decision process. This section will give you some insights to the nature and complexity of the family purchase decision process by first looking at the family as a decision making group. Second, some of the major determinants of how families make decisions will be considered, and finally some alternative decision making strategies for the family will be investigated.

Family Versus Individual Decision Making

The family decision process is often investigated in terms of the relative power of the husband and wife, but it may be better to view the family decision process in the context of the goal oriented behavior of a small group.[11]

Decision Role Structure The family roles were discussed briefly in an earlier section, but the concepts need to be refined to understand the importance of family roles in the decision process. Although purchase influence may be exerted by one family member when a decision is made, it is more likely that more than one family member will be involved. Although children and teenagers may play active roles in the decision, it is common to consider only the husband/wife interaction for the sake of simplicity, and the influence of other family members may come out in the attitudes of the husband and wife anyway.[12]

The role structure in family decision making manifests itself in the degree to which the decision is made jointly or by a spouse acting alone. This gives rise to several possibilities for role interaction: wife alone, joint—wife dominant, joint—equal influence, joint—husband dominant, and husband alone. In considering family decisions in the aggregate, it is useful to break the process into four levels of interaction based on the extent of specialization and the relative influence of husbands and wives: wife-dominant (majority of decisions dominated by wife), husband-dominant (majority of decisions dominated by husband), syncratic (more than half of family's decisions made jointly), and autonomic (less than half of family's decisions made jointly).[13]

It is not enough, however, to simply say that a decision is made jointly; we must also consider the kinds of influence each decision participant exerts and the conditions under which various kinds and amounts of influence will be brought to bear. The family is not a homogeneous unit—rather, it is essentially a collection of individuals with different needs, goals, motives, and interests.[14] Given this, circumstances will dictate who assumes a leadership, an influencing, or a passive role at any given time. Thus, the Family Financial Officer (FFO) or decision maker may be one or the other spouse or both at different times and under varying circumstances,[15] and the roles of purchasing agent and consumer or user will shift as well.

It will be difficult to predict which role a given family member will play. Prescribed husband-wife roles may be fairly good indicators of the roles each spouse will play in a decision, but in developed Western societies, norms of shared interests, give and take, and companionship will likely exist and complicate any concept of consistently assumed roles.[16]

Fig. 8-1. Family Decision Process

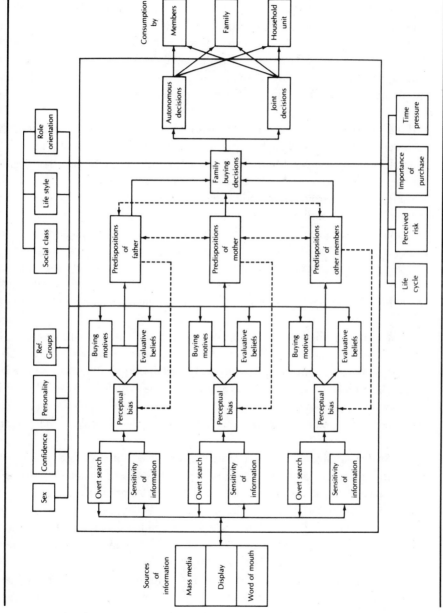

Jagdish N. Sheth, "A Theory of Family Buying Decisions." Figure 2-1 (pp. 22-23) in *Models of Buyer Behavior: Conceptual, Quantitative, and Empirical* by Jagdish N. Sheth. Copyright © 1974 by Jagdish N. Sheth. Reprinted by permission of Harper & Row Publishers, Inc.

Goals and Attitudes A given family will likely have goals existing on at least three levels: individual family member goals, goals held by more than one family member, but not all; and family goals, agreed upon and sought by all family members. When goals of family members coincide, there is a different problem than when they are in conflict. In order to function effectively, the family must achieve some degree of consensus relative to goals, objectives, and modes of operation. However, automatic agreement is rare, so negotiation is required to develop priorities all family members can accept. [17] To the extent that the attitudes and goals of the husband and wife are congruent, they will be more likely to make purchase plans and decisions jointly, and the FFO will be the husband and wife acting in concert. [18]

Effectiveness of the Family as a Decision-making Group The family unit has been compared to a business firm in microcosm, but there are several reasons for a family's decision process to be less efficient than an industrial purchasing group or the laboratory group often studied in decision research. [19]

First, the environment of family decision making may lead to poor decisions. Goals may be less well defined than those of other groups, and there may be more push for satisfaction of individual goals than in an industrial setting. Family activities, crises, and lack of firm goals may create distractions in the decision process. Deciding what car to buy while preparing a meal or watching television may not lead to an optimally satisfying decision. In addition, families often come together early in the morning and after a day's work when energy and efficiency levels are low.

A second factor leading to poor family decisions involves the maintenance needs of the family. The long-term nature of the family relationship may lead to decisions or actions aimed at preserving stable relationships rather than other goals. A purchase problem may be seen as a threat to family solidarity, particularly if it's obvious that someone will be dissatisfied. Thus, the problem may be set aside. Often families seek to reduce tension rather than to analyze a problem and potential solutions rigorously. [20]

Finally, family decisions are heavily interrelated. Families face several problems simultaneously, and the least complex problems may be satisfied at the expense of more far-reaching and significant ones. This may occur if spouses fixate on different aspects of the decision. For example, a wife may see the washing machine problem in terms of the capability of a new machine to handle different fabrics effectively and to take larger loads. Her husband may define the problem in terms of making the old machine last, avoiding payments, and the overemphasis on labor-saving features that cost more than they're worth. As a result, the question of a new washing machine may be dropped. A second factor that may delay or set aside a decision is the mutually exclusive nature of some decisions—a new washing machine may mean no new deer rifle or fishing boat, and vice versa, so both purchases may be bypassed, sometimes in favor of something that neither party wants.

Determinants of Family Decision Making

The determinants of family decision making are conditions which influence whether a decision will be made jointly or by one spouse acting as a specialist. These determinants are not exhaustive, but they do point to the wide range of influence on interaction in the decision process.[21]

Social Class It was noted earlier that social class has a significant influence on family life-style and purchasing patterns. It also seems to have an effect on family decision making. In general, higher social class families have a greater sense of control over their environment, and they are, therefore, more likely to engage in information search actively prior to a decision.[22] Joint decision making has been found to be more prevelant in middle-income levels and among better-educated couples.[23] Wives appear to have greater decision autonomy among the upper and lower social classes and less in the middle class.[24]

Role Definition Some of the variability in decision involvement can be explained by the roles family members play. This is, in part, a function of the sex of the FFO. Families in which the FFO is the husband tend to have a higher portion of income saved. In addition, husband-led families are more likely to have savings in variable-dollar assets, to own a home, and to purchase cars less frequently. On the other hand, if the wife gives more priority to saving, is more concerned with high quality, or is more economy- and bargain-conscious, she is more likely to be the FFO.[25]

Three general factors have been advanced to explain variations in role definition in families: cultural role expectations, comparative resources, and relative investment.[26] In some cases a family's culture will define certain expectations for the roles of family members. This identification of who *should* make the decision reflects legitimate power. Another cultural norm may define the degree of companionship expected between a husband and wife. If the culture approves high companionship, there might be more joint decision making.

The concept of comparative resources is referred to as exchange theory. The allocation of tasks and authority is carried out on the basis of each member's ability to reward and punish, personal attractiveness, or competence. These "resources" are exchanged for the right to make or participate in a decision (or not to be involved). Unlike cultural role expectations, exchange theory sees role determination as internal to the family itself.

Finally, it is suggested that a given decision may be of more significance to some family members than to others—namely, one party may have a greater relative investment than the other. A cost-benefit assessment of various decision outcomes may influence whether and how each spouse participates in a given purchase decision. The relative investment theory differs from the comparative resources explanation in two ways. First, resources define the *potential* for family members to exert influence, while investment defines the *motivation* for them to apply the influence. Second, the relative investment concept yields predictions about *family member involvement* in specific decisions as opposed to the *general authority structure* of the family explained by the comparative resources idea.

Life Cycle The length of time a couple has been married and the presence or absence of children in the family seem to have a direct influence on family decision making. The family life cycle seems to be a better explanatory variable than the length of time married. As the family matures, there is increased pressure for spouses to agree upon and pursue common goals. The presence of children seems to exert a major force toward family goal congruence since divergent goals are more common in families before and after they have children at home. [27]

During the early years of marriage the husband and wife begin to adjust to one another's needs. There is considerable discussion and negotiation relative to present and future family goals and priorities. During this time there is a great deal of joint decision making and purchasing.

Individual preferences and skills are learned and compromises are often made where individual goals conflict. The patterns that emerge at this time set the tone for future family operations. [28] By the second year of marriage, one spouse typically begins to emerge as the FFO, [29] and as the family moves to later stages of the family life cycle, family goals are more solidified and acceptable to both husband and wife. Decisions now move from compromise to concensus. As individual roles become more firmly established, joint decision making tends to give way to specialized decision roles. [30]

The trend toward consensus in the family may be described as a process of adjustment. This adjustment is probably the result of several forces. [31]

1. The family may be viewed as a reference group that shapes the attitudes of its members. [32]
2. A husband and wife probably share membership in other reference groups and tend to move toward views commonly held by those groups. [33]
3. Members of a family tend to share all the same information sources, such as magazines and newspapers.
4. Some obvious needs exist for most families, such as a large car for a large family that travels together.
5. The more times a family has made a decision, the greater is the probability of agreement.

Life-Style The concept of life-style is used rather broadly here to include the family's decision-making style and household structure. Some families exhibit more formality than others. In a more formal family, family councils might be held to give all members the opportunity to contribute to goals and decisions. A typology based on the compatibility of preferences, interests, and priorities, and the coordination of goal-directed activities in the family leads to four family structure types: coordinated-compatible, coordinated-incompatible, uncoordinated-compatible, and uncoordinated-incompatible.[34] Coordination is defined in terms of goal agreement and cooperation is a function of congeniality among members. The coordinated-compatible family is the ideal—they get along and they tend to make good decisions in the sense that the needs of individual family members are generally satisfied within the context of family goals. The coordinated-incompatible family is calculating, price-conscious, immune to emotional appeals, and hard bargaining. The uncoordinated-compatible family would be rather happy-go-lucky and quite susceptible to promotion and impulse buying. The uncoordinated-incompatible family is probably on the verge of collapse, and any cooperation in buying decisions would be purely a matter of necessity.

Several other life-style typologies suggest differences in decision-making style and specialization in decision making. One view types families on the basis of whether familism (family orientation), career, or consumership represents the dominant theme of living.[35] Family values may also influence decision making. Lifestyles may be based upon such values as flexible versus rigid, nonevaluative versus evaluative, objective versus family role, emancipated versus limited, and appreciated versus unappreciated.[36] For example, we might expect to see more decision autonomy in flexible, nonevaluative, objective, emancipated, and appreciative families.

The aspiration and expectation levels of the husband and wife may directly influence life-style and decision making.[36] If a husband's aspirations and expectations exceed those of his wife, we might expect him to be the prime motivator for an improved family life-style. A husband might aspire to a higher life-style but hold lower expectations than his wife. In this case, his wife would likely push for a higher standard of living, and she might seek employment outside the home to achieve it. This is suggested as a prevalent pattern for many U.S. working-class families.[37]

Nature of the Purchase Several aspects of the purchase may influence the family decision process. Important characteristics include the end use of the product, type of product, time constraints, importance of the purchase, degree of risk, and second preference.

The end use of the product in terms of individual versus group consumption will influence the decision. Joint decision making is more likely to characterize products destined for family consumption, but there might still be specialization according to individual expertise and interest. Keep in mind that many purchases do not represent a single decision but rather numerous decisions on various product features. In a study of home buying, the majority of couples reported equal influence for every element of the housing decision (seek residence, rent or buy, floor plan, style, price, location, size, and so forth). However, when one spouse had relatively more influence, husbands and wives generally agreed that the husband was dominant in the decision to rent or buy and in the price decision, while the wife was dominant in the floor plan, style, and size decisions.[38]

Husband-wife involvement in a decision varies widely by product category.[39] In consumer research, the major distinction has been drawn between durable and nondurable products. Nondurable purchase decisions tend to be more autonomous, while durable purchases are more likely to be characterized by joint decision making.

Where time pressures exist, decision making is more likely to be autonomous.[40] Individual purchases may need to be made quickly for a variety of reasons, and a working wife and the presence of children tends to increase general time pressure for the family.[41]

Both importance and risk influence family decision making. Joint decision making is more prevelant for more important and riskier purchases.[42]

A significant dimension of many purchase decisions is choosing a brand. If one spouse has a brand preference and the other does not, or if both share the same brand preference, there is little problem. However, when there is disagreement on brand preference, negotiation of some sort may be necessary. When disagreements do exist, the wife's preferred brand is more likely to be purchased than the husband's.[43]

Stage in the Decision Process So far, we have looked at family decision making as if it were merely a matter of selecting an alternative. However, as chapter 2 indicated, the decision is made up of a number of stages. In the words of one researcher, "marketers must investigate the entire decision process since relative influence may vary from one decision phase to the next . . . husband-wife influence must be investigated for each stage rather than falling prey to the assumption of stable influence across the process based upon intuition or limited inquiry into a single phase of the process."[44] Figure 8-2 shows variation that takes place over the decision process. Information search is often characterized by more specialization than other stages.[45]

Fig. 8-2. Patterns of Influence in the Decision Process

Pattern of Influence	Phase		
	Problem Recognition	Search for Information	Final Decision
Husband-dominant	2	3	2
Autonomic	10	9	5
Syncratic	7	6	13
Wife-dominant	6	7	5

Harry L. Davis and Benny P. Rigaux, "Perception of Marital Roles in Decision Processes." Reprinted with permission from *The Journal of Consumer Research* (1974), 1:55.

Participants other than the husband and wife may exert influence at various stages of the process. For example, a husband and wife may decide together about whether to buy a new car or to repair the old one, while the husband and teenage son may decide which make to buy.[46]

As the couple begins the decision process, they may be pretty much in agreement as to what they want, but as they move through the process, they may weigh product attributes quite differently. Disagreement about attribute weights and differing information that comes to participants through various sources may lead to rather major disagreements by the time the couple is ready to make the final purchase decision.[47]

Alternative Decision-making Strategies

When family members are in agreement about goals, the decision process can be described as *consensual*. A second situation exists when family members realize that priorities, preferences, and goals are irreconcilable. Under these conditions, the process is one of *accommodation*—negotiation to find a solution with which various family members can live.[48] Figure 8-3 summarizes the decision strategies likely to be used under these two conditions.

Fig. 8-3. Alternative Decision-making Strategies

Goals	Strategy	Ways of Implementing
	Role Structure	The Specialist
Consensus (Family members agree about goals)	Budgets	The Controller
	Problem Solving	The Expert The Better Solution The Multiple Purchase
Accomodation (Family members disagree about goals)	Persuasion	The Irresponsible Critic Feminine Intuition Shopping Together Coercion Coalitions
	Bargaining	The Next Purchase The Impulse Purchase The Procrastinator

Harry L. Davis, "Decision Making Within the Household." Reprinted with permission from *The Journal of Consumer Research*, (1976),2:255.

Role Structure One way to handle decisions if family members agree on goals is simply to recognize one member as a specialist who makes certain decisions without help from others. This member would be accorded legitimate power.

Budgets Here, decision responsibility is controlled by an impersonal arbitration system based on rules or budgets. The process of agreeing on a budget may elicit a good deal of conflict, but once agreed upon, it becomes a conflict-reducing guide.[49]

Problem Solving A third type of strategy for goal-congruent situations is problem solving. Experts, both within and outside the family, can be relied upon to provide inputs on the merit of various alternatives. There may be a feeling that problem solution-oriented family discussion can provide a better solution than one reached by a single family member. In the multiple solution strategy, two or more brands or products may be purchased instead of one. When family members have different preferences for toothpaste, for example, an obvious solution is to let each have his or her own brand.

When family members do not agree on goals, strategies of persuasion or bargaining are likely. The distinction between the two strategies is a little fuzzy, but persuasion can be viewed as a way of more or less forcing someone to make a decision that would not otherwise be made. Bargaining, on the other hand, relies on give and take and mutual benefit to bring about willing agreement.

Persuasion Generally, the person who makes a decision receives credit or blame, depending on the outcome. When blame is appropriate, another family member can take the role of irresponsible critic, offering criticism and suggestions without having to worry about being realistic. When a wife is dominated by her husband, she may resort to feminine intuition to predict times when her husband is vulnerable to new ideas or persuasion. Shopping together brings agreement by securing a commitment from the dissenting member while looking at the desired item. Coercion is the most extreme form of persuasion because it implies some sort of psychological duress to obtain consent from an unwilling family member. Coalitions may be formed within a family to pressure single or minority holdouts to consent to a purchase.

Bargaining Bargaining strategies typically involve longer-term solutions than persuasive strategies. Explicit or tacit agreements made in the past (precedents) may influence current purchase decisions. Waiting for the next purchase is a useful approach if a family member feels a high probability of loss of power by pushing for an immediate showdown. An impulse purchase is similar to the first move in a strategy game. A husband may buy a new car without consulting his wife. When he drives the car home, his wife may consider the purchase a *fait acompli* and let him keep it. Too, she might like it once she's seen it. The second move could be her independent purchase of an item she's wanted. Finally, when one family member is charged with the task of purchasing an item that he or she really doesn't want, the purchase may be delayed in hopes that the procrastination will defer the decision until new information appears or a new situation develops so that the choice may be changed.

The Changing Social Environment

The decades of the sixties and seventies have witnessed enormous social changes, and the eighties portend additional shifts. The trends established in the past twenty years may predict the changes of the next twenty. This section will look at a few of the major social changes that seem relevant to consumer behavior.

Economic Changes

Major economic changes have occurred in recent years that have an impact on consumer behavior. Inflation and scarce energy exert pressure on U.S. budgets. If the trend continues, we may see less discretionary income at all socioeconomic levels. This could lead to more careful deliberation and reduced purchase of luxury items. We've already seen a trend toward smaller, less powerful automobiles. The great American love affair with the automobile may be cooling, and the automobile could become less a status symbol; at least the characteristics that communicate status are likely to change.

Social and economic changes are making small families the rule. Effects of a stable population, declining youth market, and smaller families may be manifested in reduced demand for many products.

Cultural Changes

There are a number of cultural changes that may affect consumer behavior. Figure 8-4 suggests several changes in core cultural values. Part of these at least may influence consuming behavior. Figure 8-5 illustrates further social trends with some of their implications for consumer behavior.

Fig. 8-4. Changes in American Values

From	To
Self-reliance	Governmental reliance
"Hard Work"	The "easy life"
Religious convictions	Secular convictions
Husband-dominated home	Wife-dominated home
Parent-centered household	Child-centered household
Respect for individual	Dislike of individual difference
Postponed gratification	Immediate gratification
Saving	Spending
Sexual chastity	Sexual freedom
Parental values	Peer group values
Independence	Security

Philip Kotler, *Principles of Marketing*, © 1980, p.226. Reprinted by permission of Prentice-Hall, Inc., Englewood Cliffs, New Jersey.

Fig. 8-5. Social Trends and Implications

1. Psychology of affluence trends

The first group are traceable to the effects of "psychology of affluence." That is, they manifest themselves among consumers who feel sufficiently free from economic insecurity to seek the fulfillment of other needs.

Trend toward physical self-enhancement, spending more time, effort and money on improving one's physical appearance; the things people do to enhance their looks.

Trend toward personalization, expressing one's individuality through products, possessions and new life-styles. The need to be "a little bit different" from other people.

Trend toward physical health and well-being, the level of concern with one's health, diet and what people do to take better care of themselves.

Trend toward new forms of materialism, the new status symbols and extent of deemphasis on money and material possessions.

Trend toward personal creativity, the growing conviction that being "creative" is not confined to the artist. Each man can be creative in his own way, as expressed through a wide variety of activities, hobbies and new uses of leisure time.

Trend toward meaningful work, the spread of the demand for work that is challenging and meaningful over and above how well it pays.

2. Antifunctionalism trends

A second group of trends underscores a major new force in American life—the quest for excitement, sensation, stimulation, and meaning to counteract the practical and mundane routines of everyday life. There is a reaction among certain groups in the population against the drabness of modern life, giving rise to a many-faceted hunger that reaches beyond the practical.

Trend toward the "new romanticism," the desire to restore romance, mystery and adventure to modern life.

Trend toward novelty and change, the search for constant change, novelty, new experience, reaction against sameness and habit.

Trend toward adding beauty to one's daily surroundings, the stress on beauty in the home and the things people do and buy to achieve it.

Trend toward sensuousness, placing greater emphasis on a total sensory experience—touching, feeling, smelling, and psychedelic phenomena. A moving away from the purely linear, logical and visual.

Trend toward mysticism, the search for new modes of spirtual experience and beliefs, as typified by the growing interest in astrology.

Trend toward introspection, an enhanced need for self-understanding and life experiences in contrast to automatic conformity to external pressures and expectations.

3. Reaction against complexity trends

A third and important group of trends cluster around the theme of reaction against the complexity of modern life. We find more and more people changing their habits and life styles in reaction to crowded conditions, complicated products, unresponsive institutions, restrictive regulations and information overloads.

Trend toward life simplification, the turning away from complicated products, service and ways of life.

Trend toward return to nature, rejection of the artificial, the "chemical," the man-made improvements on nature; the adoption of more "natural" ways of dressing, eating and living.

Trend toward increased ethnicity, finding new satisfactions and identifications in foods, dress, customs and life styles of various ethnic groups such as Black, Italian, Irish, Polish, Jewish, German.

Trend toward increased community involvement, increasing affiliation with local, community and neighborhood activities. Greater involvement in local groups.

Trend toward greater reliance on technology versus tradition, distrust of tradition and reputation that is based on age and experience, due to the swift tempo of change. Greater confidence in science and technology.

Trend away from bigness, the departure from the belief that "big" necessarily means "good," beginning to manifest itself with respect to "big" brands, "big" stores.

4. Trends that move away from puritan values

The fourth group of trends measure the penetration of certain new values at the expense of the traditional puritanical values.

Trend toward pleasure for its own sake, putting pleasure before duty; changing life styles and what that means for product usage and communication.

Trend toward blurring of the sexes, moving away from traditional distinctions between men and women and the role each should play in marriage, work and other walks of life.

Trend toward living in the present, straying from traditional beliefs in planning, saving, and living for the future.

Trend toward more liberal sexual attitudes, the relaxation of sexual prohibitions and the devaluation of "virtue" in the traditional sense, among women.

Trend toward acceptance of stimulants and drugs, greater acceptance of artificial agents (legal and illegal) for mood change, stimulation and relaxation as opposed to the view that these should be accomplished by strength of character alone.

Trend toward relaxation of self-improvement standards, the inclination to stop working as hard at self-improvement; letting yourself be whatever you are.

Trend toward individual religions, rejection of institutionalized religions and the substitution of more personalized forms of religious experience, characterized by the emergence of numerous small and more intimate religious sects and cults.

5. Trends related to child-centeredness

Children born into the child-centered homes of the 40s and 50s are now in their twenties and teens. Although the consequences of this orientation are difficult to isolate, research indicates that a few important personality characteristics and values associated with them can be identified. These provide the source for the final group of trends—trends which have a direct impact on marketing as well as on other facets of modern life.

Trend toward greater tolerance of chaos and disorder, less need for schedules, routines, plans, regular shopping and purchasing, tolerance of less order and cleanliness in the home, less regular eating and entertaining patterns.

Trend toward challenge to authority, less automatic acceptance of the authority and "correctness" of public figures, institutions, and established brands.

Trend toward rejection of hypocrisy, less acceptance of sham, exaggeration, indirection, and misleading language.

Trend toward female careerism, belief that homemaking is not sufficient as the sole source of fulfillment and that more challenging and productive work for the woman is needed.

Trend toward familism, renewed faith in the belief that the essential life satisfactions stem from activities centering on the immediate family unit rather than on "outside" sources such as work and community affairs.

Reprinted from *Marketing News* 4 (May and June 1971), published by the American Marketing Association.

Family Changes

Many of the social and economic forces cited will directly influence the family and its purchasing behavior. Figure 8-6 summarizes some recent social trends as they are likely to influence family consuming behavior.

Possibly the most significant recent influence on the family and U.S. culture in general is the changing role of women. Although the nuclear family appears to

Fig. 8-6. Factors Affecting the Family

Trend	Impact
More leisure time	A shorter work-week will mean increased emphasis on family recreation and entertainment. There should also be a greater demand for products that make the use of time more rewarding and enjoyable.
More formal education	Better education will mean a more aware consumer, which should increase the demand for more reliable products. There should also be increased interest in products and services that satisfy the need for individualism.
More working married women	A higher total family income should mean less economic pressure and more money available for the purchase of products previously out of reach for the family. There should also be increased joint husband-wife decision making, a greater sharing of domestic responsibilities, and a continued preference for smaller families.
Increased life expectancy	As people live longer, the demand for products and services designed to cater to the health, recreation, and entertainment needs of an older population will increase. There should also be a greater emphasis placed on proper nutrition and diet.
Smaller size families	Fewer children (zero population growth) will mean that parents will be able to spend more time and money on the development of each child's skills and capabilities. There will also be more discretionary income available for parents to spend on their own development, to pursue their own interests, and to improve the general standard of the family's life-style.
Women's movement	Husbands and wives will increasingly share household responsibilities, including joint decision making. Moreover, as an outgrowth of the women's movement, traditional sex-linked roles will continue to decline, and products that have generally been aimed at either males or females will increasingly be targeted to members of both sexes.

Leon G. Schiffman and Leslie Lazer Kanuk, *Consumer Behavior*, © 1978, p.256, Fig.9-7. Reprinted by permission of Prentice-Hall, Inc., Englewood Cliffs, New Jersey.

be an enduring phenomenon, roles of husbands and wives have been changing dramatically. The trend is toward more women working outside the home, more shared or dominant roles for women, and a general shift away from what we might call traditional American attitudes toward women and their roles.

In 1950 women made up 29.6 percent of the U.S. work force. By 1975 they represented 39.9 percent of the total. Only 20 percent of all women worked at the turn of the century, but by 1975 46 percent were employed outside the home. The following predictions indicate that more and more women will enter the workforce: 1980—48.4 percent; 1985—50.3 percent; and 1990—51.4 percent. By 1985 more than half of women over fifteen are expected to be in the labor force.[50] As women enter the work force, their behavior and attitudes may change because they have more personal security, more legitimate power in family financial decisions, and less time for traditional homemaking roles.

Whether women are employed or not, many of their basic values are changing, and these changes affect consumer behavior. While the majority of young women still play the role of wife and mother, they are less likely to do so in the traditional sense of being subordinate to their husbands and following a prescribed pattern of home-oriented behavior without regard to their personal interests and abilities. The modern woman has opted for a more egalitarian sex role, which stresses similar behavior patterns for men and women and allows for goal actualization in both sexes.[51]

The suggestion is that women can be classified not only as "working" and "nonworking" but as "modern" and "traditional" as well. The traditional female orientation is no longer accepted by the majority of American women. In 1967 sixty percent of adult women agreed with the statement, "A woman's place is in the home," but by 1975 that proportion had dropped to twenty-six percent, and the decline can be expected to continue.[52] The feeling that underlies this change comes through in the following quote:

> The role of "homemaker" is undervalued in the United States, where occupation is the key to assignment of role status, and achievement and monetary value tend to provide the criteria for social ranking. In contemporary America, women tend to absorb the same values as the men with whom they are educated, and to use these men as reference persons in comparing social role rewards. Educated women in the "homemaker only" role may feel a sense of "relative deprivation" in the distribution of social status. A "homemaker-plus" role (such as the addition of employment to home duties) may promise greater social recognition.[53]

It must be noted that women do not represent a homogeneous group. In the simplest split they may be described as traditional or modern, and both types are found in the marketplace. For example, a sample of nearly 2,000 women were asked which of the following statements represented their preferred marriage style:

1. A traditional marriage with the husband assuming the responsibility for providing for the family and the wife running the house and taking care of the children.

2. A marriage where husband and wife share responsibilities more—both work and both share homemaking and child responsibilities.
3. Some other arrangement, such as staying single or living with a group of other persons. [54]

Forty-five percent of the respondents indicated that they preferred a traditional marriage, fifty-four percent chose a modern or sharing mode, and one percent selected the third choice.

Fig. 8-7. Profile of Traditional and Modern Women

Item	Traditional	Modern
Age		
Under 25	34%	66%
25-34	36	64
35-44	44	56
45-54	48	52
55+	58	42
Education		
Some college and higher	40	50
High school and lower	60	40
Employment		
Employed	26	56
Not employed	74	44
Family Income		
Under $4,000	4	4
$4,000-8,000	16	13
$8,000-10,000	10	10
$10,000-15,000	32	27
$15,000-20,000	18	24
$20,000 or over	20	22
Dwelling Unit		
Apartment	5	11
One-family home	83	76
Other	12	13

Fred D. Reynolds, Melvin R. Crask, and William D. Wells, "The Modern Feminine Life Style," *Journal of Marketing* 41(July 1977):38-45. Reprinted from the *Journal of Marketing*, published by the American Marketing Association.

As figure 8-7 indicates, modern women differ measurably from traditional women in their demographic characters. Only the age group of women over fifty-five years has a majority of traditional women. One of the key factors relating to the traditional versus modern outlook is employment, but there is also a difference between employed and unemployed traditionals and moderns. Figures 8-8, 8-9, and 8-10 indicate significant differences among the various categories.

The role of women in society is rapidly changing, and these changes will continue to influence their buying behavior. Many previous assumptions must be altered if marketing efforts are to remain effective. Figure 8-11 outlines some specific marketing implications of the changing role of women.

Fig. 8-8. Media Consumption by Women

	Percent Exposed[a]					
	Total		Working		Non-working	
Category	Traditional	Modern	Traditional	Modern	Traditional	Modern
Radio Program Format						
Heavy Rock	8%	20%	8%	19%	8%	21%
Popular music—top 40	44	56	48	58	44	55
Television Program Favorites						
Waltons	42%	32%	41%	30%	42%	34%
Little House on the Prairie	33	24	31	22	34	28
Happy Days	16	20	14	21	17	19[b]
Daytime Game Shows (in general)	12	8	14	8	11	10
Magazines (read 1+ issue in last four issues)						
Cosmopolitan	10%	16%	12%	19%	9%	12%[b]
Glamour	7	13	6	25	7	10[b]
Playboy	9	19	11	19	9	18
Psychology Today	3	6	2	6	3	6
Redbook	27	34	22	34	29	34[b]

a. p ≤ .05 unless otherwise indicated.   b. (NS) = p > .10.

Fred D. Reynolds, Melvin R. Crask, and William D. Wells, "The Modern Feminine Life Style," *Journal of Marketing* 41 (July 1977):38-45. Reprinted from the *Journal of Marketing*, published by the American Marketing Association.

Fig. 8-9. Life-style Profile of Women

Statement	Percent Agreeing[a]					
	Total		Working		Non-working	
	Traditional	Modern	Traditional	Modern	Traditional	Modern
Traditional Roles: Home & Work						
A woman's place is in the home.	68%	30%	62%	27%	69%	34%
The working world is no place for a woman.	28	9	21	8	30	10
I am a homebody.	77	62	61	55	78	70
Traditional Roles: Family Relations						
Men are smarter than women.	29%	18%	29%	19%	28%	17%
The father should be the boss in the house.	81	59	83	60	81	58
A wife's first obligation is to her husband, not her children.	74	67	71	66[b]	75	68
Children are the most important thing in a marriage.	60	45	57	47	60	43
Young people have too many privileges.	80	72	80	72	81	71
When children are ill in bed, parents should drop everything else to see to their comfort.	82	69	83	67	82	72
When making important family decisions, consideration of the children should come first.	58	52	60	50	58	53[b]
Orientation toward Housekeeping Activities						
Our home is furnished for comfort, not style.	92%	88%	91%	88%[b]	93%	89%
The kind of dirt you can't see is worse than the kind you can see.	79	74	77	75[b]	80	73
I like to save and redeem saving stamps.	78	72	75	73	79	74
My days seem to follow a definite routine—eating meals at the same time each day, etc.	70	62	66	57	71	68[b]
Meal preparation should take as little time as possible.	37	44	44	47[b]	35	42
I never eat breakfast.	30	35	28	38	30	32[b]
I always bake from scratch.	44	37	39	38[b]	46	35

I went out to breakfast instead of having it at home at least once last year.	46	57	49	63	46	51[b]
I cooked outdoors at least once during the past year.	81	85	83	91	82	79[b]
Satisfaction with Life						
I wish I could leave my present life and do something entirely different.	22%	30%	23%	29%[b]	22%	32%
My greatest achievements are still ahead of me.	56	70	62	73	54	66
Physical Attractiveness						
I like to feel attractive to members of the opposite sex.	79%	89%	80%	88%	79%	90%
I want to look a little different from others.	66	72	69	71[b]	65	73
All men should be clean shaven every day.	76	67	76	67	75	67
There are day people and night people; I am a day person.	72	67	76	66	70	67[b]
I like to think I am a bit of a swinger.	18	39	20	32	18	29
A drink or two at the end of a day is a perfect way to unwind.	18	23	16	24	19	22[b]
Had a cocktail or drink before dinner at least once last year.	56	69	55	74	64	67[b]
Had wine with dinner at least once during the past year.	53	64	52	66	54	61
Travel Proneness						
I would feel lost if I were alone in a foreign country.	75%	64%	75%	61%	74%	67%
I would like to take a trip around the world	59	74	64	77	54	71
I would like to spend a year in London or Paris.	25	39	30	37	25	38
Mobility						
We will probably move at least once in the next five years.	32%	41%	32%	40%	33%	43%
Attitudes toward Transportation						
I have often thought of buying a subcompact car.	42%	50%	42%	51%	42%	48%[c]
I like sports cars.	30	47	31	49	29	45

Fig. 8-9. Life-style Profile of Women (continued)

Statement	Percent Agreeing[a]					
	Total		Working		Non-working	
	Traditional	Modern	Traditional	Modern	Traditional	Modern
Financial Outlook						
Five years from now our family income will probably be a lot higher than it is now.	60%	70%	62%	73%[b]	59%	65%[c]
Women don't need more than a minimum amount of life insurance.	42	32	35	31[b]	44	33
I am considering buying life insurance.	13	22	15	23	13	19
Attitudes toward American Business						
Americans should always try to buy American products.	78%	68%	77%	69%	78%	66%
I admire a successful businessman more than I admire a successful artist or writer.	33	25	32	25	32	23
Views toward Events and Situations						
Everything is changing too fast today.	69%	62%	70%	59%	68%	65%[b]
There is too much emphasis on sex today.	90	81	94	79	89	84
I am in favor of very strict enforcement of all laws.	94	89	91	90[b]	95	89
Police should use whatever force is necessary to maintain law and order.	76	62	77	61	75	62
Communism is the greatest peril in the world today.	71	55	71	55	71	54
The U.S. would be better off if there were no hippies.	64	46	65	43	64	50
I think the Women's Liberation movement is a good thing.	41	61	39	60	42	62

Activity Patterns

I have somewhat old fashioned tastes and habits.	91%	81%	90%	79%	92%	84%
I went to the movies at least once in the past year.	68	79	74	81	67	76
I like science fiction.	37	53	36	53	38	54
I visited an art gallery or museum at least once last year.	45	52	42	54	47	48[b]
I gave a speech at least once during the past year.	23	30	23	34	24	24[b]
I attended school at least once during the past year.	22	32	30	39	21	24[b]
I attended church at least once during the past year.	89	82	90	84	89	81
Went to a pop concert at least once last year.	7	18	11	20	5	15
I did a crossword puzzle at least once last year.	73	78	70	79	74	77
I played cards at least once during the past year.	80	86	77	88	82	84[b]
I went swimming at least once last year.	57	67	60	71	57	62[b]
I went bowling at least once last year.	30	39	34	41[b]	30	37
I went skiing at least once during the past year.	4	7	4	8	5	5[b]

a. $p \leq .05$ unless otherwise indicated.   b. $p \geq .10$.   c. $p \leq .08$.

Fred D. Reynolds, Melvin R. Crask, and William D. Wells, "The Modern Feminine Life Style," *Journal of Marketing* 41 (July 1977):38-45. Reprinted from the *Journal of Marketing*, published by the American Marketing Association.

Fig. 8-10.   Product Usage by Women

Product	Percent Using Weekly or More Often[a]					
	Total		Working		Non-working	
	Traditional	Modern	Traditional	Modern	Traditional	Modern
Lipstick	87%	80%	91%	82%	85%	79%
Hairspray	62	56	64	61[b]	61	51
Eye makeup	48	62	54	67	46	56
Suntan lotion (Summer)	28	40	49	51[b]	31	41
Artificial sweetener	33	8	32	29[b]	33	27
Beer	9	12	7	12	9	11[b]
Flavor-filter cigarettes	8	12	8	11[b]	8	13
Menthol-filter cigarettes	7	11	7	10[b]	7	11
Cold or allergy tablets	39	48	46	48[b]	37	48
Gasoline (Personally purchased)	78	83	83	89	76	76[b]
Regular (stick) margarine	87	81	87	80	88	83[b]
Ready-to-eat cold cereal	94	90	95	89	94	91[b]
Prepared breakfast	96	93	96	91	96	95[b]

a. p ≤ .05   b. (NS) = p > .10.

Fred D. Reynolds, Melvin R. Crask, and William D. Wells, "The Modern Feminine Life Style," *Journal of Marketing* 41 (July 1977):38-45. Reprinted from the *Journal of Marketing*, published by the American Marketing Association.

Fig. 8-11. Marketing Implications of Women's Changing Role

Working women can justify economic expenditures for, and psychologically accept, expensive appliances and household equipment, such as microwave ovens and prepared foods, which may even reduce the wives' roles in important household tasks.

Working wives are often unable to shop during regular retailing hours. They might prefer that sales be held in the evening.

Some shopping may be done by wives' surrogates—daughters and sons. Shopping also becomes more of a shared husband and wife activity or even a family venture. Saturday, Sundays, and evenings become very important shopping times.

The distinction between men's and women's work in the home has blurred and a sense of shared household duties prevails. Appliances that formerly had an image of being a female appliance, such as a vacuum cleaner, tend to take on a unisex image.

Working women place a premium on a youthful appearance and on the "maintenance of self." Advancement in business is often associated with being young.

The family-dominated meal scene and the wife's role have changed. Prepared foods, convenience foods, fast-food and family-style restaurants occupy a significant position in the family feeding function.

Working women are more education-oriented and interested in self-improvement, travel, leisure and their own individualism. They tend to be more independent and confident.

Working wives tend more to become equal decision makers in the home. This change is particularly noticeable among lower social classes where wives were very subordinated.

The availability of household services beyond the usual morning and afternoon household hours (repair services during weekends) will become increasingly important.

Women dislike the way they are depicted in some advertisements, which is often at considerable variance with both their desired and actual roles.

Price for some products may become less important than convenience, availability, service, and time savings.

Women are becoming more cosmopolitan in their tastes and expectations as they become more involved with, and exposed to, the world external to the home.

William Lazer and John E. Smallwood, "The Changing Demographics of Women," *Journal of Marketing* 41 (July 1977):14-22. Reprinted from the *Journal of Marketing*, published by the American Marketing Association.

SUMMARY

The family is the basic social and consumption unit in virtually all societies. By definition, the family is a social entity minimally composed of a couple (or single parent) and children. Traditionally, the family has been characterized by formal establishment, common residence, economic cooperation, a sexual relationship, and reproduction. It acts as a socializing agent as well as an economic and social unit. Four major areas of family influence relative to consumer behavior were identified: role structure, life cycle, life-style, and family decision making.

Each individual in a family is likely to play a variety of roles relative to purchasing behavior: influencer, gatekeeper, decider, buyer, preparer, and user. The family life cycle is defined in terms of the age of the family head and the age and presence or absence of children. Stages in the life cycle were given as single, newlywed, full nest I, full nest II, empty nest, and retirement. Family life-style was defined as the system of attitudes and behaviors that influence how family members spend their time and money. Psychographic research is used to study life-style and its relationship to buying behavior systematically. Decisions made by families are often characterized by multiple influence and varying degrees of cooperation. Family decision making can be viewed as small group, goal-oriented behavior. Decisions can be autonomous or joint and goals may be agreed upon or in conflict. Several factors determine whether a decision will be made jointly or not, including social class, role definition, life cycle, life-style, nature of the purchase, and stage in the decision process.

Where family goals are agreed upon, several decision strategies may be followed, including role structure, budgets, and problem solving. If goals are in conflict, persuasion or bargaining may be employed.

Social and economic changes are occurring that are likely to influence consumer behavior strongly in the future. One of the most significant areas of change is the shift in the role of women. As women have entered the work force and become more self-sufficient, many changes in their buying habits and purchase influence have taken place.

CHAPTER 8   STUDY REVIEW

Important Terms and Concepts

Nuclear family
Extended family
Family role structure
Expressive values
Instrumental values
Family life cycle
Family life-style
Family decision making
Accomodation or consensus in family decision making
Family goals and values
Traditional versus modern family structure

Questions

1. Describe the significant purchaser-consumer roles in a family.

2. Discuss the impact of the increasing number of working women on consumer behavior.

3. Outline the stages of the family life cycle, and explain the characteristic buyer behavior patterns for each stage.

4. Discuss the differences between individual and family decision making.

5. Discuss the factors that influence family decision making.

6. Discuss the alternative decision-making strategies of the family.

7. What major social changes are likely to influence consumer behavior in the future, and what influences are they likely to have?

8. Contrast the life-styles and attitudes of modern versus traditional women, and discuss their impact on consumer behavior.

9

Consumer Research

The first eight chapters of this text have referred to the results of a number of research studies that have been generated by a variety of consumer research techniques. The chapters that follow this one draw even more heavily upon consumer research studies.

The purpose of this chapter is not to teach you to do consumer research. Most practicing marketing managers do not directly engage in data collection, but most will use research data. Because of this you will likely work with research people and research reports. This will put you in contact with the research process at several levels.

First, the marketing practitioner will often be involved in designing the research project. There is a problem inherent in this, however. Research experts often have little feel for the problems of the marketing strategist. At the same time, the marketer often has little more than a nodding acquaintance with research techniques and problems. The greater the marketer's familiarity with the research process, the better can be the communication between marketer and researcher.

Second, in order to assess the validity and applicability of any research data that you confront, you should have an idea of how such data is collected and the caveats of its application. Both as a student and as a practicing manager you are bombarded with research findings that purport to represent ways in which consumers behave. Even though you may not be actively engaged in collecting research data, you should be capable of interpreting and judging its quality.

Purposes of Consumer Research

Consumer research can be defined as collecting, analyzing, and interpreting data relevant to any buyer, consumer, or purchase influencer and any product or service acquisition, consumption, or influencing process. Consumer research, accordingly, may involve researching the demographics, including age, sex, income, and geographic location, or such behavioral characteristics as attitudes, motives, life-style, and product usage.

As in most disciplines, consumer research is carried out at two levels, pure or theoretical and applied. The research appearing in the various professional journals that deal with consumer behavior can probably be considered more theoretical, although many direct applications can be made to marketing strategy.[1] Applied research is that which is carried out relative to a specific product or company activity. Unfortunately, much of the research undertaken by marketing companies, advertising agencies, and marketing research firms is proprietary and therefore not available to advance general knowledge of consumer behavior. The companies feel that sharing such information might lessen their differential advantage. However, it might benefit all firms if some of their findings were made public.[2] Since most firms will not share information, however, a large portion of published information advancing our understanding of consumer behavior will continue to come from the academic community.

General Types of Consumer Research

If you want to know something about a consumer market, you generally have two choices. You can go to existing research sources (secondary research) or you can generate your own data (primary research). In most cases, even if the situation calls for primary research, a survey of existing literature should be undertaken before going to the field. Very often, a marketing manager will face strategic questions for which case-specific answers are required. Under these conditions, primary research will often be required.

Marketing research breaks into two broad categories, quantitative and qualitative. Consumer research may be of either type, but we tend to associate qualitative research with consumer behavior because it tries to answer the question, Why? Quantitative research gives us answers to questions like, How many? Who? Where? When? It's sometimes called nose counting, and it is generally used to collect demographic data. This chapter will concentrate essentially on qualitative techniques.

The collection of any type of data may utilize one or more types of research design. Depending on time, funds, and purpose, data may be collected through survey, experiment, or observation.

Survey Research

The most common data collection method is the survey. Survey research is based on the concept of random sampling. Using statistical techniques, characteristics of a population can be estimated from a small representative group drawn at random. Survey data is collected using a set of questions directed to a respondent. Researchers often take questionnaire development lightly, but a good questionnaire is absolutely essential to obtaining accurate and useful data.

The major objective of questionnaire design is to seek information in such a way that accurate informaton is gleaned and the respondent's true attitudes and motives are measured. This requires careful phrasing of questions as there are a number of potential problems associated with constructing questions. The major problems involve ambiguity, misperceptions, and loading.

Particularly when investigating motives and attitudes, ambiguous terminology and wording may occur. People may misperceive questions that seem quite clear to the framer of the questions. One of the most common problems involves leading the respondent. People tend to be quite cooperative, and they will often try to answer as they think the interviewer would like. Questions must be worded in such a way that the respondent is given no indication of how the question "ought" to be answered.

Individual questions may be structured or open-ended. The structured question gives the respondent several choices and asks that one or more be selected. For example, a question may ask:

Which factor is most significant when you select a brand of toothpaste?
_____ Flavor
_____ Texture
_____ Whitening ability
_____ Decay prevention
_____ Breath protection
_____ Other(please specify) _____

The open-ended question, on the other hand, allows the respondent to answer a question freely, such as, "Tell me about the factors you consider significant when you select a toothpaste brand."

Survey questionnaires may be administered via mail or telephone, or during a personal interview. Each technique has advantages that argue for its use under different circumstances. The key factors in deciding which approach to use are flexibility, amount of information needed, amount of information required, accuracy of information, speed, cost, and administration.[3]

The mail survey is relatively inexpensive but is limited in flexibility in that questions must be simple and pretty well structured, and there is no opportunity for explaining the questions further. The problem of slow questionnaire return and nonresponse can be very significant, too.

Telephone surveys can be administered quickly but tend to be more costly than mail in that interviewers must ask the questions. Calls typically must be kept short, so there is limited opportunity for open-ended response and interviewer probing. Nonresponse should be minimized through call backs, but respondents are limited to those with telephones.

The personal interview costs the most and is time consuming but represents the best in terms of flexibility. Questions can be unstructured, and intensive probing is possible, so a great deal of data can be collected. If interviewers are well trained, nonresponse can be minimized. To assure that unbiased data is collected, interviewers must be trained to ask questions and probe in such a way that respondents are not led in their answers.

Observation

Direct observation of the consumer may replace questioning the respondent which indirectly determines behavior. There is a great deal of opportunity for marketers to observe consumer behavior informally. Sometimes strategy is formulated based on casual observation, but it's a dangerous process. To reduce the risk of misinterpretation of consumer actions or false assumptions that the observed behavior of a few consumers is representative of the many, and to give the marketing strategist confidence in observational research, it should be conducted scientifically. This means that observation should (1) serve a specific research purpose, (2) be systematically planned, (3) be carefully recorded, and (4) be subjected to checks and controls on its total accuracy.[4]

Observation is probably the least used design for consumer research and is often implemented when there is no alternative, as in investigating preferences of children who cannot talk. To use observation, data must be accessible, behavior must be repetitive, frequent, or otherwise predictable, and the observed event must cover a reasonably short time span.[5]

Obviously, a great deal of consumer behavior does not lend itself to observational research. Attitudes and motives cannot be directly observed; they must be inferred from observed behavior. Brand decisions are often the result of long experience or decision processes, and, as a consequence, they are not amenable to observation.

If observation seems to be the appropriate form of research, there are a number of bases on which the design may vary: (1) natural or contrived, (2) obtrusive or unobtrusive, (3) structured or unstructured, (4) direct or indirect, and (5) human or mechanical. The most reliable observations may come under natural circumstances, but often the observed activity occurs infrequently or unpredictably and must therefore be set up. Sometimes consumers may be observed unobtrusively, as through two-way mirrors. This would mean that the consumer would be acting naturally. Consumers may also be asked to participate in studies where they know they are being observed. Even though the consumer is asked to behave normally, obtrusive observation may lead to out-of-the-ordinary behavior. Observations, like questionnaires, can be structured or unstructured. The observer may be left alone to decide what to record, or a detailed form may direct the types of behavior to be observed and recorded. Direct observation of consumer behavior is most common; however, if the behavior of interest has already occurred, indirect measurement is required. Pantry audits may be utilized, wherein buying behavior is inferred by the brands the consumer has in the home inventory. Of course, possession of a given brand does not suggest that the subject actually bought the brand and will use or repurchase it. Most observation uses human observers, but such mechanical measurement devices as the polygraph, eye movement camera, pupilometer (which measures reaction by detecting changes in pupil size), voice stress analyzer, and hidden camera may be used when appropriate.

Experimentation

In experimental research designs, the emphasis is placed on control of variables. One or more variables will be manipulated while other forces are held constant. In general, experimentation gives opportunities for more precise measurement of variables. An experiment essentially forms a micromodel of the real world. Perhaps the most common experimental design is the test market. Here a product can be placed in two or more comparable market areas with some factor, such as price, advertising copy, package, or display, varied across the test areas. If the areas are actually comparable and if no external force, such as weather or competitive efforts, enters in, any significant difference in sales, attitudes, or other response should be attributable to the experimental variable.

On a smaller scale, test stores can be set up in which various factors, such as price and display, can be altered among different test groups. Many of the research results reported in professional journals are generated with experimental groups, such as housewives or college students.

Although experimental studies can yield useful and reliable results, care must be taken in designing experiments. There are numerous approaches to be utilized and a variety of pitfalls to be avoided.[6]

Specific Types of Consumer Research

The various research designs and techniques discussed may be applied in a number of ways. Different kinds of problems have given rise to several different approaches to investigating how and why consumers buy. This section will consider four broad types of consumer research: (1) motivation research, (2) need research, (3) attitude research, and (4) psychographic research.

Motivation Research

Part of the modern study of consumer behavior has its roots in the motivation research studies of the 1940s and 1950s, and it is used today to develop and test such things as advertising appeals, brand names, packages, and store displays. A survey of 1,322 companies in 1973 revealed that thirty-three percent were using motivation research.[7]

The basic idea behind motivation research is that consumers have many reasons for their purchasing behavior of which they are not consciously aware. Motivations for purchases may not be accessible to researchers because respondents are unwilling or unable to reveal or articulate their reasons for behavior. Because of this, a number of indirect means are used to circumvent consumer defenses. The techniques have generally been borrowed from clinical psychology and psychiatry, often with less than satisfactory results. The techniques can be generally divided into depth interviewing and projective techniques.

Depth Interviewing Depth interviews are conducted on an open-ended basis. They typically last for an hour or so and generally are conducted with only a few (twenty-five to fifty) respondents. The interviewer will use indirect questions and probe for additional information as the respondent answers. The interview may be conducted with a single individual or with a group of respondents. Group depth interviews, often referred to as focus group interviews, depend on interaction among group members to generate ideas for and about new products. Figure 9–1 gives a brief example of a focus group interview.

There are some major problems with depth interviewing. First, the volume and subjectivity of the data generated makes it difficult and time consuming to analyze. Second, the small nonrandom samples and nonquantifiability of results makes it difficult to generalize data for larger populations. The nonstructured nature of the approach means that the interviewer must be very skillful.

Projective Techniques Although depth interviews can uncover hidden motives, direct questioning and probing may not penetrate respondent defense mechanisms. Projective tests use indirect techniques to relieve respondents of the responsibility for their reactions. Presumably, this will lead respondents to be more candid in their answers.

A wide variety of projective techniques are used in motivation research. Most of the techniques are structured so that the respondents can "project" their feelings onto other people. Thus, they will be able to express their own feelings without sensing that someone is learning how they personally feel. This guards against defensive responses and responses that try to reflect what the respondent perceives the interviewer wants to hear. There are numerous projective techniques, including third person, association, sentence completion, and thematic apperception tests.

Third-person Techniques A person may be asked to reveal motives indirectly by telling about the motives of others. Presumably we know our own motivations best, so we are likely to project our motivations on others. The research on instant coffee mentioned in chapter 1 utilized this technique.[8] Interviews had previously been conducted using direct questions like, "Do you use instant coffee?" and "If not, what do you dislike about it?" The majority responded that they did not use instant because they disliked the flavor.

In order to get a better picture of consumer motives; each of the two shopping lists was shown to respondents (Figure 9-2). One hundred received the first list and one hundred the second, with each group unaware of the other. Respondents were instructed as follows:

> Read the shopping list below. Try to project yourself into the situation as far as possible until you can more or less characterize the woman who bought the groceries. Then write a brief description of her personality and character. Whenever possible; indicate what factors influenced your judgment.

Fig. 9-1. Focus Group Interview on Dishwashing

Dr. S.: One thing struck me as you reported on how you wash dishes and what you use for them. You seemed to stress getting the job done quickly and efficiently. Is that right? Maybe you didn't mean to put it just that way.

Mrs. J.: Yes, that's right—it's a three-times-a-day process.

Mrs. H.: More than that, with coffee, snacks, somebody dropping in—

Mrs. J.: That's true.

Dr. S.: Maybe this is a leading question, but it has to come in some time. I have been under the impression that women are anxious to keep their hands beautiful—yet nobody has stressed that in this discussion!

Mrs. R.: A housewife doesn't worry about her hands.

Mrs. T.: I will say one thing: J———— really hurt my hands—some people are sensitive to certain things. It's not a question of gorgeous, delightful hands, but some people are more sensitive to chemicals; when it gets to the point where your hands hurt, you stop.

Dr. S.: I don't want to seem contrary, but I am not altogether convinced, because I thought women's hands were very important.

Mrs. T.: Look at all of us—I bet none of us have had manicures.

Mrs. J.: Oh, here's one over here!

Dr. S.: But don't you actually pay any attention to the claim, "Protect your hands"?

Mrs. T.: Advertising is so overplayed I don't think any of us pay attention to any of these things.

Dr. S.: I don't believe that. I am very stubborn.

Mrs. R.: I do use a hand cream after washing dishes; I don't want my hands to get rough. I don't think my hands are beautiful—they never were—but to keep them from getting rough I use a hand cream.

Mrs. T.: All of us do that.

Mrs. B.: In the cold weather every woman does.

Dr. S.: Mrs. H, do you do that?

Mrs. H.: Yes. I don't always think about it—that's why I don't believe in the claims too much. When you are in a rush, everything has to be done, and all of a sudden the baby cries; you don't worry about your hands, you just stop, that's all.

Dr. S.: You're certain about this?

Mrs. H.: Yes. Many times when I go out I say, "I should have been more careful about my hands," but when Monday morning starts out—

Mrs. T.: You have the telephone to answer and a thousand things to do. All of us would like to sit in the shade, but let's face it.

Mrs. J.: I don't think washing dishes is much worse than a lot of other things we do with our hands.

Dr. S.: For example?

Mrs. J.: When the children are in the house, things get on the floor; you pick up a glass . . . that's how I spent last week . . . you are constantly putting your hands in water and cleaning crayon off the floor with E———— or whatever you can find. Those things hurt your hands. We won't go into that—C———— and other things, probably worse than any detergent.

Mrs. T.: Let's face it! If we were really unhappy about our hands we would use rubber gloves to be perfectly practical. . . .

Mrs. H.: You just don't have time to worry about hands.

Fig. 9-2.   Shopping Lists Used in the Nescafé Instant Coffee Study

Shopping List #1	Shopping List #2
1 ½ lbs. of hamburger	1 ½ lbs. of hamburger
2 loaves of Wonder Bread	2 loaves of Wonder Bread
Bunch of carrots	Bunch of carrots
1 can Rumford's Baking Powder	1 can Rumford's Baking Powder
Nescafé Instant Coffee	1 lb. Maxwell House Coffee (drip grind)
2 cans Del Monte peaches	2 cans Del Monte peaches
5 lbs. potatoes	5 lbs. potatoes

Mason Haire, "Projective Techniques in Marketing Research," *Journal of Marketing* 24 (April 1960): 649-656. Reprinted from the *Journal of Marketing*, published by the American Marketing Association.

The results were that forty-eight percent of the people described the woman who bought Nescafé as lazy, while only four percent described the woman who bought Maxwell House as lazy. Forty-eight percent of the people described the woman who bought Nescafé as failing to plan household purchases and schedules well; twelve percent described the woman who bought Maxwell House this way. Four percent described the Nescafé woman as thrifty, and sixteen percent described the Maxwell House woman as thrifty, twelve percent described the Nescafé woman as spendthrift, while none described the Maxwell House woman this way. Sixteen percent described the Nescafé woman as not a good wife, while no one described the Maxwell House woman this way. Four percent described the Nescafé woman as a good wife, and sixteen percent described the Maxwell House woman as a good wife.

As noted previously, a later study indicated that these attitudes no longer hold, but the technique itself is still useful when consumers will not or cannot give "real" reasons for their buying actions.

Association Techniques The feelings and attitudes elicited by words, phrases, and pictures can be helpful to marketers in naming products and preparing promotion messages. Word association tests have been used for many years by psychologists. The technique involves giving a repondent a word and asking for the first idea that comes to mind. American Telephone and Telegraph used word association when they selected a name for their long-distance dialing service.[9] Among the seven names tested were Nationwide Dialing, Customer Toll Dialing, and Direct Distance Dialing. National Dialing elicited a response suggesting that consumers would confuse the word *nationwide* with *worldwide*. Customer Toll Dialing was associated with money and suggested an unfavorable perception of high cost. Direct Distance Dialing was selected because it conveyed the concept of long distance calls with no operator and had no unfavorable connotations.

Stimuli other than words can be used in association techniques. Such phrases as "eating out" and "buying a new car" may also be used to generate associations. Figure 9–3 shows pictures that have been used to elicit associations.

Sentence Completion In the completion technique, an unfinished sentence or story is given to the respondent, who is instructed to complete it. The sentence might begin, "People who drive large cars are . . ." or "A woman who uses meat extenders is . . . ." Again, the respondent can project his or her own feelings about the issue without having to admit that the attitudes or motives are personally held.

Thematic Apperception Tests The thematic (for themes that are elicited) apperception (for the perceptual-interpretive use of pictures) test—TAT for short—utilizes one or more pictures or cartoons shown to a respondent.[10] The respondent is asked to assume the role of one of the persons in the picture and tell what that person is saying, doing, or thinking.

The pictures in figure 9–3 show a thematic apperception test used to investigate the price-quality relationship for beauty cream. Each woman in the study was shown the two pictures in random order and asked to describe the woman and the beauty cream in the picture. Responses to the picture of the forty-nine-cent cream were characterized by the following:

"Any female over 18 interested in her appearance who falls for the advertising claims and doesn't have too much money to spend on cosmetics."
"It's a poor quality product that's probably greasy and oily."

Responses for the five-dollar cream were quite different:

"Someone who cares what she looks like—probably a business girl interested in her appearance."
"It's a cream that leaves your skin clear and refreshed. It probably would keep your skin young-looking by softening and cleansing your skin."[11]

The Value of Motivation Research At one time, motivation research was considered a kind of panacea for understanding consumer motivation. Today, the technique is just one of many consumer research tools that may be useful.

The major problems with motivation research revolve around the small, nonrandom samples typically used, the high degree of expertise required for interpretation, the subjectivity associated with the interpretation, and the fact that the techniques have largely been lifted from clinical applications, where they are intended for one-on-one applications. Care must be taken in selecting those who will administer and interpret motivation studies. The small sample size is inherent to in-depth motivation research, but the ideas derived from motivation research studies can often form the nucleus of a large-scale survey.

Used properly, motivation research can generate some helpful, if bizarre, data. For example, one motivation research study suggested that large doorknobs help sell houses. Presumably, the doorknob is the only way a person can caress a house. This goes back to a baby's embryonic development when the thumb fills the palm of the

Fig. 9-3.   Thematic Apperception Test

Paul E. Green and Donald S. Tull, *Research for Marketing Decisions*, 3rd Edition, © 1975, p. 146. Reprinted by permission of Prentice-Hall, Inc., Englewood Cliffs, New Jersey.

hand. Apparently, we're all still seeking that prenatal security. In any case, the results prompted one California lock maker to enlarge its doorknobs.[12]

Need Research

From your first marketing course, you have been told that product offerings and marketing activities should be based upon consumer needs. However, repeated failures in the marketplace, even when consumer needs are investigated, suggest that systematic research should be undertaken to uncover significant consumer needs. Among the more common techniques are:

1. empirical studies
2. Delphi process
3. relevance tree technique
4. need confrontation technique
5. user observation technique
6. creative thinking techniques
7. ergonomic or human factors analysis

Empirical Studies One of the more commonly used techniques for evolving an understanding of consumer needs is the use of formal and informal studies. Informally, a company may receive knowledge of consumer needs through communication from consumers themselves, salespeople, and other company employees and their families. This technique is unreliable because the company tends to work with samples of one. To provide more reliability, a company may undertake formal surveys to ask consumers what they want or need. As noted before, however, consumers often don't know what they need. It is especially unlikely that any earth-shaking new idea would emerge since consumers probably cannot conceive of problems or solutions far removed from their present situations.

Delphi Technique One variation of the Delphi Technique consists of a number of repeated written discriminatory rounds with anonymous experts interacting by mail through some intermediary.[13] The first step is to select a panel of from 10 to 1,000 persons with relevant backgrounds in the interest area. Then a number of statements are made, for instance, about inventions that may be urgently needed in the next twenty years. The interaction process is begun with a letter. Results from the first inquiry are analyzed and edited, a list of statements is sent out, and respondents are asked for a probability statement of when the innovations are likely to occur. Respondents are then asked to refine their predictions further and to explain disagreements. The process may be useful in forecasting technological and social trends along with specific future consumer needs.

Relevance Tree Concept The relevance tree concept begins with a major social or consumer objective, such as energy conservation.[14] The activities or objectives contributing to this are then broken down; and further subobjectives are generated until specific consumer needs are derived, such as needs for energy-efficient heating systems. Subjective probabilities are placed on the branches of the resulting tree, and the researcher can get ideas of future needs and their perceived probability of significance.

Need Confrontation Technique The need confrontation concept asks members of the research and development (R and D) team to use products themselves to determine areas of dissatisfaction and to uncover latent needs. The time involved will vary according to the complexity of the products, learning time, and other factors.

User Observation Technique The user observation method allows for the systematic study of what is unsatisfactory in a user situation by observing, recording, and analyzing the behavior of those involved. This generally requires some sort of simulated use system for consumer products. For example, a test kitchen could be set up, consumer volunteers could be given various products to try, and their behaviors noted. The observation could then be followed up with interviews.

Creative Thinking Techniques A great number of techniques, such as brainstorming and synectics, have been developed to foster and stimulate group creativity. Since many studies suggest that individual creativity is often more efficient and effective,[15] techniques such as attribute listing and the morphological box have been used to encourage individual creativity.[16]

Many individual and group creative thinking techniques may be used to help clarify problems by discovering latent needs. One example is a company making appliances when the sale of kitchen ranges had declined significantly. In a brainstorming session involving engineers from the R and D department, one suggestion was to develop some way to let an oven clean itself. The idea was inspired by associating the automatic defrosting of refrigerators, developed many years before.[17]

Several special creative techniques have been advanced to aid in generating new product ideas. Three that show promise are: (1) heuristic ideation technique (HIT), (2) problem inventory analysis, and (3) benefit structure analysis.

Heuristic Ideation Technique Creative output may be defined as a combination of two or more concepts in the creator's mind. If all relevant concepts that apply to a product area could be listed, all possible combinations of these concepts would represent the total set of currently possible product ideas in that area. Naturally such a procedure results in a lot of combinations. The use of heuristics makes this more manageable. Heuristics are rules of thumb often derived from trial and error experiences that have previously led to acceptable outcomes.[18] They represent principles or devices that contribute to the reduction of search time by eliminating alternatives that seem likely to give poor solutions and retaining potentially good ideas.[19]

Several useful heuristics have been developed for identifying potentially good ideas and reducing screening time in the food industry.[20] One heuristic based on the observation that the majority of positive product ideas contain two factors and can be described in two-word combinations, such as toaster tart, potato chip, and whipped cream. A second heuristic suggests that some cross-classifications are immediately more useful than others. Different technologies applied to various food forms often provide more viable ideas than crossing fruits and vegetables, for instance. Some specific heuristics include: (1) applying kitchen appliances to various foods (toaster waffles); (2) adapting foods to a different meal (breakfast milk shake); (3) applying dessert words to nondessert foods (ice cream flakes cereal); and (4) applying gaps in consumer benefits to existing food forms (nutritious coffee)

Edward Tauber cites both advantages and limitations for HIT. On the one hand, HIT is systematic, freeing management from the ills of random timing of new product ideas; enables management to consider many alternatives, thus increasing the probability of finding new ideas; is flexible (the set of factors needs to be specified only once); and is designed for use by the individual and requires no special training. On the other hand, HIT relies on management's ability to specify all "relevant" factors, itself a difficult problem; employs heuristics that do not guarantee optimal solutions; delivers only a combination of factors (imagination is required to translate combinations into workable product ideas); and may provide new product ideas that are not technically feasible.

Problem Inventory Analysis Many creative techniques focus on solving problems. Creative activity may be viewed as a "special class of problem solving activity characterized by novelty, unconventionality and persistence."[21] But to solve a problem, we must know the problem. If the problem is defined as finding a profitable new product, a fishing expedition is likely to result. Brainstorming and HIT seem to fit into this category. What is needed to increase the chance for success is a well-defined consumer problem. Problem inventory analysis has, as its objective, isolating consumer needs or problems.[22]

One of the problems with brainstorming and many other traditional creativity-inducing techniques is that consumer needs are derived from a management viewpoint. The focus group is used to overcome this problem partially. This technique places a group of consumers together to discuss their needs and problems relative to a specific product or product group. But samples are small, and the technique relies on consumers to tell their needs and problems in unstructured interviews.

The problem inventory technique reverses the focus technique by providing the customer with a list of problems and asks what products have those problems. The procedure is based on two assumptions:

1. The general ways in which products and services can improve the quality of life are rather limited.
2. It's much easier for consumers to relate known products to suggested problems than to generate problems for a given product.

Based on a set of problems, the consumer is asked to complete such statements as "Preparing_____leaves so many pots to clean."[23] Consumers are asked to indicate the product that immediately comes to mind, given the specified problem. The method is far from foolproof, however. Figure 9-4 shows the results of a problem inventory analysis in the food industry. Note that forty-nine percent of the respondents mentioned cereal as a package that does not fit well on the shelf. General Foods tried a compact cereal box that failed. Also, sixteen percent of the sample indicated that it's difficult to get catsup to pour easily. But few consumers would accept thinner catsup, and a wider opening for the bottle has already been tried without success. The marketer must not only be concerned with the question, Is there a problem? but also with whether the problem is significant and what solutions consumers would find acceptable.

Fig. 9-4. Problem Inventory Analysis of Food

Questions Asked and % of Respondents Answering

1. The package of _____ doesn't fit well on the shelf.			6. _____ makes a mess in the oven.	
cereal	49%		broiling steaks	19%
flour	6%		pie	17%
			roast/pork/rib	8%
2. My husband/children refuse to eat _____ .			7. Packaged _____ tastes artificial.	
liver	18%		instant potatoes	12%
vegetables	5%		macaroni and cheese	4%
spinach	4%			
3. _____ doesn't quench my thirst.			8. It's difficult to get _____ to pour easily.	
soft drinks	58%		catsup	16%
milk	9%		syrup	13%
coffee	6%		gallon of milk	11%
954. Packaged _____ doesn't dissolve fast enough.			9. Packaged _____ looks unappetizing.	
jello/gelatin	32%		hamburger helper	6%
bouillon cubes	8%		lunch meat	3%
pudding	5%		liver	3%
5. Everyone always wants different _____ .			10. I wish my husband/children could take _____ in a carried lunch.	
vegetables	23%		hot meal	11%
cereal	11%		soup	9%
meat	10%		ice cream	4%
desserts	9%			

Edward M. Tauber, "Discovering New Product Opportunities with Problem Inventory Analysis," *Journal of Marketing* 39 (January 1975):70. Reprinted from the *Journal of Marketing*, published by the American Marketing Association.

Benefit Structure Analysis This technique seeks to look at both the nature and significance of consumer problems. The following are basic characteristics of benefit structure analysis:

1. It was developed especially for finding new product opportunities in very broad product/service categories.
2. It determines consumer reactions to a large number of relatively specific product/service benefits and product/service features of physical characteristics.
3. These reactions reflect both desire for and perceived deficiencies in each benefit and characteristic.
4. The technique also provides rather complete information on relative conditions surrounding the use of the product (time of day used, other persons present, use or task).
5. It provides a complete cross section of current product use patterns. [24]

The technique may be illustrated by applying it to cleaning products. The study began with twenty-five to fifty depth interviews—focus groups would work as well. [25] The interviewer asked the respondent to recall occasions when she cleaned interior surfaces during the day prior to the interview. For each occasion she is asked:

1. What was the cleaning chore?
2. What types and brands of products were used?
3. What benefits were sought or what were the objectives of the cleaning? (See figure 9-5 for examples of benefits.)
4. What were the physical characteristics or attributes of the product used? (See figure 9-5 for examples of product characteristics.)
5. What applicator (if any) was used?
6. What time of day was the work done, and were other family members involved?

The next phase of the study determined the degree to which each product characteristic was desired by the consumer for each cleaning occasion and the extent to which benefits were or were not being received. To determine the significance of the benefits and product characteristics, respondents were asked whether they wanted that benefit or characteristic any more or any less than they got it. The difference was quantified by scaling the degree of desire versus receipt of benefit or characteristic. The difference was called the benefit deficiency. The higher the deficiency and the more significant the difference, the more interest the company would have in satisfying the need represented with a new product offering the desired benefits and characteristics. Thus, consumer needs can be translated into product benefits and characteristics, and these become the basis for product promotion when the product is introduced.

Ergonomic or Human Factors Analysis Ergonomic analysis is an approach for systematic study of the psychological and physiological requirements of a product from a human point of view. [26] The purpose is to provide a basis for making products that are fitted as well as possible to human capabilities and limitations. The analysis

Fig. 9-5. Product Benefits and Characteristics

Examples of Benefits

Bleaches	Chrome sparkles
Removes stains	Doesn't dull
Removes grease	Doesn't hurt hands
Removes built-up dirt	Dissolves grease
Cleans tub ring	Doesn't remove gloss from paint
Less elbow grease	Boosts detergents
Can see it work	Strips wax
Cleans cracks (grout) better	Less build-up
Doesn't leave residue	Lets color come through
No rinsing necessary	Stands up to damp mopping
Doesn't damage surfaces	Seals porous floors
Kills mildew	Doesn't yellow
Disinfects	No streaking
Removes discoloration	Does two jobs at once
Removes soap scum	Leaves it "squeaky clean"

Examples of Product Characteristics

Strong smell	Biodegradable
Abrasive/scratchy	Concentrated
Thin liquid	Self-polishing
Low suds	Can spray on
Quick drying	Attractive color
Can wipe on	Contains deodorant
Dark color	Economical
Caustic	Pine smell
Contains wax	Perfumed smell
Contains ammonia	Lemon smell
Thick liquid	Stains
Light color	Little odor
Contains antiseptic	No deterioration when stored

James H. Myers, "Benefit Structure Analysis: A New Tool for Product Planning," *Journal of Marketing* 40 (October 1976):25. Reprinted from the *Journal of Marketing*, published by the American Marketing Association.

begins by looking at such factors as sex, age, education, and use habits. Following this is an assessment of physiological load (light or heavy), psychological load (stress), and perceptual and environmental conditions (heat and noise). The technique may be applied anywhere people interact with products, as with appliances and automobiles.

If the product need is known to exist, concept or product testing should be used:

(1) to estimate whether or not the market is large enough to be profitable; (2) to determine whether the new product features or benefits are really significant to potential buyers; and (3) to analyze the competitive situation.[27] If the need is not known to exist but is suspected, then the objective would be: (1) to confirm or invalidate the suspected need; (2) to define the need in terms of buyer benfits; and (3) to achieve an estimate of market potential.[28]

Concept and Product Testing Concept testing is undertaken to determine whether or not a specific product idea or variation is likely to meet consumer needs.

Focus groups and conversational interviews are often used for concept testing. Selected consumers are exposed to statements, drawings, advertisements, or product mock-ups to communicate the physical characteristics and attributes of the product. Various aspects of the product concept, such as features, price, and promotion, should be considered for competitive products as well as for the company's potential offering.[29] It has been suggested that product concepts be presented to consumers in the same format and through the media that will be used to promote the actual product to achieve predictability.[30] However, concept testing is not a substitute for product use testing. Concept testing measures whether or not a new product idea generates interest among potential consumers. We must also know whether consumers perceive that the product would be satisfactory in use.

Product testing involves determining consumer needs and their degree of satisfaction by actually putting the product into the use situation with the consumer. This is often accomplished through consumer panels, in which a group of potential consumers is given sample products. While using these products, respondents record the product strengths and weaknesses. Consumers tend to react favorably to all products tested, and they often make erroneous comparisons between the new product and one previously used. Consequently, a variety of techniques, including multiple-brand comparisons, risk analysis, level of repeat purchases, and intensity of preference analysis, are used to determine consumer preference. Paired comparisons (two products) or monadic testing (one product-two consumer panels) are often used to force consumers to indicate product preference.[31]

Whatever techniques are used in concept and product testing, there are numerous problems in using the tests to produce new product success.[32] One problem is the question of whether consumer attitudes adequately predict consumer behavior. Validation work with concept and product testing suggests that intentions prior to trial, measured by concept tests, relate to but do not necessarily predict product trial. Posttrial intentions, measured by product tests, relate to early repeat behavior.[33] The critical factor in new product success is not trial, however, but adoption—that is, continued use and brand loyalty. The problem is that although consumers can predict trial purchase on the basis of concepts or product use, they themselves do not know whether the product will actually meet their needs.[34] Interest in a product is really what is measured by concept and product testing as traditionally carried out. It has been suggested that if we measure the degree to which the product or product concept solves a consumer problem or fills an unmet need, ultimate product adoption can be more accurately predicted. Thus, consumers may be asked, having been exposed to concept or product, a number of questions.[35]

1. Does this product solve a problem or need you or other members of your family now have that isn't being satisfied by products now on the market?
2. What is the problem or need?
3. How important is this need?
4. How likely would you be to buy this product?

Concept and product testing, then, are not foolproof in predicting consumer need satisfaction. They are effective in predicting product trial, which must precede adoption, and, with modification, they may be effective in predicting product adoption.

Attitude Research

To some extent the measurement of attitudes presents problems similar to discovering motives. Attitudes, like motives, are intangible. Also, as noted in chapter 6, there is a good deal of disagreement on the definition of attitude.

In essence, when we measure attitudes, we are trying to assess the direction and magnitude of feeling toward some object or phenomenon. From the measure derived we infer the attitude, and we can make some sort of behavioral prediction based on the attitude. As already noted, however, attitude is a very unreliable predictor of behavior.

There are basically five approaches to measuring attitudes:

1. Inferences based on self-reports of beliefs, feelings, and behaviors.
2. Inferences drawn from observation of overt behavior.
3. Inferences drawn from responses to partially structured stimuli (projective techniques).
4. Inferences drawn from the performance of objective tasks.
5. Inferences drawn from the physiological reactions to the attitudinal object.[36]

Inferences from Self-reports One thing that differentiates attitude research from other types of consumer research is its reliance on scales. Self-report attitude measures ask respondents to rate some product, brand, or store on a scale to indicate the direction and intensity of the attitude.

The most commonly used attitude scales are: Q-sort, Guttman, Thurstone, Likert, semantic differential, Stapel, and multidimensional.

Q-Sort The Q-sort technique involves sorting sets of cards into appropriate piles according to the respondents' feelings toward certain phenomena. The result is a forced rank ordering of various attitude objects from most positive to least positive. For example, a set of cards could be prepared with the brand names of various toothpastes. Respondents would then be asked to order the cards according to various questions, like, "Which brand of toothpaste would you most likely use to insure against tooth decay?" Another question might ask, "What brand of toothpaste gives the whitest teeth?" Respondents would be asked to order the cards from highest to lowest for each question. Figure 9-6 gives a hypothetical example of four respondents' rankings. Respondents can be grouped according to age, sex, and current brand used, and conclusions can be drawn relative to brand attitudes for various market segments. Q-sort scales are amenable to statistical interpretation via correlation analysis.[37]

Fig. 9-6. Hypothetical Rankings of Toothpaste on Decay Prevention Capability

	Respondent 1	Respondent 2	Respondent 3	Respondent 4
Aqua Fresh	1	2	3	3
Crest	2	1	2	4
Aim	4	3	1	2
Closeup	5	6	4	5
Gleem	3	4	6	1
Pepsodent	6	5	5	6

Guttman Scale The Guttman scale, a scalogram analysis developed by Louis Guttman, is cumulative—that is, the scale items are related and unidimensional.[38] This means that the scale should measure only one aspect of the attitude object and that the cumulative score on the scale should indicate what the attitude is.

If we use the following set of statements, a cumulative unidimensional pattern should develop.

	Respondent			
	A	B	C	D
1. Fluoride is effective in preventing tooth decay.	X	X	X	X
2. Brushing your teeth with a fluoride toothpaste will help prevent tooth decay.	X	X	X	
3. The fluoride in Crest toothpaste will help prevent tooth decay.	X	X		
4. Brushing your teeth with Crest helps prevent tooth decay.	X			

This shows that the attitude toward fluoride as a tooth decay preventive is all that is being measured and that the scale is cumulative. The score will reveal the respondents' attitude. A score of 4 shows that the respondent has a positive attitude toward brushing with Crest to prevent tooth decay. A score of 1 shows that the person has a positive attitude toward fluoride but does not have a positive attitude toward the other three concepts that were measured: brushing with a fluoride toothpaste, the fluoride in Crest, or brushing with Crest. Although the Guttman scale has had little use in consumer research, it does have value in determining question and response validity after responses have been collected.

Thurstone Equal-appearing Interval Scale The Thurstone scale attempts to develop interval scaled data by providing questions scored precisely even though the data may be qualitative in nature. To accomplish this:

1. The researcher develops a number (100 +) of statements related to the attitude being studied and ranging from one extreme to the other. Statements may come from unstructured responses of a large group or may simply be formulated by the researcher. Any statements perceived to be confusing or ambiguous are immediately discarded.
2. A group of judges (twenty or more) independently classify the statements into eleven "equal" groups ranging from most favorable to most unfavorable, with the sixth group identified as "neutral." Statements are to be arranged without respect to the judges' personal opinions.
3. A scale value is assigned to each statement from the median or mean of the scores given by the judges. Those statements on which the judges display little agreement (high variance) are discarded.
4. The ten to twenty questions with highest agreement among the judges are incorporated into a final questionnaire. The questions are randomized, and the respondent is unaware of the scale value associated with each statement. Respondents are asked to check only those statements with which they agree.
5. The subject's mean scale value is computed from the items checked, and that becomes the respondent's score on the attribute.[39]

Several problems make the Thrustone scale difficult to use in consumer research. First, the technique is time consuming and expensive. Second, identical scores may reflect very different underlying attitudes. Finally, some subjects may have such widely dispersed responses that measures of central tendency are relatively meaningless.

Likert Scale The Likert scale is widely used in consumer attitude research because it is relatively easy to develop measurement instruments, and the technique is simple for the respondent to understand. This scale asks the respondent to express his or her extent of agreement or disagreement with a number of statements on a five-point scale, using some variation of strongly agree, agree, undecided, disagree, and strongly disagree. The scale may be scored $+2$, $+1$, 0, -1, -2 or 1, 2, 3, 4, 5. The results are summed algebraically to arrive at a final score. Thus, the Likert scale is referred to as summative or cumulative.

Osgood's Semantic Differential Rather than seeking to measure attitudes by having respondents indicate the extent of agreement with various opinion statements, the semantic differential focuses on the meaning attached to a word or concept.[40] The technique assumes that there is a hypothetical semantic space of an unknown number of dimensions in which the meaning of any word or concept can be represented as a particular point. The procedure has respondents judge a particular concept on a set of semantic scales with no scale value assigned. The scales are structured with verbal opposites and a neutral midpoint (seven, nine, or eleven points are typically used, with seven the most common). Figure 9-7 illustrates a hypothetical semantic differential analysis of two brand perceptions. The points on the scale are the means of all responses. Charles Osgood originally indicated that most adjective pairs could be classified in terms of evaluative (good-bad), potency (strong-weak), and activity (active-passive).

Fig. 9-7. Semantic Differential on Brand Attitudes

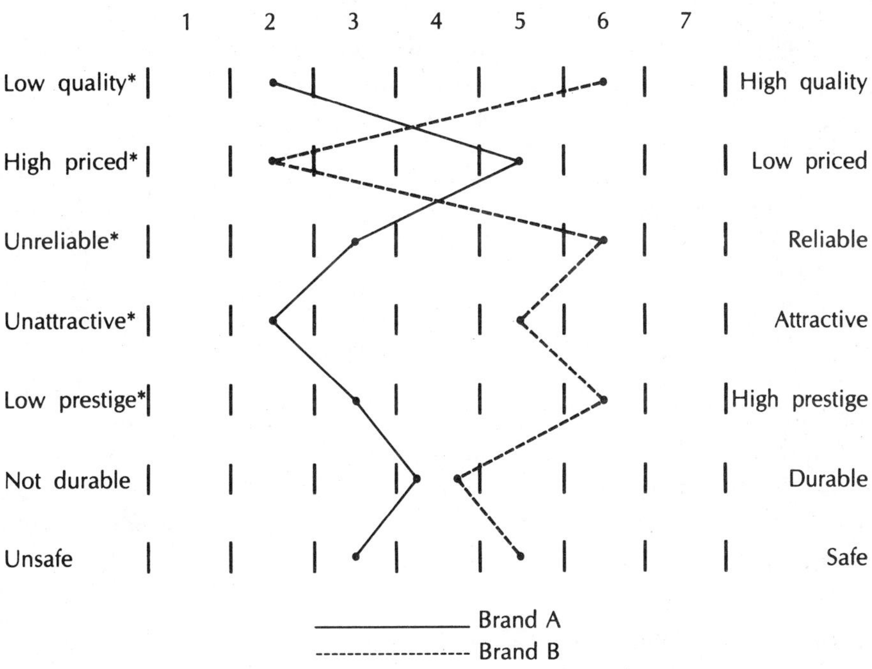

*Indicates a statistically significant difference (p.05)

The semantic differential technique is widely used in consumer research. Most researchers agree that the results can be treated as interval, thus facilitating statistical analysis. The major problem in applying this method is in generating useful adjective pairs that are both relevant to the concept studied and truly opposite.

Stapel Scale The Stapel scale is really a variation of the semantic differential, but it is unipolar while the semantic differential is bipolar. Thus, only one descriptive adjective is used and the respondent is asked to register the degree to which the adjective fits the phenomenon in question. A Stapel scale question would appear as follows:

Rate brand A on the following characteristics:

Low priced	Durable	Unattractive	Safe
+3	+3	+3	+3
+2	+2	+2	+2
+1	+1	+1	+1
−1	−1	−1	−1
−2	−2	−2	−2
−3	−3	−3	−3

Although the Staple scale seems to give responses equivalent to the semantic differential,[41] there is a problem in respondent misunderstanding when adjectives are presented in both the positive and the negative form to respondents.[42]

Multidimensional Scaling The attitude scales discussed so far are based on one of two simplifying assumptions. Some scales, like the Guttman, assume that only one attitude dimension is relevant. Scales like the semantic differential, assume that several dimensions, known to the researchers, are relevant.

Multidimensional scaling (MDS) refers to a number of scaling techniques that assume that neither the researcher nor the respondent can identify the number or nature of dimensions underlying the overall attitude toward the brand, store, or other attitude object.[43] MDS utilizes judgments of similarity or preference for brands or stores on several attitude dimensions. Two-dimensional scales can be easily plotted on a two-axis graph (see figure 9-8). More than two dimensions require computer programs.

Inferences from Observed Behavior People's attitudes may be observed from their behavior. Presumably, if a person selects a particular brand, the attitude toward that brand is positive—more positive than for other brands. In-store analysis of traffic patterns and time spent looking at displays typify this approach. Consumer panels and diary studies are variations of observation techniques. As noted in earlier chapters, caution must be exercised in inferring attitudes from behavior, since it may not accurately reflect attitudes.

Projective Techniques The projective techniques discussed earlier were developed by psychologists to test personality, but marketers have borrowed them to measure both motives and attitudes.

Fig. 9-8. Multidimensional Space for Soft Drinks

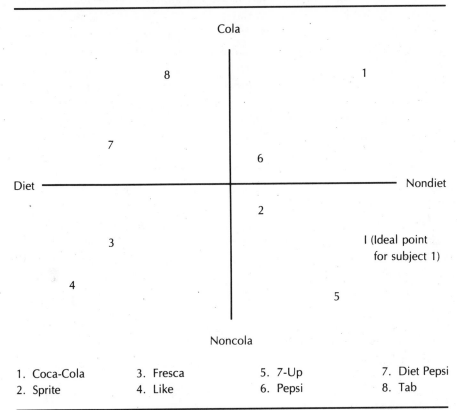

1. Coca-Cola	3. Fresca	5. 7-Up	7. Diet Pepsi
2. Sprite	4. Like	6. Pepsi	8. Tab

The above preference map was generated from one individual's ranking of his preferences for the eight brands and from the judgments about which pair of brands were most similar, next most similar, and so on until all possible pairs are ranked according to similarity. The map uses the dimensions of "Dietness" and "Colaness." The ideal point for the respondent is at "I," nearest to 7-Up.

Inferences from Performance of Objective Tasks Attitudes can be inferred from consumers' performance of various tasks. As in observing behavior, the assumption is that the respondents' attitudes may influence behavior. Respondents can be asked to spend a certain amount of money in a laboratory store setting. The brands chosen may be assumed to reflect attitudes. Another technique involves asking respondents to list favorable brands or stores.

Inferences from Physiological Response Because there is a question as to how accurately consumers describe their attitudes, many researchers seek to bypass cognitive processes altogether through various kinds of instrumentation to measure involuntary physiological responses to various stimuli. These techniques have been most widely used in consumer research for testing responses to advertising copy and package design. When exposed to a stimulus that elicits an emotional response, a person may exhibit responses of various types, including electrodermal or galvanic skin response (perspiration and electrical conductivity of the skin), brain wave patterns, respiration rate, muscle tension, voice pitch, pupil size, blood pressure, and heart rate. Presumably, measurement of these responses can give insights into a consumer's attitudes, especially if they are coupled with consumer commentaries on the stimuli.

The polygraph, psychogalvanometer, and multigraph are used to measure a number of responses simultaneously, and they have been rather extensively used in motivation and attitude research. Eye movement cameras track the consumer's eyes as they look at various parts of an ad. Presumably, longer looking times would suggest heightened interest. The pupilometer records dilation and constriction of the consumer's pupils. Some researchers have suggested that pupils will dilate when the consumer likes an ad and constrict with a nonfavored ad.[44] In general, however, researchers agree that physiological responses by themselves do not measure affect or attitude direction. Voice pitch analysis, a relatively new technique, uses a voice stress analyzer to measure emotional response as the consumer talks about various promotional stimuli.[45] Physiological response measures for consumer research are controversial, but many advertising agencies and research firms use them.

Psychographic Research

Psychographics is a term applied to a broad range of research concepts that seek to go beyond demographic research in segmenting markets. Depending on the objectives of the researcher, the dimensions added to demographics have included activities, interests, opinions, needs, values, attitudes, and personality traits.[46] Psychographics has also been called life-style research and activity and attitude research. As one writer puts it, psychographics "combines the objectivity of the personality inventory with the rich, consumer-oriented descriptive detail of the qualitative motivation research investigation."[47] Psychographics can be defined as the systematic use of relevant activity, interest, and opinion constructs (AIO's) to explore and explain quantitatively the communication, purchasing, and consuming behaviors of persons for brands, products, and groups of products.[48]

Most psychographic research is directed at combining measures of AIO's to arrive at profiles of life-style. Several typical AIO and demographic variables are found in figure 9-9. Once a life-style profile has been developed for consumers being studied, product and brand usage patterns and other shopping variables can be matched to the life-styles to determine consistent behavior patterns within psychographic segments. Figure 9-10 shows eight psychographic segments drawn from a

Fig. 9-9. Life-style Dimensions

Activities	Interests	Opinions	Demographics
Work	Family	Themselves	Age
Hobbies	Home	Social issues	Education
Social events	Job	Politics	Income
Vacation	Community	Business	Occupation
Entertainment	Recreation	Economics	Family size
Club membership	Fashion	Education	Dwelling
Community	Food	Products	Geography
Shopping	Media	Future	City size
Sports	Achievements	Culture	Stage in life cycle

Joseph T. Plummer, "The Concept and Application of Life Style Segmentation," *Journal of Marketing* 38 (January 1974):34. Reprinted from the *Journal of Marketing*, published by the American Marketing Association.

Fig. 9-10. Male Psychographic Segments

Group I. *"The Quiet Family Man"* (8% of total males)

He is a self-sufficient man who wants to be left alone and is basically shy. Tries to be as little involved with community life as possible. His life revolves around the family, simple work and television. Has a marked fantasy life. As a shopper he is practical, less drawn to consumer goods and pleasures than other men.

Low education and low economic status, he tends to be older than average.

Group II. *"The Traditionalist"* (16% of total males)

A man who feels secure, has self-esteem, follows conventional rules. He is proper and respectable, regards himself as altruistic and interested in the welfare of others. As a shopper he is conservative, likes popular brands and well-known manufacturers.

Low education and low or middle socio-economic status; the oldest age group.

Group III. *"The Discontented Man"* (13% of total males)

He is a man who is likely to be dissatisfied with his work. He feels bypassed by life, dreams of better jobs, more money and more security. He tends to be distrustful and socially aloof. As a buyer, he is quite price conscious.

Lowest education and lowest socio-economic group, mostly older than average.

Group IV. *"The Ethical Highbrow"* (14% of total males)

This is a very concerned man, sensitive to people's needs. Basically a puritan, content with family life, friends and work. Interested in culture, religion and social reform. As a consumer he is interested in quality, which may at times justify greater expenditure.

Well educated, middle or upper socio-economic status, mainly middle aged or older.

Group V. *"The Pleasure Oriented Man"* (9% of total males)

He tends to emphasize his masculinity and rejects whatever appears to be soft or feminine. He views himself a leader among men. Self-centered, dislikes his work or job. Seeks immediate gratification for his needs. He is an impulsive buyer, likely to buy any products with a masculine image.

Low education, lower socio-economic class, middle aged or younger.

Group VI. *"The Achiever"* (11% of total males)

This is likely to be a hardworking man, dedicated to success and all that it implies, social prestige, power and money. Is in favor of diversity, is adventurous about leisure time pursuits. Is stylish, likes good food, music, etc. As a consumer he is status conscious, a thoughtful and discriminating buyer.

Good education, high socio-economic status, young.

Group VII. *"The He-Man"* (19% of total males)

He is gregarious, likes action, seeks an exciting and dramatic life. Thinks of himself as capable and dominant. Tends to be more of a bachelor than a family man, even after marriage. Products he buys and brands preferred are likely to have "self-expressive value," especially a "Man of Action" dimension.

Well educated, mainly middle socio-economic status, the youngest of the male groups.

Group VIII. *"The Sophisticated Man"* (10% of total males)

He is likely to be an intellectual, concerned about social issues, admires men with artistic and intellectual achievements. Socially cosmopolitan, broad interests. Wants to be dominant, and a leader. As a consumer he is attracted to the unique and fashionable.

Best educated and highest economic status of all groups, younger than average.

William D. Wells, "Psychographics: A Critical Review," *Journal of Marketing Research* 12 (May 1975):201. Reprinted from the *Journal of Marketing Research*, published by the American Marketing Association.

study of male consumers. Some typical consumer and media consumption patterns for the segments can be seen in figure 9-11.

Measuring AIO's involves testing with a variety of statements to which respondents express agreement or disagreement. Figure 9-12 presents several sample test items taken from two psychographic studies. One set of test items includes general activity statements, while the other is built around specific product use and need factors. Results of the general test did not successfully differentiate among consumers on the basis of product usage, while the specific test yielded psychographic segments that differed substantially in their preferences for pain relievers. In general, psychographic test instruments that draw from a wide variety of life-style, physical need, and personality variables, that are custom-made for a particular study, and that relate specifically to a product's primary functions and benefits generally prove more useful than those that simply employ general activity statements.[49]

Fig. 9-11. Product and Media Use by Psychographic Group

	I	II	III	IV	V	VI	VII	VIII
				Psychographic group[a] percentages				
Drink Beer	45	56	57	51	75	59	80	72
Smoke cigarettes	32	40	40	29	54	42	51	38
Air travel outside U.S.	4	4	6	7	5	8	12	19
Air travel, domestic	14	15	14	26	19	32	20	42
Use Brand X deodorant	7	7	6	8	14	10	9	12
Used headache remedy								
in past four weeks	53	60	66	61	61	64	65	67
Read current issue of:								
Playboy	8	11	8	13	25	27	36	30
National Geographic	21	13	11	30	13	28	16	27
Time	17	8	7	16	9	26	17	29
Newsweek	17	14	8	20	11	18	13	22
Field & Stream	10	12	14	8	12	9	13	3
Popular Mechanics	11	6	9	9	9	9	8	6
Viewed in past week:								
Sanford & Son	32	35	29	19	26	25	27	23
Sonny & Cher	17	24	22	19	14	24	30	22
Marcus Welby	26	25	26	23	20	16	20	18
Rowen & Martin	21	23	17	15	22	20	23	21
New Dick Van Dyke	19	15	16	13	11	8	10	12

[a]Described in figure 9-10

William D. Wells, "Psychographics: A Critical Review," *Journal of Marketing Research* 12 (May 1975):202. Reprinted from the *Journal of Marketing Research*, published by the American Marketing Association.

Fig. 9-12.   Typical Psychographic Items

General statements used in a study of stomach remedies:	General statements used in a study of pain relievers:
My daily life is full of things that keep me interested.	I suffer headaches more severely than others do.
I prefer clothes that attract attention.	I get headaches more often than other people.
I believe a good many politicians are just a little bit crooked.	Aspirin helps me carry on with social activities.
My hands and feet are often cold.	Aspirin helps me not look ill.
I think it is true that "every cloud has a silver lining."	Regular use of aspirin can be dangerous.
I am a very energetic person.	I try to see a doctor when I have a headache.

Adapted from Joseph Pernica, "Psychographics: What Can Go Wrong," Ronald C. Carhan, ed., *1974 Combined Proceedings of the American Marketing Association*, (1975), pp. 46-47. Published by the American Marketing Association.

Summary

Numerous research techniques have been developed to measure and understand consumer behavior. This chapter has touched on some of the more significant research concepts and techniques.

Consumer research was defined as collecting, analyzing, and interpreting data relevant to any buyer, consumer, or purchase influences and any product or service acquisition, consumption, or influencing process.

Marketing research can be broken into two broad categories, quantitative and qualitative. Because qualitative research is aimed at the "whys" of buying, it characterizes consumer behavior research.

Research designs may be survey, observation, or experimental. Survey research must be concerned with questionnaire design. Questionnaires may be administered in person, by mail, or by telephone. Observation research may be used when the behavior is accessible to observation, is repetitive, frequent, or otherwise predictable, and covers a reasonably short time span. Observation designs may be natural or contrived, obtrusive or unobtrusive, structured or unstructured, direct or indirect, and human or mechanical. Experimentation emphasizes control of variables and generally provides for more precise measurement of variables. To provide useful results, marketing experiments must be carefully designed and controlled.

Several special types of consumer research include motivation, need, attitude, and psychographic. Motivation research involves depth interviews and projective techniques. Depth interviews use more or less unstructured formats and seek to get respondents to reveal their innermost feelings by probing for more and more information. Projective techniques are utilized to get at consumer motives by indirection—by allowing the respondent to project feelings onto someone else. Projective techniques include third person, association, sentence completion, and thematic apperception. Although product strategy should be based on consumer needs, discovering needs may be a difficult task. Several research techniques were suggested to uncover consumer needs: empirical studies, Delphi process, relevance tree, need confrontation, user observations, creative thinking, and ergonomic. Attitude research is broken into five categories, which infer attitudes from self-reports through a variety of attitude scaling devices, observation, partially structured stimuli, performance of objective tasks, and physiological reactions. Psychographic research is directed at measuring activities, interests, and opinions to develop life-style profiles. Life-style segments are often found to display different consuming patterns.

CHAPTER 9   STUDY REVIEW

Important Terms and Concepts

Primary research
Secondary research
Quantitative research
Qualitative research
Survey research
Questionnaire design
Observation
Experimentation
Physiological response
Motivation research
Need research
Attitude research
Psychographic research

Questions

1. Why is it important for a marketing manager to understand consumer research?

2. Describe survey, observational, and experimental research. Cite the strengths and weaknesses of each, and discuss situations in which you might use each.

3. Discuss the strengths, weaknesses, and specific techniques of motivation, need, attitude, and psychographic research, and give examples of each.

2
Strategic Applications of Consumer Behavior

10

The Diffusion
and Adoption
of New Products

A firm's product offering lies at the heart of its marketing strategy. Because of this, most firms are heavily engaged in developing new products and effectively managing existing products. The product offering is a behavioral phenomenon. From the inception of a product idea to product introduction and throughout the product life cycle, the marketing strategist must be concerned with consumer need satisfaction, product perception, and consumer attitudes toward the product.

This chapter and the two that follow are concerned with the major behavioral factors that underlie a firm's product strategy. This chapter deals primarily with the fundamental concepts of what constitutes a new product or innovation and the process by which innovations are communicated to and adopted by early buyers. Chapter 11 is devoted to strategic considerations for new and ongoing product offerings. Chapter 12 treats behavioral aspects of packaging and branding.

To understand the problems of product development, we must first adequately understand what a product is. What a customer buys must be recognized as more than simply a physical entity. Peter Drucker observes, "The customer never buys a product. By definition, the customer buys the satisfaction of a want."[1] When you buy an automobile, what do you expect to receive? Certainly the vehicle is more than a conglomeration of steel and plastic. Presumably, the buyer is looking for transportation. This may be referred to as the product's primary functional quality. Secondary functional qualities may include such factors as economy, comfort, and safety. As a buyer, you may also be interested in some primary psychological qualities relating to the nature of the car and yourself. For instance, your self-image and life-style might be embodied in the image of the car. There may be secondary psychological qualities associated with the product, too. These might include power, status, value, and appearance.

Psychological qualities may be unique to individuals, while functional qualities may be more general. In any case, it is apparent that a product may have meaning for buyers far beyond its physical character. When a product is marketed, its psychic benefits are sold along with its physical satisfactions. One writer summed up the psychological nature of products like this:

Among other things, a product is a symbol by virtue of its form, size, color, and functions. Its significance as a symbol varies according to how much it is associated with individual needs and social interaction. A product, then, is the sum of the meanings it communicates, often unconsciously, to others when they look at it or use it. Studies of different products such as coffee have illustrated the point.

Coffee has many meanings which enable it to contribute to emotional well-being. It symbolizes warmth, pleasure, leisure, luxury, intimacy, hospitality, sociability, belonging to a group, relaxation, adulthood, and an interest in homemaking. Research on the meanings of coffee and cultural trends led the Pan American Coffee Bureau to promote coffee more as a part of gracious living, of the moving away from earlier cultural restrictions on sensory pleasure, and of the trend toward expression of personality by drinking different kinds of coffee and serving it in different ways.[2]

The satisfaction derived from a product is a satisfaction of needs, as discussed in chapter 4. Thus, a product may be viewed in a behavioral sense as any need satisfier or tension reducer, whether the tension is physical or psychological. The tension may arise from any number of internal or external sources.

The process by which new products or innovations are adopted and accepted by society has been heavily researched by scholars in a variety of disciplines, including anthropology, economics, psychology, education, communication, journalism, geography, consumer behavior, and numerous fields of sociology.[3] In order to understand the complex dynamics of new product introduction and acceptance, you need to be acquainted with the adoption and diffusion process. Actually, there are four basic concepts involved.[4]

1. *Innovation* represents a complex phenomenon for which there is no single clear-cut definition. In fact, one researcher identified fifty-one different concepts of innovation.[5] For the moment, we can say that an innovation is any idea, product, or service perceived to be new.[6]
2. *Innovator* is someone who accepts something new—an innovation—quite soon after it is introduced. Innovativeness and innovation proneness are terms used to describe persons who tend to adopt new products earlier than others.
3. *Adoption* is the decision to continue to use an innovation on a regular basis.
4. *Diffusion* is the process by which the acceptance of an innovation is spread by communication to members of a social system over a period of time.

Innovation

Market survival is often dependent upon a firm's ability to develop and market innovations successfully. This means carving out a niche in the market and perhaps displacing existing products. In order to study consumer behavior's contributions to the new product development process effectively, we must first have some idea of just when a new product is really new. For example, we would have no trouble in identifying television or pocket calculators as fundamentally new products. But how new were they? Isn't television just radio with a picture? Aren't pocket calculators really just scaled-down calculators or computers, depending on their complexity? In fact, even the U.S. patent office has some problem in defining what constitutes a real innovation.[7]

As noted before, definitions of the concept of innovation seem rather inconsistent. The various approaches to defining product innovation or a new product might be classified as *product-usage* based, *market-penetration* based, and *consumer-perception* based.[8]

Product-usage based definitions generally focus on the degree of newness of a product. The best known of these configurations rests on the degree to which the innovation is likely to disrupt existing behavior patterns of consumers. A *continuous* innovation has the least disrupting influence on established patterns. It involves altering a product rather than establishing a new one. Examples: fluoride toothpaste, new model automobile changeovers, menthol cigarettes. A *dynamically continuous* innovation has more disrupting effects than a continuous innovation, but it still does not generally alter established patterns. It may involve the creation of a new product or the alteration of an existing product. Examples: electric toothbrushes, the Mustang automobile, Touch-Tone telephones. A *discontinuous* innovation involves the establishment of a new product and the establishment of new behavior patterns. Examples: television, computers.[9]

The Federal Trade Commission takes a rather narrow product-based view of what constitutes a new product. According to the FTC, a product can be called new for only a limited time—namely, six months. To be considered new, a product must be entirely new or changed in "a functionally significant or substantial respect."[10]

Another concept based on product use defines newness in terms of the potential impact of the new product on consumer satisfaction.[11] Products may be classified as artificially new, marginally new, or genuinely new. To be considered genuinely new, a product must satisfy consumer needs significantly more than previously existing products.

Market-penetration-based approaches treat newness in terms of the amount of exposure or usage of the innovation. Newness may be measured in terms of the percentage of potential customers who have purchased the new product or the length of time the product has been available to the market.

Finally, newness may logically be defined as a function of consumer perception. A product is new if a consumer perceives it to be new. The consumer's behavior rests on perception regardless of what reality may be. Thus, if a company is successful in convincing consumers that a product is new, consumers will respond as if the product were new, no matter how much real innovation is actually involved. Of course, there are legal implications, in that a marketer may not legally attempt to deceive consumers by telling them a product is new when it is, in fact, identical to current offerings. But, assuming some difference, the new product's success is determined by consumers' willingness to accept it as novel. Thus, consumers who had radios bought TV's because they were perceived as being significantly different from their radios. The pocket calculator offered previously unavailable portability and computational flexibility. In both cases, it was not the physical product with its

Fig. 10-1

Strong advertising copy can be used to drive home the idea that a new product is truly innovative.

Courtesy of the Procter and Gamble Company.

similarity to other products that led consumers to buy. Rather, it was the need-satisfying performance qualities of the new product that caused consumers to buy, even though they might have had radio and movies to satisfy their needs for entertainment and slide rules, desk calculators, and computers to perform their mathematical functions.

Innovators

There are some people who tend to accept innovations more readily than others. However, innovators for one product are not necessarily early triers of other innovations. There is a likelihood that innovators will behave consistently within product groups but not across broadly different product categories.

This section reports a wide range of research studies, in which a fair amount of confusion exists. Although the concepts most strongly suggested by research results will be treated, empirical findings to conflict with virtually every idea advanced could be found. If knowledge of innovators is so inconsistent and incomplete, why study innovators at all? There are several important reasons that make the investigation worthwhile.

1. Innovators are the people who must be reached by company promotional efforts first, and they are the ones who must be convinced to try new products before others have done so.
2. Innovators tend to be heavy users. For most products, a fairly small percentage of users consume the majority of the product. These customers constitute the most profitable target market.
3. Innovators are heavy users of informaton. They can generally be reached fairly easily by various forms of promotion and noncommercial communication.
4. Not only do innovators seek information, they also disseminate information to other potential users. They tend to be opinion leaders and can, therefore, influence others to try new products.

The process of innovation occurs over time. Innovators are, of course, those who adopt the new product or idea first. Following them are others who adopt later. Figure 10-2 indicates this distribution of adopters as normal. Obviously, actual adoption does not pattern itself so neatly, but there is a tendency toward such a distribution.

In a general sense, innovators tend to be younger, have higher social status, and be in better financial condition than noninnovators. They also tend to have broader, more cosmopolitan social relationships. In addition, they are more likely to rely on impersonal sources of information, including those external to their own social system, as opposed to personal salespeople or other word-of-mouth sources.[12]

There is another side to innovations, too. The nature of the product, or, more precisely, the way consumers perceive the product, will also influence whether and how rapidly it is adopted. As we look at the various factors that relate to innovations, keep in mind that the relationships represent tendencies. In virtually every case,

Fig. 10-2. New Product Adoption Segments ($\overline{x}$ = mean time for adoption)

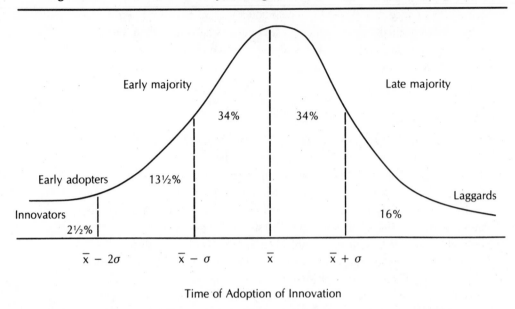

Time of Adoption of Innovation

there are research studies showing positive, negative, neutral, and conditional relationships.[13] Conclusions drawn here represent the preponderance of evidence for each factor.

Characteristics of Innovators

The variables or characteristics by which innovators may be differentiated from later adopters and nonadopters are categorized as: economic, social, communications, product-related, personality, innovativeness, attitudinal, and demographic.

Economic Variables In general, innovators tend to have higher incomes and to possess more wealth than the general population or later adopters.[14] However, income is a less significant factor for lower-priced products, purchases perceived as less significant, and purchases of items in familiar product categories. Other measures of wealth that have been associated with innovation proneness are newness of car owned, multiple car ownership, and high value of home owned.[15]

Social Variables Social variables can be viewed in terms of social integration, social class, and life-style. In general, innovators tend to be more socially active and to have higher social status than noninnovators.

Social Integration Innovators also tend to be more socially integrated within the community than noninnovators. Early adopters of push-button telephones had more social involvement with other members of the community than did noninnovators.[16] Early adopters of a new brand of coffee tended to be better integrated (i.e. considered a relatively close friend by more community residents) than noninnovators.[17]

Innovators generally belong to more social groups and organizations than others. Female fashion innovators tend to belong to more formal organizations than later adopters or nonadopters.[18] Innovators in adopting cable TV held more memberships and were more involved in social and civic clubs, professional associations, and organized church groups than later adopters.[19] Innovators in a student sample showed a greater propensity to date more frequently, spend more money on each date, and spend more on nondating social activities. They were also more likely to smoke and to play golf.[20]

On the other side of the social relationship coin is the influence of the innovator on other people. Innovators are often opinion leaders (people who influence the attitudes of other people), and they are likely to provide other potential consumers with information and advice on new products. Because others tend to follow opinion leaders' advice, consumer innovators often influence the acceptance or rejection of new products.[21]

Social Class The relationship of social class to innovativeness tends to be complex, probably because the concept of social class itself is complex and inconsistently defined from one research design to another. In an early study of social class and innovation, upper classes were found to adopt the card game Canasta more quickly, but lower classes were innovators of the more passive entertainment form, television.[22] The same study found that innovators in supermarket shopping were concentrated in the lower levels of the upper and middle classes. Blue Cross medical insurance and medical service showed no relationship between adoption and social class. Farmers of the highest social standing are innovators in implementing new farming ideas.[23]

In general, persons of higher social class are more likely to be innovators,[24] but there is the question of whether being higher in social status leads to innovation or whether being innovative causes one to be more highly regarded in society. Perhaps the best way to reach an understanding of the relationship is to view innovators relative to the various components of social class.

Although there are numerous conceptions of the factors that determine social class, amount of income, education, and occupation are pretty consistently employed as determinants. Studies have indicated a positive relationship for all three of these variables to innovation proneness.[25]

Income seems to be positively related to innovation proneness, but the relationship is complex. The concept of privilege appears to be important here.[26] Innovators tend to have higher discretionary income than their neighbors and to perceive themselves to be richer. The innovators were not necessarily from the highest income levels in society. Rather, they were from the overprivileged segments of each social class. Also, because of their perception of privilege, innovators were less concerned with the cost of the item purchased.

Occupation is the most acceptable single variable for measuring or establishing social status. Accordingly, occupational titles have been ranked and scored for status, and one study indicated that persons scoring higher in occupational status were more likely to be innovators. Education also relates positively to innovation proneness. [27]

In addition to the determinants of social class that appear to be related to innovation proneness, some characteristics of people in the various classes seem to suggest innovation proneness. Chapter 7 looked at some differences between middle-class and lower-class individuals, including the facts that the middle class tends to be more self-confident and more willing to take risks, to have a greater sense of choice making, and to have extended horizons. Innovators tend to be more venturesome and more inclined to take risks. [28] Thus, we may generally conclude that innovators are likely to be of higher social status than noninnovators.

Another aspect of social class that has received research attention is social mobility—the desire for or achievement of upward movement within the social class structure. Many people are content with their social station or even unaware of social status. Others are acutely aware of their social standing and prestige and continually behave so as to move upward on the social ladder. Often included in this behavior is conspicuous consumption and innovative purchasing. Thus, upward social mobility has frequently been associated with innovative buying. [29]

Life-style A major manifestation of social activity is life-style, defined as "the distinctive or characteristic mode of living, in its aggregate and broadest sense of a whole society or segment thereof." [30]

Many research studies have indicated that an individual's level of living relates positively to innovation proneness. [31] Some people's life-styles lead them to be savers, living within their means. Others may be living at the outer limit of their means and heavily in debt. The high livers seem to be innovators, which would suggest a possible relationship between credit use and innovation proneness.

One study of the relationship between innovation proneness and life-style was based on the idea that there might be more than one kind of innovator for a group of products, that these various types of innovators would have different media habits and different characteristics even when choosing the same products, and that adoption behavior should be analyzed over several product categories simultaneously. [32] It was felt that characteristics related to early adoption in one product class might be associated with early adoption in other product categories even though previous research had indicated that innovators for one product class may not be innovators for other unrelated products. [33]

The study identified four life-style categories of innovators based on such factors as attitude toward change, life-style venturesomeness, self-confidence, opinion leadership, and self-esteem. The four classes are summarized in figure 10-3. All of the participants in the study were innovators. Innovators of different life-styles appear to be more innovative in different ways with respect to the activities studied. Different

Fig. 10-3. Life-style Categories of Innovators

Category	Life-style Characteristics	Innovative Characteristics
Suburban Swinger	*Above average* on mobility, youth, self-esteem, self-confidence, life-style venturesomeness, and media consumption (radio and TV). *Below average* on education, income, and number of children.	*Above average* for personal grooming and apparel innovativeness.
House Husband or Established Isolate	*Above average* on education, number of children, and self-esteem. *Below average* on mobility, income, self-confidence, youth, attitude toward change, life-style venturesomeness, and media consumption.	*Above average* for home care innovativeness.
Suburban Conservatism	*Above average* on education, number of children, and income. *Below average* on mobility, self-esteem, self-confidence, attitude toward change, life-style venturesomeness, and media consumption.	*Below average* for all three areas of innovativeness.
Established Suburbanite or Permanent Nester	*Above average* on number of children, income, and media consumption. *Below average* on mobility, education, youth, self-esteem, self-confidence, attitude toward change, and life-style venturesomeness.	*Above average* for all three areas of innovativeness.

Adapted from William R. Darden and Fred D. Reynolds, "Backward Profiling of Male Innovators," *Journal of Marketing Research* 11 (February 1974):79-85.

life-styles may relate differently to innovation proneness for a wide variety of products and activities.

Communication Variables Acceptance of innovation is based upon communication of the innovation. Potential innovators must be made aware of the existence and nature of the innovation before they can be expected to accept it. The question is whether innovators have different communication receipt and transmission patterns from noninnovators. This area has been rather heavily researched, and the answer seems to be that innovators do regard and use communication differently than do noninnovators.[34]

The communication behavior patterns of innovators can be viewed in terms of both receipt and transmission of information and the kind of information passed. The information itself is either marketer-controlled or nonmarketer-controlled, and either personal or mass in character.

Receipt of Information Potential innovators may receive information about innovations from a variety of commercial and noncommercial sources. The sources of this information are extremely important to marketers of new products as they attempt to communicate with innovators and early adopters to induce product trial.

Looking first at the marketer-controlled information sources, we find a rather complex set of relationships. Mass media exposure was found to relate to innovation proneness in nearly ninety percent of research studies up to 1965.[35] In general, mass media are found to be important in making innovators aware of innovations.[36]

Television may have some influence in making innovators aware of innovations,[37] but research indicates that innovators generally watch less TV and are less likely to get information from TV than noninnovators.[38] This probably arises partly from the fact that the higher-income and higher social class groups who tend to be innovators are not heavy TV viewers and partly from the nonselective nature of TV.

Magazine readership, particularly specialized magazine readership, is, however, related to innovation proneness.[39] One study found the level of readership of virtually all mass media magazines to be substantially higher among innovators than among others. Innovators were found to be heavy readers of *Playboy.* More than half read three or more of every four issues of *Newsweek* and *Sports Illustrated,* and almost three-fourths read three or more of every four issues of *Time.* [40]

Selective publications are heavily read by innovators, especially when their editorial content is specific to the product in question. Male fashion innovators tend to be heavy readers of *Esquire* and *Gentlemen's Quarterly.* [41] Another study found a strong positive relationship between innovation proneness in packaged food items and readership of women's magazines. The same was true for women's fashion clothing innovators who were heavy readers of such women's fashion magazines as *Glamour* and *Vogue.* However, romance magazines whose editorial content appears to have little relevance for consumer products were not effective in attracting readership of innovators.[42] Such home magazines as *Better Homes and Gardens* were found to be particularly effective in reaching consumer product innovators.[43]

Another study found direct mail to be effective in inducing early trial, especially where free samples were involved.[44] The same study was one of the few that found TV to be a good means of reaching innovators. Network commercials were effective, but local spot TV commercials were not.

Personal interaction has generally been found to be important in informing consumer innovators. Although relatively little research has been done in the area, salespeople seem to play a very important role in providing information to innovators.[45]

Nonmarketer-controlled sources are also quite significant in influencing innovators. While mass media are quite influential in making innovators aware of new products, they turn to other people as they get closer to actual purchase. Other persons are looked to for their product experience or technical expertise. Most of the users of a new automobile diagnostic test center learned about the service from a *Reader's Digest* article or other semiauthoritative articles in the mass media, but the decision to use the service was often largely based on the reported experience of friends and relatives.[46] Other individuals are also consulted more often as perceived risk of purchase increases and where product differences are unclear.[47,48] Most studies of innovation that investigated the role of friends, relatives, and other individual influences showed a significant relationship.[49] Although word-of-mouth communication is not considered market-controllable, the first triers of the product or service are heavy information seekers, and the information they receive from marketers determines, in part, what they pass along. Thus, it is suggested that sellers of innovations have much to gain from providing detailed point-of-sale information and owner's manuals so that the adopter will have adequate and realistic information to communicate.[50]

In addition to personal sources, innovators may receive noncommercial information from mass sources, such as consumer test magazines. In a study of purchases of large and small appliances, readership of consumer test publications was strongly related to innovation proneness.[51]

Transmission of Information Innovators are also involved in communication to others. In one study, innovators were found to be more likely to indicate that they had recently been asked their opinions on detergents or volunteered information to others.[52] Innovators in the use of the automobile diagnostic test center were twice as likely to transmit personal opinions about new things in general than were noninnovators.[53] Both positive and negative information can be transmitted, of course, and this is significant to marketers. One study indicated that consumers who received unfavorable word-of-mouth communication were twenty-four percent less likely to purchase a new product than other consumers. At the same time, those who received favorable word-of-mouth information were twelve percent more likely to buy.[54]

Product-related Variables Although there is a tendency for innovators in one area to be innovators in other areas as well, there is evidence that consumers may be innovators for one product but not for another.[55] It has also been noted that innovation for specific products is related to the buyer's predisposition to innovate within the product category, but this may not hold true over other types of products.[56] Interest in the new product or the product category has also been found to relate positively to innovation proneness.[57]

The way consumers perceive an innovation also appears to have a marked bearing on innovative behavior. Five product perception characteristics that seem to relate to innovation proneness have been identified: relative advantage, compatibility, complexity, divisibility, and communicability.[58]

Relative Advantage Relative advantage is the degree to which an innovation is perceived as superior to the product or idea it supercedes or with which it competes in the market. As discussed later in this chapter, the innovation that has an obvious advantage over its predecessor has a much higher probability of success. Research suggests that where there is a stronger promise of need-fulfillment, the innovator is more likely to seek information about a new product, maintain interest, and try and adopt the product. When the perceived benefit of the product is more immediate, product trial is more likely.[59]

Compatibility The degree to which a new product is perceived to be consistent with existing values, habits, and past experience of the potential adopter is referred to as compatibility. Products that are too new or too different from existing products will be more slowly adopted—if they are accepted at all. But to complicate matters, a new product that is not perceived to be unique or to provide new need satisfactions may find difficulty in gaining acceptance. An acceptable innovation must be new but not too new.

Complexity A complex item may require detailed written instructions or personal explanation because consumers must learn to use the new product. These "slow-learning" products move slowly through the introductory phase of the product life cycle since innovators must not only be acquainted with the innovation but educated in its use as well.

Divisibility Divisibility or trialability refers to the degree to which a product is available for trial on a limited basis. A product that can be sampled free or at low cost can be tried with little risk and tends to be adopted more easily.

Communicability Communicability or observability is the degree to which benefits of an innovation are apparent and transmittable to potential innovators. Promotion of a new product depends on the capability to point out its advantages to potential buyers easily. If a product is visable in a social situation, it tends to be more readily adopted.

Personality Variables Several studies have investigated the relationship between innovation proneness and personality. As with most attempts to relate personality to consumer behavior, results have been equivocal at best. A few generalizations have emerged, however. One study of new product purchases across three product categories—appliances, clothing, and food—investigated the relationship between innovative behavior and the personality variables: dominance, capacity for status, sociability, social presence, self-acceptance, sense of well-being, responsibility, socialization, self-control, tolerance, good impression, commonality, achievement via conformance, achievement via independence, intellectual efficiency, psychological mindedness, flexibility, and femininity/masculinity.[60] Although the authors questioned the practical significance of the results, they did find the following traits to be positively associated with innovation proneness for at least one of the products:

Sociability—outgoing, sociable, participative temperament.

Self-acceptance—sense of personal worth.

Socialization—degree of social maturity, integrity, and rectitude that the individual has attained.

Commonality—degree to which an individual's reactions and responses correspond to the model (common) pattern established for the inventory—dependability, moderateness, tact.

Intellectual efficiency—degree of personal and intellectual efficiency that the individual has attained.

Dogmatism is another personality variable that has been related to innovation proneness. Dogmatism is defined as the degree to which a person is open- or closed-minded. The highly dogmatic person has a low tolerance for ambiguity and is more likely to be influenced by prestigious or authoritative communicators.[61] These characteristics lead to conflicting expectations as to the influence of dogmatism on innovation proneness. Low tolerance for ambiguity might make consumers less likely to accept innovation. On the other hand, it has been observed that many authoritative persons favor progress, and since dogmatic persons tend to accept authoritative communication, they might be swayed to become innovative in the interests of progress or seeming to be progressive.[62]

In general, the studies of the relationships between dogmatism and innovation suggest that open-minded persons tend to be more innovative than dogmatists.[63] However, one study suggested that although dogmatists were less likely to accept true innovations, they were early acceptors of recent products that were not greatly different from the products they displaced.[64]

Highly dogmatic individuals tend to accept information regarding innovation on the strength of the source of the information, while low dogmatic individuals tend to prefer objective information.[65] It also appears that the innovative behavior of high dogmatics results from compliance with social norms, while low dogmatics change because of general receptiveness to new information.[66]

Several other personality characteristics seem to relate positively to innovation proneness, including gregariousness (desire to associate with others), venturesomeness (willingness to accept risk), inner-directedness (relying on one's own values or standards in making a decision), broad categorizing (willingness to take the risk of a broad range of new products or ideas), impulsiveness (tendency to act quickly without extensive planning), exhibitionism (desire to show off and be noticed), narcissism (feeling of self-like, self-worth), and lower intellectual interest. [67]

In total, the innovative person seems to be more self-confident, more willing to take risks, to face the unknown or unfamiliar, and to rely on personal standards and values. From a marketing management standpoint, we probably ought to try to communicate with and promote to potential innovators differently from later adopters. The consumer innovator is more apt to relate to informative advertising that explains product benefits and that can be used to compare against personal values and needs. [68]

Innovativeness It is somewhat unclear whether some consumers are generally more innovation-prone than others. One study concluded that some buyers are generally more receptive to innovations than others, but the study was for a single product category. [69] When the question included appliance, food, and clothing innovators, there was no evidence that one consumer was more innovative than another. [70] Another study, again in a single product category, found the earliest adopters of a new automobile service to be more willing to experiment with new ideas, more likely to purchase new products (in general) earlier, less likely to switch brands because of small price changes, less interested in price, per se, and less likely to try new convenience items if the change from previous products was minor. [71]

In the final analysis, it seems that we might expect an innovator for one product to be innovative for similar products but not necessarily for dissimilar products. Intensive investigation has led to the conclusion that "the consistency of innovativeness cannot be expected across product categories, but can be expected within product categories and, sometimes, between related product categories." [72]

Attitudinal Variables Just as certain personality characteristics may be associated with innovativeness, certain attitudes people hold are associated with innovative behavior. [73] People who are more knowledgeable and more aware of the external world and what is going on in it are more innovative. Those who have a positive attitude toward change, who are achievement motivated, who have a positive orientation toward business, and who have high aspirations for their children also tend to be more likely to accept new products readily. On the other hand, consumers who are generally satisfied with their lives or who are mentally rigid (a manifestation of dogmatism) tend to be less innovative.

Demographic Variables Several demographic variables, many of which relate to social class and life-style, are associated with innovative behavior. The variables most often positively associated with innovative behavior are education, literacy, income, and level of living. [74] Age has been heavily investigated as a potential determinant of innovativeness, and several writers suggest that innovators tend to be younger than noninnovators. However, in a review of 158 studies, it was found that thirty-two percent of them showed older consumers to be more innovative, eighteen percent found younger buyers more innovative, while forty-one percent found no correlation at all.[75]

Modeling Innovative Behavior

Relatively little has been done to tie all of the variables that influence innovation into a single construct. However, at least one attempt has been made to present an integrated conceptual model of innovative behavior.[76] Figure 10-4 outlines such a model.

The model omits demographic characteristics for simplicity, but they could be shown to relate in somewhat the same way as psychological and sociological traits. Looking at the model, psychological traits would include such things as empathy, dogmatism, achievement motivation, self-monitoring, and intelligence. Sociological traits would include social participation, social integration, and cosmopolitanism. In addition to relating to innovations, these constructs might also relate to other phenomena associated with adoption. For instance, empathy or lack of dogmatism might lead a potential innovator to be more susceptible to interpersonal messages, while receipt of these messages may be a function of the individual's social integration.

Moving from the theoretical construct into observable (although not necessarily measurable) phenomena, we find intervening variables, such as interest in the product category, which may be influenced by sociological, psychological, and demographic factors. Another intervening variable is communicated experience, which represents the network of interpersonal messages relating to the product and the effects of these messages on individuals. The third intervening variable is situational effects, suggesting that the innovator may be influenced by environmental or other factors peculiar to the innovation or innovator.

Figure 10-4 is somewhat oversimplified, but it does suggest that we can view the innovative process as a whole. The model also suggests that it is probably fallacious to try to look at individual influences on innovativeness in a vacuum. We must see the high degree of interaction and interdependence of factors influencing innovation and also recognize that innovative behavior is often product or situation specific.

Adoption

The process by which consumers decide to accept or reject a new product is referred to as the adoption process. There is some similarity between the adoption process and the consumer purchase decision process discussed in chapter 2. However, the adoption process refers to the possible acceptance and continued use of an item that

Fig. 10-4. Midgley-Dowling Model of Innovativeness

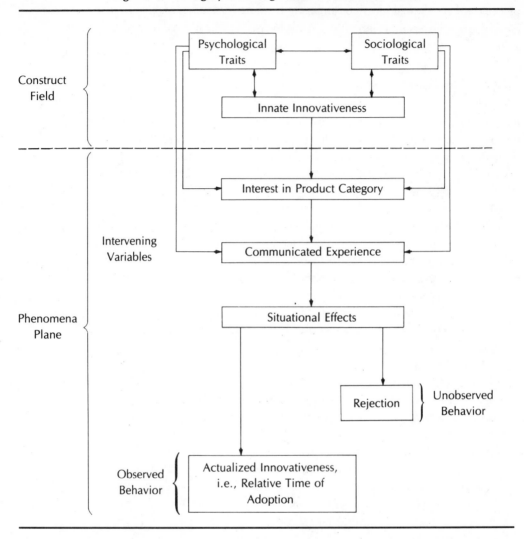

David F. Midgley and Grahame R. Dowling, "Innovativeness: The Concept and Its Measurement." Reprinted with permission from *The Journal of Consumer Research* (1978), 4:236.

has not previously been bought, while the purchase decision process generally refers to a single buying decision for a product with which the buyer may have had previous experience.[77]

In practice, the difference between the processes is not so clearly drawn. It is difficult to specify what actually constitutes adoption. The definition is partially tied to the type of product in question. For example, the adoption process and purchase process for a major appliance would be virtually synonymous, since the infrequency of purchase makes the concept of acceptance and continued repurchase questionable. For a product like a detergent, characterized by a high frequency of purchase and heavy brand switching, what number of repeat purchases would constitute adoption—three times in a row, three out of four, or what?[78] There is also a question of the degree of behavior change required to constitute an adoption decision. In switching from All to Cheer a rather minor change in behavior is involved. But for the consumer who goes through the process of adopting Procter and Gamble's Bold 3, a rather major change is involved, since the product is unique in that it includes whiteners, an anticling/antistatic agent, and a fabric softener, previously available only in two or three separate products.

The level of use may also be a significant criterion. In determining the difference in adoption for heavy versus light users, a person may look at the regular user versus the occasional user modes of adoption.[79] The regular user purchases the product at regular intervals without using competing products, while the occasional user purchases the adopted product more consistently than competing items but buys substitutes rather frequently as well.

Conceptions of the Adoption Process

Several general schemes for identifying the stages in the adoption process have been advanced. They may be treated as adoption process schemes, hierarchy of effects schemes, and a variety of others.[80]

The Adoption Process Scheme The adoption process as first defined in the 1950s consists of five sequential stages.

1. *Awareness*—the individual knows of the new idea but lacks sufficient awareness about it.
2. *Interest*—the individual becomes interested in the idea and seeks more information about it.
3. *Evaluation*—the individual mentally applies the innovation to present and anticipated situations and makes a decision for or against trial.
4. *Trial*—the innovation is used on a trial basis to determine whether or not it meets the buyer's needs.
5. *Adoption*—if the innovation is satisfactory, the individual accepts it for use on a continuing basis.

This scheme does not make allowance for any skipping of stages, and no feedback is considered. For example, after the trial stage an individual may desire more information and return to the interest stage. Also, the trial stage requires evaluating the innovation. Despite these deficiencies, the scheme does allow for rejection at any stage.

The adoption process scheme provides a useful framework for understanding information acquisition during the adoption process. Figure 10-5 indicates the relative usefulness of personal versus nonpersonal information sources during adoption.

Fig. 10-5.   Different Types of Information Sources

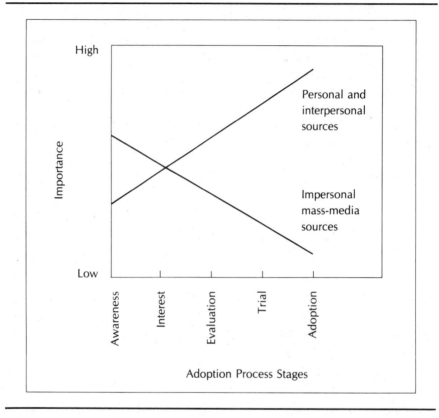

Leon G. Schiffman and Leslie Lazar Kanuk, *Consumer Behavior*, © 1978, p. 415, Fig. 14-5. Reprinted by permission of Prentice-Hall, Inc., Englewood Cliffs, New Jersey.

As indicated earlier, both mass and personal communication sources are utilized by innovators. The tendency is for personal sources to become more significant and for nonpersonal sources to become less important as the consumer moves from awareness to adoption.

The Hierarchy of Effects Scheme The hierarchy of effects, first advanced by Robert Lavidge and Gary Steiner and labeled by Kristian Palda, includes the following stages:

1. *Awareness*—the individual becomes conscious of the product's existence.
2. *Knowledge*—the individual comes to realize what the product does or what benefits it has to offer.

3. *Liking*—attitude toward the product becomes favorable.

4. *Preference*—the individual's attitude becomes positive enough that the product is considered superior to other alternatives.

5. *Conviction*—preference is strong enough that the individual gains confidence that the product would satisfy needs, leading to actual demand or desire to purchase.

6. *Purchase*—the product is actually acquired.[81]

It is assumed that all steps must occur even though they may happen virtually instantaneously and simultaneously, as in the case of an impulse purchase. No feedback loops are included, and a continuous process is envisioned. The hierarchy of effects scheme is probably the first adoption model to rely on an information-attitude-behavior theory of communication effect. The assumption is that communication functions by providing information (awareness and knowledge) and forming or changing attitudes (liking and preference), thus inducing behavior (conviction and purchase).[82]

Other Purchase Decision Schemes There are numerous additional schemes that have been advanced to explain adoption. The simple AIDA model, set down in 1925,[83] includes four elements: attract attention, create and sustain interest, arouse desire, and achieve action. Another model advanced later identified three stages: attention, comprehension, and acceptance.

Viewed as a problem-solving process, adoption may be viewed thus:

1. *Perception of the problem*—for adoption to occur, a problem must be perceived to exist. (It is assumed here that problem perception precedes awareness. We might as easily argue that awareness of the innovation could give rise to perception of a problem).

2. *Setting the stage*—a configuration of information and alternative solution is brought together.

3. *The act of insight*—an alternative solution is accepted. The innovation may be accepted or rejected.

4. *The critical revision*—the innovation is analyzed by the consumer to determine its practicality in terms of cost, availability, etc.[84]

Another problem-solving or innovation decision process model (see figure 10-6) lists four steps.

1. *Knowledge*—the individual is exposed to the innovation's existence and gains some understanding of how it functions.

2. *Persuasion*—the individual forms a favorable or unfavorable attitude toward the product.

3. *Discussion*—the individual engages in activities that lead to a choice to adopt or reject the innovation.

4. *Confirmation*—the individual seeks reinforcement for the decision process for the innovation decision made, but the decision may be reversed if there is exposure to conflicting messages about the innovation.[85]

Figure 10-6 suggests that a number of variables classified as receiver and social system variables along with various communication sources influence the receipt of information during the knowledge stage. Moving into the persuasion stage, the potential innovator continues to be influenced by communication sources and the information carried forward from the knowledge stage. In addition, the perceived characteristics of innovation (relative advantage, for example) come into play. Communication sources continue to influence the decision phase when the consumer elects to adopt or reject either permanently or temporarily. Given adoption, the decision is subject to confirmation. Here again, feedback flows are not considered, leaving the model rather inflexible.

More comprehensive flow models have been suggested to explain the adoption process. The models of Francesco Nicosia and Alan Andreasen attempt to account for the dynamics of consumer decision making and to specify the operating variables and their interrelationships.[86]

The Nicosia model (figure 10-7) assumes that a firm is introducing a new product or brand and that the consumer has no prior attitudes toward either the brand or its product class. This suggests quite a unique innovation. The decision flow for this model consists of seven components:

1. The firm's initial advertisement
2. The consumer's exposure
3. Interaction of consumer attributes with message content
4. The resulting attitude formation
5. The possibility of the attitudes' leading to search/evaluation activity, resulting in motivation
6. The conversion of motivation to a purchase/rejection decision.
7. Feedback of purchase information to the firm and to the consumer potential leading to modifications in consumer predisposition and the firm's future communication strategy.

(It should be noted that the Nicosia model presented the subfields indicated in great detail.)

Andreasen also assumes innovative consumer behavior. The process (see figure 10-8) begins with a consumer who is unaware of a product or brand and therefore has no attitude toward it. *Information* reaches the consumer, having been communicated by some *source*. The information is then filtered by the consumer, and this selectively perceived information influences consumer attitude defined in terms of belief, feeling, and disposition components. Attitude may result in a decision either to *select* the product, to *search* for additional information, or take *no action*. The decision to select will be mediated by various constraints (such as income and priorities), and other purchase decisions (such as store selection and quantity) will be made before *ownership* is accomplished. The model includes appropriate mediating variables and traces feedback flows.

Fig. 10-6. Innovation-Decision Process

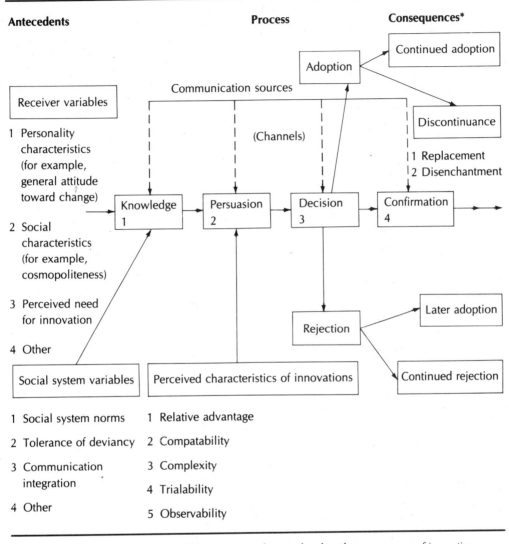

*For simplicity, only the consequences of the process are shown rather than the consequences of innovation.

Reprinted with permission of Macmillan Publishing Co., Inc. from *Communication of Innovations*, by Everett M. Rogers and Floyd Shoemaker. Copyright © 1971 by The Free Press, a Division of Macmillan Publishing Co., Inc.

Refinements of Adoption Models

Several refinements of adoption models have been suggested that may make them more useful. First, there is no single *form* to which the adoption process must conform. The form of the adoption process will vary with (1) the importance of the decision, (2) the extent of meaningful product differentiation, (3) the extent of

Fig. 10-7. Nicosia Model

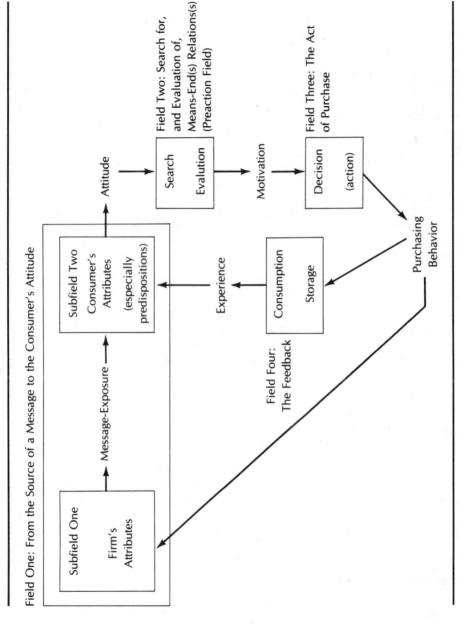

Field One: From the Source of a Message to the Consumer's Attitude

Subfield One

Firm's Attributes

Message-Exposure

Subfield Two

Consumer's Attributes (especially predispositions)

Attitude

Field Two: Search for, and Evaluation of, Means-End(s) Relations(s) (Preaction Field)

Search

Evaluation

Motivation

Field Three: The Act of Purchase

Decision

(action)

Purchasing Behavior

Field Four: The Feedback

Consumption

Storage

Experience

Francesco Nicosia, *Consumer Decision Processes: Marketing and Advertising Implications*, (Englewood Cliffs, N.J. : Prentice-Hall, 1966), p.156. Reprinted by permission.

Fig. 10-8. Andreasen Conceptualization of the Purchase Decision Process

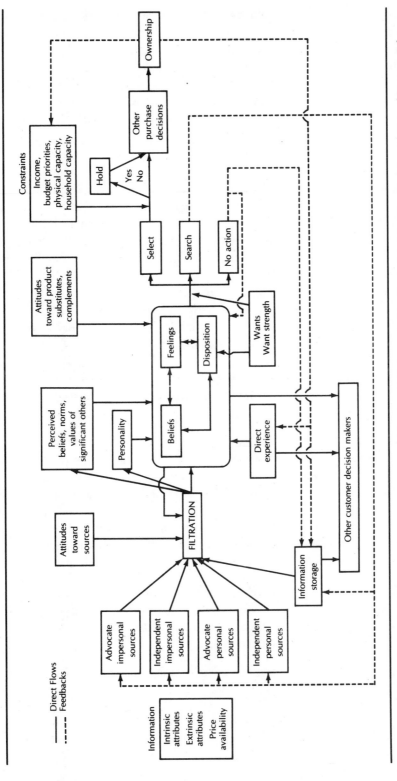

Alan R. Andreasen, "Attitudes and Consumer Behavior: A Decision Model," in Lee E. Preston, ed., *New Research in Marketing* (Berkeley: Institute of Business and Economic Research, University of California, 1965).

product conspicuousness, (4) the extent to which the consumer can afford to take risks, and (5) the decision-making ability of consumers. Second, there is no specified *number* of stages that will always occur. The minimum number of stages seems to be two, whereas the maximum number of stages is probably a function of one's ingenuity in drawing distinctions. Finally, there is no specified *sequence* of stages that must occur. Any adoption model must make allowances for consumers to skip stages and also provide feedback loops, since buyers are unlikely to follow some tightly defined set of steps consistently.[87]

Figure 10-9 shows the summary model based on these refinements. Several features of the model should be emphasized. The information-attitude-behavior conceptualization is maintained, since it seems to provide a useful format for understanding adoption. Also, it ties directly to our understanding of how advertising works. It is possible to trace the different forms of the adoption process. The rational/decision-making form follows the full awareness to trial and the nonrational/ psychosocial form moves from awareness to legitimization, to trial, or perhaps to adoption without small-scale trial. Feedback effects are noted by broken lines. Adoption is viewed as affecting legitimization and attitude, and adoption yields knowledge and heightens product awareness. Two new stages (problem perception and dissonance) are added to account more fully for possible sequences that may occur.[88] Rejection may occur at any stage of the process once the consumer is aware of the innovation. The interest stage was omitted on the grounds that it is not distinguishable but rather acts as a requisite for each stage. Evaluation was also left out since evaluation is ongoing throughout the entire process. The stages are defined as follows:

> *Problem perception*—although, as noted earlier, the reverse may be true, the adoption process often begins as the consumer becomes aware of a problem to be solved and seeks solution to the recognized problem.
>
> *Awareness*—the awareness stage assumes only that the consumer knows that the product in question exists.
>
> *Comprehension*—comprehension is based on knowledge and represents the consumer's conception or understanding of what the product is and its functions and potential benefits.

The awareness and comprehension stages are information processing stages. Together, they comprise the cognitive field of the adoption process. Comprehension, however, overlaps with attitude because knowledge, defined in terms of beliefs, is recognized as an attitude component.

> *Attitude*—attitude goes beyond comprehension in terms of the feeling (affective) and actions (behavioral) components. A favorable evaluation (attitude) is usually necessary for the adoption process to continue.
>
> *Legitimization*—if the individual has a positive attitude toward the product, trial is likely. However, whether trial occurs will largely depend on the result of the legitimization stage. The individual must become convinced that the

Fig. 10-9. Summary Adoption Decision Process Model

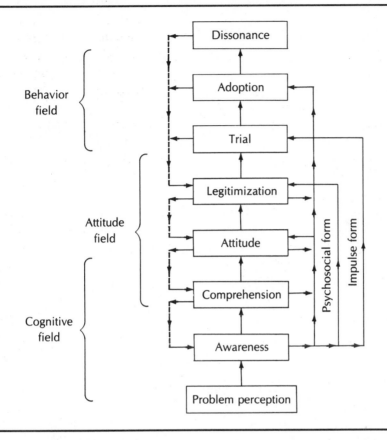

Figure 14-5 (p. 290) in *Models of Buyer Behavior: Conceptual, Quantitative, and Empirical* by Jagdish N. Sheth. Copyright © 1974 by Jagdish N. Sheth. Reprinted by permission of Harper & Row, Publishers, Inc.

purchase is appropriate. This decision may be based upon accumulated information, or additional information may be sought. The consumer may ask, "Does this product fit my self-image?" "Do, or would, my friends or others I respect use such a product?"

The comprehension, attitude, and legitimization stages comprise the attitude field of the model. There is an overlap, in that comprehension is part of the cognitive field, and legitimization may also be considered part of the behavioral field since the individual is, in a sense, active toward goal achievement.

Trial—the consumer uses the product on a limited basis. Trial may represent a commitment to adopt or a means of evaluating the product based on experience.

Adoption—the product is accepted, and the consumer continues to buy and/or use it.

The legitimization, trial, and adoption stages make up the behavioral field.

Dissonance—commitment to an adoption decision may lead to cognitive dissonance. Since dissonance is uncomfortable, the individual will seek to reduce it, perhaps by seeking social support or selectively perceiving advertisements for the product purchased. There may be a tendency to tell friends about the product to "sell" them on it, thus achieving social support. This dissonance may work for the marketer in stimulating the important word-of-mouth "promoting" discussed earlier.

Rate of Adoption

The marketing manager must be concerned not only with the stages that consumers pass through in adopting a new product but with the rapidity with which the product is accepted as well. Fad items, such as Pet Rocks or Hula Hoops, may be accepted almost instantaneously, and laggards in adoption may be those who accept thirty days after innovators. On the other hand, a product like television or in-home computers may take many years to become widely used.

Diffusion

The diffusion process is often confused with the adoption process. There is a relationship, but they are not the same. The adoption process is a microprocess. The concern is with the mental process by which a single individual comes to adopt an innovation. Diffusion, on the other hand, is a macroconcept. Diffusion is the aggregate of all individual adoptions over time. Thus, diffusion is the process by which any new idea or innovation is communicated and accepted by a social system over time.

Elements of Diffusion

There are four basic components in the diffusion process: the innovation, the communication from one individual to another, the social system that receives the innovation, and the time dimension of the process.

Innovation Innovations have already been identified as ideas or products perceived in varying degrees to be new by the potential buyer. The basis for defining "new" was shown to depend on the disrupting effects the new product has on existing behavior.

Communication The essence of diffusion lies in human interaction wherein one individual transmits information regarding an innovation to another person. This communication, which may be transmitted through either formal or informal channels, is necessary for diffusion to take place.

Social System A social system is defined as a population of individuals who are functionally differentiated and engaged in problem-solving behavior.[89] The social system for a new product is all those individuals or firms in a specified area who could use the product. The terms generally used to denote social systems in marketing are *target market* or *market segment*.

The orientation of a social system influences the acceptance of new products and, hence, the rate and extent of diffusion. For instance, a "modern" social system would tend to adopt an innovation more rapidly than a "traditional" system. The following characteristics typify a "modern" social system.

1. Positive attitude toward change
2. Advanced technology and skilled labor force
3. General respect for education and science
4. Emphasis on rational and ordered social relationships as opposed to emotional
5. Interaction with persons outside the social system, facilitating infusion of new ideas
6. Capability of members of the system to see themselves in various roles[90]

The critical issue is the climate into which an innovation enters. The United States has seen major changes in the climate for innovations of late. These are exemplified in the desire for cleaner, more energy-efficient automobiles, more nutritious, "safer," and more natural foods, and modular homes. The marketing manager must pay close attention to trends in the social system that may obsolete some products and create needs for others.

Time Not all people adopt new ideas or products at the same time. For example, figure 10-10 depicts housewife A being exposed to a commercial for Bounce, a static remover/fabric softener, in May 1976. However, she did not actually begin using this product on a regular basis until September 1976. Housewife B heard of Bounce from her neighbor in June 1976 and began using the product on a regular basis in July of that year. The time for adoption differs significantly, and the marketing manager would like to know not only why it took housewise A so long to adopt but also any individual and environmental differences between the two.[91]

Patterns of Diffusion

The general trend of diffusion may be helpful to marketers attempting to predict how readily a new product may be adopted. Figure 10-11 shows two general patterns of diffusion; logistic and exponential. The logistic or S-shaped diffusion curve is considered the most common. The S-shape results from initial slow acceptance among early innovators, followed by rapid acceptance among late innovators, followed by slower acceptance among later adopters.

Fig. 10-10. Time Spans Incurred Before Adoption

	May	June	July	August	September
Housewife A	Hears commercial		Adopts product		
Housewife B		Hears about product from neighbor			Adopts product

One-month span

Four-month span

Reproduced by permission from Hisrich, Robert D. and Peters, Michael P., *Marketing a New Product: Its Planning, Development and Control.* Menlo Park, California: The Benjamin/Cummings Publishing Company, 1978.

Fig. 10-11. Exponential and Logistic Diffusion Patterns

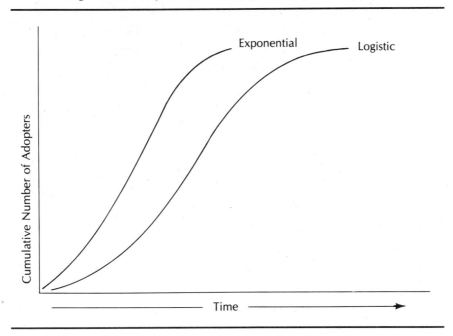

The exponential curve characterizes innovations that take place very rapidly, as with fads. These innovations tend to be short-lived, and they are often discontinued as quickly as they are accepted.[92]

If a firm is able to predict the diffusion pattern for a new product, it may be able to generate more accurate market forecasts. Simply identifying the likelihood of an exponential curve versus an S-curve is a start, but more sophisticated models—penetration, epidemiological, and deterministic—have been advanced.

Penetration Models Penetration models aim at predicting the number of persons who will adopt a new product over time from early sales results. Based on the exponential growth curve, a functional statement for new product penetration can be represented thus:[93]

$$rx\,(1-r)^{i-1} + k$$

Where: r   is the rate at which the level of penetration approaches the ceiling of penetration

         x   is the ceiling of penetration (the maximum percentage of households that can be expected to purchase the product)

         i   is the number of time periods passed

         k   is a constant representing the rate at which new customers are added once the product reaches maturity

This formula underlies the penetration curve illustrated in figure 10-12. The model was tested using data from a study on shoppers of a new dairy store (see figure 10-13).[94] The application shows an excellent fit of actual data to predicted penetration. It is important to note, however, that the success of application depends heavily on assumptions that must be made to quantify the variables.

Fig. 10-12. Penetration Function $[rx(l-r)^{i-1}+k]$

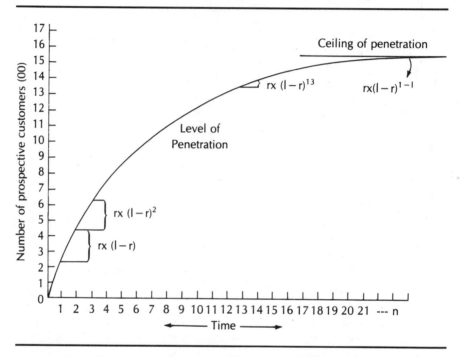

Robert F. Kelly, "The Diffusion Model as a Predictor of Ultimate Patronage Levels in New Retail Outlets," in R. M. Haas, ed., *Science, Technology and Marketing*, (1966), p. 742. Reprinted from *Science, Technology and Marketing*, published by the American Marketing Association.

Epidemiological Models As the name implies, these models are based on social interaction wherein early adopters "infect" the rest of the population. This, of course, occurs through interpersonal communication. Because the information moves slowly at first and more rapidly as more people becomes involved, these models follow the S-curve.

One model yields good predictions based on actual data.[95] The model is:

$$S(T) = mf(T) = P(T)[m-Y(T)] = [p+q\int_O^T S(t)dt/m][m-\int_O^T S(t)dt]$$

Where: S(T) is sales at time T

m is the total number purchasing during the period for which the density function was constructed (O,T)

Fig. 10-13. Comparison of Estimated and Actual Penetration Curves for a Retail Store

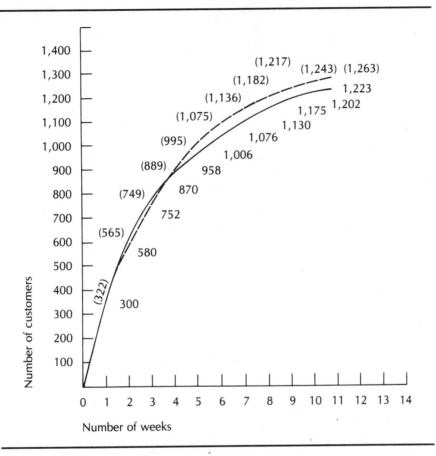

Note: Solid curve represents actual penetration; dashed curve, projected penetration.

Robert F. Kelly, "Estimating Ultimate Performance Levels of New Retail Outlets," *Journal of Marketing Research* 4(February 1967):17. Reprinted from the *Journal of Marketing Research*, published by the American Marketing Association.

P(T) is the probability of initial purchase at time T
Y(T) is the total number purchasing in the (O,T) time interval
p is the probability of purchase of the innovative product at T = O or the coefficient or innovativeness
q is the probability of purchase of an imitative product at T = O or the coefficient of imitation

Applying the model to sales of eleven products gave very good predictions. Figure 10-14 gives actual versus predicted sales of home freezers.

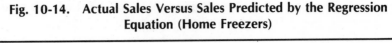

Fig. 10-14. Actual Sales Versus Sales Predicted by the Regression Equation (Home Freezers)

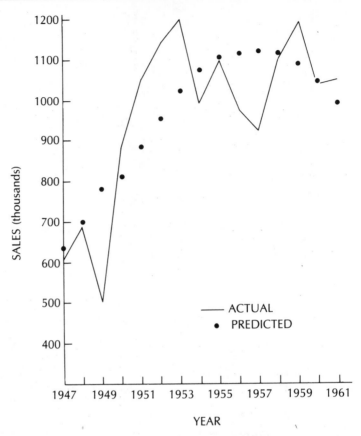

Reprinted by permission from Frank M. Bass, "A New Product Growth Model for Consumer Durables," *Management Science* 15, no. 5 (January 1969):220. Copyright 1969 The Institute of Management Sciences.

Deterministic Models Deterministic models esssentially attempt to relate product adoption to consumer variables. These variables may determine the way consumers move through the stage of adoption.

The Batton, Barton, Durstine & Osborn, Inc., advertising agency uses the Demon model (figure 10-15) to predict adoption based on advertising and promotion expenditures.[96] The model assumes that (1) consumers go through stages leading to the actual purchase of a new item, (2) probability of purchase increases with succeeding stages, and (3) virtually all variables are influenced by advertising.

Fig. 10-15.   Demon Model

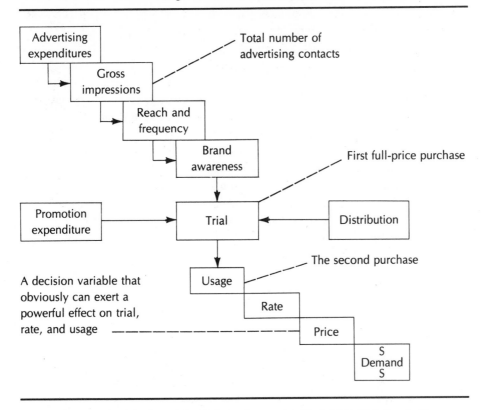

James K. DeVoe, "Plans, Profits and the Marketing Program," in Frederick E. Webster, ed., *New Directions in Marketing*, (1965). Reprinted from *New Directions in Marketing*, published by the American Marketing Association.

SUMMARY

One of a company's most important strategic functions is to generate and operationalize successful new product ideas. Many behavioral concepts are valuable in guiding this process.

A new product was defined as one that consumers perceive to be new. The degree of newness has major implications for company strategy and consumer response.

To provide a conceptual foundation for the study of new products, the product diffusion/adoption process was studied. Four significant concepts were discussed: innovation, innovator, adoption, and diffusion.

Innovation was defined as any idea or product perceived to be new and was discussed in terms of product usage, market penetration, and consumer perception classifications. An innovator was defined as someone who accepts something new soon after it is introduced. Correlates of innovative behavior were given as economic variables, social variables, communications, product-related variables, personality variables, innovativeness, and attitudinal variables. The adoption process represents the stages through which an individual passes in accepting a new product for ongoing use. Several models advanced to detail this process included adoption process schemes and hierarchy of effects schemes. Diffusion was defined as the aggregate of all individual adoptions over time. The elements of diffusion were given as the innovator, communication from one individual to another, social system, and time.

CHAPTER 10   STUDY REVIEW

Important Terms and Concepts

Innovation
Innovator
Adoption
Diffusion
Innovativeness

Questions

1. List the primary and secondary functional and psychological qualities for a new pair of jeans.

2. Evaluate the three classes of definitions of innovation.

3. Why is it important to study innovators?

4. What are the characteristics of innovators? Are they consistent across products and buying situations? Why?

5. Discuss the stages in the adoption process, and cite the reasons for disagreement among researchers as to the nature of the adoption process.

6. Describe the components of the diffusion process. How might your knowledge of this process aid you in introducing a new product?

7. Differentiate among the various models of diffusion.

11

Product:
Influences
and Strategies

The previous chapter looked at new products in a very general way. This chapter takes more of a microview, considering behavior-based concepts and strategies for both new and ongoing products. Following a discussion of new product issues, the chapter turns to positioning, personality, and interpersonal forces.

As noted earlier, the physical product is not what the consumer seeks and buys. Instead, a product represents a bundle of need satisfactions. The meaning of a product does not lie in its form but in its function and the psychological and sociological overtones of the needs that it satisfies. As such, a product may mean different things to different market segments. One objective of consumer research is to learn what products or potential products mean to various market segments. Product appeals and promotion efforts are most effective when they are relevant to consumers in terms of portraying roles and symbols that are perceived as being accurate and realistic in their own terms.[1] Product strategy can be most effective when the subjective side of products is kept in mind.

New Product Strategy

New products are the lifeblood of many firms. Consumer desires and tastes are constantly changing. Competitors constantly pressure one another as they jockey for position in the marketplace. New products fail much more often than they succeed. To minimize losses from new product failures, marketers should concentrate on learning and meeting consumer needs. However, discovering those needs and translating them into viable products is a complex and often frustrating process.

Consumer Needs

Chapter 9 outlined a number of techniques for discovering consumer needs. In general, product usage may give the best clues to unmet but significant consumer problems. This is based on two premises.

1. People seek the benefits that products provide rather than the products per se. Specific products or brands represent the available combinations of benefits and costs.
2. Consumers consider the available alternatives from the vantage point of the usage contexts with which they have experience or the specific applications they are considering. It is the usage requirement that dictates the benefits being sought. [2]

There are several reasons for basing new products on consumer needs. First, needs represent tension states and, as such, are uncomfortable for consumers. If a product is perceived as meeting an existing need, those who have the need may react fairly rapidly. Engineers and financial analysts had a strong and immediate need for rapid and convenient computational capability, something computers and slide rules were not then providing. The pocket calculator was accepted immediately upon introduction in spite of an initially high price.

Second, in order to move consumers to action, they must be effectively motivated. The motivated state is founded on need recognition, has some sort of driving force or energy mobilization, and is goal directed. Thus, for consumers to move into the motivated state, preparatory to purchase, they must become aware of an *unsatisfied* need: a satisfied need does not motivate. Marketers must search for these areas of consumer dissatisfaction.

Discovering consumer needs is no simple task since consumers may be unwilling or unable to communicate their needs. What's more, even if a company discovers a consumer need and develops a product to meet that need, the product must appeal to a sufficient number of people and be priced and promoted so as to communicate potential need satisfaction.

Some Problems in New Product Marketing

Why do some new products succeed, bringing millions of dollars to innovating companies, while others fail, often with great losses? The answer is not simple, and certainly we cannot say that "good" products succeed while "bad" products fail. Many products that function well and seem to meet consumer needs have fallen by the wayside. Sometimes, virtually identical products exist in the market at the same time with one emerging as profitable while the other fails. McNeal Laboratories' Tylenol has become successful as an aspirin substitute, yet Bristol-Meyers entered the test market at about the same time with Neotrend, also a substitute for aspirin, which quickly failed.

Of course, many products fail because they don't work or don't hold up to consumer use, but some quirk of consumer behavior is probably more likely to be the problem. Naturally, we won't concern ourselves here with engineering problems —we want to know how consumers' behavioral response patterns may catapult a product to success or doom it to failure.

The nature of the product is a factor in its success or failure, but the important

onsumer's perception of the product's need-satisfying capability. Any
onception should be aimed at meeting a customer need, and the
motion should seek to communicate that need-satisfying quality and
tomer to try the product. Often, attitude change is involved, and,
hanges in life-style may be sought.

npany walks a tightrope. A new product is more likely to be
esents a truly novel way of solving a customer problem; but this
ied too far, may ask the customer to learn new behavior patterns.
ake the change if the perceived benefit is sufficient, but inertia
ers will often not go to the effort that is required. During the
eventies Bristol-Meyers was plagued with new product failures
of these problems.[3] In 1967 and 1968 the company entered the
ion advertising campaign for Fact toothpaste, a dentifrice billed
nd an $11 million campaign to promote Resolve, a direct
eltzer. Both products failed quickly, not because they didn't
vas no consumer need but apparently because consumers just
could see shift from an already satisfactory product to a different one
that promised no new benefit. At the opposite extreme, the company asked customers to alter their life-styles drastically by switching from the time-honored bar
of soap to Moisturette, a gel to be used as a cleanser, shampoo, and bubblebath
maker. Again, a failure—consumers were just not willing to make such a radical
change.

New Products and Consumer Learning

The new product represents something of a learning problem. New products may
be classified as high learning or low learning. Low-learning products are those that
require a minor change in consumer behavior or those for which the advantage is
so obvious to the consumer that it does not need to be explained. High-learning
products may require extensive explanation before consumers will adopt. The important consideration here is that the marketer recognize which situation is faced and
develop a marketing strategy accordingly.

New product success may be a function of generalization and discrimination
in learning. Generalization, as noted in chapter 5, is the process by which we extend
what we know about one phenomenon to other phenomena. For example, although
a house, a shed, and a skyscraper are quite different, you have no difficulty in
identifying each as a building. If asked, you could explain the relationship that
categorizes these different structures together. When a new product appears on the
market, potential buyers should be able to identify it as consistent with their needs
and expectations. The product should fit—it should be identifiable and classifiable
by the consumer. Products that are too different from what consumers currently
expect and accept run high failure risk.

Philco got the idea, some years ago, of introducing a new streamlined TV set.
For the first time, a TV set was designed as a technical instrument, quite different

from anything the consumer had seen. They immediately ran into a generalization problem. The Predicta was slim, with a swivel picture tube that could be detached from the control unit and placed anywhere in the room.[4] Consumers, however, did not generalize the new set as an acceptable addition to the living room. Consumers saw TV sets as part of the living room decor, and this technical instrument was not perceived as furniture. Consumers had learned what constituted an acceptable living room addition, and the Predicta did not fit.

Discrimination represents the learned differences between phenomena. A small child may learn the word *puppy* and apply it to everything from cows to sawhorses, but the child soon learns to discriminate among various four-legged objects. Similarly, consumers learn to differentiate various products and brands. To be successful a new product should be perceived as different from existing products.

Some rules have been advanced for new product success based on principles of discrimination.[5] First, a new product is most likely to succeed if it is obviously superior to existing products. The pocket electronic calculator was an instant success because it filled a real consumer need, and its superiority over desk calculators and slide rules was readily apparent. A study of 100 new grocery brands showed that significantly better new products substantially outperformed others (see figure 11-1).[6]

Fig. 11-1. Successful and Unsuccessful New Products

Difference from Competitive Product	50 Successful New Products	50 Unsuccessful New Products
Significantly better performance, higher price	22	4
Marginally better performance, higher price	3	6
Better performance, same price	12	0
Same performance, lower price	4	0
Same performance, same price	8	15
Same performance, higher price	1	15
Worse performance, same or higher price	0	10
Total	50	50

Reprinted by permission of the *Harvard Business Review*. Exhibit from "Why Most New Products Fail" by J. Hugh Davidson (March-April 1976). Copyright © 1976 by the President and Fellows of Harvard College; all rights reserved.

Second, even if the new product is not better, it may succeed if it is demonstrated to be different from existing products. Procter and Gamble was able to communicate their product's softness by instructing people not to "squeeze the Charmin." It's debatable whether Charmin is softer, tissue for tissue, than other toilet papers, but because it's fluffed as it's rolled, it *feels* softer when you squeeze the roll. Charmin reached the number one sales position in just a few years.

Third, new products that are identical with existing products have the highest failure rate. There are identical products that succeed, but success is generally based on psychological differentiation. Undifferentiated products are vulnerable to inroads from superior products. Completely undifferentiated products, such as fresh fruits and vegetables, fall into this category. Even here, a perceptive marketer may be able to differentiate. Several years ago, the Batton, Barton, Durstine & Osborn (BBD&O) advertising agency was asked to help promote the products of the United Fruit Company. Bananas are bananas, true, but BBD&O found that United Fruit was breaking the huge banana stalks into small bunches and packaging them for easier handling. BBD&O determined that this led to fewer bruises on bananas. Since consumers often judge the quality of bananas by their external appearance, fewer bruises should mean more sales. But how do you brand a banana? With the Chiquita sticker, of course, and a commodity was turned into a successful brand.

L'Eggs panty hose is another good example. A problem with panty hose was bagginess. Little Prunes, L'Eggs, and several other brands began to promote on the basis of good fit. L'Eggs won for several reasons. Its egg-shaped packaging was distinctive. It was distributed through supermarkets where it received excellent exposure to potential buyers at a reasonable price, and the advertising communicated its benefit dramatically with, "Our L'Eggs fit your legs, they hug you, they hold you, they never let you go." The consumer need was recognized, and consumers were effectively taught to discriminate L'Eggs from other brands.

Some Principles of New Product Introduction

What else can we learn from the study of consumer behavior that will help make more product successes and fewer failures? There are really no hard and fast rules, but several general principles seem valid.

1. Solve a real problem for your prime prospect.
2. Communicate product benefits, not product attributes.
3. Prepare an adequate attitude-changing strategy.
4. Position your product effectively against competition.
5. Time your product introduction for maximum impact.

Solving Problems Solve a real problem for your prime prospect. Consumer needs are based on unsolved problems that lead to the tension state we defined as a need. In the consumer decision process model discussed in chapter 2, the consumer is pictured as entering the purchase decision process via the recognition of an un-resolved problem—actually a need state. The real question here is, What constitutes a consumer problem? Consumers have all sort of problems. The marketer's job is to identify problems that are significant enough to a sufficient number of consumers to yield profits for the innovating company. The prime prospect is sometimes referred to as the "heavy half." Generally, a very large portion of product sales come from a relatively small proportion of buyers. Gillette observed in the 1960s that with men's hair styles getting longer, the current hair dressings were likely to be inadequate. No longer would a greasy or slicked-down look do. Thus, the Dry Look was born and overtook Vitalis's twenty percent plus share of market in only four years.[7]

The Procter and Gamble Pampers story represents another company's successful bid to satisfy real customer needs.[8] A grandfather baby-sitting for his first grandchild decided there had to be something better than cloth diapers or the then-available disposables. Cloth diapers meant handling, storing, and washing soiled diapers and folding and putting away clean diapers. On the other hand, the disposables were neither as absorbent nor as strong as cloth diapers. The grandfather was not only a consumer but a Procter and Gamble engineer as well. He persuaded the company to pursue the idea, and after several years of product development, a few test market flops, and a fair number of R and D dollars, the company came up with Pampers—an absorbent, reasonably priced product. To show you just how important finding the right consumer problem is, consider Baby Scott, introduced by Scott paper company at about the same time Procter and Gamble entered the market with Pampers. The problem Scott announced and "solved" was sticking the baby with the diaper pins. While that might be a problem for some, it was not perceived as a significant problem by enough consumers, and Scott lost $12 million.[9] The promised solution "keeps baby drier," accompanied by a product that delivered the solution, gave Procter and Gamble an outstanding success.

Product Benefits versus Attributes Communicate the benefit of the product to the consumer—not a product attribute.[10] Consumers do not buy what a product is, they buy what it does. As Charles Revson, founder of the Revlon Company put it, "We're not selling cosmetics, we're selling hope and beauty." Buyers of cosmetics are not concerned with the composition or attributes of the products—they are concerned with what the products will do for them.

One recent product failure represents an excellent example of a company's promoting a product attribute. Vitamin E was the hottest wonder-cure around when the Mennen Company decided to incorporate it into their new deodorant, Mennen E. The company budgeted $12 million for the first year to tell the world in its advertising headlines, "Incredibly, Vitamin E is a deodorant." The world was not impressed. The addition of Vitamin E represented merely a meaningless product attribute. There was no benefit apparent to the consumers that would solve any significant problem. The result was a costly product failure for the Mennen Company.

The Nestlé Company, on the other hand, had a real consumer benefit in their Taster's Choice freeze-dried coffee. The coffee, although prepared instantly, tasted fresh-brewed. Their commercials told the story. Not only do you have to have a desired product benefit, you must communicate that benefit in such a way that consumers perceive the benefit and perceive that the benefit is somehow unique to the brand offered. General Foods' freeze-dried coffee offered the same consumer benefit as the Nestlé product but lost out to Taster's Choice because coffee drinkers didn't really perceive Maxim as unique and separate from Instant Maxwell House. In other words, Maxim was just another instant coffee. But Nestlé presented Taster's Choice by putting a handle and spout on the jar in the commercial and pouring coffee like fresh perked out of the jar with the words, "Looks, smells, and tastes so much like ground-roasted, fresh-perked coffee that if you didn't know the difference, you couldn't tell the difference." There was no question in the consumer's mind what the Taster's Choice product benefit was. This type of communication successfully capitalizes on a real consumer need and motivates the consumer to buy.

Prepare to Change Attitudes If you know you have a high-learning product—that is, one that requires an extensive change in consumer attitude and/or life-style, prepare an adequate attitude-changing strategy. If you have an obvious consumer benefit that will solve a significant consumer problem without seeking major changes in consumer behavior or attitude, your only real challenge is to communicate your story to the perspective buyer adequately. But, if you are asking for a major shift, use the full spectrum of attitude change strategy. In chapter 6 we looked at the structure of attitudes and cited three structural dimensions of attitude: cognitive, affective, and behavioral. An effective strategy for major attitude change logically involves working on each of these components.

One of the best examples of the application of this idea was employed by the Vicks' Company in the 1968 campaign that took Nyquil into the national market. Nyquil was really a potential flop. At the time the product entered the market, cold symptom relievers were, aside from simple cough remedies, largely pills or capsules. Taking liquid for nasal congestion represented a pretty major change, almost on a par with Analoze, the failed analgesic to be taken without water. But Nyquil represented a solution to a significant consumer problem, and Vicks' communicated the solution convincingly enough to effect major attitudinal and behavioral change.

One of the worst things about a cold is that it's hard to get a good night's sleep. The general-use cold remedies weren't really strong enough to give the level of relief needed at night when cold symptoms tend to be at their worst. One of the side effects of most antihistamines is to make you sleepy. Some products add caffeine to counter that affect. But, if you made a special-use product to be taken only at night, you could capitalize on the sleep-inducing effects of the antihistamines. So, enter Nyquil, a product specially developed for nighttime use. But how to communicate the benefit to the market? How does one change America's habits and attitudes toward cold remedies?

The strategy masterfully influenced each of the components of attitude. The first job, of course, was to influence the cognitive component. To create awareness of the Nyquil name, the company used an interesting technique that had America saying "Nyquil" back to their television sets. After explaining that Nyquil was an extra strength product to relieve nighttime cold symptoms, the announcer explained, "Nyquil" is a very difficult name to remember, so I'll say it for you three times— Nyquil, Nyquil, ... " That's right, he didn't say it the third time. After waiting a few seconds, the audience, seeking closure, repeated, mentally or aloud, "Nyquil" the third time. Nyquil was no longer a difficult name to remember—it was unforgettable.

Now for phase two. The affective component involves our like or dislike of a phenomenon. Vicks' second objective was to create positive feelings toward the product, and the company accomplished this by applying classical learning theory. By pairing an unconditioned stimulus that gives rise to an unconditioned response with a conditioned stimulus (or to-be-conditioned stimulus), a response similar to the unconditioned response can be elicited when the conditioned stimulus is presented (see figure 11-2).

Fig. 11-2. Classical Conditioning Applied to a Marketing Problem

Unconditioned Stimulus	Unconditioned Response
Husband tells his sick wife that he loves her and wants her to get well. Wife responds, "You're a good husband."	Feelings of love and understanding on the part of the viewer.

Conditioned Stimulus	Conditioned Response
A prominently displayed bottle of Nyquil and husband giving wife a dose of Nyquil.	Same warm, glowy feeling.

What happens here? In the commercial we have a wife, obviously suffering with a miserable cold. Enter hubby with much comforting and soft words. Quoting loosely here: "I know you feel terrible, dear, but I've got something here that will make you feel better. Nyquil will unclog your nose and stop those aches and pains and that fever, and it will help you sleep." Wife (strongly nasal), "Oh, thank you, dear, you're such a good husband." A tender scene—you can't help but feel warmth and love. And, of course, there's Nyquil. After you've seen this loving interlude a few times, you are conditioned. The next time you hear the word "Nyquil" or see the bottle on the shelf in the store, you will be hard-pressed not to feel a little warm and glowy inside.

So much for phase two. The market is now aware of the Nyquil name and of its benefits, and they are positively disposed toward it as well. But old habits die hard. Consumers are not automatons to be programmed and manipulated. Even at this point, many will be unwilling to put away their Dristan and Contac, even just for the night. We still need to approach the third attitude component. Consumers may know a product and even feel quite positively toward it, but they still may not buy. There is an effort and a risk associated with buying a new product, and consumers satified with their old brands may not be willing to shake the inertia that binds them to habitual buying patterns. Vicks' was not to let the behavioral challenge go unanswered. There are several alternatives for a company trying to induce trial of a new product. All seek to reduce risk. Cents-off offers, money-back offers, premiums, unconditional money-back guarantees, a strong, well-known company standing behind the product, and endorsements by well-known and reliable personalities are widely used. But Vicks' opted for an expensive but effective technique called · sampling. Vicks' sent two-dose free samples to consumers all over the United States. The product arrived at the beginning of cold season. When a cold struck, consumers didn't have to go to the store to buy a remedy and be faced by Nyquil along with a plethora of competing products on the shelf. The small bottle of Nyquil was there on the shelf to be administered on the first night of cold symptoms. Now the payoff. After taking Nyquil with its large concentration of antihistamines, pain reliever, and twenty-five percent alcohol content, cold sufferers really didn't care about the cold any more—they slept. The product worked, America went out and bought the full-sized bottles, and a product success was in full bloom.

The strategy-paid off, and Nyquil is still with us, along with its newer daytime counterpart. What could easily have been a product fiasco because of the requirement of a too drastic behavior change became a success because the company carefully led the consumer through attitude change by directly confronting each dimension of the attitude.

New Product Positioning A good product that solves a problem and communicates that solution in terms of benefits should be effectively positioned for maximum effect. Positioning and repositioning are covered in detail in the next two sections, so the concepts will be just touched upon here as they particularly relate to new product strategy. Essentially, there are three major positioning mistakes: (1) insigificant problem approached, (2) confusion in product image or function, and (3) a mismatch between the product appeal and its performance.[11]

Because companies try so hard to find consumer problems to solve, they often find problems that exist, but nobody really cares if they get solved. Or, at least, nobody is willing to pay for the solution. Several detergents that have been put into tablet form represent a good example of this. Apparently, somebody thought that having to measure detergent accurately enough to get best washing results was a difficult and time-consuming task for busy housewives. One company aimed its advertising at working wives who needed all the time they could get and shouldn't have to waste time measuring detergent. However, the time involved in measuring detergent is infinitesimal and the cost of the tablet is significantly greater than powder. Thus, tablets have never really caught on, even though more and more women are finding employment outside the home.

Confusion in product image or function can also be deadly for a product. It may arise from several sources. The name of the product can be a problem. For example, Revlon introduced Super Natural hairspray in the early 1960s and lost several million dollars in the process because super means more holding power, and natural means less holding power. The consumer couldn't figure out just what the product was supposed to do.[12]

Mismatched positioning has been called the greatest single problem in advertising communication because it is prevalent with both new and established products.[13] The challenge here is to determine the most effective combination of consumer appeal and product performance. In other words, what aspect of the product represents its most profitable need satisfier relative to what consumers want? Many products are not well matched to their market potential—some can recover if repositioned, others cannot. A good example of a product that was originally mismatched with a market and was subsequently repositioned for better profitability is Right Guard deodorant.

Right Guard deodorant was positioned as a man's deodorant until 1963. At that time a switch in advertising was made with the claim, "the perfect family deodorant because nothing touches you but the spray itself." Sales increased by $20 million annually. The new appeal was more in line with product performance. Note that the product itself did not change. Only consumer perception was changed by a shift in promotional appeal.

Timing the Introduction Timing of the product introduction can be an important factor. More than once a product has entered the market at the wrong time. Consumers could not perceive a need at the time, the promotional appeal wasn't right for the time, or there were just too many similar products coming on the market at the same time. There is a tendency for a lot of "me-too" products to follow a successful new product entry. Some of these will be successful—some even more successful than the innovator—but it is important to try to time for best impact. More important, though, may be not getting in too big a hurry to enter the market with an inferior product. Consumers' first perceptions often stick. It's generally better to wait for adequate testing and possible improvements to achieve a stronger position rather than to sacrifice image.

Obviously, there are other factors involved in applying consumer behavior knowledge to new product strategy, but consumer needs, motivation, perception, learning, and attitude covered here represent the major concepts. Some other aspects, such as social class and personality (covered in the product adoption area), are important conceptually but are not so significant in a strategic sense as those discussed here.

Positioning

The management of the firm's product offering often involves creating a specific market niche for a product. Because a product is a combination of physical attributes and perceived consumer benefits, market segmentation studies tell us that different consumer groups seek different things from the products they buy. The management of product image is referred to as positioning. The term *product positioning* is used in reference to the objective features and functions of products.[14]

There is really no universally accepted definition of positioning, but it may be considered a combination of product differentiation and market segmentation.[15] Positioning means making a product stand out from competing products—to be selectively perceived among a variety of products and marketing strategies. Influencing consumer perceptions may involve fundamental changes in the product itself, or it may mean changing package, price, image, promotion, or other strategic variables.[16] Position could be defined as the image consumers have of a given product or brand relative to their perception of similar products or brands.[17]

Positioning strategy is part product strategy and part promotion strategy. Positioning involves a six-step process:

1. Determine the wants and needs of selected market segments.
2. Analyze the benefits of your product compared with those of competitors serving the selected market segments.
3. Determine how important the identified benefits are to the target market.
4. Look at how the target market views the benefits offered by competitors.
5. Adjust your product benefits to meet the needs of the target market, especially those not currently met.
6. Promote your product to create the image you want the target segment to perceive.[18]

Positioning requires that consumer needs be analyzed relative to current product offerings from competitors. This may be accomplished by numerous techniques. Obviously, you could simply ask a consumer what product characteristics are most significant in making a purchase decision and the degree to which various brands possess those characteristics. The method is simple, but respondents may have difficulty in naming relevant purchase criteria and differentiating among brands.

Perceptual mapping may be helpful in identifying the relative positions existing brands hold and discovering areas of unmet need. A given product may have numerous attributes and potential benefits, but consumers will generally tend to judge it and competing products on relatively few characteristics.[19] Chapter 3 defined cues as stimuli that consumers have learned to use in judging purchase phenomena. For example, a friendly salesperson may be considered honest. The overall price level of a supermarket may be judged by the store's price for hamburger. A prospective buyer may try to predict the quality of a car by kicking its tires. A smile, a price, a design, or almost any physical or psychological phenomenon associated with a product may represent the differentiating characteristic that will serve as the basis for selecting a particular product or brand.

Perceptual mapping often uses multidimensional scaling (MDS). Figure 11-4 uses two variables for simplicity's sake, but computer analysis can treat several characteristics simultaneously.[20] Obviously, the various toothpastes appeal to quite different people. Figure 11-5 identifies characteristics of the users of various brands of toothpaste. These characteristics give excellent fodder for promotional appeals that could differentiate brands in the minds of various market segments.

Aim represents a superb example of successful positioning. Refer again to figure 11-4. If Aim were not in the pleasant flavor/good decay prevention quadrant, there would be no brand to serve this market segment, leaving a major gap in the market. This fact seems pretty significant, since figure 11-5 shows children to be favorably disposed to good flavor, and they also need decay prevention. Aim entered the market with strong product differentiation and good position. The product was also the first gel to attack the tooth decay problem (Close-Up is a gel, but it doesn't have

Fig. 11-3

BIG SHAMPOO NEWS!

Try the shampoo that wins over 8 leading shampoos— New Improved Agree Shampoo.

—the tests—

Hundreds of women across the country ages 14-45 recently tested New Improved Agree Shampoo against 8 leading shampoos. The results of these independent studies could change your mind about your current shampoo.

VS. **The leading balsam & protein shampoo**
Agree was preferred for lather and manageability.

VS. **The leading baby shampoo**
A majority of women tested preferred Agree for total performance.

VS. **The leading pH shampoo**
The majority of women who expressed a preference felt that their hair was cleaner with Agree.

VS. **The leading herbal shampoo**
The majority of women who expressed a preference felt that their hair was more manageable with Agree.

VS. **The leading dandruff shampoo**
The majority of women who expressed a preference felt that their hair had more body with Agree.

VS. **The leading blow dryer shampoo**
The majority of women who expressed a preference felt that their hair stayed clean longer with Agree.

VS. **The leading economy shampoo**
The majority of women who expressed a preference felt that their hair was less oily and greasy with Agree.

VS. **The leading gold formula shampoo**
Agree was significantly preferred for manageability.

VS. **All of these shampoos**
Most women said *they preferred Agree overall.*

All comparison tests were conducted by an independent research firm using national statistical samples in 1978.

New Improved Agree shampoo helps stop the greasies.
A major problem with all hair types is that hair gets oily and greasy too soon after shampooing. We call this "the greasies."

Excess oil builds up on the scalp, spreads to the hair and attracts dirt and additional oil causing hair to lose body and become stringy and oily.

Tests prove that Agree is unsurpassed in its ability to help stop the greasies.

Unlike some shampoos, Agree shampoo contains no greasy feeling additives. So it cleans hair beautifully without leaving a greasy residue. That's why regular use of Agree helps stop the greasies between shampoos.

Hate the greasies?   You'll love new improved Agree.

There's a new improved Agree shampoo for your hair type.
Because everyone's hair is not alike. Agree offers you three Shampoo formulas: Regular Formula. Balsam & Protein. Oily Hair Formula.

New Improved Agree Shampoo helps stop the greasies.

By comparing the major characteristics and benefits of Agree shampoo with those of its competitors, S. C. Johnson effectively positions Agree simultaneously against all leading shampoos.

Courtesy of S. C. Johnson & Sons, Inc.

Fig. 11-4. Example of a Two-dimensional MDS for Toothpaste

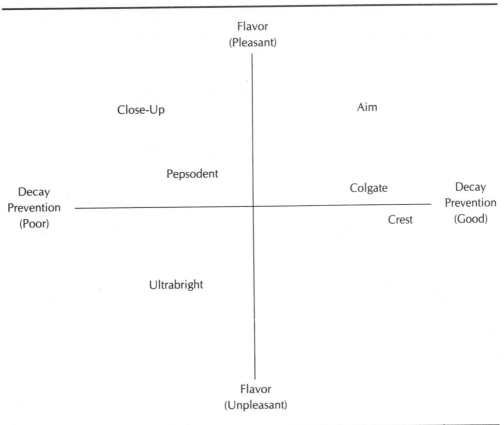

fluoride—a must for the decay prevention market). Early ads stressed that Aim's foaming action gets the toothpaste all over the teeth, and later ads played up the idea that because Aim tastes so good, children will brush longer and get more fluoride protection.

Notice that Aim actually fits two segments, but those two segments overlap heavily. The perceptual map showed that overlap very graphically, and a successful new brand could be projected from the map.

Repositioning

A company's original positioning strategy may prove less than satisfying for a variety of reasons. When a product achieves a particular image with a specific market segment it may exclude other profitable opportunities. Many product positions prove to be too narrow to afford the best profitability. Marlboro represents an excellent example of repositioning a product.[21]

When the Phillip Morris Company acquired Marlboro, the brand was perceived as feminine. Motivation research at the time indicated that smokers were

Fig. 11-5. Toothpaste Market Segment Description

Segment Name	Sensories	Sociables	Worriers	Independents
Brand(s) preferred	Aim, Pepsodent	Close-Up, Ultra Bright	Aim, Colgate, Crest	Private brands Brands on sale
Principal benefit sought	Flavor, product	Brightness, whiteness	Decay prevention	Price
Demographic characteristics	Children	Teens, young people	Large families, Children	Men
Personality characteristics	High self-involvement	High sociability	High hypochondriasis	High autonomy
Life-style characteristics	Hedonistic	Active	Conservative	Value oriented
Behavioral characteristics	Desire for good taste	Smokers, singles	Heavy users	Heavy users

Modified and adapted from Russell I. Haley, "Benefit Segmentation: A Decision Oriented Research Tool," *Journal of Marketing* 32 (July 1968):33. Reprinted from the *Journal of Marketing*, published by the American Marketing Association.

subconsciously seeking a sense of virility or potency from their cigarettes. Product image change could not be achieved by simply coming out and telling consumers that Marlboro is masculine and makes you virile. Image is created more subtly. The company approached the problem by creating advertising that pictured rugged-looking men in such masculine occupations as cowboy or sailor. The man in the ad had a tatoo and smoked a cigarette, but no suggestion was made in advertising copy that smoking Marlboro made you masculine or even that the model was smoking a Marlboro.

Since items in close proximity are perceived as being related, consumers naturally assumed that the virile man in the picture was smoking a Marlboro, and the logical conclusion was that Marlboro is for virile, masculine types. Since consumers drew their own conclusion, the ad was credible and they learned a new image for Marlboro. The cigarette soon achieved and still retains the most masculine image of any brand.

Lava soap, long perceived as a strong, hard-working soap for extremely dirty hands, recently used advertising appeals aimed at broadening its market by attracting family use. Johnson's Baby Shampoo successfully expanded its market by appealing to adults. For many years attempts have been made, with little success, to increase the cigar market by appealing to women ("Shouldn't a gentleman offer a Tipperillo to a lady?").

Personality and Product Use

The relationship between personality and product use has been researched with somewhat mixed results. The basic question is, What can we say about product selection and use given a consumer's personality? A great deal of research has been directed at identifying a relationship between personality and brand preference and selection. Chapter 12 will look at brand relationships.

The basic concepts of personality were covered in chapter 4, and you may want to refresh your memory on these ideas. One of the problems in trying to correlate consumer behavior with personality is to decide on just what definition and measurement device to adopt.

From a logical standpoint, a consumer's personality ought to predict buyer behavior. If personality represents a consistent response to stimuli, knowing these responses should allow some prediction of product use. However, there are several reasons why a person would expect the strength of relationships between product use and personality to be low. First, the size of relationship that can be obtained is partly dependent on the reliability of the measurement instrument. This is in turn dependent on the number of items contained in the instrument. Because of time and cost limitations, most marketing studies tend to use short, easily administered instruments that lead to low reliability. Second, the maximum correlation that can be achieved depends to a large extent on the reliability with which the buying behavior to be predicted is measured. Again, the tendency has been to use brief measures of questionable reliability. Third, many studies have attempted to predict specific actions or events based on personality. In trying to predict an individual's purchase of a particular brand, adoption of a specific new product, or purchase of a certain car, there is a problem of the reliability or consistency of the behavior itself. As mood, health, need states, and other extraneous factors change, a person can't expect to predict individual behavior on the basis of general predispositions. Fourth, personality theory itself suggests the following about relationships between personality and consumer behaviors:

1. The same personality trait can manifest itself in many ways, depending upon temporary conditions and circumstances. A high-esteem need could conceivably be met by purchasing a Cadillac or a Volkswagen.

2. Identical behavior in two individuals may be grounded in entirely different traits. Purchase of new fashion clothing may be based on exhibition needs, esteem needs, or need for conformity.

3. A personality trait can be expressed by behavior opposite to that expected. Freud calls this *reaction formation*. A mother who feels deep hostility toward her son may push him out of the way, or she may overprotect him, showering him with gifts and attention.

4. Behavior is seldom the product of a single need or personality trait; rather, it grows out of a complex mixture of needs. A housewife who bakes frequently may be fulfilling a need to show love to her family. She may also be seeking recognition, approval, and economical savings. Any one of these needs by itself might be insufficient to trigger behavior.

5. We all play roles. The roles we play may determine the way we manifest need satisfaction. For example, an artist seeking satisfaction of an achievement motive may dress shabbily or extremely to "play the role." A business person, on the other hand, may reflect achievement motivation through fashionable and conservative dress.

6. People are members of varying cultures and subcultures. Seeking to conform to the informal dictates of particular social strata may lead to a working-class person satisfying recreation needs through hunting while an upper-status person may turn to golf or reading for recreation. [22]

When you consider all these limitations it's a wonder that anything correlates. Actually, finding any significant correlation between personality and product usage may be a major discovery.

With these limitations in mind, let's look at some specific findings relating product use to personality. One study, which used the Thurstone Temperament Schedule to investigate personality differences among owners of different types of autos, found owners of convertibles to be more active, impulsive, and sociable than standard car owners and more active, impulsive, vigorous, and sociable than compact car owners. No significant differences were found between standard and compact owners. [23]

Another study investigated the relationship between personality and cigarette smoking using the Edwards Personal Preference Scale. [24] A significant difference among nonsmokers, smokers, and heavy smokers was discovered in a research study that rated smokers according to five personality characteristics. Individuals who scored higher on sex, aggression, and achievement were more likely to smoke and more likely to be heavy smokers. At the same time, those who scored higher on order and compliance tended to be nonsmokers or light smokers. The same study found smokers who scored high on dominance and change were more likely to be filter smokers, while those who scored high on aggression and automony tended to be nonfilter smokers.

Using the personality model advanced by Karen Horney in which people are typed as compliant (desire to be loved, wanted, appreciated, needed), aggressive (desire to excel and to achieve success, prestige, and admiration), or detached (desire to put emotional distance between themselves and others),[25] Joel Cohen investigated personality effects on the purchase of a number of products.[26] As in the studies previously cited, the product usage factor related to use or nonuse and usage rate. Compliant individuals were more likely to use mouthwash. Aggressive consumers were more prone to use manual as opposed to electric razors and to be heavy users of tea. The remainder of the relationships were either not significant or were related to specific brands.

Over the years, there have been many other studies that have suggested relationships between various personality variables and product decisions. In a comprehensive review of the topic, forty-three separate personality characteristics measured by seven different standardized personality tests and a number of nonstandard instruments were identified.[27] Most of the relationships were found to be quite weak, but even weak relationships may provide valuable insights to behavior and clues for strategy. Marketing decisions and strategies are based on group, not individual, behavior. The knowledge that certain personality traits are associated with specific kinds of buying behavior may lead to better promotion or packaging, for example, just as knowledge that consumers in a particular income class tend to behave in a certain way may guide marketing strategy.[28] Psychographic research, as discussed in chapters 3 and 9, holds a good deal of promise for research into relationships between personality and products. Since much psychographic research relates to brand preference and selection, discussion of specific applications is deferred to chapter 12.

Interpersonal and Group Influence

From the influence of another individual to the impact of our overall culture, we often find the selection and perception of the products we buy and use to be influenced by enculturation or socialization—the influence of significant others or social agents. Although we might like to think of our choice of products as the satisfaction of our own unique needs, we tend to conform to what we feel others think or expect of us.

Social influence may be manifested in a variety of ways, as discussed in chapters 7 and 8. Informational influence is accepted (internalized) if people perceive it to enhance their knowledge of their environment and/or their ability to handle that environment, e.g., purchasing a product. ~~Utilitarian influence~~ occurs when an individual complies with the preferences or expectations of another individual or group if that person perceives that they may give significant rewards or punishments, believes that behavior will be visible or known to them, and is motivated to receive the reward or avoid the punishment. Value-expressive influence relates to an individual's motive to enhance or support self-concept because the reference group may bolster that person's ego or because of a simple liking for the group.[29]

A reference group may be defined as any person or group that serves as an example of what an individual would like to do or be. Thus, reference group influence on consumer product decisions may come from other individuals, family, friends, social class, subcultures or the overall culture. The nature and degree of social influences from reference groups seem to vary by product category.

It has been suggested that a marketer should first determine the classification into which a product falls and then, if neither product nor brand appears to be associated strongly with reference group influence, advertising should emphasize the product's attributes, intrinsic qualities, price, and advantages over competing products. If reference group influence is operative, the advertiser should stress the kinds of people who buy the products, reinforcing and broadening where possible the existing stereotypes of users. The strategy of the advertiser should involve learning what the stereotypes are and what specific reference groups enter into the picture so that appeals can be "tailored" to each main group reached by the different media employed.[30]

With these basic notions in mind, the following sections consider some specific areas of social influence: culture, subculture, social class, and family.

Culture

Although culture has received less specific attention than other reference groups, it probably lies at the heart of product consumption. Fundamental cultural values and themes can determine the importance of products in general and the kinds of products preferred and consumed.[31] U.S. culture has tended to be quite materialistic and accepting of novelty. This has led to an expectation of an endless stream of new and improved products. However, it is important to recognize that U.S. cultural values are not universal. To be successful in cross-cultural marketing efforts, we must be careful to note cultural differences. The problem is that the very nature of enculturation makes our values so "natural" that we have difficulty in recognizing our own ethnocentricity. A product that is heavily used in one culture may be virtually nonexistent in another. Furthermore, a product used in one culture may be used in another culture but with an entirely different meaning. An example is the automobile and bicycle. In the U.S. culture, the automobile is a virtual necessity of life, providing transportation to nearly everyone. In fact, it has become a fundamental symbol of our society. On the other hand, the bicycle is used for recreation and conditioning. In many cultures, the bicycle is a staple of transportation, while automobiles are used by a very few.

Failure to understand cultural and language differences has led to many marketing debacles as U.S. firms attempt to market abroad. Colgate-Palmolive introduced Cue toothpaste in French-speaking countries, unaware that the word "cue" is an obsenity in French. When Goodyear sought to demonstrate the strength of its "3T" tire cord by showing it to be stronger than a steel chain (quite acceptable in the United States), Germans considered it to be uncomplimentary to steel manufacturers and therefore unacceptable.[32]

In a study of the relationship between commonly held cultural values and product usage, a value orientation matrix (figure 11-6) based upon four basic value dimensions and three alternative orientations for each was used to evaluate purchasing patterns for automobiles. The study evaluated full-size, intermediate, compact, subcompact, and sports models in terms of number of units owned.[33]

Fig. 11-6. Value Orientation Matrix

Value Dimension	Alternative Orientations		
Man's Relation to Nature	Subjugated by	In harmony with	Mastery over
Time Dimension	Past	Present	Future
Personal Activity	Being	Becoming	Doing
Man's Relation to Others	Lineal	Collateral	Individualistic

Walter A. Henry, "Cultural Values Do Correlate With Consumer Behavior," *Journal of Marketing Research*, 13 (May 1976):122. Reprinted from the *Journal of Marketing Research*, published by the American Marketing Association.

The alternative orientations for mankind's relation to nature suggest that people can simply take events as they come (subjugated by), can plan for contingencies (in harmony with), or overcome the environment (mastery over). The time orientation alternatives emphasizes tradition (past), living for today (present), or investing in the future (future). Alternatives for personal activity suggest the possibilities of being nonmaterialistic and enjoying life (being), learning and self-fulfillment (becoming), or results orientation (doing). In relation to others, mankind can be oriented to family or patriarchal structure (lineal), collective democracy (collateral), or basic individualism (individualistic).

The study found that these cultural values did relate to automobile ownership. Essentially, owners of full-sized cars tended toward lineal and subjugated orientations, owners of intermediate and subcompacts were collateral in relation to others, while nonowners of compacts were lineal. Sports car owners were oriented to the past, in harmony with their environment, and had a strong self-fulfillment (doing) perspective. Orientation toward patriarchial relations with others and a subjugated outlook toward the world and its events were associated with ownership of more automobiles on the average. For one- and two-automobile families, high auto ownership was associated with a becoming orientation, while for three- or more automobile families, being was correlated with heavier ownership.

In a broader sense, Montrose Sommers and Jerome Kernan treat the relationship between products and culture in terms of six categories of cultural patterns, identified by Talcott Parsons and Seymore Lipset.[34,35,36] According to them, cultural patterns can be distinguished by the degree to which people:

1. are either egalitarian or elitist
2. are prone to lay stress on accomplishment or inherited attributes
3. expect material or nonmaterial rewards
4. evaluate individuals or products in terms of objective norms or standards
5. focus on the distinctiveness of the parts (intensiveness) rather than the general characteristics of the whole (extensiveness)
6. are oriented toward personal, rather than group, gain

These values may have significant effects upon product consumption. Although we might consider U.S., Canadian, British, and Australian cultures to be similar, figure 11-7 suggests that some very distinct differences appear when viewed in terms of these values.

Fig. 11-7.   Rankings of Countries According to Six Variables

Pattern Variable	U.S.	Australia	Canada	Britain
Equal-Elite	2	1	3	4
Performance-Quality	1	2.5	2.5	4
Material-Nonmaterial	1	3	2	4
Objective-Subjective	1	3	2	4
Intensive-Extensive	1	2.5	2.5	4
Individual-Collective	1	3	2	4

Montrose Sommers and Jerome Kernon, "Why Some Products Flourish Here, Fizzle There," *Columbia Journal of World Business* (New York: Columbia University, March-April, 1967).

In the United States, where performance, not family origin, counts, there is a heavy emphasis on doing things—thus the abundance of leisure-related products. Since U.S. consumers perceive many distinct needs and ways of satisfying them (intensive orientation), they tend to be much more "gadget" oriented and acquire a great array of household and kitchen appliances, along with extras for cars and boats. The high level of materialism in the United States leads many products to become symbols of success. Because of an intensive value orientation, American consumers are most likely to notice small product differences, thus making great opportunities for product differentiation. On the other hand, Britain's extensive value orientation leads its consumers to be less interested in details and more concerned with make, manufacturing process, or accepted use.

Strategically, knowledge of a culture's values can aid a marketer moving into a foreign country in two ways. First, cultural values may indicate whether a given product will be acceptable. Second, if the product is deemed to be marketable, cultural values may indicate how the product should be marketed. Virtually all cultures are ethnocentric, and almost no product (the most notable exception being Coca-Cola) can be dropped into a culture without special attention to its unique characteristics.

Subcultures

Most cultures are not homogenous. They are made up of various subgroups that often exhibit different consumption patterns. As noted in chapter 7, there are numerous subcultures in the United States, including ethnic, age, and geographic.

Various ethnic subcultures in the United States characteristically prefer certain types of products and may have somewhat unique perceptions of products. While the specific relationships indicated in figure 11-8 may no longer hold, they do show the kinds of differences that might be expected.

Fig. 11-8. Acceptance of Products by Ethnic Subcultures

Product	Degree of Acceptance by			
	Italian Homemakers	Jewish Homemakers	Puerto Rican Homemakers	Black Homemakers
Frozen dinners	Low	Very Low	High	Moderate
Frozen red meat	Very Low	Low	Mod. High	Low
Frozen fruit pie	Very Low	Very Low	High	Low
Instant coffee	Very Low	High	Mod. High	Very Low
Cake mixes	Low	Very Low	High	Low
Dehydrated soups	Moderate	Low	High	Very Low

Milton Alexander "The Significance of Ethnic Groups in Marketing," in Lynn H. Stockman, ed., *Advancing Marketing Efficiency*, (1959). Reprinted from *Advancing Marketing Efficiency*, published by the American Marketing Association.

Several underlying forces seemed to cause the differences.[37] Italian homemakers had a strong ethnic preference for fresh meat and vegetables that led them to reject frozen meat and dinners. Black and Jewish homemakers also rejected these foods, but blacks rejected these along with the other foods in the study because of cost and a lack of freezer space. Jewish housewives did so because of dietary laws. Puerto Rican housewives were favorably disposed to all types of convenience foods because a large proportion of them were employed outside the home. Frozen fruit pies and cake mixes were rejected by Italian and Jewish homemakers because the sweets they consumed were either made at home or purchased at local ethnic bakeries.

Because blacks represent the largest of the ethnic subcultures, they have received special attention from researchers. There is some disagreement as to whether blacks really represent a unique consuming group. Certainly, there are wide variations in spending behavior among blacks, especially of varying income levels. Overall, when income level is held constant, there seems to be little consistent racial difference in expenditures for recreational goods (although blacks go to movies more and spend less on such expensive leisure products as boats and skis), home furnishings and appliances, personal hygiene products, and soft drinks. Blacks apparently spend less on food, housing, medical care, and automobile transportation and more on clothing, liquor (especially Scotch), tobacco, milk, and butter.[38] It should be noted that there is a fair amount of disagreement in the findings of the studies cited. Also, it seems that as time passes and as black incomes rise, they will become more and more similar in their product-purchasing behavior to middle-class whites.

Religious subcultures may have significant product demand differences—Orthodox Jews consume kosher foods, Mormons may not use coffee, tobacco, or alcohol, Christian Scientists may not use over-the-counter drugs. Specialized books, tapes records, pictures, and even tours may be specifically aimed at these subcultures.

The obvious age subcultures in the United States are children, teens, adults, and the elderly. The product needs of these groups vary considerably. Although the spending of children is strongly influenced by parents, they may, in turn influence adult spending. They are heavy consumers of toys, games, and candy. Teens are particularly heavy spenders in such areas as records and tapes, clothing, and entertainment.

The elderly as a target market also have unique product requirements. They tend to be heavy consumers of special housing, health products, diet and health foods, travel, leisure goods and services, special insurance, and investments. However, aside from promoting laxatives and dental adhesives, American marketers seem to largely ignore this segment. One note of caution should be extended here. Older people probably don't like to be reminded of their station in life by such items as "special old people shoes."[39]

There are distinct differences in product demand from one part of the country to another. Part of these differences derive from climatic variations, but part of the differences come from variations in local norms, as suggested in chapter 7. These factors result in the kinds of variations in product consumption shown in figure 11-9.

Social Class

An individual's social standing relative to others is strongly reflected in products owned and consumed. Social class is not created by the products a person owns, but the types of possessions that person will acquire are to some degree dictated by social

Fig. 11-9. Regional Consumption Differences

Product	Percentage reporting using once a week or more					
	Total	East	South	Mid-west	West	South-west
Regular chewing gum	26	17	40	30	24	26
Mouthwash	51	48	62	47	40	54
Men's cologne	61	58	72	61	55	71
Shaving cream in a can	55	55	54	55	45	54
Toothpaste	88	89	92	89	90	82
Regular coffee (nondecaffeinated)	62	59	63	58	72	66
Instant coffee (nondecaffeinated)	36	40	33	36	31	24
Hot tea	29	44	14	30	30	24
Iced tea (summer)	69	73	84	69	52	76
Regular soft drinks	53	46	67	53	35	63
Artificial sweetener	18	19	30	19	11	21
Nondairy powdered creamer (Coffee-mate, Cremora, etc.)	23	23	33	23	20	15
Potato chips	35	21	48	41	26	43
Fresh sausage	18	15	30	15	11	22
Bologna	33	30	23	36	31	28
Cottage cheese	32	27	17	41	40	30
Yogurt	5	9	2	4	11	3
Vitamin tablets	35	36	21	36	44	35
Domestic wine	14	15	5	16	28	8
Blended whiskey	11	16	4	13	13	7
Scotch	7	12	5	7	8	2

Product	Percentage owning					
	Total	East	South	Mid-west	West	South-west
Automatic dishwasher	43	44	42	42	56	56
Garbage disposal	28	11	8	35	50	44
Freezer	58	48	68	62	58	60
Water softener	13	6	1	21	14	9
Room air conditioner	41	45	45	42	28	37
Color TV set	77	79	65	83	83	77

Courtesy of Needham, Harper & Steers Advertising, Inc.

class. There is a dichotomy of influence between income and social class. Income determines what a person is able to buy, but social class can be a major influence on what product that person selects. A number of years ago it was suggested that occupational class was a better predictor than income in determining expenditure patterns for food and shelter.[40] Another study showed social class to be a better predictor than income in the purchase of dry instant milk, instant coffee, variety bread, powdered detergent, facial tissues, paper towels, and cottage cheese. However, for eighty-two other products studied, income was a better predictor than social class.[41] In a later study of thirty-six products, including furniture, appliances, clothing, and travel, only black and white TV and air travel were found to be more sensitive to social class than income.[42] It has been observed that income may be more influential than social class in determining participation or nonparticipation in a number of activities and possibly for products as well, but social class is a better predictor of frequency of participation.[43]

Whatever the case, it seems that the relationship between social class and product purchase and use is rather complex. Certainly, income does dictate the purchase of many products, but social class analysis seems to give the opportunity for fine tuning. Each social class has its over- and underprivileged segments, and social class and income may interact here to influence the products to be purchased. The overprivileged member of the upper-middle class may drive a Mercedez, while the underprivileged may buy a new Ford or Chevrolet (probably near the top of the line).[44] One researcher found the "average" income group in each social class tended to buy more foreign, economy, intermediate, and compact cars, while the overprivileged of each class owned more medium-sized and large cars and fewer foreign economy cars.[45]

Looking further at the relationship between specific products and social class, it has been noted that the way a person dresses correlates with social class, probably because of the high visibility of clothing.[46] Much of the difference comes in the way a person perceives clothing. One study found that working class women were more likely to consider a dress for a special occasion a luxury item than were middle-class women.[47] Because of mass distribution, fashion tastes are really not markedly different among different social classes,[48] but there is a tendency for people in the higher social classes to be more aware of fashion.[49]

Home furnishings and appliances are also sensitive to social class effects. Lower-class housewives tend to express themselves through their appliances as opposed to clothing.[50] The way the living room is furnished seems particularly influenced by social class. Lower-class families tend to place the TV in the living room and furnish around it, while higher status families tend to organize the living room for conversation and relegate the TV to a family room. Figure 11-10 shows the results of one study that viewed the differential furnishing habits of higher-versus lower-status families.

In addition to the specific products purchased, social class seemed to affect the way people acquire products. Higher social class families are heavier users of credit cards,[51] and the kinds of goods considered acceptable to charge differ among classes.[52] Lower-class consumers prefer to use bank credit cards for necessary and durable

Fig. 11-10. Analysis of Living Room Objects by Social Class

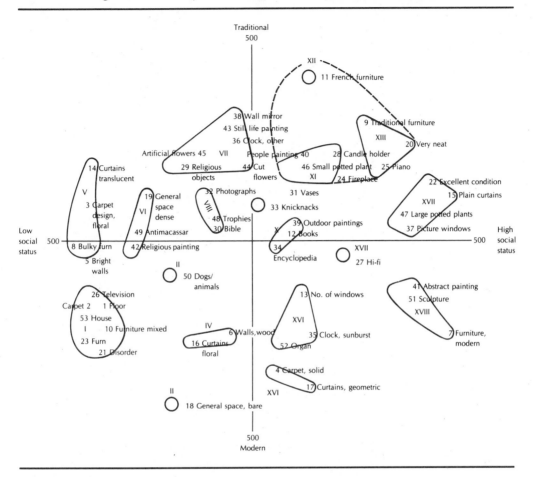

Edward O. Laumann and James S. House, "Living Room Styles and Social Attributes: The Patterning of Material Artifacts in a Modern Urban Community," *Sociology and Social Reseach* 54(April, 1970):326.

goods, such as appliances, furniture, and clothing. On the other hand, upper-class consumers tend to use their cards for luxury items, such as luggage and restaurant meals.

In general, it seems that markets for various products can be segmented along social class lines. Also, social class is a determinant of life-style, and it thus influences product-purchasing behavior. Although many products are not sensitive to social class, some seem to be, and the marketing manager must be aware of social status factors in designing product strategy.

Family

The family is often a strong force in determining the products to be purchased. In looking at the influences of various aged children in families, we have already noted

Fig. 11-11. Husband/Wife Influence on Nondurable Product Purchase Decisions

Product	Purchases By:		Share of Influence							
			Direct Influence				Indirect Influence			
			Product Decision		Brand Decision		Product Decision		Brand Decision	
	Wife	Husband	Wife	Husband	Wife	Husband	Wife	Husband	Wife	Husband
Baby food	82%	18%	91%	9%	91%	9%	89%	11%	89%	11%
Instant coffee	79	21	60	40	59	41	54	46	54	46
Cold/allergy tablets	73	27	68	32	66	34	65	35	65	35
Deodorant	73	27	61	39	63	37	61	39	61	39
Toothpaste	77	23	70	30	68	32	64	36	63	37
Gasoline	42	58	32	68	30	70	33	67	31	69
Gin	41	59	42	58	36	64	45	55	38	62
After-shave	51	49	16	84	18	82	18	82	18	82

Adapted from *Purchase Influence: Measures of Husband/Wife Influence on Buying Decisions*, Haley, Overholser & Associates, Inc., New Canaan, Conn., Sponsored by: *Family Weekly, Reader's Digest, Sports Illustrated, Time*, and *TV Guide*, (1975), pp. 13, 19, 21, & 23.

Fig. 11-12.   Husband/Wife Influence on Service and Durable Product Purchase Decisions

Share of Influence

Product	Purchase Decision Influence				Initiation				Information Gathering			
	Product Decision		Brand Decision		Product Decision		Brand Decision		Product Decision		Brand Decision	
	Wife	Husband	Wife	Husband	Wife	Husband	Wife	Husband	Wife	Husband	Wife	Husband
Automobile	38%	62%	33%	67%	22%	78%	22%	78%	18%	82%	18%	82%
Color TV	46	54	42	58	38	62	30	70	41	59	37	63
Washer	54	46	51	49	70	30	57	43	57	43	55	45
Vacuum cleaner	60	40	60	40	80	20	69	31	66	34	65	35
Camera	50	50	51	49	54	46	49	51	47	53	46	54
Life insurance	36	64	34	66	25	75	23	77	27	73	27	73
Vacation w/spouse	47	53	41	59	44	56	37	63	47	53	44	56

Adapted from *Purchase Influence: Measures of Husband/Wife Influence on Buying Decisions*, Haley, Overholser & Associates, Inc., New Canaan, Conn., Sponsored by *Family Weekly, Reader's Digest, Sports Illustrated, Time,* and *TV Guide,* (1975), pp. 27-29.

some significant influences. It is difficult to generalize about the roles of husband and wife in making purchase decisions. Traditionally, each spouse has played a fairly consistent role in evaluating products. The husband has tended to evaluate the more mechanical product attributes while his wife was more concerned about aesthetic factors. These are referred to as instrumental and expressive values; discussed in chapter 8. However, as marital roles change with women taking increasingly active roles outside the home and becoming more independent in the home, we are likely to see these relationships change.

Recognizing the dynamics of today's family, look at the roles in product decisions suggested in figures 11-11 and 11-12. Judging from the examples given, which incidentally represent only a small portion of the products studied, it is apparent that there is a major variation from product to product in the influence exerted by each spouse. Further development may change these relationships rather dramatically.

Product decisions are thus influenced by other persons. The more visable a product is and the more it tends to represent the self-image and personality of an individual, the more likely it is to be influenced by important others. We are socialized from childhood to learn to buy and consume products, and the influence of this socialization as it continues through life heavily influences our choice of product.[53]

SUMMARY

Product strategy is a significant aspect of the marketing manager's responsibility. Much of this strategy is based on consumer behavior.

New product decisions should be based upon unsatisfied consumer needs. These needs are satisfied by the benefits that products offer. Failure to consider needs that are relevant to consumer needs leads to many new product failures. Recognizing that consumers must learn about new products, a marketer can utilize the concepts of generalization and discrimination.

Five principles of new product introduction were advanced: solve a real problem for your prime prospect; communicate product benefits, not product attributes; prepare an adequate attitude-changing strategy; position your product effectively against competition; and time your product for maximum impact.

Positioning relates directly to consumer perception and learning. The image created by the marketer and communicated to the consumer is a vital determinant of product success or failure. Often, if a product is mispositioned, subsequent consumer anlaysis can suggest a new position that will be more viable.

Correlating personality with any aspect of consumer behavior tends to be frustrating and to lead to ambiguous findings. However, there is an indication that a person's personality may suggest the ways in which products are perceived and the kinds of products preferred.

Finally, the relationships that we have with others—from the overall culture to interaction with other individuals—may influence the products we buy. Products that are not universally owned may become symbolic of membership in or identification with particular groups. Also, our product-purchasing decisions are not made in a vacuum; we are often heavily influenced by significant others.

CHAPTER 11   STUDY REVIEW

Important Terms and Concepts

Product
New product
Product perception
Product benefits versus attributes
Positioning
New product positioning
Repositioning
Perceptual mapping

Questions

1. Why should new product development concentrate on reaching unsatisfied consumer needs?

2. Discuss the marketing problems associated with high-learning versus low-learning products.

3. Summarize the rules for new product success based on principles of discrimination.

4. Summarize the principles of new product introduction.

5. To what degree does personality seem to be related to product usage? Why?

6. How do other people influence our product purchase and usage?

7. Discuss the relationship between culture and product usage.

8. Why does product usage and acceptance vary across subcultures?

9. Discuss social class as it influences product purchase and consumption.

10. Why and how does product purchase influence vary across family members?

12

Branding
and Packaging

Product strategy is carried out at two levels. New products are conceived and marketed, and existing products and product lines are manipulated and modified to meet changing consumer needs and competitive activities. Part of this strategy revolves around cues that communicate the source, function, and quality of products. The product's brand, package, price, and physical characteristics are important cues the market strategist can control to influence consumer perceptions and attitudes.

This chapter will consider the major behavioral dimensions of the first two of these strategic variables. Three aspects of branding will be treated: brand image, brand loyalty, and brand strategy. Following this, the chapter considers packaging as a behavioral phenomenon. Pricing will be treated in chapter 13.

Brand Image

As you will probably remember from your basic marketing course, a brand is defined as a name, term, symbol, or design that identifies the products of a particular marketer and differentiates them from the products of others. A brand, however, is really more than this. As a cue to consumers, it communicates an image of quality, prestige, usefulness, and value. The brand image is not inherent to the product or brand; rather, it exists in the minds of consumers. Many companies set out very deliberately to create a particular brand image. In other cases, a brand image may be developed by consumers, and the marketer may discover the nature of the image through consumer research. Many brands try to be all things to all people, and they may end up with many inconsistent and fragmented images held by different consumers.

Brand image seems to be composed of at least six factors: (1) the nature of the product itself; (2) the price of the product; (3) the appeals used in promoting the brand; (4) the package; (5) the brand name; and (6) the stores that sell the brand. The combination of these factors lead consumers to perceive branded products as quite different from one another, even if they are objectively identical. Beer drinkers often form very strong perferences for "their" brands. Ask beer drinkers why they prefer a particular brand and you are likely to hear something about taste. However, experimentation shows that most beer drinkers cannot pick their favorite brand from among several brands without package or brand cues.[1]

Almost anything can act as a cue for consumers when judging a product. If there is no discernable quality difference between products, consumers often "create" something. A cola manufacturer advertises that consumers have chosen its brand as better tasting than its chief competitor in blind taste tests. However, the competing brand cried "foul." The brands were identified only by letters of the alphabet, but the advertiser's brand had been identified by a "favored" letter while competitors were given a "nonfavored" letter. The letter acted as a cue, and consumers were subconsciously picking the brand with the favored letter, even though they really couldn't tell the difference. Several experiments have shown that price and smell can also act as cues for judging product quality.[2,3]

Self-image and Brand Image

We all have perceptions of what we are and what we'd like to be. This perception is referred to as self-image or self-concept. An individual really has two self-images. The actual self-image is what the consumer thinks he or she is really like. The ideal self-image represents what the consumer would like to be.

As noted in the previous section, brands have images, too. In general, brand image is created by marketers through their positioning strategy. Given this, several ideas are relevant in explaining the relationships between symbolic brand image and self-image:

1. An individual has a self-concept.
2. The self-concept has value.
3. Because this self-concept has value, an individual will direct behavior toward furthering and enhancing self-concept.
4. An individual's self-concept is formed through the interaction process with parents, peers, teachers, and significant others.
5. Goods serve as social symbols and, therefore, are communication devices for the individual.
6. Using these goods as symbols communicates meaning to the individual and to others, causing an impact on the interaction and/or the interaction process and an effect on the individual's self-concept.
7. The consuming behavior of an individual will be directed toward furthering and enhancing self-concept through the consumption of goods as symbols.[4]

In general, research indicates that consumers do, in fact, buy brands to fit their self-image. One study found that buyers of a particular automobile brand perceive themselves to be similar to others who buy the same brand and different from owners of other brands.[5]

Fig. 12-1

Et Cetera

China
582-802 Nouveau Finish
W42 D17 H80 3/4
Two lights and three adjustable glass shelves
   behind leaded glass doors and glass end
   panels at top.
Two lights and one adjustable glass shelf
   behind leaded glass doors and glass end
   panels at bottom.
Adjustable glides.

Drexel is attempting to communicate the opportunity of expressing one's self-image through various styles of furniture. A single brand may thus fit a variety of self-images through different styles and models.

Courtesy of Drexel Heritage Furniture Inc.

There is a question of whether consumers seek to match their actual or ideal self-concept. Some buyers apparently match brand image with self-image, while others tend to match product image with ideal self-image.[6]

Brand Name

The brand name selected for a product is often significant in determining the success of a product. There are numerous rules and characteristics brand names should fit. A brand name should: (1) fit the product's design, color, and use; (2) help create and sustain the brand image; (3) distinguish the product from competing brands; (4) be descriptive of the product's attributes or benefits; and (5) motivate the consumer to buy. In addition, the brand name should be short, easy to say and remember, and communicate some sort of appropriate meaning when read. A good brand name can generate such feelings as security, reliability, trust, status, speed, power, sex appeal, confidence, strength, and gentleness.

The rules don't appear to be hard and fast, though. Some brand names seem to work even though they don't follow the rules. For instance, Orville Redenbacher's Gourmet Popping Corn certainly bends the rules a bit.

The brand name is an important component of the brand image, and it should contribute positively to the positioning of the brand. It should create a positive image while distinctly identifying the product and setting it apart from competitors. The importance of this distinct and unique position is evidenced by the fact that the Daniel Starch Corporation reports that twenty-five percent of people who noted TV commercials attributed them to the wrong company.[7] The brand name is so significant in communicating to the consumer that it often takes the place of information search, with the consumer relying almost totally on the brand in making a selection.[8]

Examples of poorly named products are Colgate 100, Mennon E, Williams W, Breck One, and Revlon Flex, Balsam, and Protein. These names do nothing to position the product, and they really have little potential to create a brand image. On the other hand, some well-named products include Dial soap, (for 24-hour protection), Close-Up toothpaste, Slender diet drink, Intensive Care skin lotion, and Head and Shoulders shampoo.[9] These brand names have the potential for clearly and distinctly positioning a product in the consumer's mind.

Animal names are among the earliest a child learns, and they arouse strong and consistent images within all of us. Names like Mustang, Bronco, Cougar, Cobra, Wildcat, and Pinto have successfully positioned automobiles. Mustang suggests freedom and individuality; cougar has speed, strength, and stamina; and a pinto is small but has strength and stamina.[10]

Some words and combinations of words are more strongly associated with and representative of certain product categories than others. Plural words seem to be more representative of cereals than singular words. One-syllable words are associated with cereals, while three-syllable words don't fit. Laundry detergents, on the other hand, are better represented by a singular word.[11]

With the enormous number of registered brand names in use, there is a problem of finding a name that's available for use and that elicits the right image.

As a result, coined words that have no existing image are often used. Nyquil, Novahistine, Comtrex, and Datril are examples of words that arouse no image in and of themselves, so the marketer must create an image through promotion. But there are some problems. An extremely ambiguous and novel brand name can arouse negative feelings in the minds of consumers.[12] This initially hostile reaction can be explained by the concept of "response uncertainty." The individual really doesn't know how to respond to the unfamiliar stimulus. If exposure has been minimal and if the brand name is totally unfamiliar, the consumer's ability to reduce the uncertainty through associative generalization (applying what is known about a familiar stimulus to the unfamiliar stimulus) is inhibited. The extreme ambiguity and novelty results in psychological discomfort (cognitive dissonance), which is translated into dislike.[13]

A negative attitude toward the new brand name can negatively influence a consumer's response to information about the product.[14] This problem, however, can be alleviated by repeated exposure to the brand name through promotion. Simply making a brand name familiar to the consumer will generally erase the negative feelings and replace them with a positive reaction. Liking a product is directly related to the amount of exposure to the brand name.[15] Coupling the new brand name with favorable or pleasant stimuli can further create positive image through classical conditioning.[16] Once a brand name has come to be preferred, it will tend to be more readily perceived than competing brands.[17] Thus, a familiar, preferred brand name will be selectively perceived, insulating it from competitors' promotional efforts.

Brand Attitude

Brand attitude overlaps brand image. Brand attitude relates specifically to the positive and negative feelings a consumer has toward a brand. In general, the proportion of people with favorable attitudes toward a brand is higher among its current users than among former users and lowest among those who have never used it. Attitude depends, in part, on how recently a consumer has used a brand.[18]

One question that is often raised is the degree to which brand buying behavior is related to brand attitude. Chapters 2 and 6 noted that purchasing behavior does not necesssarily follow attitude. Consequently, we cannot say that the purchase of a brand necessarily indicates a favorable attitude toward the brand. Conversely, positive attitude will not necessarily lead to brand purchase. Research does suggest that attitude change precedes new brand purchase, but attitude changes more after the purchase.[19]

Brand attitude can be changed from negative to positive by following the strategy of appealing to each of the three attitude components as outlined in the previous chapter. In addition, preference changes can be effected by providing information dissonant to present preferences and invoking the *majority effect.* If consumers believe that the majority of other people use a particular brand, they may switch preference. The weaker the preference is for the preferred brand and the higher the nonfavored brand is in the preference hierarchy, the more likely the damage. Preference switching is inversely related to age, socioeconomic status, and number of strong preferences indicated.[20]

Personality and Brand Selection

In general, efforts to correlate brand selection with personality have not been particularly successful. To the extent that brands have strongly differentiated images, we might suspect that various personality traits and types would be associated with certain brands.

The earliest study of brand usage and personality did not show a relationship, so there has been less attention to personality's influence on brand selection than there might otherwise have been.[21] Subsequent research has shown significant relationships, although the results are somewhat spotty and rather weak. Results are hard to categorize and compare since different researchers use different personality scales.

One study of brand and product use found some significant relationships with the personality types: (1) compliant (those who move toward people); (2) aggressive (those who move against other people); and (3) detached (those who move away from other people).[22,23] Figure 12-2 shows that some brand preferences were differentiated on personality, but not many. Old Spice users were more aggressive, while Right

Fig. 12-2. Study of Personality and Brands/Products

Product	Within-trait comparison[a]	Brand or category	N	Percent of high grouping in each brand or product category		
				C (n = 66)	A (n = 67)	D (n = 75)
Cigarettes	NS	Smoker	47	40	40	32
		Nonsmoker	83	60	60	68
Men's dress shirts	NS	Arrow	26	20	15	22
		Van Heusen	21	16	25	20
		Brand not known	15	8	5	12
		Other	67	56	55	46
Mouthwash	Compliant	Used	91	74	64	56
		Not used	54	26	36	44
Men's deodorant	Aggressive	Old Spice	33	34	41	24
		Right Guard	53	45	38	52
		Other	33	21	21	24
Men's cologne and after shave lotion	Aggressive	At least several times a week	119	88	91	82
		Several times a month or less	25	12	9	18

Toilet or bath soap	Compliant	Dial	50	47	36	31
		No preference	39	19	23	38
		Other	46	34	41	31
Men's hair dressing	NS	Not used	46	41	43	39
		Other	65	59	57	61
Toothpaste	NS	Crest	77	61	60	60
		Colgate	28	16	24	20
		Other	29	23	16	20
Razors	Aggressive	Electric	48	38	25	38
		Manual	92	62	75	62
Beer	NS	Coors	54	41	49	35
		Not consumed	29	19	19	24
		Other	60	40	32	41
Tea	Detached	At least several times a week	41	26	22	33
		Several times a month or less	116	74	78	67
Wine	Compliant	At least several times a month	38	35	33	23
		Several times a year or less	119	65	67	77
Metrecal and similar diet products	NS	At least a few times a year	18	15	12	11
		Never	139	85	88	89
Gasoline	NS	Standard	32	17	23	19
		Shell	32	28	18	23
		Other	83	55	59	58
Headache remedies	NS	Bayer aspirin	44	32	38	30
		Other aspirin	33	13	23	21
		Bufferin	23	18	11	15
		Other remedy	47	37	28	34

[a]High and low groupings on each trait were compared using the chi-square test. Differences significant at the .05 level are reported by trait designation.

Joel B. Cohen, "An Interpersonal Orientation to the Study of Consumer Behavior," *Journal of Marketing Research* 4 (August 1967):276. Reprinted from the *Journal of Marketing Research*, published by the American Marketing Association.

Guard users were more detached and less aggressive. Users of Dial soap were more compliant. Old Spice has been positioned with a strong he-man image. Dial soap, with its emphasis on making a person completely clean and odor free, would be likely to appeal to a person with a strong desire to be accepted by others.

In a test of several personality variables relative to cigarette brand choice (achievement, affiliation, aggression, antonomy, dominance, femininity, change, social recognition, and self-confidence), the brands were categorized by brand image.[24] Group I brands (Belvedere, DuMaurier, Matinee, Peter Jackson, and

Rothmans) were characterized as milder, more feminine, and more elegant than Group 2 brands (Export and Player). Femininity in males was significantly related to preference for Group I brands. More feminine women also preferred the brands, but the relationship was less pronounced. Need for social recognition was positively related to whichever brand associates preferred. High change scores for males and high affiliation scores for females were associated with preference for Group I brands.

In a psychographic study combining personality, life-style, and physiological needs, definite brand preferences were established based on the relative potency (or perceived potency) of various brands. Four psychographic types were identified (See figure 12-3). Extreme sufferers would likely use Excedrin. Active medicators might prefer Vanquish or Bufferin. Because Anacin emphasizes that it contains the ingredient doctors recommend most for pain, it might fit the hypochondriac segment. Practicalists might prefer Bayer, or, if they are more economy minded, they might buy St. Joseph's or a less expensive brand.

Fig. 12-3. Psychographic Segments in the Pain Reliever Market

Segment	Characteristics
Severe sufferers	Young people with children, well educated, living at a fast pace. Anxious and irritable. Believe they suffer more severely than others. Heaviest product users. Take the ailment seriously, pamper themselves when sick. Keep searching for new, more effective products, extra potency, extra ingredients, and new formulas.
Active medicators	Typical, middle-class suburbanites, leading active lives. Emotionally well adjusted. Accept the contemporary beliefs of getting help for all minor ills. Look for the remedy to improve their general well-being and help them relax and recover, look better and do better in their social activities. Satisfied with their brand and brand loyal. Look for extra potency and restorative benefits, as well as a modern, reputable, and well-advertised product.
Hypochondriacs	Older, female, down-scale in education. Deeply concerned over their health. Very cautious in self-treatment. Worry over side effects and see possible dangers in frequent use of remedies, new ingredients, and extra potency. Look to their doctors to tell them how to treat sickness and what remedies to use. Disciplined in their choice of products and frequency of use. Want a safe, single-purpose remedy that is backed by doctors or a reputable company.
Practicalists	Older, well educated, emotionally stable. Accept pain as a part of life, without fuss or concern for safety. Use a remedy as a last resort and are skeptical of complicated, modern remedies and of advertising claims. Seek a simple, inexpensive product with proven effectiveness.

Adapted from Joseph Pernica, "Psychographics, What Can Go Wrong?," Ronald C. Curhan, ed., *1974 Combined Proceedings of the American Marketing Association*, (1975), pp. 45-50. Published by the American Marketing Association.

Personality apparently can be related to brand use. The strongest association is likely to be between personality characteristics and brand image, especially if the brand image is well developed and consistently held.

Social Variables and Brand

The social environment of an individual may influence brand choice and image. The amount of influence a small group has on its members' brand-related attitudes and behavior is a function of a number of factors, including the relevance of the group to the product purchased, the cohesiveness of the group, the reward or punishment power of the group, the degree of attraction the group has for the individual, the susceptibility of the individual to group influence, the awareness of group members of one another's behavior, and the perception of the group's judgment relative to the individual's expertise.[25]

An individual's social class is likely to influence the types of brands that person buys, the meanings brands hold, and the importance of branding in general (brand saliency). In one study of supermarket products, it was found that upper-class women placed significantly less importance on brand name than middle- or lower-class women. For soft drinks and laundry detergent, upper-class women were more brand-conscious than lower-class women. In general, lower and middle classes were more sensitive to brand name than the upper class, and upper-class women were most likely to buy dealer brands.[26] Overall, social class seems to influence brand choice, but the relationship appears to be quite product specific.

Brand Loyalty

The questions of what constitutes brand loyalty and who is brand loyal have been heavily researched. One problem in studying brand loyalty is that there is no single acceptable definition of it. One early definition used the sequence of brand selections to indicate loyalty. Four types of loyalty were identified: (1) undivided loyalty—AAAAAA; (2) divided loyalty—ABABAB; (3) unstable loyalty—AAABBB; and (4) no loyalty—ABCDEF.[27] Research found numerous patterns that did not fit these four models, however. Other measures, including preference over time, proportion of purchases, and a combination of the two, have been advanced. The result of the lack of agreement is that many research findings cannot be cross-compared.

A distinction should be made between repeat purchase behavior and true brand loyalty. Some people who may repeatedly buy a brand because nothing else is available or out of habit or convenience rather than from real preference are susceptable to new brand entries.[28] Consequently, it is suggested that brand loyalty include not only a consistent pattern of brand purchase, but positive attitude toward the brand as well.[29]

An expanded definition contains six necessary and collectively sufficient conditions. These are that brand loyalty is: biased—that is, it involves nonrandom patterns;

a behavioral response—that is, a purchase (as opposed to merely an attitude); expressed by some decision-making unit (not merely a purchaser); expressed over time; related to one or more alternative brands out of a set of such brands; a function of psychological processes—that is, a decision-making, evaluative (attitudinal) process.[30]

Numerous studies have tried to uncover consistent characteristics of brand-loyal consumers. In general, these studies have found that brand loyalty correlates more to product and situation than to consumer characteristics. Correlates and characteristics of brand loyalty include the following:

1. The greater a consumer's brand loyalty, the less sensitive that person will be to price changes of the preferred brand relative to alternatives.

2. The greater a consumer's brand loyalty, the less frequently that person will try new brands.[31]

3. Personal characteristics of consumers explain differences in store loyalty, which is the best single predictor of brand loyalty.

4. Loyalty is positively correlated with the extent to which a housewife socializes with her neighbors.[32]

5. Brand loyalty tends to increase with cognitive dissonance.[33]

6. In cohesive groups, members tend to prefer the same brand as the leader, and members of groups with brand-loyal leaders also tend to be brand loyal.[34]

7. Brand loyalty varies substantially over products, and much of that variation can be explained on the basis of structural variables. For example, consumers tend to be less loyal toward a single brand when many brands are available, when number of purchases and dollar expenditures are high, when prices are relatively active, and when consumers might be expected to use a number of brands simultaneously. Consumers are also more brand loyal in markets where brands tend to be widely distributed and where market share is concentrated heavily in the leading brand.[35]

8. In keeping with the importance of brand as a perceptual cue, consumers can be loyal to a particular brand, even if it is not objectively different from competing brands.[36]

9. Brand loyalty varies negatively with education.[37]

The process of becoming brand loyal is a learning phenomenon. Obviously, one way to learn brand loyalty is favorable experience over time with a particular brand. Brand loyalty may also be learned through generalization and information processing. In brand generalization the consumer transfers a learned brand loyalty from one product or brand to another. The role of information processing in learning brand loyalty relates to the complex cognitive process whereby a consumer learns by actively seeking information about various brands. Initial trial may lead directly to brand loyalty. This effectively reduces the time and effort of actually trying alternate brands.[38] Consumers may also learn that any of several brands may be satisfying. In this case, the consumer may be loyal to several brands and more or less oblivious to alternate brands.[39]

Brand Strategy

Any brand strategy involves trying to create a strong preference for the firm's brand over time. Although the end is the same, there are a number of strategies a firm may follow, including line extension, broadening the base, family branding, individual branding, and retail branding.

Line Extension

If a firm has a line of products, it can introduce new brands as additions to or extensions of the line. However, the firm runs the risk of diluting the brand name or *cannibalization* (taking business away from its own brands).[40]

Diluting the brand's image can be very damaging because consumers may lose sight of what the brand means. The more products placed under the same brand name or image, the weaker that image becomes. Scott Paper Company put product after product under the same name (ScotTowels, ScotTissue, Scotties, Scotkins, and Baby Scott). The strategy seemed successful. In the early 1970s Scott had forty percent of the $1.2 billion market for towels, napkins, toilet tissues, facial tissue, and other consumer paper products. However, because Scott's brand image was so weak, Procter and Gamble was able to enter the market with Charmin—strongly positioned on softness—and within a few years, Charmin displaced Scott as the leading brand.[41]

Consumers perceive phenomena in such a way as to give them meaning. Because the world we perceive is extremely complex, perception tends to introduce a kind of shorthand to identify things as simply as possible. Thus, the brand name often becomes the only name by which a product is identified. This can lead to problems, as when the brand name becomes so firmly entrenched as a generic descriptor for a product that all products of the type come to be called by the brand name. Two things may result. First, a company may lose the right to exclusive use of the brand name. Cellophane and aspirin were once brand names that fell victims to "genericide." Second, consumers may learn to identify all similar products by the brand name. Thus, the company loses its unique image as consumers accept any product without realizing that they are not receiving the authentic item. The Coca-Cola company goes to great lengths in making sure that consumers do not receive a substitute when they ask for Coke. A team goes from place to place asking for Coke, then chemically analyzing it to be sure that it's "the real thing." If not, the seller is advised that the product is being misrepresented and that if the deception is not stopped, a lawsuit will be filed.

Brand image and identification is a two-edged sword. The brand name should be well known, but it must be uniquely identified with a particular product of a specific marketer. The 3M Company has tried hard to preserve its Scotch Tape brand by referring to it as Scotch brand cellophane tape. When you see brand names like Kleenex, Vaseline, Jello, Band-Aids, Crisco, and Crayola, a specific product comes to mind. Can you name the companies that make each of these? The images of these brands are strongly engrained, and an attempt to line extend off of any of them would likely be unsuccessful. For example, the image of Kleenex as a facial tissue is so strongly held that Kleenex paper towels did not fare well. When the company entered the disposable diaper market, they didn't make the same mistake. They named the new product Kimbies.

Oh, the names of those companies? Kimberly-Clark, Chesebrough-Pond's, General Foods, Johnson and Johnson, Procter and Gamble, and Binney Smith, Inc., in that order. How did you do?

Broadening the Base

While it can be a mistake to try to line extend, a single brand may be promoted for a variety of uses. Suppose you have a product that has sold well, but most people used only a small amount. Now suppose that you could convince people to pour a whole box full down the drain regularly. That would really expand your market. Well, that's just what Arm & Hammer did with their baking soda. In addition to using the product a teaspoon or so at a time, consumers were convinced to stick a whole box in the refrigerator to deodorize it and to pour the contents of the box down the kitchen drain monthly to deodorize it. The company became so impressed with itself that it introduced Arm & Hammer deodorant for people. This line extension strategy did not work as well as broadening the base.

Johnson's Baby Shampoo was the number one baby shampoo because of its mildness. However, many adults who wash their hair frequently are interested in mildness, so Johnson's became the number one adult shampoo when it was promoted as good for both adult and baby hair.

Family Branding

Family or blanket branding is a type of line extention in which a manufacturer places all or part of its products under the same brand name. The logic is that family branding leads to a connection in consumer minds, which generalizes consumer preferences to all existing and future products under the brand name.[42] Generalized preference is better achieved when products are similar in distribution channels, promotion form, target market, and end use. Family branding as used by Heinz, Hunt, Campbell, Green Giant, and others can facilitate the adoption process and the acceptance of new products, again because of generalization of the existing brand quality and image to new products.

Of course, there is the potential for image dilution, but if the products are similar, the strategy can be effective. Also, a firm must take care to maintain consistent quality. If expectations are not fulfilled, the generalization may boomerang, a quality decline may be attributed to the line, and sales of all products in the family may be affected.

Individual Branding

When all company products are given different brand names, firms may give each brand a separate brand image. Positioning then becomes an appropriate strategy. Procter and Gamble markets ten different brands of laundry detergent—Tide, Cheer, Bold 3, Gain, Dash, Oxydol, Duz, Bonus, Salvo, and Era—and two soaps—Ivory Flakes and Ivory Snow. Each brand has a unique character. Together they account for more than half of all laundry product sales.

Since the addition of each new product increased total sales, one could conclude that the strategy afforded Procter and Gamble a greater market share than any one brand could by itself. There are two major reasons for this. First, each brand receives at least one shelf facing in the store, and more exposure means more sales. Second, most people are not singularly loyal to one brand. People switch brands for a variety of reasons, and if a company has a large portion of all available brands, odds are that a consumer will switch *from* one of its brands *to* one of its brands, thus conserving total market share. This only works, though, if each brand has a unique position, completely separate from the company as a whole. Notice that the company almost never associates its brand names with its name. (How many Procter and Gamble products can you name?)

Retail Branding

In order to take advantage of the image of their store name, many retailers have adopted their own brands, called private or dealer brands. Again, there is a generalization in which the image of a retail store is transferred to its brands.

Private brand proneness refers to the question of the conditions and characteristics of private brand purchases and purchasers. Research results are a little sketchy on these questions, but a few results are relevant. First, consumers tend to develop loyalty to private brands in general, without respect to store. This suggests that the price advantage of private brands is more important to many consumers than the store's image. However, loyalty to a particular store does increase loyalty for that store's brands.[43] Second, a great deal of private brand purchasing behavior is product specific. For example, one study found that suburban shoppers were more inclined to buy private brands of soft drinks and paper products than were consumers from other parts of the city. However, there was no difference for laundry and cleaning products, packaged goods, and desserts.[44] Another study found that upper-class shoppers were heavy buyers of private brands in general, but lower-class consumers were heavier private brand buyers for soft drinks and laundry products.[45]

The ultimate private brand is the generic brand or no-brand-name product. Many stores, particularly grocery stores, offer unbranded items at a low price. Here, nothing but the image of the store stands behind the product, and product image should be identical to store image.

Relatively little research has been conducted on generic brand buying behavior. Generic brands were first introduced in early 1976 in France by the Carrefour supermarket chain, and the concept quickly spread throughout Europe, Canada, and the United States.[46] The major appeal of generic brands is low price—up to thirty-three percent below national brands and ten to twenty percent below dealer brands.[47]

Generic brands have caught on rapidly, probably in part because of increased consumer price sensitivity resulting from inflationary pressures. It was first thought that generic brands would draw business primarily from private brands, but early research shows that only twenty-four percent of generic purchasers switched from private brands; twenty-two percent indicated that they had previously bought private and national brands in equal amounts; and fifty-five percent switched from national brands.[48]

In general, generic brand users perceived the no-name products to be as good as those they had previously used and indicated that they would continue to buy them,[49] in spite of the fact that government standards actually allow for lower-grade quality in generic brands.[50] Age, marital status, family income, and occupation do not differ between buyers and nonbuyers of generics. However, consumers over age fifty-five showed some reluctance to try generic brands, and households headed by managers and professionals indicated a slightly higher preference for generics than others. This probably reflects the fact that higher education is associated with generic brand usage. In addition, larger families show a preference for generic products over branded items.[51]

Packaging

In a sense, the package is part of the product. It encloses and protects the product. In today's self-service world, the package becomes a major communication medium from manufacturer or retailer to consumer. In general, the package acts as a perceptual cue, much as the brand does, to communicate symbolic meaning to consumers. As such, the package imparts a certain personality and quality image to shoppers.

The Package and Product Personality

A product has a personality much like a person does. The product personality has two parts—the physical image and the personality image. The consumer perceives a unified image, and a negative aspect of either image is likely to affect the consumer's total perception of the product. A package that plays a promotional role needs prominent design features to capture and hold attention, making the product stand out on the shelf.

For a given product, a consumer has an image of the ideal package. The image is more than a simple picture of how the product looks. It's a dramatic visualization of the feel of the package as it's turned in the consumer's hand, of its fit on the shelf at home, and of its functional utility and convenience.

Packaging requirements are based on the consumer's emotional and rational needs. They may be listed as follows:

Convenience—Does the package hold enough of the product to satisfy the consumer's needs without being too bulky or heavy?

Adaptability—How well does the package fit into the consumer's freezer, cupboard, glove compartment, or dresser drawer?

Security—Does the package communicate quality?

Status or prestige—Does the package allow the consumer to feel as though the purchase allows self expression?

Dependability—Does the package give the consumer the feeling that the seller is reliable?

Aesthetic satisfaction—Is the impact of the design, color, and shape of the package appealing to the eye?

According to Ernest Dichter, a pioneer in motivation research,

> The core of all successful packaging meets the emotional and psychological needs of today's consumer, as expressed in his daily purchasing patterns and his conceptions of the ideal package—a good package does not *create* the personality of a product. Like a good cosmetic on a beautiful girl, the desirable package merely expresses personality in a dramatic, easily recognizable way. On the other hand, a bad package or design contradicts, underplays, or undermines a product's personality.[52]

Packaging and Product Perception

A package can influence a consumer's perception of a product's quality. This influence may result from information found on the package, the design and composition of the package, and the package color.

Package Information What the marketer prints on a package communicates a great deal to consumers. In selecting a package size, for example, consumers generally rely on price. However, research indicates that many consumers really do not have a clear idea of a product's relative value in terms of cents per pound. When provided with accurate unit prices, many consumers exhibit much different behavior, switching to larger, more economical sizes.[53] However, if too much information is provided on the package, consumers may actually use information less than they otherwise would. As a result, too much information can actually lead to more impulsive behavior.[54] Many consumers feel more satisfied and less confused when provided with more information. However, they make poorer decisions with more information because of confusion.[55]

Of the types of information found on packages, brand name and price tend to be most heavily used (see figure 12-4). In general, less information is sought from the package when the brand name is known, possibly because the brand name is a quality surrogate acting as an information chunk in decision making.[56]

One kind of information often included on packages is the promotional message "New" or "Improved." Of course, the marketer hopes that such claims will cause

Fig. 12-4. Package Information Dimension Selection Frequencies

Information Dimension	Brand and Manufacturer Name AVAILABLE (n = 42)		Brand and Manufacturer Name UNAVAILABLE (n = 42)	
	Frequency Selected	Rank	Frequency Selected	Rank
Brand name	41	1	X	X
Price	24	2	35	1
Size (in ounces)	24	3	31	2
Flavor	16	4	28	3
ADA Seal of Approval	14	5	23	4
Whitening powers	14	6	18	7
Mouthwash properties	11	7	19	6
Special active ingredients	5	8	21	5
Good Housekeeping seal and/or money back guarantee	5	9	10	10
Date contents placed in package	5	10	7	12
Container type	4	11	14	9
Manufacturer's name	4	12	X	X
Artificial flavoring or color	3	13	14	8
Safety information/cautions on use	3	14	7	13
Preservatives to extend product life	2	15	4	15
Color of paste	1	16	9	11
Storage instructions	1	17	2	16
Usage instructions	1	18	4	14
No. of Dimensions Selected	178		246	
Mean No. of Dimensions Selected	4.24		5.86	

Overall mean number of dimensions selected = 5.05; rho = .93.

Jacob Jacoby, George J. Szybillo, and Jacqueline Busato-Schach, "Information Acquisition Behavior in Brand Choice Situations." Reprinted with permission from *The Journal of Consumer Research* (1977), 3:212.

a perception of novelty and thereby induce trial. However, one study found that such claims have no effect in consumer evaluations of household and personal care products. These terms have apparently been so overused that they have little meaning to many consumers. Perhaps, too, past expectations of newness may not have been fulfilled. [57]

Another information cue that may appear on a package is the seal of certification, such as the Good Housekeeping Seal of Approval. The seal could be used as a cue for product evaluation similar to a brand name. One study of nine branded products investigated the effects of seals. The Good Housekeeping Seal was tested against no seal and a dummy seal. The results were as follows:

1. A widely recognized seal (the Good Housekeeping Seal) has no greater influence on ratings of or preference for products than does an unknown (dummy) seal.
2. The presence of a seal (widely known or unknown) has no significant influence on product evaluations.
3. Brand, advertising, product characteristics, and other attributes influence ratings and preferences to a greater degree than do seals of certification.
4. Readers of *Good Housekeeping* magazine do not appear to be influenced to a greater degree by the presence of a Good Housekeeping Seal than nonreaders of the magazine.[58]

Package Design and Composition The design of a package may communicate an image to a consumer: a plain package, economy; an extravagent package, luxury. The materials from which the package is made may act as a quality cue to the consumer. One early study found that consumers perceived bread of equal freshness to be fresher when wrapped in cellophane as opposed to wax paper.[59]

A more recent study found that product quality was subjectively perceived as better depending on packaging material even when the better package was more difficult to open.[60] Potato chips of equal freshness were packaged in wax paper bags and polyvinyl bags. Consumers consistently (eighty-seven percent of the time) rated the chips in the polyvinyl bag as superior in taste and crispness to those in the wax paper bags, even though the polyvinyl bags were much more difficult to open.

> Interviewers observed utter frustation on the part of many subjects attempting to open the polyvinyl bags. A number of people ultimately bit the bag to open it, and one female respondent finally placed the package on the floor, stood on the edge of the top seam and pulled with both hands. The package ripped and the chips scattered on the floor. One elderly male interviewee struggled for several minutes with the polyvinyl bag and finally handed it back.[61]

Ninety-three percent of the respondents preferred the difficult-to-open packages. It seems that the perceived higher quality led to the willingness to sacrifice convenience in favor of quality.

Package Color The color used in a package conveys definite meaning about a product. This is partly cultural. Colors mean different things in different cultures. Black is seldom used as a predominant package color in the U.S. because of its association with death. For the same reason, white might be avoided in Japan, purple in South America, and blue in Iran. In China, bright colors symbolize quality. When Scott entered Taiwan with its American blend of pastel-colored toilet tissue, the product did poorly. When the company switched to bright red, yellow, and gold, sales turned around, and Scott was soon the market leader.[62] Can you visualize bright red toilet paper in bathrooms in the United States?

In the United States white packages may be used to connote purity and cleanliness, green packages indicate nature and natural ingredients, blue package color indicates coolness (thus the use of blue in menthol cigarette packaging and Cold Water All detergent). On the other hand, red and yellow in packaging are suggestive of a "hot" new product commanding shopper attention. [63]

Several years ago an experiment was conducted in which housewives were given the identical detergent in three different colored packages; red, yellow, and blue. They were asked their opinions of the three "different" detergents, unaware that all three boxes contained the same product. When the results came back, the three detergents were evaluated quite differently. The yellow detergent was mild, too mild, really. The blue detergent was a good all-around laundry product. The red detergent was powerful—good for difficult stains and the like.

Of course, none of this is lost on America marketers. Notice Procter and Gamble's three main detergents—Tide, Cheer, and Bold (before it was Bold 3). Tide is in an orange box, half way between yellow (mild) and red (strong). Cheer is blue (for all-around washing—"All Tempacheer"). The Cheer box also has red and yellow on it to suggest that it is hard-working, yet mild. Bold is red; even the "l" in Bold is a stick of dynamite (strong, hard-working stuff). Tide "gets clothes white," Cheer gets clothes "whiter than white," and Bold gets clothes "all the way to bright."

Packaging Strategy

Package design may be a major factor in the success of consumer products. The original package design decision is significant, but subsequent design changes may be required to fine tune product promotion strategy. Although changes may be necessary, they can be risky. Because the package is an integral part of a product and its brand image, any change in a package has the potential for changing that image. Or course, that can be good or bad. A changed image can lead to more or fewer sales. The package is considered by some to be the most sensitive indicator and influencer of a product's personality. [64]

Factors that are relevant in determining the degree of risk involved in package change include the product's market share, the specific change made, and how the change is handled. [65] When a package is changed, some consumers will respond positively while others will react negatively. With a large market share, chances of negatively influencing a present customer are great, while the odds of attracting new customers is greater if market share is relatively small.

Obviously, a package can be changed in a variety of ways. Some types of package changes are riskier than others, as noted in figure 12-5. The addition of caution and warning labels on products is often necessary and involves a low risk *if* it is not unexpected. In general, it is wise to be sure that consumers are apprised of any potential problems as they develop so that they will not feel deceived or betrayed by warning labels.

Generally speaking, minor changes in side panels or the use of special premiums (such as cents-off offers) on the package carry little risk. Major risks come with

Brand attitude overlaps brand image and relates specifically to positive or negative feelings of a consumer toward a brand. Information about or purchase of a brand may affect brand attitude. Influencing attitude components or invoking the majority effect may also be effective. The majority effect will be stronger if brand preference for the most preferred brand is weak and if the less preferred brand is higher in the preference hierarchy. Switching is inversely related to age, socioeconomic status, and the number of strong preferences held.

Although positive results are spotty, brand image does seem to correlate with at least some aspects of consumer personality. The relationship tends to be stronger when brand image is particularly strong and unique. Psychographic profiles can be developed to relate to brand image.

Small groups and social class can influence members' brand perception. Effects tend to be on brands preferred and purchased, brand image, and brand saliency.

Although definitions of brand loyalty are varied, the concept is useful. Brand loyalty is biased, behavioral, expressed by some decision-making unit, expressed over time, related to one or more alternative brands out of a set of such brands, and a function of psychological processes.

Brand strategy involves the creation of a strong preference for a brand over time. Potential brand strategies were discussed as line extension, broadening the base, family branding, individual branding, and retail or private branding.

Packaging is an extension of product and branding strategy. In a sense, the package helps create the product personality. Package requirements based on consumer needs involve convenience, adaptability, security, status or prestige, dependability, and a esthetic satisfaction. A package may influence product perception through package information, design and composition, and color. Changes in packages may carry varying degrees of risk, and careful consumer research should precede high-risk changes.

CHAPTER 12   STUDY REVIEW

Important Terms and Concepts

Brand image
Brand loyalty
Brand strategy
Brand name
Brand attitude
Line extention
Broadening the base
Family branding
Private brand proneness
Generic brands
Behavior-based packaging requirements

Questions

1. Discuss the relationship between self-image and brand image.

2. How does a product's brand name contribute to brand image?

3. Discuss the relationship between brand attitude and product purchase.

4. Explain the relationship between consumer personality and brand selection.

5. How is a person's social class likely to influence brand selection?

6. Describe the correlates of brand loyalty.

7. How might a product's package contribute to the product's "personality"?

8. How is package information used by consumers, and how does this information contribute to product image?

9. How do package design, composition, and color communicate product image?

10. Discuss the risks of package design change and approaches to reducing those risks.

13

Behavioral Concepts
for Pricing

As noted in the previous chapter, price is a cue that imparts meanings to consumers. Pricing is also a major strategic tool for the marketing manager, and, as such, it is one of the four elements of the marketing mix. This chapter will look at pricing as a behavioral concept, beginning with the economist's view and continuing with pricing behavior in the business firm. The topics of price perception and consumer response to pricing complete the chapter.

Economic Price Theory

The first scholars to deal with consumer behavior systematically were the economists. Microeconomics is basically a theory of the firm or price theory. Classical economics made several limiting assumptions about consumers and the market, which led to a simple model of market behavior. It was assumed that: there were so many buyers and sellers that none could influence either supply or demand; products were homogeneous; buyers and sellers had perfect knowledge of the market; and there were no barriers to entry for firms. (These are the assumptions of the "economic man" theory that were touched on in chapter 1.)

Given these four assumptions of classical economics, there could be only one price, the market price, determined by the forces of supply and demand. The theory fit a relatively simple agrarian economy, but it fell short for a complex industrial economy where most prices are administered by firms rather than determined by market forces. To deal with the complexity, monopolistic competition theory was developed. The theory relaxed the assumption of product homogeneity and resulted in the downsloping demand curve, which recognizes that raising a price will not cause a firm to lose all of its sales and lowering the price will attract more customers. It is assumed that consumers will demand more of an item if price decreases and less if price goes up. The concept of demand elasticity further refines the theory by noting that demand is elastic if a lowering of price results in an increase in total revenue, and vice versa. Demand is inelastic if a price cut leads to a decline in total revenue and a price increase leads to an increase in total revenue.

Economic theory is useful, but by assuming a completely rational consumer, it fails to account adequately for psychological product differentiation, advertising effects, differences in individual perception and motivation, and "nonrational" responses to price, such as discontinuous and backward bending demand schedules. The remainder of this chapter will treat pricing concepts not fully considered in economic price theory.

Business Pricing Behavior

As indicated earlier, most pricing practice involves administered pricing as opposed to market determined pricing. Given this, price may become a very active strategic marketing variable. The marketing manager has a full range of pricing options available, from the unit cost of a product to the peak of what the market will bear. Price may be set to follow competition. On the other hand, more volume may be sought through lower-than-market prices. In this instance, profit per sale will likely be lower than what competitors' prices yield, but the low-price firm will typically turn its capital faster, resulting in a higher return on investment, assuming it is able to maintain a positive per-unit profit. Companies must undertake closer expense management here, since the small profit margin could easily turn to a loss. A higher-than-market price can lead to a prestige situation in which the marketer is able to achieve a higher per-unit margin. With the high-price strategy, satisfactory profit may flow from a lower sales volume.

A major task of any marketing strategy is to motivate consumers to buy. Price is often used as an incentive motivator to induce trial or to increase purchase rates. Price reductions, cents-off coupons and packages, free samples, and rebates fall into this category.

Price setting typically is based on cost factors rather than demand. Firms generally use both a price level policy and a simple percentage markup or some sort of formula to arrive at a price. Understanding how consumers perceive and react to various prices will aid a firm in deciding upon a price strategy.

New Product Pricing

One of the more difficult price decisions involves unique new products. When there is no competitor's price to serve as a point of departure, almost any price may be selected. Consumers, however, react differently to different price levels, as you will see in later sections, so even here the pricing strategist does not have a completely free reign.

One way to determine a reasonable base for setting prices is to establish an expected price. Consumers can be shown the new product or be given a description of what the product will do and asked what they would expect to pay for the item or what they think a fair price might be. This could be accomplished during concept testing. The midpoint of the expected prices would be the price level used to determine a new product price. Because any product embodies benefits, the consumer should be able to give a good estimation of what the benefits would be worth. It should be noted that for new products, consumers may have little or no basis for quality assessment other than price, so the price may determine perceived quality.[1]

Broadly, two philosophies may guide new product pricing: skimming and penetration. When there are no close substitutes for a product, and where technology or patents assure some time in the market free of competition, a firm may elect to price high to gain large profits and early payback of development costs. Hewlett-Packard priced its pocket calculator very high relative to slide rules when they were first introduced. Later, when competitive calculators entered the market, prices were lowered. Hewlett-Packard has retained the image of the "quality" product, and the premium price this company commands relative to other brands is consistent with its market position.

One of the problems with a skimming price strategy is that the wide profit margin invites competition, and it's unusual for a company to maintain a unique market position for long. Polaroid, however, was able to protect its position for years by maintaining hundreds of separate patents. The concept behind penetration pricing is that a firm, to discourage competition, may set a low price to enter the market. In this way, the product may have a strong preference position before competition can enter.

Pricing to Induce Trial

One of the barriers consumers face in trying new or untried products is the perceived risk of parting with money in exchange for uncertain benefits. A marketer's pricing policy can reduce that risk and encourage trial. Such price incentives range from free samples to cents-off coupons, premiums, combination offers, and cash rebates.

The ultimate price inducement is the free sample. This is an expensive strategy, but dollars normally spent for advertising can logically be diverted to free samples where product trial is important to positive attitude formation, as in the Nyquil introduction. Prime candidates for a free sample strategy are normally low-priced, frequently purchased consumer goods, such as toothpastes, deodorants, and mouthwashes. Care must be taken that only enough of the product is distributed free to achieve initial trial. Colgate sampled so much of their Colgate 100 mouthwash a few years ago that a person could have accumulated several months' supply at no cost.

Some sort of introductory price reduction can be used as a lower cost alternative to sampling. There are some potential problems with such a strategy, however. In the first place, the reduction may not lessen risk enough to induce trial. On the other hand, if the incentive price is offered over too long a time period, it may come to be perceived as the regular price, and there may be resistance over what is perceived to be a price increase when the regular price is instituted. In addition, price can signal quality to a consumer, and an unrealistically low price may suggest low quality. Use of a cents-off label or a coupon rebate may emphasize the price saving and communicate the regular price as well. A firm may actually rebate an amount over and above the purchase price. Chrysler recently utilized a fifty-dollar incentive to encourage prospective buyers to take test-drives with the knowledge that the probability of purchase is increased through the behavioral attitude dimension and the potential positive attribution that may come from a given action. Use of some sort of factory rebate may have the added advantage of being attributed to the manufacturer rather than to the retailer, thus establishing and reinforcing brand loyalty.

Psychological Pricing

Many firms utilize pricing strategies that recognize the complex and often seemingly nonrational consumer response to price stimuli. Rather than seeing a single type of demand curve, psychological pricing strategy is based on the assumption that there are numerous curves associated with different products, purchase situations, and consumers. Psychological pricing strategy assumes that consumers are perceptually sensitive to certain prices so that deviation above or below the critical price will result in decreased demand. Psychological pricing is broken into customary pricing, odd pricing, price lining, multiple-unit pricing, leader pricing, and prestige pricing.[2] Figure 13-1 suggests the demand curves that may underlie the various psychological pricing strategies.

Customary Pricing Some products have been priced at a certain level for so long that there is strong resistance to any price change. For years candy bars sold for a nickel. As production costs increased, the candy bar got smaller and smaller. Only when it became apparent that the choice was between miniscule pieces of chocolate and a ten-cent bar did the candy bar size and price increase. In times of rapid inflation there is so much cost and demand pressure on prices that there is little opportunity for customary prices to develop or hold.

Odd Pricing A price strategy with which you are undoubtedly familiar involves ending a price with an odd number (1,3,5,7,9) or near a round number (98,99). The assumption is that price sensitivity at these levels is greater or that the consumer will perceive the price to be lower ($5.95 perceived as $5.00 rather than $6.00). Another purpose for odd pricing is to force retail clerks to make change so that they cannot pocket the money from an exact change transaction. The odd price may also create the illusion of precision in price setting, thus discouraging price haggling.

Research on the effects of odd pricing is sparse. One study of mail-order selling found no sales advantage of using odd prices over even.[3] Another researcher concluded that any effectiveness of odd pricing lies in the fact that they are so widely used they have the effect of customary prices. Thus, odd prices may lead to increased sales not because they are perceived to be lower but because they fit consumer expectations.[4]

Fig. 13-1. Demand Curves Underlying Psychological Pricing Strategies

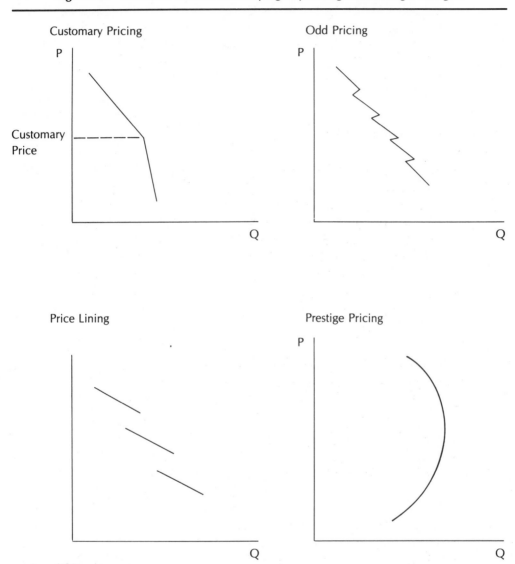

Price Lining In order to take advantage of various levels of purchasing power and desire for quality, marketers often price products at different levels. Price is one way to interpret the quality of a product. Different price levels in a price line identify quality levels (good, better, best). There is some evidence to support the idea that consumers tend to select a medium-priced item.[5] Price lining positions an "average" quality, moderately priced item for consumers along with economy and premium priced products.

Multiple-unit Pricing Pricing items in multiples (2 for 29¢, 6 for $1.39) is a widely used psychological pricing tool, particularly in food stores. Studies have indicated that using multiple unit pricing can generate substantial sales increases.[6] Even though true price savings may be minimal, consumers seem to perceive multiple-unit prices as lower, or they perceive greater convenience in buying larger amounts.

Apparently, there is some limit to the multiple-unit pricing effect. Higher multiples, such as six, may result in a drop in sales, depending on the product. There is just so much of a product a family can consume. The trend toward smaller families may accentuate this effect. Multiple-unit pricing is relatively ineffective on high-unit price products, new or unknown products, and items that are not consumed rapidly.[7] For such products the consumer would likely seek to reduce risk and investment.

Leader Pricing Stores, particularly grocery stores and discount stores, often reduce price substantially on certain items to build traffic. These items are frequently purchased and widely distributed products for which prices can be readily compared. The theory is that the leader price will act as a cue to suggest that overall prices are low. Since supermarkets and discounters carry thousands of items, it is reasonable to think that perceptions of a store will be based on a few easily distinguished cues.

Prestige Pricing Many products are status symbols. One factor that contributes to a product's being considered a prestige item is that relatively few people can possess it. People in higher social strata may buy high-priced items as symbols of their social status. The most common way to monitor ownership is limited supply and attendant high price. Automobiles such as Lincoln, Cadillac, and Mercedes are symbolic of prestige in the United States. The high price of the autos lends them prestige and assures limited ownership. Part of the price paid for the cars is for prestige—it's doubtful that the incremental quality is equal to the incremental price over a less prestigious car. On an individual basis, the ability to pay high prices may reflect a consumer's self-image or ideal self-image.

Effects of Psychological Pricing There seems to be a consistency among pricing strategies in supermarkets that suggests that psychological prices are widely used and believed to be effective. Multiples of twelve are the most popular number of selling units packed in a carton, accounting for 74.5 percent of all test items. Prices ending in nine or five account for as much as 80 percent of retail food prices. There is also extensive multiple-unit pricing, with the multiples never dividing evenly into the price.[8]

Using only odd prices in multiple-unit sales is inconvenient for the consumer who wants to compare prices. If the multiple-unit price is too complex, consumers are likely to reject it in favor of a more easily calculated purchase quantity.[9] Unit pricing has been advanced as a practical remedy for the problem of accurately comparing prices across products. This is relevant not only to multiple-unit pricing but to any sort of packaging where price can be compared by ounce, pound, and so on. Unit pricing is now available in many supermarkets, even though marketers fought it at first on the grounds that it was too costly and would be little used. In addition, early research showed that low-education, low-income families, who presumably needed the benefits of unit pricing more than others, were not using it. [10] However, there is evidence indicating that, over time, a large proportion of consumers of all types come to use the service. [11] Low-income and low-education consumers were apparently slower to utilize unit pricing, but this is probably a function of their general slowness to accept innovations of all types rather than a rejection of unit price information per se.

Research indicates that unit pricing leads to consumers' making lower-unit price decisions within categories. For example, buyers of all-meat dog food might select a lower-unit price all-meat dog food, but they would be unlikely to switch to an even lower unit price nonmeat dog food. Likewise, buyers of national brands are unlikely to switch to store brands on the basis of lower-unit price alone. [12] Given that price confusion may lead consumers not to buy, unit pricing strategy may lead to differential advantage for stores that first use it. Nearly fifty percent of all special off-price promotions were in multiples of five, even-numbered discounts were more predominant, one-cent discounts were not found, and two-cent and nine-cent discounts were very rare.

Although research has not specifically supported the effectiveness of psychological pricing, retailer practice suggests widespread belief in the strategy. Success of the strategy suggests underlying behavioral principles that are not yet understood.

Price Perception

Perception of any phenomenon is subjective, and price perception is no exception. Because price perception is subjective, many of the assumptions about pricing and consumer response to pricing must be reevaluated from a behavioral viewpoint. This section will consider price consciousness, price thresholds, and the price-quality relationship.

Price Consciousness

Economic theory suggests that consumers are very sensitive to price. At the extreme, price is considered the only relevant variable, and consumers seek the lowest price consistent with the utilities or benefits they want. This theory can only be correct to the extent that the consumer is actually aware of the prices paid and sensitive to price level. A consumer's degree of price consciousness may be significant to a marketing strategist in that price can be more easily raised if consumers are less price sensitive. At the same time, if consumers are more price-conscious, price decreases are likely to be more effective in increasing sales revenue. As an indication of product cost, price is assumed to influence the purchase selection process. [13]

One study used the following measures of price consciousness:

1. Eighty-two percent of the 640 housewives interviewed indicated that they recalled the price most recently paid for fifteen supermarket products.
2. Fifty-seven percent of prices were correctly identified.
3. Of 184 incorrectly named prices, fifty-two percent were no more than ten percent from the correct price. [14]

In this study, price consciousness and the accuracy of price recall were inversely correlated with income, except at the lowest income level. Housewives in the highest social class were more willing to state a price paid than lower-class wives, but lower-class wives more often *correctly* identified the price paid. Price consciousness was also found to be lower for branded items, suggesting that brand preference was more relevant than price in many cases.

While another study found that income and social class (based on the occupation of the head of the household) were positively associated with the average price paid per unit for supermarket items, suggesting an inverse relationship with price sensitivity,[15] other studies have found no such relationship.[16] One problem in analyzing price consciousness is that it varies considerably across products.[17] Among sixty advertised and price-competitive branded grocery products, the percentage of correctly identified prices ranged from a low of two percent for shortening to a high of eighty-six percent for Coca-Cola.[18]

An extensive study of more than 1,000 customers in twenty-seven supermarkets in five communities sought to determine the nature of consumers who perceive prices most accurately.[19] Shopping variables correlated more strongly with perceptual validity than socioeconomic variables. The number of stores shopped, shopping for price, and use of a shopping list were among the most relevant variables. Not only did perceptions and determinants vary across products, they varied across communities as well.

In some instances more shopping activity led to *less* valid price perception, apparently because of confusion. Older, higher-income consumers had more accurate price perceptions. Married, full-time housewives had low price perception validity. Males had more valid price perceptions than females, and single shoppers were better price perceivers than marrieds. Those who were employed had more accurate price perception than those who were employed part-time or unemployed. Perceptual validity was better for those who were critical of their own and others' shopping ability, who used price as a major cue for store selection, and who used automobiles for shopping.

The following tentative explanations have been advanced for unexpected findings:

1. The female food shopper is doing the job expected of her; the male food shopper has more often chosen the task, and so is part of a self-selected group. (This kind of motivation and interest might well explain more valid perceptions, but it does not warrant a conclusion that males will be, in general, more valid perceivers.)

2. Either part-time or full-time employment implies less time for shopping and possibly more concern for its financial side, perhaps producing a more organized and efficient approach with more valid perceptions. The full-time housewife may view price as one of the least important characteristics to consider.

3. Those who think they are better shoppers have a false sense of security, perhaps not recognizing the complexity of the situation, and so do not perceive price as validly as others. [20]

Price consciousness is an indication of price sensitivity or concern. One study found that the degree of concern for prices varies with the product. Concern over price paid was found in thirteen percent of cereal buyers, seventeen percent of candy buyers, and twenty-five percent of detergent buyers. [21]

There is some indication that advertising increases price consciousness. One goal of advertising is to differentiate products on nonprice grounds, thus insulating a product against price competition. This has led many economists to conclude that advertising is counterproductive to a competitive environment. However, advertising often makes consumers more aware of reasonable prices and allows for more convenient price comparison. [22] Recent trends to advertise prescription drug prices and medical and legal fees give the consumer far better opportunities for price comparison and should lead to heightened price sensitivity.

Price Thresholds

Perception is subject to thresholds of awareness. As noted in chapter 3, there are upper and lower boundaries to human perceptual capability, as well as differential thresholds that relate to the ability to perceive that a stimulus has changed. In addition to physical thresholds, there are psychological thresholds that involve acceptable and unacceptable levels and selective perception of levels and differences. Consumer perception seems to be influenced by both absolute limit and differential thresholds.

Absolute Price Thresholds It certainly comes as no surprise that there is an upper limit to acceptable price for products. This upper limit may vary from consumer to consumer depending on a variety of factors. Contrary to what a person might intuitively think, there is also a *lower* acceptability threshold on price. [23] A major implication of this is that cost does not necessarily represent the lower limit of price. Thus, the cost-plus price-setting technique (the most common practice) may lead to pricing errors in spite of the fact that it satisfies cost and upper price limit (competition and demand) requirements. [24]

The price-limit concept makes many of the established procedures of demand estimation suspect. Such procedures are based upon an implicit inverse price-quantity assumption, which leads to the familiar downsloping demand curve. The price-limit concept, however, suggests that part of the demand curve is positively sloped (see figure 13-2).[25]

Fig. 13-2.   Demand Curve for the Price-Limit Concept

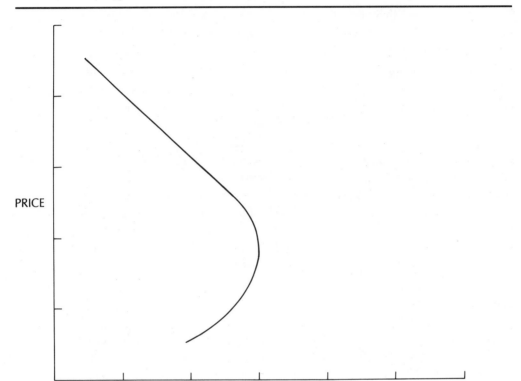

PRICE

MEDIAN QUANTITY DEMANDED

Kent B. Monroe, "Measuring Price Thresholds by Psychophysics and Latitudes of Acceptance," *Journal of Marketing Research* 8 (November 1971):463. Reprinted from *The Journal of Marketing Research*, published by the American Marketing Association.

The reason for the lower price limit seems to lie in consumers' suspiciousness of "too good a deal" and the feeling that "you get what you pay for." In view of the lower price threshold, marketers must be aware that too low a price may elicit negative reactions from consumers. The lower price threshold may vary from customer to customer and product to product. If someone were to offer you a fourteen karat gold chain for $1.98, you would likely think the chain was stolen or fake. In buying aspirin, Bayer customers are willing to pay a substantial premium for a product that in fact works no better in relieving pain than the much less expensive brands. Presumably, the lower price threshold for the Bayer customer is higher than for those who buy the cheaper brands. Possible explanations may include the effectiveness of Bayer advertising or Bayer customers' fear of an inferior product.

Since price limits represent psychological rather than physical thresholds, both upper and lower price thresholds can be changed through marketing efforts. Advertising appeals and personal selling efforts may lead consumers to believe that a given brand is worth more, thus raising the upper price limit. Obviously, some consumers may be more readily sold than others. On the other hand, unusually low prices should be justified to the consumer. If they are to accept an unusually low price, consumers must be led to attribute the price reduction to the selling situation rather than to product quality. This, of course, is easier if the price reduction involves a well-known, branded item, and it argues strongly for using branded items with well-established, regular prices as price leaders.

In times of inflation, upper price limits must be constantly shifted upward. What is perceived as a normal price today may be only a fond memory tomorrow. Think how good gasoline at fifty cents a gallon would look now and how bad it would have looked when it was selling for thirty-five cents a gallon. This upward shifting of price limits means that the customary price is constantly being shifted upward, and it explains, in part, why a tripling of gasoline prices has not brought about drastic cuts in driving. Until income effects become relevant, consumers will alter their spending patterns to accomodate rising gasoline prices by cutting costs in areas other than travel.

As prices are rapidly bid upward, consumers may develop an inflationary psychology of buying now before the price goes up again. The upward price trend probably increases price consciousness but lowers price sensitivity and resistance to higher prices. Think how you reacted to the first twenty percent increase in gasoline prices compared with your feeling about the most recent increase; after a while you get a little numb. At this point, consumers may come to adapt to price increases and become more sensitive to price decreases.

Differential Price Thresholds Even though two prices may be objectively different, it cannot be assumed that customers actually perceive the prices to be different. You will recall from chapter 3 that the difference between two stimuli must reach a critical level before a difference is perceived. This critical level is called the just noticeable difference (j.n.d.). Weber's law states that the j.n.d. is a function of the size of the stimulus, and is given as:

$$\Delta\ S/S = k$$

Where: S is the magnitude of the stimulus
       Δ is the incremental change in the stimulus
       k is a constant

When considering price changes, Weber's law suggests that the change in price required to cause consumers to perceive that a change has taken place is a function of the magnitude of the price. While you might readily perceive a five-cent change in the price of a candy bar, such a change in the price of an automobile would almost certainly go unnoticed.

The change relevant to price may not be price itself. A change in product size or quality may indirectly effect a price change. For example, as inflation has driven the price of candy bars relentlessly upward, the bar gets smaller while the price stays the same for a while. The bar can get somewhat smaller before consumers notice the difference.

A complication of the concept of Weber's law comes with stimuli near the absolute thresholds. When stimuli are close to the lower thresholds, k may become considerably greater, and it may increase for high stimulus values as well. On the strength of this, it has been suggested that subjective sensations should be measured indirectly using differential increments. This reasoning led to the Weber-Fechner law, given as:

$$R = k \log S + a$$

Where: R is the magnitude of response
             S is the magnitude of the stimulus
             k is the constant of proportionality
             a is the constant of integration

The Weber-Fechner law implies that the relationship between price and price response is logarithimic with consumers more sensitive to price changes at the extremes of their price limits. [26]

The j.n.d. for a price decrease depends on the consumer's motivation to receive a better price and the effort required to get the lower price. In addition, research indicates that consumers are more sensitive to price increases than to price decreases. [27] This research, however, predates the intense inflation we have experienced. There may be a tendency to become somewhat accustomed to price increases so that there would be less sensitivity at the upper limit.

The value of k tends to vary over products. For some products, such as prestige items, a relatively large price change in either direction might occur without its being perceived as relevant. [28]

The concept of differential threshold has been further refined through the application of adaptation level theory. [29] This theory suggests that the relevant price on which the consumer bases perceptions is the last paid price, or the fair price. [30] There are several relevant implications of adaptation level theory on price perception.

1. Price perceptions are relative to other prices and to associated use values.
2. There is a standard price for each discernible quality level for each product category.
3. The standard price serves as an anchor for judgment of other prices.
4. There is a region of indifference about a standard price such that changes in price within this region produce no change in perception.
5. The standard price will be some average of the prices for similar products.

6. Buyers do not judge each price singly, but rather each price is compared with the standard price and the other prices in the price range.
7. The standard price need not correspond with any actual price nor the price of the leading brand. [31]

The Kamen-Toman study of the effect of fair prices as opposed to Weber's law concluded, "The evidence in support of the 'fair price' theory over Weber's law seems overwhelming." [32] Researchers contended that increased gasoline prices induce some motorists to cut back on recreational driving, to look at economy cars, to form car pools, to tune their engines, or to use motorcycles or public transportation. However, the adaptation effect noted earlier takes over as consumers become accustomed to the higher prices, and they then abandon their cost-cutting ways.

Joseph Kamen and Robert Toman further illustrate the fair price concept with the following example:

> A person ordering a meal may have a 'fair price' estimate for a steak of $3.50 with an acceptable range from $2.50 to $4.50; for coffee, the estimate might be 20 cents with an acceptable range from 15 cents to 25 cents. We would predict that, for example, a 30 cent charge (or 20% over the maximum fair price) would have a greater negative effect than a similar absolute or proportionate reduction from the price of the steak. [33]

This same study also indicated that as the price levels of gasoline go up, motorists tend to favor: independent brands at any given major-independent price differential, regular over premium grade at any given regular-premium price differential, and independent-regular over major-premium at any combination of major-independent and regular-premium differentials. [34]

The results of the Kamen-Toman study were heavily challenged by other researchers. [35] Kent Monroe observed that the Kamen-Toman assumption that fair price theory negates Weber's law was fallacious and cites the following evidence in support of the subjective perception of price:

> (1) The subjective price scale of the buyer seems to follow a logarithmic scale, and (2) there is a range of acceptable prices for certain products. As Kamen and Toman recognize, the second conclusion is similar to the fair price notion. The first conclusion can be derived from Weber's law, and both conclusions are compatible. [36]

In support of their fair price concept, Kamen and Toman quote James Engel, David Kollat, and Roger Blackwell:

> Since consumers are often unaware of the exact prices for many products, it may be that in many instances there is a range of acceptable prices. So long as the price of the product falls within the acceptable zone, price may not be a criterion. However, if price exceeds the upper or lower range of acceptable prices, price becomes important and the product in question is rejected. [37]

Kamen and Toman further defended their position in a journal article, in which they wrote that "under certain conditions the price differences would bear an *inverse* relationship to price, particularly, where price exceeds a "fair" level. There simply is no j.n.d. for price, and our methodology shows we were testing not discrimination, but preference behavior."[38]

Jon Stapel contended that what Kamen and Toman observed was a substitution effect of inferior lower-priced alternatives as the price of a favored alternative increased.[39] Looking at it another way, it seems that the controversy revolves around overt behavior versus perception. Weber's law indicates that a difference will become *noticeable* at some critical level of change. Real changes may occur without being noticed. This leaves room for psychological effects. If a person were to measure carefully any stimulus before and after a change, the change could be detected, but might not be noticed by a person not making such careful measurements.

If a change is noticed, Weber's law says nothing about whether that change will be acted upon. Within some range of indifference the consumer may not act upon a price change, but the change may be noticed. The key is whether the consumer is consciously aware of a price change, not whether some act will take place because of the change. It is recognized that Weber's law holds only over limited ranges and that the constant (k) will change as stimuli move closer to absolute thresholds.

Based on all the evidence, it seems logical to conclude:

> The logarithmic nature of the subjective price scale is characteristic of group attitude, and thus fully compatible with the "fair price" theory. Kamen and Toman were therefore not justified in considering the latter to be contradictory to the relevant aspects of the principle of which Weber's law is a special case.[40]

The Price-Quality Relationship

As noted several times in this chapter, consumers often equate high price with high quality, and vice versa. This is in keeping with the earlier discussion of the consumer's use of cues to signal information about various phenomena. Brand name, product features, package design or color, price, or almost anything can be seized upon by the consumer to communicate product quality. However, the working of any cue in the presence of other cues may become quite complex. If the consumer has only one cue to rely on, that cue will generally be assimilated and interpreted as a differentiating factor, but the actual purchase situation is almost never characterized by isolated cues.

The earliest studies of the price-quality relationship all reported a strong tendency for consumers to judge product quality by the product's price. The first of these studies asked respondents to choose between two imaginary brands of moth flakes, cooking sherry, razor blades, and floor wax, differentiated only by price. Subjects were asked to indicate their degree of satisfaction with their choices. Those who chose the lower-priced brand tended to be less satisfied with their choice.[41] A subsequent study using salt, aspirin, floor wax, and liquid shampoo found that respondents tended to choose the higher-priced alternative if they believed the brands to be different from one another.[42] A later study also found that consumers use price as an indicator of quality, even when their senses indicated that there was not a positive relationship between price and quality.[43]

Several reasons have been advanced to explain the relationship between price and perceived quality.[44]

1. _Ease of measurement_—price is a concrete, measurable variable for the shopper. In most retail outlets price is fixed, not subject to bargaining. If the shopper were to buy in a store where price was set through bargaining, the price-quality relationship would not hold. Since price is concrete and measurable, the consumer views it with more confidence than other cues more closely related to quality, but more difficult to judge. Also, self-service shopping makes it more difficult to receive other quality cues.

2. _Effort and satisfaction_—consumer satisfaction depends, in part, on the amount of effort expended in obtaining the product.[45] It seems reasonable that the expenditure of money is similar to the expenditure of effort, and, if so, it could be said that the more money the consumer invests in the product, the greater will be the satisfaction with the purchase.

3. _Snob appeal_—a consumer may want friends and neighbors to know that he or she can afford to spend a lot. It may be felt that his or her prestige and social position require that the most expensive item be purchased.[46] To the extent that high price is associated with scarce products, it might be indicative of individuality.

4. _Perceptions of risk_—the prospective buyer balances the dollar cost of the higher-priced product against the possibility of losing out because of the assumed lower quality of the lower-priced alternative. Buying a higher-priced product will generally be perceived as a risk-aversive strategy. In purchasing a gift, consumers may be more likely to purchase a high-priced alternative to ensure that it will be appropriate. The cost and quality of a component part also can have an impact on the consumer's attitude toward risk. The less important the cost of a component in the finished product and the more important the quality contribution of the component, the more likely the consumer is to buy a high-priced component to ensure that the finished product will be acceptable. Pressure to conform can also be a factor. A consumer may pay a high price in the interest of reducing the risk of failure to conform.

Given all these reasons why there is a relationship between price and perceived quality, attention can now be focused on more recent research, which casts some doubt on the existence of a simple, direct price-quality relationship. The early studies that found a strong relationship between price and perceived quality were single-cue studies—that is, price was the only cue consumers had to indicate product quality. In addition, consumers were generally in a situation where they were required to select what they perceived to be the highest quality item. Under such conditions, the consumer really had no alternative since there was no other relevant information. An additional problem has been noted, particularly for the single-cue studies.

> The validity of quantitative relationships between price and perceived quality depends heavily on the interval scale properties of the quality measure and the assumption that equal price intervals are perceived as equal by the consumer.

Evidence is not plentiful for either assumption. Therefore, before such findings are inbued with external validity and generalized to other products and other situations, they should be cross-validated.[47]

Further studies have used multiple cues, with mixed results. At the extreme, one researcher observed, "It must be concluded that price, except for unique but as yet unspecified circumstances, does not influence perception of product quality."[48] Another study found that price by itself did influence quality perception, but when combined with brand image, brand image affected quality perception while price did not.[49] Another study of the perception of carpet quality found a direct relationship with price but none with store information. There was, however, an interaction effect between price and store information.[50] Some multiple-cue studies have supported the price-quality relationship,[51] while others have not.[52]

In general, as more information cues are available to the consumer, less relevance is attributed to price. However, when the consumer is provided with too many information cues, there is a tendency to return to price as a major cue to quality.[53] Apparently, as consumers are perceptually overloaded, often with subjective information, some return to the objective price cue.

Resolving the conflict among price-quality studies is probably impossible at this point. There is enough evidence to conclude that price probably does have an impact on quality perception during the purchase process. Additional evidence suggests that the price paid for an item also influences quality perceptions after the purchase.[54] The relationship appears to be somewhat product specific, explaining some of the conflicting results.[55]

The price-quality relationship seems to be rather complex and influenced by a number of factors, including the following:

1. Type of product.[56]
2. Risk and uncertainty leads to greater price reliance.[57]
3. Brand preference often influences the perception of quality. Sometimes price overrides brand, and sometimes the reverse occurs.[58]
4. Trust in the competency and honesty of price makers is correlated with generalized price reliance.[59]
5. People who are "snobs" rely on price to connote quality.[60]
6. Lower-income and education consumers are more sensitive to the price-quality relationship.[61]
7. Brand experience tends to lessen reliance on the price cue.[62]
8. Consumers low in self-confidence and/or high in anxiety tend to rely on price as a quality cue.[63]
9. Consumers who find it difficult to judge price tend to rely more on price image than those who find it easy to judge whether a price is reasonable.[64]

Whatever the exact nature of the relationship between price and perceived quality, market experience suggests that consumers do use price as an indicator of quality. For years the Sony brand communicated high quality and high price in television sets. In a market where low-priced TV sets became the rule, Sony concentrated on quality emphasized by advertising and price level. The strategy paid off as Sony's share of the U.S. market more than doubled in the five years from 1971 to 1976, capturing 7.5 percent of the 8.2 million-set market and $2.9 billion in sales. Then, in the late seventies, retailers began sharply cutting prices on Sony TV's. Not only did the Sony quality image slip, but they sold fewer sets as well.[65] Low price is not always the best avenue to higher sales volume.

Consumer Response to Price

The previous section dealt largely with the relationship between consumer perception and price. This section is concerned with consumers' actual response to price. The concept that consumers perceive price and product quality to be positively related really doesn't say much about actual product selection, since many consumers may be unable or unwilling to pay for the highest quality. The following discussion covers the topics of price paid and response to price changes.

Price Paid

A consumer may elect to pay a high price, a low price, or some price between the extremes when making a purchase. Research has indicated that those who pay high prices are different from those who pay low prices.[66]

Sales of products and brands at different prices suggest that consumers respond to prices differently. This is contrary to economic theory, which assumes objective and consistent price perception. Perhaps different consumer perceptions of price information lead to different interpretations and price responses. Thus, price selection may be affected by preconceived beliefs and perceptions of self and products. These factors can be general (physical product features) or specific (company and brand images).

Generally, consumers who choose high-priced items perceive large quality variations among products and brands. They see the consequences of a poor choice as being undesirable. As noted earlier, this is the case in such high-risk situations as gift giving. Some years ago, when I was selling in a retail store at Christmas time, the importance some people place on paying a high price was graphically demonstrated. The store was well known as a high-price, high-prestige operation. A customer asked for a table lighter, priced $20.00 (not $19.95). We normally carried the item but had sold the last one. I explained to her that we were out, but told her that a nearby discount store had the same lighter on sale for $9.98. She krinkled her nose and said, "But that's a discount house. What else do you have?" Her interest was in obtaining a high-priced item from a quality store to be sure that her gift was "right."

"High-price payers" are confident that quality is related to price and see themselves as good judges of product quality. They often perceive that their experience with the product purchased is high, and they tend to feel that their brand choice is likely to influence other people's social judgments of them. Additional research indicates that higher prices are paid in buying situations in which consumers perceived that they had adequate information.[67]

Those who select low-priced items have much less confidence in a price-quality relationship. They tend to think that quality variation is limited and that brand choice has relatively little social meaning. They perceive minimal consequences to be associated with an unsatisfactory purchase. They believe that their ability to judge product quality and their purchasing experience are relatively low.[68]

Many consumers follow a strategy of selecting a middle-level price. In this way the consumer can feel that the purchase is of acceptable quality but reasonably priced. Hotel managers report that patrons tend to select a middle price when given a choice, and selection from a restaurant menu also shows a mid-range preference.[69]

Managers can influence this mid-range selection by controlling what product choices buyers perceive to be middle-priced. Such perceptions can be generated by providing a range of prices with a concentration in the mid-range. Sellers with price lists or catalogs can more readily influence price perceptions.[70]

Price Change

Economic logic indicates that a price increase should lead to reduced purchases, and vice versa. However, the relationship is not this simple. In general, brand preference tends to be more sensitive to price decreases than to price increases. If preference is a predictor of purchase behavior, small price increases should not lead to decreased demand.[71] This, of course, relates to the differential threshold.

When a consumer has had experience with a brand, the experience is likely to be a dominant factor in choice, even in the face of price change. The more consumers know about their preferred brand, the greater is the price change required to change their purchase behavior.[72]

SUMMARY

Although economic price theory is useful as a tool in understanding price, it often fails to represent true consumer price response resulting from psychological product differentiation, advertising effects, differences in individual perception and motivation, and nonrational price response.

Because most prices in a complex industrialized economy are administered rather than directly determined by the forces of supply and demand, price is an important variable in a firm's marketing strategy. Most administered prices are set with consideration of costs and what price limits the market will bear, and most actual prices are based on product cost. Price can be set at, above, or below prevailing market prices. Firms engage heavily in nonprice competition through product differentiation. Price can create an image for a product or firm from discount to prestige. Special price allowances or reductions can act as incentive motivations for consumers.

Pricing a new product presents special problems, particularly if no relevant market price exists for the particular item. Firms may follow a penetration or skimming price strategy here, and initial market price can be set based on what consumers indicate they would expect to pay for the benefits provided by the product. The price the marketer initially establishes will often have a direct bearing on consumer perceptions of quality, since people may have nothing else on which to base that perception.

Marketers of new products must elicit initial product trial if they are to establish a market share. Price cuts may be used as an incentive motivation and as a means of risk reduction to gain trial. The free sample represents the greatest price cut but is an expensive strategy. Coupons, low introductory prices, cents-off offers and rebates are less costly and can be effective.

Psychological pricing recognizes the seemingly nonrational price response of consumers. Psychological pricing techniques include: customary pricing, odd pricing, price lining, multiple-unit pricing, leader pricing, and prestige pricing. Psychological pricing seems to be widely used and is thought to be effective. However, psychological pricing may sometimes lead to confusion. Since a confused consumer will often refrain from buying, unit pricing may actually lead to increased sales.

Consumers' subjective perception of prices is generally more important than the price itself. Price perception relates to price consciousness, price thresholds (absolute and differential), and price-quality relationship.

Consumers pay different prices for the items they buy. Price selection may be affected by preconceived beliefs and perceptions of self and products. Many consumers follow a decision rule of selecting a middle-priced item to assure them adequate quality at a reasonable price. Price changes may or may not lead to changed buying behavior. Brand preference, experience, and knowledge may insulate against brand switching in the face of higher-priced or lower-priced alternative products.

CHAPTER 13 STUDY REVIEW

Important Terms and Concepts

Economic price theory
New product pricing
Price incentives
Psychological pricing
Customary pricing
Odd pricing
Price lining
Prestige pricing
Multiple-unit pricing
Price leaders
Price perception
Price consciousness
Price thresholds
Fair price concept
Price-quality relationship

Questions

1. Why might economic price theory not provide an adequate basis for understanding buyer response to price?

2. How might price strategy be used to induce product trial?

3. What are the practical implications of perceptual thresholds for price strategy?

4. What is the nature of the price-quality relationship? Why should such a relationship exist? To what degree do you feel that it actually exists?

5. Differentiate between consumers who pay high prices and those who pay low prices for items.

14

Interpersonal
Communication

The communication process involves transmitting and receiving information. Meanings are encoded and exchanged through decoding—processing, categorizing, and interpreting information. Virtually all areas of behavioral study are potentially relevant to the understanding of the communication process, but perception and learning theory probably offer the greatest insights.

Marketing communication involves all purchase-related information to, from, and among consumers. This communication is categorized as personal versus mass and advocate (marketer-controlled) versus neutral (nonmarketer-controlled). This chapter covers the personal side of marketing communication, and chapter 15 treats nonpersonal or mass communication, essentially advertising.

Interpersonal communication as it relates to consumer behavior consists of personal selling and personal customer service on the controllable (advocate) side and personal interactions among such persons as friends, relatives, and associates on the noncontrollable (neutral) side. Chapter 2 considered some interpersonal communication effects along with the consumer decision process. This chapter expands that treatment to consider word-of-mouth influences among consumers and some behavioral implications of personal selling effort.

Interpersonal Influence

Marketing communication involves the dissemination of various types of purchase-related information, but the marketer is not so much concerned with information flows per se as with the influence that communication may have upon consumer buying attitudes and responses. The impact that personally shared information has upon consumers' attitudes, perceptions, and behavior is referred to as interpersonal influence. We are all heavily influenced by people around us. Virtually all human behavior is sensitive to the influence of other persons, and consumer behavior is no exception.

For many buying decisions, personal influence has the major impact. For example, one study indicated that personal influence was seven times as effective as advertising in persuading women to switch kinds of household products.[1] Another study found that only forty-eight percent of housewives who indicated that they had been heavily exposed to advertising that urged a switch to a new supermarket actually changed, while eighty percent of those who had been influenced by other people changed.[2]

Many business firms consider personal selling and sales management to be substantially more important than advertising. On the average, the industrial firms studied indicated that personal selling was 5.2 times as important as advertising, while firms selling consumer products cited personal selling as 1.8 times as important for durables and 1.1 times as important for nondurables.[3]

Literally hundreds of other research studies have found that personal influence is considered to be the greatest single factor in consumer buying decisions. One reason for the significance of personal influence is the effect of social power (referent, legitimate, coercive, expert, and reward). Both noncommercial and commercial information sources can exercise various kinds of social power to influence individual consumer behavior.

Noncommercial Influence

Noncommercial sources, such as friends, neighbors, relatives, and associates, represent significant others to whom we turn for advice and support in buying decisions. Such interaction may be initiated either by the prospective purchaser or by one who is moved to impart unsolicited information and advice. Influence may be one-way or mutual in an interaction. Personal influence may also occur as the result of observation of the behavior of others. The actions of significant others may become cues from which consumers model their own buying behavior. Fashions and styles may be transmitted without verbal interaction. Upwardly mobile individuals may find observed cues from those after whom they pattern their behavior to be particularly significant.

Noncommercial personal influence is generally treated as opinion leadership or word-of-mouth communication (sometimes referred to as word-of-mouth advertising, or simply word-of-mouth). Purchase information of all types may be transmitted through personal influence channels, but the bulk of it probably centers around new or untried products, the quality of specific brands, prices, and experiences with various retailers. A great deal of the information shared is negative, since consumers relate problems with products and stores to other interested parties.

Motivations for Informal Market Communications Motivation for consumers to become involved in interpersonal communication and influence is two-sided. On the one hand is the motivation to communicate with and influence others (dominance need), and on the other hand is the motivation to seek or follow advice (deference need).

Communicator Motivation The motives that lead a person to communicate with others about products can be classified as follows:

1. *Product involvement.* Experience with the product (or service) produces a tension that may not be reduced by the use of the product alone but that must be channeled by way of talk, recommendation, and enthusiasm to restore the balance (provide relief). One researcher found this motivation to be present for thirty-three percent of the consumers studied.

2. *Self involvement.* For twenty-four percent of the consumers studied, the accent was more on the self than on the product, with the latter serving as a means through which the speaker can gratify emotional needs, categorized as self-confirmation needs, including:

   Gaining attention—The products and services that, in their totality, represent what could be called the machinery of living take the place of topics centered around people or ideas. (Introducing a product into a conversation can be a way of "having something to say.")

   Showing connoisseurship—Talking about certain products can serve as proof of being in the know or having refined judgment.

   Feeling like a pioneer—Newness and difference of products provide the speaker with an opportunity to identify with them and their makers.

   Having inside information—Some products or services permit the speaker to feel clever—that is, to know more about them and their production than the listener is expected to know.

   Suggesting status—Talking about products with social status provides an "elevator" for the talker by which he can reach the level of the product and its users.

   Spreading the gospel—Converting the listener to using a product can provide the speaker with occasion to enlist the listener in a good cause.

   Seeking confirmation of personal judgment—The more people there are who follow the speaker's advice, the more justified will that person feel in personal judgments; the speaker needs followers to feel reassured about making a personal decision.

   Asserting superiority—Recommending of products can be a tool for assuming leadership and exercising power over listeners and may even serve as a sort of test to determine whether listeners really respect the speaker (Will they or won't they heed my advice?).

3. *Other involvement.* Twenty percent of those studied said the product chiefly fills the need to give something to the other person, to share their pleasure with that person, or to express care, love, or friendship. In these instances the recommendation takes the place of a gift, just as a thoughtful gift often expresses a tacit recommendation. ("Because I have had pleasure in this, I want you, too, to have it. Here it is.")

4. *Message involvement.* This refers to talk that is mainly stimulated by the way the product is presented through advertisements, commercials, or public relations but is not necessarily based on the speaker's experience with the product proper. Message involvement motivated twenty-three percent of the consumers studied. Several forces operate here that are based on people's interest in and exposure to advertisements: "the show is the thing," shop talk, and verbal play.

Since it is difficult for consumers to avoid exposure to advertising, many people have turned to accepting it for its independent attraction and entertainment value. They are inclined to lean back and let the advertisers compete with the shows. Thus, entertainment value and originality of ads have become topics of talk.

Knowing that hundreds of highly paid brains are competing for their favor, readers and listeners have become judges and experts of advertising effectiveness. They assume the critical attitude of an advertising manager and tell each other about clever ads.

Whether or not the product is desired or the content of the sales message is of interest, readers and listeners like to quote playfully and apply verbally ad lines and slogans. (Remember "I can't believe I ate the whole thing." In addition some advertising songs become hits, like "No Matter What Shape Your Stomach Is In" (Alka Seltzer), and "I'd Like to Teach the World" (Coca-Cola). Even when the original mood is one of mockery or irony in the ad, the advertiser or the product, it is usually superseded by the pleasure gained in the act of perhaps often-repeated and varied application. A certain gratefulness is the price one pays for the opportunity offered by the ad to play with it.[4]

Listener Motivation There is an involvement and motivation for the recipient of word-of-mouth information that transcends the desire to know more about a product or service from an unbiased source. Some people have a need to follow or to be influenced by other people. Recipients may feel that to listen to or follow the advice of another will cause that person to accept them more.

There is a certain satisfaction derived from knowing that someone else is interested enough in you or your well-being to give information about products when there is no perceived selfish motivation on the part of the communicator. This, of course, assumes that the recipient attributes the communication to an unselfish desire to be helpful. Attribution theory potentially offers insights into the perceived motives and qualifications of those who communicate informal market information.[5]

Consumers may seek information from other persons to reduce purchase risk. If other people with whom the consumer identifies use or approve a product, perceived social risk is reduced. If others express satisfaction with the function of a product, perceived economic risk may be minimized. Research findings suggest that consumers high in perceived risk are more likely to initiate purchase-related conversations and to ask for product information than those low in perceived risk.[6] When a product purchase is perceived to be risky, consumers may seek information from personal sources, and, if this is inadequate, other information sources will be consulted. Thus, other persons are likely to represent the primary information source in a risky decision, and other sources may be consulted only if personal channels are inadequate.[7]

Opinion Leadership Many years ago it was hypothesized that "ideas often flow from radio or print media to opinion leaders and from these to the less active sections of the population."[8] Subsequent research has cast some doubt on the notion of a simple two-step flow of information.[9] Actually, no simple explanation for information flows exists. People seem to act as both receivers and transmitters of information, and the concept of generalized opinion leadership is very questionable.[10] We are more likely to find opinion discussers than opinion leaders, since leadership is largely a function of the situation and individual interest and experience.

Even though there is some question as to the significance or even the existence of opinion leaders, a considerable amount of research has been done to determine who opinion leaders are. Results suggest that some people are more active in discussing their opinions than others, and some people seem to be more influential than others in getting their opinions accepted. Because innovators seem to be active in influencing later adopters to accept innovations, research on innovators and opinion leadership overlaps substantially. This research has largely centered on personal characteristics of opinion leaders and situational factors.

Personal Characteristics In general, demographic characteristics have not successfully discriminated between opinion leaders and nonopinion leaders, but research suggests that younger housewives and larger families are associated with opinion leadership.[11] Opinion leaders are generally more socially outgoing than other consumers.[12] In keeping with their innovative nature, opinion leaders have more favorable attitudes toward new products.[13] Findings on the personality of opinion leaders are mixed. While some researchers report no differences between the personality of leaders and nonleaders, others have found opinion leaders to be more self-confident, more venturesome, more emotionally stable, likeable, and assertive, and less self-deprecating and depressive.[14] Opinion leaders appear to be more attentive to mass media than others, and they tend to use more objective information (such as test reports), while nonleaders tend to use more personal sources.[15] Consumer life-style variables, including leadership, information exchanges, innovation, community and club involvement, independence, price consciousness, occupation, and fashion consciousness, have been found to relate to opinion leadership.[16]

The question of whether there are general opinion leaders across a wide variety of products is still unanswered, but it would seem that generalized opinion leadership is limited. Opinion influence appears to be two-way, and people identified as opinion leaders seem only slightly more influential than others. The opinion leader is in turn influenced and is not a dominant leader influencing a passive set of followers.[17]

Situational Factors Given that there are probably no general opinion leaders, influence would appear to be situational. While a certain amount of overlap in influence across related products does exist, this depends upon knowledge and interest and does not seem to apply necessarily to a broad range of unrelated topics.[18] Although no relationship was found between generalized self-confidence and opinion leadership, one study suggested that the level of confidence in ability to judge a specific product was positively associated with word-of-mouth activity.[19]

Opinion leaders are generally heavier users of mass media. They also are more heavily exposed to specialized sources and to more technically accurate sources relevant to their particular areas of expertise and interest.[20]

There is evidence to suggest that opinion leadership, particularly with respect to the types of products most subject to opinion influence, varies across cultures. There is also research indicating that opinion leadership varies by section of the country.[21]

Sources of information in general and opinion leadership in particular have been found to vary with the stage of the purchase process. In a study of opinion leadership in the adoption of the Mazda automobile, opinion leaders differed substantially from nonleaders in their initial information sources. Leaders were more likely to use magazines, while nonleaders were more likely to receive information from friends. However, as additional information was sought, leaders switched to reliance on personal sources.[22]

Personal Influence in Marketing Strategy For the marketing strategist the question is, How can personal influence that is beyond direct control be used to influence prospective buyers? Of course, strategic use is somewhat limited, but influence does seem possible. Probably one of the most important things is to make sure that products and services meet customer expectations so that negative word-of-mouth can be curtailed.

A particularly difficult question is how to reach opinion leaders through mass media. One author suggested that opinion leaders are high in mobility, status, and confidence.[23] Presumably, advertising that appealed to such types would reach opinion leaders. In general, however, research indicates that opinion leadership is not person specific so much as it is situation specific, so segmenting through media selection and advertising appeals may be rather difficult.

Since there seem to be few universal opinion leaders in informal consumer interactions, and opinion leaders really seem to have little more influence than others, perhaps it isn't really necessary to try to reach opinion leaders at all. A more important goal would seem to be simply to get people talking about a brand, store, or new product without any concern for who is leading whom. Anyone who tries a product and is satisfied with it can potentially influence others to try that product. Fabergé has used an advertisement encouraging word-of-mouth. The television commercial explained the benefits of the brand and closed with the words, "Tell two of your friends about Fabergé Organic Wheat Germ and Honey and they'll tell two more, and they'll tell two more, and so on, and so on, and so on. . . ." The video showed the user multiply to two, four, eight, and sixteen frames (see figure 14-1). Ernest Dichter suggests that advertisers can both simulate and stimulate word-of-mouth.[24]

Simulating Word-of-Mouth Advertisers cannot fully escape the attribution that a product is recommended for monetary gain. We accept the opinions of friends because we attribute no ulterior motive to their product information and recommendations. There are some ways in which consumer attributions can be influenced,

Fig. 14-1. Advertisement Encouraging Word-of-Mouth Influence

"Organic Reaction"

GIRL: I told two friends about Faberge Organics Shampoo with pure wheat germ oil and honey.

And they told two friends.

And so on...

and so on...

ANNOUNCER (VO): That's the organic reaction...you'll want to tell your friends about super rich Faberge Organics Shampoo.

For fresh smelling hair with super shine and super body...give it a try!!
GIRL: You'll tell two friends about it.

And they'll tell two friends

And so on...and so on...

With pure Wheat Germ Oil and Honey.

Faberge Organics Shampoo with pure wheat germ oil and honey.

Courtesy of Fabergé.

since attributions are based on perceptions, and perceptions can be altered. In general, attributing advertising to other-than-profit motives can be accomplished by moving perceptions of the advertiser closer to the position of the consumer's friend, thereby "proving" altruistic and friendly intentions, and making the advertiser's relation to the product seem authentic.

Everyone wants to be liked; consumers would like to think that an advertiser is personally concerned about them. Essentially, advertisers can prove their intentions and ally themselves with their customers in the following ways:

Anticipate customer attitudes—Knowing that customers are likely to be suspicious of an advertiser's intent, they can be invited to join the fun of advertising, even at the advertiser's expense. Humor in advertising may accomplish this. Advertisers can poke fun at themselves or their product but never their customer. Thus, the consumer, in a sense, joins the advertiser at the same level.

Gift package the sales message—By expressing a sales message in an entertaining, agreeable fashion, the advertiser reveals a concern for the customer, who is free to benefit from this thoughtfulness whether or not the recommendation is followed. Entertainment alone will not sell a product, but it can create a more receptive environment for communicating an effective selling message.

Establish audience kinship—Establishing a common ground with the consumer heightens a feeling of identification and mutual trust. The style of an ad, its artwork, language, and the situation it portrays all contribute to a base of identification. The slice-of-life commercial, widely used by marketers of packaged goods, can convey this feeling, if the situation is not too far-fetched or contrived. Using "real" people in ads instead of actors can also create this kinship bond, as can testimonials from satisfied consumers.

Initiate an exclusive club—Suggesting that a product is not for everybody can give the consumers the feeling that purchase initiates the buyer into an exclusive group. The desires to belong and to be unique may lead the consumer to seek the advertiser's initiation and acceptance.

Be a humanitarian—Institutional advertising that casts the firm in a positive role through its gifts, foundations, donations, and research may be perceived as acts of friendship and thus can warm consumers to the advertiser's commercial messages.

Convey personal experience—Word-of-mouth advertising is effective partly because communicators have had experience with the product in question. Advertisements that show a genuine love for a product and an understanding of its role in the consumer's life engender positive reactions. The advertiser's feeling and communication must be based on real understanding if this tactic is to be successful. Life-style research can often yield useful results here. Some time ago, the Kellogg Company studied the behavior patterns of families in the morning. The result was the advertising campaign that used the theme of "wakin' up." Ads showed all sorts of waking-up events in a fast-action sequence. Viewers could readily identify with the scenes and could really believe that Kellogg understood what went on as Americans prepared for their day.

The advertiser must also communicate an authentic relationship with the product. This brings the advertiser alive for the customer in a number of ways.

Become a consumer—Often the best selling is done when a salesperson slips out of role and becomes a consumer, explaining personal successes in using the product. The consumer should attribute the information in the selling message as arising from the personal experience of the seller.

Personalize the producer—The company needs to personalize itself with the consumer, emphasizing its concern for product and consumer. Often this can be done by using company employees. The Union Pacific Railroad could easily be perceived as a distant giant, but its TV commercials with its people singing and being identified by name and home town make the company seem human.

Trace company myths—Often the roots of a company make great fodder for advertising. The Kraft Cheese Company traces its beginnings in its ads to J. L. Kraft, who hand-made and delivered quality cheese to his customers. That same tradition, we are told, lives on in the company today.

Describe the organization climate—An advertiser who can find something about the product or its creation that is unique or exciting can turn this aspect into effective appeals to bring customers to identify with the company and its products. This can reflect a company climate of caring, appreciation, and love for the product. Ads for Paul Mason wine use the dramatic voice and talent of Orson Wells to convey the message, "We will sell no wine . . . before its time." Johnny Carson's humorous take-offs on that theme also help to foster discussion of the commercial and the product.

Reflect on adventure—Avoiding the polished anonymity of the typical copy-writer, an advertisement can be turned into a personal statement about an adventure with a product. The product can take on a life of its own and be personified in the eyes of consumers as a kind of hero.

Stimulating Word-of-Mouth A marketer may directly stimulate consumers to talk about products, but the audience must be provided with motivations and information that will get them talking. Contests, premiums, special sales, innovative products, and creative promotion appeals can all stimulate discussion. People generally don't talk without reason. An advertiser can use a number of tactics to stimulate discussion.

Use the "shock of difference" with a purpose—Consumer attention and interest can be gained with an unusual, off-beat appeal, but the appeal should be relevant to the customer's needs. The Bic pen on the end of a jackhammer, the Timex watch that keeps getting retrieved from so many out-of-the-way places, and other products fit the criterion. The incongruity, extremity, or unusualness of the ad creates a climate that psychologically moves the audience to form the desired image. The shock of difference may produce a sort of tension in the consumer that can be relieved by talking about the product or ad.

Use "heightened reality"—Talked-about commercials tend to use staged situations that symbolically heighten reality and make the product bigger than life. Artistic creation may use "the suspense of drama, the lilts and moods of poetry, the relief of comedy, the irony of anecdote, the bluff of paradox, and the startling truth of a documentary close-up." Some care has to be taken to avoid deception, and sometimes it's a little hard to predict just what the FTC will consider deceptive. All detergent staged an ad in which a stain on a man's shirt was removed when the room he was in filled with water and a little All was added. The ad was held to be deceptive because that small amount of detergent in that much water could not get the stain out. But there is still some room for creative license. Cat food commercials with piano-playing, singing, and dancing cats are effective attention getters using bigger-than-life appeals.

Invite consumers to poke fun at ads—When the advertiser jokes about the product or the company, the consumer can feel "let in" to the advertiser's trust and confidence. Volkswagen Beetle ads masterfully portrayed the Volkswagen driver as smart and thrifty, while the car was made fun of unmercifully. One ad showed the car as a lemon on wheels. Buyers loved it, and they bought huge windup keys for their cars and affectionately referred to their cars as bugs.

Equip the message with "wings"—Use of catchy slogans, tunes, and appeals that are easy to remember and easy to quote sometimes creates a compulsiveness for repetition. (How often have you caught yourself humming a tune from an ad?) To achieve this end, the sequence of words and sounds should provoke verbal play through its rhythm, alliteration, and pointedness. The ad should apply to a wide variety of life-styles and situations, and it should employ symbolism, figurativeness, irony, aggression, or suggestiveness. Perhaps you remember the Noxema ad where the lovely Swedish woman cooed to a man, "Take it off, take it *all* off." Of course, she was talking about the fellow's beard, but it was hard to keep that in mind.

Leave room for the consumer's wit and ingenuity—Good humor often leaves something to the audience's imagination through omitted words or double meanings. Advertisements that allow the consumer to improvise or provide meanings can often stimulate discussion. The commercial that shows a housewife going through the drudgery of her day and says that she's had a full day of motherhood, but now she's going to have an "Aviance night" leaves us with all sorts of possibilities as she (now glamorous) greets her husband at the door.

Do not leave the customer alone with the product—Almost the antithesis of the previous point is the suggestion that the customer be shown specifically what benefits the product provides, particularly those that might not be immediately obvious. Feeling that they may have insights nobody else has, consumers may tell their friends. There is a certain satisfaction in being the first to bear news.

Link the product with the trends and needs of the times—Advertising appeals should be timely if they are to relate to the audience. Humor is often tied to what's happening. Even old products can be kept fresh if their selling-appeals and packaging are constantly updated. People talk about what's new, so this can be important.

Give the consumer a change—Unusual and interesting twists on a product and its uses can get people talking. The product or company can form a backdrop for the story, but it must be inextricably tied in so that when people tell the story, the product is in it.

Make the consumer feel that product recommendation is a gift—The recommendation to buy a cherished product may be viewed as a kind of gift. Ads may express the fact that friends will appreciate being told about the product and will express their gratitude. Thus, talking about a product may be seen as a reward to both the communicator and the recipient.

Offer a bridge of friendship—The seller can make it easy to send a product as a gift. When people ask what might make a good gift, the product may be mentioned. The gift giver who is on the lookout for appropriate gifts will likely appreciate the suggestion and may pass the information along to others.

Commercial Influence

Although the marketer may be able to influence the informal word-of-mouth information channel, generally a more direct and controllable communication is also required. The personal selling process has been much less researched than advertising, but it is a vital component of many marketing strategies. The concern here is not with the selling process per se. Rather, the discussion will center on personal selling as an interpersonal process and consumer response to sales strategies.

Theories of Personal Selling Several theories have evolved that seek to explain successful selling strategies.[25] The earliest theories revolved around personal characteristics and traits of successful salespeople. However, successful salespeople seem to be of all types; there seems to be no such thing as a born salesperson or an archetypically successful salesperson.

Another theory focuses upon the salesperson's actions. The classic concept of selling action is the AIDA model. The salesperson first captures the prospect's attention, then builds interest, creates a desire for the product and, finally, elicits action in the form of a purchase. Along with the AIDA concept, numerous lists of steps in the selling process have been advanced.

Fig. 14-2.   Dyadic Interaction in Personal Selling

Salesperson		Prospect	
Role concept and expectations:		*Role concept and expectations:*	
Self		Self	
Prospect		Salesperson	
Prospect's reactions to salesperson		Salesperson's reactions to prospect	
Knowledge of:		*Knowledge of:*	
Product		Product	
Company		Company	
Selling and salespeople		Selling and salespeople	
Prospect		Salesperson	
Attitudes toward:	Verbal and Nonverbal Communication	*Attitudes toward:*	
Selling and salespeople	Social Distance	Selling and salespeople	
Company		Company	
Prospect		Salesperson	
Personality structure:		*Personality structure:*	
Salesperson's		Prospect's	
Prospect's		Salesperson's	

Objective and physical characteristics (Salesperson):

Education	Politics	Weight
Income	Family	Appearance
Religion	Age	Personal habits
Occupation	Height	Social class

	Company
Training	Reputation
Support	Advertising

Objective and physical characteristics (Prospect):

Education	Politics	Weight
Income	Family	Appearance
Religion	Age	Personal habits
Occupation	Height	Social class

Influencers	
Spouse	Friends
Family	Experts

Adapted from Franklin B. Evans, "Dyadic Interaction in Selling—A New Approach," (unpublished manuscript, University of Chicago, 1964), p. 26.

The stimulus-response theory posits that the salesperson has only to find the right stimulus or appeal and the customer will respond with a purchase. A variation on this is the need satisfaction theory. As in the preceding theories, the customer is viewed in a passive role. The salesperson determines what the customer needs and makes the sale by choosing the right selling points that show the prospect how buying will satisfy expressed needs.

All of the theories fail to explain why a given salesperson using the same approach with persons of similar needs succeeds in selling some prospects and fails with others. One plausible explanation is that the selling process is not simply a presentation to a passive prospect.

Selling as an Interpersonal Process Personal selling can be best understood if it is viewed as social behavior or interpersonal interaction rather than one person unilaterally influencing another. In social behavior, the power, perceptions, motives, personality, and attitudes of each party involved are relevant in determining the outcome of an interaction.

Personal selling interaction can be viewed as a dyad in which the interaction of two persons depends on the economic, social, physical, and personality characteristics of each party, and understanding the outcome requires a study of the interface of the two parties rather than the individual characteristics of the customer and salesperson. Figure 14-2 presents an early model of dyadic influences in personal selling. The probability of a sale taking place is influenced by the degree to which the prospect's and salesperson's characteristics, including age, height, income, political opinions, religious beliefs, and smoking behavior, are perceived by the prospect to be similar to his or her own.[26] Sales success, therefore, is partially the result of a blend of salesperson and customer characteristics, not simply salesperson skill or characteristics (see figures 14-3 and 14-4).

Fig. 14-3.   Sales Representative Characteristics that Improve Sales Effectiveness

1. A sales representative's *initial impression* upon his customer largely determines his future interactions with the customer and the degree to which the customer will *like* him.
2. Up to some point, the more *familiar* a sales representative becomes to his customer, the more his customer will like him.
3. The more a sales representative *rewards* his customer (particularly, psychological rewards), the more his customer will *like* him.
4. The more *similar* a sales representative is to his client, the more likely the client will *like* him.
5. The sales representative is more persuasive if he is perceived by his customer as highly *credible* (i.e., trustworthy, prestigious, expert, honest, etc.)
6. The sales representative is more persuasive if he is perceived by his client as *similar* to himself.
7. The sales representative is more persuasive if he is *empathetic* toward his customer.

From *The Marketing Communication Process* by M. Wayne DeLozier. Copyright © 1976 by McGraw-Hill Book Company. Used with the permission of McGraw-Hill Book Company.

Fig. 14-4.   Customer Characteristics that Improve Sales Representative Effectiveness

1. A customer low in *self-esteem* is more persuasible than someone high in self-esteem, especially where social approval is involved.
2. A customer with an *authoritarian* personality is more susceptible to persuasion when the sales message is attributed to authority figures than when it is attributed to anonymous sources.
3. A customer with a *nonauthoritarian* personality is more susceptible to persuasion when a sales message is attributed to anonymous figures.
4. A customer with a highly *dogmatic* personality tends to be persuaded more by authority figures whom he trusts than by authority figures whom he does not trust.
5. A customer who is *"open-minded"* is persauded on the merits of an argument, rather than on the basis of who delivers the message.
6. Customers who exhibit *social withdrawal* tendencies are less susceptible to persuasion than those who do not display this tendency.
7. Customers who *inhibit* their *aggressive feelings* are very persuasible, whereas those who display aggressiveness are less persuaded by majority opinion.
8. Customers high in *anxiety* tend to be hard to persuade.
9. Customers who are high in *rich-imagery* and *fantasy* tend to be more persuasible than those who exhibit less of these traits.
10. Due to their ability to make valid inferences, customers with *high intelligence* are influenced more by logical argumentation than customers with low intelligence.
11. Due to their superior critical ability, customers with *high intelligence* are influenced less than people with low intelligence when presented with a "false, illogical, irrelevant" argument.
12. *Women* tend to be more persuasible than men.
13. Sales messages are more influential when directed at *specific* customer *interests, goals,* and *problems* than when directed at the "public at large."
14. Sales message which attack a customer's centrally held *belief* on some subject are almost always ineffective.
15. Customers high in *popularity* or *prestige* tend to resist attitude change, especially when it might affect their group status.

There is evidence that successful salespeople concentrate on prospect types who are perceived as most likely to buy from them.[27] As research in the area has progressed, influences on the outcome of the personal selling interaction have been viewed as being quite complex, with the success of the salesperson dependent upon attention, attractiveness, credibility, and communication.

Attention Attention is treated as the first stage in some of the consumer decision-making models covered in chapter 2. It is essentially the same as the problem perception stage of the decision process. Attention puts the consumer in a receptive state of mind for acquiring product information and interacting with salespeople. This corresponds to the perceptual concept of mental readiness in which the consumer becomes selectively perceptive of relevant information. Readiness is a concept drawn from educational psychology that relates to an individual's ability and desire to interact or communicate with another person.[28]

Presumably, the prospect who enters a retail store is ready to communicate about product needs or search for potential solutions. The in-home or industrial sales call probably requires an approach aimed at creating customer readiness, which is related to buyer predispositions and intentions. If a buyer enters a transaction ready and willing to buy, the probability of purchase is likely to be higher, regardless of the characteristics of the salesperson and prospect.

The success of a sale appears to be quite situational.[29] If the consumer is pressed for time or if a purchase is not deemed important enough to warrant extensive shopping, a purchase is more likely when contact is made with a salesperson. In addition, the presence of *purchase pals* (friends who have come along to help with the decision) seems to reduce the importance of salesperson characteristics and leads to a higher portion of successful sales.[30] Purchase pals are often sought when customer self-confidence is low because their presence seems to raise the customer's self-confidence.[31]

Attractiveness The perceived attractiveness of a salesperson may increase the likelihood of a successful transaction. Attraction is a function of similarity, empathy, likability, and role congruence.

Customers apparently respond better to salespeople who are similar to themselves. Although subsequent research and analysis has challenged this conclusion,[32] there seems to be evidence that similarity may raise the probability that a sale will be consumated.

The general attitudes toward selling and salespeople that a prospect brings to a selling situation provide the framework for judging an individual salesperson.[33] At the same time, the salesperson has attitudes that affect the selling message. Successful sales tend to occur when prospect attitudes are positive and when there is a high degree of attitudinal similarity between the prospect and the salesperson.[34] Perceived similarity in ideas and attitudes may be more important than other factors because similar attitudes provide a basis for cooperation, and dissimilar attitudes are more likely to lead to friction.[35] A salesperson who is a good actor may be able to communicate similar attitudes by agreeing with the prospect's tastes and opinions.

Similarity in appearance may be achieved by being sure that salespeople are paid enough to dress as well as their customers. Other types of similarity, such as social class, may be more difficult to achieve because of regulations against discrimination in hiring.

Empathy is achieved by letting a customer know that the salesperson understands his or her problem or point of view. Thus, even though there may be no real similarity between the two, there can be a bond of understanding.[36]

Even though a salesperson may not be similar to a customer, the customer's self-esteem may be raised by the salesperson who shows friendship, approval, and support of the prospect's projected self-image.[37] This can be especially significant in long-term associations, since frequent interaction is likely to increase interpersonal liking.

Attractiveness influences are significant because they relate to the consumer's real or ideal self-image. One of the benefits of social interaction is that the participants can develop distinct, consistent, and satisfactory self-concepts. If the customer perceives that the salesperson does not accept and support his or her self-image, there may be a resulting loss of face. One of the functions of the individual's attitudes is ego defense, which may cause the customer to develop a negative attitude toward the salesperson, the product represented, or both if the salesperson communicates disapproval.

Salespeople who are more skillful in interpreting their customer's self-image and projecting attractiveness through establishing common characteristics, empathetic communication, and a friendly posture tend to be more successful. Consumers give feedback that should act as a cue for modifying or reinforcing approaches used. Although what the customer says, along with the choice of words "the product seems inexpensive" as opposed to "it looks cheap", provides significant feedback, feedback is often nonverbal and may come in the form of a nod, smile, or frown. Salespeople, however, are often insensitive to customer feedback, assuming selling to be a one-way process.[38]

In a dyadic relationship each party has a conception of what the other's role should be, and a judgment is made during and after the interaction as to how well that role is fulfilled. This critical factor in determining the success of a sale is the degree to which the salesperson meets the prospect's role expectations. The degree of pressure the salesperson is expected to exert, the amount of familiarity and friendliness exhibited, and the amount of expertise displayed are examples of role components. Thus, the salesperson whose behavior fits the prospect's perceived ideal role is more likely to make the sale.[39]

Salespeople, then, need to "size up" prospects early in the communication and watch carefully for positive and negative feedback. The following guidelines are suggested for salespeople to enhance their attractiveness:

1. Seek some genuine common ground so that mutual interests are established (likely reference groups—family, community—leisure activities, state of the world).
2. Mention in favorable terms something the salesclerk has noticed about the customer.
3. Be supportive of the customer; voice agreement or give praise (such as, "I hadn't thought of that"), but particularly be supportive of the image projected by the customer.[40]

Above all, the salesperson must appear genuine in relating to customers. Salespeople are often perceived as being biased and as having ulterior motives, and prospects may very well be skeptical of a salesperson's flattery. Consequently, many people will react negatively to a salesperson's overfamiliarity. It's probably best to underplay social overtures, balancing "low key" with enthusiasm.

Credibility A variety of research results indicate that the credibility (trustworthiness, believability, and expertise) of any information source is an important factor in how effective the source is in changing attitudes and influencing behavior. One study of the relative effects of expertise and similarity in the personal selling situation found that the perceived expertise of salespeople was substantially more important to sales success than perceived similarity.[41]

The importance of perceived credibility should be emphasized. The extent to which an argument is perceived to be credible is, in part, dependent upon the prospect's beliefs and experience. Thus, similarity plays some part in perceived credibility, and the role of the salesperson may lend some expectation of credibility that will likely influence the prospect, especially the naive customer.

It has been suggested that some customers will rely on salesperson expertise, while others will be influenced by attractiveness, depending on personality. An inner-directed person is guided by internalized values and may be more susceptible to the influence of expertise and truthfulness. On the other hand, an other-directed person is likely to be more responsive to an attractive salesperson.[42]

Communication Although source effects are important to the success of a selling effort, message effects are also significant (see figure 14-5). Two message-related concepts seem significant in determining the success of a buyer seller interaction.

> The first dimension is the "content of communication" representing the substantive aspects of the purpose for which the two parties have got together. It entails suggesting, offering, promoting or negotiating a set of product-specific utilities and their expectation. . . . A second dimension of buyer-seller interaction is the "style of communication." It represents the format, ritual or mannerism which the buyer and seller adopt in their interaction.[43]

Interaction Process Analysis Although personal selling has often been viewed as a dyadic interaction, there is some question as to whether many personal selling situations, particularly at the retail level, can legitimately be considered a two-person group with the characteristics required of a true dyad.[44] A dyad has been defined in terms of the length of association. The relationship must persist over a long enough time for a pattern of interacting personalities to develop, and it is assumed that the dyad's existence will continue over time, resulting in an ongoing relationship.[45] To the extent that personal selling situations do not meet this criterion, much of the research in social psychology relative to dyadic groups may be inapplicable.

The personal selling process that is not part of an ongoing relationship may more realistically be viewed as a less formal relationship, referred to as a focused gathering or encounter. The encounter is unique in that embarrassment, maintenance of poise, capacity for verbal communication, exchange of speaker role, and

Fig. 14-5.   Message Characteristics that Improve Sales Representative Effectiveness

1. A sales presentation which appeals to the customer's permanent interests or his immediate concerns attracts and holds attention.

2. A sales presentation which is supportive of the customer's presently held attitudes and opinions attracts and holds attention.

3. A sales presentation which appeals to customer needs tends to gain and maintain attention.

4. A sales presentation which promotes a product requiring mechanical skills is learned best if the customer actively participates in the demonstration of the product.

5. The major product benefits are best learned by a customer if they are presented at the beginning and at the end of the sales presentation.

6. A sales presentation which is unique or unusual is better remembered than a commonplace presentation.

7. Repeating the major benefits of the product in a sales presentation enhances the customer's learning of those benefits.

8. A customer will learn a simple sales presentation more easily than a complex one.

9. A sales presentation is more persuasive if a one-sided message is presented to customers who (a) initially approve of the sales representative's brand, (b) are poorly educated, or (c) are not expected to see or hear subsequent counterarguments.

10. A sales presentation is more persuasive if a two-sided message is presented to customers who (a) initially disapprove of the product, (b) are well educated, or (c) are likely to see or hear counterarguments.

11. A sales presentation is more persuasive if it uses an *anticlimax order* for customers who have a low level of interest in the product.

12. A sales presentation is more persuasive if it uses a *climax order* for customers who have a high level of interest in the product.

13. A sales presentation is more persuasive if it uses a *primary order* for controversial, interesting, and highly familiar products.

14. A sales presentation is more persuasive if it uses a *recency order* for uninteresting or moderately unfamiliar products.

particularly maintenance of continuous focus on the official activity of the encounter are not properties of social groups in general.[46]

Analysis of the transitory sales encounter might be best described using Interaction Process Analysis (IPA).[47] In essence, the interaction is viewed as a mutual problem-solving effort where both buyer and seller contribute to the solution. IPA helps in understanding an act by analyzing an interaction.

An analysis of sales transactions based in part on IPA focuses on the length, velocity, content, and interaction roles in the buyer-seller interaction.

> *Length.* Retail transactions varied from one minute to more than two hours, averaging twenty-three minutes, with seventy-five percent less than thirty minutes.

> *Velocity.* On the average there were ten acts per minute, with more than half of transactions producing six to eleven acts per minute.

15. A sales presentation is more persuasive if it arouses a need first, then offers the product as a means of satisfying the need.

16. A sales presentation is more persuasive if it uses a strong fear appeal which poses a threat to the consumer's loved ones, or is presented by a highly credible source, or concerns topics somewhat unfamiliar to the customer, or is directed to consumers high in self-esteem.

17. A sales presentation is more persuasive if it uses highly affective language to describe the product.

18. A sales presentation is more persuasive if it associates the product with popular ideas.

19. A sales presentation is more persuasive if it uses nonverbal communications to enhance the product's meaning, especially nonverbal cues which elicit positive consumer feelings and emotions.

20. For products aimed at the "young-marrieds" market, the sales presentation should be designed and directed toward both husband and wife. (They exhibit more joint purchase decisions.)

21. Sales messages which emphasize instrumental functions of a product should be directed toward the husband in a family, whereas those emphasizing aesthetic features should be directed toward the wife.

22. When product or brand purchase decisions are not influenced strongly by reference groups, the sales message should emphasize brand features, intrinsic qualities, and benefits over competing brands.

23. When a reference group does influence consumer purchase decisions, the sales message should emphasize the kind of people who use the brand and reinforce these stereotypes in the minds of consumers.

24. For new products, the sales message should stress the relative advantages of the new brand over existing brands, show how it fits into the consumer's present ways of doing things (i.e., be compatible), demonstrate the product's ease of use (i.e., reduce perceived complexity), and show the results of using the product (observability).

25. Where opinion leaders for a product can be identified, the sales representative should direct considerable effort toward this group, so that the opinion leaders might, in turn, favorably influence their followers.

From *The Marketing Communication Process* by M. Wayne DeLozier. Copyright © 1976 by McGraw-Hill Book Company. Used with the permission of McGraw-Hill Book Company.

Content. More than seventy-five percent of the interaction involved orientation and opinion. Orientation (information and clarification) was most common. These acts simply laid the groundwork for effective communication. Suggestions and agreement accounted for most of the remainder of the acts and were more significant to the actual decision even though less time-consuming.

Interaction roles. Study of the relative contribution of each party in the transactions showed that salespeople performed twice as many acts as the customer. Salespeople were most active in the attempted answer and the disagreement, tension, and antagonism areas (negative reactions accounted for less than two-tenths of one percent of all acts). Customers were four times as active in the question categories.[48]

Social Power In any interaction the concept of social power is likely to be relevant. Although a salesperson could conceivably exert any type of social power in a selling interaction, expert and referent power influences have been studied thoroughly. Because the customer has control of the final decision, his or her power is likely to be strongest in the reward area.

In reality, the influence of expert and referent power is analogous to the concepts of attractiveness and credibility discussed earlier. Consistent with earlier findings on the effects of similarity and expertise, expert power is generally more influential than referent power, but there are some qualifications on this conclusion that should be considered.[49]

A major problem the salesperson has is winning the customer's trust. Both expert and referent power of the salesperson enhance the buyer's trust, but expert power is more significant. Although the salesperson can win confidence through friendly concern, product knowledge has more weight. Expert power may be achieved through product knowledge. Greater referent power can be achieved by creating a feeling that the purchase problem is shared by the salesperson.

Referent power seems to give a salesperson a wider range of influence, possibly because liking the salesperson transcends specific purchase situations. Salespeople who sell a wide variety of products or services (typical in the retail situation) need strong referent power. Although sales training can impart expert power, referent power may have to be sought in the selection process by seeking congenial, outgoing persons. In ongoing sales relationships, the salesperson can exert reward power by gratifying the customer's ego, entertaining and "favor doing." Over time, this may lead to a strong referent power base.

The Salesperson/Consumer Decision Interface

In models of consumer decision making the consumer is considered to be in control of the process as alternatives are determined, information is sought, and the final decision is made. However, the interactive nature of the selling process suggests that the consumer is often substantially less than autonomous in making the decision when salespeople are involved. In many cases the salesperson will suggest a major portion of the alternatives to be considered and will control a good deal of the information that the prospect receives—and does not receive—about alternative products.

To the degree that the salesperson understands the buyer decision process, a greater degree of success in closing sales can be achieved.[50] The sales transaction tends to follow a sequence of stages that coincide with the stages of the decision process. The selling process often involves bargaining to culminate in the decision. In order to gain control of the selling situation, the salesperson may employ techniques of persuasion and behavior modification.

One researcher studying transactions in retail refrigerator and color TV sales identified three phases in a transaction: orientation, evaluation, and consummation.[51] In the orientation phase, information flow is primarily directed at establishing customer needs. The phase may be initiated by either the salesperson's inquiry or the customer's request. Research on the phase indicates that surprisingly little information is actually transmitted during orientation. In more than half the transactions the salesperson asked no questions of prospects to ascertain customer needs. Salespeople tend to rely on one or two attributes customers mention. In a sense, this is not bad, since relatively few attributes will generally act as cues for the customer's evaluation. The orientation phase contains virtually no mention of nonproduct attributes, like credit or warrantee. In a few instances the orientation phase is entirely bypassed with the interchange launching immediately into evaluation.

The evaluation phase begins when the salesperson shows the first alternative to the customer. The phase is characterized by the exchange of information pertaining primarily to specific alternatives considered. Evaluation accounts for the bulk of transaction time and effort.

In the consummation phase the transaction is terminated with a purchase or a break-off. This phase is primarily concerned with discussion of nonproduct attributes.

Investigating this process reveals the relationship between the structure of the transaction and the consumer decision process. The salesperson appears to be a significant force in guiding and influencing the decision process. In most cases the salesperson, not the customer, determines the extent of search and evaluation of alternatives. The salesperson typically selects the order and number of alternatives evaluated and seems to dominate the evaluation of each alternative in that the semiprepared presentation guides the customer's attention to various product attributes. The salesperson also clearly influences the evaluation of alternatives, especially with respect to such attribute characteristics as style appropriateness, brand quality, and capacity or size requirements. In some cases, the customer completely abdicated responsibility for such evaluation and simply asked for the salesperson's recommendation. Moreover, the salesperson could and often did influence the salience of particular attributes. Finally, product attributes were of paramount importance to the decision. Nonproduct attributes, such as credit availability and terms, delivery and set up, and service, appeared to be secondary, and references to them typically occurred only after the decision to purchase was made.[52] We may conclude that in purchase situations where a salesperson is involved, the consumer decision process can be substantially influenced and guided by a knowledgeable salesperson.

Bargaining A unique situation exists when some dimensions of a sale are not firmly set prior to buyer-seller interaction. Points amenable to bargaining may include price, delivery, options or special features, and trade-in. In these situations relative power and negotiating skill may become quite important. One view suggests the following components of the bargaining process:

1.   *Direct offers*—Any concession by the salesman, such as reduction of price, more rapid delivery, or extended credit terms; the customer's offer to purchase for concessions such as above.
2.   *Presentation of concession limits*—Statement of expectations from the transaction by either salesman or customer, such as statement of prices, desired style, or service policies.
3.   *Determination of concession limits*—Attempts to determine expectations of the other person in the transaction, such as a salesman's attempt to determine

the customer's credit wishes or a customer's attempt to determine a salesman's delivery schedule.

4.   *Attempts to change concession limits*—Attempts by either customer or salesman to get the other to change his expectations of the transaction.[53]

Several significant conclusions can be drawn from a study of bargaining across
several stores and products. As figure 14-6 indicates, the greatest bargaining activity
occurred in the presentation of concession limits. Customers who were very active
in this area were high in purchase intention, spent more time in shopping, had
price-oriented patronage motives, and had previously owned the product. Figure
14-7 gives the points on which bargaining activities turned.

Fig. 14-6. Structural Components of Bargaining

Bargaining Component	Mean number of acts per transaction	Proportion of acts per transaction
Presenting concession limits	17.9	58.8%
Determining concession limits	7.0	23.1
Attempts to change concession limits	4.8	15.6
Direct offer	.8	2.5
All bargaining acts	30.4	100.0%

Allan L. Pennington, "Customer-Salesman Bargaining Behavior in Retail Transactions," *Journal of
Marketing Research* 5 (August 1968):256. Reprinted from the *Journal of Marketing Research*, published
by the American Marketing Association.

Fig. 14-7. Frequencies of References for Bargaining Acts

Referent	Mean number per transaction
Price	11.2
Product features	6.5
Timing of purchase	3.0
Brand	1.9
Terms	1.7
Delivery	1.7
Service	1.2
Guarantee	.9
Product quality	.6
Styling	.6

Allan L. Pennington, "Customer-Salesman Bargaining Behavior in Retail Transactions," *Journal of
Marketing Research* 5 (August 1968):257. Reprinted from the *Journal of Marketing Research*, published
by the American Marketing Association.

Better-educated consumers, those shopping more stores, considering several brands, and replacing an existing product, made more attempts to change the salesperson's concession limits. Direct offers did not correlate with shopping behavior, but the frequency of direct offers was significantly higher in multiline operations than in either department or specialty stores. Consumers high in purchase intention were more active in determining concession limits, and they were also much more likely to buy. A salesperson working with a prospect active in seeking concession limits may reasonably expect the prospect to be close to a purchase decision.

The bargaining study found eleven shopping or bargaining variables to be associated with actual purchase (see figure 14-8). Bargaining behavior is not a particularly common phenomenon, and the trend has been away from bargaining. However, bargaining is still found in automobile, housing, and some appliance and furniture sales. The salesperson who is able to interpret customer bargaining behavior will find important clues to identifying high-intention customers, predicting the time of purchase, and adapting the sales presentation to the unique characteristics of individual consumers.[54]

Fig. 14-8.   Relationships Between Key Shopping and Bargaining Variables and Purchase

Shopping or bargaining variable	Correlation of variable with purchase at time observed (Point-Biserial r)
Number of stores shopped by customer	−.27[c]
Frequency of direct offers	+.18[b]
Relative frequency of attempts to change concession limits	−.25[c]
Frequency of commitment to concession limits	+.33[c]
Frequency of attempts to change concession limits by devaluating other's product	−.17[a]
Frequency of reference to product quality	−.17[a]
Frequency of reference to delivery	+.25[c]
Frequency of reference to styling	+.21[b]
Relative frequency of reference to price	−.24[c]
Relative frequency of reference to warranty	+.18[b]
Relative frequency of reference to brand	−.16[a]

[a]Significant at .05 level.
[b]Significant at .01 level.
[c]Significant at .001 level.

Allan L. Pennington, "Customer-Salesman Bargaining Behavior in Retail Transactions," *Journal of Marketing Research* 5 (August 1968):261. Reprinted from the *Journal of Marketing Research*, published by the American Marketing Association.

Behavior Modification Personal selling, of course, seeks to change or influence buyer behavior. Essentially this can be accomplished in two ways: through persuasion and through direct behavior influence strategies. Persuasion is aimed at modifying customer response indirectly by influencing attitudes and intentions. Behavioral influence, on the other hand, concentrates on directly modifying behavior. In particular, two behavioral influence strategies have been studied relative to buyer behavior. These are called foot-in-the-door (FITD) and door-in-the-face (DITF).

Foot-in-the-Door The FITD approach is based on the idea that inducing a person to commit to or agree to some relatively small request will increase the likelihood that subsequent, larger requests will elicit positive response. This sort of approach is often used in personal selling strategy. A life insurance salesperson will often take a prospect through a series of minor commitments in filling out an insurance application. The final request for the prospect's signature on the contract is then easier to secure. It is not necessary that the prospect's attitude toward the policy be changed at all. Behavior is affected directly. After the purchase, the buyer's attitude may come to agree with the behavior.

The use of free gifts and premiums are also used to give the salesperson a foot-in-the-door. Having accepted the gift, a prospect may feel some obligation to buy.[55] Simply taking a salesperson's time, inviting the seller into the home, or attending a selling party may serve as the initial act potentially leading to purchase.

The effectiveness of FITD has been explained by applying self-perception and attribution theories.[56] The theories suggest that, having complied with a small initial request, the prospect is lead to self-attribute a favorable disposition toward such behavior, thereby increasing the probability of compliance with a second, larger request.[57]

A number of studies have supported the idea that FITD is more effective than attempts at cold calling or persuasion.[58] Source credibility apparently plays a role here. One study found that FITD and persuasion associated with high credibility sources were about equally effective.[59] There is also evidence to suggest that FITD may be less effective when the larger request immediately follows the initial request. It is possible that psychological reactance is aroused if the prospect perceives that the small request is being used to get the larger commitment. Rejection may allow the prospect to demonstrate independence from perceived manipulation.[60]

Door-in-the-Face DITF is the antithesis of FITD. Here the prospect is presented with a large request that is almost sure to be refused. After the refusal, a second, smaller request is made. Having refused the larger request, the prospect feels somewhat compelled to give in to the smaller request.[61] In this technique the salesperson's movement from an initial, extreme request to a second, more moderate one is seen by the prospect as a concession. Research indicates that rejection of the large request led to significantly greater compliance with the smaller request than when only the small request was made.[62] However, one study found DITF to be inferior to either

FITD or persuasion.[63] The effectiveness of DITF may lie in the societal rule of reciprocation of concession, which posits, "You should make concessions to those who make concessions to you."[64]

In a sense, the "assumptive close" used by the salesperson is related to this concept. Some years ago when in my first management training position, I often attempted to close a tire sale with, "Will you want all five tires, or just the four." The customer didn't buy all five tires very often, but the concession to buy fewer often netted a four-tire sale when I might have sold only two, or two when I might have sold none.

Sometimes the two strategies can be used in tandem. This may be done in seeking add-on sales. Having sold one item (FITD), the salesperson may come back with a suggestion for a large, additional purchase. Having turned this down, the customer may be amenable to a less expensive add-on. One example stands out from my experience selling in a men's clothing store. A customer approached me and asked for a package of handkerchiefs ($1.50 for a package of three). I then advised him that he really needed a new suit to go with the handkerchiefs. We both laughed, and then I said, "But we do have some sport coats that just came in today, let me try one on you." To make a long story short, he wound up with the sport coat, three pairs of pants, several shirts and ties, and assorted socks—the total came to about $300. Obviously, the results are not always so spectacular, but the salesperson who suggests specific items—even high-priced ones—as add-ons will probably sell more goods.

After a study of FITD, DITF, and persuasion, researcher Alice Tybout concluded the following:

1. Foot-in-the-door should be used only when two contacts can be made efficiently, unless methods for increasing the effectiveness of foot-in-the-door when both requests are made in one contact can be developed.

2. Increasing the salience of compliance with the small request under foot-in-the-door does not increase the effectiveness of this strategy when both requests are made in the same interaction. Thus, no method for increasing the effectiveness of foot-in-the-door when only one contact can be made is currently available.

3. The argument that door-in-the-face may not be effective when the source is perceived to be motivated by self-interest suggests that this technique may be of limited utility in most marketing contexts where the communicator's advocacy is often viewed as being guided by selfish interests.

4. The effectiveness of door-in-the-face may be a function of the size of the second request. Evidence shows that if the second request is relatively large, individuals may be reluctant to reciprocate by accepting it and instead may search for a less binding way to reciprocate. Thus, marketers using this technique should pretest the size of their second request to insure that it is not too large.[65]

Relative to the source credibility and appeal salience Tybout observes:

1. Factors in the environment that enhance acceptance of the arguments in a persuasive appeal, such as high source credibility, may also operate as

discounting cues for internal attribution of compliance with requests under foot-in-the-door, thereby undermining effectiveness of this strategy. Thus, when marketers are working with a new product or issue that requires elaboration prior to making any requests, it may be impractical to combine the initial communication about the issue with a foot-in-the-door strategy.

2.   The finding that the self-perception process only occurred under high salience foot-in-the-door suggests the importance of making salient the cues needed for consumers to make the desired belief inferences. In some instances, it may be necessary to draw consumers' attention to the cues explicitly, whereas in other situations they may attend to the cues spontaneously. Regardless, the marketer must insure that the self-perception process occurs if the foot-in-the-door is to offer any advantage over straight persuasion.

3.   Assuming that the self-perception process occurs the foot-in-the-door strategy is maximally effective when delivered by a low credibility source. As a result, this strategy may be particularly useful in marketing situations where the source often is perceived to be of low credibility.[66]

Response to Some Specific Selling Strategies

Consumer response to various sales appeals seems to be a function of the consumer, the salesperson, and the situation. Given this, a salesperson is often faced with altering the selling approaches to fit differing circumstances and prospects. What works well in one case may not work at all in others. A salesperson may have to play different roles ranging from passive adviser to active persuader. One set of criteria suggests analyzing the sales situation in terms of the customer's choice criterion. As indicated in figure 14-9, the customer's product choice criteria may be absent or inactive, inadequate or vague, in conflict, or explicit.[67]

Absent or Inactive It is possible for a consumer to reach the purchase decision point with no specific product or brand attributes in mind. The customer may be relying on faith in a brand name, intuition, or the advice of a more knowledgeable person. Here the salesperson's strategy could be to *educate* the customer. Having established that the customer has no specific criterion in mind, the salesperson might first try to discover what particular use the product will serve. Given this, the salesperson can instruct the customer as to the attributes a "good" product should have and suggest a brand with the appropriate characteristics. Credibility may be established by suggesting the brand or product that will minimally meet the customer's needs. It is possible for the prospect to then be sold up to an item that will more fully meet needs (presumably at a higher price).

Inadequate and Vague The prospect may have a vague idea about the product desired and may open the conversation with something like, "I'd like to buy a more economical car." The term economical gives some guidance here, but the question is, More economical than what? What other features are needed—power, size, style? In this situation the salesperson has two potential strategies. First, since criteria are quite broad, any product not specifically excluded by the criteria can be suggested.

Fig. 14-9. Product Choice Criteria and Selling Strategy

	Choice Criteria Inactive or Nonexistent	Choice Criteria Vague and Inadequate	Choice Criteria in Conflict	Choice Criteria Explicit
Strategy	Educate	Solve (Recommend*)	Depreciate (Enhance Gain*)	Match
Attitude Theory Emphasis	Learning	Perceptual and Functional	Consistency	
Product Purchasing Characteristics	Low-Price Convenience Product; New Product	Technical Product and Infrequent Purchase		Important Purchase with Specific Application

* Less effective strategies.

John O'Shaughnessy, "Selling As an Interpersonal Process," *Journal of Retailing* 47, no. 4 (Winter 1971-72):42. Reprinted by permission of the *Journal of Retailing*.

There is a potential problem here, however. The salesperson will probably be doing more recommending than selling, and the customer may become aware of the vagueness of his or her needs and decide to look around more to sharpen the criteria.

The second potential strategy here is similar to that recommended for the previous choice criteria state. The salesperson helps the customer to diagnose and define the problem. Assuming that the salesperson has a range of products available, the right one can be offered to solve the customer's problem. The emphasis here is not on recommending what the salesperson considers a good product but in discovering the benefits the customer desires. Only after the customer's needs have been firmly identified is a product solution offered.

In Conflict Chapter 4 discussed the condition a person encounters when needs are in conflict. The following list reviews the three possibilities:

1. The approach-approach condition exists for mutually exclusive but desirable goals. Typically, this condition is unstable because the indecision is transitory. The individual will generally resolve which positive alternative to follow quite quickly.
2. Avoidance-avoidance is represented where two negative, mutually exclusive goals exist. Since the prospect seeks to avoid both, the situation is considered stable.
3. In approach-avoidance goals are both positive and negative. The strength of an individual's tendency to approach a positive goal and at the same time to avoid a negative outcome are decreasing functions of the distance from the goal. The tendency to approach predominates at a distance from the goal while moving near the goal arouses avoidance. Because the individual is likely to remain at the point where the tendencies intersect, the situation is considered stable. Inducing movement toward the goal by emphasizing its positive qualities increases fear and anxiety, while reducing its perceived negative features is likely to be more effective, since it moves the prospect toward the less feared goal.[68]

Situations 1 and 3 are particularly relevant to personal selling. In approach-approach, the customer must choose from two or more alternatives with some mutually exclusive attributes. The salesperson can stimulate the customer's decision by playing up one alternative while depreciating the other. This reinforcement on one or more cues helps the consumer to perceive a difference between the alternatives, with one emerging as superior.

In approach-avoidance, the product or attribute is accompanied by negative features. The most common is the price-desire conflict. The prospect approaches purchase, but guilt or other negative reaction to parting with the money increases as the prospect moves closer. The salesperson can either concentrate on making the item seem more attractive or deemphasize the negative feature. Presumably decreasing negative feelings, assuaging the consumer's guilt, and leaving attention focused on desirable consequences of the purchase would represent the more successful strategy.

Explicit When the customer's purchase criteria are clearly formulated, the selling strategy involves learning the criteria and matching product attributes to customer criteria. As each of the criteria is met, the salesperson seeks agreement from the prospect. At the end of the presentation, the prospect will have agreed on each point, and any disagreement from the customer will arouse the dissonance of denying a previously agreed upon point. To close the sale the salesperson may summarize each point with the customer again, affirming agreement. After agreeing with each element, the customer will have a hard time refusing to buy.

SUMMARY

Communication strategy lies at the heart of a firm's marketing strategy. Some communication to consumers is under the control of marketing management while some is independent. This chapter has been concerned with interpersonal communication and influence, some of which is directly under marketer control and some of which can be influenced only indirectly, if at all.

Interpersonal *communication* consists of personal selling and personal customer service (controllable) and interactions among friends, relatives, and associates (noncontrollable). Interpersonal *influence* relates to the impact of personally shared information on consumer behavior. For many, perhaps most, buying decisions, personal influence has a greater impact than mass-marketing efforts.

Noncommercial personal influence may be initiated by either information seekers or transmitters, may be one-way or two-way, may be verbal or nonverbal, centers largely around new or untried products, the quality of specific brands, and experience with retailers, and is very often negative in nature. Noncommercial personal influence is often referred to as opinion leadership or word-of-mouth communication or advertising. Both communicators and receivers are motivated to become involved in the interpersonal influence process.

Some researchers have suggested a two-step communication process whereby marketing information flows from mass communication media through opinion leaders to the majority of persons. However, it seems that information flows are not that simple. Most people both influence and are influenced by other persons, leadership being a function of the situation.

Although opinion leadership and word-of-mouth communication are beyond the direct control of marketers, they can be influenced to some degree. While it is difficult to pinpoint opinion leaders, the marketer may be able to get consumers talking about products by simulating and stimulating word-of-mouth.

Through personal selling the marketer can directly influence consumer behavior and attitudes. Several theories of personal selling effects have been advanced, but the dynamic interaction (dyad) theory seems to offer the most promise in understanding consumer response to personal selling effort. As an alternative to dyadic analysis, interaction process analysis provides insights to the selling interaction as a brief, transitory encounter. The interaction may be viewed in terms of length, velocity, content, and interaction roles. Social power is also important to the selling process. Expert and referent power are particularly significant in long-term sales relationships.

Three phases were identified as components of a sales transaction: orientation, evaluation, and consummation. The selling process often involves negotiation or bargaining on various points. Salespeople may also seek to influence customers through persuasion to change attitudes or through direct behavior modification. Direct influence may be exerted through the foot-in-the-door technique or by the door-in-the-face method. Finally, sales strategies were suggested for various states of customer product choice criteria: inactive, inadequate or vague, in conflict, or explicit.

CHAPTER 14   STUDY REVIEW

Important Terms and Concepts

Interpersonal communication
Word-of-mouth communication
Personal influence
Noncommercial personal influence
Opinion leadership
Commercial personal influence
Personal selling dyad
Interaction process analysis
Transaction
Bargaining
Behavior modification
Foot-in-the-door
Door-in-the-face

Questions

1. Why is personal influence so important in purchase decisions?

2. Summarize the motives that lead consumers to communicate with others about products and to listen to that communication.

3. What are the correlates of opinion leadership?

4. How can marketing strategists encourage word-of-mouth communication about their products?

5. Summarize the theories of personal selling.

6. Discuss the salesperson characteristics that lead to success in a personal selling dyad.

7. Discuss the customer characteristics that are likely to lead to success in a selling situation.

8. Discuss message characteristics that influence the success of a selling situation.

9. What is interaction process analysis, and how does it relate to the personal selling situation?

10. Discuss ways in which social power may influence the personal selling process.

11. To what extent can behavior modification techniques be employed in actual selling situations?

12. Discuss the selling approach appropriate to each of the customer choice criteria.

15

Behavioral Implications for Advertising

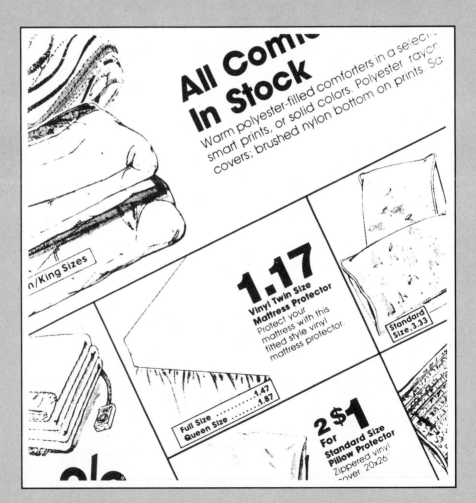

Probably no area of marketing strategy has been more heavily influenced by the study of consumer behavior than advertising. Many of the advertisements you see each day are based on behavioral research and principles, and many of the examples used throughout this text relate to advertising.

This chapter is devoted to advertising strategy as influenced by consumer behavior. Most of the observations will also apply to noncommercial public relations efforts of firms. Although point-of-purchase advertising could fit into this chapter, this topic is covered in chapter 16, along with retailer considerations.

Advertising is the major promotional device used by manufacturers to reach consumers. Although it may play a relatively less significant role in the retailer's promotion mix, it is still a vital force. Firms use advertising to change buyer attitudes and behavior, so it is fundamentally a behavioral process. The discussion here will draw upon perception, learning, attitudes, motivation, personality, and social forces.

The chapter begins with an overview of the attention/awareness/interpretation nature of advertising influence. The section is built around the concept of perception. The remainder of the chapter is organized around four areas of influence on advertising response. Source effects relate to the impact of the origin (or perceived origin) of an advertising message. Media effects are based on the mechanism that carries the message to the consumer. Message effects are the forces in the advertisements themselves that influence consumer reaction. Finally, receiver effects derive from internal characteristics of consumers as they influence advertising response.

Perception of Advertising

The effectiveness of advertising depends on the extent to which and the way in which the audience receives and interprets an advertisement. Consumers must receive and interpret an advertising message before it can be acted upon. Consumers' perception of advertising can be expected to be both selective and person specific (subjective).

411

Attention to Advertising

Although it appears that information may be received and interpreted at an unconscious level,[1] evidence continues to argue that conscious awareness of an advertisement precedes its effect on attitudes and behavior. As a result, the concepts of exposure and attention are significant in understanding advertising response.

Selective Exposure and Attention As noted in chapter 3, consumers tend to be selective in the advertising messages to which they expose themselves. Early research indicated that people were not likely to allow themselves to be exposed willingly to persuasive messages discrepant with their existing attitudes.[2]

Selective exposure may be the result of several forces. First, it seems obvious that with the many buying decisions that must be made, the consumer is likely to limit information search only to those messages relevant to current purchase problems. Furthermore, many purchases are just not important enough to warrant information search or processing. Finally, many consumers are satisfied with current solutions and don't want discrepant information ("Don't bother me with the facts, my mind is made up."). There are three reasons for this phenomenon.

1. An individual self-censors his intake of communication so as to shield his beliefs and practices from attack.
2. An individual seeks out communications which support his beliefs and practices.
3. The latter is particularly true when the beliefs or practices in question have undergone attack or the individual has otherwise been made less confident of them.[3]

There are those who contend that selective exposure is not so much a function of receiver interest or attitudes as of certain intervening variables, such as income, social class, education, background, or life-style.[4] Whatever the reason, selective exposure seems to be a major factor in determining what information the advertiser is able to place before consumers. Although there seems to be little the advertiser can do in directly motivating consumers to expose themselves to messages, attention can be gained even if consumers do not purposely expose themselves to the message.

Attention refers to a conscious awareness of a stimulus, and may be classified as follows:

1. *Involuntary attention*—A stimulus intrudes upon consumers' consciousness even though they do not want it to do so. In this case, attention may be based on the intensity (loudness, etc.) of the advertisement.
2. *Nonvoluntary attention*—A person is spontaneously attracted to an advertisement and attends to it because it arouses and holds interest. The consumer neither resists nor willingly attends to the advertisement. Once attention is attracted, the individual's interest is held because of a perceived benefit or relevancy. Since consumers are often watching, reading, and listening to the media that carry advertising messages for reasons other than the ads themselves, this type of attention may be the most common.

3. *Voluntary attention*—Consumers may consciously and willingly attend to advertisements when they have been sensitized to particular types of advertising by interest in specific products. This may occur either prior to or following a purchase. The mechanism here is similar to selective exposure.[5] Whether consumers willingly or unwillingly attend to advertisements, selective attention operates to increase or decrease the likelihood of conscious reception of particular ads.

Determinants of selective attention will vary according to the type of attention. Interest and experience will probably be the primary determinants of the ads to which a consumer will voluntarily attend. Attending can be considered a function of one or more stimulus (message) or individual (receiver) factors, many of which were discussed in chapter 3. Stimulus factors include the following:

1. *Size.* Large ads generally have greater attention-getting potential than smaller ones. However, the square root law indicates that a printed ad must increase four times in size to double its attention-getting value.
2. *Movement.* Movement or the *appearance* of movement attracts attention. Obviously, television commercials can directly employ movement, but the illusion of movement can be created in print ads through the use of blurred photographic techniques.
3. *Intensity.* Intensity can be employed to capture nonvoluntary attention. Brightly colored print ads, large headlines, and loud or penetrating radio or TV commercials can achieve this. Special papers and colors that seem to glow may achieve the desired effect. Care must be taken to avoid receiver irritation, however. Irritating stimuli may be physically or mentally tuned out.
4. *Novelty.* When stimuli are unusual or unexpected, consumers may be more likely to notice them. All human senses have the capacity to adapt to stimuli resulting in a kind of conditioned nonawareness. As we process information, a familiar or expected stimulus will likely be ignored. We tend to notice by exception. When a new perfume called Whisper was advertised on television, the commercial invited the viewer to whisper rather than shout to get attention. Part of the message was whispered, and attention was gained. The message further suggested the same subtlety was desirable in a scent.
5. *Contrast.* Closely related to the idea of novelty is a stimulus that contrasts with its background. Anything that makes an advertisement stand out will increase its attention value.
6. *Color.* In general, color ads receive more attention than black and white. However, as noted in chapter 3, a black and white ad may get attention among color ads because of its novelty and contrast.
7. *Position.* As noted in chapter 3, the upper and left-hand portions of a page get more attention than the rest of the page. Presumably, the upper left-hand quadrant of a page is the best place for an ad or the major attention-getter in an ad.
8. *Shape.* Advertisements that are taller than wide receive more attention than

those wider than tall. This may be explained by the fact that people generally scan across a page and are therefore more apt to see a vertical ad than a wide or square one of the same size.

9. *Isolation.* Chapter 3 indicated that a message or illustration in isolation may have great attention-gathering value.

10. *Multiple-sensory Messages.* The more senses an advertisement can involve, the better its attention value. TV can combine sight, sound, and movement. Print ads are more limited, but through "Scratch and Sniff" or other scent microencapsulations, fragrance can be introduced. Samples of some products can also be included to invoke touch. Records cut on thin, flexible plastic can also bring sound to a print ad. Special paper stock can be employed to give the page on which the ad appears a different feel or look from other pages in the publication. This can be particularly useful in newspaper, where the regular paper is low quality.

Individual factors involve:

1. *Permanent interests.* Almost any significant and basic motive may serve as a basis for attention, including love, sex, hunger, and status.

2. *Immediate concerns.* Current needs of a person may lead to perceptual vigilance and selective attention to certain ads.

3. *Attention span.* The human span of attention in terms of both time and number of items may limit attention. A person can process a maximum of about eleven information bits at a time. A person's attention tends to shift about once every four or five seconds. Advertisements, therefore, should provide stimulus variety, and the length of time consumers' attention can be held is limited.

4. *Attitudes and opinions.* People notice advertisements consistent with their own predispositions and filter out noncongruent messages.

Awareness The logical result of attention to advertising is awareness. In order to consider a product or brand for purchase, the consumer must be aware of it. This awareness may occur spontaneously on seeing a product displayed or through advertising. Awareness alone may be sufficient to lead a consumer to select one brand over another.

Interpretation of Advertising

Perception does not simply involve receiving and recognizing stimuli. Stimuli are also processed to allow the recipient to organize, interpret, and categorize information content. Selective perception extends to the interpretation of advertising in that the advertising message is likely to be selectively distorted and retained.

Whatever the message that is intended for communication by the advertiser, the receiver will tend to modify it to fit his or her motives, needs, attitudes, and opinions. As a result, it matters little what the advertiser intends to convey. What the consumer interprets is the determinant of any attitude or behavioral change that may occur as a result of the advertisement. This means, of course, that the advertiser must engage in research to determine whether the desired meanings are being communicated by advertising.

In addition to the immediate distortion that may occur when an advertising message is received, the recall of the message may be altered over time, or the message may be forgotten entirely. Messages that are more relevant may be retained longer and more accurately. Many messages pass by consumers and are retained for only a few moments at most. Others may be mentally filed in such a way that they will not be freely recalled, but some other stimulus, such as a store display, may trigger an "aided" recall. Although the main selling points in a message may be recalled in some circumstances, they usually aren't. The selling points may become part of the overall brand image and the information chunked for easy retrieval later on. The consumer buying a particular brand may have an overall favorable image but may be unable to recall specific brand features from advertising.

There may be some long-term distortion of information. Over a period of time the source of an advertising message may become irrelevant. There is also a potential for the advertising recipient to attribute the advertisement to other brands. In this case, an advertiser can end up advertising for its competitors as much as for itself. The potential for this is especially high in comparative advertising where the advertiser identifies its competitors by name. Over time the receiver may come to attribute the message to one of the other brands in the ad.[7] For this reason the brand leader probably should not use comparative advertising. It is likely that a leader-sponsored ad would result in increased awareness of competing brands without materially altering the leader's brand awareness. On the other hand, the less well known brand may benefit from its comparative ads through increased exposure and identification with and differentiation from the better-known brand or brands.

Behavioral Effects of Advertising

There are a number of factors that influence the exposure to, interpretation of, and reaction to advertising. These are generally categorized as source, media, message, and receiver effects.

Source Effects

One of the most significant factors influencing the consumer to respond to advertising favorably is credibility or believability. If the consumer does not believe what an ad is saying, the probability of positive attitude or behavior change is greatly reduced. The source that communicates the advertising message will have a major impact on how the message is received and interpreted. In general, a source is more persuasive if its credibility is high. Figure 15-1 cites some major findings on source effects.

Credibility is the result of a wide variety of source characteristics, including perceived honesty, prestige, expertise, and attractiveness, likableness, and similarity.

Fig. 15-1. Source Principles in Persuasion

1. In general, a source is more persuasive when his audience perceives him high, rather than low, in credibility.

2. A source's credibility, and thus his persuasiveness, is reduced when his audience perceives that the source has something to gain from his persuasive attempts (intention to manipulate).

3. Over time, the opinion change attributed to a high-credibility source decreases, whereas the opinon change induced by a low-credibility source increases, resulting in about the same level of retained opinion change for both low- and high-credibility sources.

4. Reinstatement of a high-credibility source some time after his initial message presentation results in *higher* opinion change retention than if no reinstatement occurs; whereas reinstatement of a low-credibility source some time after his message presentation results in *lower* opinion change retention than if no reinstatement occurs.

5. The low-credibility source can increase his influence by arguing for a position which is against his own self-interest.

6. A communicator increases his influence if at first he expresses *some* views already held by his audience, followed by his intended persuasive communication.

7. A communicator increases his persuasiveness if at the begining of his message he states that his position on the topic is the same as that of his audience, even though he may argue against that position.

8. The more similar members of an audience perceive the source to be to themselves, the more persuasive the communicator will be.

9. What people think of a communicator's message affects what they think of him (his image).

10. A source is more persuasive when he holds a positive, rather than a negative, attitude toward himself, his message, and his receiver.

11. The more powerful and attractive a source is perceived to be, the more influence he has on a receiver's behavior.

A wide range of research has demonstrated that audience reactions to identical messages will vary according to the source to which they are attributed.[8]

Honesty Honesty or trustworthiness is often considered the most significant determinant of source credibility. In general, consumers are likely to perceive that the purpose of any advertising message is to persuade them to accept the brand. The advertiser will be considered biased and apt to say anything to convince the consumer to buy. Under such conditions, low honesty will be attributed to the source. Advertisers have used several strategies in attempting to change consumer attributions. One commonly used technique is to create a situation in which the consumer overhears a conversation between individuals in the ad. This is referred to as a slice of life ad. The idea is to lead consumers to attribute an actual preference and use pattern to the characters in the advertisement, thereby reducing the feelings of being manipulated.

A second technique is the hidden camera ad. Here, someone has used the product and is now reporting the results of that usage in an unbiased way to an interviewer. The effect of this may be enhanced if the interviewee is initially skeptical of the brand. Procter and Gamble has used a good (effective, not necessarily entertaining) ad for Oxydol. A woman is being interviewed about a group of detergents she has just tried. A voice-over tells us that she has tried many detergents without being aware of what she was using and that the interview has discussed so many brands that she will not be influenced by the mention of Oxydol. The interviewer asks her if she would consider using Oxydol. She would not. She is then shown (to her surprise) that the detergent she picked as best is, in fact, Oxydol. Asked if she will now consider using Oxydol, she replies that she will. This ad is aimed specifically at consumers for whom Oxydol is not part of their evoked set. Having seen the ad, they are now aware that this consumer (who, *like them,* never considered Oxydol) will now consider and probably use the product. The attribution here is that the consumer in the ad is similar to the viewer of the ad, she has nothing to gain from the viewer's use of the product, and she wasn't even aware that she was in a position to influence others.

The basic problem a consumer has in judging the credibility of an advertisement is in determining whether the information in the ad—announcement, endorsement, or testimonial—represents the true feelings of the spokesperson.[9] If the spokesperson is perceived as having a choice between saying something positive or negative about the product, the consumer is more likely to attribute sincerity and credibility to that person. So, a third technique for creating credibility involves admitting a competitor's superiority on a minor point that may lead to an attribution of source independence and, therefore, credibility.[10] This concept could be extended to suggest that at least some testimonial ads should include a person with a negative attitude toward the product or some aspect of it. Rapid Shave has used a spoof ad in which a pile of shaving cream is placed in the middle of a road and the question is asked, "Will this pile of Rapid Shave stop this speeding car?" Of course, it won't, but then, as the announcer is quick to point out, it really doesn't have to.

A fourth common device for establishing trustworthiness is the product endorsement or testimonial. Both the celebrity and the ordinary consumer endorser can be effective here. Such a spokesperson may have both referent power and trustworthiness.

A celebrity may play four different roles.

1. *Testimonial*—A celebrity who has personally used a product or service and is in a position to attest to its quality may be asked to give a testimonial. Sports figures often give testimonials for products they use.
2. *Endorsement*—A celebrity who may or may not be an expert with regard to a product or service may be asked to lend his or her name and physical person to an advertisement for the product or service. Debbie Reynolds's endorsement of GE dishwashers is an example (see figure 15-2).

Fig. 15-2. Celebrity Endorsement

"THE NEW POTSCRUBBER III IS THE BEST DISHWASHER GE HAS EVER MADE. WHO COULD ASK FOR ANYTHING MORE?"
—Debbie Reynolds

IT WASHES DISHES CLEANER. The Potscrubber III dishwasher features the new exclusive Multi-Orbit™ Wash Arm, engineered to direct

a constantly changing pattern of water up through the dishes. This arm, combined with a Power Shower on top, and a Power Tower in the middle, gives you 3-level washing action that gets dishes and glasses cleaner than ever.

And the special Power Scrub·· Cycle, while it may not do everything (such as remove burned-on soils), is designed to remove heavy dried-on and baked-on foods from pots and casseroles.

IT SAVES WATER AND SAVES ENERGY. Almost 80% of the energy used in a dishwasher is in the hot water it consumes.

The Potscrubber III dishwasher has been specially designed to use less hot water. In fact, you could save hundreds of gallons a year.

You can also save energy by letting the dishes dry naturally, simply by pressing the Energy Saver button. And you can cut down on the number of washings you do because the new Super Racks hold more dishes.

AND IT RUNS QUIETLY, TOO. Our PermaTuf™ tub is not only tough (it won't chip, crack, peel or rust in normal use), but it's actually a sound-dampening material too.

And we didn't stop there. We even surrounded the PermaTuf tub with a blanket of sound insulation.

The Potscrubber III dishwasher from General Electric. Who could ask for anything more?

THE APPLIANCES AMERICA COMES HOME TO.

GENERAL ⚡ ELECTRIC

Courtesy of the General Electric Co.

3. *Actor*—A celebrity may be asked to present the product or service dramatically as a part of a character enactment rather than as a personal testimonial or endorsement. Robert Young has made many TV and print ads in which he acts as a friend in recommending Sanka coffee.

4. *Spokesperson*—A celebrity who represents a brand or company over an extended period of time, often in print or television and in personal appearances, can be called a company spokesperson. Eventually, the spokesperson's appearance becomes closely associated with the brand or company. Michael Landon has been a spokesperson for Kodak cameras in magazine and TV ads for some time.[11]

"Ordinary" people in advertisements may also lend to source credibility because of an attribution of their expressing true personal opinions and having nothing to gain from the consumer's accepting their word. Consumers may be able to identify with someone like themselves more readily than a celebrity who is hard to think of as the person next door (see figure 15-3).

The endorsement may be effective because of either identification or internalization. Identification occurs as individuals conform to an attitude or behavior advocated by another person to derive satisfaction from the feeling of being similar to the model. The individual may believe in the advocated behavior or attitude but primarily draws satisfaction from conformity. Internalization occurs when individuals follow the attitudes or behavior of another primarily because they have come to believe in the action or opinion enough to want to accept (internalize) it into their personal value/action system.[12] It should be noted that endorsement advertising has come under close scrutiny of the Federal Trade Commission. New FTC guidelines for endorsement and testimonial advertising are summarized in figure 15-4.

Prestige The status of an individual may lend credibility to an advertisement. Role models who are of higher prestige generally have more impact on other persons. The prestige of a source may vary from product to product, and prestige figures must be carefully selected.[13]

Expertise Closely related to the concept of prestige, expertise of a source may have significant influence on the receiver's perception of the credibility of an ad. An advertisement may use an acknowledged expert to endorse a product. The expert can be an individual or a group. For example, Crest toothpaste achieved its immediate success because of the endorsement of the American Dental Society, which stated that Crest with fluoride reduced tooth decay.

There is evidence to suggest that the type of product advertised is a significant determinant of the best type of endorser to employ.[14] Celebrities, by using the identification process, should be most effective for products that demonstrate the need for good taste, such as jewelry or clothing. Experts seem to work through internalization. They should be most effective for complex or technical products, such as appliances or automobiles. Average consumer endorsers, since they are likely

Fig. 15-3.   Ordinary Person Testimonial

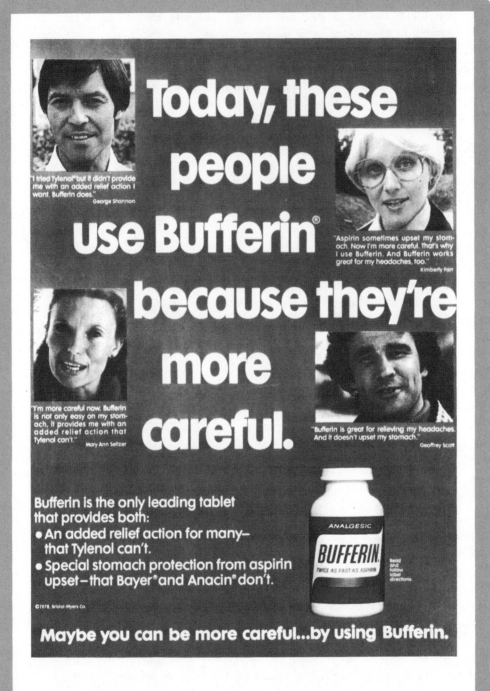

Courtesy of Bristol-Myers Co.

Fig. 15-4. Federal Trade Commission Guidelines for Endorsement Advertising

In January 1980 the Federal Trade Commission issued guidelines indicating that celebrities who endorse products should use the products and tell the truth about them. In addition, companies using consumer endorsement claims must be able to prove that the average person can expect the satisfaction or results or admit to lesser results. The guidelines are not laws per se, but they set FTC policy, and a violation may lead the FTC to issue a formal complaint and publicize the action.

Specifically, the guidelines state:

(1) Any consumer endorsement of drugs in ads must be consistent with what the Food and Drug Administration has determined for the drug relative to safety and effectiveness.

(2) Ads featuring "actual consumers" must use real consumers or admit that actors are involved. For example, if an ad features a hidden camera approach showing people in a cafeteria line trying a new breakfast cereal, the use of any actors must be disclosed since the viewer may think they are actual consumers.

(3) Advertisers must have good reason to believe that celebrities or experts who endorse products actually believe what they are saying.

(4) Endorsers must actually use the product if the ads represent that they do, and the advertiser must have reason to believe the endorser continues to use the product so long as the endorsement is used.

(5) Endorsers need not use the product if the ad does not say or imply that they do. For example, consumers who praise a product following a blind comparison test would not be subject to this requirement.

to be perceived as similar to the viewer, should be effective in promoting everyday low-risk products, like cookies or other well known food items.

Attractiveness, Likability, and Similarity As noted before, many people are more likely to respond to persuasive efforts of other persons perceived as similar to themselves. These similar models inspire identification ("That person is like me so I should do what he does.").

Identification is also related to likableness and attractiveness, so a celebrity should be useful in causing the consumer to perceive a source as credible. In general, people perceive others who are attractive in a more favorable light than those who are considered plain.[15] Concepts from person perception and attribution theory may explain this phenomenon.

Person perception involves ways in which people form impressions of and make inferences about others.[16] Perceptual cues again become significant here. Almost anything can be a cue, so the physical attractiveness of models or spokespersons in ads could signal product quality, spokesperson trustworthiness, and ad credibility. In addition to other person perception, self-concept may be relevant. If the ad recipient sees the person in the ad as representative of the typical brand user, and if that person fits the real or ideal self-concept of the viewer, the brand may be seen as supportive of the receiver's self-concept.

It has been suggested that attribution theory may give insights into the effects of attractive versus unattractive persons in ads.[17] Attribution of the internal state made from the behavior of an attractive individual may be different from the inferences made from the behavior of an unattractive person.[18] Persons perceived as unattractive tend to be rated as more "external" on the Rotter internal-external dimension than moderately or very attractive persons. The internal individual is believed to have outcomes directly under his or her own control, while externals are seen as having little control over events. On the basis of this, physically attractive individuals are more likely to be perceived as independent. Independent persons tend to draw more attributions of credibility and trustworthiness than those who are perceived as being compelled to say what someone else directs. Research on this effect is limited, but one study found that the presence of an attractive model, although positively influencing evaluations of the aesthetic qualities of the ad itself, had no impact on cognitive acceptance of an advertising message. However, the study employed a scantily clad, attractive model from *Playboy,* and the test group was made up of college students. The authors suggested that the student group was naturally skeptical of advertising in general.[19] It seems more likely that the sexy model distracted their attention from the message. Other research does suggest that sex in an ad may inhibit message acceptance and recall.[20]

Further research may provide more definitive answers on the effects of physically attractive models on advertising perception. The preponderance of evidence to date, however, does suggest that attractive models are favorably perceived and that attraction is likely to influence source perception.

Media Effects

The media that carry advertising messages may influence consumer perceptions in much the same way as does the source of the message. In general, the printed word has more credibility than broadcast messages. Certain magazines have more prestige than others, and that image can be transferred to the ads they carry and the brands they advertise.[21]

The attitude with which a consumer approaches a medium may influence both attention and receptiveness to the message communicated. Consumers tend to be tolerant of advertising in magazines and newspapers, and they may even actively seek out and read the ads. In broadcast media, commercials are apt to be viewed as intrusive interruptions in the entertainment flow. Although TV commercials can reach large audiences, the majority of viewers either physically or mentally tune out the advertising. TV is cluttered with a large number of commercials. People tend to perceive the first commercial in a string, but attention fades until the programming resumes.[22]

Message Effects

In addition to external cues that may influence the consumer's perception of an advertisement, the message itself will have an effect. Keep in mind that it is not the content of the advertising message but the consumer's *perception* of the message that determines any response behavior. This section will consider both message design and message appeals. See figure 15-5 for a summary of message effects.

Message Design The way an advertising message is put together influences the consumer's perception of the message content. Several topics are relevant here: advocacy, order, closure, complexity, size, wording, and nonverbal cues.

Advocacy Presumably every ad is aimed at persuading consumers to accept and act upon it. However, many people react negatively to a high-pressure persuasive effort. In order to convey an impartial or low-key image, a communicator can present two sides of an argument. This technique has been little used in advertising for fear of arousing questions about product quality. Attribution theory suggests that higher credibility can be achieved through two-sided communications.

The two-sided argument is not applicable to all communication situations. People of higher education levels are most positively affected by a two-sided argument.[23] If consumers are already in agreement with the advertiser's message, a one-sided message is better. On the other hand, if the audience is negative, a two-sided appeal is likely to be more effective.[24] The two-sided commercial is likely to be more effective in appealing to users of competitive products.[25] When there is an expectation that the consumer will be exposed to counterarguing in the future, a two-sided argument may innoculate against accepting the conflicting information.[26]

Order Whatever message strategy an advertiser uses, there is a question of how the message components should be ordered. Should the strongest points be made at the beginning, in the middle, or at the end of the message? In a two-sided argument, where should the positive points be positioned relative to the negative point or points? The topic is usually treated in terms of *primacy* (strongest message first) and *recency* (strongest message last), or *climax order* (best arguments last), *anticlimax order* (best arguments first), and *pyramidal order* (best arguments in the middle).[27]

Originally, it was felt that information presented first in any argument would have the greatest impact.[28] Subsequent research, however, suggests that the significance of primacy versus recency is largely situational. Nonsalient, controversial topics, interesting subject matter, and highly familiar issues favor the primacy effect. Salient topics, uninteresting subject matter, and moderately unfamiliar issues are more sensitive to recency effects.[29] Highly credible communicators induce more

Fig. 15-5. Message Principles

---

1. One-sided versus two-sided messages
   (a) A one-sided message is more effective when (1) the audience initially agrees with the communicator's position, (2) the audience is poorly educated, (3) the audience is unlikely to hear counterarguments.
   (b) A two-sided message is more effective when the (1) the audience initially disagrees with the communicator's position, (2) the audience is well educated, (3) the audience is likely to hear counterarguments.

2. Climax versus anticlimax order
   (a) Neither a climax nor an anticlimax order is generally superior to the other.
   (b) Where audience interest is *low* for the material presented, the anticlimax order is superior to the climax order.
   (c) Where audience interest is *high* for the material presented, the climax order is superior to the anticlimax order.
   (d) The pyramidal order is the least effective order of presentation.

3. Recency-Primacy
   (a) Neither a recency nor a primacy order is generally superior to the other.
   (b) Controversial topics, interesting subjects, and highly familiar issues favor the primacy order.
   (c) Uninteresting subjects and moderately unfamiliar issues favor a recency order.

4. A message arrangement which first arouses a need and then provides information relevant to the satisfaction of the need is superior to an arrangement which is opposite in order.

5. A message which presents highly desirable material followed by less desirable material is better in changing opinions than a message which arranges these components in an opposite order.

6. A highly credible source induces more opinion change when he presents his pro arguments first, followed by his con arguments, rather than vice versa.

7. Generally, a communicator is more effective in changing opinions in the desired direction by drawing a conclusion.

8. For less intelligent people, the communicator will achieve greater opinion change in the desired direction if he draws a conclusion; for highly intelligent people, drawing a conclusion or leaving the conclusion to the audience is about equally effective in changing opinions.

9. If people perceive that the communicator has an intent to manipulate by stating a conclusion, or if people might feel an insult to their intelligence by having a conclusion drawn for them, a communicator is more effective by leaving the conclusion to the audience.

10. In a communication dealing with highly personal or ego-involving issues, the communicator may be more effective by allowing receivers to draw a conclusion themselves; for impersonal topics, stating a conclusion is generally more effective.

11. For highly complex issues, the communicator is more effective if he states a conclusion for his audience; for simple issues, the approach makes little difference.

12. Fear appeals
    (a) Sometimes a mild fear appeal is more persuasive than a strong one; at other times a strong fear appeal is better than a mild one.
    (b) In general, strong fear appeals appear to be superior to mild ones when they "pose a threat to the subject's loved ones; are presented by a highly credible source; deal with topics relatively unfamiliar to the subject; aim at subjects with a high degree of self-esteem and/or low perceived vulnerability to danger."

13. "It seems that fear appeals are most effective when (1) immediate action can be taken on

recommendations included in the appeal; (2) specific instructions are provided for carrying out recommendations included in the appeal."

14. "Pleasant forms of distraction can often increase the effectiveness of persuasive appeals."
15. Active participation can increase the effectiveness of the persuasive appeals.
16. Emotional appeals are enhanced by:
    (a) Using highly affective language to describe a situation
    (b) Associating the proposed idea with either popular or unpopular ideas
    (c) Associating the proposed idea with visual or nonverbal stimuli that might arouse emotions
    (d) The communicator displaying "nonverbal emotional cues"
17. Arousing feelings of aggression, followed by suggestions of how to reduce those feelings, may be an effective appeal in certain situations.
18. In general, humor appears to be a very effective means of attracting attention and aiding in recall and comprehension; however, its effectiveness in persuasion is doubtful.
19. In persuasive communications "emotionally charged" language is more effective on an audience who already agrees with a communicator; however, it may produce effects opposite to those intended, especially on an audience who initially disagrees with the communicator.
20. In general, when highly favorable words are associated with a concept, an audience will view the concept as favorable; when associated with unfavorable words, the concept will be generally viewed as unfavorable.
21. Nonverbal communication is often more important in communicating an idea than the verbal message it accompanies.
22. The nonverbal code is primarily instrumental in eliciting feelings and emotions within an audience.

From *The Marketing Communication Process* by M. Wayne DeLozier. Copyright © 1976 by McGraw-Hill Book Company. Used with the permission of McGraw-Hill Book Company.

opinion change when pro arguments are presented first, followed by con arguments.[30] A message in which need is aroused first, followed by information on satisfaction of the need, leads to higher message acceptance than the reverse.[31] When a message contains both desirable and undesirable information, opinion change is more likely to accompany presentations in which the good news comes first, followed by the bad.[32] Anticlimax order is more effective when the topic is unfamiliar or the audience is not interested in the topic. Uninterested or unknowledgeable peoples' attention must be gained with a strong approach before they will listen at all.[33] Information coming either at the beginning or at the end of a message has greater impact than that in the middle. Several factors may confound order effects, including the attitude of the communicator, audience predisposition, audience commitments, and importance of the message.[34]

Closure There is a question as to whether or not an advertisement should draw conclusions for the consumer. In general, participation in communication tends to lead to greater message acceptance.[35] Thus, it could be argued that the message should be open-ended, allowing the consumer to reach his or her own conclusions. However, this must be qualified, since the consumer may reach the wrong conclusion. An extreme example of the open-ended ad was one in which the receiver was told to buy both Wilkenson Sword and Gillette blades and shave one side of his face with one blade and the other side with the other blade. Having done so, he would know who paid for the ad. Obviously, Wilkenson was attempting to induce Gillette users to try Wilkenson, since Gillette was the market leader and Wilkenson the relative newcomer.

As with order, closure seems to be quite situational. Several tentative generalizations can be advanced.[36] In general, communicators are more effective in changing opinions in the desired direction if they draw a conclusion for their audience.[37] For less intelligent people, communicators will achieve greater opinion change in the desired direction if they draw a conclusion; for highly intelligent people, drawing a conclusion or leaving the conclusion to the audience produces about the same degree of change in opinion.[38] If people perceive that communicators have an intent to manipulate or something to gain by stating their conclusion, or if people might feel an insult to their intelligence by having a conclusion drawn for them, the communication would be more effective by leaving the conclusion to the audience. In a communication dealing with highly personal issues or those involving the ego, communicators may be more effective if they allow the receivers to draw a conclusion themselves; for impersonal topics, stating a conclusion is generally more effective.[39] For highly complex issues, the communicator is more effective by stating a conclusion for the audience; for simple issues, the approach makes little difference.[40]

Complexity The degree of complexity in an ad has an effect on a perceptual construct referred to as looking time. Ads that are visually more complex elicit longer looking time than simple ads. Consumers who look at advertisements longer tend to recall ad content better than those with short looking times. Ease of product identification within an ad appears to be an important determinant of looking time as well as ad recall. Consumers may look longer at ads with difficult-to-identify products, but they are more likely to remember easy-to-identify products.[41]

Size There is a feeling that the relationship between product purchase and advertisement exposure will decline with increased advertisement size.[42] The logic is that because large ads stand out on the page, predispositions and intentions toward product purchase have little relation to who notices and recalls large ads. Smaller ads, on the other hand, are likely to be filtered out by those not interested in the product, while those in the market for the advertised product will notice them. The idea is that selective perception works for small, not large, ads.[43] One research study found that usage and exposure were unrelated for both the largest and smallest ads, but in the small to medium range there was a tendency for ads to be noted and read more by users than by nonusers.[44]

Wording Words elicit mental responses. The perception of any advertising is influenced by the type and order of words used to convey the message. For instance, compare the following product descriptions:

1. The new plastic product resembling leather will soon be available to show manufacturers.

2. The fabulous new plastic product which out-leathers leather will soon replace all other products used in the manufacture of superior-quality shoes.[45]

The information contained in both messages is essentially the same, but the superlatives, adjectives, and imagery used in the second convey excitement and novelty to the consumer. Words that are synonymous in purely technical terms can elicit quite different reactions from consumers. Adjectives can be moderate (trusting, unattractive) or intense (gullible, revolting).

Thus, a message is low key or emotional depending on the adjectives selected. The use of highly emotional phrasing is generally more effective with audiences who are current users or who agree with the advertiser's statements because the strong language reinforces their currently held attitudes. Even so, most people react negatively to extremely intensive communication. The skeptical audience is unlikely to be won over by intense language. Subtle phrasing, moving from points of agreement to points of disagreement, and a low-key, nonemotional approach will be best for the hostile or skeptical viewer. Intense language or overly emotional appeals are likely to raise consumers' cognitive defenses.

Nonverbal Cues Nonverbal communication can be important in advertising. Such factors as gestures, eye contact, illustrations, and colors can act as cues by which the advertising recipient subjectively judges the communicator and the communication. It was found that the pupil size and eye direction of persons in advertisements influenced viewer attitudes toward both the source and the message. Larger pupil sizes in the models increase the favorableness of attitude and increased interest in ad content. Models who were looking left were favored by consumers who were predominantly left-lookers, and vice versa.[46] Research indicates that left-lookers are "more relaxed, sociable, imaginative, subjective, yielding to suggestion, less quantitative, and more affectionate than right-lookers.[47] In addition, left-lookers are "more emotional, subjective, and hence more susceptible to suggestion; whereas those characterized primarily by right eye movements are more rational, objective, and influenced more by logic and precision.[48]

Research suggests that an advertiser using objective appeals should employ right-looking models, while left-looking models should be used with emotional appeals. This may be true, but research is somewhat limited on the subject, so caution should be exercised in applying the concept.

Message Appeals The appeals that are utilized in an advertisement become the link to consumer motivation. Appeals must be appropriate to the consumer's needs and motives before they will have an effect on attitudes or buying behavior. Several factors are relevant to a discussion of appeals, including use of emotion, distraction, and humor in advertising.

Emotion Advertising appeals can be economic or rational in nature or they can be directed at consumer emotions. There seems to be no best appeal, but advertising practice has traditionally been more inclined to favor emotional appeals. Use of a fear appeal has been heavily researched (see chapter 4), and results suggest that the appropriateness and effectiveness of fear appeals are, in part, situational and person specific.[49]

In general, moderate fear appeals seem to be more effective than either very strong or very weak appeals.[50] Strong fear appeals might be appropriate when the fear appeal threatens one's loved ones, is presented by a highly credible source, relates to topics with which the audience is unfamiliar, or is directed toward subjects with a high degree of self-esteem and/or low perceived vulnerability to danger. Fear appeals appear to be most effective in changing behavior when immediate action can be taken on the message recommendation, and specific instructions are given for carrying out the recommendations.[51]

Other emotional appeals relate to love, acceptance, power, and popularity, to name a few. Suggestions for employing emotional appeals include the following:

1. "Use highly affective language to describe a situation." That is, use highly emotional language to report the facts. Often this is achieved by using words that are highly connotative or personal in nature.
2. "Associate proposed ideas with other popular or unpopular ideas." When an idea is unknown, it is advantageous to associate it with a well-known idea.
3. "Associate ideas with visual or nonverbal stimuli that might arouse emotions." In presenting your ideas, depict emotionally charged scenes or symbols.
4. "The communicator should display nonverbal emotional cues." That is, exhibit body and hand movements, facial expressions, and vocal characteristics consistent with your message.[52]

Distraction Anything that draws attention from a communication may be considered a distraction. Many external factors may distract a consumer's attention from an advertising message. Although one might surmise that distraction would be detrimental to advertising effectiveness, there is some evidence that distraction might be beneficial under some circumstances.[53] Although external distraction is not controllable, advertisers can include distracters in the ads themselves, such as music and attention-getting models.

Essentially, the distraction hypothesis says that in situations where a persuasive message is aimed at an audience that doesn't agree with the communicator, distractions may block counterarguing. If this can be accomplished without substantially blocking message reception, persuasibility may be increased. Although some marketing studies have failed to demonstrate this distraction effect, there is evidence that just the right amount of distraction directly related to the ad itself can improve receptivity to a persuasive message.[54]

Humor Humor has been widely used in advertising, but many marketers hardly understand its effectiveness. Success stories of the use of humor to sell products may lead a person to believe that humor alone can do the job. Stan Freeberg's advertising campaigns for Sunsweet Prunes, Ballentine Beer, Chung King Chow Mein, Geno's Pizza Rolls, Salada Tea, and many others are classic examples of humor that sells. Alka Seltzer and Excedrin, however, learned that humor may not be effective in selling some products.

After a thorough review of the literature on humor in advertising, the following conclusions were made:

1. Humorous messages attract attention.
2. Humorous messages may detrimentally affect comprehension.
3. Humor may distract the audience, yielding a reduction in counterargumentation and an increase in persuasion.
4. Humorous appeals appear to be persuasive, but the persuasive effect is at best no greater than that of serious appeals.
5. Humor tends to enhance source credibility.
6. Audience characteristics may confound the effect of humor.
7. A humorous context may increase liking for the source and create a positive mood. This may increase the persuasive effect of the message.
8. To the extent that a humorous context functions as a positive reinforcer, a persuasive communication placed in such a context may be more effective.[55]

Receiver Effects

In a discussion of consumer behavior and advertising, we must be concerned with the role played by the consumer in the communication process. In a sense, source, message, and media effects are receiver effects because their influence is a function of consumer attitudes, motives, needs, and perception. However, there are several aspects of the consumer as a mass information receiver and processor that have not been touched on and that seem to be better handled individually: learning, attitudes, personality, and social forces. A summary of some important receiver effects is found in figure 15-6.

Learning Consumer response to advertising has long been viewed as a learning process. In a sense, the marketer attempts to teach consumers about brands and product features. In particular, the various learning theories suggest different ways in which consumers may be influenced by advertising. This section will consider some specific applications of learning principles drawn from the various theories.

Wearout Advertising wearout refers to the point at which repeated exposures to an advertisement no longer have a positive effect on consumer attitudes, behavior, or recall.[56] This reflects the S-shaped advertising response curve, which suggests an ultimate saturation of a market with advertising effort after initial slow growth of sales followed by rapid growth.

Fig. 15-6. Receiver Principles in Persuasion

1. In general, a person low in self-esteem is more persuasible than someone high in self-esteem, especially where social approval is involved.

2. An authoritarian personality is more susceptible to messages attributed to authority figures than to those attributed to anonymous sources.

3. A nonauthoritarian personality is more susceptible to messages attributed to anonymous sources than to those attributed to authority figures.

4. Highly dogmatic personalities are more susceptible to persuasion by authority figures whom they trust than by authority figures whom they do not trust.

5. The "open-minded" individual is persuaded on the merits of an argument rather than on the basis of who delivers the message.

6. People who exhibit social withdrawal tendencies are less susceptible to persuasion than those who do not display these tendencies.

7. People who inhibit their aggressive feelings are very persuasible, whereas those who display aggressiveness are less persuaded by majority opinion.

8. People high in anxiety tend to be hard to persuade.

9. People who are high in rich-imagery and fantasy tend to be more persuasible than others who exhibit less of these traits.

10. No consistent relationship exists between *general* intelligence and persuasibility.

11. Due to their *ability to make valid inferences,* people with high intelligence are influenced more by logical argumentation than people with low intelligence.

12. Due to their superior *critical ability,* people with high intelligence are influenced less than people with low intelligence when presented with a "false, illogical, irrelevant" argument.

13. "In our society, women are more persuasible than men."

14. Messages directed at specific customer interests, goals, and problems are more influential on opinions than when directed at the "public at large."

15. "Successful persuasion takes into account the reasons underlying attitudes as well as the attitudes themselves."

16. Centrally held opinions are extremely resistant to change.

17. Derived beliefs (those tied to centrally held beliefs) are more difficult to change than peripheral beliefs which exist apart from centrally held beliefs.

18. Highly popular or prestigious persons tend to resist change, especially when it might affect their group status.

From *The Marketing Communication Process* by M. Wayne DeLozier. Copyright © 1976 by McGraw-Hill Book Company. Used with the permission of McGraw-Hill Book Company.

In dealing with the problem of wearout, advertisers have historically accepted a weak effects hypothesis, based on verbal learning theory, to explain the impact of repetition.[57] The weak effects theory may be summarized as follows:

> The consensus is that commercials do wear out and lose their initial effectiveness. Marketing factors contribute to wearout as well as psychological ones. People must perceive what a commercial means before they can evaluate the appeal of the product and act on it.

Viewing television is for the most part a passive and receptive pastime. Viewers pay or withdraw various amounts of attention depending upon their interest or involvement in what is shown. Repeated exposure is needed for a viewer to learn all he cares to from a commercial. Generally, the subject of most commercials is of little vital interest to him, and at some point in time he will recognize a commercial, feel that it no longer is of interest to him, and turn his attention elsewhere. At that time, the viewer, in spite of additional exposure to the commercial, will begin to lose what he learned from the commercial. The attitudes formed on the basis of the commercial, though, are more resistant to wearout and can persist after the viewer has forgotten the content of what a commercial said.

Based on these concepts and other research, several generalizations about wearout can be advanced.

1. Repetition aids consumer learning. A commercial, then can be scheduled fairly often at the start of a new campaign when the purpose is to establish the appeal for the product.

2. Repetition should also help establish (build awareness, etc.) products or brands that are new to television.

3. A group or pool of commercials should not wear out as fast as a single commercial given the same overall frequency of exposure. But there are always production costs to consider.

4. When the number of commercials to be produced is limited and thus in danger of wearing out quickly, one might consider using a subtle approach, introducing nuances or several claims in a commercial to lengthen the learning process—the point being to maintain interest while striking a balance between a straightforward, single claim and a more complicated one.

5. Frequently, several commercials are produced on a single creative theme, and the rate that the commercials will wear out does not depend as much on the actual number produced as on viewer perception of how similar or dissimilar they are. If the viewer discounts the variation from one commercial to another, the group may behave like a single commercial.

6. Commercials whose single point of humor is a gag or punch line apparently wear out quickly.

7. Commercials for infrequently purchased products (a major appliance, an automobile, a camera, carpeting, etc.) may wear out slower than those for everyday products because there is a natural turnover in the market and the commercial audience. At any given time, only a small portion of the population is actively interested in a major purchase, and as these people buy, they are replaced by others for whom, in effect, the commercial takes on an air of newness.

8. The greater the time span between commercial airings (or frequency of viewing), the longer a single commercial can run.

9. A commercial that has been running for a while can be removed and reintroduced after a time and take on a sense of newness. But, as we can expect some viewers to recall the earlier flight, we can expect the second flight to wear out faster than the first.

10. Commercials may wear out faster among those who are heavy TV viewers, providing, of course, that these people learn equally as fast as light TV viewers.

11. If an advertising budget is light, a single commercial to reinforce learning

spread out over time may be better than a pool of commercials which could dissipate the effective presentation of the creative idea.

12.   Commercials that seek to involve the viewer and increase his active participation should be effective over a longer time than those which simply present a straightforward product story.

13.   As learning generally increases with repeated exposure, copy testing methods predicated on a single viewing usually will not measure the commercial's maximum performance.

14.   Studies which measure a commercial's "penetration" at a single point in time do not indicate whether it is in the "generation" or "satisfaction" phase. Ideally, commercial or campaign performance should be tracked with periodic studies.

15.   Only *good* commercials wear out. If wearout means a loss in effectiveness, a commercial that was ineffective to start with cannot lose what it never had.

The weak effects hypothesis, then, argues that the effect of any one commercial exposure is light and only very large amounts of repetition can "ingrain a stimulus in the mind."[58]

A strong effects hypothesis has been advanced as more appropriate than the incremental (weak effects) theory of association.[59] Essentially, the strong effects concept says that the effectiveness of an ad is dependent upon the events surrounding a consumer's first few exposures. Although further effect is possible through additional repetition, it is unlikely to be significant because of inhibiting factors in the communication process. This concept is related to low-involvement learning as discussed in chapter 5. However, the strong effects hypothesis does not fit what psychologists say about the positive effects of repetition even at high levels. Research has found that advertising recall tends to increase initially and then drop at some level of repetition.[60] Ads consumers rate as better experience this turndown at higher repetition levels than those rated average or below.[61] Message or brand recall appears to be more enduring over time with heavy repetition.[62]

Apparently there is a wearout effect when ad repetition goes beyond that required for brand comprehension. With higher degrees of repetition (what is "high" depends on the consumer, distraction levels, and the quality of the ad itself), there may be a turndown in the advertising/response curve, what I refer to as the nauseation level. Consumers can become sick of a commercial after seeing it too many times and tune it out or, at the extreme, switch brands.

It is suggested that advertisers use strategies to enhance attention to an ad in high-frequency campaigns. Such strategies might include humor, variety in theme and brand features, or a slow unfolding of brand features through a campaign, including several settings or various consumer problems that the brand might solve.[63] Research suggests however, that strategies that raise attention will not necessarily retard wearout. Wearout may occur as consumers process information. In the first few exposures to an ad the consumer's thoughts tend to be message-related, while later exposures tend to elicit nonmessage-related thoughts.[64] This suggests that a message should be changed fairly frequently to continue to stimulate message-related thoughts.

Learning Principles Psychological learning theory has developed numerous principles to explain the learning process. Several years ago Steuart Henderson Britt set down the learning principles that he saw as relevant to the development of advertising strategy. Britt's article is a classic and contains some useful suggestions for advertising strategy.[65]

1. Unpleasant things may sometimes be learned as readily as pleasant things, but the most ineffective stimuli are those that arouse little or no emotional response. Those "bad" ads you see are, perhaps, not as effective in some cases as entertaining ones, but any ad that gets your attention and elicits an emotional response is better than one that arouses no emotion at all.)

2. The capacities of learners are important in determining what can be learned and how long it will take. (The complexity of an ad is important to its effectiveness, but what is complex to one consumer is simple to another, so care must be taken in message design and media selection so the advertiser's approach will fit its audience.)

3. Things that are learned and understood tend to be better retained than things learned by rote. (Understanding a message and what a product can do for the consumer is more important than simply recalling a brand or slogan.)

4. Practice distributed over several periods is more economical in learning than the same amount of practice concentrated into a single period. (This principle suggests that advertising campaigns spread over several weeks or months are likely to achieve higher consumer learning than short, intense advertising blitzes.)

5. When teaching people to master mechanical skills, it is better to show the performance in the same way that they would see it if they were doing the job themselves. (If a television commercial seeks to show the consumer how to do something, an over-the-shoulder or subjective camera angle can be helpful in getting the consumer to see the task from the doer's perspective.)

6. The order of presenting materials to be learned is very important. (The significance of order was discussed under message effects. Essential material presented at the beginning or end of a message is more likely to be recalled than that in the middle.)

7. If material to be learned is different or unique, it will be better remembered. (This goes back to the figure-ground discussion of chapter 3. The product advertised should become figure; all other stimuli should be ground for maximum effect.)

8. Showing errors in how to do something can lead to increases in learning. (Ads that show both right and wrong product use can enhance learning.)

9. Learning situations that are rewarded only occasionally can be more efficient than those where constant reward is employed. (This relates back to the reinforcement schedule discussion presented in chapter 5. As noted there, premiums and deals should not become a permanent promotional strategy.)

10. It is easier to recognize something than it is to recall it. (Including brand name

and package in all ads will help consumers recognize the product in the store, even though the name and package might not be subject to unaided recall.)

11. The rate of forgetting tends to be very rapid immediately after learning. (Repetition is necessary to maintain a share of the consumer mind.)

12. Messages attributed to persons held in high esteem influence change in opinion more than messages from persons not so well known, but after several weeks both messages seem equally effective. (Source effects were discussed earlier in this chapter. The sleeper effect was advanced in chapter 5. To the extent that the principle is true, expensive celebrities could be replaced by ordinary people.)

13. Repetition of identical materials is often as effective in getting things remembered as repeating the same story but with variation. (This principle relates to the strong effects hypothesis as it relates to wearout. Psychological experiments have noted the effectiveness of nonvaried materials in learning, but, as noted earlier, this does not seem to hold in actual advertising practice. Although Britt suggests that this principle means identical ads could be run over and over with good sales results, advertising research argues against the effectiveness of such a strategy.)

14. In a learning situation, a moderate fear appeal is more effective than a strong fear appeal. (While relating to earlier discussions, this statement is probably an oversimplification.)

15. Knowledge of results leads to increases in learning. (Feedback is important to learning. Some commercials use participative quizzes to make consumers aware of what they know and don't know about a product. You may have seen the Biz Quiz on television.)

16. Learning is aided by active practice rather than passive reception. (Many firms use contests to get consumers to do something—write a jingle, go to the store to see if they've won something, write the company or brand name. Coupons, rebates, and test drives accomplish the same thing.)

17. A message is more easily learned and accepted if it does not interfere with earlier habits. (Ads may be more effective when they build on existing behavior and attitudes than when they seek major behavioral changes. On the other hand, if major changes can be induced, the consumer may self-attribute the change to a change in attitude and follow up with continuing the new behavior, such as new brand use.)

18. The mere repetition of a situation does not necessarily lead to learning. Two things are necessary—"belongingness" and "satisfiers." (Belongingness refers to the fit of stimulus objects. It's easier, for example, to learn a sequence of numbers than a random group of figures. An ad message should fit the consumer's expectations. The concept of positioning is relevant here. If an ad message directly challenges strongly held consumer notions, the message doesn't fit and is likely to be rejected. If the consumer is told that Sperry-Rand computers are best and firmly believes that IBM computers are best, the message is likely to be rejected. Worse than that, the consumer may coun-

terargue by affirming that IBM computers are best. Not only will the consumer's mind be unchanged, but the conviction toward the competing product is apt to be strengthened.)

19. When two ideas are of equal strength but of unequal age, new repetition increases the strength of the earlier idea more than that of the newer idea. (If there are two brands—one older and one newer—that have equal association with a product, and if both brands are given the same amount of advertising, the older brand will probably benefit more than the newer one. Positioning a new product in the market requires intense advertising effort if the product is to gain market share and share of mind at the expense of existing brands.)

20. Learning something new can interfere with remembering something learned earlier. (This retroactive inhibition means that if new products can gain a share of mind, established brands may be forgotten. When faced with the onslaught of a new brand, an established brand will need increased advertising support.)

Attitude For many years it has been suggested that advertising objectives should be tied to the efforts of communication to change attitudes rather than to directly produce sales.[66] In part this is because attempts to relate advertising efforts directly to sales have generally proved fruitless. The hierarchy of effects model states that a purchase is the result of moving through a sequence of awareness, comprehension, attitude or conviction, and purchase. Interpreting the model suggests that advertising can influence sales by influencing the consumer's awareness, understanding, and preferences for a product.[67] Each of these stages could be measured prior to and following an advertising effort in order to determine the effectiveness of the advertisement. Using an advertising strategy directed at developing positive attitudes toward a brand coupled with the rest of the marketing mix would ultimately lead to increased sales and profits.[68]

The concept of a hierarchy of effects foundation for advertising strategy can be strongly criticized, however. Some people argue that if the end goal is sales and profit, sales should be measured directly.[69] The problem, of course, is that many forces other than advertising influence sales, but wouldn't many of the same nonadvertising forces shape consumer attitudes?

A second, more condemning objection can be raised on the grounds of the connection between attitudes and behavior. As noted in chapters 2 and 6, research indicates a complex and often inconsistent link between a person's attitudes and subsequent behavior. Actually, the whole hierarchy of effects scheme has been challenged on the grounds that learning does not necessarily result in attitude change, and attitude change does not necessarily lead to behavior change.[70]

The controversy is not settled, and many advertisers today continue to design advertising to influence attitudes. One example was developed in chapter 11 to approach a consumer on the cognitive, affective, and behavioral levels simultaneously or sequentially in order to strengthen the attitude-sales relationship. Richard Reiser, executive director of the market research department of the Grey Advertising Agency, expressed the thinking of the time on the attitude-advertising question.

Our reason for selecting attitudes as our basic way of looking at a market is based on more than the fact that one function of advertising is to affect attitudes. There is considerable evidence to show that the way a person thinks and feels about a brand—his attitude set—determines how he will behave. His reasons for wanting a product determine his selection. We have always found a close relationship between opinion toward a product and probability of purchase.[71]

Several thoughts can be advanced that relate to the relationship between product attitudes and sales. First, given recent research, we have to ask whether attitude or behavior comes first. The suggestion is that either can be the case. Thus, advertising might stimulate product trial and the satisfaction or dissatisfaction with the product will direct attitude formation, thereby influencing future purchases.

Second, as noted in chapter 6, the attitude toward purchasing a product is a more reliable precursor to purchase than simple brand or product attitude. Given this, advertising should concentrate on attitude toward purchase as opposed to attitude toward brand.

A third view suggests that attitude is a variable that links psychological and behavioral components.[72] Since attitudes reflect consumer perceptions of products, they invariably indicate predispositions as well.[73] This means that advertisers should design messages that will affect product perceptions and subsequent purchase predispositions, which is what positioning attempts to do. A product is described or presented in such a way that the consumer perceives and categorizes the product or brand image in a particular way. A predisposition is thus formed to buy, not to buy, or to consider the brand. The perceptual shift would, therefore, place the product inside or outside the consumer's evoked set.

Given an advertising goal of changing consumer attitudes, one of several potential broad strategies could prove useful.[74]

1. Affect those forces that influence strongly the choice criteria used for evaluating brands belonging to the product class.
2. Add characteristic(s) to those considered salient for the product class.
3. Increase/decrease the rating for a salient product class characteristic.
4. Change perception of the company's brand with regard to some particular salient product characteristic.
5. Change perception of competitive brands with regard to some particular salient product characteristic.

The foregoing represents a conventional view of the attitude-advertising question. Thomas Robertson suggests, "Advertising has long needed new perspectives on communication effects. The prevailing 'active audience' view, with its emphasis on selective processes, and stepwise information-processing, reflects only part of the total reality."[75] The traditional view of attitudes or active audience view of advertising effects suggests that consumer attitudes are generally strongly held and, therefore, difficult to change through advertising.[76] The active audience view is correct if we are assuming a highly committed audience dealing with issues considered very important. However, if consumers do not fit this mold and if a large portion of consumer decisions are unimportant and noncommitting, advertising-initiated change may not be particularly difficult.[77]

Commitment is defined as "the *strength of the individual's belief system* with regard to a product or brand (that) . . . will be maximized under conditions of (1) a high number of perceived *distinguishing attributes* among brands and (2) a high level of *salience* attached to these attributes.[78] It seems obvious that a great deal of consumer behavior is not associated with high-commitment behavior. In addition, television is a low-involvement medium where information from advertising is received and processed in a low-drive, relaxed state.[79]

Given that a good deal of consumer behavior is low commitment, attitudes may be rather easily changed. In fact, many brands may be used without much attitudinal commitment, and brand loyalty is a matter of habit rather than true preference. Low-commitment conditions suggest the following:

1. A relative lack of active information seeking about brands.
2. The use of trial as the main informational means of brand evaluation.
3. Routinized brand purchase behavior and relatively high brand loyalty.
4. Brand switching based on variety seeking or stimulus variation, especially toward new brands.
5. The relative inoperability of selective processes, since beliefs are not strongly held.
6. The relative lack of other cognitive defenses, such as counterargument.
7. Minimal learning requirements before brand trial may occur.
8. A simple and collapsed hierarchy of effects purchase sequence.
9. The relative lack of personal influence as a source of information or social support.
10. The relative absence of cognitive dissonance.[80]

Given these low-commitment conditions, two implications can be offered for advertising strategy. Under high-commitment conditions, advertising must be designed with greater information content since the consumer is likely to deliberate over purchase and to go through a "learning" hierarchy. Under low-commitment conditions, weight of advertising may be the key to sales, rather than content. Maximizing exposure levels may be the relevant objective, rather than maximizing recall (learning) levels. Exposure may have to be used in combination with promotion and deals in order to encourage high trial rates. Given the relative lack of differentiating among brands . . . trial reinforced by further advertising exposure should logically maximize sales.[81]

Personality Several personality variables have been found to relate to advertising effects. These are particularly relevant to the consumer's persuasibility. Self-confidence, authoritarianism, aggressiveness, dogmatism, anxiety, and sociability are the variables considered here.

Self-confidence Self-confidence is a personality trait reflecting a person's self-assurance in various situations. In a study of general social confidence (GSC) and information-processing confidence (IPC) it was found that in high-involvement purchase situations, the relationship between GSC and counterarguing was stronger than between IPC and counterarguing. The reverse was true in low-involvement situations.[82]

Some studies report that people high in GSC are low in message acceptance.[83] Others find a curvilinear relationship with greatest message acceptance coming from those with intermediate GSC scores.[92] There are two chief reasons for this relationship. First, persons high in GSC view an influence attempt as a challenge to their self-esteem and prefer to discredit it, thereby blunting its challenge. Those low in GSC are motivated to study and assimilate the discrepant information because it may help them perform better in the future.[94] In information-processing terms, this view proposes that persons with high GSC are more highly motivated to counterargue than those with low GSC.[84] Second, self-confidence "is related to attention and comprehension since lack of self-esteem is usually associated with distractibility, lack of intelligence, and social withdrawal," and self-confidence is negatively related to yielding.[85]

Authoritarianism The authoritarian trait is associated with power and status. Research indicates that an authoritarian personality tends to be more susceptible to persuasive messages attributed to high-credibility sources; a nonauthoritarian personality tends to be more susceptible to persuasive messages attributed to anonymous sources than those attributed to authority figures; and an authoritarian personality tends to rely on source, while a nonauthoritarian depends on the strength of the argument in the message.[86]

Aggressiveness The aggressive person is critical, hostile, and irritable. "The more hostility, irritability, and overt aggression a person displays, the less likely is he to be persuaded by communications which stress the majority opinion."[87]

Dogmatism Since the dogmatic person is closeminded, he or she would be less persuasible than the low dogmatic. Highly dogmatic people tend to accept information from credible sources. Nondogmatics tend to prefer objective information and facts.[88]

Anxiety Anxiety is associated with feelings of apprehension and uncertainty. People who are high in anxiety are low in persuasibility.[89] This would suggest that care should be taken in using anxiety-arousing appeals in advertisements.

Sociability In general, sociable people are more persuasive than social isolates.[90] Unsociable people are especially insensitive to persuasion citing affiliation drives or using personal appeals.

Social Forces In addition to the internal psychological variables that influence the consumer's reaction to advertising, social factors like social class and cultural values can yield insights for advertising strategy. Major contributions relate to both media selection and message design.

Social Class Because each social class has its own values, what appeals to one class will often be lost on another. For example, what is considered humorous varies by social class. Upper-class humor tends to be much more subtle and to employ different themes than lower-class humor. Consumers should be able to relate to and comprehend the symbols, themes, and appeals in an advertising message for maximum impact.

Some years ago an advertising campaign for beer was built around a fox hunter appearing in every ad dressed in a velvet cap, red coat, and black patent leather boots.[91] Compare the fox hunter to the following profile of the typical beer drinker:

> The life-style findings suggest that the male heavy user of beer is a total hedonist: He exerts effort only when it results in his personal pleasure, or when it in some way furthers his fantasy-view of himself as the hard-drinking, swinging he-man. Being extremely self-indulgent (heavy eating, heavy smoking), he gives no indication that he is concerned with the everyday responsibilities of job, wife or family. In fact, he prefers to live dangerously, playing poker, betting at the races, taking chances, etc.
>
> While he is far from avant-garde, he does reject religious and "old-fashioned" values. He doesn't think movies should be censored and he doesn't think there is too much emphasis on sex today. Indeed, he seems to think that, "you only go around once in life, so you have to grab with all the gusto you can."
>
> The heavy beer drinker sees himself in a masculine role, but it is masculinity in the sense of "one of the boys" rather than as a lady-killer. Although he is a girl watcher and unfolds the monthly *Playmate,* masculinity to him is sports, cars, bowling, poker and horse races. With the exception of bowling, his interest in sports seems to be limited to the role of the observer rather than the participant.
>
> Finally, drinking is a very important part of his masculine role: He sees himself as a *real beer drinker* and real beer drinkers as *real men.*

Consider yet another profile of the heavy beer drinker. It was written by one of the Burnett writers on the Schlitz account who put on an old pair of dungarees and spent the weekend doing some personal research at bars on the Northwest side of Chicago where blue-collar men congregate. He came back to the office the following Monday and wrote:

> Who is our heavy beer drinker? Let's forget about demographics for a moment and talk about psychology. The heavy beer drinker is a dropout from life. He is a guy who is not making it and probably never will. He is a dreamer, a wisher, a limited edition of Walter Mitty. He is a sports nut because he's a hero worshipper. He goes to the tavern and has six or seven beers with the boys. What does he talk about? Chances are it's not sex. It's. . . .

Inappropriate language does not permit me to finish the quote, but the point is this: The two approaches to identifying the heavy beer drinker produced remarkably similar profiles. Actually, the creative man's profile was completed first. The style-of-life research served to verify, modify slightly, corroborate and elaborate on the writer's view of his target.[92]

Needless to say, the heavy beer drinker didn't relate to the fox hunter image.

Media consumption also varies considerably by social class. Various magazines aim their editorial styles at different social levels. Upper-class families tend to be heavy newspaper readers and FM radio listeners and light television viewers. Magazines like *Fortune, Atlantic Monthly, New Yorker, House Beautiful,* and *Vogue* are heavily read by upper-class consumers. Although the upper-middle class consumers watch a good deal of television, they tend to be critical of it and of advertising as well. Advertising appeals should be "different, individualistic, witty, sophisticated, stylish, and appeal to good judgment, discriminating taste, and offer the kinds of objects and symbols that are significant to their status and self-expression goals.[93]

The lower-middle class reads morning newspapers and magazines like *Good Housekeeping* and other medium-level shelter magazines, *Reader's Digest,* and *Sports Illustrated.* The best advertising appeals are built around home and family.

The upper-lower class is more likely to read evening newspapers, listen to AM radio, and be heavy TV viewers. Program preferences run to variety shows, situation comedies, game shows, and soap operas. *True Story* and other confession magazines are preferred. Suggestions for advertising to this social level include the following:

> They are quite receptive to advertising that has a strong visual character, showing activity, energy, ongoing work and life, and solutions to practical problems in everyday situations and social relationships.
>
> Advertising should convey an image of the gratifying world in which products fit functionally into the drive for a stable and secure life.
>
> It should communicate a feeling of confidence and safety about the product and its operation.
>
> Advertising should counteract the suspicion and distrust they have of business people.
>
> The advertising setting is important. It should make the item *seem desirable*— that is, the item should be portrayed as part of the average woman's living and consuming, an expected item in the good life. It could also serve to educate the woman as to how she might use the product and how she might relate it to her own situation.
>
> Advertising should reassure the woman that the product is within her reach socially, psychologically, and economically.
>
> Advertising that emphasizes easing the housewife's burdens should at the same time communicate a sense of her continuing importance to the family and offer fruitful ways to use her idle time to gain more love from them.
>
> Advertising that communicates a "prettied-up" atmosphere gains a good reception.[94]

Culture People in various subcultures also can be expected to react differently to various advertising appeals and media. People in different regions of the country exhibit different media consumption patterns. (see figure 15-7).

Ethnic subcultures often exhibit unique media and appeal acceptance patterns. Blacks prefer black magazines, such as *Ebony, Essence, Encore, Black Creation, Relevant,* and *Black Sports,* and black radio and TV (although specialized black programming on TV is limited). Blacks listen to more radio, and half of their

Fig. 15-7. Regional Media Differences

Category	Percentage exposed						
	Total	East	South	Mid-west	West	South-west
Newspapers						
Sunday newspaper (read 4+ issues in past 4 weeks)	68	73	63	69	65	74
Daily morning (read 9+ issues in past 10 days)	31	34	31	30	30	37
Daily evening (read 9+ issues in past 10 days)	45	54	48	52	35	39
Radio station types						
Popular music—top 40	46	47	51	52	46	35
All talk—telephone discussion/news	40	43	51	44	38	24
Country and western	53	38	70	56	42	54
Magazines						
TV Guide	37	41	47	28	49	38
National Geographic	33	37	30	31	42	44
Penthouse	17	19	7	15	24	14
TV programs[a]						
"Hawaii Five-O"	35	36	41	31	26	35
"Sanford and Son"	40	37	48	38	32	41
"All in the Family"	46	55	47	34	40	40

[a]Rated "very good" to "one of my favorites."

Courtesy of Needham, Harper & Steers Advertising Inc.

listening is to black radio.[95] There are a large number of Hispanic stations, especially in areas of heavy population concentration.

Blacks tend to look at ads in terms of both selling the product and contributing to improving the image of blacks. Advertisers are well advised to consider this in their campaigns. Public relations efforts to show contributions of companies to social improvements for blacks and emphasizing a significant contributions from blacks is also important.

Different age groups, of course, have different media consumption patterns, and different advertising appeals may have to be directed at various levels. There are specialized magazines aimed at virtually any age segment. Because special concern has developed relative to television advertising to children, special care must be given to following FTC guidelines without sacrificing message effectiveness.

Cross-cultural advertising presents many challenges in terms of language and value differences. Cultures vary from one another—often greatly—in terms of customs, mores, sanctions, and social, ethical, and political values, themes, and taboos. Although rapid communication, increased cross-cultural travel, and increased education and quality of life combine to create an increasingly worldwide community, marketers must be aware that there are still significant differences across cultures that may require different message and media strategies in advertising. Although a few advertising campaigns can be used cross-culturally by simply translating the language, many require major modifications. Several problems with cross-cultural application of brand names were noted in chapter 13. There are also numerous examples of problems with advertising.

Listerine has long shown men and women in ads reacting to the problem of bad breath in maintaining romantic relationships, with Listerine as the solution. However, the traditional boy-girl theme didn't work in Thailand because public display of male-female relationships is unacceptable by Thais. When the ad was changed to a discussion between two women, the ad and the product were accepted.[96]

The marketer has to take special care in promoting to cultures that may speak fundamentally the same language but for which certain words and phrases may have unique meaning. For example, a laundry product marketer entered the French-Canadian market with a product that was billed as good for especially dirty parts of the wash. This translates in French to *les parts de sale,* and in France that would probably be OK, but in Quebec, it translated to mean about the same as the American slang phrase "private parts." Needless to say, the product had an image problem.[97] General Mills tried to enter the British cereal market with a campaign featuring an all-American youngster appeal. It failed because the British view children in a much different—more formal—way than do Americans.[98]

All of the problems an international or intercultural marketer might face cannot be enumerated here. Suffice it to say that rather than taking the ethnocentric view, which says, "People in other cultures are like me," the marketer should assume that cross-cultural differences exist and investigate product usage and image patterns along with differences in consumer information processing. Campaigns can then be designed accordingly.

SUMMARY

Receiving and interpreting advertising is fundamentally a perceptual process. As such, consumers' perception of advertising is both subjective and selective. Consumers tend to expose themselves to and attend to only advertisements that are in some way relevant to their needs. The relevance may be the need for a particular product or the pure entertainment value of an ad. Messages that are not in consonance with consumer attitudes will tend to be selectively ignored, distorted, or forgotten.

Attention to an ad may be gained, even though consumers do not selectively expose themselves to it. Attention can occur at three levels: involuntary, nonvoluntary, and voluntary. Attention is a function of both stimulus (message) and individual (receiver) factors. The logical result of attention is awareness or conscious recognition of the product advertised.

Advertising perception involves attention and awareness, but it also is concerned with organizing and categorizing (interpreting) information in an ad. At the interpretation level, advertising may be selectively distorted and retained. Interpretation, not actual or objective ad content, determines consumer response. Much specific information is internalized and stored as an overall product or brand image.

Four behavioral effects of advertising were noted: source, media, message, and receiver. Source effects are generally translated into ad credibility. In general, a source is more credible if consumers perceive it as trustworthy. Several source factors contribute to source credibility: honesty, prestige, expertise, and the attractiveness, likability, and perceived similarity between the spokesperson and the consumer. Consumer reactions to advertising can be influenced by the media that carry the message. Print ads are generally more credible than broadcast commercials. Individual magazines and programs can also lend credibility and favorable image. The message conveyed in an ad will have a major impact on consumers. The message effect can come from message design or message appeal. Receiver effects include perception, learning, attitude, personality, and social forces.

CHAPTER 15   STUDY REVIEW

Important Terms and Concepts

Attention to advertising
Selective exposure to advertising
Selective attention to advertising
Stimulus factors in selective attention
Individual factors in selective attention
Awareness of advertising
Interpretation of advertising
Source effects
Message effects
Media effects
Receiver effects
Credibility
Wearout

Questions

1. Describe the classes of attention, and discuss ways in which advertising may stimulate each kind of attention.

2. Discuss the determinants of selective attention to advertising.

3. Discuss the factors that contribute to perceived credibility of advertising.

4. Describe the roles a celebrity may play in an advertisement, and discuss the effects these roles may have on consumer perception and buying.

5. Why might a product endorsement be effective?

6. How might fear appeals be effectively used in advertising?

7. What is advertising wearout, and how can it be minimized?

8. Summarize learning principles that may relate to advertising.

9. Discuss the relationship between attitudes and sales as influenced by advertising.

10. Discuss the relationship between personality and advertising response.

11. How does advertising response vary across social classes?

12. In what ways might we expect advertising response to vary across subcultures and cultures?

16

Behavioral Dimensions of Channel Strategy

A marketing channel is composed of the institutions through which title to or control over goods pass from producer to user or final consumer. Strategic channel decisions flow in two directions. On the one hand, the manufacturer attempts to determine the optimal combination of wholesalers, retailers, and direct distribution efforts to move its products to final users. On the other hand, the retailer must assemble a salable array of products from various sources and attempt to communicate an image that is consistent with its inventory and marketing style.

The behavior of final consumers is an important input to the channel strategy decisions of manufacturers and retailers. The majority of consumer goods are sold through retail stores, with a relatively small portion sold directly by manufacturers to household consumers. For this reason, the retail institution generally forms the physical interface between the manufacturer and the consumer. The manufacturer can directly control the advertising interface, but retail efforts can usually be influenced only by providing promotional material, by carefully selecting retail outlets or, at the extreme, by creating a vertical marketing system (VMS) in which one member owns or contractually controls some or all institutions in the channel structure.

This chapter will begin by looking at the manufacturer's channel decision as influenced by consumer behavior. Following this, behavioral inputs to the retailer will be treated.

Channel Strategy

The manufacturer's basic channel problems relate to the number and types of retail outlets used to reach the final consumer. In addition, changes in consumer behavior may signal the need for innovative variations in channel strategy.

Distribution Intensity

Distribution intensity refers to the number of retail outlets a manufacturer uses to reach its customers. In general, there are three levels of distribution intensity:

447

intensive, selective, and exclusive. Intensive distribution involves selling through all retail outlets that will stock an item. In selective distribution, the manufacturer markets through only those outlets that are considered best able to sell the product. Exclusive distribution uses a single dealer in a defined geographic area.

Consumers' behavior and attitudes dictate the appropriate distribution level as indicated in figure 16-1. A manufacturer who can determine the way in which the majority of consumers view a given product or brand, may facilitate a distribution intensity decision.

Fig. 16-1.　Intensity of Distribution and Consumer Behavior

Consumer Behavior	Suggested Distribution Intensity
The consumer prefers to buy the most readily available brand of product at the most accessible store.	Intensive
The consumer selects a purchase from among the assortment carried by the most accessible store.	Intensive
The consumer selects a purchase from among the most accessible store carrying the item in stock.	Selective or Exclusive
The consumer is indifferent to the brand of product bought but shops different stores to secure better retail service and/or price.	Intensive
The consumer makes comparisons among both retail-controlled factors and factors associated with the product or brand.	Intensive
The consumer has a strong preference as to product brand but shops a number of stores to secure the best retail service and/or price for this brand.	Selective or Exclusive
The consumer prefers to trade at a specific store but is indifferent to the brand of product purchased.	Selective or Exclusive
The consumer prefers to trade at a certain store but is uncertain as to which product to buy and examines the store's assortment for the best purchase.	Selective or Exclusive
The consumer has both a preference for a particular store and for a specific brand.	Selective or Exclusive

Adapted from Louis P. Bucklin, "Retail Strategy and the Classification of Consumer Goods," *Journal of Marketing*, 23 (January 1963):50-55. Reprinted from the *Journal of Marketing*, published by the American Marketing Association.

Outlet Selection

Because a retail store tends to have a specific image or personality, a manufacturer might want to seek retailers who will fit the brand image created through the manufacturer's promotion efforts. In practice, it may be difficult for a manufacturer to exercise close control over which stores carry its products without a VMS.

However, since retailers are likely to be seeking products and brands to fit their own images, the problem may not be critical.

Channel Dynamics

Both the retailer and the manufacturer may find it useful to understand current and developing consumer behavior trends. The desires and expectations of consumers often dictate major changes in the structure of channels.

Life-style determines how people shop and the kinds of stores in which they shop. Life-style changes can be used as predictors of new types of distribution systems and retail stores. Psychographics, of course, can be employed to understand shopper life-styles. Psychographic research has been applied relatively seldom to distribution problems "because distribution tends to be perceived as a separate entity bearing no relationship to the other marketing activities. But there is a critical need to synthesize all parts of the marketing program, and to apply life style and psychographic methods to distribution as an essential part of the marketing process."[1]

Consider the following example of how life-style research might aid in formulating distribution strategy:

> A manufacturer with a line of expensive frozen foods was confronted with the problem of convincing supermarkets to stock it. The line moved well when it was stocked in stores, but the premium prices the line required tended to discourage interest on the part of supermarket chain buyers.
>
> The manufacturer initiated a study to learn how consumers purchase various food products. The study concentrated on attitudes, motivations, purchase practices and life style. Through discriminant analysis it was discovered that people in certain neighborhoods were the first to try new products. A subscription list of a prestigious national magazine was obtained. It was discovered that a good match existed between the publication's readers in areas where early new product purchases tended to occur.
>
> The manufacturer elected to buy a regional edition of the magazine for his advertising campaign. The frozen food line was distributed only in neighborhoods where people tended to try new products. The line moved in the specially selected neighborhoods. With this brisk movement, the chains proceeded to stock the line in other stores.
>
> At least part of this success can be attributed to strategic use of psychographics. The product introduction took into consideration both the consumer and distribution implications inherent in the problem.[2]

In addition to attention to prevailing life-styles, the marketer should look at clues that current life-style trends may offer for future distribution strategy. The concept of self-service grocery shopping was introduced in 1916 by Clarence Saunders in a Piggly Wiggly Market in Memphis.[3] Prior to that time groceries were purchased in a personalized full-service environment. Population growth and increased urbanization began to lead retailers away from personalization. With the depression of the 1930s, consumers were ready for low prices, and Michael Cullen responded with the King Kullen supermarket in Jamaica, Long Island.[4] Combining low prices (a third of the items were sold at cost) and semi-self-service, a new retailing form was born in response to a large market segment with diminished purchasing power and the desire to stretch their shrinking dollars.

In contrast, the discounting revolution occurred in response to life-style changes of the booming post-World War II era. Consumers had abundant dollars, and they also had tremendous pent-up demand. Gasoline and automobiles were once again available, and the age of consumer mobility and the rush to the suburbs began. In response, discount stores, able to operate on low margins with the huge volume of business available, sprang up everywhere, cutting deeply into the business of conventional department stores. Coupled with the demand was the emergence of the better educated, more self-confident consumer who felt capable of judging product quality without having to rely on the security of the well-known manufacturer's brand or department store name.

The future is likely to present life-style changes just as significant in their influence on retailing. We've already seen something of a backlash to the fast-paced life-style. The advent of more specialty stores and boutiques through the seventies, along with the surge in do-it-yourself stores, reflects the desire for self-sufficiency and evidence the volatile nature of consumer buying and retail response. Certainly the scarcity of fuel can have a major impact on outlying shopping centers which depend upon the use of the family automobile. We could see more in-home shopping in the future as the telephone and television become the consumer's route to retail shopping.

The trend to more and more women being employed outside the home may also have serious implications for retailers. This has already led to a tremendous demand for convenience foods and, coupled with affluence and mobility, has spawned the multi-billion-dollar, fast-food industry.

A phenomenon called out-shopping or interurban shopping has been a constant thorn in the side of local retailers as they see large volumes of retail customers from their trade areas shopping in other cities. Out-shoppers tend to be younger, better educated, have higher incomes, and fewer children. Out-shoppers are attracted to superior selections and better or more current fashion offerings outside the local area.[5] Out-buyers tend to be more gregarious, active, and flexible than in-shoppers.[6]

One study of out-shopping identified the following natural out-shopping groups:

1. In-shopper group (64.4%)
2. Big ticket out-shopper (4.3%)
3. Furniture out-shopper (14.4%)
4. Appearance (fashion) out-shopper (12.2%)
5. Home entertainment out-shopper (4.7%)[7]

Figure 16-2 gives some of the characteristics of these groups.

The question, of course, arises as to how the increasing cost of gasoline is likely to affect out-shopping. As late as 1976 improved local retail facilities and increased gasoline prices seemed to have little effect on out-shopping.[8]

Fig. 16-2. Outshopper Characteristics

---

1. Age significantly differentiates among the outshopping groups, but outshoppers are not necessarily younger. Instead it is the product-specific outshoppers who are younger.
2. Stage in the consumer life cycle also relates to outshopping. Outshoppers for big-ticket home products tend to be in earlier stages of the life cycle.
3. Neither occupation, household size, nor education of either spouse is related to the outshopping groups in this study. In prior studies education was found to relate to outbuying.
4. Distance residential moves over the last five years and expectations of moving in the coming year are related to the outshopping groups in the study. The authors find that big-ticket home product outbuyers (group 2) are extremely mobile.
5. In general, interurban outshoppers have higher incomes; but outshoppers for home entertainment products (group 2) have incomes no higher than those of outshoppers.
6. Lifestyle measures generally relate to kinds of outbuying. For example, the authors found that (1) outshoppers are more fashion conscious; (2) appearance and home entertainment outshoppers are more self-confident; (3) outshoppers demonstrate greater patronage innovative behavior; (4) except for appearance outshoppers, outbuyers are more optimistic about their financial future; (5) outbuyers are more weight conscious; and (6) some outshopper types dislike housekeeping.

William R. Darden and William D. Perrault, Jr., "Identifying Interurban Shoppers: Multiproduct Purchase Patterns and Segmentation Profiles," *Journal of Marketing Research*, 13 (February 1976):59. Reprinted from the *Journal of Marketing Research*, published by the American Marketing Association.

Obviously, the marketer must be aware that as consumer life-styles and attitudes change, their shopping behavior and expectations change as well. In the past there has been a tendency for conventional retailers to greet innovation with cool disdain. However, with rapid changes in consumer behavior, manufacturers and retailers will have to be sensitive to innovative distribution opportunities suggested by new consumer life-styles and attitudes.

Retailer Strategy

As the channel member generally closest to the final consumer, the retailer must be particularly sensitive to consumer behavior in its strategy formulation. In this section, several aspects of consumer behavior relevant to retail strategy will be explored. In the first part, some general aspects of retail customer behavior will be treated. Several specific store strategy areas will be covered in the second part.

The Retail Customer

Many of the general concepts of consumer behavior discussed in earlier sections are applicable to the behavior of the retail customer. In addition, some of the ideas advanced relative to brand response apply to store choice and image. These and some topics that more specifically relate to retail buying behavior are treated here.

Fig. 16-3. Life-Style Characteristics of Shoppers

Life Style Profile	F-ratio	Group Means (overall F-ratio = 1.41)*							
		Apathetic Shopper	Demanding Shopper	Quality Shopper	Fastidious Shopper	Stamp Preferer	Convenient Location Shopper	Stamp Haters	Total Means
Shopping center activity	1.12	27.4	25.8	26.6	25.9	29.6	26.6	27.1	27.0
Venturesome shopper	.59	18.3	16.4	17.4	18.6	17.1	17.5	19.3	17.8
Discount store activity	.47	24.1	26.2	23.3	23.7	25.4	24.2	24.8	24.3
Browser	1.34	21.2	24.9	21.1	20.1	21.6	19.7	21.4	21.2
Special shopper	5.37†	24.7	25.3	23.9	21.2	28.6	19.6	16.8	23.1
Quality shopper	2.35‡	30.8	30.8	35.1	33.4	33.1	31.7	32.1	32.5
Apathetic shopper	.82	16.0	15.5	16.6	16.6	13.2	15.2	17.3	15.8
Economic shopper	1.14	25.0	27.5	23.8	25.2	28.1	25.6	27.3	25.7
Depersonalizing shopper	.38	24.8	26.0	23.7	24.8	23.9	24.3	25.3	24.6
Support local retailer	1.04	9.5	9.4	8.1	9.7	9.8	8.5	9.4	9.1
Small store shopper	1.31	20.9	22.0	19.0	23.0	22.3	20.8	23.4	21.3
One-store shopper	1.51	11.7	10.3	11.6	12.9	12.4	13.5	12.0	12.1
Brand loyal shopper	1.22	9.2	7.3	9.1	9.3	8.6	9.0	8.1	8.8

Brand innovator	1.12	10.8	13.0	10.8	12.1	12.3	10.5	10.8	11.3
General self-confidence	2.27‡	14.5	16.4	16.5	18.1	14.8	15.7	16.2	16.0
Credit shopper	1.00	12.9	15.0	15.5	15.8	16.1	15.8	16.3	15.3
Opinion leadership—furniture	.27	14.5	14.9	13.8	15.3	14.8	15.5	12.8	14.6
Opinion leadership—cake mixes	.88	11.5	12.6	10.9	11.4	12.5	11.1	6.5	11.1
Opinion leadership—gifts	.84	15.1	15.1	15.1	14.7	13.4	15.5	9.5	14.4
Age (years)	.83	34.2	37.5	38.3	40.6	36.0	34.1	35.2	36.5
Education§	1.84	2.4	1.9	2.3	3.1	2.0	3.5	2.5	2.6
Number of children	1.25	2.4	3.1	2.1	2.3	3.1	2.4	2.3	2.5
Income‖	.30	3.7	3.7	3.9	4.1	3.8	4.1	3.5	3.9
Mobility#	.51	1.2	1.3	1.2	1.3	1.1	1.2	.7	1.2

* Using Multivariate Analysis of Variance (MANOVA), overall discrimination among supermarket preference groups is significant at the .01 level.
† Univariate F-ratio significant at the .001 level.
‡ Univariate F-ratio significant at the .05 level.
§ Coded as follows: grammar school or less (1), at least some high school (2), at least two years of college or less (3), college graduate (4), at least some graduate school (5).
‖ Coded as follows: $5,000 or less (1), $5,001 through $14,999 (2), $15,000 through $24,999 (3), $25,000 and above (4).
Measured in number of geographic moves over the last five years.

William R. Darden and Dub Ashton, "Psychographic Profiles of Patronage Preference Groups," *Journal of Retailing*, 50, no. 4 (Winter 1974-75):108-109. Reprinted by permission of the *Journal of Retailing*.

Shopper Typologies Several attempts have been made to categorize retail buying behaviors. Given some fairly consistent profiles, market segmentation strategies can be developed for promotion, display, and design.

Using a psychographic technique, supermarket customers were categorized according to the seven following segments:

1. *The apathetic shopper.* This is the largest segment, with nearly 22 percent of the sample. Most consumers in this group do not express preferences for any supermarket attribute. The exceptions include competitive prices and brand variety; 60 percent demand competitive prices and 52 percent prefer supermarkets with a wide brand variety. Nevertheless, other patronage segments express even stronger preferences for these two supermarket segments.

2. *The demanding shopper.* Only 8.6 percent of shoppers demand excellence on all dimensions except trading stamps. They want quality products at competitive prices. They demand clean supermarkets with friendly personnel at convenient locations; they expect wide brand variety with quality meat cuts.

3. *The quality shopper.* Comprising 19 percent of the shoppers, this group demands fresh produce and quality meat cuts. They appear to expect little more from a supermarket.

4. *The fastidious shopper.* (15 percent.) All shoppers in this group prefer supermarkets with spic-and-span facilities. They also expect a wide assortment of brands for most products.

5. *The stamp preferer.* Female shoppers in this group prefer supermarkets offering trading stamps. Only 12 percent of the sample falls into this category. A majority in this segment also expect quality products, competitive prices, brand variety, friendly personnel, and clean stores.

6. *The convenient location shopper.* These shoppers require only one attribute of a supermarket: that it be conveniently located. Since only 14.7 percent of the housewives fall into this category, the data suggest that this segment is not as dominant as might be expected.

7. *The stamp haters.* Over 8 percent of the suburbanite housewives actually prefer stores *not* offering trading stamps. Other than this negative preference, customers in this segment have preference profiles which resemble the total sample.[9]

Of course, these categories come from a single sample, so we wouldn't expect supermarket shoppers in general to necessarily fit these profiles, but they may suggest that all shoppers are not alike, and retailers should have an awareness of what customer groups they are serving. Each of the profiles exhibited different life-style characteristics as noted in figure 16-3. Information such as this could effectively guide a retailer in promotion, inventory, and image strategies. Note that such traditional marketing variables as age, education, number of children, income, and mobility did not differ significantly among the groups.

Looking at figure 16-3, several consistencies emerge.[10] The segments vary more on the degree to which they shop for "specials" than on any other characteristic. The trading stamp group scored highest as special shoppers, while stamp avoiders scored lowest. The quality shopper was highest on the quality scale, while the apathetic and demanding shoppers scored lowest. The fastidious shopper was highest in self-confidence, while the stamp haters were lower in mobility and opinion leadership.

As noted previously, many different typologies could be constructed to categorize retail shoppers. One such division that has been investigated looks at the difference between department store shoppers and those who do not shop department stores. Figure 16-4 details the life-style characteristics that differentiate frequent department store shoppers from light department store shoppers.

Figure 16-5 displays yet another typology. This one is based on shopping orientation, including (1) source of information used in learning about new products, (2) source credibility, (3) preferences for kinds of information, (4) quantity of media used, and (5) types of media used. [11]

Shopping Motivation Why do people engage in retail shopping? Obviously, they are trying to accumulate a required inventory of products for their own use. But this does not entirely explain why people often engage in shopping for the fun of it.

Actually, there seem to be many motives—personal and social—that lead people to shop. Among the personal motives are:

Role Playing. Many activities are learned behaviors, traditionally expected or accepted as part of a certain position or role in society—mother, housewife, husband, or student.

Diversion. Shopping can offer an opportunity for diversion from the routine of daily life and thus represents a form of recreation.

Self Gratification Different emotional states or moods may be relevant for explaining why (and when) someone goes shopping. Some people report that often they alleviate depression by simply spending money on themselves. In this case, the shopping trip is motivated not by the expected utility of consuming, but by the utility of the buying process itself.

Learning about New Trends. Products are intimately entwined in one's daily activities and often serve as symbols reflecting attitude and life-styles. An individual learns about trends and movements and the symbols that support them when the individual visits a store.

Physical Activity. Shopping can provide people with a considerable amount of exercise at a leisurely pace, appealing to people living in an urban environment. Some shoppers apparently welcome the chance to walk in centers and malls.

Sensory Stimulation. Retail institutions provide many potential sensory benefits for shoppers. Customers browse through the store looking at the merchandise and at each other; they enjoy handling the merchandise, the sounds of background music, the scents of perfume counters and prepared food outlets.

Social motives include the following:

Social Experience Outside the Home. The marketplace has traditionally been a center of social activity and many parts of the United States and other countries still have "market days," "county fairs," and "town squares" that offer a time and place for social interaction. Shopping trips may result in direct encounters with friends (e.g. neighborhood women at a supermarket) and other social contact.

Fig. 16-4. Life-style Dimensions of Frequent Department Store Shoppers

Demographics	Activities	Interests	Opinions	Media Usage
Younger	Vacationing	Fashion	Modern Family Oriented	Magazine Readers
Better Educated	Traveling	Appearance	Financially Secure	Radio Listeners
Higher Income	Golf	Cleanliness	Satisfied with Life	Television Viewing
	Tennis	Foreign Cultures	Physically Attractive	News Viewing
	Water Sports	Music	Innovative	
	Picnics	Arts and Crafts	Opinion Leader	
	Hiking	Health	Self Indulgent	
	Walking	Nutrition	Liberal	
	Jogging	Cooking	Urbanite	
	Community Involvement	Production Satisfaction	Pro-Business	
	Socializing		Pro-Advertising	
	Games and Cards		Careful Shopper	
	Cultural-Educational		Price Conscious	
	Shopping			

Melvin R. Crask and Fred D. Reynolds, "An Indepth Profile of the Department Store Shopper," *Journal of Retailing*, 54, no. 2 (Summer 1978):28. Reprinted by permission of the *Journal of Retailing*.

Fig. 16-5.   Shopping Orientation Types

Orientation	Representative Psychographic Characteristics
Special Shopper	I shop a lot for specials.
Brand-loyal Shopper	I prefer buying only specific brands of cosmetics.
Store-loyal Shopper	I would buy my cosmetics from any store that happened to be carrying them. (reverse score)
Problem-solving Shopper	I often find it hard to decide which cosmetic products best suit me.
Psycho-socializing Shopper	I often decide to buy those cosmetic products that I see my friends using.
Name-conscious Shopper	I judge some brands of cosmetics on the basis of the store that sells them.

George P. Moschis, "Shopping Orientations and Consumer Uses of Information," *Journal of Retailing*, 52, no. 2 (Summer 1976):65. Reprinted by permission of the *Journal of Retailing*.

Communications With Others Having a Similar Interest.   Stores that offer hobby-related goods or services such as boating, collecting stamps, car customizing, and home decorating, provide an opportunity to talk with others about their interests and with sales personnel who provide special information concerning the activity.

Peer Group Attraction.   The patronage of a store sometimes reflects a desire to be with one's peer group or a reference group to which one aspires to belong. For instance, record stores may provide a meeting place where members of a peer group may gather.

Status and Authority.   Many shopping experiences provide the opportunity for an individual to command attention and respect or to be "waited on" without having to pay for this service. A person can attain a feeling of status and power in this limited "master-servant" relationship.

Pleasure of Bargaining.   Many shoppers appear to enjoy the process of bargaining or haggling, believing that with bargaining, goods can be reduced to a more reasonable price. An individual prides himself in his ability to make wise purchases or to obtain bargains.[12]

Patronage Factors Essentially, a consumer decides which store or stores to shop by comparing store characteristics with some criterion of acceptability. Patronage factors consist of evaluative criteria (defined as the specifications used to judge and compare one store with another), perceived characteristics of the store or store image, comparison processes, and acceptable and unacceptable sources.[13]

For stores with which the consumer is familiar this whole process would likely be unnecessary. However, if a consumer is looking for a particular product or brand, it may become necessary to evaluate several known stores to determine such factors as availability and price for that product. Given that a person evaluates a store, the process may appear as in figure 16-6.

Fig. 16-6.   Store Choice Processes

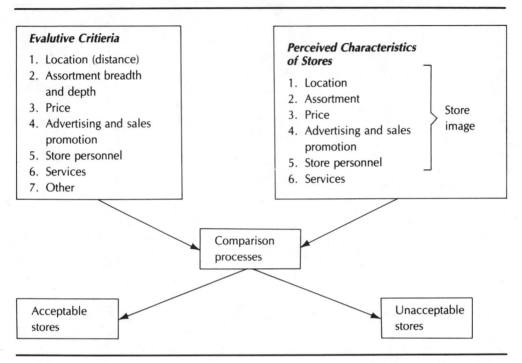

The question of what factors actually determine which stores a customer shops is difficult to answer. There has been a great deal of research on the determinants of brand choice but relatively little on store choice. Some of the reasons for store choice seem to relate to individual consumers and some to the products purchased.

If a consumer has a strong brand preference and relatively few stores stock the favored brand, choice may be immediately limited to those few stores. There are some complicating factors in understanding store choice. For one thing, a given store may be preferred for purchasing some items and not others. In addition, consumers may be indifferent as to which of several stores they shop at, and resulting store selection may occur as much by chance as by choice. Also, consumers may shop from store to store for variety and recreation as much as for anything else.

In spite of the complications and limited research, there seem to be some consistencies in store choice that may offer clues for effective market segmentation by various types of stores. As noted previously, relevant choice factors may vary substantially across store types. Figure 16-7 indicates some choice criteria for department stores and grocery stores. Department store shoppers are more concerned about the quality of the store's merchandise, the degree of ease of the shopping process, and posttransaction satisfaction. Grocery shoppers are more concerned about the merchandise mix of the store, the ease of shopping, and store cleanliness.[14]

Fig. 16-7.   Store Attributes for Department and Grocery Stores

---

TOP TEN ATTRIBUTES

Department Store	Grocery Store
1. Dependable products	1. Dependable products
2. Fair on adjustments	2. Store is clean
3. High value for money	3. Easy to find items you want
4. High-quality products	4. Fast check out
5. Easy to find items you want	5. High-quality products
6. Fast check out	6. High value for the money
7. Helpful personnel	7. Fully stocked
8. Easy to return purchases	8. Helpful store personnel
9. Easy to exchange purchases	9. Easy to move through store
10. Store is clean	10. Adequate number of store personnel

BOTTOM FIVE* ATTRIBUTES

Department Store	Grocery Store
1. Store is liked by friends	1. Easy to get home delivery
2. Many friends shop there	2. Lay-away available
3. Store is known by friends	3. Easy to get credit
4. Company operates many stores	4. Many friends shop there
5. Lay-away available	5. Store is liked by friends

---

*"1" indicates Least Important.

Robert A. Hansen and Terry Deutcher, "An Empirical Investigation of Attribute Importance in Retail Store Selection," *Journal of Retailing* 53, no. 4 (Winter 1977-78):69. Reprinted by permission of the *Journal of Retailing*.

There are differences between the patronage motives of department store and specialty store buyers. In a study of stereo component purchases, department store buyers were primarily interested in store location convenience and guarantee policies. Specialty store patrons, on the other hand, considered salesperson expertise and brand/model assortment most significant.[15] Price was equally important to both groups.

In addition to differences in the patronage motives across stores, different persons display different motives and prefer different stores. For example, age and education are related to store choice for certain products.[16] Social class is also a determinant of patronage motives. As noted in figure 16-8, lower-class shoppers are attracted by price appeals, middle-class shoppers are disposed to broad appeal stores, and high fashion stores appeal to upper-class customers.[17] Department stores tend to appeal to all social levels, while discount and downtown stores are more heavily patronized by lower-class shoppers. Upper-middle class and upper-class consumers seem to enjoy the *act* of shopping, including store atmosphere and displays, and they tend to shop more often than lower-class shoppers. The *acquisition* of new clothing and household items provides the major shopping enjoyment for lower-class consumers. Home shopping also tends to vary by social class with heavy mail-order and telephone buyers coming from upper income and social classes.[18]

Fig. 16-8. Department Stores Favored Across Social Classes

| Kind of Department Store | Social Class | | | | | |
	L-L	U-L	L-M	U-M	L-U	U-U
High fashion store	4%	7%	22%	34%	70%	67%
Price appeal store	74	63	36	24	19	18
Broad appeal store	22	30	42	42	11	15
Total	100%	100%	100%	100%	100%	100%
Number of cases	67	208	204	71	32	10

Stuart U. Rich and Subhash C. Jain, "Social Class and Life Cycle as Predictors of Shopping Behavior," *Journal of Marketing Research* 5 (February 1968):48. Reprinted from the *Journal of Marketing Research*, published by the American Marketing Association.

Stage in life cycle is also a factor in store choice as noted in figure 16-9. Department stores are more heavily shopped by older shoppers. Discount and mail-order firms are favored by the younger shopper.[19]

Fig. 16-9. Favorite Store by Stage in Life Cycle

| Favorite Store Type | Stage in Life Cycle | | | |
| | Under 40 | | 40 and over | |
	No Child	Child	No Child	Child
Department	65%	57%	83%	79%
Discount	9	13	2	2
Mail Order	5	11	2	7
All others	21	19	13	12
Total	100%	100%	100%	100%
Number of Cases	66	474	240	276

Stuart U. Rich and Subhash C. Jain, "Social Class and Life Cycle as Predictors of Shopping Behavior," *Journal of Marketing Research* 5 (February 1968):48.

Figure 16-10 details some demographic-based differences in store attribute importance. Neighborhood A is an established area, with relatively low-income, older, less well educated residents. Neighborhood B is relatively new, with the majority of its residents well educated, younger, and higher in income. A tends to place more weight on store advertising and adjustment policy, while B emphasizes price-related and efficiency components. Given a demographic profile for a neighborhood, a store could be established or altered to fit the neighborhood profile.[20]

Fig. 16-10. Benefit Segments Based on Demographics

DEMOGRAPHICS	NEIGHBORHOOD A (N = 118)	NEIGHBORHOOD B (N = 140)
Age	35 or more	44 or less
Income	$15,000 or less	$10,000 or more
Education	Not a college graduate	At least some college
Length of Time in Area	Seven or more years	*

ATTRIBUTE IMPORTANCE RANKS†	NEIGHBORHOOD A (N = 118)	NEIGHBORHOOD B (N = 140)
Fast Checkout	14	3
Wide Selection	18	12
Low Prices vs. Competition	26	17
High Value for Money	9	2
Many Specially-priced Items	28	22
Advertising is Informative	20	25
Advertising is Helpful	24	29
Advertising is Believable	13	21
Fair on Adjustments	3	9

*This variable was not used in establishing the segment.
†These ranks are based upon the average importance scores for 41 attributes.

Robert A. Hansen and Terry Deutcher, "An Emperical Investigation of Attribute Importance in Retail Store Selection," *Journal of Retailing* 53, no. 4 (Winter 1977-78):70. Reprinted by permission of the *Journal of Retailing*.

The same study showed significant differences between store attribute importance for customers who enjoy shopping as opposed to those who do not (see figure 16-11). Consumers who don't enjoy shopping want to spend as little time as possible doing it. They want to get to the store quickly and easily, to get out of it quickly, and they want to have returns and adjustments handled without problem. The shopping enjoyer concentrates on low prices, specials, advertising, and quality of salespeople.[21]

Psychological profiles can be developed for consumers who tend to shop in specific types of retail stores. For example, compared with department store buyers, specialty store buyers are more self-confident, consider the purchase more important, and, while they perceive less purchase risk, they consider a purchase error to be more serious than department store shoppers.[22]

Fig. 16-11.   Benefit Segments Based Upon Shopper Interests

Attribute	Importance Ranks* for Those Who	
	Do Enjoy Shopping (N = 159)	Do Not Enjoy Shopping (N = 56)
Fast Checkout	11	4
Store is Nearby	27	15
Short Time to Reach Store	24	16
Easy Drive to Store	23	5
Easy to Return Purchase	26	19.5
Fair on Adjustments	15	9
Low Prices vs. Competition	17	23
High Value for Money	4	11
Many Specially Priced Items	18	27
Courteous Sales Personnel	8.5	13
Advertising is Informative	20	25
Advertising is Helpful	22	26
Advertising is Believable	14	21

*Ranks are based upon 41 attributes.

Robert A. Hansen and Terry Deutcher, "An Emperical Investigation of Attribute Importance in Retail Store Selection," *Journal of Retailing* 53, no. 4 (Winter 1977-78):71. Reprinted by permission of the *Journal of Retailing.*

Discount store buyers have some distinctive characteristics, but differences among products purchased are often more significant than variations among individual consumers. Although discount store patronage is heavy among the blue-collar class, white-collar families are also frequent discount buyers.[23] The two social classes, however, tend to buy somewhat differently. Although the two classes tend to behave the same in purchases of staple clothing items and appliances, the higher social class buyer is more likely to shop elsewhere for more fashion-related items.[24] In general, higher social class shoppers have less favorable attitudes toward discount stores, and they tend not to shop discounters for products that they perceive to have high social risk.[25]

In some instances, at least, consumers may shop a given store simply because it is considered the least negative alternative. The store avoidance hypothesis suggests that consumers may not have strong patronage motives in many cases and, in these instances, any patronage pattern may be quite easily upset by new retailers.[26]

Store Image The consumer's total perception of a retail store, based on the various patronage factors, forms the store's image. In general, most retail stores have an identifiable and distinct image. A retailer cannot be all things to all people. The discussions on consumer types and patronage motives should make it clear that different consumers look for different things in the stores they shop. A store's management must decide which market segments it will serve and attempt to match the store's offering to the requirements of the identified segment.[27] This may present problems because the impression that management has of its store very often does not match the consumer's image.[28]

Store image is variously defined by different writers. Pierre Martineau defined store image as "the way the store is defined in the shopper's mind, partly by its functional qualities and partly by an aura of psychological attributes."[29] Note the terms *functional qualities* and *psychological attributes.* Functional relates to attributes like merchandise selection, price ranges, credit policies, store layout, and similar qualities that can be objectively compared across retailers. Psychological qualities refers to such things as a sense of belonging or welcome, the feeling of warmth or friendliness, or possibly an attitude of interest or excitement. More than one quality may be relevant, and it is assumed that each quality can be visualized on a subjective scale ranging from good to bad. Store image is thus subjectively formed on both functional and psychological planes simultaneously.[30]

A second definition of image advanced relative to the influence of television viewing influences on store image and shopping frequency says that store image is "a complex of meanings and relationships serving to characterize the store for people."[31] A third definition emphasizes the effects of experience and image modification over time, saying that store image "may be defined as discriminative stimuli for an action's expected reinforcement that a person associates with shopping at a particular store. . . . An image is acquired through experience and is thus learned."[32]

Store image is a perceptual construct and, as such, is highly subjective. Since consumers really cannot effectively process information relative to all attributes of a store, they simplify and combine many dimensions and ideas into a single construct. Thus, a store may have a favorable image because it is friendly, or it may have an unfavorable image because it is dirty. The stated image may, then, be quite simple, even though the underlying attitudes may be quite complex and based on a wide range of store attributes. As a result, an image may be based on largely irrelevant data as consumers rely on indirect cues rather than actual observation of what they presumably want to know.[33]

Like price and other cues, store image may serve as a surrogate for quality, and the consumer may come to view the items sold in a store with a favorable image as being of higher quality than those sold in a store with a negative image. Moreover, a consumer may actually hold varying store images, depending on the product sought.[34]

In general, it is felt that consumers seek retail stores with images that fit their own self-images.[35] Thus, a store communicating a high-class image would likely have a clientele of upper social strata and upwardly mobile customers. However, some research suggests that a person may actually shift his or her store image so that self-image is seen to be congruent with stores shopped.[36] In attribution theory terms

Fig. 16-12

*"Once in a while
I just get away
from everyone and go
off by myself.
I never really do anything.
But still
I accomplish so much."*

*You have a special way
of getting down to basics.
So do our clothes.* The Talbots
Since 1947

*Simple. Understated. That's the beauty of our superb classic clothes. Why not see for yourself? Visit our stores
in Massachusetts, Connecticut, New York and Pennsylvania. And don't forget to ask for a subscription to our free catalog. Or call toll-free 800-225-8200
(in Massachusetts call 800-232-8181) or write The Talbots, Dept. QM, Hingham, MA 02043.*

A store may communicate its image and seek to match it to specific personality types as in this ad which appeals to a reflective personality type.

Courtesy of The Talbots.

the customer would be saying, in effect, "I'm shopping in this store, and I have this self-image, so the store must have this image." If this notion is correct, the results of any in-store image study might be suspect.

Although image components are variously designated from one study to another, nine more or less universal store image attribute groups have been identified as follows:

Merchandise—The five attributes considered here are quality, selection or assortment, styling or fashion, guarantees, and pricing. Merchandise itself is taken to mean the goods and services offered by a retail outlet.

Service—The attribute areas are service-general, salesclerk service, self-service, ease of merchandise return, delivery service, and credit policies of the store.

Clientele—Social class appeal, self-image congruency, and store personnel are included as attributes of this factor.

Physical Facilities—These facilities include such things as elevators, lighting, air conditioning, and washrooms. It may also be used by a customer to include store layout, aisle placement and width, carpeting, and architecture.

Convenience—Three factors have been identified that fit into this classification —namely, convenience-general, locational convenience, and parking.

Promotion—Within this summary grouping are sales promotions, advertising, displays, trading stamps, and symbols and colors.

Store Atmosphere—This attribute category consists of what can be called atmosphere-congeniality. This refers to a customer's feeling of warmth, acceptance, or ease.

Institutional Factors—Within this grouping is the conservative-modern projection of the store; the attributes of reputation and reliability enter the picture.

Posttransaction Satisfaction—This classification of attributes would include such areas as merchandise in use, returns, and adjustments. In essence, was the consumer satisfied with the purchase and with the store?[37]

Store image is measured in a number of ways. Probably the most common technique involves asking the respondent to rate several competing stores on a number of image factors using a semantic differential scale. This would yield results similar to those found in figure 16-13. Such data must be used with caution, however, as the following example shows.

A small western saddlery and apparel store operated successfully for years with the same wooden floors, ancient, home-made fixtures, and crowded layout. An image study revealed that consumers viewed the store as old-fashioned in comparison with its two major competitors. Taking these findings as a personal affront, the owner expanded the store and modernized it with new tiled floors, modern fixtures, additional lighting, etc. After several months business had not improved—actually it decreased. A follow-up study indicated that the store's customers actually preferred the store's previous atmosphere. Under the former arrangement customers felt more comfortable and perceived that they received greater value for their dollars. Thus old-fashioned was not perceived as detrimental. Rather, the "old-fashioned" store

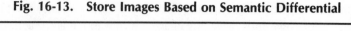

Fig. 16-13.   Store Images Based on Semantic Differential

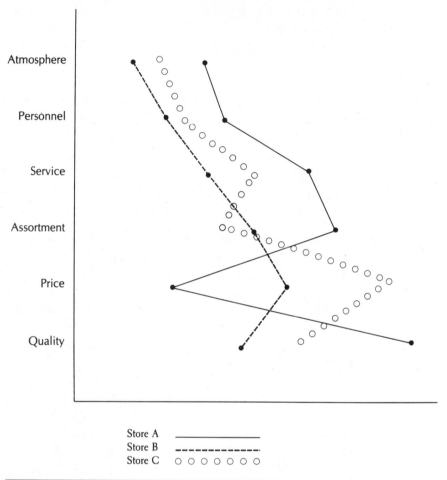

Don L. James, Richard M. Durand, and Robert A. Dreves, "The Use of a Multi-Attribute Model in a Store Image Study," *Journal of Retailing*, 52, no. 2 (Summer 1976):29. Reprinted by permission of the *Journal of Retailing*.

met the needs of store customers better than a modern, more sterile, spacious store. The problem is that the semantic differential did not provide this retailer with enough information to develop a marketing plan.[38]

The semantic differential may be applied to image components that really are not particularly relevant to the consumers. If the semantic differential is applied without considering the significance and direction of consumer attitude on the image attributes, we may find the following situation:

> people are encouraged to respond to characteristics that do not necessarily comprise the image they have of the store being studied. For example, respondents might be asked to evaluate a store on the basis of whether it has a pleasant or unpleasant

atmosphere. The problem is that the consumer may or may not think of "atmosphere" when he thinks about a particular store. When he is required to make an evaluation of such characteristics, they become part of the image of the store that he is concluded to have. The resulting "image" then is likely to be more highly correlated with the instrument than with reality.[39]

To overcome the weaknesses of the semantic differential, a multi-attribute attitude model for assessing the salience of each characteristic is suggested in which various attributes are weighted according to desirability.[40] In addition, multidimensional scaling, similar to that used in assessing brand image, is also often used, resulting in perceptual maps like that found in figure 16-14.[41]

Store Loyalty Consumer loyalty is defined as "the tendency for a person to continue over time to exhibit similar behaviors in situations similar to those he has previously encountered: e.g. to continue to purchase the same brand and product in the same store each time he needs or wants an identical or similar item."[42] The same problems relevant in dealing with brand loyalty are faced in studying store loyalty. A particular difficulty lies in defining what constitutes store loyalty. Probably very few customers are totally store loyal in the sense that they buy all of a particular item in a single store. However, many consumers are probably partially store loyal—that is, they make the majority of a given type of a purchase from a relatively few stores out of all those available.

The value of the store-loyal customer to a retailer is open to some question. One study of store loyalty reported that nonloyal customers spend more than loyal customers.[43] The same study, however, reported that the amount a family spends in a year in a grocery store is closely tied to the number of trips made to the store, suggesting a benefit in trying to build store loyalty. Other research that is more direct in pointing up the value of store loyalty suggests that: (1) store-loyal behavior is independent of the total amount of food expenditures; (2) more loyal consumers allocate much larger expenditures to their first-choice stores than do less loyal customers; (3) stores with the largest number of loyal customers have the largest share of the market; and (4) loyal customers are no more expensive to serve than nonloyal customers.[44]

Another author ties the sales performance of a store directly to store loyalty:

> For every highly loyal family you can attract, you will get on the average 62.3 percent of its total food purchases (half again as much as the average family).
>
> In sum, your greatest opportunities lie in getting the best possible mix of consumer loyalties for the traffic that your store will carry. In a shopping area with many competitors, in fact, your best bet for holding and increasing sales volume is to improve the quality of your consumer loyalty mix.[45]

In food shopping, at least, the store-loyal consumer seems to be a powerful market force. The same may not be true with respect to the department store. Although overall sales and sales of items complementary to those for which customers are store loyal are likely to be enhanced by increasing the number of

Fig. 16-14. Perceptual Map of Store Image

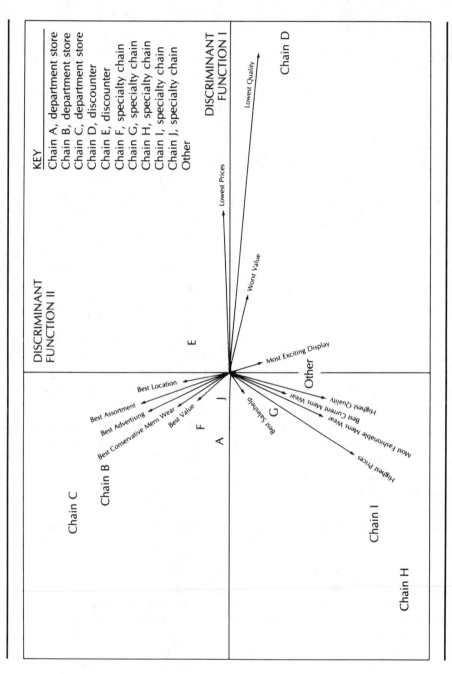

Lawrence J. Ring, "Retail Positioning: A Multiple Discriminant Analysis Approach," *Journal of Retailing*, 55, no. 1 (Spring 1979):52. Reprinted by permission of the *Journal of Retailing*.

store-loyal customers, research suggests that department store loyalty, in general and with respect to specific items, is likely to be quite rare.[46]

When we consider the factors associated with consumer loyalty, a mixed picture emerges. In general, consumer loyalty is related to the product itself and the structure of its market, the buyer's information sources, the customer's purchase patterns, and the purchaser's personal characteristics. Store loyalty has received less research attention than brand loyalty, so specific data is a little sketchy.[47]

Store loyalty has been positively linked to time-conciousness, entertainment media use, attitude toward local shopping conditions, and age. It has been found to correlate negatively with fashion opinion leadership, credit use, urban orientation, venturesomeness, attitude toward out-shopping and shopping conditions in other towns in the trading area, education, and family income.[48] In addition, store loyalty differs according to the benefits sought from the store, and the benefits sought are correlated with various demographic characteristics of consumers.[49]

Subcultural Influences on Retail Shopping Behavior Most of the research that looks at differences in retail response across subcultures has been directed at blacks versus whites. In general, shopping patterns and attitudes of middle-class blacks are the same as those of middle-class whites.[50] The major differences come from lower-income younger blacks. This group tends to be substantially different from both lower-income and middle-income whites. A study of the perceptions of suburban versus ghetto blacks for a ghetto food store as opposed to a suburban store determined the following:

1. Few perceptual differences were found between all black ghetto and all black surburban residents with respect to either store. Further, it was the ghetto resident who often had a generally favorable response when there were differences.

2. When comparing all ghetto and all suburban blacks, the few differences that did exist were based on store atmosphere rather than quality or price variables.

3. Comparison of perceptions between older and younger respondents revealed several differences on price and quality variables. The younger blacks were less favorable than older blacks in every instance but one.

4. In the age analysis within each resident group, many more perceived differences were found between younger and older ghetto respondents than between suburban age groups in their specific residence stores.

5. Education was generally not an important variable in explaining differences in perceptions.

6. Few systematic perceptual differences with reference to price, quality, and atmosphere appeared to be associated with both of the stores.

7. Most of the factors which evoked perceptual differences were those centering on store atmosphere and cleanliness. Differences in perceptions of price and quality were fewer than expected.[51]

Another study of the actual shopping behavior across subcultures viewed differences in age, race, and place of residence. The study drew five conclusions.

1. While white city and mixed city area shoppers appeared to fragment their shopping trips—buying different products in stores of different affiliations, suburban and black city area shoppers confined their purchases of all products chiefly to a particular class of store-behavior consistent with buying food on one or two major shopping trips each weeks.

2. Black city area shoppers shopped at certain stores for about the same proportion of their purchases as white, city area shoppers and for a higher proportion than suburban shoppers. Since chain stores were less dense in the black city area, the black city area shoppers must have traveled relatively further to shop than other residents of the city.

3. For beverages and paper products, blacks bought proportionately fewer private brands; for other product groups no systematic differences emerged. The observed differences seemed more due to taste than availability.

4. The average package sizes bought by shoppers in various areas did *not* systematically differ.

5. The proportion of nonshoppers among black city area families was relatively large for all product groups. Although black city area shoppers may have traveled further to reach a particular chain store, they were relatively less likely to shop among stores than were the suburban shoppers.[52]

Apparently there are some differences in the ways various subcultures perceive and behave toward retail stores. Image and shopping habits vary, so retailers should take the effort to learn how relevant subcultures see their stores. Stores in locations heavy in concentrations of specific subcultures should try to merchandise and manage in such a way as to meet their primary target markets' expectations.

Retail Customer Decision Making The consumer decision process is manifested in a buyer's shopping behavior. A good deal of the consumer's information search and processing, along with alternative evaluation, takes place within and between retail stores. The consumer's contact with salespeople at the retail level takes place in stores, so concepts from previous discussions on store patronage motives, shopping styles, store image, and store loyalty can be brought to bear in investigating the nature and significance of retail customer decision making.

Consistent with other types of information search and alternative evaluation, most consumers shop relatively few stores for any given purchase. The majority of retail customers shop only one or two stores even prior to making major purchases.[53] Often, however, customers visit the store of purchase several times prior to the purchase.[54] In general, price and store comparisons are subject to the evoked set principle in the same way as are brands.[55] Customers of higher education, income, and social class shop more stores, on the average, than other consumers.

Different retail customer types appear to use quite different information-processing and decision-making strategies. One writer identified four shopping orientations underlying different kinds of decision behavior.

1. *The economic shopper* probably the most active information seeker and processor, was highly sensitive to price, quality, and merchandise assortment, and these factors were decisive in store selection. For this shopper, the store and its personnel were instruments for purchase of goods. This shopper is likely to exhibit little store loyalty.

2. *The personalizing shopper* bases store patronage on relationships with store personnel. This shopper seeks information from friends, and store personnel in preferred stores are seen as friends. Store loyalty will be a significant force for this shopper.

3. *The ethical shopper* is the champion of the small retailer. "Help the little guy" or "the chain store has no soul" underlies this shopper's decision criterion. The ethical shopper is likely to be fairly store loyal.

4. *The apathetic shopper* is one whose decision style is to "get it over with." Shopping is aimed at reducing expenditure of effort. Location convenience is more important than price, quality, assortment, or personnel. This shopper may patronize only a few stores, but out of convenience rather than loyalty.[56]

Consumers with different shopping orientations tend to have different information needs and decision styles.[57] Life-style characteristics can be used to predict shopper communication needs and to suggest effective promotion strategies. Consumers may have different buying goals, influencing their evaluation and use of information.[58] Shopper psychological makeup and life-style leads to both differential exposure and preference for mass media.[59]

Several shopping orientations based on life-style factors provide a basis for differentiating among various patterns of decision making (refer back to figure 16-5). Consumers of different shopping orientations tend to seek information from varying sources.[60] The brand-loyal and name-conscious shoppers use advertising heavily. Friends and neighbors are the prime sources for the psychosocializing shopper who tends to follow others' consumption behavior. People who are brand loyal more often consult salespeople.

In addition to differences on information use, shoppers have varying degrees of trust for different media. The special shopper relies on free samples more than any other shopper type. The brand-loyal shopper is heavily oriented toward salespeople and newspaper/magazine ads, while the store-loyal shopper depends on salespeople. The problem solver has greater trust for personal sources. The psychosocializer is oriented toward advertising and friends. The name-conscious shopper is a heavy user of print advertising (see fig 16-15).

Figure 16-16 shows how information preferences vary across shopping orientations. The special shopper seems to prefer more objective types of information. Shoppers who seek to emulate the behavior of others prefer more social types of information, such as their friends' opinions, and try to learn of the preferences of others.

Shoppers with different orientations use the media differently. Problem solvers and psychosocializers tend to spend a lot of time watching television. Name-conscious shoppers read more fashion, news, and business magazines, while special shoppers prefer home-oriented magazines.

Shopper decision making apparently varies across stores. In a study of the purchase of audio equipment it was found that, as opposed to department store buyers, specialty store buyers were more knowledgeable, had more product experience, read more product-oriented special-interest magazines, examined manufac-

Fig. 16-15. Shopping Orientation and Source Credibility*

Information Source	Shopping Orientation						
	Special Shopper	Brand-Loyal Shopper	Store-Loyal Shopper	Problem-Solving Shopper	Psycho-socializing Shopper	Name-conscious Shopper
Television Advertisements	.06	.00	-.03	-.05	.16[b]	-.01
Friends or Neighbors	.02	.04	-.02	.16[b]	.41[a]	.03
Newspaper/Magazine Advertisements	.12[c]	.12[c]	.07	-.02	.15[b]	.20[a]
Salespersons	-.06	.21[a]	.22[a]	.27[a]	-.03	.22[a]
On-the-Counter Testers	-.05	-.10	-.17[b]	-.07	-.10	-.08
Free Samples	.19[a]	-.03	-.08	-.03	-.09	-.08

* Numbers are correlation coefficients.
[a] $p < .01$.
[b] $p < .05$.
[c] $p < .10$.

George P. Moschis, "Shopping Orientations and Consumer Uses of Information," *Journal of Retailing*, 52, no. 2 (Summer 1976):67. Reprinted by permission of the *Journal of Retailing*.

Fig. 16-16. Shopping Orientation and Information Preferences*

Kinds of information	Shopping Orientation					
	Special Shopper	Brand-Loyal Shopper	Store-Loyal Shopper	Problem-Solving Shopper	Psycho-socializing Shopper	Name-conscious Shopper
"Friends' opinions of various brands"	.06	-.01	.03	.14[b]	.49[a]	.21[a]
"Main differences between brands"	.15[b]	.04	.11	.12[c]	-.06	.08
"Available brands on the market"	.07	.23[a]	.11	.22[a]	-.00	.24[a]
"Salesperson's opinion on various brands"	-.01	.13[c]	.27[a]	.31[a]	.08	.17[b]
"Brands carried by a particular store"	.09	.28[a]	.18[a]	.17[b]	.01	.35[a]
"What kind of people buy certain brands"	.04	.01	.18[a]	.26[a]	.17[b]	.13[c]

* Numbers are correlation coefficients.

[a] $p < .01$.
[b] $p < .05$.
[c] $p < .10$.

George P. Moschis, "Shopping Orientations and Consumer Uses of Information," *Journal of Retailing*, 52, no. 2 (Summer 1976):68. Reprinted by permission of the *Journal of Retailing*.

turer's literature more often, visited more stores, and more often sought advice from friends and neighbors.[61]

Finally, postpurchase activities are significant. For example, postpurchase communication with retail customers can lead to improved customer satisfaction and increased recommendation of the retailer to others.[62]

Customer Satisfaction Customer satisfaction with both stores and products is a critical issue for retailers. If the store avoidance hypothesis is at all correct, any degree of relative dissatisfaction could send a retail customer to competing stores on a regular basis. Retailers, particularly larger ones, have adopted very liberal adjustment policies for unsatisfactory goods. However, since this policy is costly, it is important to try to be certain that most customers are satisfied with no follow-up adjustment. Knowledge of how to please shoppers must be based on an understanding of the nature of customer satisfaction.

Essentially, satisfaction is a function of the degree to which the outcome of a transaction conforms to customer expectations going into the purchase. It has been suggested that customer expectations, because of sustained affluence, are high and get continually higher.[63] Given this, general customer satisfaction would decline even if retail service stayed the same.

In addition, it has been suggested that satisfaction (or dissatisfaction) is more a function of the shopper's personality than of problems with a store or its products.[64] Several personal characteristics of shoppers are found to relate to the degree of satisfaction expressed toward retailers. Findings include the following:

1.   Satisfaction increases with age.
2.   Satisfaction increases with the personal competence of the shopper.
3.   Satisfaction tends to decrease with education.
4.   Satisfaction has been shown to vary negatively with family income and social class.
5.   Satisfaction is related to sex, race, marital status, household size, years of residence in community, years married, life cycle stage, and moves during married years.[65]

Retail Store Strategy

Having investigated several aspects of the consumer relative to retail strategy, discussion turns to some behavioral dimensions of retail store strategy. Beginning with store location, this section covers strategies for store layout and design, display, and store positioning (image building).

Location Retail store location is fundamentally a behavioral phenomenon. A good location is the lifeblood for many retailers. Strategies utilized in finding a good location include traffic counts, retail gravitation techniques, and cognitive mapping.[66] What constitutes a profitable location for one retailer may be unprofitable for another, so it is difficult to draw many useful generalizations.

The previous discussion of life-style and shopping behavior from different neighborhoods suggests that the socioeconomic and life-style characteristics of a trading area should be investigated prior to establishing a store.[67] In addition, the character of retail trade areas is constantly changing, so relevant variables should be monitored from time to time to determine whether the location and merchandising strategy are still appropriate.

The concept of convenience is important in location. A good location can be just a few feet away from a poor one. In analyzing a location, the main concerns are how shoppers will perceive and react to the location and whether the location is easy to get to. People tend to move to their right when driving, probably because of the difficulty and time involved in making a left turn across traffic. A store in which I was located for management training some years ago is a case in point. The store was a medium-sized home and auto establishment located in a large western city. A new shopping center had opened, and occupancy costs for the center were quite high, so management elected to locate directly across the street from the center. The center was large and successful, so this sounded like a good strategy. It was not, however. As you look at the store location in figure 16-17, what problems do you see?

The store did not show a profit in its first fourteen years of operation. Location wasn't the store's total problem, but it was part of it. Note that the main city lies to the east of the store. Any traffic coming from that direction will tend to turn right into the center rather than trying to cross eastbound traffic. Traffic coming from the west will be siphoned into the center at the left turn light. This leaves the store easy access only from the south, where the street does not go through. Little traffic other than local moved on that street. The upshot was that the store was hard to get to, and shopping traffic was light even during peak times for the center.

Store Layout and Design In general, the problem of store layout and design has been treated as a question of engineering. Maximizing the display available from a given space or laying out a floor plan to achieve the most efficient traffic flows might be considered important design goals. Store planners often use the phrase "form follows function," noting that the design of a particular store space is dependent upon the job that must be performed (displaying, selling, cashiering, receiving, or marking).

In a sense, however, the allocation and design of store space is fundamentally based upon behavioral considerations. Consider, for example, the way you feel when you enter a particular store. Go to several stores and note the image that they communicate and the feelings that they elicit. How do you feel when you enter a discount department store? Why? Now consider a prestige department store or a high-class specialty shop. How do your emotional reactions differ? Why?

Part of the difference will, of course, come from the type of merchandise sold. A good deal of it, however, will derive from the colors used, the lighting, the height and shape of displays, and the traffic flow (aisles—wide or narrow—versus free flow). Harsh lighting, light-reflecting walls, and tightly arranged merchandise displays in the discount store create a reaction of urgency and economy. The subdued lighting,

Fig. 16-17. Store Location

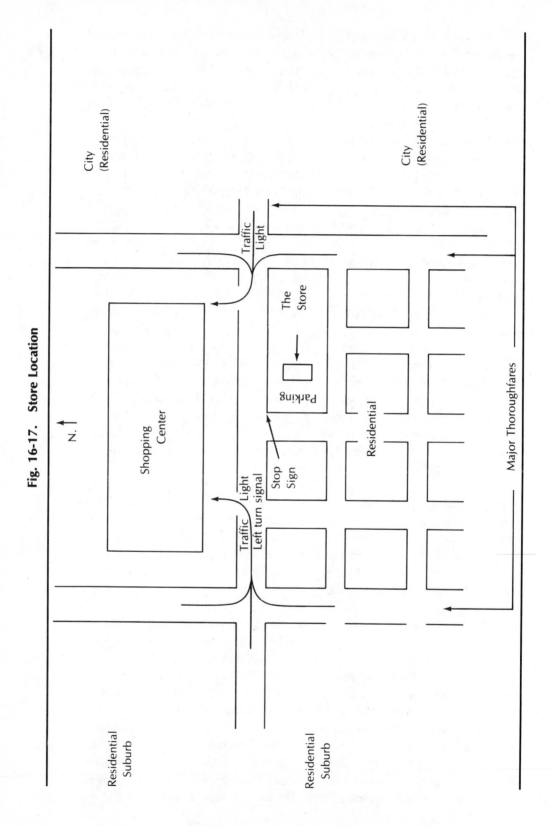

scattered and tasteful displays, and the light- and sound-absorbing walls, floors, and ceilings of the prestige store create a relaxed atmosphere that encourages browsing, conversation with salespeople, and possibly a desire for self-gratification and extravagance.

To quote one group of authors:

> A subtle dimension of in-store customer shopping behavior is the environment of the space itself. Retail space, i.e., the proximate environment that surrounds the retail shopper, is never neutral. The retail store is a bundle of cues, messages, and suggestions which communicate to shoppers. Retail store designers, planners, and merchandisers shape space, but that space in turn affects and shapes customer behavior. The retail store is not an exact parallel to a Skinner box, but it does create mood, activate intentions, and generally affect customer reactions.
>
> Retail merchandisers are avowed behavior shapers. In a market economy, freedom to compete implies freedom to organize, to shape, and to modify customer demand, buying habits, and store patronage in an effort to increase sales and profits. Retailers strive to accomplish these objectives through the manipulation of product and merchandise tactics, pricing and store location, design and space utilization. Yet too frequently, store design and space utilization are not well integrated into the overall merchandising plan, nor does the merchandiser-marketer always appreciate the significance of space utilization, overall store design, color, and lighting as dynamic parts of his selling strategy. There are vague notions that space affects behavior, but until very recently little was known about this important social psychological phenomenon, and the result has been inadequate attention to the significance of space.[68]

Given these considerations, the article goes on to state four tentative propositions about store space:

1. Space is an important modifier and shaper of behavior.
2. The retail store as a proximate environment affects behavior by a process of a psychology of stimulation.
3. The retail store, like other aesthetic surroundings, affects customers' perceptions, attitudes, and images.
4. Space utilization and store design can be deliberately and consciously programmed to create desired customer reactions.

Behavioral Effects of Space The amount and type of space in which we find ourselves have a significant effect on mood which, in turn, influences behavior. We have a sense of territoriality. We seek to protect that which we consider our own. "A customer hovering over a counter of sale merchandise, spreading her packages, her coat, and her purse over the counter while she examines a host of colors or styles, is engaged in a form of displaced aggression as obvious as a small bird whose territory has been invaded by an intruder and who pretends to be eating or pecking while demonstrating both frustration and possession."[69]

The amount of space available is an important contributor to mood. Intruding on someone's personal space through crowding leads to irritability, conceivably resulting in at least two effects. It might cause customers to move through the store hurriedly to avoid the irritation (punishment), or it could lead to hostility toward the store or its personnel which may result in generalized dissatisfaction.

To a degree, the amount of space required or expected is a function of social class, with higher social strata demanding more personal space. Thus, the social identification and image of a store is raised by wide aisles and low displays. At the same time, however, a feeling of exclusiveness can be achieved through boutique-type arrangements, which give consumers the feeling that store space is their own, adding to the store's status image.

Behavior Shaping by the Store Stores may vary in character from being sterile and impersonal to "exciting, vibrant person-environment systems which accentuate merchandising efforts and generate large positive measures of customer rewards and satisfaction."[70] If we perceive a retail environment as comfortable and rewarding, we are likely to see the activities and transactions that transpire therein as similarly pleasant. Through such continued rewards, customers identify favorite or preferred stores.

The retail store is a bundle of cues and stimuli. The customer can't escape substantial impact on perceptions and attitudes from store surroundings.

> Retail space creates expectations through stimulation. For example, if a retailer wants to capitalize on high turnover, he will probably use high illumination and not worry too much about using sound deadening materials. On the other hand, if he wants customers to linger or browse he uses dim lighting and sound-proofing surfaces such as carpets, drapes, and padded or acoustical ceilings. The physical environment of a retail store, like other buildings, creates certain expectations about how one should act—people lower their voices and stop smiling when they enter banks and church. Customers in retail stores often "feel" a sense of belonging or they sometimes feel like aliens in a strange aversive environment. In restaurants, retail stores, libraries, and other public spaces, cutting down movement in the peripheral field via layout or traffic flow patterns can reduce the sense of crowding, whereas maximizing peripheral stimulation can build up a sense of activity, crowding and business.[71]

Shaping and Affecting Perceptions, Attitudes, and Images Retail store layout and design communicate vast amounts of information to consumers via the image and atmosphere they create. Consumers process the cues and form perceptions through which they subjectively evaluate stores and form appropriate attitudes.

> Through effective design and space utilization, customer behavior can often be affected by changing or by modifying attitudes and images. Via design features, attitudes and images are created; that is, store personalities are created and shaped, and these personalities (images)—friendly, upper-class, aloof, high quality, low priced, convenient, warm, inviting, cool, haughty, etc.—are in turn meant to affect customer attitudes and images and hence to shape behavior. Store images are designed to create a dynamic interplay of interstimulation between the customer and his store. An image that is believed by customers becomes a self-fulfilling prophecy.[72]

3. Determine how other stores rank.
4. Determine the opinions, impressions, and images different types of customers hold of a store.
5. Decide what kind of images and impressions you would like to create ideally.
6. Decide what kind of impression/image you should *realistically* try to convey— taking account of present image and cost of change.
7. Select the tools to employ—taking account of cost-effectiveness and risk. (All retailers are especially interested in whether certain tools exist that are highly effective, low cost, and fast. There are no magic cures for poor store images, but some measures are far better than others for each individual store.)
8. Monitor the results.[82]

SUMMARY

The marketing channel decision flows in two directions. The manufacturer seeks an optimal mix of intermediaries to move a product to final customers, while an intermediary seeks sources of products from which to build an inventory.

Several behavioral considerations are relevant to the manufacturer's channel strategy. The manufacturer's distribution intensity is, in part, dependent upon consumer behavior relative to the product sold. Intensive distribution is appropriate when the consumer prefers and buys from the most convenient retailer, is low in brand loyalty or preference, and may shop from store to store for the best price or service (but not for a particular brand). Selective or exclusive distribution is suggested in situations where customers have brand or store loyalties, even if they shop for the best price.

Channel structure form and change may be dictated by changing buying habits of consumers. Psychographics may lead to an understanding of life-styles that influence reaction to channels and institutions. Recent trends toward service industries, including fast-food chains, reflect such life-style changes. Out-shopping may be influenced by the increase in numbers of working women and increases in fuel prices.

Numerous attempts have been made to categorize retail shoppers into various subgroups. Among these were apathetic shopper, demanding shopper, quality shopper, fastidious shopper, stamp preferer, and convenient location shopper.

In addition to the obvious need to buy certain goods, people have a number of personal and social motives for shopping. A customer decides which store or stores to shop at through a four-step process: evaluative criteria formulation, perceived store image, comparison processes, and acceptable and unacceptable source determination. Patronage motives tend to vary from one type of store of another. They also vary across consumers according to such factors as social class, demographic characteristics, stage in life cycle, benefits sought, product purchased, life-style, personality, and perceived risk.

The totality of shopper attitudes and motives toward a given store represents that store's image. Retail store image may communicate a perceived quality for all the items it sells. In general, customers seek store images that match their self-images.

Store loyalty can be defined as the tendency for a person to continue to shop a specific store or set of stores in similar product and need situations over time. Although most consumers will not be loyal to just one store, many will be loyal to a few stores. Store-loyal customers and postpurchase satisfaction are valuable to retailers trying to establish a favorable image and seeking to capture and hold loyal customers. Satisfaction is a function of how well customer expectations are met and of the personality of the shopper. Several aspects of store strategy were discussed, including location, store layout and design, store display, and store positioning.

CHAPTER 16   STUDY REVIEW

Important Terms and Concepts

Out-shopping
Store patronage
Store choice criteria
Patronage motives
Store image
Store image attributes
Store loyalty
Retail customer decision making
Store avoidance hypothesis
Behavioral effects of store space
Retail store positioning

Questions

1. How might a manufacturer use psychographic research findings in making marketing channel decisions?

2. Summarize the major retail shopper typologies, and explain how they might aid in formulating marketing strategy.

3. Why do people shop?

4. How does a consumer decide which stores to shop in?

5. What is store image, how is it formed, and how is it likely to influence store choice?

6. What is store loyalty, and what is its significance?

7. Discuss the major subcultural influences on retail shopping behavior.

8. What factors influence customer satisfaction with retail stores?

9. Discuss the major behavioral implications for store location.

10. How can buyer behavior be shaped by in-store layout, display, and design?

17

Consumer Behavior and Public Policy

Up to this point the text has been directed toward understanding consumer behavior for the benefit of the firm's marketing strategy. In this chapter, however, emphasis shifts to an investigation of what our knowledge of consumer behavior suggests to the public policy maker. The chapter will also aid the marketing manager in understanding the philosophy and direction of public policy as it influences and is influenced by actual consumer behavior and what public policy makers assume to be true about consumer behavior. At the same time, policy makers might see implications of consumer behavior for directing future efforts in consumer protection and education.

The business and public policy environment has changed noticeably over the century. As Howard K. Smith, ABC newsman, observed recently,

> Real power in this country—not power as written in the constitution, but real power of special interests to get their will—has been segmented in this country. The first third of the century, business ran things, electing politicians, passing laws at will. . . . In the second third, labor was able to elect politicians and pass its laws. In the final third, now, the consumer is knocking on the door.[1]

The power shift has been rather dramatic. At first we operated from a philosophy of caveat emptor—let the buyer aware. Now the pendulum seems to have swung to caveat venditor—let the seller beware. Public policy emphasis has moved from fostering competition to protecting competitors to protecting consumers. As government agencies, law makers, and the courts have shifted their thinking, they have relied on a set of assumptions about consumer behavior. Often these assumptions come through implicitly in legislation, policies, and interpretations, but they are seldom explicitly stated. An even greater problem lies in the fact that the assumptions that underlie the current direction of public policy formulation often do not seem to square with the results of consumer research.

General Problems

Looking at the issue of developing and implementing public policy oriented toward buying behavior, several general problems emerge.

1. Public policy makers typically come from legal backgrounds and so have relatively little knowledge of consumer behavior.
2. Many times public policy makers have a kind of built-in antagonism toward business—often growing out of direct experience or observation of shoddy marketing practice.
3. On the other hand, the business community generally reacts negatively toward virtually any consumer legislation. Lobbying efforts often block or alter regulations that could truly benefit consumers.
4. Although a great deal of laudable legislation has recently been implemented, it often does not get at the real consumer problems.
5. There are some genuine differences in philosophy as to what consumer rights and responsibilities should be.
6. Often there is no consumer research undertaken prior to policy implementation. Research is frequently carried out after policy adoption, but at that time it is difficult to determine the effects of the policy, because there is no opportunity to test before and after policy implementation. Also, it is often difficult and time consuming to change policy once it is in effect.
7. It has proved extremely difficult to communicate protection availability and other policy-related information to consumers in such a way that they become aware of it and avail themselves of its benefits.

Certainly these are not exhaustive of the problems that face consumer-oriented public policy, but they are representative of the overall challenges facing those who seek to improve the buying environment for consumers. This chapter will address some of these problems. After regulation and the potential for consumer research are discussed, the rest of the chapter will treat policy from the standpoint of consumer information processing, deceptive advertising, consumer dissatisfaction, and some selected areas of consumer legislation and public policy that stand to gain from consumer research.

Regulation

The assumptions and thinking that underlie public policy have changed markedly in recent years. For many years, for example, it was more or less assumed that a company would overstate its product benefits in its advertising. Puffery—often a great deal of it—was allowed, presumably on the premise that if consumers knew they were being misled it was all right. But restrictions on puffery are growing tighter as many firms are required to present specific evidence that their advertising claims are literally and completely true. The increase in advertising that cites results of laboratory tests and consumer trials, along with comparative advertising in which firms compare their products with those of competitors by name, is an outgrowth of this philosophy.

Assumptions about Consumers Part of the problem with public policy is that consumer-oriented legislation has developed without a firm underpinning of empirically derived theory. Any attempt to discuss the assumptions of consumer behavior on which policy and legislation are based must be pretty much inferred from the policy itself. By observation and inference, the assumptions about consumer behavior are as follows:

1. Consumers are ill-informed about products, credit, and the like.
2. The more information consumers have, the better.
3. Consumers should base their purchase decisions on technical, rational information rather than on potential satisfaction of psychological needs.
4. Information for intelligent decision making is not readily available to consumers.
5. Marketers cannot or will not make objective information available to consumers without legal requirements to do so.
6. If information is made readily available to consumers, they will automatically use the information to make better buying decisions.
7. Price, brand, store, advertising, and quality are assumed to be completely independent of each other. "The idea that a person would be willing to pay more for a certain brand, even though the almost identical product is available at less cost is thought by many to signal some flaw in the system and represent anticompetitive behavior on the part of some business firms."
8. "The consumer has unlimited shopping time to make numerous comparisons and unlimited time to acquire the necessary information to achieve the lowest economic cost. This belief, unfortunately ignores total economic cost."[2]

Because these assumptions are more implicit than explicit, there may be a wide variation from time to time, agency to agency, and individual to individual.

Objectives of Regulation One of the major concerns in any regulatory program must be a statement of objectives. Unfortunately, the objectives of public policy on marketing practices and consumer welfare have really not been well stated and well defined. At times the objectives that have been stated are unrealistic or slanted toward either consumers or business.

It is unfortunate that in many instances consumers and businesses find themselves in an adversary position. In general, consumers want to have their needs served and marketers want to satisfy them—at a profit. The exchange, however, turns out to be not quite so simple in reality. Consumer expectations are often unrealistically high (too often because marketers have raised them to an unrealistic level). Also, there are some unscrupulous individuals and firms who prey on the unsuspecting consumer.

In order to function properly, a free enterprise, free consumer-choice economy depends upon an informed consumer. This is not necessarily the perfect-knowledge consumer of economic theory, but at least an aware, problem-solving consumer is needed. For a variety of reasons the consumer is often ill-equipped for effective problem solving. In order to create a knowledgeable consumer policy makers have followed several objectives.

One objective is to educate or protect the "least sophisticated" consumer.[3] Achieving this goal has proved difficult since unsophisticated consumers are generally not heavy readers, typically of low education and aspiration, and often apathetic to attempts to upgrade their buying capabilities. With these difficulties in mind the objective often changes to one of making the information available, whether or not it will be used. The idea is that the consumer will at least have the *opportunity* to receive information. Such a goal may be quite wasteful, however. In the words of John Howard and Lyman Ostlund,

> The (Federal Trade) Commission must . . . aim primarily at correcting those cases of unfairness, that is, information imbalance, that will result in a behavioral change by the consumer. No purpose is served in requiring the marketer to disseminate information a given consumer segment will not or cannot use. To do so would represent a waste of resources by both the FTC and the marketer. Rather the commission should first attempt to establish through consumer behavior research the types of information that consumers currently use, or would use if available and a clear understanding of the decision making process in a given product category before drafting regulations or legislative recommendations.

Another objective that seems to guide thinking is achieving full and truthful disclosure about products in advertising. In a sense, there are really two objectives here, one that is probably impossible to achieve, and one that is probably possible, although not easy, to reach.

No matter how much information a manufacturer discloses about a given product, it is likely that more *could* be said. In addition, it seems too much to ask

Reprinted by permission. © 1980 NEA, Inc.

an advertiser to buy time or space to reveal all of a product's bad points. It is unlikely that the consumer would take the trouble to internalize all of the information, in any case.

On the other hand, it is possible for marketers to make what they say about their products truthful. Truth, however, can sometimes be an elusive concept. Marketers may not be fully aware of all relevant characteristics of their products, and part of the truth can sometimes be as deceitful as a lie. Also, genuine attempts to meet the spirit of the law can result in unintended violations.

In the first place, there is great pressure on advertising copywriters to be creative and to present product features in a high-impact way so as to break through the selective unawareness and resistance to advertising. For example, it is possible that the creators of the Listerine ads that recently netted Warner-Lambert the biggest deceptive advertising judgment ever levied on a company (an $18,000,000 fine and corrective ads) could have been quite innocent of deceptive intent. (Keep in mind that the FTC does not have to show *intent* to deceive, or even deception—only the capacity to deceive.) Imagine the creative people trying to come up with some new ideas for ads. For years, the company had promoted that Listerine stopped bad breath (halitosis) by killing germs. Someone may well have said something like, "Hey, if Listerine kills germs, why wouldn't it stop sore throats and colds?" And so a new campaign was born. The germs that Listerine kills, however, are bacteria, and colds are caused by viruses. Therefore, Listerine has no effect on colds. Corrective ads have carried the message, "Listerine will not stop colds or sore throats, nor lessen their severity."

Another kind of problem is illustrated as companies try to demonstrate something undemonstratable. For example, think of a TV commercial for ice cream. Visualize a bowl of vanilla ice cream with rich, dark chocolate syrup pouring down the sides, whipped cream and nuts, topped off by a big juicy red maraschino cherry.

Now, did you ever stop to think of what would be likely to happen to all that cold ice cream under the hot TV lights. It would melt, right? Right. What to do? Well the FTC says it's okay to substitute if you *can't* show your product in its true form or setting. Substitute mashed potatoes for the vanilla ice cream and you get a somewhat different mental image.

Armed with this policy knowledge, L.O.F.—manufacturers of automobile glass—planned their campaign for a new, nondistorting glass. If you looked directly through the old glass and the new glass, there was a noticeable difference. But the resolution of the TV camera would not show the difference. Again, creativity to the rescue. Following (or so they thought) the FTC guideline, they smeared the old-fashioned glass with petroleum jelly and shot the commercials through this smeared glass and the new, improved glass demonstration was shot with the car window rolled down. Even though this seemed to meet the criterion, the FTC said no, and the ads were pulled.[4]

More recent policy efforts have come in the areas of product quality and safety. For example, efforts are underway to raise awareness of the nutritional level of food through disclosures on food packages. Product safety is also a major issue. Pressure is placed on companies to eliminate, modify, or at least warn consumers of unsafe products. The burden here often seems to be on companies, in spite of the fact that most consumer injuries come as the result of misuse of fundamentally safe products as opposed to faulty product design.[5]

The major objectives of public policy on marketing practices, then, seem to be:

1. To provide for an adequate level of information for consumer decision making.
2. To educate and protect the least sophisticated consumer.
3. To seek full disclosure of product characteristics.
4. To combat deceptive promotion and generally protect consumers from "unfair" marketing practices.
5. To make available safer and more beneficial products.

As we shall see, achieving these goals is difficult in view of current knowledge and theory of consumer behavior.

Consumer Research: Problems and Opportunities

Although consumer behavior theory and research have been little used in the formulation of public policy, they seem to hold great promise and are actually being used more and more to guide the thinking and actions of policy makers. There are problems, too, however, of which we must be aware.

The historical attitude of marketing researchers toward policy makers' receptiveness to and use of consumer research is summed up in the following:

The most severe disadvantage researchers must overcome is that most public policy makers have neither the training nor experience in the use of research evidence.

It appears that consumer research is often not appreciated by policy makers.

For too long now the public policy maker has been relying primarily on economists, lawyers, and journalists for information.

It still be up to the agencies and courts to decide what evidence and what research procedures to use, but at present they have only legal procedures, so they operate on the basis of "fireside" inductions.

This . . . policy has not been advanced with even rudimentary supporting consumer evidence.[6]

It has been noted that "the discipline of consumer behavior has the *potential* to be a powerful boundary spanning agent (to resolve some of the conflict that arises between business, government, and consumer groups) by providing a rigorous framework for the investigation of issues in consumerism."[7] This capability could lead to better policy decisions, and there is evidence that policy makers are increasingly receptive toward the use of consumer research *prior* to the formulation of public policy, as opposed to the common practice of implementing policy first and conducting research later.[8]

Even with the more favorable climate for the application of consumer theory and research, numerous problems remain. It has been suggested that negative public statements by marketing researchers are antagonistic to policy makers who subsequently refuse to listen to experts in consumer behavior.[9]

Several additional problem areas complicate the application of consumer research. Although the study of consumer behavior has repeatedly shown that the economic man assumption is fallacious, the policy maker, trying to reduce a complex behavior to a simple one, often relies on the theory. No single model of consumer behavior is widely accepted. In the absence of such a general model personal ideas of what is or should be are often adopted as bases for policy and legislation. Consumer use of cues, such as price, brand, and store image, is often interpreted by policy makers as an indication that information available to consumers is inadequate. In fact, cues allow consumers to integrate a wide range of learned information, making decision making simple and efficient. Much of what policy makers see as inadequate information search and use is simply the result of habit based on past experience and information processing. The most serious misconception is the belief that consumers are highly impressionable and that by saying the right words an advertiser can lead the consumer to obey the admonitions in advertisements blindly. There is a problem when the concept of protecting or informing the least sophisticated consumer is followed. Unscrupulous marketers have consistently proved that there are numerous gullible consumers who can be duped into spending money foolishly. On the other hand, policy might more logically seek to educate these consumers in more intelligent buying behavior rather than in forcing more information disclosure, which will be little used. The legal background of most policy makers is generally lacking in training in the behavioral sciences. Their unfamiliarity with behavioral concepts makes it difficult for them to incorporate behavioral principles or to accept behavioral research results. A final constraint is that policy makers consider that business-conducted or sponsored research is suspect. Because of their lack of expertise in conducting and interpreting behavioral research, they tend to dismiss all business research as inherently biased. Unfortunately, there is some legitimacy in the assumption. For that reason consumer agencies need to sponsor more unbiased consumer research prior to policy formulation and implementation.[10]

Consumer Information Processing

A great deal of public policy turns on the concepts of consumer information processing. However, public policy makers often do not understand the nature and limitations of consumer information processing. The policy maker's view of information processing leads to three conclusions, which may be erroneous: (1) more information is better; (2) the quality and content of information is irrelevant; and (3) information is processed in the same way by all consumers in all circumstances and at all stages of the decision process.[11]

Policy Intent

There is considerable question as to what public policy should try to accomplish and how it should be enacted to protect consumers. Others suggest that rather than making more laws, more information should be made more readily available to more consumers.[12] However, from an information-processing standpoint, it could be argued that present information is adequate, and all that is needed is to teach consumers to use currently accessible information better.

It is really quite difficult to assess just what the goals of policy relative to consumer behavior should be.[13] There is little evidence on the behavioral effects of information disclosure because of the relative newness of most of the requirements and the inherent difficulties of designing and implementing appropriate evaluative research (especially after disclosure requirements have been implemented). Notwithstanding increasing research in the area, there is a lack of conceptual basis for understanding how buyers actually use information. There is confusion as to the objectives to be served through the provision of additional information. There is general disagreement as to whether new disclosure requirements should simply enhance the consumer's right to know, improve the quality of products and needs, and thus increase purchase satisfaction, or pursue broad educational goals like creation of general public awareness of and interest in nutrition or increased sensitivity to energy conservation.

Information Issues

When considering the problem of information disclosure, three major issues must be considered: what information should be presented, how should the information be presented, and to whom should the information be presented?

What Information Should Be Presented? The question of what information should be presented becomes one of considering what information *must* be disclosed, what *may* be said in promotion, and what *may not* be said in promotion. Each of these issues presents special problems.

The overriding criterion in information disclosure should be concerned with what is relevant to the consumer. The question of relevance becomes difficult because what matters to one consumer is irrelevant to another. Policy makers must have a pretty clear idea of how consumers actually make buying decisions to determine the types of information they need or will use. Unfortunately, consumers do not often use what policy makers see as needed information. For example, improved knowledge of rates and charges that could be attributed to disclosures resulting from truth in lending legislation has had relatively little effect on credit search and usage behavior.[14] The credit decision typically comes at the end of the purchase decision and is considered by many consumers to be incidental. The source and terms of credit are typically determined by the store of purchase or dictated by available and accepted credit cards.

Even with full disclosure many consumers, particularly those at the low end of the education and income spectrum, often do not attend to the credit information or understand the implications of the annual percentage rate. Credit goals of lower-income consumers tend to involve seeking credit terms that minimize the down payment and monthly payments rather than reducing the rate of interest.[15] The educational task here is not so much one of making information available as it is bringing consumers to an understanding of the information and persuading them to use it.[16] On the other hand, we might give some consideration to the idea that low interest is not, and perhaps should not be, the primary concern of the low-income shopper. In the short run, at least, low payments may be the most viable objective for the lower-income consumer. Any change in the attitudes underlying the behavior will have to be based on major value changes, since low-income, low-status consumers tend to live for the short term.

By the same token, American consumers are little motivated to utilize nutritional information when it is made available. They do, however, seem to feel more confident in their decisions when they have nutritional and freshness-dating information.[17]

Including energy consumption information on new appliances does not seem to stimulate consumers to increase the number of alternatives for seeking information nor to engage in a greater amount of total information acquisition. However, there does seem to be a tendency for consumers to shift away from energy-inefficient appliances with the knowledge of differences among the appliances.[18]

Initial reactions to unit pricing were disappointing to policy makers. Consumers, particularly those of lower income and education, used unit prices relatively little. However, as time has passed, more and more consumers at all levels have come to use the unit pricing information more frequently in their grocery shopping.

Overall, it seems that many consumers will use price and product information. However, time must be allowed for new information usage patterns to develop. At the same time, consumers must be sold on the use of information if it is to have maximum effect.[19] Given that a wide variety of information should be made known to consumers, figure 17-1 provides a model of the effects of information disclosure. However, it must be emphasized that "more reliance on 'clear and conspicuous disclosure' is not, in and of itself, likely to lead to a successful information program. The program must be realistic in its recognition of the limitations of the consumer's motivation and capacity to seek, receive, and process new information."[20]

There is a further question as to whether nonrational product information should be allowed. It is often argued that consumer interests would be better served by permitting only objective facts to be presented in ads. However, this ignores the many psychological satisfactions that consumers derive from products. Also, many desirable products, such as cosmetics, deodorants, colognes, and perfumes, have their benefits *only* in psychic satisfactions.

How Should Information Be Presented? There are numerous ways in which information can be presented to consumers. It can come through advertisements,

Fig. 17-1. Effects of Information Disclosure Requirements

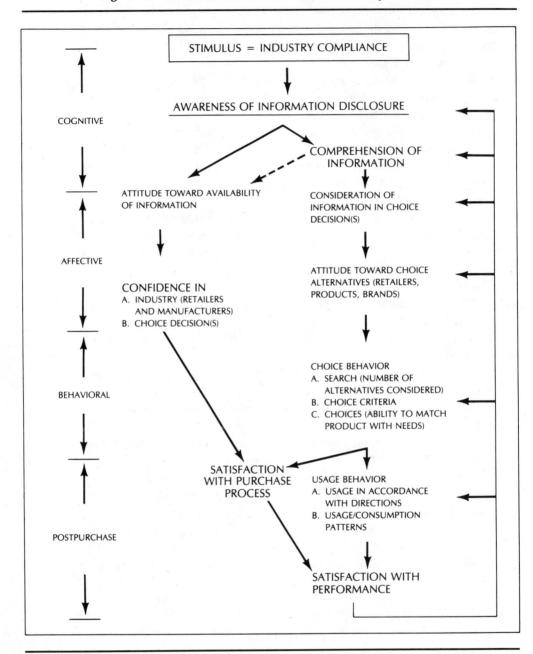

George S. Day, "Assessing the Effects of Information Disclosure Requirements," *Journal of Marketing* 40 (April 1976):45. Reprinted from the *Journal of Marketing*, published by the American Marketing Association.

government and consumer group publications, and salespeople. Advertising contains a good deal of information, but it is, of course, slanted toward the advertiser's interests. Only strict government control of what can be included (or what must be excluded) in an ad could force exclusively objective and even negative information into advertising, and this seems undesirable in a free enterprise, free-choice economy. Therefore, it seems that some types of information should be delivered through government agency and consumer group-sponsored communications. This means, however, that such messages should be as carefully and effectively developed as consumer advertising, and they should use a persuasive format to influence consumer behavior in desirable directions or to at least make consumers aware of alternative information and product choices.

There is another question of when information should be made available—prior to the sale or at the point of purchase. Information disclosure "will have the maximum effect when the buyer (a) has easy access to the information at the point of sale, (b) can readily comprehend and process the information, and (c) can use it to make direct comparisons of the choice alternatives along relevant attributes—in short, when the information is easy to use and relevant to the consumer"[21] The greater efficacy of information availability at the place of purchase is largely a function of the ease of recognition as opposed to recall. Consumers are not likely to recall relevant product information from nonadvertising sources because the message quality is typically low and the messages are unlikely to be repeated with the frequency of a commercial message.

To Whom Should Information Be Presented? On the surface it might be said that product information should be provided to and directed at all consumers. In reality, there are certain consumer groups that policy makers believe require special treatment. Among these groups are children, the elderly, and the underpriviledged. Public policy aimed at children generally involves protection from specific types of advertising and limitations on the amount permitted. Traditional thinking has led to the philosophy that low-income, low-education segments of the society should receive special treatment because they have virtually no understanding of their rights and because they are no match for the sophisticated marketer.[22] Some research, however, suggests that low-income consumers are only slightly less knowledgeable than other consumers.[23] Actually, virtually all consumers appear to be underinformed, so information dissemination and consumer education effort should probably be broadly directed rather than narrowly dispersed. It should be noted that consumer problems and information needs will vary across market segments, so consumer information programs should be designed accordingly.

Information Processing Issues

Consumer information processing has limitations and characteristics that must be considered in public policy decisions. These generally break into the areas of processing capacity, processing efforts, and readiness.

Processing Capacity The basic notion that more information is better has been both defended and challenged by various researchers. There are several issues here that must be considered. First, what is the policy objective? If the objective is simply to give consumers the *opportunity* to gain desired information on any product or purchase factor, we could say the more information, the better. If the consumer is actually to be made *aware* of relevant facts, the information must be framed and delivered in appropriate ways and be limited to an amount and relevance such that the consumer will not overload and so that the information can be easily recognized and internalized. If the objective is to lead consumers to make better decisions, some optimum amount of information should be supplied. If consumer satisfaction is to be maximized, the amount of information available should be increased.

A good deal of research underlies these observations. For example, increasing amounts of information may cause a consumer to divide processing time among the pieces of information leading to an apparent information overload. Simplifying information allows more accurate selection of the objectively best brand, but consumers are left feeling dissatisfied and wanting more information. Consumer utilization of product information in purchase decisions depends on the availability of information, information processibility (simplicity/complexity), and usefulness of the information to the consumer.[24]

Evidence on the effects of information overload suggests that as the number of dimensions of available information increases, consumer decision accuracy likewise increases. However, as the number of brands on which information is available increases, decision accuracy begins to decrease. Combining the two factors (brands multiplied by dimensions per brand) to generate a measure of total information load shows that decision accuracy increases at first and then decreases measurably. As the decision accuracy declines, consumers feel more satisfied and less confused with the increased amount of information.[25] Apparently consumers can be lulled into a sense of false security by large amounts of information, while the volume of information overloads their processing capabilities.

The notion that more information may not be better created a good deal of controversy.[26] It seems logical that, although there is a minimum level of information required for good consumer decisions, there is likewise an upper limit of information at which consumers will become confused and turn to less rational cues for decision aids.

Psychologically, consumers can overload with too much information, but there is no reason to conclude from the overload concept that consumers should not be provided with adequate information. Care should simply be taken not to provide *too much* information. Particular consideration should be given to the probability that low-income, low-education consumers may have more limited information-processing capability than those of greater educational experience. Again, there may be problems in helping those consumers who presumably need help the most.

Consumers do absorb and retain objective information from advertisements. Public policy's objective of making sure that product information is available to consumers seems to be advanced by commercials containing objective information.

Reprinted by permission. © 1980 NEA, Inc.

It may be possible to change what consumers know or believe about products (cognitive attitude dimension) through provision of objective information, but if the objective is *attitude* (affective) or *behavioral* change toward the objectively best brand, one-time exposure to relatively unfamiliar information will not be sufficient.

Influencing consumer attitudes and behavior requires that policy be implemented through repeated communication of effective messages. Educational programs that seek to inform consumers and modify their behavior over an extended period of time are likely to be successful in disseminating large amounts of information. There is evidence that suggests that information-processing limitations are more a function of the time available for processing than of the volume of information per se.[27]

Processing Efforts Not all of the limitations in consumer information processing arise from the inability to process large amounts of information. Unwillingness to process is also a factor. It takes both time and effect to seek and interpret information. Consumers are often not interested in making a heavy investment in information processing. Many times purchases are simply not important enough to warrant extensive information search.

Policy makers seem to assume that the reason consumers use subjective product cues in making purchase decisions is frustration or lack of objective information. Many times consumers use brand name, price, or another cue simply because it is easy and their experience may tell them that such cues are fairly reliable. To the extent that subjective cues are used out of lack of objective information, policy implementation must take two directions. First, objective information must be provided for ready access, and second, consumers must be educated as to its availability, relevance, and use.

Readiness Closely associated with consumer willingness to make information-processing efforts is the concept of attitudinal and cognitive readiness.[28] Where consumer legislation requires consumers to take the initiative in seeking redress for fraudulent or deceptive marketplace activities, the effectiveness of the statute must rely on consumers who have both a sufficient understanding of the law to recognize illegal activities (cognitive readiness) and sufficient confidence in the legal system to be willing to seek legal recourse (attitudinal readiness).

Research has repeatedly shown a low awareness among all types of consumers of both laws and legal remedies relating to consumer problems.[29] Particular problems are found again among low-income consumers who strongly feel that consumer protection laws are primarily for upper-income groups. Of course, the opposite is true, but the perceptions that these consumers hold form the basis for their behavior. Low-income consumers generally feel that laws cannot stop unfair business practices, and they have not been as attitudinally and cognitively ready to use "cooling-off" laws for in-home selling as have higher-income consumers.

Based on these problems several suggestions can be advanced. Where consumers do not display a readiness and willingness to use a proposed law, the law probably ought to be redesigned to operate at a low degree of consumer initiative. Some current statutes may have to be restructured to prevent unfair practices from entering the marketplace rather than simply providing opportunity for recourse to victims. In the long run, consumers should be educated to the existence and applicaton of laws. In other words, consumers' cognitive readiness should be raised.

Deceptive Advertising

One of the major public policy issues to which the FTC has given special attention is deceptive advertising. As in all areas of consumer legislation there are difficult problems. The two major behavioral questions treated here are what is deception and what remedies are most effective?

What is Deception?

On the surface the nature of deceptive advertising seems obvious. However, there is a great deal of controversy surrounding the topic. To say that advertising containing any false statement is deceptive is an oversimplification. First, the concept of "false" is difficult to define. Many product characteristics are open to interpretation. Also, there is the question of whether an omission of fact constitutes deception. Deception can be defined from both a legal and a behavioral standpoint.

Legal Definitions of Deception The FTC has, in general, held that deception occurs when "an objectively ascertainable fact is presented falsely, is ambiguous, or is misleading."[30] Historically, the FTC has been concerned with protecting competition, so deception was defined in terms of advertising practices that allowed a competitor to generate business at the expense of other business organizations through untruthful advertising. As the FTC has applied the concept of unfairness to deceptive advertising, the emphasis has switched to protecting consumers.[31] Even with this, however, there has been little concern for incorporating consumer behavior concepts into the understanding of deceptive advertising. Most evidence in deceptive advertising cases comes from people who testify based on their special expertise and training. They testify as to their expectations of what consumers are likely to perceive and believe.

The FTC works on the thesis that an advertisement that has the capacity or potential to deceive is unfair. This puts the FTC in the position of having to make a hypothetical supposition about how a consumer might interpret an ad, making the process highly subjective. What the consumer actually sees and believes seems to have little relevance. Qualified experts can be found for both sides of an issue, so the facts of the case often get lost as each side tries to discredit the other's witnesses and to win the case on legal grounds.[32]

Behavioral Definitions Obviously the real issue in a case of deception is one of whether the consumer is inclined to think or behave differently because of false statements in an ad. Such a behavioral view should underlie policy, but as one author notes,

> Many consumers think they recognize deception in advertising. However, their understanding of deception must be translated into appropriate legal terms and practices if deceptive practices are to be stopped by legal procedures. The problems of translation are immense and at least twofold. First, what is deception? Is a lie that virtually every one recognizes as a lie deception? Conversely, is an advertisement that contains no literal lies but that results in deceptive perceptions deceptive? . . . Past efforts to define and measure deception suffer from the lack of consideration of how consumers process and use information available to them in advertisements.[33]

Behavior-based definitions of deception are based on such concepts as the following:

> a skilled writer can effectively create a total impression which is misleading by careful phrasing and presentation of statements which may be quite literally true when considered individually. The phenomenon, which is called a *Gestalt* effect, occurs commonly in the interpretation of many perceptual stimuli. The meaning a person attaches to a total package of stimuli is often something different from the simple cumulation of the meaning attached to the stimuli individually. This effect usually results from either the sequencing or the omission of some stimuli. In the advertising case, the reader fills in the missing phrase, reads between the lines, or completes the logical argument, adding something to what is literally stated and thereby creating his own deception (albeit with the help of the copy writer).[34]

A typical behavior-based definition of deception says that it is "found when an advertisement is the input into the perceptual process of some audience and the output of that perceptual process (a) differs from the reality of the situation and (b) affects buying behavior to the detriment of the consumer.[35] Or, "if an advertisement (or advertising campaign) leaves the consumer with an impression(s) and/or belief(s) different from what would normally be expected if the consumer had reasonable knowledge, and that impression(s) and/or belief(s) is factually untrue or potentially misleading, then deception is said to exist."[36]

The concept of deception is extended by the fact that consumer perceptions are based on cues. Advertisers often use various cues in ads, such as color or size, to communicate various subjective product qualities. It is possible for these cues to deceive the consumer. The FTC has recognized this capacity to deceive relative to such cues as color, symbols, endorsements, and magnitude.[37]

Color often communicates nonobjective product features, as noted in chapter 12. Recognizing this, the FTC required the manufacturers of two denture cleaners to provide documentation for the claims, "The green shows speed as powerful cleaning bubbles scrub dentures fast," and "Bubbles are scrubbing away at stain and odor; when the blue disappears . . . dentures are clean."[38]

Symbols, particularly brand names, can be deceptive if they provide a false image. Coca-Cola came close to losing the right to use its trade name Hi-C because the name symbolized a product high in vitamin C.[39]

As noted in chapter 15, product endorsements have the capacity to deceive. A trustworthy, credible, or prestigious communicator tends to be perceived as non-manipulative, and an audience is more likely to accept what he or she says as true.[40] Even though the FTC has guidelines for endorsements, enforcing them can be difficult. How, for example, can one determine whether a celebrity who says, "I really like Crunchy Flakies" is telling the truth?

The magnitude of difference between one product and another may be questionable, too. An obvious source of deception is overstating differences. Even if one product is technically different from another, is the difference enough to matter, and is the point of difference relevant to the consumer?

The FTC issued a complaint against the Borden Company for a Kava ad that showed the difference in acidity between Kava and regular coffee on a pH meter. The complaint was based on the fact that Borden showed the difference on a scale that depicted the difference of 2 units as if it covered the entire 14-unit pH scale.[41]

When Schick advertised that its Kronachrome razor blades showed less wear under microscopic examination than competing stainless steel blades, the FTC agreed but contended that it made absolutely no difference to the quality of shave received.[42]

Moves of the FTC toward ad claim substantiation are based on the *meaning* communicated by an ad as interpreted by the FTC.[43] Even though meanings are based on consumer perceptions, the FTC is not required to research consumer perceptions to establish meaning in cases involving potential deception or the need for substantiation. The commission believes, however, that consumer research can be useful, and when Firestone was able to show survey results that indicated that only 1.4 percent of those surveyed selected the tire called Safety Champion as one with special performance or safety characteristics, the company was allowed to continue to apply the name to its product.[44]

In order to be truly effective, then, policy relating to deceptiveness should consider not only what an advertisement says but also the image or perception created by the message. Such an approach should be research based if perceptions are to be correctly understood. At the time this book was written, however, the FTC considered consumer research to be too imprecise to be relied upon, although the commission would consider research findings.

If the role of public policy is considered to be one of making the market system work better for consumers, three classes of public policy issues arise that differ considerably from conventional questions involving unfairness, deception, and untruthfulness.

1. In a particular setting, is any information lacking that, if it were made available at some cost, would cause consumers (or some subset of consumers) to act differently and/or to consider themselves better off after making some sort of choice, such as purchase?
2. Is there any technically and economically feasible way to deliver the appropriate data through appropriate media so that it is available at the point of decision (which often is not the point of purchase)? Is there any reason to believe that sellers or other institutions will not do so on their own? Are there any obvious restrictions on the ability of members or new entrants to an industry to communicate important or potentially important product characteristics efficiently to buyers?
3. Can a necessary information provision either be done or required without harmful side effects, such as the possibility of the regulatory process itself imposing unnecessary rigidities? In particular, accomodation to pressure from special groups (public and private) for supplying certain types of information when consumers really prefer other kinds of information may impose substantial costs (particularly on smaller producers) without much promise of benefit to consumers.[45]

Remedies for Deception

Initial remedies for deceptive advertising were directed at stopping the deception and possibly punishing offenders. An additional remedy that is aimed at correcting false impressions in consumer minds has been advanced. The corrective advertising remedy has been used by the FTC with mixed results. Given the short retention span for most advertising messages, damage from deceptive ads may be rather short-lived, obviating the necessity for corrective messages.

Consumer Dissatisfaction

Both marketers and public policy makers must be concerned with consumer dissatisfaction. In order to provide relevant legislation and policy, policy makers should have a high degree of understanding of the dynamics of consumer dissatisfaction and the significance of consumer complaints. Dissatisfaction may come from many sources, some of which are logically the direct concern of the business sector, while others fall in the public sector.

The Nature of Dissatisfaction

Essentially, dissatisfaction can occur any time a consumer's expectations are not met.[46] Only the consumer can decide whether he or she is dissatisfied. At least three situations can be identified relative to dissatisfaction. Dissatisfaction is felt and appears to be justified by the circumstances. This is the typical case, when the consumer recognizes defects or poor performance. In another situation, dissatisfaction appears to be justified but is not felt. This is characteristic when defects or poor performance occur but are not recognized by the consumer because of ignorance or inexperience. Finally, dissatisfaction is felt but does not seem to be justified. This situation occurs when the consumer misuses or abuses the item or evaluates performance in terms of totally inappropriate expectations.

The exact way in which expectations influence the evaluative process is really not well understood. Three of the psychological theories that have been advanced are as follows:

1. *Cognitive dissonance*—When the performance of a product or service does not conform with expectation . . . the theory of cognitive dissonance predicts a state of psychological tension that leads consumers to adjust their perceptions to conform with their expectations.
2. *Contrast theory*—The prediction of contrast theory is exactly the opposite, suggesting that a discrepancy between expectations and performances will be magnified. Thus, if the performance exceeds expectations, the reaction will be highly favorable, and, if it falls short, the reaction will be highly unfavorable.
3. *Assimilation-contrast theory*—The combination of the assimilation and contrast theories predicts that at moderate levels of disconfirmation of expectancies (within a "latitude of acceptance") the difference will be assimilated, and at high levels the difference will be magnified.[47]

When a product fails to meet consumer expectations, the resulting dissatisfaction may arise from any of several sources. These may include the feelings that: The product is not faulty but doesn't meet the consumer's needs, the product is faulty, the product was used improperly, the whole marketing system is faulty, and so on. Types of dissatisfaction might be categorized as macromarketing system dissatisfaction, which covers the marketing system as a whole, and micromarketing system dissatisfaction, which treats specific aspects of the marketing system—shopping system dissatisfaction, buying system dissatisfaction, and consuming system dissatisfaction.[48]

In a given situation in which a consumer experiences dissatisfaction, an attribution is typically made as to the reason for the dissatisfaction. A success or failure with a product may be attributed to the user (internal) or to the situation or product itself (external). The outcome of the purchase-use situation can also be attributed to something temporary (unstable) or something that is likely to occur each time the product is purchased or used (stable).[49]

A firm would want any attributions for dissatisfaction to be unstable or internal. If the attribution is unstable, the consumer will view it as a one-time problem. An internal attribution would lead the consumer to blame something other than the product, manufacturer, or retailer for any difficulties. There is an inherent problem relative to external/internal attributions. An observer of a product-use situation will tend to attribute product performance to the consumer (internal), while the user will be more likely to attribute success or failure to an external factor, such as the product or retailer.[50] Thus, a retailer faced with a complaining customer will likely consider the problem the fault of the customer, while the customer insists that the problem is with the product.

On a larger scale, the public policy maker must be attuned to the fact that many customer dissatisfactions and complaints are not the fault of marketers and manufacturers. A consumer is naturally slow to accept any blame for product misuse, poor selection, or unrealistic expectations. Therefore, a large number of complaints coming from consumers related to the micromarketing system may be the result of differences in perception. Although consumers may have a fair idea of what they want, they will often have an unrealistic set of understandings and expectations relative to what firms can deliver. Often, consumers are not knowledgeable as to what constitutes an unfair business practice. For example, they tend to equate deception in advertising with advertisements described as annoying, offensive, and insulting to the intelligence.[51] This is not to suggest that marketers are guiltless, but certainly care should be taken to deal only with situations in which consumers suffer some real or tangible economic or physical harm. A major objective in this area should be education as to product use and legitimate expectations for products and marketers. This should come from both public agencies and from marketers themselves.

Complaining Behavior

The consumer activity of complaining deserves special attention.[52] One view holds that the traditional concept of consumer satisfaction (the confirmation or disconfirmation of the consumer's specific expectations of product performance) is of little value to business firms or consumer protection agencies.

> This view of satisfaction does not appear to be especially useful as the basis of developing operational measures of satisfaction for direct use by business firms or consumer protection agencies. If expectations are measured in advance of the consideration of alternatives, the avoidance of testing effects seems impossible in a realistic setting. If expectation is gauged retrospectively, the vagaries of memory and rationalization are invited. Whatever the measures of expectation and satisfaction used, the results obtained will vary with time and various environmental factors. Someday we may overcome the difficulties involved in evaluating expectations, tracking "real world" consumers through the choice process to assess the post-purchase confirmation or disconfirmation of expectations, and finally translating the results into a measure of satisfaction that can be compared over individuals. In the present state of the art, they are mind boggling.

When we look at the overall concept of consumer dissatisfaction, there is a tendency to see it as a postpurchase reaction to the quality of a product or service. Considering consumer complaints, however, this view is quite limited. Complaints may be directed at the advertisements or pricing policies even when no purchase is involved. When a purchase is involved, consumers may be fundamentally satisfied with the product itself but complain about service, credit, delivery, and so on. There are many potential complaint areas other than the product itself (see figure 17-2).

Fig. 17-2. Complaints to a Consumer Hotline

Type of Complaint	Percentage of Sample
Prepurchase (advertising)	14%
Purchase transaction/delivery	27
Product performance	17
Guarantee/warrantee/contract	11
Service/repairs	26
Deposits/credit/collections	4

S. L. Diamond, S. Ward and R. Faber, "Consumer Problems and Consumerism: Analysis of Calls to a Consumer Hot Line," *Journal of Marketing* 40 (January 1976):58-62. Reprinted from the *Journal of Marketing*, published by the American Marketing Association.

Alternatives for Complaining Behavior When faced with dissatisfaction, consumers may seek compensation, redress, restitution, or other such remedy. This might be sought through (1) personal persuasion in the form of claims, complaints, threats of unfavorable word-of-mouth, or termination of patronage; (2) collective pressure, such as actions of various consumer groups and business-sponsored groups, like Better Business Bureaus; (3) institutional coercion involving government agency investigations and court suits; and (4) failing all these solutions, additional legislation may be sought by individual consumers, consumer action groups, or elected officials. Figure 17-3 provides a summary model of the alternatives open to dissatisfied consumers. The direction such action may take depends on a number of things including marketing-, consumer-, and situation-related factors.

Marketing-related Factors The reputation of the manufacturer or seller of a product may strongly influence a consumer's complaining behavior. Firms of high reputation who invite complaints and are quick to offer redress will likely receive more complaints than low-reputation firms, but the result is likely to be satisfactory to the consumer as the complaint usually offers an opportunity to increase consumer loyalty. Complaints against low-reputation firms are likely to be less frequent but more serious, and they are apt to be more aggressively pursued by dissatisfied consumers.

Fig. 17-3. Postdissatisfaction Alternatives

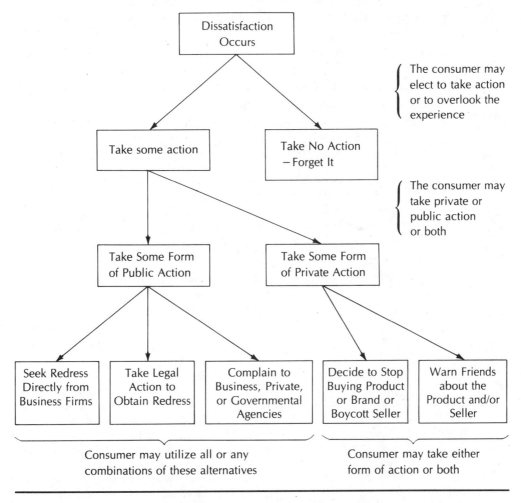

Reprinted by permission of the publisher from "Toward a Theory of Consumer Complaining Behavior," by Ralph L. Day and E. Laird Landon, Jr., in *Consumer and Industrial Buying Behavior*, by Arch G. Woodside, Jagdish N. Sheth, and Peter D. Bennett, eds., p 437. Copyright 1977 by Elsevier North Holland, Inc.

Sales resulting from hard-sell efforts by the marketer seem more likely to lead to recognized dissatisfaction and redress than those in which the seller offers help and multiple purchase alternatives. Almost any element in the sale that could lead to postcognitive dissonance could be expected to increase the probabilities of dissatisfaction and subsequent complaint.

The attitude of the marketer is likely to have a major impact on postpurchase dissatisfaction. It's hard to be angry with a marketer who is genuinely interested in the consumer's problem and cheerfully offers immediate refund, exchange, or other appropriate reaction. On the other hand, the consumer is likely to approach the

complaint situation with some apprehension, and any reluctance or blame forthcoming from the marketer is likely to evoke strong negative response from the
consumer.

Consumer Factors Some consumers appear to be more likely to be dissatisfied, and
some seem to be more likely to complain. Effective, well-informed consumers may
have more dissatisfactory buying experiences simply because they know what to
expect and are more likely to spot a problem.

There seems to be a propensity to complain. People who write complaint letters
are not typical of the overall population.[53] Aggressiveness and leisure time availability
are positively associated with the propensity to complain. Active complainers are also
highly educated, have a higher income, are younger than average, have negative
attitudes toward business, and are politically liberal.[54]

Situational Factors Several factors in the circumstances surrounding the purchase
will influence complaining behavior. More expensive, more essential, and more
visible items are more subject to complaint. Also, ease of redress is positively
associated with complaining. Products that have received unfavorable attention and
publicity are more likely to generate complaints.

Theory of Complaining Behavior Several steps in complaining have been identified as part of a theory of consumer complaining behavior (see figure 17-4).

1. The importance of obtaining redress or voicing his or her dissatisfaction is
    evaluated by the consumer after he has experienced dissatisfaction. If he
    concludes that the value of obtaining redress or complaining about the
    incident is so slight that it is not worth the effort, the process ends and the
    incident is ignored. If the value of obtaining reparations or registering a
    complaint is seen as being worth considering further, the process continues.

2. An evaluation of the availability of direct compensation and the effort re-
    quired to obtain it is made. If redress seems easy to obtain, an effort to obtain
    replacement, refund, free repairs, or some other form of atonement will be
    made. If not, some form of indirect public action may be considered. Also,
    private or personal actions such as boycotting the product class or brand
    and/or warning friends may be considered. Private or personal actions may
    be undertaken in addition to any of the following steps.

3. Consumers who elect to take public action will consider and evaluate alterna-
    tive methods of attempting to obtain redress. If feasible and reasonably
    convenient, a direct effort will be made to obtain compensation within the
    channels of distribution. If this is not feasible or if an effort to directly obtain
    redress is made and proves unsuccessful, advice and assistance may be sought
    through the Better Business Bureau, consumerist organizations, or govern-
    mental agencies.

4. If redress is still not forthcoming after assistance has been sought, legal action
    may be initiated and/or complaints registered directly to business firms or
    through private organizations (e.g., better business bureaus) or governmental
    agencies at local, state, or national levels.

Fig. 17-4. Postdissatisfaction Decision Process

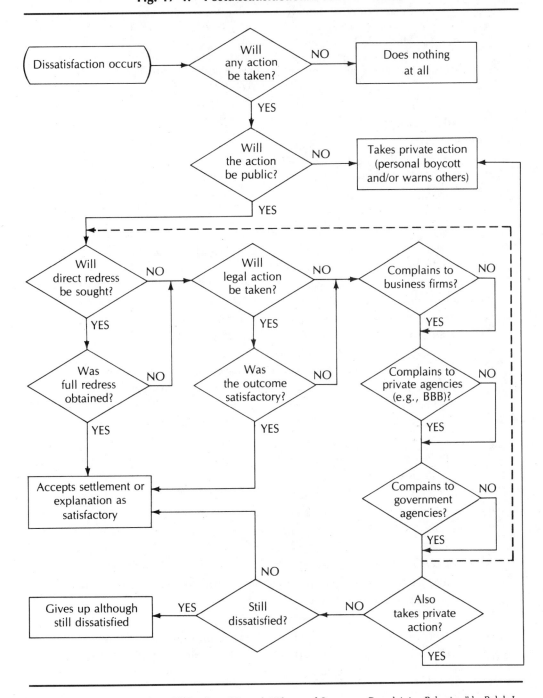

Reprinted by permission of the publisher from "Toward a Theory of Consumer Complaining Behavior," by Ralph L. Day and E. Laird Landon, Jr., in *Consumer and Industrial Buying Behavior*, by Arch G. Woodside, Jagdish N. Sheth, and Peter D. Bennett, eds., p. 436. Copyright 1977 by Elsevier North Holland, Inc.

5. If legal action fails to obtain a favorable settlement and/or no satisfactory response to complaints is forthcoming, the dissatisfied consumer who is not willing to give up may continue to exercise his boycott of the unsatisfactory item and to urge friends to do likewise. He may also write to consumer protection agencies and consumerist organizations in the hope of having pressures applied to the offending company or possibly influencing the passage of new consumer protection legislation.[55]

Specific Policy Issues

This section highlights a few problem areas for public policy. No attempt is made to be comprehensive; the section simply cites some behavioral issues that seem relevant to marketing strategists and policy makers.

Trademarks and Brands When two trademarks or brand names appear to be too similar to one another, the case must be decided, usually by the Court of Customs and Patent Appeals. In the past such decisions have been so unpredictable as to seem almost capricious. The issue is not whether two brands are identical but rather whether they are too similar. One way to settle the issue would seem to be to conduct tests of consumer perceptions. If the trademarks give rise to essentially the same brand image, they could be considered too close. Otherwise, they might be found dissimilar enough to be used by two companies.

In the same vein, brand names that have become generic descriptors can no longer be protected. The test again could involve consumer perceptions. If a brand name generates precisely the same image as the product itself, it could be said to be generic.

Energy Labels The use of energy labels seems to be useful. Given these labels, consumers appear to be able to make better appliance selection decisions.[56]

Product Safety The vast majority of product-related injuries are directly traceable to poor use of safe products as opposed to products that are themselves unsafe.[57] Simply informing a customer of risks may not deter unsafe use, and warnings do not necessarily release the marketer from legal liability.[58] It therefore behooves the marketer to seek to alter consumers' unsafe behavior through carefully conceived and implemented consumer education efforts.

Credit Credit terms and interest rates are areas of major confusion for consumers. Truth in lending legislation has not, in and of itself, solved these problems. This area requires large-scale consumer education.

Unit Pricing Although consumers, particularly those at lower socioeconomic levels, were slow to use unit pricing, after several years it seems to be catching on. Since this is an excellent point-of-sale device, consumers should be further educated as to its availability and use. This education should probably take place at the point of sale.

Children's TV Advertising This type of advertising continues to be a hotbed of debate. Even after extensive research it remains unclear as to the nature and degree of harm (if any) that may come to children through viewing TV commercials. Strong movements are afoot to remove advertising from children's television completely. Marketers, of course, strongly resist this.

More research is needed, but having to use and evaluate advertising is an important part of the child's socialization process in becoming an effective consumer. However, children should probably receive special consideration and protection from some advertising. The schools should continue their efforts to teach children to be better consumers.

Drug Abuse Although many people have protested that television and other forms of advertising for over-the-counter drugs may have a tendency to lead to drug abuse, research evidence does not support that contention.[59]

Nutrition Labeling Although packages containing nutrition information are available for some products, there is a push to expand this. However, consumers do not seem to use the information, although they do seem to be more satisfied and more confident when the information is available.[60]

Advertising Substantiation There is a feeling that requiring advertisers to substantiate advertising claims made lead them to drop the use of allegedly factual claims in favor of "nebulous puffery" bordering on fantasy.[61] This has already been noted in (1) recent Lincoln Continental ads showing that "38 out of 40 airline pilots" prefer Continental's ride to Cadillac's, and (2) RCA's ads claiming that TV engineers prefer the RCA picture. To both of these a person could easily say, "So what."

Warning Messages Many products require warning messages in ads and on labels. The cigarette experience suggests limitations to the strategy. Although consumers may perceive products to be more dangerous when they carry a warning message, this perception often does not change their buying intentions or behavior. In addition, the perception of danger may be carried over from the dangerous product to related but safe products.[62]

SUMMARY

Public policy is often formulated and administered without carefully and accurately considering consumer behavior. In many policy areas understanding consumer behavior is essential to effective implementation. In recent years policy direction has shifted from preserving competition and protecting competitors to educating and protecting consumers and creating a high-information buying environment. At the same time, the general philosophy of policy has moved in the direction of requiring full and accurate disclosure on the part of advertisers.

Although the objectives of public policy are often not explicitly spelled out, there are several underlying implicit goals that seem to guide policy decisions. Not only is there an attempt to create well-informed consumers through education and disclosure, but policy may seek to protect ill-informed consumers as well. In addition, there is impetus toward safer and more beneficial products.

Although consumer research seems to hold great promise for improving public policy decisions, there are several problems in its application. In general, there is a lack of awareness and understanding of behavioral principles on the part of policy markers, which often leads consumer researchers to be openly critical of their capabilities and decisions. This, in turn, creates a defensiveness on the part of the policy makers. At the same time, policy makers may operate from some erroneous assumptions about consumer information processing in that they seem to ignore the context of information, to hold that all information is processed in the same way, and to believe that more information is always better for the consumer. To alleviate some of these problems, policy makers should consider what information is relevant to consumers, the best ways of presenting information, and the people who most need information. In addition, consumer information processing capacities and their readiness to receive information must be considered.

Deception in advertising has been a particular concern of policy makers. Deception is difficult to define, and it should be viewed in terms of the consumer's perceptions and behavior rather than simply legalistically. Remedies have involved stopping the deception and correcting misconceptions that have been formed.

Public policy makers must understand consumer satisfaction and dissatisfaction if their efforts are to be fully effective. Dissatisfaction occurs when consumer expectations are not met. Dissatisfaction may lead to complaints to companies, complaints to other agencies, negative word-of-mouth, appeal to courts, and pushing for protective legislation. Complaining behavior tends to be quite problem specific. The direction of complaints tends to vary according to market-related, consumer-related, and situation-related factors.

CHAPTER 17   STUDY REVIEW

Important Terms and Concepts

Public policy
Caveat emptor
Caveat venditor
Deception
Cognitive readiness
Attitudinal readiness
Consumer dissatisfaction
Complaining behavior

Questions

1. Discuss the major problems in generating and implementing public policy for marketing activities. Which of these problems are related to consumer behavior considerations?

2. What assumptions about consumers seem to underlie public policy decisions? To what degree do you think they are valid?

3. Discuss the objectives of regulation. Are they realistic in view of what you know about consumer behavior? Explain.

4. Why has it been difficult to apply consumer behavior knowledge to public policy formulation?

5. What insights does our knowledge of consumer information processing hold for public policy formulation and administration?

6. Differentiate between legal and behavioral conceptions of deception in promotion.

7. What is consumer dissatisfaction, how does it arise, and how can it be avoided or minimized?

8. Discuss the nature and significance of consumer complaining behavior.

Some Problems
and Prospects
in the Study of Consumers

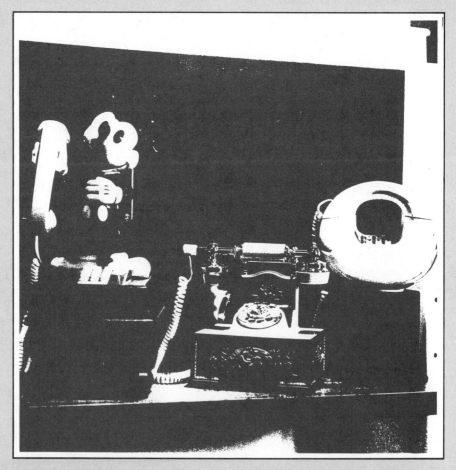

© Walt Disney Productions—housing produced by American Telecommunications Corp.

Consumer behavior has been heavily studied for many years, and major strides have been made in the field. Nevertheless, unanswered questions abound. It is not surprising that so diverse a study as consumer behavior has been the source of so many viewpoints and theories. Understanding consumer behavior is, of necessity, based upon the various social science disciplines that study and attempt to explain human behavior. These social sciences, however, are badly fragmented in their approach to studying human behavior. Since there is no study of human behavior as a total system of action, consumer researchers have pursued numerous directions for theory and research that generally correspond to the various behavioral disciplines, resulting in the maze of concepts and theories confronting the student of consumer behavior.

A consumer behavior textbook must somehow cut across the various concepts and theories to acquaint the student with the diversity of the subject. At the same time, some attempt should be made at bringing the quantity of information into some sort of integrated whole. Early texts in the field were, with a few exceptions, collections of readings. Some authors tried to deal with the concepts in a text format prior to 1968, but the first major book on consumer behavior appeared that year, dealing with the various behavioral dimensions developed in the first chapters of this text and one of the flow models of buyer decision making presented in chapter 2 (figure 2-8).[2] The attempt at integrating theoretical and empirically derived concepts was useful, but it made the 1968 book somewhat narrow in following only one of many possible models. The model, like most others that have been advanced prior to and since that one, represent careful thought in trying to simplify and organize a vast body of knowledge and speculation. The various models, however, have received little empirical testing, and their predictive values are therefore somewhat suspect. There is a problem associated with any attempt to model consumer behavior, since some of the buying process is observable while some is purely cognitive in nature and difficult to test. New techniques, such as the electroencephalogram (EEG), are providing better access to the cognitive side. Although the models are useful in organizing thinking about buying behavior, they often have little practical value for the marketing strategist.

513

In spite of the problems, consumer behavior study has great potential value, not only for the student and practitioner of marketing but for the general study of human behavior as well. The fragmented nature of the study of human behavior gives little opportunity or impetus for a holistic approach. However, the student of consumer behavior focuses on a rather narrow area of human behavior while at the same time being interested in the whole spectrum of behavior. In that respect, consumer behavior has the potential for becoming a focal point on which to base an integrated study of human behavior.

This text has purposely avoided the comprehensive model approach in favor of looking at the body of knowledge that has grown up around the study of consumers and its interface with the formation of marketing strategy and accompanying tactical decisions. The thrust of this book has been to investigate various behavioral concepts as they relate to consumer buying activity and to integrate these insights with various aspects of the marketing management process. In essence, the traditional structure of marketing strategy planning (identify a target market and formulate a marketing mix) was used as the framework for organizing the diverse behavioral concepts. This is in contrast with the more usual approach of developing the behavioral concepts and providing examples of how they might apply to strategy or looking at behavior from the standpoint of how the consumer decision process operates with some attempts at exploring ways of influencing that process.

The marketing manager is, to some degree, concerned with broad theoretical issues of consumer decision making and the behavioral and environmental forces that influence it, but, for the most part, formulating and implementing a marketing strategy tend to be problem oriented—that is, any conceptual knowledge of buyer behavior will likely become relevant in solving specific problems relating to such issues as the promotional program, package design, or store image. Approached from the theoretical standpoint, consumer behavior researchers and theorists have tended to ask several questions. How does consumer personality influence brand selection? How do people in various social classes respond to various advertising appeals and media? How are consumer attitudes formed and changed?

The marketing manager will probably approach consumer behavior from a different perspective, with a different set of appropriate questions. How is my product perceived relative to competing brands by buyers in this market segment? How can my promotional strategy be altered to give this group of potential buyers a more favorable image of my brand? How will this price change affect the way in which buyers perceive my brand relative to others? What impact will distribution through these retail stores have on the image and sales volume of this item? What life-style or personality characteristics do readers of this magazine have that will help in designing the advertisements that will run next year?

Sometimes the value of understanding buyer behavior lies simply in knowing what questions to ask. For example, Singer elected to broaden the product line in their sewing machine stores. With women buying sewing machines in the stores, it seemed logical to think that they could be induced to make other major household appliance purchases at the same time. A knowledge of the structure of family decision making should have led the company to ask whether the sewing machine purchase decision was somehow unique. The company, however, did not seek an answer to that question and lost money on the expanded sales project. Women may make the sewing machine decision alone, but other major appliance decisions tend to be made jointly. Answers to specific strategic questions will often come only from specially designed research efforts. Behavioral concepts, however, will often suggest which questions to ask, of whom they should be asked, and how they are to be asked and interpreted.

One of the problems we have in the study of consumer behavior and its applicaton to marketing strategy is the proprietary nature of much of the commercial applications of behavioral tools and concepts. Unfortunately, some of the most valuable and interesting behavioral applications are the property of business firms, research companies, and advertising agencies. With relatively few exceptions these firms are unwilling to share their current knowledge. In medicine, for example, academic research tends to precede medical practice, and research results tend to be readily shared. In consumer behavior, academic research generally addresses broad and often strategically irrelevant questions, while commercial applications and success stories often come out only long after the fact. Marketing strategies can be studied to try to infer what behavioral research results may underlie them, but such inefficiency and speculation can lead to wrong conclusions.

Unfortunately, there is no easy solution for this problem. The proprietary knowledge may give firms a profitable competitive edge they are unwilling to relinquish by providing the information for student use. In addition, the research results that underlie a great deal of product design, packaging, branding, and promotion decisions smack of manipulation and exploitation and would likely be subject to a good deal of criticism from some observers. A case in point is current research in the relationship between brain waves and consumer response. The human brain is divided into two cerebral hemispheres. The right side is involved with images and shapes, while the left brain deals with verbal concepts. In addition, the brain registers alpha and beta waves. An EEG oscilloscope measures beta activity and left/right brain activity. The proportion of beta waves to alpha waves measures the degree to which an individual is activated—presumably in the direction of product purchase.[3] Although a fair number of advertisers test and develop brand names, package designs, and advertisements through EEG analysis, most are unwilling to talk about it.[4] Whether or not such techniques allow marketers to influence behavior more effectively can only be the subject of conjecture without careful and unbiased testing. Claims for success often come from those who sell the service, and, as with subliminal advertising, results may be overstated.

Strategy-Behavior Interface

With all these ideas in mind, we may now turn to the problem of integrating consumer behavior theory with marketing operations and management practice. In a sense, consumer theory is a tool that marketers can apply in a variety of circumstances. Faced with the prospect of somehow tying together the vast array of conceptual material covered in this text, it seems appropriate to fall back upon the marketing strategy model. The question essentially boils down to, How might the consumer's behavior impact upon or be influenced by this action?

The problem of teaching marketing has been approached in a variety of ways, including the consideration of how individual commodities are marketed and the identification of functions and principles. Most contemporary texts use a marketing management approach, following the activities of the manager. This basically involves the formulation of a marketing mix. Many strategic decisions are not directly related to consumer behavior, but many decisions relative to elements of the marketing mix can potentially draw upon behavioral concepts. The development of a marketing plan often involves the use of a checklist to assure that all relevant issues are covered. The following checklist is specific to the behavioral side of the marketing plan. Each element of the marketing mix includes suggested consumer behavior issues that should be considered when appropriate.

Product

Product planning is concerned with all decisions associated with new and existing products and services. Major behavioral considerations include the following:

1. What needs does my product satisfy?
2. What motivates buyers to try my product?
3. What needs do competitive products satisfy?
4. Do people who use my brand exhibit unique personality characteristics?
5. How do the attitudes toward my brand differ between those who use my brand and those who do not?
6. What is the self-image of those who buy my brand?
7. Do buyers of my brand tend to be of a particular social class?
8. Is my product threatened or potentially strengthened by changing sociocultural conditions?
9. How did buyers of my brand learn about it?
10. Are those who buy my brand loyal? If so, do they buy only my brand or others as well?
11. Does the image projected by my package reflect the brand image?
12. Are the attitudes of users of competing products readily subject to change?
13. How is my brand positioned relative to competing brands?
14. What psychographic profile fits users of my brand? Are the profiles of users of competing brands different?
15. How long a decision process typically precedes the purchase of my product?
16. Does the design of my product fit the image I am trying to project for it?
17. Are buyers of my brand generally satisfied with it?
18. Is my brand used by a given buyer in some circumstances and not in others?

19. What image does my brand name project to buyers versus nonbuyers of my brand?
20. Which family members buy, use, and decide upon purchasing my product?
21. Is my brand used more by some subcultures than others? Do members of different subcultures perceive my product differently?
22. How are products like mine diffused and adopted in the marketplace? Who have been the early adopters of other products similar to the one I am about to launch in the market?
23. To what degree is risk associated with the purchase of my product? Can I reduce that risk?

Price

Price plays numerous roles. In practice, product cost often plays the major role in price decisions, even though it probably shouldn't. Actually, from the standpoint of the marketing manager, customer demand should be the most important determinant, not cost. Given this, behavioral dimensions of consumer response to price should be critical to the price decision. The following questions might be relevant:

1. Does my brand have unique features that might make customers willing to pay a premium for it?
2. To what degree is my product's brand image dependent upon the price I charge?
3. Would my brand's image be influenced by a price change? How much could price be changed without influencing my brand's image?
4. How much can I change my price before by customers will perceive that the price has significantly changed?
5. Is there some sort of expected price associated with my product?
6. Are the buyers of my brand relatively more or less price sensitive than buyers of other brands?
7. What pricing tactics can I use to reduce my buyers' perceived risk, especially in first-time product trial?

Promotion

Promotion strategy involves communicating to and influencing consumers. Because of its persuasive objective, promotion strategy probably draws more heavily from behavioral concepts than any other element of the marketing mix. In developing advertising and promotional strategies, the marketing manager might ask the following questions:

1. What consumer motives can be translated into advertising appeals for my brand?
2. What relevant life-style factors can be incorporated into my advertising messages?
3. What brand image should my advertisements project?

4. What needs do consumers have that can be communicated to them in terms of product benefits?
5. What learning principles can be applied in formulating specific advertisements?
6. How can promotion efforts be structured to bring about appropriate attitude changes most effectively?
7. To what social classes does my product appeal, and how can their values be reflected in my advertising messages and media selection?
8. What specific advertising tactics will most effectively retard advertising wearout?
9. What personal selling approach will be most likely to persuade a customer to buy without being antagonized?
10. What advertising strategy can be used to move my brand into the evoked set of nonusers of my brand?
11. How can my advertising or personal selling strategy effect problem recognition so as to trigger the buyer's decision process?
12. Is purchase of my product likely to stimulate postcognitive dissonance, and, if so, can my advertising message minimize that dissonance?
13. What persons influence the buyers in the purchase of my product? Can my promotional strategy stimulate favorable word-of-mouth communication relative to my brand?
14. How can my promotional effort minimize the impact of competing promotional messages?
15. What current social trends should be reflected in my media selection and message design?
16. To what degree can or should reference persons be used in my ads to exert various forms of power on buyers?

Channel Strategy

Determining the type of channel and selecting specific institutions to move a manufacturer's products to the final consumer is a significant decision that may be improved by a knowledge of behavioral concepts. The retailer may also benefit from application of behavioral principles. Appropriate questions here might include the following:

1. Given the image of my brand, what store image should I look for in distributors?
2. What sort of consumer response may be expected from my in-store displays?
3. Are some of my customers store loyal? If so, what special characteristics do they have that differentiate them from nonstore customers?
4. Is my product likely to be purchased on impulse, and, if so, how can impulse purchases be stimulated?

5. What specific personality, demographic, life-style, and social characteristics do my customers have that should be reflected in my store design, layout, location, merchandising, and personnel?

6. To what degree are purchase decisions made inside versus outside the store?

7. Do my customers hold the same image of my store as I do?

8. How do attitudes of those who shop in my store differ from those who do not?

9. What subcultural and cultural values are reflected in store selection and shopping behavior that are significant as I move into new geographical regions and foreign markets?

10. To which family members does my store appeal, and what is their role in the family purchase decision process?

Obviously, these questions do not exhaust the possibilities for behavioral applications in marketing strategy, but the marketing manager should be asking questions like these constantly in formulating and adjusting a marketing strategy. Recent research suggests that the situation is a major factor in the degree and direction of applicability of behavioral concepts. Thus, although it is possible to provide a background in theories and concepts of consumer behavior, the strategic value of any given concept or empirical finding may become relevant only in a given decision situation.

This text offers a good foundation for understanding and applying behavioral concepts to consumers. The learning process should not stop here, however. The study of consumer behavior is a lifetime project, perhaps multi-lifetime. We will probably never fully understand the buyer's behavior; let's hope not, at least, for that would deny us the pleasure of practicing the art of marketing.

Footnotes

Chapter 1

1.   Charles R. Wasson, *Consumer Behavior: A Managerial Viewpoint* (Austin, Tex.: Austin Press, 1975), p. 27.
2.   Leon G. Schiffman and Leslie Lazar Kanuk, *Consumer Behavior* (Englewood Cliffs, N.J.: Prentice-Hall, 1978), p. 4.
3.   David L. Loudon and Albert J. Della Bitta, *Consumer Behavior* (New York: McGraw-Hill, 1979), p. 5.
4.   "So We Built a Better Mousetrap," *President's Forum,* Fall 1962, pp. 26–27.
5.   Burt Schorr, "Many Products Fizzle Despite Careful Planning, Publicity," *Wall Street Journal,* 5 April 1961.
6.   Mason Haire, "Projective Techniques in Marketing Research," *Journal of Marketing* 14 (April 1950): 649–52.
7.   Frederick E. Webster, Jr., and Frederick Von Peckman, "A Replication of the 'Shopping List' Study," *Journal of Marketing* 34 (April 1970): 61–63.
8.   Edward C. Bursk and Stephen A. Greyser, *Advanced Cases in Marketing Management* (Englewood Cliffs, N.J.: Prentice-Hall, 1968), pp. 6–7.
9.   "Stan Freberg Prospers by Browbeating Clients, Poking Fun at Products," *Wall Street Journal,* 20 June 1969.
10.   At present, *The Journal of Consumer Research* is sponsored by the American Anthropological Association, American Association for Public Opinion Research, American Economic Association, American Home Economics Association, American Marketing Association, American Psychological Association (div. 23), American Sociological Association, American Statistical Association, Association for Consumer Research, Institute for Management Sciences, International Communication Association.
11.   Theodore Leavitt, "The New Markets: Think Before You Leap," *Harvard Business Review,* May-June 1969, pp. 53–67.
12.   Lee A. Iacocca, "Some Kind of Animal," *Nation's Business,* February 1969, pp. 62–67.
13.   Alfred R. Oxenfeldt, *Executive Action in Marketing* (Belmont, Calif.: Wadsworth, 1966), pp. 70–77; Philip Kotler, "Behavioral Models for Analyzing Buyers," *Journal of Marketing* 24 (October 1965): 37–45; Philip Kotler, *Marketing Management: Analysis Planning and Control,* 3d ed. (Englewood Cliffs, N.J.: Prentice-Hall, 1976), pp. 74–81.
14. Oxenfeldt, *Executive Action in Marketing,* p.75.
15.   *Consumer Buying Habit Studies* (Wilmington, Del.: E. I. duPont deNemours and Co., 1965), pp. 3–4.
16.   Frank M. Bass, "The Theory of Stochastic Preference and Brand Switching," *Journal of Marketing Research* 11 (February 1974): 1–20.

Chapter 2

1.   See Francesco M. Nicosia, *Consumer Decision Processes* (Englewood Cliffs, N.J.: Prentice-Hall, 1966), pp. 8–12.
2.   John Dewey, *How We Think,* (New York: D. C. Heath, 1910), p. 72.
3.   George Katona and Eva Mueller, "A Study of Purchase Decisions," in Lincoln H. Clark, ed., *Consumer Behavior: The Dynamics of Consumer Reaction* (New York: New York University Press, 1955), pp. 30–87.
4.   Harold H. Kassarjian, "Presidential Address, 1977: Anthropomorphism and Parsimony," *Advances in Consumer Research,* vol. 5 (Chicago: Association for Consumer Research, 1978), pp. xii–xiv;

521

Richard W. Olshavsky and Donald H. Granbois, "Consumer Decision Making: Fact or Fiction?" *Journal of Consumer Research* 6 (September 1979): 93–100; Frank M. Bass, "The Theory of Stochastic Preference and Brand Switching," *Journal of Marketing Research* 9 (February 1974): 1–20; M. Venkatesan, "Cognitive Consistency and Novelty Seeking," in Scott Ward and Thomas S. Robertson, eds., *Consumer Behavior: Theoretical Sources* (Englewood Cliffs, N.J.: Prentice-Hall, 1973), pp. 354–84.

5. William R. King, *Quantitative Analysis for Marketing Management* (New York: McGraw-Hill, 1967), p. 16.

6. John A. Howard, *Marketing Management: Operating, Strategic and Administrative,* 3d ed. (Homewood, Ill.: Richard D. Irwin, 1973), pp. 61–74.

7. See especially John A. Howard and Jagdish N. Sheth, *The Theory of Buyer Behavior,* (New York: John Wiley and Sons, 1969); James F. Engel, Roger D. Blackwell, and David T. Kollat, *Consumer Behavior,* 3d ed. (Hinsdale, Ill.: Dryden Press, 1978).

8. Donald H. Granbois, "A Study of the Family Decision-making Process in the Purchase of Major Durable Household Goods" (D.B.A. diss., Indiana University, 1962).

9. Ruby T. Norris, "Processes and Objectives of House Purchasing in the New London Area," in Lincoln H. Clark, ed., *The Dynamics of Consumer Reactions* (New York: New York University Press, 1955), pp. 25–29.

10. George Katona, *The Mass Consumption Society* (New York: McGraw-Hill, 1964), pp. 289–90; Paul E. Green, Michael Halbert, and J. Sayer Minas, "An Experiment in Information Buying," *Journal of Advertising Research* 4 (September 1964): 17–23; C. K. Hawkins and J. T. Lanzetta, "Uncertainty, Importance, and Arousal as Determinants of Predecisional Information Search," *Psychological Reports* 17, (December 1965): 791–800. Louis P. Bucklin, "The Informative Role of Advertising," *Journal of Advertising Research* 5 (September 1965): 11–15; George Katona, *Psychological Analysis of Economic Behavior* (New York: McGraw-Hill, 1951), pp. 67–68; Katona, *Mass Consumption Society,* pp. 289–90.

11. B. T. Ratchford and Alan R. Andreasen, "A Study of Consumer Perceptions of Decisions," *Advances in Consumer Research,* vol. 1 (Urbana, Ill.: Association for Consumer Research, 1974), pp. 242–46.

12. Hawkins and Lanzetta, "Predecisional Information Search," p. 799

13. Ratchford and Andreasen, "Consumer Perceptions," pp. 242–46.

14. J. W. Payne, "Heuristic Search Processes in Decision Making," *Advances in Consumer Research,* vol. 3 (Cincinnati: Association for Consumer Research, 1976), pp. 321–27.

15. Ratchford and Andreasen, "Consumer Perception," pp. 242–46.

16. John D. Claxton, Joseph N. Fry, and Bernard Portis, "A Taxonomy of Prepurchase Information-Gathering Patterns," *Journal of Consumer Research* 1 (December 1974): 35–42; James F. Engel, "Psychology and the Business Sciences," *Quarterly Review of Economics and Business* 1 (1961): 75–83; William P. Dommermuth and Edward W. Cundiff, "Shopping Centers, and Selling Strategies," *Journal of Marketing* 31, (October 1967): 32–36; Joseph W. Newman and Richard Staelin, "Prepurchase Information Seeking for New Cars and Major Household Appliances, *Journal of Marketing Research* 9 (August 1972): 249–257; Donald F. Cox and Stuart U. Rich, "Perceived Risk and Consumer Decision Making: The Case of Telephone Shopping," *Journal of Marketing Research* 1 (November 1964): 32–39. Although higher-perceived risk may lead to more active information search, greater-perceived risk and greater purchase importance may block information search. See Raymond Bauer, "Consumer Behavior as Risk Taking," in Robert S. Hancock, ed., *Dynamic Marketing for a Changing World: Proceedings of the Forty-third Conference of the American Marketing Association* (Chicago, 1960), pp. 389–400; Joseph W. Newman and Richard Staelin, "Multivariate Analysis of Differences in Buyer Decision Time," *Journal of Marketing Research* 8 (May 1971): 192–98; Peter Wright and Barton Weitz, "Time Horizon Effects on Product Evaluation Strategies," *Journal of Marketing Research* 14 (November 1977): 429–43; Katona and Mueller, "Purchase Decisions," pp. 30–87; Ratchford and Andreason, "Consumer Perceptions," pp. 242–46; Newman and Staelin, "Prepurchase Information Seeking," pp. 249–57.

17. John A. Howard, *Consumer Behavior: Applications of Theory* (New York: McGraw-Hall, 1977), p. 9.

18. Katona and Mueller, "Purchase Decisions," pp. 30–87; Newman and Staelin, "Prepurchase Information Seeking," pp. 249–57; Paul E. Green, "Consumer Use of Information," in Joseph W. Newman, ed., *On Knowing the Consumer* (New York; John Wiley and Sons, 1966), pp. 67–80.

19. Louis P. Bucklin, "Consumer Search, Role Enactment, and Market Efficiency," *Journal of Business* 42 (October 1969): 416–38.

20. Sidney J. Levy, "Social Class and Consumer Behavior," in Newman, ed., *On Knowing the Consumer,* pp. 146–60; D. J. Hempel, "Search Behavior and Information Utilization in the Home-buying

Process," in P. R. McDonald, ed., *Marketing Involvement in Society and the Economy* (Chicago: American Marketing Association, 1969), pp. 241–49; Katona and Mueller, "Purchase Decisions," pp. 30–87; Newman and Staelin, "Prepurchase Information Seeking," pp. 249–57.

21. Newman and Staelin, "Prepurchase Information Seeking," pp. 249–57.

22. A large number of research studies have reported the types and importance of information in consumer decision making. Among the studies are: Granbois, "Family Decision-making Process;" Katona and Mueller, "Purchase Decisions," pp. 30–87; Newman and Staelin, "Prepurchase Information Seeking," pp. 249–57; Alderson and Sessons, "Basic Research Report on Consumer Behavior: Report on a Study of Shopping Behavior and Methods for Its Investigation," in Ronald E. Frank, Alfred A. Kuehn, and William F. Massey, eds., *Quantitative Techniques in Marketing Analysis* (Homewood, Ill.: Richard D. Irwin, 1962), pp. 129–45; Jon G. Udel, "Pre-Purchase Behavior of Buyers of Small Appliances," *Journal of Marketing* 30 (October 1966): 50–52; Hugh W. Sargent, *Consumer Product Rating Publications and Buying Behavior*, (Urbana, Ill., Bureau of Business and Economic Research, University of Illinois, 1959); Elihu Katz and Paul F. Lazarsfeld, *Personal Influence* (Glencoe, Ill.: Free Press, 1955); Carol A. Kohn Berning and Jacob Jacoby, "Patterns of Information Acquisition in New Product Purchases," *Journal of Consumer Research* 1 (September 1974: 18–22; Claxton, Fry, and Portis, "Information-gathering Patterns," pp. 35–42; Bruce LeGrand and Jon G. Udell, "Consumer Behavior in the Market Place," *Journal of Retailing*, Fall 1964, pp. 32–40; Terrell G. Williams, "Problem Recognition and Deliberation in the Purchase of Consumer Durables" (Ph.D. diss., University of Arizona, 1973).

23. E. Scott Maynes, "Decision-making for Consumers, "*A Guide to Consumer Economics,* (New York: Macmillan, 1976), cited in Loren V. Geistfeld, "Consumer Decision Making; The Technical Efficiency Approach," *Journal of Consumer Research* 4 (June 1977): 48.

24. Robert A. Westbrook, Joseph W. Newman, and James R. Taylor, "Satisfaction/Dissatisfaction in the Purchase Decision Process," *Journal of Marketing* 42 (October 1978): 54–60.

25. Ibid., p. 57.

26. Jacob Jacoby, Donald E. Speller, and Carol A. Kohn, "Brand Choice Behavior as a Function of Information Load: Replication and Extention," *Journal of Consumer Research* 1 (1974): 33–42.

27. Del I. Hawkins, Kenneth A. Coney, and Roger J. Best, *Consumer Behavior: Implications for Marketing Strategy* (Dallas: Business Publications, 1980), p. 244.

28. Ibid., p. 245.

29. Peter L. Wright, "Consumer Choice Strategies: Simplifying vs. Optimizing," *Journal of Marketing Research* 12 (February 1975): 60–67; Gerald Zaltman and Melanie Walendorf, *Consumer Behavior: Basic Findings and Management Implications* (New York: John Wiley and Sons, 1979), pp. 310–12.

30. Katona and Mueller, "Purchase Decisions," p. 74.

31. David T. Kollat, "A Study of Unplanned Purchasing in Self Service Food Supermarkets" (Ph.D. diss., Indiana University, 1966), p. 360.

32. Katona and Mueller, "Purchase Decisions," pp. 48–49.

33. William P. Dommermuth, "The Shopping Matrix, and Marketing Strategy," *Journal of Marketing Research* 2 (May 1965): 128–32.

34. Katona and Mueller, "Purchase Decisions," p. 48.

35. Westbrook, Newman, and Taylor, "Purchase Decision Process," p. 56.

36. Chem L. Naryona and Rom J. Markin, "Consumer Behavior and Product Performance: An Alternative Conceptualization," *Journal of Marketing* 39 (October 1975): 1–6, cited in David L. Louden and Albert J. Della Bitta, *Consumer Behavior: Concepts and Applications* (New York: McGraw-Hill, 1979), p. 461.

37. Brian M. Campbell, "The Existence and Determinants of Evoked Set in Brand Choice Behavior" (Ph.D. diss., Columbia University, 1969); Brian M. Campbell, "The Existence of Evoked Set and Determinants of Its Magnitude in Brand Choice Behavior," in John A. Howard and Lyman E. Ostlund, eds., *Buyer Behavior: Theoretical and Empirical Foundations* (New York: Knopf, 1973), pp. 243–44.

38. Terrell G. Williams and Michael J. Etzel, "An Investigation and Extension of the Evoked Set Concept Applied to Consumer Durables." *Proceedings of the Southern Marketing Association* (Atlanta, 1976), pp. 237–39.

39. Naryona and Markin, "Consumer Behavior," p. 2.

40. Claxton, Fry, and Portis, "Information-gathering Patterns," pp. 35–42.

41. Robert A. Westbrook and Claes Fornell, "Patterns of Information Source Usage Among Durable Goods Buyers," *Journal of Marketing Research* 16 (August 1979): 303–12.

42. Russell W. Belk, "An Exploratory Assessment of Situational Effects in Buyer Behavior," *Journal of Marketing Research* 11 (May 1974): 156–63; Russell W. Belk, "Situational Variables and Consumer

Behavior," *Journal of Consumer Research* 2 (December 1975): 157–64.

43. Martin A. Fishbein, "Some Comments on the Use of 'Models' in Advertising Research," *Proceedings: Seminar on Translating Advanced Advertising Theories into Research Reality* (The Netherlands: European Society of Market Research, 1971), pp. 297–318.

44. Jon Stapel, "Predictive Attitudes," in Lee Adler and Irving Crespi, eds., *Attitude Research on the Rocks* (Chicago: American Marketing Association, 1968).

45. Idem, "Sales Effects of Print Ads," *Journal of Advertising Research* 11 (June 1971): 98.

46. Peter D. Bennett and Gilbert D. Hanell, "The Role of Confidence in Understanding and Predicting Buyers' Attitudes and Purchase Intentions," *Journal of Consumer Research* 2 (September 1975): 110–17.

47. Howard and Sheth, *Theory of Buyer Behavior,* pp. 35–144.

48. Belk, "Buyer Behavior," pp. 156–63.

49. Richard J. Lutz and Pradeep Kakkar, "The Psychological Situation As a Determinant of Consumer Behavior," *Proceedings of the Association for Consumer Research,* vol. 2 (Chicago: 1975), pp. 439–53.

50. Belk, "Buyer Behavior," pp. 156–63.

51. Kenneth E. Miller and James L. Ginter, "An Investigation of Situational Variation in Brand Choice Behavior and Attitude, *Journal of Marketing Research* 16 (February 1979): 111–23.

52. Belk, "Situational Variables," p. 159.

53. Engel, Blackwell, and Kollat, *Consumer Behavior,* p. 483.

54. *Consumer Buying Habit Studies* (Wilmington, Del.: E.I. duPont deNemours, 1959, 1965); Vernon T. Clover, "Relative Importance of Impulse Buying in Retail Stores," *Journal of Marketing* 15 (July 1959): 66–70.

55. *Consumer Buying Habits Studies.*

56. James D. Shaffer, "The Influence of Impulse Buying or In-The-Store Decisions on Consumers' Food Purchases," *Journal of Farm Economics,* May 1950.

57. Hawkins Stern, "The Significance of Impulse Buying Today," *Journal of Marketing* 26 (April 1962): 59–62.

58. David T. Kollat, "A Decision Process Approach to Impulse Purchasing," in Raymond M. Haas, ed., *Science, Technology, and Marketing,* (Chicago: American Marketing Association, 1966), pp. 626–39.

59. Ibid.

60. Belk, "Buyer Behavior," p. 160.

61. Leon Festinger, *A Theory of Cognitive Dissonance* (New York: Harper and Row, 1957).

62. Robert Mittelstaedt, "A Dissonance Approach to Repeat Purchasing Behavior," *Journal of Marketing Research* 33 (October 1969): 444–46.

63. Sadaomi Oshikawa, "Can Cognitive Dissonance Theory Explain Consumer Behavior?" *Journal of Marketing* 33 (October 1969): 44–49.

64. Idem, "Consumer Pre-Decision Conflict and Post-Decision Dissonance," *Behavioral Science* 15 (March 1970): 132–40.

65. George Brown, "The Automobile Buying Decision Within the Family," in Nelson N. Foote, ed., *Household Decision Making* (New York: New York University Press, 1961), pp. 193–99.

66. William H. Cummings and M. Venkatesan, "Cognitive Dissonance, and Consumer Behavior: A Review of the Evidence," *Journal of Marketing Research* 13 (August 1976): 303–8.

67. Westbrook, Newman, and Taylor, "Purchase Decision Process," p. 54.

68. Hiram C. Barksdale and William R. Darden, "Consumer Attitudes Toward Marketing and Consumerism," *Journal of Marketing* 36 (October 1972): 28–35; Thomas P. Hustad and Edgar A. Pessemier, "Will The Real Consumer Activist Please Stand Up: An Examination of Consumers' Opinions About Marketing Practices," *Journal of Marketing Research* 10 (August 1973): 319–24.

69. Donald A. Hughes, "An Investigation of the Relationship of Selected Factors to Consumer Satisfaction" (Paper presented in the Marketing Science Workshop on Consumer Satisfaction/Dissatisfaction Research, April 11–13, 1976); Rex H. Warland, Robert O. Hermann, and Jane Willits, "Dissatisfied Consumers: Who Gets Upset and Who Takes What Action," *Journal of Consumer Affairs* 9 (Winter 1975): 148–63.

70. Westbrook, Newman, and Taylor, "Purchase Decision Process," p. 59.

71. Ibid.

72. Hustad and Pessemier, "Real Consumer Activist," pp. 319–24.

73. James F. Engel, David T. Kollat, and Roger D. Blackwell, *Consumer Behavior* (New York: Holt, Rinehart, and Winston, 1968).

74. John A. Howard, *Marketing Management: Analysis and Planning* (Homewood, Ill.: Richard D. Irwin, 1963), pp. 31–113.

75. Howard and Sheth, *Theory of Buyer Behavior,* p. 31.

76. Howard, *Consumer Behavior,* p. 138.

Chapter 3

1. Robert E. Siverman, *Psychology,* 2d ed., (Englewood Cliffs, N.J.: Prentice-Hall, 1974), p. 113.

2. Bernard Berelson and Gary A. Steiner, *Human Behavior: An Inventory of Scientific Findings* (New

York: Harcourt, Brace and World, 1964), p. 87.

3. Ibid., p. 88.

4. Ibid.

5. Harry C. Triandis, "Cultural Influences Upon Cognitive Processes," *Advances in Experimental Social Psychology,* vol. 1 (New York: Academic Press, 1964), pp. 1–48.

6. Leo Postman, Jerome S. Bruner, and Elliott McGinnies, "Personal Values as Selective Factors in Perception," *Journal of Abnormal and Social Psychology* 43 (April 1948): 142–52.

7. George A. Miller, "The Magical Number Seven, Plus or Minus Two: Some Limits on our Capacity for Processing Information," *Psychological Review* 63 (1956): 81–97.

8. Brian M. Campbell, "The Existence and Determinants of Evoked set in Brand Choice Behavior" (Ph.D. diss., Columbia University, 1969).

9. Jack Trout and Al Ries, "The Positioning Era Cometh," *Advertising Age,* 24 April 1972, pp. 35, 38.

10. James R. Bettman, *An Information Processing Theory of Consumer Choice* (Reading, Mass.: Addison-Wesley, 1979), p. 97.

11. Sheldon S. Zalkind and Timothy W. Costello, "Perception: Some Recent Research and Implications for Administrators," *Administrative Science Quarterly* 7 (September 1962): 218.

12. Donald A. Laird, "How the Consumer Estimates Quality by subconscious Sensory Impressions —with Special Reference to the Role of Smell," *Journal of Applied Psychology* 16 (June 1932): 241–46.

13. "Toilet Tissues: Softness, Strength or Price?" *Consumer Reports* 42 (August 1977): 466–68.

14. "Are Color Television Commercials Worth the Extra Cost?" (New York: Association of Color Advertisers, 1966).

15. Paul F. Secorn, "Facial Features and Inference Processes in Interpersonal Perception," in Renato Tugiuri and Luigi Petrullo, eds., *Person Perception and Interpersonal Behavior* (Stanford, Calif.: Stanford University Press, 1958), pp. 300–315.

16. Lee Iacocca, "Some Kind of Animal," *Nation's Business,* February 1969, pp. 62–67.

17. James H. Myers and William H. Reynolds, *Consumer Behavior and Marketing Management* (Boston: Houghton Mifflin, 1967), p. 22.

18. Ibid., p. 7.

19. "How Important is Position in Consumer Magazine Advertising?" *Media/Scope* 8 (June 1964): 52–77.

20. H. J. Rudolph, *Attention and Interest Factors in Advertising* (New York: Funk & Wagnalls, 1947).

21. Jerome S. Bruner and Cecile C. Goodman, "Value and Need as Organizing Factors in Perception," *Journal of Abnormal and Social Psychology* 42 (January 1947): 33–44.

22. Robert Levine, Isidor Chain, and Gardner Murphy, "The Relationship of the Intensity of a Need to the Amount of Perceptual Distortion: A Preliminary Report," *Journal of Psychology* 13 (1942): 283–93.

23. James F. Engel, "The Influence of Needs and Attitudes on the Perception of Persuasion," in Stephen A. Greyser, ed., *Toward Scientific Marketing* (Chicago: American Marketing Association, 1964), pp. 18–29.

24. A. Gimelli and A. Coppallini, "The Influence of the Subject's Attitudes in Perception," *Acta Psychology* (1958): 12–14.

25. Thomas L. Parkinson, "The Use of Seals of Approval in Consumer Decision Making as a Function of Cognitive Needs and Style," *Advances in Consumer Research,* vol. 2 (Chicago: Association for Consumer Research, 1975), pp. 1933–40.

26. Rom J. Markin, Jr., *Consumer Behavior: A Cognitive Orientation* (New York: Macmillan, 1974), p. 216.

27. Ibid.; Myers and Reynolds, *Consumer Behavior,* pp. 72–73.

28. S. Asch, "Opinions and Social Pressure," *Scientific American* 193 (November 1955): 31–35.

29. Thomas C. Kinnear and James R. Taylor, "The Effect of Ecological Concern on Brand Perceptions," *Journal of Marketing Research* 10 (May 1973): 191–97.

30. V. F. Ray, "Human Color Perception and Behavior Response," *Transactions of the New York Academy of Sciences,* vol. 16 (1953): 98–104.

31. Charles Winick, "Anthropology's Contributions to Marketing," *Journal of Marketing* 25 (July 1961): 53–60.

32. Thomas R. Donahue, Timothy P. Meyer, and Lucy L. Henke, "Black and White Children: Perceptions of TV Commercials," *Journal of Marketing* 42 (October 1978): 34–40.

33. George S. Day, "Attitude Change, Media, and Word of Mouth, *Journal of Advertising Research* 11 (December 1971): 31–39.

34. Fritz Heider, *The Psychology of Interpersonal Relations* (New York: John Wiley and Sons, 1958).

35. Gerald Zaltman and Melanie Walendorf, *Consumer Behavior: Basic Findings and Management Implications* (New York: John Wiley and Sons, 1979), p. 426.

36. Fritz Heider, "Social Perception and Phenomenal Causality," *Psychological Review* 51 (1944): 358–74; Heider, *Interpersonal Relations.*

37. Edward E. Jones and Keith E. Davis, "From Acts to Dispositions: The Attribution Process in Person Perception," *Advances in Experimental Social Psychology,* vol. 2 (New York: Academic Press, 1965), pp. 219–66.

38. Richard W. Mizerski, Linda L. Golden, and

Jerome B. Kernan, "The Attribution Process in Consumer Decision Making." Reprinted with permission from *Journal of Consumer Research* (1979) 6: 125.

39. Robert B. Settle and Linda L. Golden, "Attribution Theory and Advertiser Credibility," *Journal of Marketing Research* 9 (May 1974): 181–85; Robert A. Hansen and Carol Scott, "Comments on Attribution Theory and Advertiser Credibility," *Journal of Marketing Research* 13 (May 1976): 193–97; Linda L. Golden, "Attribution Theory Implications for Advertisement Claim Credibility," *Journal of Marketing Research* 14 (February 1977): 115–17; Robert E. Smith and Shelby D. Hunt, "Attributional Processes and Effects in Promotional Situations," *Journal of Consumer Research* 5 (December 1978): 149–58.

40. Richard W. Mizerski, "Causal Complexity: A Measure of Consumer Causal Attribution," *Journal of Marketing Research* 15 (May 1978): 220–28.

41. Bobby J. Calder and Robert E. Burnkrant, "Interpersonal Influence on Consumer Behavior: An Attribution Theory Approach," *Journal of Consumer Research* 4 (June 1977): 29–38.

42. Daryl J. Bem, "An Experimental Analysis of Self-Persuasion," *Journal of Experimental and Social Psychology* 1 (1965): 199–218; idem, "Self Perception: An Alternative Interpretation of Cognitive Dissonance Phenomenon," *Psychological Review* 74 (1967): 183–200; idem, "Self Perception Theory," Advances in Experimental Social Psychology, vol. 9 (New York: Academic Press, 1972).

43. Harold Kelley, "Attribution Theory in Social Psychology," in David Levine, ed., *Nebraska Symposium on Motivation* (Lincoln, Neb.: University of Nebraska Press, 1967); idem, *Attribution in Social Interaction*, (Morristown, N.J.: General Learning Press, 1971); idem, *Causal Schemata and the Attribution Process*, (Morristown, N.J.: General Learning Press, 1972); idem, "The Processes of Causal Attribution," *American Psychologist* 28 (February 1973): 107–28.

44. Mizersky, Golden, and Kernan, "Attribution Process," pp. 126–27.

45. Kelley, "Attribution Theory in Social Psychology," p. 197.

46. Mizersky, Golden, and Kernan, "Attribution Process," p. 127.

47. Raymond A. Bauer, "Consumer Behavior as Risk Taking," in Robert S. Hancock, ed. *Dynamic Marketing for a Changing World: Proceedings of the Forty-Third Conference of the American Marketing Association* (Chicago, 1960), p. 389.

48. Donald F. Cox, "Risk Handling in Consumer Behavior: An Intensive Study of Two Cases," in Donald F. Cox, ed., *Risk Taking and Information Handling in Consumer Behavior* (Boston: Division of Research, Graduate School of Business Administration, Harvard University, 1967), pp. 36–38.

49. Ibid., pp. 5–7.

50. Donald H. Granbois, "The Role of Communication in the Family Decision Making Process," in Stephen A. Greyser, ed., *Toward Scientific Marketing* (Chicago: American Marketing Association, 1963), pp. 44–57.

51. Jacob Jacoby and Leon Kaplan, "The Components of Perceived Risk," in M. Venkatesan, ed. *Proceedings of the Third Annual Conference of the Association for Consumer Research* (Chicago, 1972), pp. 282–93.

52. Ted Roselius, "Consumer Rankings of Risk Reduction Methods," *Journal of Marketing* 35 (January 1971): 56–61; Jagdish N. Sheth and M. Venkatesan, "Risk Reduction Processes in Repetitive Consumer Behavior," *Journal of Marketing Research* 5 (August 1968): 307–10.

53. Vance Packard, *The Hidden Persuaders* (New York: McKay, 1957).

54. N. F. Dixon, *Subliminal Perception,* (London: McGraw-Hill, 1971), p. 320.

55. R. Wilhelm, "Are Subliminal Commercials Bad?" *Michigan Business Review* 8 (January 1956): 26.

56. Richard P. Barthol and Michael J. Goldstein, "Psychology and the Invisible Sell," *California Management Review* 1 (Winter 1959).

57. James V. McConnell, Richard L. Cutler, and Elton B. McNeil, "Subliminal Stimulation: an Overview," *The American Psychologist* 13 (1958): 229–42.

58. M. L. DeFleur and R. M. Petronoff, "A Television Test of Subliminal Persuasion," *Public Opinion Quarterly* 23 (Summer 1959): 170–80.

59. Del Hawkins, "The Effects of Subliminal Stimulation on Drive Level and Brand Preference," *Journal of Marketing Research* 7 (August 1970): 322–26.

60. Markin, *Consumer Behavior,* p. 216.

61. Kenneth E. Runyon, *Consumer Behavior and the Practice of Marketing* (Columbus, Oh.: Charles E. Merrill, 1977), p. 312.

62. Wilson Bryon Key, *Subliminal Seduction* (New York: Signet, 1975).

63. Harold W. Berkman and Christopher C. Gilson, *Consumer Behavior, Concepts, and Strategies* (Encino, Calif.: Dickenson, 1978), p. 262.

Chapter 4

1. Dennis Coon, *Introduction to Psychology: Exploration and Application* (St. Paul: West, 1977), p. 271.

2. Edward L. Thorndike, *Animal Intelligence* (New York: Macmillian, 1911).

3. Coon, *Introduction to Psychology*, p. 273

4. Robert C. Bolles, *Theory of Motivation* (New York: Harper and Row, 1967).

5. Abraham H. Maslow, *Motivation and Personality* (New York: Harper, 1954); ibid., Harper and Row, 1970.

6. Ibid.

7. C. Glenn Walters, *Consumer Behavior: Theory and Practice* (Homewood, Ill.: Richard D. Irwin, 1974), p. 125.

8. Leon Festinger, *A Theory of Cognitive Dissonance* (Stanford, Calif.: Stanford University Press, 1958), p. 37.

9. C. Glenn Walters and Gordon W. Paul, *Consumer Behavior: An Integrated Framework* (Homewood, Ill.: Richard D. Irwin, 1970), p. 245.

10. James U. McNeal, "Cognitive Dissonance and Consumer Behavior," in McNeal, ed., *Dimensions of Consumer Behavior*, 2d ed. (New York: Appleton-Century-Crofts, 1969), pp. 119–23, citing Leon Festinger, *A Theory of Cognitive Dissonance* (Evanston, Ill.: Row, Peterson, 1957).

11. Leon Festinger, "Cognitive Dissonance," *Scientific American* 207 (October 1962): 93.

12. McNeal, "Cognitive Dissonance," p. 120. The spelling in this quotation has been reproduced as it appeared in the original source. Coke as a registered trademark of the Coca-Cola Company should be capitalized.

13. Donald O. Hebb, *A Textbook of Psychology*, 2d ed. (Philadelphia: Saunders, 1966).

14. Coon, *Introduction to Psychology*, p. 273.

15. Rom J. Markin, "Motivation in Buyer Behavior Theory: From Mechanism to Cognition," in Arch Woodside, Jagdish N. Sheth, and Peter D. Bennett, eds., *Consumer and Industrial Buying Behavior* (New York: North-Holland, 1977), pp. 37–48.

16. Rom J. Markin, *Consumer Behavior: A Cognitive Orientation* (New York: Macmillan, 1974).

17. Ibid., pp. 108–10.

18. Robert E. Silverman, *Psychology*, 2d ed. (Englewood Cliffs, N.J.: Prentice-Hall, 1974), p. 306.

19. Markin, "Buyer Behavior Theory," p. 41.

20. Ibid., p. 43.

21. John A. Howard and Jagdish N. Sheth, *The Theory of Buyer Behavior* (New York: John Wiley and Sons, 1967), pp. 106–7.

22. Kurt A. Lewin, *Dynamic Theory of Personality* (New York: McGraw-Hill, 1935).

23. John Lamberth, John C. McCullens, and Roger L. Mellgren, *Foundations of Psychology* (New York: Harper and Row, 1976), p. 295.

24. W. H. Sheldon, *The Varieties of Temperment* (New York: Harper and Row, 1942).

25. Silverman, *Psychology*, p. 414.

26. David Reisman, *The Lonely Crowd* (New York: Doubleday, 1953), pp. 32–34.

27. See Sanford M. Dornbusch and Lauren C. Hickman, "Other-Directedness in Consumer Goods Advertising: A Test of Riesman's Historical Theory," *Social Forces* 38 (December 1959): 99–103; Joel B. Cohen, "An Interpersonal Orientation to the Study of Consumer Behavior," *Journal of Marketing Research* 4 (August 1967): 270–78; Joel B. Cohen, "Toward an Interpersonal Theory of Consumer Behavior," *California Management Review* 10 (Spring 1968): 73–80.

28. Daniel W. Green, Montrose S. Sommers, and Jerome B. Kernan, "Personality and Implicit Behavior Patterns," *Journal of Marketing Research* 10 (February 1973): 63–69.

29. Silverman, *Psychology*, p. 411.

30. Gordon W. Alport and J. S. Odbert, "Trait Names: A Psycholexical Study," *Psychological Monographs* 47, no. 211 (1936).

31. Joy P. Guilford, *Personality* (New York: McGraw-Hill, 1959).

32. Franklin B. Evans, "Psychological and Objective Factors in the Predicting of Brand Choice," *Journal of Business* 32 (October 1959): 340–69.

33. Ralph Westfall, "Psychological Factors in Predicting Product Choice," *Journal of Marketing* 26 (April 1962): 34–40.

34. Arthur Koponen, "Personality Characteristics of Purchasers," *Journal of Advertising Research* 1 (September 1960): 6–12.

35. Raymond L. Horton, "Some Relationships Between Personality and Consumer Decision Making," *Journal of Marketing Research* 16 (May 1979): 233–46.

36. Karen Horney, *Our Inner Conflicts: A Constructive Theory of Neurosis* (New York: Norton, 1945).

37. Roger Rickles, "Ernest Dichter Thrives Selling Firms Research on 'Hidden' Emotions," *Wall Street Journal*, 20 November 1972.

38. Silverman, *Psychology*, p. 411.

39. Carl R. Rogers, On Becoming a Person: A Therapist's View of Psychotherapy (Boston: Houghton Mifflin, 1961).

40. Edward L. Grubb and Gregg Hupp, "Perception of Self, Generalized Stereotypes, and Brand Selection," *Journal of Marketing Research* 5 (February 1968): 58.

41. John Dollard and Neal E. Miller, *Personality and Psychotherapy* (New York: McGraw-Hill, 1950).

42. B. F. Skinner, *Beyond Freedom and Dignity* (New York: Bantam, 1971), p. 5.

43. Edwin P. Hollander, *Principles and Methods of Social Psychology* (London: Oxford University Press, 1967), p. 292.

44. Markin, "Buyer Behavior Theory," p. 45.

45. Emanuel Demby, "Psychographics and From Whence it Came," in William D. Wells, ed., *Life*

Style and Psychographics (Chicago: American Marketing Association, 1974), pp. 11–30.

46. Ibid., p. 18.

47. Joseph Pernica, "Psychographics: What Can Go Wrong," in Ronald C. Carhan, ed., *1974 Combined Proceedings of the American Marketing Association* (Chicago, 1975), pp. 45–50.

48. Raymond L. Horton, "Some Relationships Between Personality and Consumer Decision Making," *Journal of Marketing Research* 16 (May 1979): 283–46.

Chapter 5

1. James F. Engel, David T. Kollat, and Roger Blackwell, *Consumer Behavior,* 2d ed. (New York: Holt, Rinehart, and Winston, 1973), p. 229.

2. Edward L. Thorndike, "The Law of Effect," in *Selected Writings from a Connectionist's Psychology* (New York: Appleton-Century-Crofts, 1949).

3. Dennis Coon, *Introduction to Psychology* (St. Paul: West, 1977), p. 777.

4. John B. Watson and R. Rayner, "Conditioned Emotional Reaction," *Journal of Experimental Psychology* 3 (1920): 1–14.

5. Albert Bandura and Theodore L. Rosenthal, "Vicarious Classical Conditioning as a Function of Arousal Level," *Journal of Personality and Social Psychology* 3 (January 1966): 54–62.

6. Edwin R. Guthrie, *The Psychology of Learning* (New York: Holt, Rinehart, and Winston, 1935).

7. Idem, "Conditioning: A Theory of Learning in Terms of Stimulus, Response and Association," in *The Psychology of Learning,* Forty-first yearbook of the National Society for the Study of Education, pt. 2, 1942.

8. Joe Kent Kerby, *Consumer Behavior: Conceptual Foundations* (New York: Dun, Donneley, 1975), p. 305.

9. Alfred A. Kuehn, "Consumer Brand Choice as a Learning Process," *Journal of Advertising Research* 2 (December 1962): 10–17.

10. Clark L. Hull, *Principles of Behavior* (New York: Appleton-Century-Crofts, 1943); idem, *A Behavior System* (New Haven: Yale University Press, 1952).

11. B. F. Skinner, *The Behavior of Organisms* (New York: Appleton-Century-Crofts, 1938).

12. "Stan Freberg Prospers by Browbeating Clients, Poking Fun at Products," *Wall Street Journal,* 20 June 1969.

13. Michael L. Ray, "Psychological Theories and Interpretations of Learning," *Consumer Behavior: Theoretical Sources* (Englewood Cliffs, N.J.: Prentice-Hall, 1973), pp. 47–117, especially pp. 55–58.

14. Kenneth E. Runyon, *Consumer Behavior* (Columbus, Oh.: Charles E. Merrill, 1977), p. 209.

15. Kurt Lewin, "Field Theory and Learning," in *The Psychology of Learning,* Forty-first Yearbook of the National Society for the Study of Education, 1942, pp. 215–42.

16. Edward C. Tolman, *Purposive Behavior in Animals and Men* (New York: Appleton-Century-Crofts, 1932).

17. Edward C. Tolman, "Cognitive Maps in Rats and Men," *Psychological Review* 55 (July 1948): 189–208.

18. Rom J. Markin, *Consumer Behavior: A Cognitive Orientation* (New York: Macmillan, 1973), p. 239.

19. John Lamberth, John C. McCullers, and Roger L. Mellgren, *Foundations of Psychology* (New York: Harper and Row, 1976), p. 203.

20. Ibid., p. 230.

21. Jacob L. Gerwitz, "Mechanisms of Social Learning," in David Goslin, ed., *Handbook of Socialization Theory and Research* (Chicago: Rand McNally, 1969), pp. 57–212.

22. Albert Bandura, "Vicarious Processes: A Case of No-Trial Learning," Advances in Experimental Social Psychology, vol. 2 (New York: Academic Press, 1965), pp. 1–55.

23. U.S. National Commission on the Causes and Prevention of Violence, 1970.

24. Albert Bandura, "Social Learning Through Imitation," in M. Jones, ed., *Nebraska Symposium on Motivation* (Lincoln, Neb.: University of Nebraska Press, 1962), pp. 211–74; idem, "Social Learning Theory of Identificatory Processes," in David Goslin, ed., *Handbook of Socialization Theory and Research* (Chicago: Rand McNally, 1969), pp. 213–62; idem, *Social Learning Theory* (Morristown, N.J.: General Learning Press, 1971).

25. The discussion in the remainder of this section follows Charles A. Atkin, "Children's Social Learning from Television Advertising: Research Evidence on Observational Modeling of Product Consumption," *Advances in Consumer Research,* vol. 3 (Chicago: Association for Consumer Research, 1976): 513–19.

26. Charles A. Atkin, "The Effects of Television Advertising on Children" (Final report submitted to the office of Child Development, 1975).

27. Atkin, "Children's Social Learning," pp. 513–19.

28. Talcott Parsons, Robert F. Bales, and Edward A. Skils, *Working Papers in the Theory of Action* (Glencoe, Ill.: Free Press, 1953); David Riesman and Howard Roseborough, "Careers and Consumer

Behavior," in Lincoln Clark, ed., *Consumer Behavior: Vol II., The Life Cycle and Consumer Behavior* (New York: New York University, 1955); Albert Bandura, "Modeling Influences on Children" (Testimony to the Federal Trade Commission, October 1971).

29. Scott L. Ward and Daniel Wackman, "Children's Purchase Influence Attempts and Parental Yielding," *Journal of Marketing Research* 9 (August 1972): 316–19; Andre Caron and Scott Ward, "Gift Decisions by Kids and Parents," *Journal of Advertising Research* 15 (August 1975): 15–20; James S. Frideres "Advertising, Buying Patterns and Children," *Journal of Advertising Research* 13 (February 1973): 34–35; Pat Burr and Richard M. Burr, "Product Recognition and Premium Appeal," *Journal of Communication* 27 (1977): 115–17; Scott Ward and Daniel Wackman, "Family and Media Influences on Adolescent Consumer Learning," *American Behavioral Scientist* 14 (January-February 1971): 415–27; Roy L. Moore and Lowndes F. Stephens, "Some Communication and Demographic Determinants of Adolescent Consumer Learning," *Journal of Consumer Research* 2 (September 1975): 80–92.

30. Gilbert A. Churchill and George A. Moschis, "Television and Interpersonal Influences on Adolescent Consumer Learning," *Journal of Consumer Research* 6 (June 1979): 23–25.

31. Moore and Stephens, "Adolescent Consumer Learning," 80–92; Scott Ward and Daniel Wackman, "Effects of Television Advertising on Consumer Socialization," (Cambridge, Mass.: Marketing Science Institute, 1974); Scott Ward, Daniel Wackman, and Ellen Wartella, *How Children Learn to Buy* (Beverly Hills: Sage, 1977).

32. Leon Festinger, "A Theory of Social Comparison Processes," *Human Relations* 7 No. 2 (May 1954): 117–40.

33. Riesman and Roseborough, "Careers and Consumer Behavior;" Parsons, Belez, and Skill, *Working Papers.*

34. Josephine Saunders, A. Coskun Samli, and Enid F. Tozier, "Congruence and Conflict in Buying Decisions of Mothers and Daughters," *Journal of Retailing* 49 (Fall 1973): 3–18.

35. Riesman and Roseborough, "Careers and Consumer Behavior;" Roy L. Moore, George P. Moschis, and Lowndes F. Stephens, "An Exploratory Study of Consumer Role Perceptions in Adolescent Consumer Socialization" (Paper presented to the International Communication Association, Chicago, 1975).

36. Lamberth, McCullers, and Mellgren, *Foundations of Psychology,* 154.

37. Richard C. Atkinson and R. M. Shiffrin, "Human Memory: A Proposed System and Its Control Processes," in Kenneth W. Spence and Janet T. Spence, eds., *The Psychology of Learning and Motivation: Advances in Research and Theory,* vol. 2 (New York: Academic Press, 1968), pp. 89–195.

38. James R. Bettman, "Memory Factors in Consumer Choice: A Review," *Journal of Marketing* 43 (Spring 1979): 37–53. This is an excellent review article and should be consulted for a more detailed treatment of consumer memory processes. This section is largely grounded in this article.

39. Leo Postman, "Verbal Learning and Memory," *Annual Review of Psychology* 26 (1975): 291–335; Fargus Craik and Robert S. Lockhart, "Levels of Processing: A Framework for Memory Research," *Journal of Verbal Learning and Verbal Behavior* 11 (1972): 671–84; Fargus Craik and Endel Tulving, "Depth of Processing and the Retention of Words," *Journal of Experimental Psychology: General* 1 (1975): 268–94; Thomas O. Nelson, "Repetition and Depth of Processing," *Journal of Verbal Learning and Verbal Behavior* 16 (1977): 151–71; Alan D. Baddeley, "The Trouble with Levels: A Re-examination of Craik and Lockhart's Framework for Memory Research," *Psychological Review* 85 (May 1978): 139–52.

40. Bettman, "Memory Factors," p. 44. The discussion here follows Bettman's article, pp. 45–50.

41. Peter L. Wright, "Analyzing Media Effects on Advertising Responses," *Public Opinion Quarterly* 38 (Summer 1974): 192–205.

42. Walter R. Reitman, "What Does it Take to Remember?" in Donald A. Norman, ed., *Models of Human Memory* (New York: Academic Press, 1970), pp. 469–509.

43. Walter Kintch, "Models for Free Recall and Recognition," in Norman, *Models of Human Memory,* pp. 331–73; Roger N. Shepard, "Recognitive Memory for Words, Sentences and Pictures," *Journal of Verbal Learning and Verbal Behavior* 6 (1967): 156–63.

44. Moris Eagle and Eli Leiter, "Recall and Recognition in Intentional and Incidental Learning," *Journal of Experimental Psychology* 68 (1964): 58–63; Barbara Tuesky, "Encoding Processing in Recognition and Recall," *Cognitive Psychology* 5 (November 1973): 275–87.

45. Gordon H. Bower, "Organizational Factors in Memory," *Cognitive Psychology* 1 (January 1970): 18–46; Herman Buckle, "Learning is Organized by Chunking," *Journal of Verbal Learning and Verbal Behavior* 15 (1976): 313–24.

46. Gordon H. Bower and Fred Springston, "Pauses as Recoding Points in Letter Series," *Journal of Experimental Psychology* 53 (1953): 189–98.

47. Donald M. Thomson and Endel Tulving, "Associative Encoding and Retrieval: Weak and Strong Cues," *Journal of Experimental Psychology* 86 (1970): 255–62.

48. Eric J. Johnson and J. Edward Russor, "The Organization of Product Information in Memory Identified by Recall Times," *Advances in Consumer Research,* vol. 5 (Chicago: Association for Consumer Research, 1978), pp. 79–86.

49. Catherine G. Penny, "Modality Effects in Short-Term Verbal Memory," *Psychological Bulletin,* 82 (January 1975): 68–84.

50. Allen Paivio, *Imagery and Verbal Processes* (New York: Holt, Rinehart, and Winston, 1971); Kathy A. Lutz and Richard J. Lutz, "Effects of Interactive Imagery on Learning: Application to Advertising," *Journal of Applied Psychology,* 62 (August 1977): 493–98.

51. John R. Rossiter, "Visual and Verbal Memory in Children's Product Information Utilization," *Advances in Consumer Research,* vol. 3 (Cincinnati: Association for Consumer Research, 1976), pp. 523–27.

52. John R. Rossiter, "Cognitive Phenomena in Contemporary Advertising" (Paper presented at the 1975 Conference on Culture and Communication, Temple University, March 1975).

53. Alan G. Sawyer, "The Effects of Repetition: Conclusions and Suggestions about Experimental Laboratory Research," in G. David Hughes and Michael L. Ray, eds., *Buyer/Consumer Information Processing* (Chapel Hill: University of North Carolina, 1974), pp. 190–219.

54. Hubert A. Zielske, "The Remembering and Forgetting of Advertising," *Journal of Marketing* 23 (January 1959): 239–43.

55. Herbert E. Krugman, "Why Three Exposures May Be Enough," *Journal of Advertising Research* 12 (December 1972): 11–14.

56. Marvin E. Goldberg and Gerald J. Gorn, "Children's Reaction to Television Advertising: An Experimental Approach," *Journal of Consumer Research* 1 (September 1974): 69–75.

57. Addison E. Woodward, Jr., Robert A. Bjork, and Robert H. Jongeward, Jr., "Recall and Recognition as a Function of Primary Rehearsal," *Journal of Verbal Learning and Verbal Behavior* 12 (1973): 608–17; Robert J. Chabot, Timothy J. Miller, and James F. Juola, "The Relationship Between Repetition and Depth of Processing," *Memory and Cognition* 4 (1976): 677–82; Leo Postman, "Verbal Learning and Memory," *Annual Review of Psychology* 26 (1975): 291–335.

58. Meryl P. Gardner, Andrew A. Mitchell, and J. Edward Russo, "Chronometric Analysis: An Introduction and an Application to Low Involvement Perception of Advertisements," *Advances in Consumer Research,* vol. 5 (Chicago: Association for Consumer Research, 1978), pp. 581–89.

Chapter 6

1. Robert E. Silverman, *Psychology,* 2d ed. (Englewood Cliffs, N.J.: Prentice-Hall, 1974), p. 518.

2. Robert A. Baron and Donn Byrne, *Social Psychology: Understanding Human Interaction,* 2d ed. (Boston: Allyn and Bacon, 1977), p. 95; C. A. Kiesler and P. A. Munson, "Attitudes and Opinions," *Annual Reviews of Psychology,* vol. 26 (Palo Alto, Calif., 1975).

3. Martin Fishbein and Icek Ajzen, *Belief, Attitude, Intention and Behavior: An Introduction to Theory and Research* (Reading, Mass.: Addison-Wesley, 1975), p. 6.

4. Carolyn W. Sherif, Muzafer Sherif, and Roger Nebergall, *Attitude and Attitude Change* (Philadelphia: Saunders, 1965), p. 4.

5. Milton Rokeach, *Beliefs Attitudes, and Values* (San Francisco: Jossey-Bass, 1968), p. 112.

6. Leonard Berkowitz, *Social Psychology* (Glenview, Ill.: Scott, Foresman, 1972), pp. 46–47.

7. Silverman, *Pscyhology,* p. 579.

8. Daniel Katz, "The Functional Approach to the Study of Attitudes," *Public Opinion Quarterly* 24 (Summer 1960): 163–204.

9. Berkowitz, *Social Psychology,* p. 49.

10. Muzafer Sherif and Carolyn W. Sherif, *An Outline of Social Psychology,* rev. ed. (New York: Harper and Row, 1956).

11. Milton J. Rosenberg, "An Analysis of Affective Cognitive Consistency," in Milton J. Rosenberg et. al., eds., *Attitude Organization and Change* (New Haven, Conn.: Yale University Press, 1960).

12. David Krech, Richard S. Crutchfield and Egerton G. Ballachey, *Individual in Society: A Textbook of Social Psychology* (New York: McGraw-Hill, 1962).

13. Rosenberg, "Cognitive Consistency," p. 22.

14. Katz, "Study of Attitudes," pp. 163–204.

15. See, for example, Lawrence S. Wrightsman, Jr., "Wallace Supporters and Adherence to Law and Order," *Journal of Personality and Social Psychology* 13 (September 1969): 17–22; Allan W. Wicker, "An Examination of the 'Other Variables' Explanation of Attitude-Behavior Inconsistency," *Journal of Personality and Social Psychology* 19 (July 1971): 18–30.

16. Irving Crespi, "The Challenge to Attitude Research," in Lee Adler and Irving Crespi, eds., *Atti-*

tude Research at Sea (Chicago: American Marketing Association, 1966), pp. 187–89.

17. Martin A. Fishbein, "Some Comments on the Use of 'Models' in Advertising Research," *Proceedings: Seminar on Translating Advanced Advertising Theories into Research Reality* (Amsterdam: European Society of Market Research, 1971), p. 301.

18. Peter D. Bennett and Harold H. Kassarjian *Consumer Behavior* (Englewood Cliffs, N.J.: Prentice-Hall, 1972), p. 93.

19. Baron and Byrne, *Social Psychology,* p. 145.

20. Herbert Krugman, "The Impact of Television Advertising: Learning Without Involvement," *Public Opinion Quarterly* 30 (Fall 1965): 583–96.

21. Benjamin Lipstein, "Anxiety, Risk, and Uncertainty in Advertising Effectiveness Measurements," in Lee Adler and Irving Crespi, eds., *Attitude Research on the Rocks* (Chicago: American Marketing Association, 1968), pp. 11–27.

22. Chester A. Insko and William H. Melson, "Verbal Reinforcement of Attitude in Laboratory and Nonlaboratory Contexts," *Journal of Personality* 37 (March 1969): 25–40.

23. Terence R. Mitchell and Anthony Biglan, "Instrumentality Theories: Current Uses in Psychology," *Psychological Bulletin* 76 (December 1971): 432–54.

24. Helen Peak, "Attitude and Motivation," in M. R. Jones, ed., *Nebraska Symposium on Motivation* (Lincoln, Neb.: University of Nebraska Press, 1955), pp. 149–88.

25. See Philip G. Zimbardo, Ebbe E. Ebbesen, and Christian Maslock, *Influencing Attitudes and Changing Behavior,* 2d ed. (Reading, Mass.: Addison-Wesley, 1977), pp. 55–84. The section that follows draws from this reference.

26. Morris B. Holbrook, "Beyond Attitude Structure: Toward the Informational Determinants of Attitude," *Journal of Marketing Research* 15 (November 1978): 545–56.

27. T. J. Crawford, "Beliefs About Birth Control: A Consistency Theory Analysis," *Representative Research in Social Psychology* 4 (1973): 54–65.

28. Zimbardo, Ebbesen, and Maslock, *Influencing Attitudes,* pp. 57–88.

29. Ibid., pp. 59–60.

30. Mona A. Clee and Robert A. Wicklund, "Consumer Behavior and Psychological Reactance," *Journal of Consumer Research* 6 (March 1980): 389–405.

31. Roderick R. Hart, Gustav W. Friedrich, and William D. Berolas, *Public Communication* (New York: Harper and Row, 1975).

32. Leon Festinger, *A Theory of Cognitive Dissonance* (Evanston, Ill.: Row, Peterson, 1957).

33. Elliot Aronson, Judith A. Turner, and J. Merrill Carlsmith, "Communicator Credibility and Communication Discrepancy as Determinants of Opinion Change," *Journal of Abnormal and Social Psychology* 67, No. 1 (July 1963): 31–36.

34. Judson Mills and John Harvey, "Opinion Change as a Function of When Information about the Communicator is Received and Whether He is Attractive or Expert," *Journal of Personality and Social Psychology* 21 (January 1972): 52–55.

35. Brian Sterthal, Ruby Dholakia, and Clark Leavitt, "The Persuasive Effect of Source Credibility: Tests of Cognitive Response," *Journal of Consumer Research* 4 (March 1978): 252–60.

36. Carl I. Hovland, Arthur A. Lumsdaine and Fred D. Sheffield, *Experiments on Mass Communication* (Princeton: Princeton University Press, 1949).

37. Paulette M. Gillig and Anthony G. Greenwald, "Is it Time to Lay The Sleeper Effect to Rest?" *Journal of Personality and Social Psychology* 29 (January 1974): 132–39.

38. Elaine Walster, Elliot Aronson, and Darcy Abrahams, "On Increasing the Persuasiveness of a Low Prestige Communicator," *Journal of Experimental Social Psychology* 2 (October 1966): 325–42; Elliot Walster and Leon Festinger, "The Effectiveness of Overheard Persuasive Communications," *Journal of Abnormal and Social Psychology* 65 No. 6 (December 1962): 395–402.

39. Ellen Berscheid, "Opinion Change and Communication-Communicator Similarity and Dissimilarity," *Journal of Personality and Social Psychology* 4 (December 1966): 670–80; Mills and Harvey, "Opinion Change," pp. 52–55.

40. Charles E. Osgood and Percy H. Tannenbaum, "The Principles of Congruity on the Prediction of Attitude Change," *Psychological Review* 62 (January 1955): 42–45.

41. Donn E. Byrne, *The Attraction Paradigm* (New York: Academic Press, 1971); Ellen Berscheid and Elaine Walster, "Physical Attractiveness," *Advances in Experimental Social Psychology,* vol. 7 (New York: Academic Press, 1974), pp. 158–215.

42. H. Loudon, *Psychology of the Persuader* (Morristown, N.J.: General Learning Press, 1973).

43. Berkowitz, *Social Psychology,* p. 308.

44. Alice H. Eagly and Kathleen Telaak, "Width of the Latitude of Acceptance as a Determinant of Attitude Change," *Journal of Personality and Social Psychology* 23 (September 1972): 388–97.

45. Aronson, Turner, and Carlsmith, "Communicator Credibility," pp. 31–36.

46. Irving L. Janis and Seymour Feshbach, "Effects of Fear Arousing Communications," *Journal of Abnormal and Social Psychology* 48 (January 1958): 78–92.

47. John R. Stuteville, "Psychic Defenses Against High Fear Appeals: A Key Marketing Variable," *Journal of Marketing* 34 (April 1970): 39–45.

48. Howard Leventhal, "Findings and Theory in the Study of Fear Communication," *Advances in Experimental Social Psychology,* vol. 5 (New York: Academic Press, 1970): pp. 120–186; Ronald W. Rogers and C. Ronald Mewborn, "Fear Appeals and Attitude Change: Effects of the Threat's Noxiousness, Probability of Occurance, and the Efficacy of Coping Responses," *Journal of Personality and Social Psychology* 34 (July 1976): 54–61.

49. Michael L. Ray and William L. Wilkie, "Fear: The Potential of an Appeal Neglected by Marketing," *Journal of Marketing* 34 (January 1970): 54–62; Philip Kotler, *Marketing Management: Analysis, Planning and Control,* 3d ed. (Englewood Cliffs, N.J.: Prentice-Hall, 1976).

50. Howard Leventhal, "Fear Communication in the Acceptance of Preventive Health Practices; *Bulletin of the New York Academy of Medicine,* vol. 41 (1965), pp. 144–68.

51. P. Niles, "The Relationship of Susceptibility and Anxiety to Acceptance of Fear-Arousing Communication" (Ph.D. diss., Yale University, 1964); Mina Zemach, "The Effects of Guilt-Arousing Communications on Acceptance of Recommendations" (Ph.D. diss., Yale University, 1966).

52. Niles, "Fear-Arousing Communication."

53. Leonard Berkowitz and Donald R. Cottingham, "The Interest Value and Relevance of Fear Arousing Communications," *Journal of Abnormal and Social Psychology* 60 (January 1960): 37–43; Brian Sternthal and Samuel Craig, "Fear Appeals: Revisited and Revised," *Journal of Consumer Research* 1 (December 1974): 22–34.

54. Kenneth L. Higbee, "Fifteen Years of Fear Arousal: Research on Threat Appeals, 1953–68," *Psychological Bulletin* 72 (December 1969): 426–44.

55. John J. Burnett and Richard L. Oliver, "Fear Appeal Effects in the Field: A Segmentation Approach," *Journal of Marketing Research* 14 (May 1979): 181–90.

56. Ibid., p. 188.

57. Paul Skolnik and Richard Heslin, "Quality Versus Difficulty: Alternative Interpretations of the Relationship Between Self Esteem and Persuasibility," *Journal of Personality* 39 (June 1971): 242–51.

58. William J. McGuire, "The Nature of Attitudes and Attitude Change," in Gardner Lindsey and Elliot Aronsan, eds., *Handbook of Social Psychology,* Vol. 5 (Reading, Mass.: Addison-Wesley, 1969), pp. 87–93.

59. Miriam Zellner, "Self Esteem, Reception, and Influenceability," *Journal of Personality and Social Psychology* 15 (May 1970): 87–93.

60. Paul Skolnik and Richard Heslin, "Approval, Dependence and Reactions to Bad Arguments and Low Credibility Sources," *Journal of Experimental Research in Personality* 5 (September 1971): 199–207.

61. Irving L. Janis, Donald Kaye, and Paul Kirshner, "Facilitating Effects of 'Eating-While-Reading' on Responsiveness to Persuasive Communications," *Journal of Personality and Social Psychology* 1 (1965): 181–86; Mark Galizio and Clyde Hendrick, "Effect of Musical Accompaniment on Attitude: The Guitar as a Prop for Persuasion," *Journal of Applied Social Psychology* 2 (1972): 350–59.

62. John P. Keating and Timothy C. Brock, "Acceptance of Persuasion and the Inhibition of Counter Argumentation under Various Distraction Tasks," *Journal of Experimental Social Psychology* 10 (July 1974): 301–9.

63. Norma D. Feshbach, "Nonconformity to Experimentally Induced Group Norms of High-Status Versus Low-Status Members," *Journal of Personality and Social Psychology* 6 (May 1967): 55–63.

64. Gordon A. Haaland and M. Venkatesan, "Resistance to Persuasive Communications: An Examination of the Distraction Hypothesis," *Journal of Personality and Social Psychology* 9 (June 1968): 167–74; John L. Vohs and Roger L. Garrett, "Resistance to Persuasion: An Integrative Framework," *Public Opinion Quarterly* 32 (Fall 1968): 445–52; Paul Zimbardo et. al., "Modifying the Impact of Persuasive Communications With External Distortion," *Journal of Personality and Social Psychology* 16 (December 1970): 669–80; Dennis T. Regan and Joan B. Cheng, "Distraction and Attitude Change: A Resolution," *Journal of Experimental Social Psychology* 9 (March 1973): 138–47.

65. Jack W. Breham, *Responses to Loss of Freedom: A Theory of Psychological Resistance* (Morristown, N.J.: General Learning Press, 1972).

66. Jonathan L. Freedman and David O. Sears, "Warning, Distraction, and Resistance to Influence," *Journal of Personality and Social Psychology* 1 (September 1965): 262–66.

67. Eunice Cooper and Marie Jahoda, "The Evasion of Propoganda," *Journal of Psychology* 23 (1947): 15–25.

68. Robert P. Abelson and James C. Miller, "Negative Persuasion Via Personal Insult," *Journal of Experimental Social Psychology* 3 (October 1967): 321–33.

69. Breham, *Responses to Loss of Freedom;* Michael B. Mazis, Robert B. Settle, and Dennis C. Leslies, "Elimination of Phosphate Detergents and Psychological Reactance," *Journal of Marketing Research* 10 (November 1973): 390–95.

70. William J. McGuire, "Resistance to Persuasion Confirmed by Active and Passive Prior Refuta-

tions of the Same and Alternative Counterarguments," *Journal of Abnormal and Social Psychology* 63 (September 1961): 326–32.

71. Demetrious Papageorgis and William J. McGuire, "The Generality of Immunity to Persuasion Produced by Pre-Exposure to Weakened Counter-arguments," *Journal of Abnormal and Social Psychology* 61 (June 1961): 475–81; Alan G. Sawyer, "The Effects of Repetition of Refutational and Supportive Advertising Appeals," *Journal of Marketing Research* 16 (February 1973): 23–33; Stuart W. Bither, Ira J. Dolich, and Elaine B. Nell, "The Application of Attitude Immunization Techniques in Marketing," *Journal of Marketing Research* 8 (February 1971): 56–61; George J. Szybillo and Richard Heslin, "Resistance to Persuasion: Innoculation Theory in a Marketing Context," *Journal of Marketing Research* 10 (November 1973): 396–403.

72. William L. Wilkie and Edgar A. Pessemier, "Issues in Marketing's Use of Multi-Attribute Attitude Models," *Journal of Marketing Research* 10 (November 1973): 428–41.

73. Frank M. Bass and W. Wayne Talarzyk, "An Attitude Model for the Study of Brand Preference," *Journal of Marketing Research* (February 1972): 93–96; Albert V. Bruno and Albert R. Wildt, "Toward Understanding Attitude Structure: A Study of the Complementarity of Multi-Attribute Attitude Models," *Journal of Consumer Research* 2 (September 1975): 137–45.

74. George S. Day, "Theories of Attitude Structure and Change," in Scott Ward and Thomas S. Robertson, eds., *Consumer Behavior: Theoretical Sources* (Engelwood Cliffs, N.J.: Prentice-Hall, 1973), pp. 303–53.

75. Martin Fishbein, "An Investigation of the Relationships Between Beliefs about an Object and the Attitude toward that Object," *Human Relations* 16 (August 1963): 233–40.

76. Martin Fishbein, "Attitude, Attitude Change and Behavior: A Theoretical Overview," in Philip Levine, ed., *Attitude Research Bridges the Atlantic* (Chicago: American Marketing Association, 1976), p. 12.

77. Fishbein and Ajzen, *Belief, Attitude, Intention and Behavior,* pp. 301ff.

Chapter 7

1. Edward Zigler and Irvin L. Child, "Socialization," in G. Lindsay and Elliot Aronson, eds., *The Individual in a Social Context,* vol. 2 of *The Handbook of Social Psychology,* 2d ed. (Reading, Mass.: Addison-Wesley, 1969), p. 474.

2. Orville G. Brim and Stanton Wheller, *Socialization After Childhood: Two Essays* (New York: John Wiley and Sons, 1966).

3. Scott Ward, "Consumer Socialization," *Journal of Consumer Research* 1 (September 1974): 2.

4. Robert D. Hess and Judith V. Torney, *The Development of Political Attitudes in Children* (Chicago: Aldine, 1967).

5. John R. P. French and Bertram Raven, "The Bases of Social Power," in Dorwin Cartwright, ed., *Studies in Social Power* (Ann Arbor: Institute for Social Research, 1959), pp. 150–67.

6. Ellen Graham, "Tupperware Parties Create a New Breed of Super Saleswomen," *Wall Street Journal,* 21 May 1971.

7. Tamotsu Shibutani, *Society and Personality* (Englewood Cliffs, N.J.: Prentice-Hall, 1961), p. 46.

8. Lawrence S. Wrightsman, *Social Psychology* (Belmont, Calif.: Brooks/Cole, 1977), p. 17.

9. Tamotsu Shibutani, "Reference Groups as Perspectives," *American Journal of Sociology* 60 (May 1955): 562–69.

10. C. Whan Park and V. Parker Lessig, "Students and Housewives: Differences in Susceptibility to Reference Group Influence," *Journal of Consumer Research* 4 (September 1977): 102–10.

11. Robin M. Williams, Jr., *American Society: A Sociological Interpretation,* 3d ed. (New York: Alfred A. Knopf, 1970), p. 442.

12. Ibid., p. 415.

13. Gerald Zaltman, *Marketing: Contributions from the Behavioral Sciences* (New York: Harcourt, Brace and World, 1965), p. 8.

14. Riele Tack, "Numbers Don't Tell Minority Buying Power," *Advertising Age,* 16 April 1979, p. S22

15. Eugene Jackson, "Black America: Challenging New Frontier for Marketers," *Advertising Age,* 16 April 1979, p. S23.

16. "America's Rising Black Midde Class," *Time,* 17 June 1974, pp. 19–20.

17. Jackson, "Black America," p. S23.

18. D. Parke Gibson, "Black Middle Class Emerges as Dominant Consumer Force," *Advertising Age,* 16 April 1979, p. S24.

19. McKinley Dillingham, "To Hike Profit Margins, Learn to Tap Black Market," *Advertising Age,* 16 April 1979, p. S29.

20. Leon Morse, "Black Radio Market Study," *Television/Radio Age,* 28 February 1977, pp. A–1—A–31.

21. Dillingham, "Profit Margins," p. S29.

22. Ibid.

23. Robert L. Brown, "Social Distance Perception as a Function of Mexican-American and other Ethnic Identity," *Sociology and Social Research* 57 (April 1973): 273–87.

24. John H. Burma, ed., *Mexican Americans in the United States: A Reader* (Cambridge, Mass.: Schenkman, 1970), pp. xvi–xvii.

25. The Newest Americans: A Second 'Spanish Invasion,'" *U.S. News & World Report,* 8 July 1974, p. 34.

26. Richard A. Jacobs, "Jewish Media Provide What Others Don't," *Advertising Age,* 16 April 1979, p. S28.

27. Ed Meyer, "It's a Tough Challenge, but the Teen Market Has Its Rewards," *Advertising Age,* 19 February 1979, pp. 62–63.

28. Ibid.

29. Ben J. Wattenberg, "The Forming Families: The Spark in the Tinder, 1975–1985," *1974 Combined Proceedings of the American Marketing Association* (Chicago, 1975).

30. Pat Sloon, "Market for Elderly is Often Neglected," *Advertising Age,* 2 April 1979, pp. S14–S15.

31. Don't Neglect Women over 50, DDB Advises," *Advertising Age,* 26 February 1979, p. 47.

32. Williams, *American Society,* p. 114.

33. Ibid., p. 115.

34. Richard P. Coleman, "The Significance of Social Stratification in Selling," in Martin L. Bell, ed., *Marketing: A Maturing Discipline* (Chicago: American Marketing Association, 1960), pp. 171–84.

35. W. Lloyd Warner, Marchia Meeker, and Kenneth Eels, *Social Class in America: A Manual of Procedure for the Measurement of Social Status* (Chicago: Science Research Associates, 1949), p. 124.

36. Nan Lin and Daniel Yauger, "The Process of Occupational Status Achievement: A Preliminary Cross-National Comparison," *American Journal of Sociology* 81 (November 1975): 543–61.

37. This figure and others used in the section are drawn from Coleman, "Social Stratification," pp. 171–84; James M. Carman, *The Application of Social Class in Market Segmentation* (Berkeley: Institute of Business and Economic Research, University of California Graduate School of Business, 1965). The major shift that seems to be taking place is that the lower-lower class is getting smaller while the upper-lower class gets larger; the other classes tend to remain proportionately constant over time.

38. Values for the various classes are drawn from Coleman, "Social Stratification," pp. 171–84.

Chapter 8

1. Carol R. Ember and Melvin Ember, *Anthropology,* 2d ed. (Englewood Cliffs, N.J.: Prentice-Hall, 1977), p. 295.

2. Leon G. Schiffman and Leslie Lazar Kanuk, *Consumer Behavior* (Englewood Cliffs, N.J.: Prentice-Hall, 1978), p. 238.

3. Hazel Kyrk, *The Family in the American Economy* (Chicago: University of Chicago Press, 1953).

4. Morris Zelditch, Jr., "Role Differentiation in the Nuclear Family: A Comparative Study," in Talcott Parsons et. al., eds., *Family, Socialization, and Interaction Process,* (New York: Free Press, 1955), pp. 347–48.

5. Elizabeth A. Wolgast, "Do Husbands or Wives Make the Purchasing Decisions?" *Journal of Marketing* 23 (October 1958): 151–58.

6. U.S., Bureau of Labor Statistics, BLS 78–357, *Labor Force Development,* First Quarter 1978.

7. U.S., Bureau of Labor Statistics, Special Labor Force Report No. 211, "Multiple Job Holders in May 1977."

8. Scott Ward and Daniel Workman, "Children's Purchase Influence Attempts and Parental Yielding," *Journal of Marketing Research* 9 (August 1972): 315–19.

9. See, for example, John B. Lansing and Leslie Kish, "Family Life Cycle as an Independent Variable," *American Sociological Review* 22 (October 1957): 512–19; Robert O. Blood, Jr., and Donald M. Wolf, *Husbands and Wives* (Glencoe, Ill.: Free Press, 1960); William D. Wells and George Gubar, "Life Cycle Concept in Marketing Research," *Journal of Marketing Research* 3 (November 1966): 355–363; C. Milton Coughenour, "Functional Aspects of Food Consumption Activity and Family Life Cycle Stages," *Journal of Marriage and the Family* 34 (November 1972): 656–64.

10. Adapted from Wells and Gubar, "Life Cycle Concept," pp. 355–63; George Katona, *The Powerful Consumer* (New York: McGraw-Hill, 1960); George Katona, Charles A. Lininger, and Eva Mueller, *1963 Survey of Consumer Finances,* University of Michigan Survey Research Center, Monograph No. 34 (Ann Arbor, 1964); John B. Lansing and James N. Morgan, "Consumer Finances Over the Life Cycle," in Lincoln H. Clark, ed., *Consumer Behavior,* vol. 2 (New York: New York University Press, 1955).

11. Elis P. Cox III, "Family Purchase Decision Making and the Process of Adjustment," *Journal of Marketing Research* 12 (May 1975): 189–95.

12. Gary M. Munsinger, Jean E. Weber, and Richard W. Hansen, "Joint Home Purchasing Decisions by Husbands and Wives," *Journal of Consumer Research* 1 (March 1975): 60–66.

13. Harry L. Davis and Benny P. Rigaux, "Perception of Marital Roles in Decision Processes," *Journal of Consumer Research* 1 (June 1974): 51–62.

14. Robert Ferber and Lucy Chao Lee, "Husband-Wife Influence in Family Purchasing Behavior," *Journal of Consumer Research* 1 (June 1974): 4–50.

15. Ibid.

16. Harry L. Davis, "Decision Making Within the Household," *Journal of Consumer Research* 2 (March 1976): 241–60.

17. Cox, "Family Purchase," p. 189.

18. Ferber and Lee, "Husband-Wife Influence," pp. 46–47.

19. Davis, "Decision Making," pp. 253–54.

20. Joan Aldous, "A Framework for the Analysis of Family Problem Solving," in Joan Aldous et. al., eds., *Family Problem Solving: A Symposium on Theoretical Methodological, and Substantive Concerns,* (Hinsdale, Ill.: Dryden Press, 1971), pp. 265–81.

21. These determinants are suggested by Jagdish N. Sheth, "A Theory of Buying Decisions," in Jagdish N. Sheth, *Models of Buyer Behavior* (New York: Harper and Row, 1974), pp. 17–33.

22. Pierre Martineau, "Social Classes and Shopping Behavior," *Journal of Marketing* 23 (October 1958): 121–30.

23. Mirra Komarovsky, "Class Differences in Family Decision Making and Expenditures," in Nelson N. Foote, ed., *Household Decision Making* (New York: New York University Press, 1961), pp. 255–65.

24. Paul Converse and Merle Crawford, "Buying Habits in the Home," *Advertising Age,* February 1950, pp. 46–47, 144–50; Martin Zober, *Marketing Management* (New York: John Wiley and Sons, 1964).

25. Ferber and Lee, "Husband-Wife Influence," pp. 47–49.

26. Davis, "Decision Making," p. 250.

27. Cox, "Family Purchase," p. 194.

28. Ibid., p. 190.

29. Ferber and Lee, "Husband-Wife Influence," p. 45.

30. Reuben Hill, "Decision Making and the Family Life Cycle," in Ethel Shanas and Gordon F. Streib, eds., *Social Structure and the Family: Generational Relations* (Englewood Cliffs, N.J.: Prentice-Hall, 1965), pp. 113–39.

31. Cox, "Family Purchase," p. 190.

32. Morton Deutch and Harold B. Gerald, "A Study of Normative and Informational Influence Upon Individual Judgment," *Journal of Abnormal and Social Psychology* 51, no. 3 (November 1955): 629–36; Leon Festinger, "Informal Social Communication," *Psychological Review* 57 (September 1950): 271–82; Harold H. Kelly, "The Two Functions of Reference Groups," in Guy E. Swanson, Theodore M. Newcomb, and Eugene L. Hartley, eds., *Readings in Social Psychology* (New York: Holt, 1952), pp. 410–40; John W. Thibaut and Lloyd H. Strickland, "Psychological Set and Social Conformity," *Journal of Personality* 20 (December 1956): 115–29.

33. Elizabeth Bott, "Urban Families: Conjugal Roles and Social Networks," *Human Relations* 8, no. 4 (November 1955): 345–84; Leon Festinger, "Informal Social Communication," *Psychological Review* 57 (September 1950): 271–82.

34. Wroe Alderson, *Marketing Behavior and Executive Action: A Functionalist Approach to Marketing Theory* (Homewood, Ill.: Richard D. Irwin, 1957), p. 179.

35. Wendell Bell, "Social Choice, Life Styles, and Suburban Residence," in William Dobriner, ed., *The Suburban Community* (New York: Putnam, 1958), pp. 276–83.

36. Irving S. White, "The Perception of Value in Products," in Joseph N. Newman, ed., *On Knowing the Consumer* (New York: John Wiley and Sons, 1966), pp. 90–106.

37. John H. Scanzoni, "The Conjugal Family and Consumption Behavior," McCahan Foundation Occasional Paper Series, no. 1 (Bryn Mawr, Penn., 1966).

38. Munsinger, Weber, and Hansen, "Joint Decisions," p. 62.

39. Davis and Rigaux, "Perceptions of Roles," pp. 51–62; Davis, "Decision Making," p. 246.

40. Sheth, "Buying Decisions," p. 80.

41. "Working Women: Why Do They Do What They Do?" *Media/Scope* 12 (July-December 1968): 9–28.

42. Sheth, "Buying Decisions," p. 80.

43. Nowland and Company, *Family Participation and Influence in Shopping and Brand Selection: Phase I,* (Report prepared for *Life* magazine, 1964); idem, *Phase II* (1965).

44. Robert Wilkes, "Husband-Wife Influence in Purchase Decisions—A Confirmation and Extension," *Journal of Marketing Research* 12 (May 1975): 224–27.

45. Davis and Rigaux, "Perceptions of Roles," p. 59.

46. Davis, "Decision Making," p. 248.

47. David J. Curry and Michael B. Menasco, "Some Effects of Differing Information Processing Strategies on Husband-Wife Joint Decisions," *Jour-*

nal of Consumer Research 6 (September 1979): 192–203.

48.   Davis, "Decision Making," p. 252. The discussion of family decision-making styles follows Davis, "Decision Making," pp. 254–56.

49.   Robert O. Blood, Jr., "Resolving Family Conflicts," Journal of Conflict 4 (June 1960): 209–19.

50.   Rena Bartos, "The Moving Target: The Impact of Women's Employment on Consumer Behavior," Journal of Marketing 41 (July 1977): 31–37.

51.   Fred D. Reynolds, Melvin R. Crask, and William D. Wells, "The Modern Feminine Life Style,"

Journal of Marketing 41 (July 1977): 38–45.

52.   John S. Coulson, "How Much has the Consumer Changed?" (paper presented at the meeting of the American Association for Public Opinion Research, 1974); Needham, Harper and Steers Advertising Agency, as quoted in Reynolds, Crask, and Wells, "Feminine Life Style," p. 38.

53.   Catherine Arnott and Vern L. Bengtson, " 'Only a Homemaker': Distributive Justice and Role Choice Among Married Women," Sociology and Social Research 54 (July 1970): 495–507.

54.   Reynolds, Crask, and Wells, "Feminine Life Style," p. 39.

Chapter 9

1.   Although many other behavior journals regularly publish articles dealing specifically with consumer behavior, the major forums for research are: Journal of Consumer Research, Journal of Marketing Research, Journal of Marketing, Journal of Applied Psychology, Journal of Advertising Research, and Journal of Consumer Affairs.

        Jacob Jacoby, "Consumer Research: Telling It Like It Is," Advances in Consumer Research, vol. 3 (Cincinnati: Association for Consumer Research, 1976), pp. 1–11.

3.   John Cipkala, "Research Methods in Consumer Behavior," in Melanie Wallendorf and Gerald Zaltman, eds., Readings in Consumer Behavior: Individuals, Groups and Organizations (New York: John Wiley and Sons, 1979), pp. 423–35.

4.   Claire Sellitz et. al., Research Methods in Social Relations (New York: Holt, Rinehart, and Winston, 1959), p. 200.

5.   Donald S. Tull and Del I. Hawkins, Marketing Research: Meaning, Measurement, and Method (New York: Macmillan, 1976), p. 303.

6.   Ibid., pp. 435–36.

7.   Dik Warren Twedt, ed., 1973 Survey of Marketing Research (Chicago: American Marketing Association, 1973), p. 41.

8.   This discussion is drawn from Mason Haire, "Projective Techniques in Marketing Research," Journal of Marketing 14 (April 1950): 649–56.

9.   Paul E. Green and Donald S. Tull, Research for Marketing Decisions, 3d ed. (Englewood Cliffs, N.J.: Prentice-Hall, 1975), p. 144.

10.   Ibid., p. 145.

11.   Ibid.

12.   Roger Rickles, "Ernest Dichter Thrives Selling Firms Research on 'Hidden' Emotions," Wall Street Journal, 20 November 1972.

13.   Olaf Helmer, Social Technology (New York: Basic Books, 1966), p. 122.

14.   Marvin J. Cetron, Technological Forecasting: A Practical Approach (New York: Gordon and Breach, 1969), p. 345.

15.   Norman R. F. Maier, Problem Solving and Creativity in Individuals and Groups (Belmont, Calif.: Brooks/Cole, 1970); Thomas J. Bouchard, "Personality, Problem Solving Procedure and Performance in Small Groups," Journal of Applied Psychology Monograph 53 (February 1969): 1–29; Donald W. Taylor, Paul C. Berry, and Clifford H. Block, "Does Group Participation When Using Brainstorming Facilitate or Inhibit Creative Thinking?" Administrative Science Quarterly 3 (June 1958): 23–47; Omar K. More and Scarvia B. Anderson, "Search Behavior in Individual and Group Problem Solving," American Sociological Review 19 (December 1954): 702–14.

16.   Fritz Zwicky, Discovery, Invention, Research Through the Morphological Approach (New York, Macmillan, 1969).

17.   Knut Holt, "Need Assessment in Product Innovation," Research Management, July 1976, pp. 24–28.

18.   Edward M. Tauber, "HIT: Heuristic Ideation Technique—A Systematic Procedure for New Product Search," Journal of Marketing 36 (January 1972): 58–61.

19.   Allen Newell, J. C. Shaw, and Herbert A. Simon, "The Process of Creative Thinking," in Howard E. Gruber, Glenn Terrell, and Michael Werthlimer, eds., Contemporary Approaches to Creative Thinking (New York: Atherton Press, 1962), p. 78; Alfred Kuehn, "Complex Interactive Models," in Ronald E. Frank, Alfred Kuehn, and William F. Massy, eds., Quantitative Techniques in Marketing Analysis (Homewood, Ill.: Richard D. Irwin, 1962), p. 117.

20.   Tauber, "HIT," p. 60.

21.   George M. Prince, The Practice of Creativity (New York: Harper and Row, 1970), p. 45.

22. Tauber, "Discovering New Product Opportunities with Problem Inventory Analysis," *Journal of Marketing* 39 (January 1975): 67–70.

23. Tauber, "Discovering New Product Opportunities," p. 70.

24. James H. Meyers, "Benefit Structure Analysis: A New Tool of Product Planning," *Journal of Marketing* 40 (October 1976): 23–32.

25. Ibid.

26. Holt, "Need Assessment," pp. 24–28. See also Thomas Cannon and Ronald W. Hasty, "Managing for New Products—The Additional Dimension of Human Factors Research," in Kenneth L. Bernhardt, ed., *Marketing 1776–1976 and Beyond* (Chicago: American Marketing Association, 1976), pp. 488–92.

27. William J. Stokes, "Researching the New Product," *Industrial Marketing* (June 1948): 33, 135ff.

28. Ibid.

29. Robert D. Hisrich and Michael P. Peters, *Marketing a New Product: Its Planning, Development and Control* (Menlo Park, Calif.: Benjamin/Cummings, 1978), pp. 87–88.

30. Edward M. Tauber, "What Is Measured by Concept Testing?" *Journal of Advertising Research* 12 (December 1972): 35–37.

31. Hisrich and Peters, *Marketing a New Product,* pp. 88–90.

32. Edward M. Tauber, "Why Concept and Product Tests Fail to Predict New Product Results," *Journal of Marketing* 39 (October 1975): 69–73; idem, "Reduce New Product Failures: Measure Needs as Well as Purchase Interest," *Journal of Marketing* 37 (July 1973): 61–64; Russell I. Haley and Ronald Gatley, "Trouble with Concept Testing," *Journal of Marketing Research* 8 (May 1971): 230–32.

33. Tauber, "Why Concept and Product Tests Fail," p. 70.

34. Ibid., p. 71.

35. Tauber, "Reduce New Product Failures," p. 62.

36. Stuart W. Cook and Claire Sellitz, "A Multiple Indicator Approach to Attitude Measurement," *Psychological Bulletin* 62 (July 1964): 36–55.

37. See Fred N. Kerlinger, *Foundations of Behavioral Research* (New York: Holt, Rinehart, and Winston, 1964), pp. 581–99.

38. For a detailed treatment of scalogram analysis, see Allen L. Edwards, *Techniques of Attitude Scale Construction* (New York: Appleton-Century-Crofts, 1957), pp. 172–200; Gene F. Summers, *Attitude Measurement* (Chicago: Rand McNally, 1970), pp. 174–213.

39. Adapted from Tull and Hawkins, *Marketing Research,* pp. 347–48; Green and Tull, *Research for Marketing Decisions,* p. 196; Philip G. Zimbardo, Ebbe B. Ebbesen, and Christina Maslach, *Influencing Attitudes and Changing Behavior,* 2d ed. (Reading, Mass.: Addison-Wesley, 1977), pp. 214–15.

40. Charles E. Osgood, George J. Suci, and Percy H. Tannenbaum, *The Measurement of Meaning* (Urbana: University of Illinois Press, 1957).

41. Del I. Hawkins, Gerald Albaum, and Roger Best, "Stapel Scale or Semantic Differential in Marketing Research," *Journal of Marketing Research* 11 (August 1974): 318–22.

42. Michael J. Etzel and Terrell G. Williams, "The Comparability of Three Forms of the Stapel Scale in a Marketing Setting" (Unpublished paper, Utah State University, Logan, 1977).

43. Based on Tull and Hawkins, *Marketing Research,* pp. 355–58.

44. Ronald G. Nelson and David Schwartz, "Voice Pitch Analysis," *Journal of Advertising Research* 19 (October 1979): 55–59.

45. William S. Gelbfarb, "Ocular Measurements in Advertising Research," Young and Rubicam Advertising Agency, New York, 1967.

46. William D. Wells, "Psychographics: A Critical Review," *Journal of Marketing Research* 12 (May 1975): 196–213.

47. Ibid., p. 196.

48. Fred D. Reynolds and William R. Darden, "An Operational Construction on Life Style," in M. Venkatesan, ed., *Proceedings of the Third Annual Conference of the Association for Consumer Research* (Chicago, 1972), p. 482.

49. Joseph Pernica, "Psychographics: What Can Go Wrong," *Proceedings of the American Marketing Association* (Chicago, 1974), pp. 45–50.

Chapter 10

1. Peter Drucker, *Management* (New York: Harper and Row, 1974), p. 84.

2. Joseph W. Newman, "New Insights, New Progress for Marketing," *Harvard Business Review,* 35 (November-December 1957): 95–102.

3. Everett M. Rogers and J. David Stanfield, "Adoption and Diffusion of New Products: Emerging Generalizations and Hypotheses," in Frank M. Bass, Charles W. King, and Edgar A. Pessemier, eds., *Application of the Sciences in Marketing Management* (New York: John Wiley and Sons, 1968), pp. 227–50.

4. Robert J. Kegerries, James F. Engel, and Roger D. Blackwell, "Innovativeness and Diffusion: A

Marketing View of the Characteristics of Earliest Adopters," in David T. Kollat, Roger D. Blackwell, and James F. Engel, eds., *Research in Consumer Behavior* (New York: Holt, Rinehart, and Winston, 1970), pp. 671–701.

5.   Douglas K. Hawes, "An Inspection of Innovation" (Unpublished paper submitted for a graduate course in consumer behavior, Ohio State University, Columbus, 1968), cited in James F. Engel, Roger D. Blackwell and David T. Kollat, *Consumer Behavior,* 3d ed. (New York: Holt, Rinehart, and Winston, 1978), p. 304.

6.   This is similar to the definition advanced in Everett Rogers, *Diffusion of Innovations* (Glencoe, Ill.: Free Press, 1971).

7.   Robert G. Hammerstone, "How the Patent System Mousetraps Inventors," *Fortune,* May 1973, pp. 262–74.

8.   Leon G. Schiffman and Leslie Lazar Kanuk, *Consumer Behavior* (Englewood Cliffs, N.J.: Prentice-Hall, 1978), p. 403.

9.   Thomas S. Robertson, "The Process of Innovation and the Diffusion of Innovation," *Journal of Marketing* 31 (January 1967): 15.

10.   *Business Week,* 22 April 1967, p. 120.

11.   James H. Donnelly, Jr. and Michael J. Etzel, "Degrees of Product Newness and Early Trial," *Journal of Marketing Research* 19 (August 1973): 295–300.

12.   Roman R. Andrus, John Knutsen, and Kenneth Uhl, "The Shopping Behavior of Innovators," *University of Washington Business Review,* Summer 1971, pp. 71–75.

13.   Rogers and Stanfield, "New Products," pp. 227–50.

14.   William E. Bell, "Consumer Innovators: A Unique Market for Newness," in Stephen A. Greyser, ed., *Toward Scientific Marketing* (Chicago: American Marketing Association, 1963), pp. 85–95; Rogers and Stanfield, "New Products," pp. 227–50; James S. Coleman, Elihu Katz, and Herbert Menzel, *Medical Innovation: A Diffusion Study* (Indianapolis: Bobbs-Merrill, 1966); Richard P. Coleman, "The Significance of Social Stratification in Selling," in Martin L. Bell, ed., *Marketing: A Maturing Discipline* (Chicago: American Marketing Association, 1960), pp. 171–84.

15.   Kegerries, Engel, and Blackwell, "Innovativeness and Diffusion," p. 676.

16.   Thomas S. Robertson, "Purchase Sequence Responses: Innovators versus Non-Innovators," *Journal of Advertising Research* 8 (March 1968): 47–52.

17.   Johan Arndt, "Role of Product-related Conversations in the Diffusion of a New Product," *Journal of Marketing Research* 4 (August 1967); 291–95.

18.   John J. Painter and Max L. Pinegar, "Post-High Teens and Fashion Innovation," *Journal of* *Marketing Research* 8 (August 1971): 368–69; Charles W. King, "Communicating with the Innovator in the Fashion Adoption Process," in Peter D. Bennett, ed., *Marketing and Economic Development* (Chicago: American Marketing Association, 1965), p. 428.

19.   Louis E. Boone, "The Search for the Consumer Innovator," *Journal of Business* 43 (April 1970): 138.

20.   Steven A. Baumgarten, "The Innovative Communicator in the Diffusion Process," *Journal of Marketing Research* 12 (February 1975): 12–18.

21.   Arndt, "Product-related Conversations," pp. 291–95.

22.   Saxon Graham, "Class and Conservatism in the Adoption of Innovations," *Human Relations* 9 (February 1956): 91–100.

23.   Joe M. Bohlen et al., "Adopters of New Farm Ideas: Characteristics and Communications Behavior," North Central Regional Extension Publication no. 13 (East Lansing: Michigan Cooperative Extension Service, 1961).

24.   Lyman E. Ostlund, "Perceived Innovation Attributes as Predictors of Innovativeness," *Journal of Consumer Research* 1 (September 1974): 23–29.

25.   Bell, "Consumer Innovators," pp. 85–95; Thomas S. Robertson, *Innovation and the Consumer* (New York: Holt, Rinehart, and Winston, 1971).

26.   Thomas S. Robertson, "Consumer Innovators: The Key to New Product Success," *California Management Reveiw* 10, no. 2 (Winter 1967): 23–30.

27.   Kegerries, Engel, and Blackwell, "Innovativeness and Diffusion," p. 679.

28.   Thomas S. Robertson and James N. Kennedy, "Prediction of Consumer Innovators: Application of Multiple Discriminate Analysis," *Journal of Marketing Research* 5 (February 1968): 64–69; Arndt, "Product-related Conversations," p. 294; Leon G. Schiffman, "Perceived Risk in New Product Trial by Elderly Consumers," *Journal of Marketing Research* 9 (February 1972): 106–8; Jagdish N. Sheth, "Perceived Risk and Diffusion of Innovations," in Johan Arndt, ed., *Insights into Consumer Behavior* (Boston: Allyn and Bacon, 1968), pp. 173–88.

29.   For example, see Robertson and Kennedy, "Prediction of Consumer Innovators," pp. 64–69; Robertson, *Innovation and the Consumer,* p. 29; John J. Painter and Kent L. Granzin, "Profiling the Male Fashion Innovator—Another Step," *Advances in Consumer Research,* vol. 3 (Cincinnati: Association for Consumer Research, 1976), p. 43; Boone, "Search for the Consumer Innovator," p. 138.

30.   William Lazer, "Life Style Concepts and Marketing," in Greyser, ed., *Toward Scientific Marketing,* p. 130.

31.   Rogers and Stanfield, "New Products," pp. 227–50.

32. William R. Darden and Fred D. Reynolds, "Backward Profiling of Male Innovators," *Journal of Marketing Research* 11 (February 1974): 79–85.

33. John O. Summers, "Generalized Change Agents and Innovativeness," *Journal of Marketing Research* 8 (August 1971): 313–16; Thomas S. Robertson and James H. Myers, "Personality Correlates of Opinion Leadership and Innovative Buying Behavior," *Journal of Marketing Research* 6 (May 1969): 164–68.

34. Rogers, *Diffusion of Innovations,* pp. 148–207.

35. Rogers and Stanfield, "New Products," pp. 227–50.

36. Everett Rogers, *Communication Strategies for Family Planning* (New York: Free Press, 1973).

37. Robert T. Green, Eric Langeard, and Alice C. Favell, "Innovation in the Service Sector: Some Empirical Findings," *Journal of Marketing Research* 11 (August 1974): 323–26.

38. John O. Summers, "Media Exposure Patterns of Consumer Innovators," *Journal of Marketing* 36 (January 1972): 43–49; King, "Communicating with the Innovator," p. 428; Painter and Granzin, "Male Fashion Innovator," p. 43; Painter and Pinegar, "Teens and Fashion Innovation," p. 369.

39. Summers, "Media Exposure Patterns," pp. 43–49; James F. Engel, Robert J. Kegerries, and Roger D. Blackwell, "Word of Mouth Communication by the Innovator," *Journal of Marketing* 33 (July 1969): 15–19.

40. Baumgarten, "Innovative Communicator," pp. 12–18.

41. Ibid.; Darden and Reynolds, "Profiling of Male Innovators," pp. 79–85.

42. Summers, "Media Exposure Patterns," p. 47.

43. Darden and Reynolds, "Profiling of Male Innovators," pp. 79–85; Summers, "Media Exposure Patterns," p. 47.

44. Masao Nakanishi, "Advertising and Promotion Effects on Consumer Response to New Products," *Journal of Marketing Research* 10 (August 1973): 242–49; George H. Haines, Jr., "A Study of Why People Purchase New Products," in Raymond M. Haas, ed., *Science, Technology and Marketing* (Chicago: American Marketing Association, 1966), pp. 665–84.

45. Ronald P. Willett and Allan L. Pennington, "Customer and Salesman: The Anatomy of Choice and Influence in a Retail Setting," in Haas, ed., *Science, Technology and Marketing,* pp. 665–84.

46. Engel, Kegerries, and Blackwell, "Word of Mouth Communication," pp. 15–19.

47. See, for example, Donald T. Popielarz, "An Exploration of Perceived Risk and Willingness to Try New Products," *Journal of Marketing Research* 4 (November 1967): 368–72; Johan Arndt, "Perceived Risk, Sociometric Integration, and Word of Mouth

in the Adoption of a New Food Product," in Donald F. Cox, ed., *Risk Taking and Information Handling in Consumer Behavior* (Boston: Division of Research, Graduate School of Business Administration, Harvard University, 1967), pp. 289–316.

48. James Coleman, Herbert Menzel, and Elihu Katz, "Social Processes in Physicians' Adoption of a New Drug," *Journal of Chronic Diseases* 9 (January 1959): pp. 1–19.

49. See, for example, Engel, Kegerries and Blackwell, "Word of Mouth Communication," pp. 15–19; Carol A. Kohn Berning and Jacob Jacoby, "Patterns of Information Acquisition in New Product Purchases," *Journal of Consumer Research* 1 (September 1974): 18–22; Edgar A. Pessemier, Philip C. Burger, and Douglas J. Tigert, "Can New Product Buyers Be Identified?" *Journal of Marketing Research* 4 (November 1967): 349–54.

50. Engel, Kegerries, and Blackwell, "Word of Mouth Communication," pp. 15–19.

51. Summers, "Media Exposure Patterns," p. 47.

52. Pessemier, Burger, and Tigert, "Can Buyers Be Identified?" pp. 349–54.

53. Engel, Kegerries, and Blackwell, "Word of Mouth Communication," pp. 15–19.

54. Johan Arndt, "Product-related Conversations, pp. 291–95.

55. Darden and Reynolds, "Profiling of Male Innovators," pp. 79–85.

56. Summers, "Media Exposures Patterns," p. 44.

57. Laurence P. Feldman and Gary M. Armstrong, "Identifying Buyers of a Major Automotive Innovation," *Journal of Marketing* 39 (January 1975): 33–47.

58. Everett Rogers and F. Floyd Shoemaker, *Communication of Innovations* (New York: Free Press, 1971), pp. 137–57; Lyman E. Ostlund, "Identifying Early Buyers," *Journal of Advertising Research* 12 (April 1972): 25–30; Lyman E. Ostlund, "Predictors of Innovative Behavior," in John A. Howard and Lyman E. Ostlund, ed., *Buyer Behavior* (New York: Alfred A. Knopf, 1973); Lyman E. Ostlund, "Perceived Innovation Attributes as Predictors of Innovativeness," *Journal of Consumer Research* 1 (September 1974): 23–29.

59. Engel, Blackwell, and Kollat, *Consumer Behavior,* p. 315.

60. Thomas S. Robertson and James H. Myers, "Personality Correlates of Opinion Leadership and Innovative Buying Behavior," *Journal of Marketing Research* 6 (May 1969): 164–68.

61. Milton Rokeach, *The Open and Closed Mind* (New York: Free Press, 1962).

62. Brian Blake, Robert Perloff, and Richard Heslin, "Dogmatism and Acceptance of New Products," *Journal of Marketing Research* 7 (November 1970): 483–86.

63. Jacob Jacoby, "Personality and Innovation Proneness," *Journal of Marketing Research* 8 (May 1971): 244–47; Kenneth A. Coney, "Dogmatism and Innovativeness: A Replication," *Journal of Marketing Research* 9 (November 1972): 453–55; J. M. McClurg and I. R. Andrews, "A Consumer Profile Analysis of the Self-service Gasoline Customers," *Journal of Applied Psychology* 59, no. 1 (February 1974): 119–21; Bernard Mikol, "The Enjoyment of New Musical Systems," in Rokeach, *Open and Closed Mind;* Robert Frumken, "Sex, Familiarity and Dogmatism as Factors in Painting Preference," *Perceptual and Motor Skills* 17 (August 1963): 12–18.

64. Blake, Perloff, and Heslin, "Dogmatism and Acceptance," pp. 483–86.

65. Jacob Jacoby, "Multiple-Indicant Approach for Studying New Product Adopters," *Journal of Applied Psychology* 55, no. 4 (August 1971): 384–88.

66. J. F. Jamias and V. C. Trodahl, "Dogmatism, Tradition and General Innovativeness" Unpublished manuscript cited in Milton Rokeach, *Beliefs, Attitudes and Value* (San Francisco: Jossey-Bass, 1968), p. 145.

67. Thomas S. Robertson, "The Effect of the Informal Group Upon Member Innovative Behavior," in Robert L. King, ed., *Marketing and the Science of Planning* (Chicago: American Marketing Association, 1968); Schiffman, "Perceived Risk," p. 107; Robertson, "Consumer Innovators," p. 28; Pessemier, Burger, and Tigert, "Can Buyers Be Identified?" p. 352; James H. Donnelly, Jr., and John M. Ivancevich, "A Methodology for Identifying Innovator Characteristics of New Brand Purchasers," *Journal of Marketing Research* 11 (August 1974): 331–34; Popielarz, "Willingness to Try New Products," pp. 368–72; Donnelly and Etzel, "Degrees of Product Newness," pp. 295–300; James H. Donnelly, Jr., Michael J. Etzel, and Scott Roeth, "The Relationship Between Consumers' Category Width and Trial of New Products," *Journal of Applied Psychology* 57, no. 3 (May 1973): 335–38; Baumgarten, "Innovative Communicator," p. 17.

68. Shiffman and Kanuk, *Consumer Behavior,* p. 420.

69. Johan Arndt, "Profiling Consumer Innovators," in Arndt, ed., *Insights into Consumer Behavior,* pp. 173–88.

70. Robertson and Myers, "Personality Correlates," pp. 164–68.

71. Kegerries, Engel, and Blackwell, "Innovativeness and Diffusion," pp. 671–701.

72. Robertson, "Innovative Behavior," p. 111.

73. Rogers and Stanfield, "New Products," pp. 227–50.

74. Ibid.

75. Ibid.

76. David F. Midgley and Graham R. Dowling, "Innovativeness: The Concept and Its Measurement," *Journal of Consumer Research* 4 (March 1978): 229–42.

77. Thomas S. Robertson, "A Critical Examination of 'Adoption Process' Models of Consumer Behavior," in Jagdish N. Sheth, ed., *Models of Buyer Behavior* (New York: Harper and Row, 1974), pp. 271–95.

78. Ibid., p. 272.

79. Masao Nakanishi, "A Model of Market Reactions to New Products," (Ph.D. diss., Graduate School of Business Administration, University of California, Los Angeles, 1968).

80. Robertson, "A Critical Examination," pp. 272–75.

81. Robert J. Lavidge and Gary A. Steiner, "A Model for Predictive Measurements of Advertising Effectiveness," *Journal of Marketing* 25 (October 1961): 59–62; Kristian S. Palda, "The Hypothesis of a Hierarchy of Effects: A Partial Evalution," *Journal of Marketing Research* 5 (May 1968): 131–45.

82. Robertson, "A Critical Examination," p. 274.

83. Harry Tosdal, *Principles of Personal Selling* (Chicago: Shaw, 1925), p. 61.

84. Robertson, "A Critical Examination," pp. 274–75.

85. Rogers and Shoemaker, *Communication of Innovations,* p. 103

86. Francesco M. Nicosia, *Consumer Decision Processes: Marketing and Advertising Implications* (Englewood Cliffs, N.J.: Prentice-Hall, 1969); Alan R. Andreasen, "Attitudes and Consumer Behavior: A Decision Model," in Lee E. Preston, ed., *New Research in Marketing* (Berkeley: Institute of Business and Economic Research, University of California, 1965), pp. 1–16.

87. Robertson, "A Critical Examination," pp. 281–82.

88. This section follows Robertson, "A Critical Examination," pp. 288–92.

89. Robert D. Hisrich and Michael P. Peters, *Marketing a New Product: Its Planning, Development and Control* (Menlo Park, Calif.: Benjamin/ Cummings, 1978), p. 179.

90. Rogers and Shoemaker, *Communication of Innovations,* pp. 32–33.

91. Hisrich and Peters, *Marketing a New Product,* pp. 179–81.

92. Fred D. Reynolds and William D. Wells, *Consumer Behavior* (New York: McGraw-Hill, 1977), pp. 307–8.

93. Louis A. Fourte and Joseph W. Woodlock, "Early Prediction of Market Success for New Grocery Products," *Journal of Marketing* 25 (October 1960): 31–38.

94. Robert F. Kelly, "Estimating Ultimate Performance Levels of New Retail Outlets," *Journal of Marketing Research* 4 (February 1967): 13–19.

95. Frank M. Bass, "A New Product Growth Model for Consumer Durables," *Management Science* 15 (January 1969): 215–27.

96. James K. DeVoe, "Plans, Profits, and the Marketing Program," in Frederick E. Webster, Jr., ed., *New Directions in Marketing* (Chicago: American Marketing Association, 1965).

Chapter 11

1. Joseph W. Newman, "New Insights, New Progress for Marketing," *Harvard Business Review* (November-December 1957): 100.

2. George S. Day, Allan D. Shocker, and Rajendra K. Srivastava, "Customer-Oriented Approaches to Identifying Product-Markets," *Journal of Marketing* 43 (Fall 1979): 8–19.

3. Fred Danzig, "Bristol-Myers Turns Out Parade of Clinkers," *Advertising Age,* 2 August 1971, pp. 1, 50.

4. Burt Schorr, "Many New Products Fizzle Despite Careful Planning, Publicity," *Wall Street Journal,* 5 April 1961, 1, 20.

5. Kenneth E. Runyon, *Consumer Behavior and the Practice of Marketing* (Columbus, Oh.: Charles E. Merrill, 1977), pp. 213–14.

6. J. Hugh Davidson, "Why Most New Consumer Products Fail," *Harvard Business Review* 54 (March-April 1976): 117–22.

7. Theodore G. N. Chin, "New Product Successes and Failures—How to Detect them in Advance," *Advertising Age,* 24 September 1973, pp. 61–64.

8. "P & G Uses Pampers Story to Teach the Consumer about Marketing," *Advertising Age,* 4 April 1977, pp. 41–42, 44.

9. Chin, "New Product Successes and Failures," p. 67.

10. Ibid.

11. Theodore L. Angelus, "Why Do Most New Products Fail?" *Advertising Age,* 24 March 1969, pp. 85–86.

12. Ibid., p. 85.

13. Ibid., pp. 85–86.

14. Robert E. Smith and Robert F. Lusch, "How Advertising Can Position a Brand," *Journal of Advertising Research* 16 (February 1976): 37–43.

15. Douglas J. Dalrymple and Leonard J. Parsons, *Marketing Management: Text and Cases* (New York: John Wiley and Sons, 1976), p. 152.

16. William G. Nichols, *Marketing Principles* (Engelwood Cliffs, N.J.: Prentice-Hall, 1978), p. 98.

17. John H. Holmes, "Profitable Product Positioning," *MSU Business Topics,* Spring 1973, pp. 27–28.

18. Nichols, *Marketing Principles,* p. 99.

19. James H. Myers and Mark I. Alpert, "Determinant Buying Attitudes: Meaning and Measurement," *Journal of Marketing* 32 (October 1968): 13–20.

20. See, for example, Paul E. Green and Vithala R. Rao, *Applied Multidimensional Scaling* (New York: Holt, Rinehart, and Winston, 1962).

21. The discussion here is drawn from Chester R. Wasson, *Consumer Behavior: A Managerial Viewpoint* (Austin, Tex.: Austin Press, 1975), pp. 130–33.

22. "Personality and Consumer Behavior," by William D. Wells and Arthur D. Beard, in Scott Ward and Thomas S. Robertson, *Consumer Behavior: Theoretical Sources,* © 1973, pp. 178–179. Reprinted by permission of Prentice Hall, Inc., Englewood Cliffs, New Jersey.

23. Ralph Westfall, "Psychological Factors in Predicting Product Choice," *Journal of Marketing* 26 (April 1962): 36.

24. Arthur Koponen, "Personality Characteristics of Purchasers," *Journal of Advertising Research* 1 (September 1960): 6–12.

25. Karen Horney, *Neurosis and Human Growth* (New York: Norton, 1950).

26. Joel B. Cohen, "The Role of Personality in Consumer Behavior," in Harold H. Kassarjian and Thomas S. Robertson, *Perspectives in Consumer Behavior* (Glenview, Ill.: Scott, Foresman, 1968), pp. 220–34.

27. Wells and Beard, "Personality and Consumer Behavior," pp. 179–89.

28. Ibid., p. 190.

29. C. Whan Park and V. Parker Lessig, "Students and Housewives, Differences in Susceptibility to Reference Group Influence," *Journal of Consumer Research* 4 (September 1977): 102–10.

30. Francis S. Bourne, "Group Influences in Marketing and Public Relations," in Rensis Likert and Samuel P. Hayes, Jr., eds., *Some Applications of Behavioral Research* (Paris: UNESCO, 1961).

31. Donald E. Vinson, Jerome E. Scott, and Lawrence M. Lamont, "The Role of Personal Values in Marketing and Consumer Behavior," *Journal of Marketing* 41 (April 1977): 44–50.

32. David A. Risk, Jeffrey S. Ayson, and Marilyn Y. Fu, *International Business Blunders* (Columbus: Grid Publishing, 1975).

33. Walter A. Henry, "Cultural Values Do Correlate with Consumer Behavior," *Journal of Marketing Research* 13 (May 1976): 121–27.

34. Montrose Sommers and Jerome Kernan, "Why Products Flourish Here, Fizzle There," *Columbia Journal of World Business,* March-April 1967.

35. Talcott Parsons, *The Social System* (New York: Free Press, 1964), pp. 101–12.

36. Seymore Lipset, "The Value Patterns of Democracy: A Case Study in Comparative Values," *American Sociological Review* 28 (August 1962): 515–31.

37. Milton Alexander, "The Significance of Ethnic Groups in Marketing," in Lynn H. Stockman, ed., *Advancing Marketing Efficiency* (Chicago: American Marketing Association, 1959).

38. Marcus Alesia, "Some Negro-White Differences in Consumption," *American Journal of Economics and Sociology* 21 (January 1962): 11–38; James E. Stafford, Keith K. Cox, and James B. Higginbotham, "Some Consumption Pattern Differences between Urban Whites and Negroes," *Social Science Quarterly* 49 (December 1968): 619–30; Raymond O. Oladipudo, "How Distinct is the Negro Market?" Ogilvy and Mather, Inc., Advertising, New York, 1970); Kelvin A. Wall, "Positioning Your Product in the Black Market," *Advertising Age,* 18 June 1973, p. 75.

39. Charles Winick, "Anthropology's Contributions to Marketing," *Journal of Marketing* 25 (July 1961): 53–60.

40. Chester R. Wasson, "Is it Time to Quit Thinking of Income Classes?" *Journal of Marketing* 33 (April 1969): 54–56.

41. James H. Myers, Roger R. Stanton, and Arne F. Hango, "Correlates of Buying Behavior: Social Class vs. Income," *Journal of Marketing* 35 (October 1971): 8–15.

42. James H. Myers and John F. Mount, "More on Social Class vs. Income as Correlates of Buying Behavior," *Journal of Marketing* 37 (April 1973): 71–73.

43. Robert D. Hisrich and Michael P. Peters, "Selecting the Superior Segmentation Correlate," *Journal of Marketing* 38 (July 1974): 60–63.

44. See Richard P. Coleman, "The Significance of Social Class in Selling," in *Marketing: A Maturing Discipline* (Chicago: American Marketing Association, 1960).

45. William H. Peters, "Relative Occupational Class Income: A Significant Variable in the Marketing of Automobiles," *Journal of Marketing* 34 (April 1971): 74–77.

46. Thomas Ford Hoult, "Experimental American Measurement of Clothing as a Factor in Some Social Ratings of Selected American Men," *American Sociological Review* 19 (June 1954): 324–25; Arlene Bjorngoard Ostermeier and Joanne Bubolz Eicher, "Clothing and Appearance as Related to Social Class and Social Acceptance of Adolescent Girls," *Michigan State University Quarterly Bulletin* 48 (February 1966): 431–36.

47. "A study of Working-Class Women in a Changing World," Social Science Research, Inc., May 1973.

48. Thomas E. Lasswell, *Class and Stratum* (Boston: Houghton Mifflin, 1965), p. 231.

49. Stuart U. Rich and Subhash Jain, "Social Class and Life Cycle as Predictors of Shopping Behavior," *Journal of Marketing Research* 5 (February 1968): 43–44.

50. Montrose S. Sommers, "Product Symbolism and the Perception of Social Strata," Stephen A. Greyser, ed., *Toward Scientific Marketing,* (Chicago: American Marketing Association, 1964), 200–16.

51. John W. Slocum and H. Lee Mathews, "Social Class and Income as Indicators of Consumer Credit Behavior," *Journal of Marketing* 34 (April 1970): 69–74; Joseph T. Plummer, "Life Style Patterns and Commercial Bank Credit Card Usage," *Journal of Marketing* 35 (April 1971): 35–41; Douglass K. Hawes, Roger D. Blackwell, and W. Wayne Talarzyk, "Attitudes Toward Use of Credit Cards: Do Men and Women Differ?" *Baylor Business Studies,* January 1977, pp. 57–71.

52. Slocum and Mathews, "Social Class and Income," p. 73.

53. George P. Moschis and Gilbert A. Churchill, Jr., "Consumer Socialization: A Theoretical and Empirical Analysis," *Journal of Marketing Research* 15 (November 1978): 599–609.

Chapter 12

1. Ralph I. Allison and Kenneth P. Uhl, "Influence of Beer Brand Identification on Taste Perception," *Journal of Marketing Research* 1 (August 1964): 36–39.

2. J. Douglas McConnell, "The Development of Brand Loyalty: An Experimental Study," *Journal of Marketing Research* 5 (February 1968): 13–19.

3. Donald A. Laird, "How the Consumer Estimates Quality by Subconscious Sensory Impressions —with Special Reference to the Role of Smell," *Journal of Applied Psychology* 16, no. 3 (June 1932): 241–46.

4. Edward L. Grubb and Harrison L. Grathwohl, "Consumer Self-Concept, Symbolism and Market Behavior: A Theoretical Approach," *Journal of Marketing* 31 (October 1967): 22–27.

5. Edward L. Grubb and Gregg Hupp, "Perception of Self, Generalized Stereotypes, and Brand

Selection," *Journal of Marketing Research* 5 (February 1968): 58–63.

6. E. Laird Landon, Jr., "Self Concept, Ideal Self Concept, and Consumer Purchase Intentions," *Journal of Consumer Research* 1 (September 1974): 44–49.

7. The Daniel Starch Corporation is a leader in advertising research. A "noted viewer" is one who remembers seeing an advertisement but did not pay attention to the whole ad.

8. Jacob Jacoby, George J. Szybillo, and Jacqueline Busato-Schach, "Information Acquisition Behavior in Brand Choice Situations," *Journal of Consumer Research* 3 (March 1977): 209–16.

9. "The Positioning Era" (Slide presentation prepared by Ries Cappiello Colwell, Inc., New York, 1975).

10. Walter P. Margulies, "Animal Names on Products May be Corny, but Boost Consumer Appeal," *Advertising Age,* 23 October 1972, p. 78.

11. Robert A. Peterson and Ivan Ross, "How to Name New Brands," *Journal of Advertising Research* 12 (December 1972): 29–34.

12. Steven J. Miller, Michael B. Mazis, and Peter L. Wright, "The Influence of Brand Ambiguity on Brand Attitude Development," *Journal of Marketing Research* 8 (November 1971): 455–59.

13. Margaret W. Mathin, "Response Competition as a Mediating Factor in the Frequency—Affect Relationship," *Journal of Personality and Social Psychology* 16 (November 1970): 536–52.

14. Miller, Mazis, and Wright, "Brand Ambiguity," p. 459.

15. Robert Zajonc, "Attitudinal Effects of Mere Exposure," *Journal of Personality and Social Psychology Monograph Supplement* 9 (June 1968): 1–27.

16. Sadaomi Oshikawa, "Changing Brand Beliefs and Preferences by Classically Conditioning Brand Affect and Meaning," *1976 Proceedings of the American Marketing Association* (Chicago, 1976), pp. 503–6.

17. Homer E. Spence and James F. Engel, "The Impact of Brand Preference on Brand Names: A Laboratory Analysis," in David T. Kollat, Roger D. Blackwell, and James F. Engel, eds., *Research in Consumer Behavior* (New York: Holt, Rinehart, and Winston, 1970), pp. 61–70.

18. M. Bird, C. Channon, and A. S. C. Ehrenberg, "Brand Image and Brand Usage," *Journal of Marketing Research* 7 (August 1970): 307–11.

19. James L. Ginter, "An Experimental Investigation of Attitude Change and Choice of a New Brand," *Journal of Marketing Research* 11 (February 1974): 30–40.

20. Jean E. Weber and Richard W. Hansen, "The Majority Effect and Brand Choice," *Journal of Marketing Research* 9 (August 1972): 320–23.

21. Franklin B. Evans, "Psychological and Objective Factors in the Prediction of Brand Choice: Ford versus Chevrolet," *Journal of Business* 32 (October 1959): 340–69.

22. Karen Horney, *Our Inner Conflicts* (New York: Norton, 1945).

23. Joel B. Cohen, "An Interpersonal Orientation to the Study of Consumer Behavior," *Journal of Marketing Research* 4 (August 1967): 270–78.

24. Joseph N. Fry, "Personality Variables and Cigarette Brand Choice," *Journal of Marketing Research* 8 (August 1971): 298–304.

25. Robert E. Witt, "Informal Social Group Influence on Consumer Brand Choice," *Journal of Marketing Research* 6 (November 1969): 473–76.

26. Patrick E. Murphy, "The Effect of Social Class on Brand and Price Consciousness for Supermarket Products," *Journal of Retailing* 54, no. 2 (Summer 1978): 33–42.

27. George Brown, "Brand Loyalty—Fact or Fiction?" *Advertising Age,* 19 June 1952, pp. 53–55; 30 June 1952, pp. 45–47; 14 July 1952, pp. 46–48; 11 August 1952, pp. 56–58; 1 September 1952, pp. 80–82; 6 October 1952, pp. 82–86; 11 December 1952, pp. 76–79; 25 January 1953, pp. 75–76.

28. Yoram Wind, "Brand Loyalty and Vulnerability," in Arch G. Woodside, Jagdish N. Sheth, and Peter D. Bennett, eds., *Consumer and Industrial Buying Behavior* (New York: North-Holland, 1977), pp. 313–19.

29. George S. Day, "A Two-Dimensional Concept of Brand Loyalty," *Journal of Advertising Research* 9 (September 1969): 29–35.

30. Jacob Jacoby and David B. Kryner, "Brand Loyalty vs. Repeat Purchasing Behavior," *Journal of Marketing Research* 10 (February 1973): 1–9.

31. Lance P. Jarvis and James B. Wilcox, "Repeat Purchasing Behavior and Attitudinal Brand Loyalty: Additional Evidence," in Kenneth Bernhardt, ed., *Proceedings of the 1976 Fall Conference of the American Marketing Association* (Chicago, 1976), pp. 151–52.

32. James M. Carman, "Correlates of Brand Loyalty: Some Positive Results," *Journal of Marketing Research* 7 (February 1970): 67–76.

33. Robert Mittelstaedt, "A Dissonance Approach to Repeat Purchasing Behavior," *Journal of Marketing Research* 6 (November 1969): 444–46.

34. James E. Stafford, "Effects of Group Influences on Consumer Brand Preferences," *Journal of Marketing Research* 13 (February 1966): 68–75.

35. John U. Farley, "Why Does 'Brand Loyalty' Vary Over Products?" *Journal of Marketing Research* 1 (November 1964): 9–14.

36. William T. Tucker, "The Development of Brand Loyalty," *Journal of Marketing Research* 1 (August 1964): 32–35.

37. Ronald E. Frank, Susan P. Douglas, and Rolando E. Polli, "Household Correlates of 'Brand Loyalty' for Grocery Products," *Journal of Business* 41 (April 1968): 237–45.

38. Jagdish N. Sheth, "How Adults Learn Brand Preference," *Journal of Advertising Research* 8 (September 1968): 25–36.

39. Eli Siggev, "Brand Assortment and Consumer Brand Choice," *Journal of Marketing* 34 (October 1979): 18–24.

40. Parts of this and the following section are based on "The Positioning Era."

41. Jack Trout and Al Ries, "The Positioning Era," *Advertising Age,* 24 April 1972, pp. 35, 38.

42. Joseph N. Fry, "Family Branding and Consumer Brand Choice," *Journal of Marketing Research* 4 (August 1967): 237–47.

43. Tanniru R. Rao, "Are Some Consumers More Prone to Purchase Private Brands?" *Journal of Marketing Research* 6 (November 1969): 447–50.

44. Donald E. Sexton, Jr., "Differences in Food Shopping Habits by Area of Residence, Race, and Income," *Journal of Retailing* 50, no. 1 (Spring 1974): 37–48.

45. Murphy, "Effect of Social Class," p. 42.

46. Barbara Keddy, "No-brands Invade Canada," *Advertising Age,* 3 April 1978, pp. 3, 78; Paul Webster, "French Go for No-name Brands," *Milwaukee Journal,* 20 April 1977, p. 20; "No Brand Groceries," *Time,* 21 November 1977, p. 80.

47. Isodore Barmash, "Inflation Puts the Squeeze on Supermarkets, Too," *New York Times,* 4 June 1978, pp. 1–9; "Jewel's Generic Label Line: Giving the Consumer Another Choice," *Chain Store Age Supermarkets,* October 1977, pp. 29–31.

48. Patrick E. Murphy and Gene R. Laczniak, "Generic Supermarket Items: A Product and Consumer Analysis," *Journal of Retailing* 55, no. 2, (Summer 1979): 1–14.

49. Ibid.

50. Charles Handy and Haaman Seigle, "Generic Labeling," *National Food Review,* September 1978, pp. 17–20.

51. Murphy and Laczniak, "Generic Supermarket Items," pp. 1–14.

52. This quote and the previous section are developed from Ernest Dichter, "The Man in the Package" (Pamphlet developed for the Paraffined Carton Research Council, 1957).

53. C. W. J. Granger and A. Billson, "Consumers' Attitudes Toward Package Size and Price," *Journal of Marketing Research* 9 (August 1972): 239–48.

54. Jacob Jacoby, Donald E. Speller, and Carol Kohn Berning, "Brand Choice Behavior as a Function of Information Load, Replication and Extension," *Journal of Consumer Research* 1 (June 1974): 33–42.

55. Jacob Jacoby, Donald E. Speller, and Carol A. Kohn, "Brand Choice Behavior as a Function of Information Load," *Journal of Marketing Research* 11 (February 1974): 63–69.

56. Jacob Jacoby, George J. Szybillo, and Jacqueline Busato-Schach, "Information Acquisition Behavior in Brand Choice Situations," *Journal of Consumer Research* 3 (March 1977): 209–16.

57. Michael L. Dean, James F. Engel, and W. Wayne Talarzyk, "The Influence of Package Copy Claims on Consumer Product Evaluations," *Journal of Marketing* 41 (April 1977): 34–39.

58. Beverlee B. Anderson, "The Influence of Seals of Certification on Selected Product Evaluations" (Paper presented at the Southwestern Marketing Association Meeting, San Antonio, March, 1976).

59. Robert L. Brown, "Wrapper Influence on the Perception of Freshness of Bread," *Journal of Applied Psychology* 42 no. 4 (August 1958): 257–60.

60. Carl McDaniel and R. C. Baker, "Convenience Food Packaging and the Perception of Product Quality," *Journal of Marketing* 41 (October 1977): 57–58.

61. Ibid., p. 58.

62. Scott Watterson and Gary Stevenson, "Chinese Consumer Behavior" (Unpublished paper, Utah State University, Logan, 1979).

63. James F. Engel, Martin R. Warshaw, and Thomas C. Kinnear, *Promotional Strategy,* 4th ed. (Homewood, Ill.: Richard D. Irwin, 1979), p. 463.

64. Stephen M. Barker, "When to Change Your Package—and When Not To," *Advertising Age,* 23 May 1977, pp. 49, 58.

65. Ibid.

66. Ibid.

Chapter 13

1. J. Douglas McConnell, "The Price-Quality Relationship in an Experimental Setting," *Journal of Marketing Research* 5 (August 1968): 300–303.

2. The discussions of customary and odd pricing are derived from Kent B. Monroe, "Buyers' Subjective Perception of Price," *Journal of Marketing Research* 10 (February 1973): 70–80.

3. Eli Ginzberg, "Customary Prices," *American Economic Review* 26 (June 1936): 52–58.

4. Andre Gabor and Clive W. J. Granger, "Price Sensitivity of the Consumer," *Journal of Advertising Research* 4 (December 1964): 40–44.

5. Kent B. Monroe and David M. Gardner, "An Experimental Inquiry into the Effect of Price and

Brand Preference," in Kenneth L. Bernhardt, ed., *Marketing: 1776–1976 and Beyond, 1976 Educators Proceedings of the American Marketing Association* (Chicago, 1976), pp. 552–56.

6. Milton Alexander, ed., *Display Ideas for Super Markets* (New York: Progressive Grocer, p. 73; "How Multiple Unit Pricing Helps . . . and Hurts," *Progressive Grocer* 50 (June 1971): 52–58.

7. "How Multiple Unit Pricing Helps," pp. 52–58.

8. Lawrence Friedman, "Psychological Pricing in the Food Industry," in Almarin Phillips and Oliver Williamson, eds., *Prices: Issues in Theory, Practice, and Public Policy* (Philadelphia: University of Pennsylvania Press, 1967), pp. 187–201.

9. "How Multiple-Unit Pricing Helps," pp. 52–58.

10. Hans R. Isakson and Alex R. Maurizi, "The Consumer Economics of Unit Pricing," *Journal of Marketing Research* 10 (August 1973): 277–85.

11. Bruce F. McElroy and David A. Aaker, "Unit Pricing Six Years After Introduction," *Journal of Retailing* 55, no. 3 (Fall 1979): 24–37.

12. J. Edward Russo, Gene Krieser, and Sally Miyashita, "An Effective Display of Unit Price Information," *Journal of Marketing* 39 (April 1975): 11–19.

13. Monroe, "Subjective Perception of Price," p. 71.

14. Andre Gabor and Clive W. J. Granger, "On the Price Consciousness of Consumers," *Applied Statistics* 10 (November 1961): 170–88.

15. Ronald E. Frank, "Correlates of Buying Behavior for Groceries," *Journal of Marketing* 32 (October 1967): 48–53.

16. Patrick E. Murphy, "The Effect of Social Class on Brand and Price Consciousness," *Journal of Retailing* 54, no. 4 (Summer 1978): 33–42; Howard Trier, Henry Clay Smith, and James Shaffer, "Differences in Food Buying Attitudes of Housewives," *Journal of Marketing* 25 (July 1960): 66–69.

17. Gabor and Granger, "Price Sensitivity," pp. 40–44.

18. "How Much Do Customers Know About Retail Prices," *Progressive Grocer* 43 (February 1964): 104–6.

19. F. E. Brown, "Who Perceives Prices Most Accurately?" *Journal of Marketing Research* 8 (February 1971): 110–12.

20. Ibid., p. 112.

21. William Wells and Leonard LaSciento, "Direct Observation of Purchasing Behavior," *Journal of Marketing Research* 3 (August 1966): 227–33.

22. Dick R. Wittnik, "Advertising Increases Sensitivity to Price," *Journal of Advertising Research* 17 (April 1977): 39–42.

23. Andre Gabor and Clive W. J. Granger, "The Pricing of New Products," *Scientific Business* 3 (Au-

gust 1965): 141–50; idem, "Price as an Indicator of Quality: Report on an Enquiry," *Economics* 46 (February 1966): 43–70; Kent B. Monroe and M. Venkatesan, "The Concept of Price Limits and Psychophysical Measurement: A Laboratory Experiment," *Proceedings of the Fall Conference of the American Marketing Association* (Chicago, 1969), pp. 345–51; Carolyn W. Sherif, "Social Categorization as a Function of Latitude of Acceptance," *Journal of Marketing Research* 8 (November 1971): 460–64; Joseph Kamen and Robert Toman, "Psychophysics of Price," *Journal of Marketing Research* 7 (February 1970): 27–35.

24. Kent B. Monroe, "Measuring Price Thresholds by Psychophysics and Latitude of Acceptance," *Journal of Marketing Research* 8 (November 1971): 460–64.

25. Ibid.

26. Monroe, "Subjective Perception of Price," p. 74.

27. Joseph Uhl, "Consumer Perception of Retail Food Price Changes" (Paper presented at the First Annual Meeting of Association for Consumer Research, 1970); Edgar Pessemier, "An Experimental Method for Estimating Demand," *Journal of Business* 33 (October 1960): 373–83.

28. Peter Cooper, "Subjective Economics: Factors in a Psychology of Spending," in Bernard Taylor and Gordon Wills, eds., *Pricing Strategy* (London: Staples Press, 1970), pp. 112–21; idem, "The Begrudging Index and the Subjective Value of Money," ibid., pp. 122–31.

29. Harry Nelson, *Adaptation-Level Theory* (New York: Harper and Row, 1964); Kent B. Monroe, "Objective and Subjective Contextual Influences on Price Perception," in Arch G. Woodside, Jagdish N. Sheth, and Peter D. Bennett, eds., *Consumer and Industrial Buying Behavior* (New York: North-Holland, 1977) pp. 287–96.

30. Monroe, "Subjective Perception of Price," p. 74.

31. Fred Emery, "Some Psychological Aspects of Price," in Taylor and Wills, eds., *Pricing Strategy,* pp. 98–111.

32. Kamen and Toman, "Psychophysics of Price," p. 34.

33. Ibid., p. 35.

34. Ibid.

35. See Andre Gabor, Clive Granger, and Anthony P. Sowter, "Comments on 'Psychophysics of Prices'," *Journal of Marketing Research* 8 (May 1971): 251–52; Kent B. Monroe, " 'Psychophysics of Price': A Reappraisal," ibid., pp. 248–50; Jon Stapel, " 'Fair' or 'Psychological' Pricing?" *Journal of Marketing Research* 9 (February 1972): 109–10.

36. Monroe, " 'Psychophysics of Prices'," pp. 248–50.

37. James F. Engel, David T. Kollat, and Roger D. Blackwell, *Consumer Behavior* (New York: Holt, Rinehart, and Winston, 1968), p. 429.

38. Joseph M. Kamen and Robert J. Toman, "Psychophysics of Price: A Reaffirmation," *Journal of Marketing Research* 8 (May 1971): 252–57.

39. Stapel, " 'Fair' or 'Psychological' Pricing?" pp. 109–10.

40. Gabor, Granger, and Sowter, "Comments on 'Psychophysics of Prices'," pp. 251–52.

41. Harold Leavitt, "A Note on Some Experimental Findings About the Meanings of Price," *Journal of Business* 27 (July 1954): 205–10.

42. Donald Tull, R. A. Boring, and M. H. Gonsior, "A Note on the Relationship of Price and Imputed Quality," *Journal of Business* 37 (April 1964): 186–91.

43. Gabor and Granger, "Price as an Indicator of Quality," pp. 43–70.

44. Benson P. Shapiro, "The Psychology of Pricing," *Harvard Business Review* 46 (July-August 1968): 14–25, 160. Reprinted by permission of the Harvard Business Review. Excerpt from "The Psychology of Pricing" by Benson P. Shapiro (July-August 1968). Copyright © 1968 by the President and Fellows of Harvard College; all rights reserved.

45. Richard N. Cardozo, "An Experimental Study of Customer Effort, Expectation, and Satisfaction," *Journal of Marketing Research* 2 (August 1965): 244–49.

46. Tibor Scitovsky, "Some Consequences of the Habit of Judging Quality By Price," *The Review of Economic Studies* 12 (1944–45): 100–105.

47. Jerry C. Olson, "Price as an Informational Cue: Effects on Product Evaluations," in Woodside, Sheth, and Bennett, eds., *Buying Behavior,* pp. 267–86.

48. David M. Gardner, "Is There a Generalized Price-Quality Relationship?" *Journal of Marketing Research* 8 (May 1971): 241–43.

49. Jacob Jacoby, Jerry C. Olson, and Rafael A. Haddock, "Price, Brand Name, and Product Composition Characteristics as Determinants of Perceived Quality," *Journal of Applied Psychology* 55, no. 6 (December 1971): 570–79.

50. Ben Enis and James Stafford, "Consumers' Perception of Product Quality as a Function of Various Information Inputs," *Proceedings of the Fall Conference of the American Marketing Association* (Chicago, 1969), pp. 340–44; idem, "The Price Quality Relationship: An Extension," *Journal of Marketing Research* 6 (November 1969): 256–58.

51. P. R. Andrews and F. R. Bajens, "Combining Price, Brand and Store Cues to Form an Impression of Product Quality" (Paper presented at the Conference of the American Psychological Association, 1971); Edward Smith and Charles Broome, "A Laboratory Experiment for Establishing Indifferent Prices Between Brands of Consumers' Brand Preferences," *Proceedings of the Fall Conference of the American Marketing Association* (Chicago, 1966), pp. 511–19; Edward Smith and Charles Broome, "Experimental Determination of the Effect of Price and Market-Standing Information on Consumers' Brand Preferences," ibid., pp. 520–31; Albert Della Bitta, "An Experimental Examination of Conditions which May Foster the Use of Price as an Indicator of Relative Product Attractiveness" (Ph.D. diss., University of Massachusetts, 1971).

52. Kent Monroe, "The Influence of Price and the Cognitive Dimension of Brand Attitudes and Brand Preferences" (Paper presented at the Attitude Research and Consumer Behavior Workshop, 1970); Vithala R. Rao, "Salience of Price in the Perception of Product Quality: A Multidimensional Experiment," *Proceedings of the Spring and Fall Conference of the American Marketing Association* (Chicago, 1971), pp. 571–77.

53. Vithala R. Rao, "Marginal Salience of Price in Brand Evaluations," in M. Venkatesan, ed., *Proceedings of the Association for Consumer Research* (Iowa City, 1972), pp. 125–44.

54. Michael J. Etzel, "The Price-Perceived Quality Relationship after the Purchase" (Paper presented at the Southwestern Marketing Association Meetings, San Antonio, 1976).

55. David M. Gardner, "An Experimental Investigation on the Price-Quality Relationship," *Journal of Retailing* 46 no. 3 (Fall 1970): 39–40; John J. Wheatley and John S. Y. Chiro, "The Effects of Price, Store Image, and Product and Respondent Characteristics on Perceptions of Quality," *Journal of Marketing Research* 14 (May 1977): 181–86.

56. Wheatley & Chiro, "Effects of Price," pp. 181–86.

57. Tull, Boring, and Gonsoir, "Price and Imputed Quality," pp. 186–91; Donald F. Cox and Raymond A. Bauer, "Self-Confidence and Persuasability in Women," in Cox, ed., *Risk Taking and Information Handling in Consumer Behavior* (Boston: Division of Research, Harvard Business School, 1967); Benson P. Shapiro, "Price Reliance: Existence and Sources," *Journal of Marketing Research* 10 (August 1973): 286–94.

58. Tull, Boring, and Gonsoir, "Price and Imputed Quality," pp. 186–91; Shapiro, "Price Reliance," pp. 286–94; Monroe and Gardner, "Price and Brand Preference," pp. 552–56.

59. Shapiro, "Price Reliance," pp. 286–94.

60. Ibid.

61. Wheatley and Chiro, "Perceptions of Quality," pp. 181–86.

62. Smith and Broome, "Experimental Determination of Price," pp. 520–31.

63. Raymond L. Horton, "Some Relationships Between Personality and Consumer Decision Making," *Journal of Marketing Research* 16 (May 1979): 233–46.

64. Harry Nystrom, Hans Tamsons, and Robert Thams, "An Experiment in Price Generalization and Discrimination," *Journal of Marketing Research* 12 (May 1975): 177–81.

65. Paul Ingrassia, "In a Color-TV Market Roiled by Price Wars, Sony Takes a Pounding," *Wall Street Journal,* 16 March 1978.

66. Zarrel V. Lambert, "Price and Choice Behavior," *Journal of Marketing Research* 9 (February 1972): 35–40.

67. James R. Bettman, "Perceived Price and Product Perceptual Variables," *Journal of Marketing Research* 10 (February 1973): 100–102.

68. Lambert, "Price and Choice Behavior," pp. 35–40.

69. Monroe and Gardner, "Price and Brand Preference," pp. 552–56.

70. Nonyelu Nwokoye, "An Experimental Inquiry into the Effects of Parameters of Price Structure on Buyers' Price Judgments" (Ph.D. diss., University of Massachusetts, 1975).

71. Kent B. Monroe, "The Influence of Price Differences and Brand Familiarity on Brand Preferences," *Journal of Consumer Research* 3 (June 1976): 42–49.

72. Ibid.

Chapter 14

1. Elihu Katz and Paul Lazarsfeld, *Personal Influence: The Part Played by People in the Flow of Mass Communications* (Glencoe, Ill.: Free Press, 1955), p. 176.

2. Kenward L. Atkin, "Advertising and Store Patronage," *Journal of Advertising Research* 2 (December 1962): 18–23.

3. Jon G. Udell, *Successful Marketing Strategies in American Industry* (Madison: Mimir, 1972).

4. Adapted from Ernest Dichter, "How Word of Mouth Advertising Works" *Harvard Business Review* 44 (November-December 1966): 147–66. Reprinted by permission of the Harvard Business Review. Adapted from "How Word-of-Mouth Advertising Works," by Ernest Dichter (November-December 1966). Copyright © 1966 by the President and Fellows of Harvard College; all rights reserved.

5. Bobby J. Calder and Robert E. Burnkrant, "Interpersonal Influence on Consumer Behavior: An Attribution Theory Approach," *Journal of Consumer Research* 4 (June 1977): 29–38.

6. Scott M. Cunningham, "Perceived Risk as a Factor in the Diffusion of New Product Information," in Raymond M. Haas, ed., *Science, Technology and Marketing* (Chicago: American Marketing Association, 1966), pp. 698–721.

7. Arch G. Woodside and M. Wayne Delozier, "Effects of Word-of-Mouth Advertising on Consumer Risk Taking," *Journal of Advertising* 5 (Fall 1976): 12–19.

8. Paul F. Lazarsfeld, Bernard Berelson, and Hazel Gaudet, *The People's Choice,* 2d ed. (New York: Columbia University Press, 1948).

9. Elihu Katz, "The Two-Step Flow of Communication: an Up-to-Date Report on an Operating Hypothesis," *Public Opinion Quarterly* 21 (Spring 1957): 61–78.

10. Charles W. King and John O. Summers, "Dynamics of Interpersonal Communication: The Interaction Dyad," in Donald F. Cox, ed., *Risk Taking and Information Handling in Consumer Behavior* (Boston: Division of Research, Graduate School of Business Administration, Harvard University, 1967), pp. 240–64.

11. James H. Myers and Thomas S. Robertson, "Dimensions of Opinion Leadership," *Journal of Marketing Research* 9 (February 1972): 41–46.

12. John O. Summers, "The Identity of Women's Clothing Fashion Opinion Leaders," *Journal of Marketing Research* 7 (May 1970): 178–85.

13. John O. Summers and Charles W. King, "Interpersonal Communication and New Product Attitudes," in Philip R. McDonald, ed., *Proceedings of the American Marketing Association* (Chicago, 1969), pp. 292–99.

14. Thomas S. Robertson and James H. Myers, "Personality Correlates of Opinion Leadership and Innovative Buying Behavior," *Journal of Marketing Research* 6 (May 1969): 164–68; Fred D. Reynolds and William R. Darden, "Mutually Adaptive Effects of Interpersonal Communication," *Journal of Marketing Research* 8 (November 1971): 449–54; William R. Darden and Fred D. Reynolds, "Predicting Opinion Leadership for Men's Apparel Fashions," *Journal of Marketing Research* 9 (August 1972): 324–28; Summers, "Clothing Fashion Opinion Leaders," pp. 180–81.

15. Katz, "Two-Step Flow of Communication," pp. 61–78; Elihu Katz and Paul F. Lazarsfeld, *Personal Influence* (New York: Columbia University Press, 1962); Everett M. Rogers and David G. Cartano, "Methods of Measuring Opinion Leadership," *Public Opinion Quarterly* 26 (Fall 1962): 435–41; Summers, "Clothing Fashion Opinion Leaders," pp. 180–81; Gary M. Armstrong and Lawrence P. Feldman, "Exposure and Sources of Opinion Leaders," *Journal of Advertising Research* 16 (August 1976): 21–27.

16. Douglas J. Tigert and Stephen J. Arnold, "Profiling Self Designated Opinion Leaders and Self

Designated Innovators Through Life Style Research," (Paper presented at the School of Business, University of Toronto, Ontario, June 1971.

17. Myers and Robertson, "Dimensions of Opinion Leadership," p. 46.

18. Ibid.

19. Shlomo I. Lampert, "Word of Mouth Activity During the Introduction of a New Food Product," in John U. Farley, John A. Howard, and L. Winston Ring, *Consumer Behavior Theory and Applications* (Boston: Allyn and Bacon, 1974), pp. 67–88.

20. Francesco Nicosia, "Opinion Leadership and the Flow of Communications," *Proceedings of the Winter Conference of the American Marketing Association* (Chicago, 1964), pp. 324–40; Thomas S. Robertson, *Innovative Behavior and Communication* (New York: Holt, Rinehart, and Winston, 1971).

21. Robert T. Green and Eric Langeard, "A Cross-National Comparison of Consumer Habits, in the Adoption Process," *Journal of Marketing* 39 (July 1975): 35–41; Armstrong and Feldman, "Opinion Leaders," pp. 21–27.

22. Armstrong and Feldman, "Opinion Leaders," pp. 21–27.

23. Joseph R. Moncuso, "Why Not Create Opinion Leaders For New Product Introduction?" *Journal of Marketing* 33 (July 1969): 20–25.

24. Techniques for simulating and stimulating word-of-mouth advertising are drawn from Dichter, "Word of Mouth Advertising," pp. 147–66.

25. See Frederick E. Webster, Jr., "Interpersonal Communication and Salesman Effectiveness," *Journal of Marketing* 32 (July 1968): 7–13.

26. Franklin B. Evans, "Selling as a Dyadic Relationship," *American Behavioral Scientist* 65 (May 1963): 76–79.

27. M. S. Gadel, "Concentration by Salesmen on Congenial Prospects", *Journal of Marketing* 28 (April 1964): 64–66.

28. Joseph W. Thompson and William W. Evans, "Behavioral Approach to Industrial Selling," *Harvard Business Review* 47 (March-April 1969): 137–51.

29. R. J. Lutz and P. Kakkar, "Situational Influence in Interpersonal Persuasion," *Advances in Consumer Research* vol. 2 (Chicago: Association for Consumer Research, 1975), pp. 439–53.

30. Arch G. Woodside and R. E. Pitts, "Consumer Response to Alternative Selling Strategies," *Advances in Consumer Research,* vol. 3 (Cincinnati: Association for Consumer Research, 1975), pp. 398–404; Arch G. Woodside and J. Taylor Sims, "Retail Sales Transactions and Customer 'Purchase Pal' Effects on Buying Behavior," *Journal of Retailing* 52, no. 3 (Fall 1976): pp. 57–64.

31. Gerald D. Bell, "Self Confidence and Persuasion in Car Buying", *Journal of Marketing Research* 4 (February 1967): 46–52.

32. Noel Capon, Morris B. Holbrook, and James M. Hulbert, "Selling Processes and Buyer Behavior," in Arch G. Woodside, Jagdish N. Sheth, and Peter D. Bennett, eds., *Consumer and Industrial Buying Behavior* (New York: North-Holland, 1977), pp. 323–32.

33. Franklin B. Evans, "Dyadic Interaction in Selling—A New Approach," (Unpublished manuscript, University of Chicago, 1964).

34. Edward A. Riordan, Richard L. Oliver, and James H. Donnelly, Jr., "The Unsold Prospect: Dyadic and Attitudinal Determinants," *Journal of Marketing Research* 14 (November 1977): 530–37.

35. John O'Shaughnessy, "Selling as an Interpersonal Influence Process," *Journal of Retailing* 47 no. 4 (Winter 1971–72): 32–46.

36. David T. Wilson, "Dyadic Interactions," in Woodside, Sheth, and Bennett, eds., *Consumer and Industrial Buying Behavior,* pp. 355–68.

37. This discussion is adapted from O'Shaughnessy, "Selling as Influence Process," pp. 35–37.

38. L. E. Crane, "The Salesman's Role in Household Decision Making," in George L. Smith, ed., *Proceedings of the American Marketing Association* (Chicago, 1964).

39. Ibid., p. 532.

40. O'Shaughnessy, "Selling as Influence Process," p. 36.

41. Arch G. Woodside and J. William Davenport, Jr., "The Effect of Salesman Similarity and Expertise on Consumer Purchasing Behavior," *Journal of Marketing Research* 11 (May 1974): 198–202.

42. O'Shaughnessay, "Selling as Influence Process," p. 38.

43. Jagdish N. Sheth, "Buyer-Seller Interaction: A Conceptual Framework," *Advances in Consumer Research,* vol. 3 (Cincinnati: Association for Consumer Research, 1975), pp. 383–86.

44. This section is drawn from Ronald P. Willett and Allan L. Pennington, "Customer and Salesman; The Anatomy of Choice and Influence in a Retail Setting," in Raymond M. Haas, ed., *Science, Technology and Marketing* (Chicago: American Marketing Association, 1966), pp. 598–616.

45. Howard Becker and Ruth Hill Useem, "Sociological Analysis of the Dyad," *American Sociological Review* 7 (January 1942); 13.

46. Erving Goffman, *Encounters* (Indianapolis: Bobbs-Merrill, 1961), pp. 9–14.

47. Robert F. Bales, "A Set of Categories for the Analysis of Small Group Interaction, *American Sociological Review* 15 (April 1950); idem, "Task Roles and Social Roles in Problem Solving Groups," in Elenor E. Maccoby, Theodore M. Newcomb,

and Eugene L. Hartly, eds., *Readings in Social Psychology* (New York: Holt, Rinehart, and Winston, 1958); idem, "How People Interact in Conferences," *Scientific American* 192, no. 3 (March 1955); 31–35.

48. Willett and Pennington, "Customer and Salesman," pp. 598–616.

49. Paul Busch and David T. Wilson, "An Experimental Analysis of a Salesman's Expert and Referent Bases of Social Power in the Buyer-Seller Dyad," *Journal of Marketing Research* 13 (February 1976): 3–11.

50. Barton A. Weitz, "Relationship Between Salesperson Performance and Understanding of Consumer Decision Making," *Journal of Marketing Research* 15 (November 1978): 501–16.

51. The discussion follows Richard W. Olshavsky, "Customer-Salesman Interaction in Appliance Retailing," *Journal of Marketing Research* 10 (May 1973): 208–12.

52. Ibid., p. 212.

53. Allan L. Pennington, "Customer-Salesman Bargaining Behavior in Retail Transactions," *Journal of Marketing Research* 5 (August 1968): 255–62.

54. Ibid., p. 262.

55. Carol A. Scott, "The Effects of Trial and Incentives on Repeat Purchase Behavior," *Journal of Marketing Research* 13 (August 1976): 263–69.

56. Mark Synder and Michael R. Cunningham, "To Comply or Not to Comply: Testing the Self-Perception Explanation of the 'Foot-in-the-Door' Phenomenon," *Journal of Personality and Social Psychology* 31 (January 1975): 64–67; Daryl J. Bem, "Self Perception Theory," in Leonard Berkowitz, ed., *Advances in Experimental Social Psychology* 6 (New York: Academic Press, 1972) pp. 1–62; Harold H. Kelly, "The Process of Causal Attribution," *American Psychologist* 28 (February 1973): 107–28.

57. Peter H. Reingen and Jerome B. Kernan, "More Evidence on Interpersonal Yielding," *Journal of Marketing Research* 16 (November 1979): 588–93.

58. Jonathan L. Freedman and Scott C. Fraser, "Compliance Without Pressure: The Foot-in-the-Door Technique," *Journal of Personality and Social Psychology* 4 (August 1966): 195–202; Richard L. Miller, Philip Brickman, and Diana Bolen, "Attribution Versus Persuasion as a Means of Modifying Behavior," *Journal of Personality and Social Psychology* 31 (March 1975): 430–41; Patricia Pliner, et. al., "Compliance Without Pressure: Some Further Data on the Foot-in-the-Door Technique," *Journal of Experimental Social Psychology* 10 (1974): 17–22.

59. Alice M. Tybout, "Relative Effectiveness of Three Behavior Influence Strategies as Supplements to Persuasion in a Marketing Context," *Journal of Marketing Research* 15 (May 1978): 229–42.

60. Reingen and Kernan, "Interpersonal Yielding," pp. 588–93.

61. Robert B. Cialdini and Karen Ascani, "Test of a Concession Procedure for Inducing Verbal, Behavioral and Further Compliance With a Request to Donate Blood," *Journal of Applied Psychology* 61, no 3 (March 1976): 295–300.

62. Robert B. Cialdini et. al., "Reciprocal Concessions Procedure for Inducing Compliance: The Door-in-the-Face Technique," *Journal of Personality and Social Psychology* 31 (February 1975): 206–15.

63. Tybout, "Three Behavior Influence Strategies," pp. 229–42.

64. Cialdini, et. al., "Reciprocal Concessions," pp. 206–15.

65. Tybout, "Three Behavior Influence Strategies," pp. 239–40. Reprinted from the *Journal of Marketing Research* published by the American Marketing Association.

66. Ibid.

67. This section is based on O'Shaughnessy, "Selling as Influence Process," pp. 38–43.

68. Ibid., p. 40.

Chapter 15

1. Joel Saegert, "Another Look at Subliminal Perception," *Journal of Advertising Research* 19 (February 1979): 55–57.

2. Paul F. Lazarsfeld, Bernard B. Berelson, and Hazel Gaudet, "Radio and the Printed Page as Factors in Political Opinion and Voting," in William Schramm, ed., *Mass Communications* (Urbana: University of Illinois Printers, 1949), pp. 481–95; Wilber Schramm and Richard F. Carter, "Effectiveness of a Political Telethon," *Public Opinion Quarterly* 23 (Spring 1959): 121–27; Charles F. Cannell and James C. MacDonald, "The Impact of Health News on Attitudes and Behavior," *Journalism Quarterly* 33 (Summer 1956): 315–23; David Patetz et. al., "Selective Exposure: The Potential Boomerang Effect," *Journal of Communication* 22 (1972): 48–53.

3. Elihu Katz, "On Reopening the Question of Selectivity in Exposure to Mass Communications," in Robert P. Abelson et. al., eds., *Theories of Cognitive Consistency: A Sourcebook* (Chicago: Rand McNally, 1968), p. 789.

4. David O. Sears, "Paradox of De Facto Selective Exposure without Preferences for Supportive Infor-

mation," in Abelson et. al., eds., *Theories of Cognitive Consistency,* pp. 777–87; Stuart H. Surlin and Thomas F. Gordon, "Selective Exposure and Retention of Political Advertising," *Journal of Advertising Research* 16 (February 1976): 32–37.

5. M. Wayne De Lozier, *The Marketing Communications Process* (New York: McGraw-Hill, 1976): pp. 35–36. Copyright © 1976 by McGraw-Hill Book Company. Used with the permission of McGraw-Hill Book Company.

6. Ibid., pp. 37–43; "Starch/Tested Copy," *The Starch Advertisement Readership Service,* vol. 566, no. 108, p. 2.

7. Terrell G. Williams, "An Experiment in the Effects of Comparative Advertising on Brand Awareness, Comprehension and Preference," *Southern Business Review* Spring 1978, pp. 30–42.

8. See, for example, Carl I. Hovland and Walter Weiss, "The Influence of Source Credibility on Communication Effectiveness," *Public Opinion Quarterly* 15 (Winter, 1951–52): 635–50; Herbert Kelman and Carl Hovland, "'Reinstatement' of the Communicator in Delayed Measurement of Opinion Change," *Journal of Abnormal and Social Psychology* 48 (July 1953): 327–35.

9. Michael J. Baker and Gilbert A. Churchill, Jr., "The Impact of Physically Attractive Models on Advertising Evaluations," *Journal of Marketing Research* 14 (November 1977): 538–55.

10. Robert B. Settle and Linda Golden, "Attribution Theory and Advertiser Credibility," *Journal of Marketing Research* 11 (May 1974): 181–85.

11. Joseph M. Kamen, Albert C. Azhari, and Judith R. Krogh, "What a Spokesman Does for a Sponsor," *Journal of Advertising Research* 15 (April 1975): 17. Reprinted from the *Journal of Advertising Research* © Copyright 1975, by the Advertising Research Foundation.

12. Herbert C. Kelman, "Processes of Opinion Change," *Public Opinion Quarterly* 25 (Spring 1961): 57–78.

13. See Erwin P. Bettinghaus, *Persuasive Communication,* 2d ed. (New York: Holt, Rinehart, and Winston, 1973), pp. 107–8.

14. Hershey H. Friedman and Linda Friedman, "Endorser Effectiveness by Product Type," *Journal of Advertising Research* 19 (October 1979): 63–71.

15. Daniel B. Wackman, "Theories in Interpersonal Perception," in Scott Ward and Thomas Robertson, eds., *Consumer Behavior: Theoretical Sources* (Englewood Cliffs, N.J.: Prentice-Hall, 1973): pp. 200–229.

16. See Ellen K. Beracheid and Elaine Walster, "Physical Attractiveness," *Advances in Experimental Social Psychology,* vol. 1 (New York: Academic Press, 1974). This is a good review article of the wide range of research that has been done on the effects of the degree of physical attractiveness.

17. Baker and Churchill, "Impact of Models," pp. 539–40.

18. Arthur G. Miller, "Social Perception of Internal-External Control," *Perceptual and Motor Skills* 30, no. 1 (February 1970): 103–9.

19. Baker and Churchill, "Impact of Models," p. 553.

20. See, for example, Major Steadman, "How Sexy Illustrations Affect Brand Recall," *Journal of Advertising Research* 9 (March 1969): 15–19.

21. Douglas A. Fuchs, "Two Source Effects in Magazine Advertising," *Journal of Marketing Research* 1 (August 1964): 59–62.

22. Burke Marketing Research, Inc., "Viewer Attitudes Toward Commercial Clutter on Television and Media Buying Decisions" (Paper presented at the Eighteenth Advertising Research Foundation Conference, New York, 1972); Peter H. Webb, "Consumer Initial Processing in a Difficult Media Environment," *Journal of Consumer Research* 6 (December 1979): 225–36.

23. Carl I. Hovland, Arthur A. Lumsdaine, and Fred D. Sheffield, *Experiments on Mass Communications,* vol. 3 (Princeton University Press, 1948).

24. Elliott McGinnies, "Studies in Persuasion: III. Reactions of Japanese Students to One-Sided and Two-Sided Communications," *Journal of Social Psychology* 70 (October 1966): 87–93.

25. Edwin W. J. Faison, "Effectiveness of One-Sided and Two-Sided Mass Communications in Advertising," *Public Opinion Quarterly* 25 (Fall 1961): pp. 468–69.

26. Arthur A. Lumsdaine and Irving L. Janis, "Resistance to 'Counter-Propaganda' Produced by One-Sided Versus Two-Sided 'Propaganda' Presentation," *Public Opinion Quarterly* 17 (Fall 1953): 311–18.

27. Bettinghaus, *Persuasive Communication,* pp. 152–53.

28. Frederick H. Lund, "The Psychology of Belief: A Study of Its Emotional and Volitional Determinants," *Journal of Abnormal and Social Psychology* 20 (July-September 1925): 124–96.

29. Ralph Rosnow and Edward J. Robinson, eds., *Experiments in Persuasion* (New York: Academic Press, 1967), p. 101.

30. Irving L. Janis and Rosalind L. Feierabend, "Effects of Alternative Ways of Ordering Pro and Con Arguments in Persuasive Communication," in Carl I. Hovland et. al., eds., *The Order of Presentation in Persuasion* (New Haven: Yale University Press, 1957), pp. 79–97.

31. Rosnow and Robinson, *Experiments in Persuasion,* pp. 101–2.

32. William J. McGuire, "Order of Presentation as a Factor in 'Conditioning' Persuasiveness," in Hovland et. al., eds., *Presentation in Persuasion,* pp. 98–114.

33. Carl I. Hovland, Irving L. Janis, and Harold H. Kelley, *Communication and Persuasion* (New Haven: Yale University Press, 1953), pp. 112–20.

34. William G. Nickels, *Marketing Communication and Promotion,* 2d ed. (Columbus: Grid Publishing, 1980), p. 95.

35. William A. Watts, "Relative Persistence of Opinion Change Induced by Active Compared to Passive Participation," *Journal of Personality and Social Psychology* 5 (January 1967): 4–15.

36. De Lozier, *Marketing Communications Process,* pp. 98–99.

37. Hovland, Janis, and Kelly, *Communication and Persuasion,* pp. 103–5; Carl I. Hovland, and Wallace Mandell, "An Experimental Comparison of Conclusion-Drawing by the Communicator and His Audience," *Journal of Abnormal and Social Psychology,* 47 (July 1952): 581–88.

38. Donald L. Thistlewhite, Henry DeHaan, and Joseph Kamenetzky, "The Effects of 'Directive' and 'Nondirective' Communication Procedures on Attitudes," *Journal of Abnormal and Social Psychology* 51 (July 1955): 107–13.

39. Hovland, Janis, and Kelley, *Communication and Persuasion,* p. 104.

40. Jonathan L. Freedman, J. Merrill Carlsmith, and David O. Sears, *Social Psychology* (Englewood Cliffs, N.J.: Prentice-Hall, 1970), p. 314.

41. Bruce John Marrison and Marvin J. Dainoff, "Advertisement Complexity and Looking Time," *Journal of Marketing Research* 9 (May 1972): 392–400.

42. Leo Bogart, "How Do People Read Newspapers?" *Media/Scope* 6 (January 1962): 53–56.

43. Leo Bogart, *Strategy in Advertising* (New York: Harcourt, Brace and World, 1967), pp. 146–47.

44. Alvin J. Silk and Frank P. Geiger, "Advertisement Size and the Relationship Between Product Usage and Advertising Exposure," *Journal of Marketing Research* 9 (February 1972): 22–26.

45. Bettinghaus, *Persuasive Communication,* p. 135.

46. Albert S. King, "Pupil Size, Eye Direction, and Message Appeal: Some Preliminary Findings," *Journal of Marketing* 36 (July 1972): 55–58.

47. Ibid., p. 56, citing Merle E. Day, "An Eye Movement Phenomenon Relating to Attention, Thought and Anxiety," *Perceptual and Motor Skills* 19, no. 2 (October 1964): 443.

48. King, "Message Appeal," citing Paul Bakan, "Hypnotizability, Laterality of Eye-Movements, and Functional Brain Asymmetry," *Perceptual and Motor Skills* 28, no. 2 (March 1969): 927–32.

49. John J. Burnett and Richard L. Oliver, "Fear Appeal Effects in the Field: A Segmentation Approach," *Journal of Marketing Research* 16 (May 1979): 181–90.

50. Michael L. Ray and Wendell L. Wilkie, "Fear: The Potential of an Appeal Neglected by Marketing," *Journal of Marketing* 34 (January 1970): 54–62.

51. Marvin Karlins and Herbert I. Abelson, *Persuasion: How Opinions and Attitudes Are Changed,* 2d ed. (New York: Springer, 1970), pp. 9–10.

52. Bettinghaus, *Persuasive Communications,* pp. 160–61.

53. Leon Festinger and Nathan Maccoby, "On Resistance to Persuasive Communications," *Journal of Abnormal and Social Psychology* 68 (November 1964): 359–66.

54. David M. Gardner, "The Effect of Divided Attention on Attitude Change Induced by a Persuasive Marketing Communication," *Proceedings of the Fall Conference of the American Marketing Association,* (Chicago, 1966), pp. 532–40; M. Venkatesan and Gordon A. Haaland, "Divided Attention and Television Commercials: An Experimental Study," *Journal of Marketing Research* 5 (May 1968): 203–5; Stewart W. Bither, "Effects of Distraction and Commitment on the Persuasiveness of Television Advertising," *Journal of Marketing Research* 9 (February 1972): 1–5.

55. Brian Sternthall and C. Samuel Craig, "Humor in Advertising," *Journal of Marketing* 37 (October 1973): 12–18.

56. Leon G. Shiffman and Leslie Lazar Kanuk, *Consumer Behavior* (Englewood Cliffs, N.J.: Prentice-Hall, 1978), p. 468.

57. C. Samuel Craig, Brian Sternthal, and Clark Leavitt, "Advertising Wearout: An Experimental Analysis," *Journal of Marketing Research* 13 (November 1976): 365–72; the following summary of and generalizations about wearout are from Allen Greenberg and Charles Suttoni, "Television Commercial Wearout," *Journal of Advertising Research* 13 (October 1973): 47–54. Reprinted from the *Journal of Advertising Research* © Copyright 1973, by the Advertising Research Foundation.

58. Greenberg and Suttoni, "Television Commercial Wearout," pp. 47–54.

59. Clark Leavitt, "Strong Versus Weak Effects of Mass Communications: Two Alternative Hypotheses," in G. D. Hughes and Michael L. Ray, eds., *Buyer/Consumer Information Processing* (Chapel Hill: University of North Carolina Press, 1974).

60. Valentine Appel, "The Reliability and Decay of Advertising Measurements" (Speech to The National Industrial Conference Board, October 28, 1966), cited in Greenberg and Suttoni, "Television Commercial Wearout," pp. 47–54; Robert C. Grass, "Satiation Effects of Advertising," *Proceedings of the Fourteenth Annual Conference of the Advertising Research Foundation* (New York, 1968).

61. Appel, "Advertising Measurements."

62. Craig, Sternthal, and Leavitt, "Advertising Wearout," pp. 365–72.

63. Robert C. Grass and Wallace H. Wallace, "Satiation Effects of TV Commercials," *Journal of Advertising Research* 9 (September 1969): 3–8.

64. Bobby J. Calder and Brian Sternthal, "Television Commercial Wearout: An Informative Processing View," *Journal of Marketing Research* 17 (May 1980): 173–86.

65. Steuart Henderson Britt, "How Advertising Can Use Psychology's Rules of Learning," *Printers' Ink* 252 (September 23, 1955): 74, 77, 80.

66. Harry Deane Wolfe, James K. Brown, and G. Clark Thompson, *Measuring Advertising Effectiveness* (New York: National Industrial Conference Board, 1962).

67. See, for example, Rosser Reeves, *Reality in Advertising* (New York: Alfred A. Knopf, 1961); Darroll Blaine Lucas and Steuart Henderson Britt, *Measuring Advertising Effectiveness* (New York: McGraw-Hill, 1968); Robert J. Lavidge and Gary A. Steiner, "A Model for Predictive Measurements of Advertising Effectiveness," *Journal of Marketing* 25 (October 1961): 59–62.

68. Harper W. Boyd, Jr., Michael L. Ray, and Edward C. Strong, "An Attitudinal Framework for Advertising Strategy," *Journal of Marketing* 36 (April 1972): 27–33.

69. Kristian S. Palda, "The Hypothesis of Hierarchy of Effects: A Partial Evaluation," *Journal of Marketing Research* 3 (February 1966): 13–24; Charles K. Ramond, "Must Advertising Communicate to Sell?" *Harvard Business Review* 43 (September-October 1965): 148–61; Ambar G. Rao, *Quantitative Theories in Advertising* (New York: John Wiley and Sons, 1970).

70. Leon Festinger, "Behavioral Support for Opinion Change," *Public Opinion Quarterly* 28 (Fall 1964): 404–17; Jack B. Haskins, "Factual Recall as a Measure of Advertising Effectiveness," *Journal of Advertising Research* 4 (March 1964): 2–8; Herbert E. Krugman, "The Impact of Television Advertising: Learning Without Involvement," *Public Opinion Quarterly* 29 (Fall 1965): 349–56.

71. *Advertising Age,* 19 December 1966, p. 1.

72. See Martin Fishbein, ed., *Readings in Attitude Theory and Measurement* (New York: John Wiley and Sons, 1967); Marie Jahoda and Neil Warren, eds., *Attitudes* (Baltimore: Penguin Books, 1966); and Gene F. Summers, ed., *Attitude Measurement* (Chicago: Rand-McNally, 1970).

73. Boyd, Ray, and Strong, "Attitudinal Framework," pp. 27–33.

74. Ibid.

75. Thomas S. Robertson, "Low-Commitment Consumer Behavior," *Journal of Advertising Research* 16 (April 1976): 19–24.

76. Raymond A. Bauer and Alice H. Bauer, "America, Mass Society, and Mass Media," *Journal of Social Issues* 16 no. 3 (1960): 3–66; Joseph T. Klapper, *The Effects of Mass Communication* (Glencoe, Ill.: Free Press, 1960); Raymond A. Bauer, "The Obstinate Audience," *American Psychologist* 19 (May 1964): 319–28.

77. Robertson, "Low-Commitment Consumer Behavior," p. 20.

78. Ibid., p. 19.

79. Krugman, "Impact of Television Advertising," pp. 349–56.

80. Robertson, "Low-Commitment Consumer Behavior," p. 23.

81. Ibid.

82. Peter Wright, "Factors Affecting Cognitive Resistance to Advertising," *Journal of Consumer Research* 2 (June 1975): 1–9.

83. Solomon E. Asch, "Effects of Group Pressures Upon Modification and Distortion of Judgments," in Eleanor E. Maccoby, Theodore M. Newcomb, and Eugene L. Hartley, eds., *Readings in Social Psychology* (New York: Holt, Rinehart, and Winston, 1958), pp. 174–78; Leonard Berkowitz and Richard M. Lundy, "Personality Characteristics Related to Susceptibility to Influence by Peers or Authority Figures," *Journal of Personality* 25, no. 3 (March 1957): 306–16; Irving L. Janis, "Personality and Susceptibility to Persuasion," *Journal of Personality* 22 no. 4 (June 1954): 504–18; Irving L. Janis and Peter B. Field, "Sex Differences and Personality Factors Related to Persuasibility," in Carl I. Hovland and Irving L. Janis, eds., *Personality and Persuasibility* (New Haven: Yale University Press, 1959), pp. 55–68.

84. Jeffery A. Barach, "Self-Confidence and Reactions to Television Commercials," in Donald F. Cox, ed., *Risk Taking and Information Handling in Consumer Behavior* (Boston: Graduate School of Business Administration, Harvard University, 1968), pp. 428–41; Donald F. Cox and Raymond A. Bauer, "Self-Confidence and Persuasibility in Women," *Public Opinion Quarterly* 28 (1964): 453–66; Alice H. Eagly, "Sex Differences in the Relationship Between Self-Esteem and Susceptibility to Social Influences," *Journal of Personality* 37, no. 4 (December 1969): 581–91; Kenneth J. Gergen and Raymond A. Bauer, "Interactive Effects of Self-Esteem and Task Difficulty on Social Conformity," *Journal of Personality and Social Psychology* 6, no. 1 (May 1967): 16–22; Irwin Silverman, "Differential Effects of Ego Threat Upon Persuasibility for High and Low Self-Esteem Subjects," *Journal of Abnormal and Social Psychology* 69 (1964): 567–72.

85. Wright, "Cognitive Resistance to Advertising," p. 1.

86.   Arthur R. Cohen, "Some Implications of Self-Esteen for Social Influence," in Hovland and Janis, eds., *Personality and Persuasibility*, pp. 102–20.

87.   William J. McGuire, "Personality and Susceptibility to Social Influence," in Edgar F. Borgatta and William W. Lambert, eds., *Handbook of Personality Theory and Research* (Chicago: Rand McNally, 1968), pp. 1130–87; Stewart Bither and Peter Wright, "The Self-Confidence Advertising Response Relationship: A Function of Situational Distraction," *Journal of Marketing Research* 10 (May 1973): 146–52. De Lozier, *Marketing Communications Process*, p. 116. James H. Myers and William H. Reynolds, *Consumer Behavior and Marketing Management* (Boston: Houghton Mifflin, 1967), p. 273.

88.   Jacob Jacoby, "Multiple-Indicant Approach for Studying New Product Adopters," *Journal of Applied Psychology* 55, no. 4 (August 1971): 384–88; Carol A. Kohn Berning and Jacob Jacoby, "Patterns of Information Acquisition in New Product Purchases," *Journal of Consumer Research* 1 (September 1974): 18–22.

89.   D. P. Haefner, "Some Effects of Guilt-Arousing and Fear-Arousing Persuasive Communications on Opinion Change" (Ph.D. diss., University of Rochester, New York, 1956); Irving L. Janis and Seymour Feshbach, "Effects of Fear-Arousing Communications," *Journal of Abnormal and Social Psychology* 48 (January 1953): 78–92; Jum C. Nunnally and Howard M. Bobren, "Variables Governing the Willingness to Receptive Communications on Mental Health," *Journal of Personality* 27 (March 1959): 38–46.

90.   Hovland, Janis, and Kelley, *Communication and Persuasion*, p. 195.

91.   Pierre Martineau, "Social Classes and Spending Behavior," *Journal of Marketing* 23 (October 1958): 121–30.

92.   Douglas J. Tigert, "A Research Project in Creative Advertising Through Life-Style Analysis," in Charles King and Douglas Tigert, eds., *Attitude Research Reaches New Heights* (Chicago: American Marketing Association, 1970). Reprinted from *Attitude Research Reaches New Heights*, published by the American Marketing Association.

93.   David L. Loudon and Albert J. Della Bitta, *Consumer Behavior: Concepts and Applications* (New York: McGraw-Hill, 1979), p. 210.

94.   Lee Rainwater, Richard P. Coleman, and Gerald Handel, *Workingman's Wife* (New York: Oceana Publication, 1959), p. 105.

95.   Leon Morse, "Black Radio Market Study," *Television/Radio Age*, 28 February 1977, pp. A-1–A-31.

96.   Robert S. Diamond, "Managers Away from Home," *Fortune*, 15 August 1969, 56–62.

97.   Charles Winick, "Anthropology's Contribution to Marketing," *Journal of Marketing*, (July 1961): 53–60.

98.   David Ricks, Jeffrey S. Arpan, and Marilyn Y. Fu, *International Business Blunders*, (Columbus: Grid Publishing, 1975).

Chapter 16

1.   Calvin Hodock, "Use of Psychographics in Analysis of Channels of Distribution," in William D. Wells, ed., *Life Style and Psychographics* (Chicago: American Marketing Association, 1974), pp. 205–21. Reprinted from *Life Style and Psychographics*, published by the American Marketing Association.

2.   Ibid., pp. 206–7. See also David L. Appel, "Market Segmentation: A Response to Retail Innovation," *Journal of Marketing* 34 (April 1970): 64–67.

3.   Hodock, "Channels of Distribution," p. 209.

4.   Ibid.

5.   Robert O. Herrman and Leland L. Beik, "Shoppers' Movements Outside Their Local Retail Area," *Journal of Marketing* 32 (October 1963): 45–51; John R. Thompson, "Characteristics and Behavior of Out Shopping Consumers," *Journal of Retailing* 47, no. 1 (Spring 1971): 70–80.

6.   Fred D. Reynolds and William R. Darden, "Intermarket Patronage: A Psychographic Study of Consumer Outshoppers," *Journal of Marketing* 36 (October 1972): 50–54.

7.   William R. Darden and William D. Perreault, Jr., "Identifying Interurban Shoppers: Multi Product Purchase Patterns and Segmentation Profiles," *Journal of Marketing Research* 8 (1976): 51–60.

8.   Ibid.

9.   William R. Darden and Dub Ashton, "Psychographic Profiles of Patronage Preference Groups," *Journal of Retailing* 50, no. 4 (Winter 1974–75): 99–112. Reprinted by permission of the *Journal of Retailing*.

10.   Ibid., p. 107.

11.   George P. Moschis, "Shopping Orientation and Consumer Uses of Information," *Journal of Retailing* 52, no. 2 (Summer 1976): 61–70, 93.

12.   Edward M. Tauber, "Why Do People Shop?" *Journal of Marketing* 36 (October 1972): 46–59. Reprinted from the *Journal of Marketing*, published by the American Marketing Association.

13. James F. Engel, Roger D. Blackwell, and David T. Kollat, *Consumer Behavior* 3d ed. (Hinsdale, Ill.: Dryden Press, 1978), pp. 504–5.

14. Robert A. Hansen and Terry Deutscher, "An Empirical Investigation of Attribute Importance in Retail Store Selection," *Journal of Retailing* 53, no. 4 (Winter 1977–78): 59–72, 95.

15. Leon G. Schiffman, Joseph F. Dash, and William R. Dillon, "The Contribution of Store-Image Characteristics to Store-Type Choice," *Journal of Retailing* 52, no. 2 (Summer 1977): 3–14, 46.

16. Danny N. Bellinger, Dan H. Robertson, and Elizabeth C. Hirschamm, "Age and Education as Key Correlates of Store Selection for Female Shoppers," *Journal of Retailing* 52, no. 4 (Winter 1976–77): 71–78.

17. The following observation, based on figure 16-8, can be found in Stuart U. Rich and Subhash C. Jain, "Social Class and Life Cycle as Predictors of Shopping Behavior," *Journal of Marketing Research* 5 (February 1968): 41–49.

18. Peter L. Gillett, "A Profile of Urban In-Home Shoppers," *Journal of Marketing* 34 (July 1970): 40–45.

19. Rich and Jain, "Social Class and Life Cycle," pp. 41–49.

20. Hansen and Deutcher, "Attribute Importance," p. 70.

21. Ibid., p. 71.

22. Joseph F. Dash, Leon C. Schiffman, and Conrad Berenson, "Risk and Personality-Related Dimensions of Store-Choice," *Journal of Marketing* 4 (January 1976): 32–39.

23. *Discount Store Study* (Cleveland: Cleveland Press, 1970), p. 20; "The True Look of the Discount Industry," *Discount Merchandiser* 11 (June 1971): 29-TL.

24. Stuart U. Rich, *Shopping Behavior of Department Store Shopper* (Boston: Division of Research, Graduate School of Business, Harvard University, 1963), p. 114; Rachel Dardis and Marie Sandler, "Shopping Behavior of Discount Store Customers in a Small City," *Journal of Retailing* 47, no. 2 (Summer 1971): 60–72.

25. V. Kanti Prasad, "Socioeconomic Product Risk and Patronage Preferences of Retail Shoppers," *Journal of Marketing* 39 (July 1975): 42–47.

26. V. Parker Lessig, "Consumer Store Image and Store Loyalties," *Journal of Marketing* 37 (October 1973): 72–74; Ernest B. Uhr and Ernest C. Horick, "The Store Avoidance Hypothesis: Additional Evidence" (Paper presented at the Southwestern Marketing Association Conference, San Antonio, April 1976).

27. Eleanor G. May, "Practical Applications of Recent Image Research," *Journal of Retailing* 50, no. 4 (Winter 1974–75): 15–20, 116.

28. Dev S. Pathak, William J. E. Crissy, and Robert W. Sweitzer, "Customer Image Versus the Retailer's Anticipated Image," *Journal of Retailing* 50, no. 4 (Winter 1974–75): 21–28, 116.

29. Pierre Martineau, "The Personality of the Retail Store," *Harvard Business Review* 36 (January-February 1958): 47.

30. Jay D. Lindquist, "Meaning of Image," *Journal of Retailing* 50, no. 4 (Winter 1974–75): 29–38, 116.

31. Leon Arons, "Does Television Viewing Influence Store Image and Shopping Frequency," *Journal of Retailing* 37, no. 3 (Fall 1961): 1–13.

32. John H. Kunkel and Leonard L. Berry, "A Behavioral Conception of Retail Image," *Journal of Marketing* 32 (October 1968): 21–27.

33. Alfred R. Oxenfeldt, "Developing a Favorable Price-Quality Image," *Journal of Retailing* 50, no. 4 (Winter 1974–75): 8–16.

34. These ideas have their origin in John J. Wheatley and John S. Y. Chiu, "The Effects of Price, Store Image and Product and Respondent Characteristics on Perceptions of Quality," *Journal of Marketing Research* 14 (May 1977): 181–186; Richard N. Cardozo, "How Images Vary by Product Class," *Journal of Retailing* 50, no. 4 (Winter 1974–75): 85–98.

35. Danny N. Bellenger, Earle Stienberg, and Wilbur W. Stanton, "The Congruence of Store Image," *Journal of Retailing* 52, no. 1 (Spring 1976): 17–32.

36. Joseph Barry Mason and Morris L. Mayes, "The Problems of The Self-Concept in Store-Image Studies," *Journal of Marketing* 36 (April 1970): 67–69.

37. Lindquist, "Meaning of Image," pp. 31–32. Reprinted by permission of the *Journal of Retailing*.

38. Don L. James, Richard M. Durand, and Robert A. Dreves, "The Use of a Multi-Attribute Attitude Model in a Store Image Study," *Journal of Retailing* 52, no. 2 (Summer 1976): 23–32.

39. Kunkel and Berry, "Retail Image," pp. 21–27.

40. James, Durand, and Dreves, "Multi-Attribute Attitude Model," pp. 23–32.

41. See, for example, Ricardo L. Singson, "Multidimensional Scaling Analysis of Store Image and Shopping Behavior," *Journal of Retailing* 51, (Summer 1975): 38–53; Arun K. Jain and Michael Etgar, "Measuring Store Image Through Multidimensional Scaling of Free Response Data," *Journal of Retailing* 52, no. 4 (Winter 1976–77): 61–70, 95.

42. Fred D. Reynolds, William R. Darden, and Warren S. Martin, "Developing an Image of the Store-Loyal Customer," *Journal of Retailing* 50, no. 4 (Winter 1974–75): 73–84.

43. Russel S. Tate, "The Supermarket Battle for Store Loyalty," *Journal of Marketing* 25, (October 1961): 10.

44. Ben M. Enis and Gordon W. Paul, "'Store Loyalty' as a Basis For Market Segmentation," *Journal of Retailing* 46, no. 3 (Fall 1970): 42–56.

45. Ross M. Cunningham, "Customer Loyalty to Store and Brand," *Harvard Business Review* 39 (November-December 1961): 136.

46. Alan S. Donnahoe, "Research Study of Consumer Loyalty," *Journal of Retailing* 1, no. 1 (Spring 1956): 15.

47. The ideas in this paragraph can be found in Kenneth E. Miller and Kent L. Granzin, "Simultaneous Loyalty and Benefit Segmentation of Retail Store Customers." *Journal of Retailing* 55, no. 1 (Spring 1979): 47–60; William F. Massey and Ronald E. Frank, "Short-Term Price and Dealing Effects in Selected Market Segments," *Journal of Marketing Research* 2 (May 1965): 171–85; Joseph W. Newman and Richard A. Weikel, "Multivariate Analysis of Brand Loyalty for Major Household Appliances," *Journal of Marketing Research* 10 (November 1973): 404–9; James E. Staffor, "Effect of Group Influences on Consumer Brand Preferences," *Journal of Marketing Research* 3 (February 1966); 68–75; Reynolds, Darden, and Martin, "Developing an Image," pp. 73–84; John H. Farley, "Why Does 'Brand Loyalty' Vary Over Products?" *Journal of Marketing Research* 1 (November 1964): 9–14; James M. Carmen, "Correlates of Brand Loyalty: Some Positive Results," *Journal of Marketing Research* 7 (February 1970): 67–76; A. Coskin Samli, "Use of Segmentation Index to Measure Store Loyalty," *Journal of Retailing* 51, no. 1 (Spring 1975): 51–60, 113ff.

48. Reynolds, Darden, and Martin, "Developing an Image," pp. 73–84.

49. Miller and Granzin, "Simultaneous Loyalty," pp. 47–60.

50. Lawrence P. Feldman and Alvin D. Star, "Racial Factors in Shopping Behavior," in Keith Cox and Ben M. Enis, eds., *A New Measure of Responsibility for Marketing* (Chicago: American Marketing Association, 1968), p. 226.

51. Gerald E. Hills, Donald E. Hills, and James M. Patterson, "Black Consumer Perceptions of Food Store Attibutes," *Journal of Marketing* 37 (April 1973): 47–57. Reprinted from the *Journal of Markeking*, published by the American Marketing Association.

52. Donald E. Sexton, "Differences in Food Shopping Habits by Area of Residence, Race and Income," *Journal of Retailing* 50, no. 1 (Spring 1974): 37–48, 91. Reprinted by permission of the *Journal of Retailing*.

53. Joseph W. Newman and Richard Staelin, "Prepurchase Information Seeking for New Cars and Major Household Appliances," *Journal of Marketing Research* 9 (August 1972): 249–57.

54. Jon G. Udell, "Prepurchase Behavior of Buyers of Small Electrical Appliances," *Journal of Marketing* 30 (October 1966): 50–52.

55. Terrell G. Williams and Michael J. Etzel, "An Investigation and Extension of the Evoked Set Concept Applied to Consumer Durables," *Proceedings of the Southern Marketing Association* (Atlanta, 1976), pp. 237–39.

56. Gregory P. Stone, "City Shoppers and Urban Identification: Observations on the Social Psychology of City Life," *American Journal of Sociology* 60 (July 1954): 36–45.

57. Moschis, "Shopping Orientation," pp. 61–70, 93.

58. John Wilding and Raymond A. Bauer, "Consumer Goals and Reactions to a Communication Source," *Journal of Marketing Research* 5 (February 1968): 73–77.

59. Harold Kassarjian, "Social Character and Preference for Mass Communication," *Journal of Marketing Research* 2 (May 1965): 146–53.

60. Information use patterns for the shopping orientations are all drawn from Moschis, "Shopping Orientation," pp. 61–70, 93.

61. Joseph F. Dash, Leon G. Schiffman, and Conrad Berenson, "Information Search and Store Choice," *Journal of Advertising Research* 16 (June 1976): 35–40.

62. Eldon M. Wirtz and Kenneth E. Miller, "The Effect of Post Purchase Communication on Consumer Satisfaction and on Consumer Recommendation of the Retailer," *Journal of Retailing* 53, no. 2 (Summer 1977): 39–46.

63. John A. Miller, "Store Satisfaction and Aspiration Theory: A Conceptual Basis for Studying Consumer Discontent," *Journal of Retailing* 52, no. 3 (Fall 1976): 65–84.

64. Ralph L. Day, "Extending the Concept of Consumer Satisfaction," *Advances in Consumer Research,* vol. 10 (Atlanta: Association for Consumer Research, 1977), pp. 149–54.

65. The list of findings is based on the following sources: Miller, "Store Satisfaction," pp. 65–84; Donald A. Hughes, "An Investigation of the Relation of Selected Factors to Consumer Satisfaction" (Paper presented to the Marketing Science Institute Workshop on Consumer Satisfaction/Dissatisfaction, Chicago, April 11–13, 1976); Hal B. Pickle and Robert Bruce, "Consumerism, Product Satisfaction/Dissatisfaction: An Empirical Investigation," *Southern Journal of Business* 7 (November 1972): 87–100; Robert A. Westbrook and Joseph W. Newman, "An Analysis of Shopper Dissatisfaction for Major Household Appliances," *Journal of Marketing Research* 15 (August 1978): 456–66; Joseph Barry Mason and Samuel H. Hines, Jr., "An Exploratory Behavioral and Socioeconomic Profile of Consumer

Action About Dissatisfaction with Selected Household Appliances," *Journal of Consumer Affairs* 7 (Winter 1973): 121–27; Anita B. Pfaff, "An Index of Consumer Satisfaction," in M. Venkatesan, ed., *Proceedings of the Third Annual Conference of the Association for Consumer Research* (Iowa City, 1972), pp. 713–37.

66. See, for example, Paul D. Converse, "New Laws of Retail Gravitation," *Journal of Marketing* 13 (October 1949): 379–88; David B. McKay and Richard W. Olshavsky, "Cognitive Maps of Retail Locations: An Investigation of Some Basic Issues," *Journal of Consumer Research* 2 (December 1975): 197–205.

67. Also see Jerome B. Kernan and Grady D. Bruce, "The Socioeconomic Structure of an Urban Area," *Journal of Marketing Research* 9 (February 1977): 15–18.

68. Rom J. Markin, Charles M. Lilis, and Chem L. Narayona, "Social-Psychological Significance of Store Space," *Journal of Retailing* 52, no. 1 (Spring 1976): 43–53, 94. Reprinted by permission of the *Journal of Retailing*. The remainder of this section, including the tentative propositions, draws heavily from this article.

69. Ibid., p. 46.

70. Ibid., p. 48.

71. Ibid., p. 49.

72. Ibid., p. 51.

73. George J. Kress, *The Effect of End Displays on Selected Food Product Sales* (New York: Point of Purchase Advertising Institute, n.d.)

74. Ronald C. Curhan, "The Relationship Between Shelf Space and Unit Sales in Supermarkets,"

Journal of Marketing Research 9 (November 1972): 406–12.

75. "Ways to Make Every Foot of Shelf Space Pay Off," *Progressive Grocer* 50 (March 1971): 40–49.

76. Ronand C. Curhaı, "Shelf Allocation and Profit Maximization in Mass Retailing," *Journal of Marketing* 37, (July 1973): 54–60.

77. Ibid.

78. William M. Brown and William T. Tucker, "Vanishing Shelf Space," *Atlanta Economic Review* 9 (October 1961): 9–13ff, as quoted in Curhan, "Shelf Allocation," p. 55.

79. Engel, Blackwell, and Kollat, *Consumer Behavior,* p. 263.

80. This summary is largely drawn from ibid., pp. 263–67; *Awareness, Decision, Purchase* (New York: Point of Purchase Advertising Institute, 1961), p. 14; *Drugstore Brand Switching and Impulse Buying,* ibid; *Motion Moves More Merchandise,* ibid., n.d., p. 3): *Increasing Spice Sales with Point-of-Purchase Advertising,* ibid., p. 9; Peter J. McClure and E. James West, "Sales Effects of a New Counter Display," *Journal of Advertising Research* 9 (March 1969): 29–34; "How In-store Merchandising Can Boost Sales," *Progressive Grocer* 50 (October 1971): 94–97; "How the Basics of Special Display Affect Sales and Profits," *Progressive Grocer* 50 (January 1971): 34–45; "How to Make Displays More Sales Productive," *Progressive Grocer* 50 (February 1971): 34–45.

81. "Make Displays More Sales Productive," *Progressive Grocer,* pp. 34–45.

82. Oxenfeldt, "Developing a Favorable Image," pp. 8–16.

Chapter 17

1. Quoted in John U. Farley and John A. Howard, "Current Consumer Policy and Advertising," in Yoram Wind and Marshall C. Greenberg, eds., *Moving A Head With Attitude Research* (Chicago: American Marketing Association, 1977), pp. 179–84.

2. These two quotes are taken from William L. Wilkie and David M. Gardner, "The Role of Marketing Research in Public Policy," *Journal of Marketing* 38 (January 1974): 38–47.

3. This idea and the following quote appear in John A. Howard and Lyman E. Ostlund, "Applying Buyer Behavior Theory to Public Policy," in John A. Howard and Lyman E. Ostlund, eds., *Buyer Behavior: Theoretical and Empirical Foundations* (New York: Alfred A. Knopf, 1973), pp. 569–80.

4. William L. Trombetta and Timothy L. Wilson, "Foreseeability of Misuse and Abnormal Use of Products by the Consumer." *Journal of Marketing* 39 (July 1975): 48–55.

5. Richard Staelin, "The Effects of Consumer Education on Consumer Product Safety Behavior," *Journal of Consumer Research* 5 (June 1978): 30–40.

6. Quoted in Robert F. Dyer and Terence A. Shimp, "Enhancing the Role of Marketing Research in Public Policy Decision Making," *Journal of Marketing* 41 (January 1977): 63–67, and based on Wilkie and Gardner, "Role of Marketing Research," p. 46; William L. Wilkie, "Research on Counter and Corrective Advertising," in S. F. Dirita, ed., *Advertising and the Public Interest* (Chicago: American Marketing Association, 1973), p. 189; Paul N. Bloom and Nikhilesh Dholakia, "Marketing Behavior and Public Policy: Some Unexplored Territory," *Journal of Marketing* 37 (October 1973): 67; David M. Gardner, "Deception in Advertising: A Conceptual Approach," *Journal of Marketing* 39 (January 1975): 45–46.

7. James F. Engel, David Kollat, and Roger Blackwell, *Consumer Behavior,* 2d ed. (New York: Dryden Press, 1974), p. 619.

8. Dyer and Shimp, "Enhancing Marketing Research," p. 63.

9. Ibid.

10. Wilkie and Gardner, "Role of Marketing Research," pp. 40–43. Reprinted from the *Journal of Marketing,* published by the American Marketing Association.

11. Ibid., pp. 40–41.

12. William H. Cunningham and Isabella C. M. Cunningham, "Consumer Protection: More Information or More Regulation," *Journal of Marketing* 40 (April 1976): 63–68.

13. The reasons that follow are taken from George S. Day and William K. Brandt, "Consumer Research and the Evaluation of Public Policy: The Case of Truth in Lending," *Journal of Consumer Research* 1 (June 1974): 21–32; William L. Wilkie, "Assessment of Consumer Information Processing Research in Relation to Public Policy Needs," Report to the National Science Foundation, 1974; George S. Day, "Assessing the Effects of Information Disclosure Requirements," *Journal of Marketing* 40 (April 1976): 42–52.

14. Day and Brandt, "Consumer Research," pp. 21–32.

15. Orville C. Walker, Jr., and Richard F. Santer, "Consumer Preferences for Alternative Retail Credit Terms: A Concept Test of the Effects of Consumer Legislation," *Journal of Marketing Research* 11 (February 1974): 70–78.

16. Day and Brandt, "Consumer Research," pp. 21–32.

17. Tyzoon Tyebjek, "Affirmative Disclosure of Nutrition Information and Consumers' Food Preferences," *Journal of Consumer Affairs* 13 (Winter 1979): 206–23; Day, "Effects of Information Disclosure," pp. 42–52.

18. Dennis L. McNeill and William L. Wilkie, "Public Policy and Consumer Information: Impact of the New Energy Labels," *Journal of Consumer Research* 6 (June 1979): 1–11.

19. Noel Capon and Richard J. Lutz, "A Model and Methodology for the Development of Consumer Information Programs," *Journal of Marketing* 43 (January 1979): 58–67.

20. G. Scott Hutchinson, *Public Policy and Consumer Information: Summary of Findings from Consumer Research* (National Science Foundation, n.d.), p. vii.

21. Day, "Effects of Information Disclosure," p. 47.

22. David Caploritz, *The Poor Pay More* (Toronto: Free Press, 1963), pp. 170–78; Frederick D. Sturdivant, "Better Deal for Ghetto Shoppers," *Harvard Business Review* 46 (March-April 1968): 130–39.

23. Cunningham and Cunningham, "Consumer Protection," pp. 63–68.

24. Debra L. Scammon, "'Information Load' and Consumers," *Journal of Consumer Research* 4 (December 1977): 148–55.

25. Jacob Jacoby, Donald E. Speller, and Carol A. Kohn, "Brand Choice Behavior as a Function of Information Load," *Journal of Marketing Research* 11 (February 1974): 63–69; idem, "Brand Choice Behavior as a Function of Information Load: Replication and Extension," *Journal of Consumer Research* 1 (June 1974): 33–42.

26. See, for example, J. Edward Russo, "More Information is Better: A Reevaluation of Jacoby, Speller and Kahn," *Journal of Consumer Research* 1 (December 1974): 68–72; John O. Summers, "Less Information is Better?" *Journal of Marketing Research* 11 (November 1974): 467–68.

27. Many of the ideas in the preceding two paragraphs are from Scammon, "'Information Load' and Consumers," pp. 148–55.

28. This section is based on Dennis H. Tootelian, "Attitudinal and Cognitive Readiness: Key Dimensions for Consumer Legislation," *Journal of Marketing* 39 (July 1975): 61–63.

29. Virginia Anne Dickenson, "The Consumer Awareness of Adults" (Ph.D. diss., Utah State University, 1980).

30. Gardner, "Deception in Advertising," pp. 40–46.

31. Dorothy Cohen, "The Concept of Unfairness as it Relates to Advertising Legislation," *Journal of Marketing* 38 (July 1974): 8–13.

32. Gardner, "Deception in Advertising," pp. 40–46.

33. Ibid., p. 41.

34. Richard W. Pollay, "Deceptive Advertising and Consumer Behavior: A Case for Legislative and Judicial Reform," *Kansas Law Review,* June 1969, pp. 625–37.

35. David A. Aaker, "Deceptive Advertising," in David A. Aaker and George S. Day, eds., *Consumerism,* 2d ed. (New York: Free Press, 1974), pp. 137–45.

36. Gardner, "Deception in Advertising," p. 42.

37. Dorothy Cohen, "Surrogate Indicators and Deception in Advertising," *Journal of Marketing* 36 (July 1972): 10–15.

38. Block Drug Company and Warner-Lambert Company, *3 Trade Regulation Reporter,* December 1971, no. 19,879.

39. Coca-Cola Company et. al., *3 Trade Regulation Reporter,* April 1971, no. 19,603.

40. Bernard Berelson and Gary A. Steiner, *Human Behavior: An Inventory of Scientific Findings* (New York: Harcourt, Brace and World, 1964), p. 537.

41. Borden, Inc., *3 Trade Regulation Reporter,* December 1970, no. 19,399.

42. Eversharp, Inc., *3 Trade Regulation Reporter,* April 1970, no. 19,219.

43. Robert Pitofsky, "Beyond Nader: Consumer Protection and the Regulation of Advertising," *Harvard Law Review* 90 (February 1977): 675–85.

44. Much of this paragraph is based on Dorothy Cohen, "The FTC's Advertising Substantiation Program," *Journal of Marketing* 44 (Winter 1980): 26–35.

45. Neil E. Beckwith, John U. Farley, and John A. Howard, "Marketing Communications and Public Policy," in Arch G. Woodside, Jagdish N. Sheth, and Peter D. Bennett, eds., *Consumer and Industrial Buying Behavior* (New York: North-Holland, 1977), pp. 409–14.

46. The following discussion is based primarily on Ralph L. Day and E. Laird Landon, Jr., "Toward a Theory of Consumer Complaining Behavior," in Woodside, Sheth, and Bennett, *Buying Behavior,* pp. 425–37.

47. Yves Renoux, "Consumer Dissatisfaction and Public Policy," in Fred C. Allvine, ed., *Public Policy and Marketing Practices* (Chicago: American Marketing Association, 1973): pp. 53–68.

48. B. Weiner et. al., "Perceiving the Causes of Success and Failure," in E. E. Jones et. al., eds., *Attribution: Perceiving the Causes of Behavior* (Morristown, N.J.: General Learning Press, 1971), pp. 95–120; Gerald Zaltman and Melanie Wallendorf, *Consumer Behavior: Basic Findings and Management Implications* (New York: John Wiley and Sons, 1979), pp. 442–44.

49. E. E. Jones and R. E. Nisbett, "The Actor and the Observer: Divergent Perceptions of the Causes of Behavior," in Jones et. al., eds., *Attribution,* pp. 79–94.

50. James Haefner, "The Perception of Deception in Television Advertising: An Exploratory Investigation" (Ph.D. diss., University of Minnesota, 1972).

51. Renoux, "Consumer Dissatisfaction," p. 54.

52. This section is largely drawn from Day and Landon, "Consumer Complaining Behavior," pp. 425–37.

53. R. C. Stokes, "Consumer Complaints and Consumer Dissatisfaction," (Speech at the Food and Drug Law Institute, Phoenix, April 1974).

54. Rex H. Warland, Robert O. Herrmann, and Jane Willits, "Dissatified Consumers: Who Gets Upset and Who Takes Action," *Journal of Consumer Affairs* 9 (Winter 1975): 148–63.

55. Day and Landon, "Consumer Complaining Behavior," pp. 435–36.

56. McNeill and Wilkie, "Public Policy and Consumer Information," pp. 1–11.

57. Staelin, "Effects of Consumer Education," pp. 30–40.

58. Trombetta and Wilson, "Foreseeability of Misuse," p. 50.

59. James Hulbert, "Applying Buyer Behavior Analysis to Social Problems: The Case of Drug Abuse," *1974 Combined Proceedings of the American Marketing Association* (Chicago, 1974), pp. 287–92.

60. Tyebjek, "Nutrition Information," pp. 206–23.

61. Howard and Ostlund, "Applying Buyer Behavior Theory," pp. 569–80.

62. Terrell G. Williams, "Effects of an Advertising Warning Message on Consumer Attitudes and Buying Intentions," in Kenneth L. Bernhardt, ed., *Marketing 1776–1976 and Beyond: 1976 Educators' Proceedings of the American Marketing Association* (Chicago, 1976), pp. 362–67.

Chapter 18

1. See, for example, John A. Howard, *Marketing: Executive and Buyer Behavior* (New York: Columbia University Press, 1963); James H. Myers and William H. Reynolds, *Consumer Behavior and Marketing Management* (Boston: Houghton Mifflin, 1967).

2. James F. Engel, David T. Kollat, and Roger D. Blackwell, *Consumer Behavior* (New York: Holt, Rinehart, and Winston, 1968).

3. Bibi Wern, "Psychographics," *Omni,* July 1980, pp. 54–56, 96–97.

4. Ibid.

Name Index

Subject Index

†